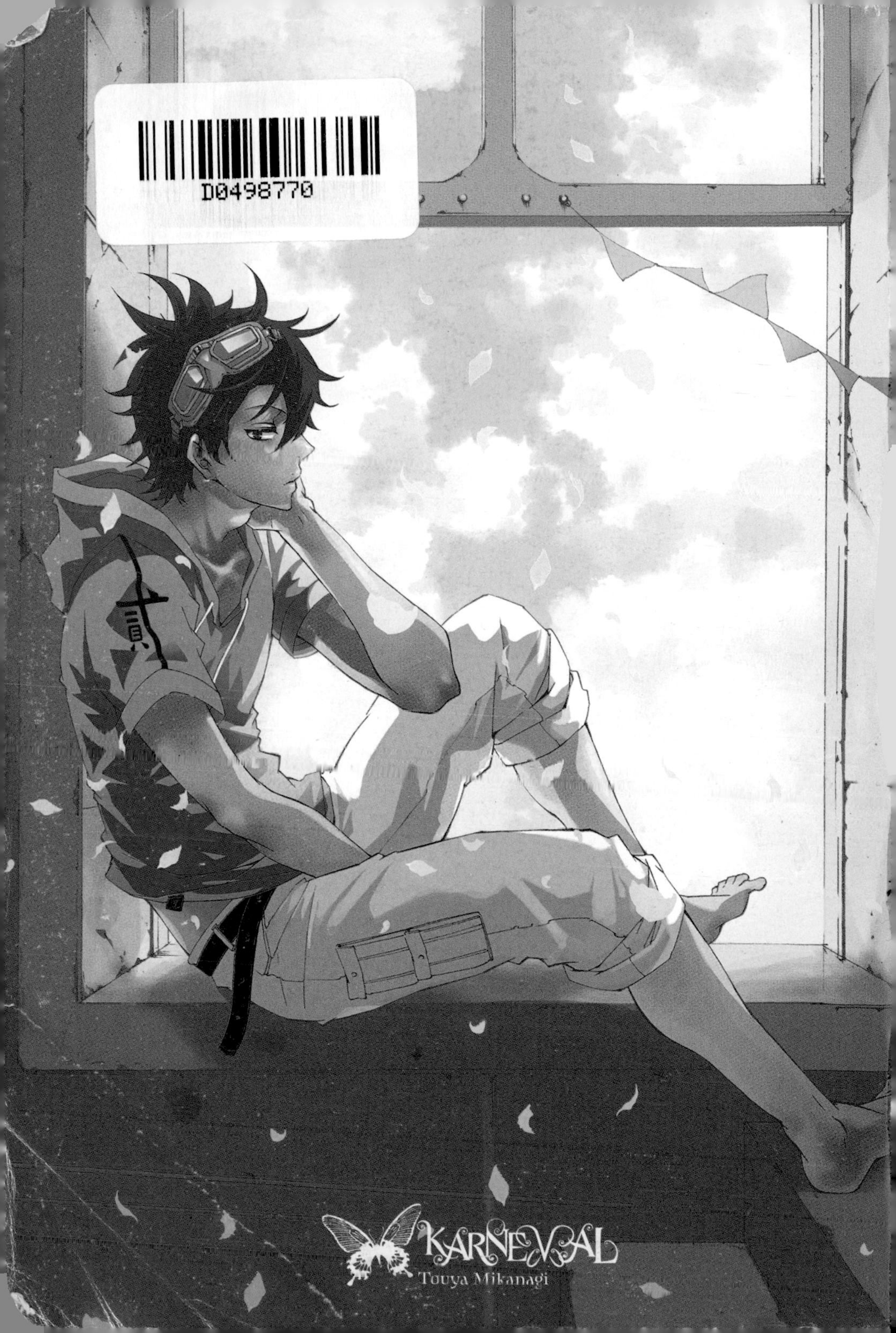
KARNEVAL
Touya Mikanagi

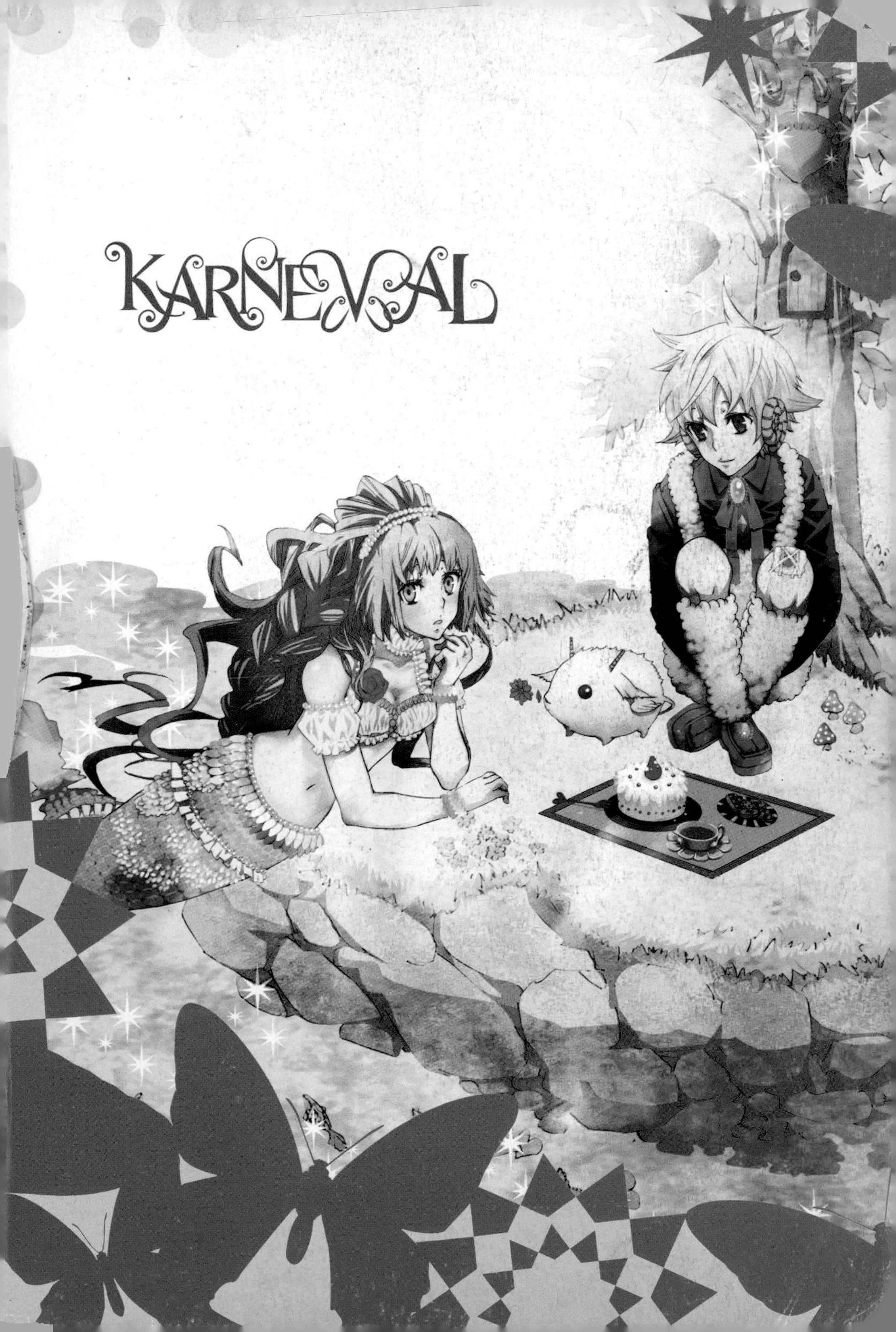
KARNEVAL

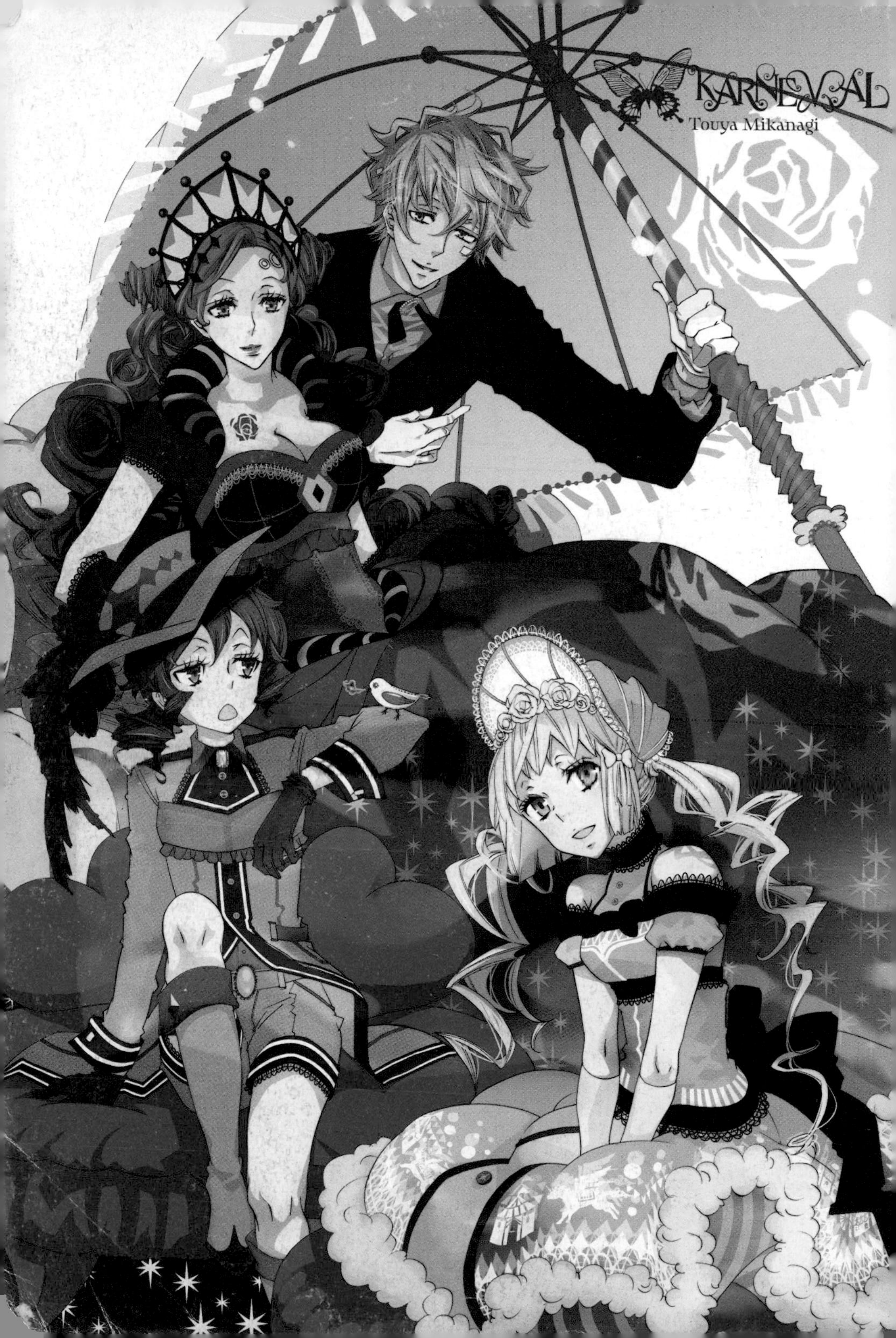
KARNEVAL
Touya Mikanagi

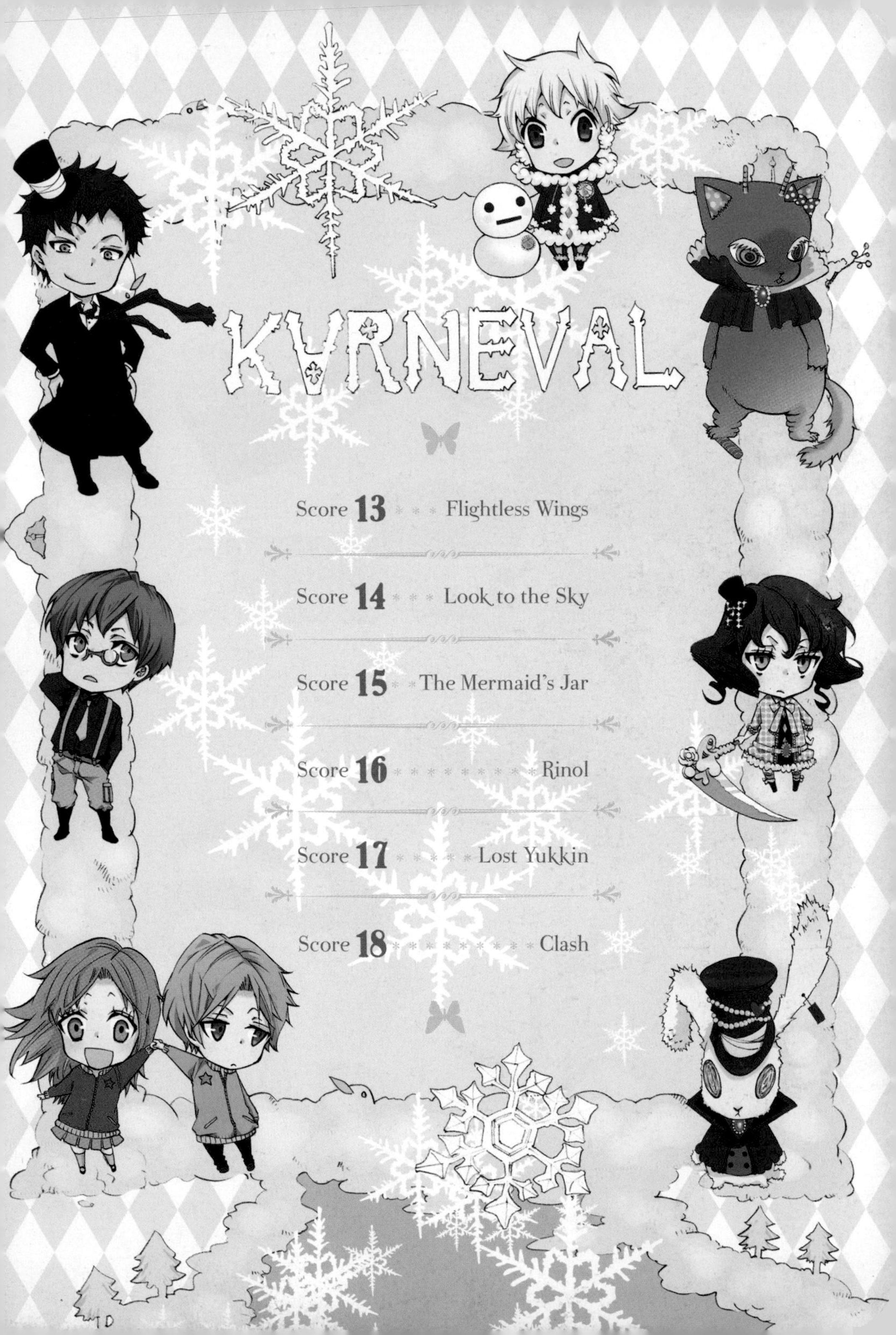

KARNEVAL

KARNEVAL

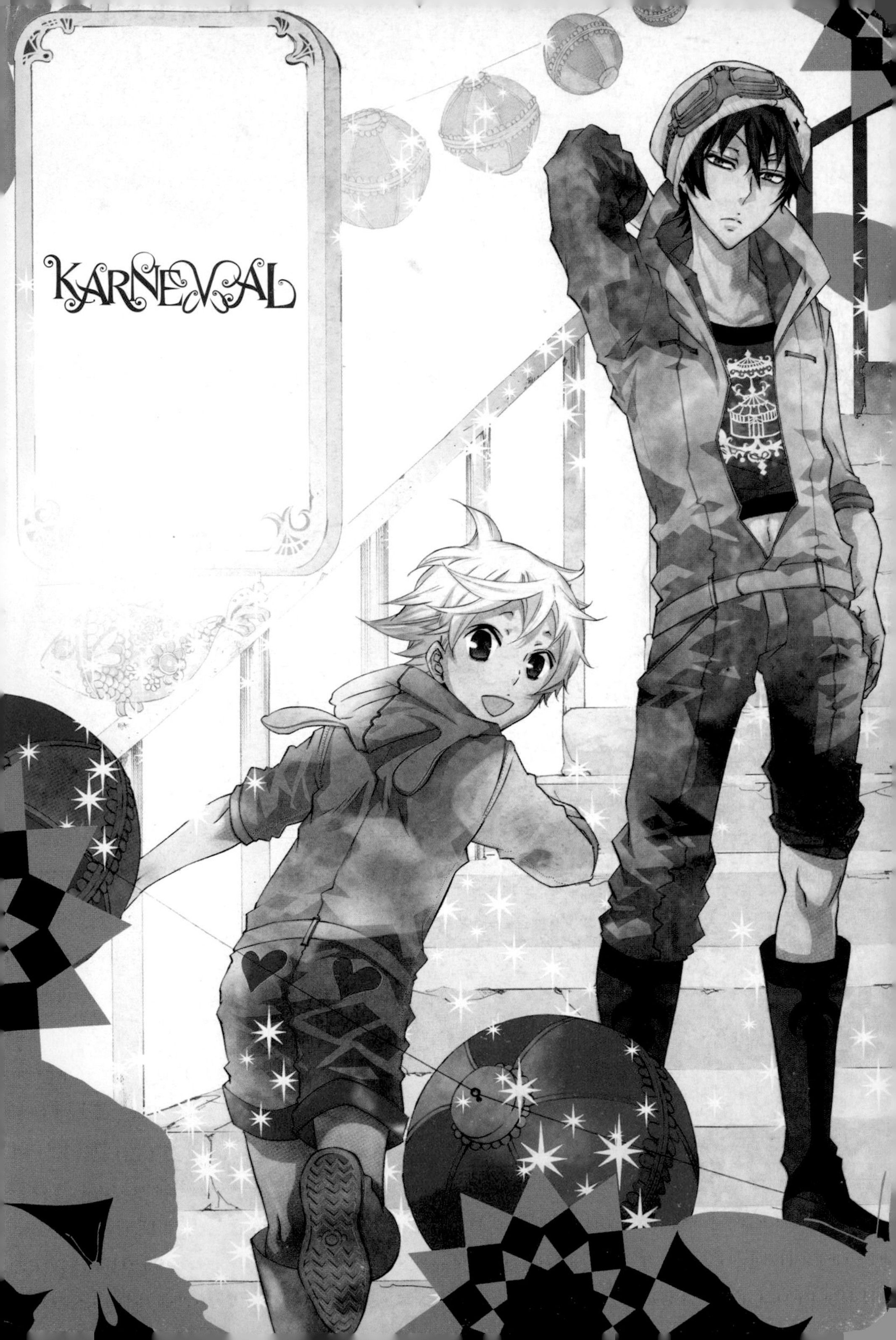
KARNEVAL

KARNEVAL 2

Touya Mikanagi

STORY.

NAI JOURNEYS IN SEARCH OF KAROKU ALONG WITH HIS RESCUER, GAREKI. AFTER SEVERAL TUMULTUOUS TWISTS AND TURNS, THEY NOW FIND THEMSELVES UNDER THE PROTECTION OF THE AGENTS OF CIRCUS'S 2ND SHIP, HUNTING FOR CLUES AS TO KAROKU'S WHEREABOUTS. AFTER HAVING HIS BODY EXAMINED BY CIRCUS, NAI LEARNS THAT HE IS NOT "HUMAN," BUT A SPECIAL LIFE FORM CREATED FROM AN ANIMAL CALLED A "NIJI." AS THE PERSON WHO "CREATED" NAI, KAROKU HAS NOW BECOME A PERSON OF INTEREST TO CIRCUS AS WELL, ALLOWING NAI AND GAREKI TO WIDEN THEIR SEARCH TO THE FOREST OF THE NIJIS ALONGSIDE RESEARCHERS FROM CIRCUS. AFTER COMPLETING THEIR EXCURSION, NAI AND YOGI ACCOMPANY GAREKI TO HIS HOMETOWN OF KARASUNA, WHERE THE THREE ENCOUNTER GAREKI'S CHILDHOOD FRIEND TSUBAME. HOWEVER, TSUBAME CONFESSES TO THEM THAT SHE HAS COMMITTED MURDER...

CHARACTERS OF KARNEVAL

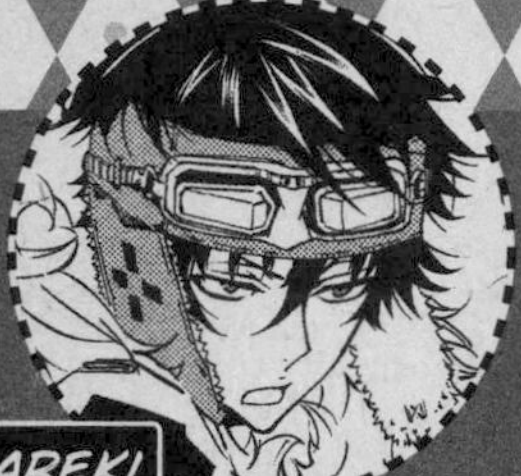

RESCUED →

← ATTACHED

GAREKI

HE MET NAI INSIDE AN EERIE MANSION THAT HE HAD INTENDED TO BURGLARIZE. INTRIGUED BY THE BRACELET NAI CARRIES, HE HAS JOINED FORCES WITH THE BOY.

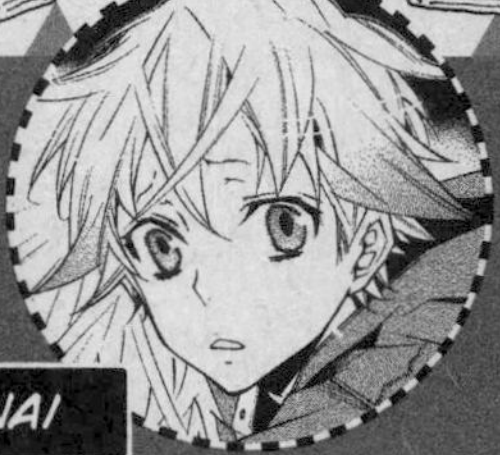

NAI

A BOY SEARCHING FOR "KAROKU" WITH A BRACELET AS HIS ONLY CLUE. THOUGH HIS ABILITY TO SURVIVE ON HIS OWN SEEMS VERY LOW, HE HAS AMAZINGLY SHARP HEARING.

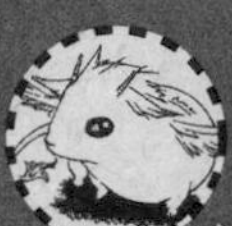

NIJI

THE ANIMAL FROM WHICH NAI WAS CREATED. THEY EXIST ONLY IN THE RAINBOW FOREST, A HIGHLY UNUSUAL ECOSYSTEM THAT ALLOWED THE NIJI TO EVOLVE AS THEY DID.

ON THE TRAIL OF

GUARDING

HIRATO

CAPTAIN OF CIRCUS'S 2ND SHIP. NAI (AND GAREKI), WHO BROUGHT THEM A BRACELET BELONGING TO CIRCUS, ARE CURRENTLY UNDER HIS PROTECTION.

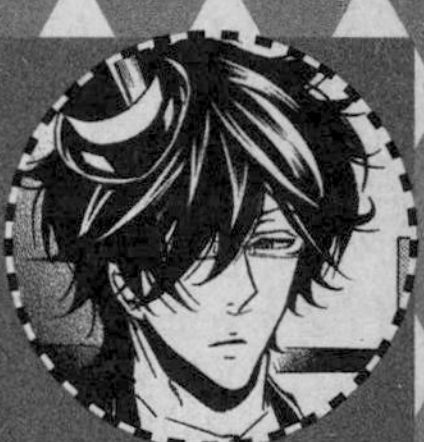

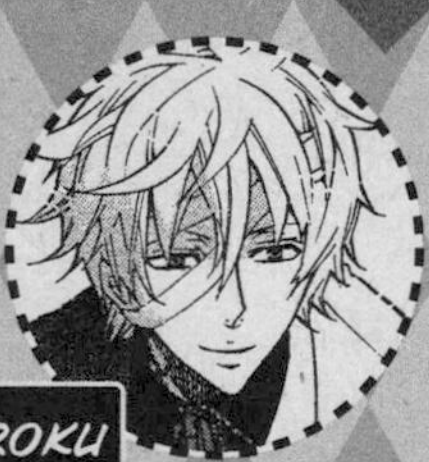

KAROKU

WENT MISSING, LEAVING BEHIND ONLY HIS BRACELET IN A POOL OF BLOOD BEFORE VANISHING. HE SEEMS TO BE ABLE TO CONTACT NAI TELEPATHICALLY...

← ? →

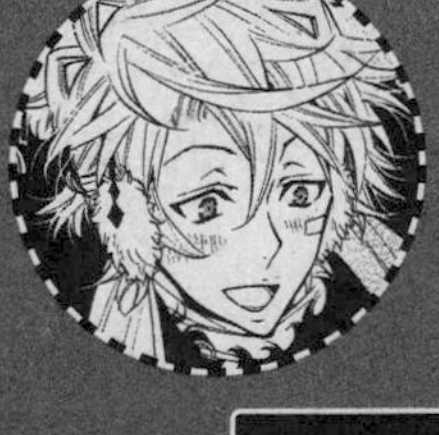

YOGI

CIRCUS'S 2ND SHIP COMBAT SPECIALIST. HE HAS A CHEERFUL, FRIENDLY PERSONALITY. FOR SHOWS, HE WEARS AN ANIMAL MASCOT SUIT.

TSUKUMO

CIRCUS'S 2ND SHIP COMBAT SPECIALIST. A BEAUTIFUL GIRL WITH A COOL, SERIOUS PERSONALITY. AS A SHOW PERFORMER, SHE IS VERY POPULAR DUE TO HER DAZZLING ACROBATICS AND BEAUTY.

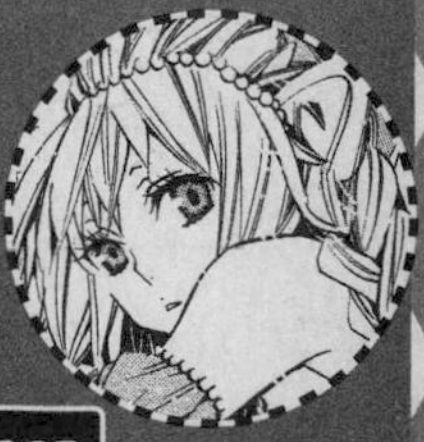

Q: WHAT IS CIRCUS?

A: THE EQUIVALENT OF THE REAL-WORLD POLICE. THEY CONDUCT THEIR LARGE-SCALE "OPERATIONS" WITHOUT FOREWARNING TO ENSURE THEIR TARGETS WILL NOT ESCAPE ARREST, UTILIZING COORDINATED POWERFUL ATTACKS!! AFTER AN OPERATION, CIRCUS PERFORMS A "SHOW" FOR THE PEOPLE OF THE CITY AS AN APOLOGY FOR THE FEAR AND INCONVENIENCE THEIR WORK MAY HAVE CAUSED. IN SHORT, "CIRCUS" IS A CHEERFUL (?) AGENCY THAT CARRIES OUT THEIR MISSION DAY AND NIGHT TO APPREHEND EVIL AND PROTECT THE PEACE OF THE LAND.

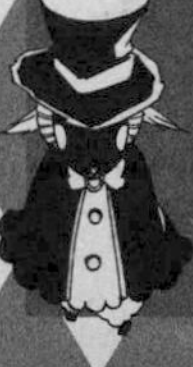

SHEEP

A CIRCUS DEFENSE SYSTEM. DESPITE THEIR CUTE APPEARANCE, THE SHEEP HAVE SOME VERY POWERFUL CAPABILITIES.

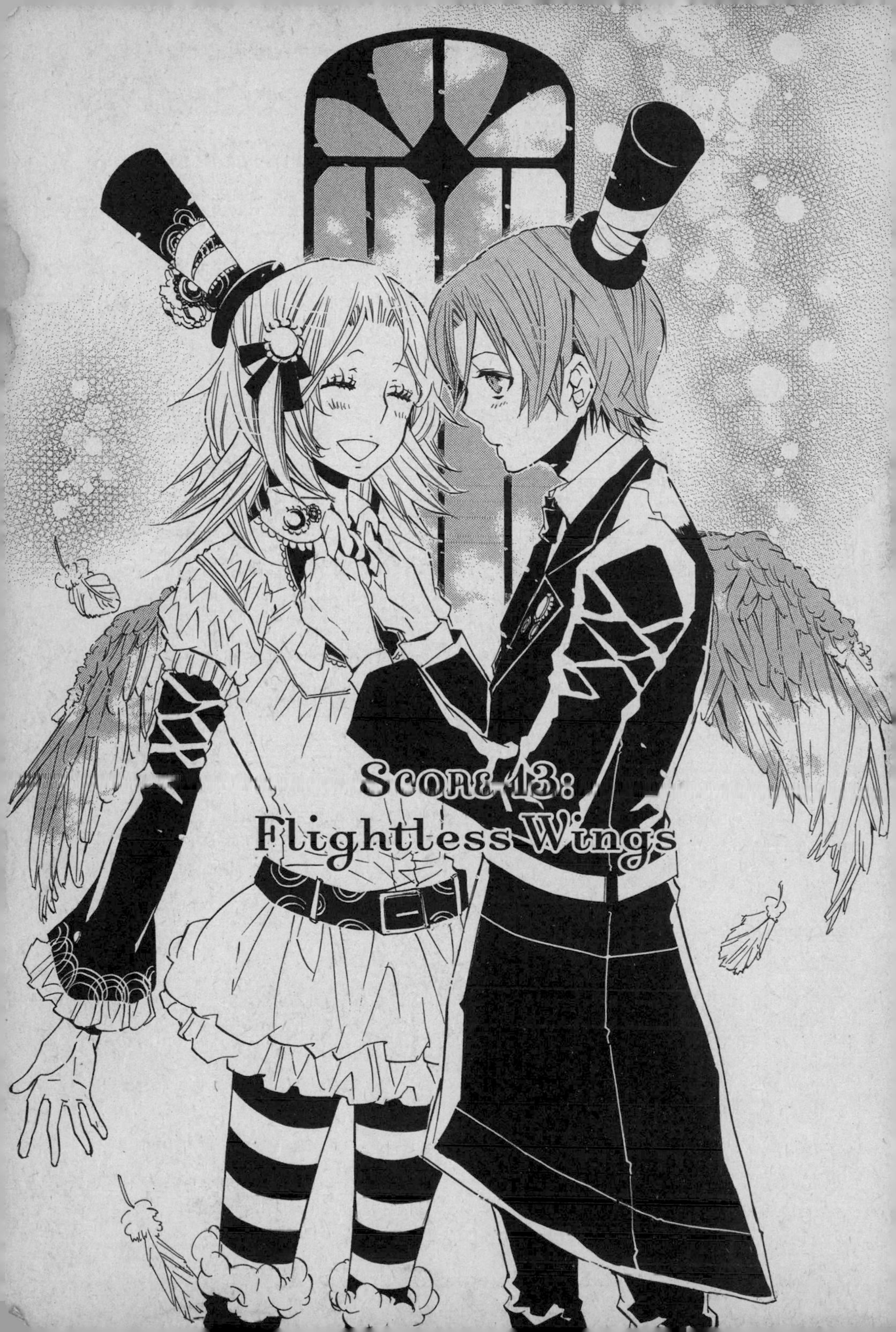
Score 13:
Flightless Wings

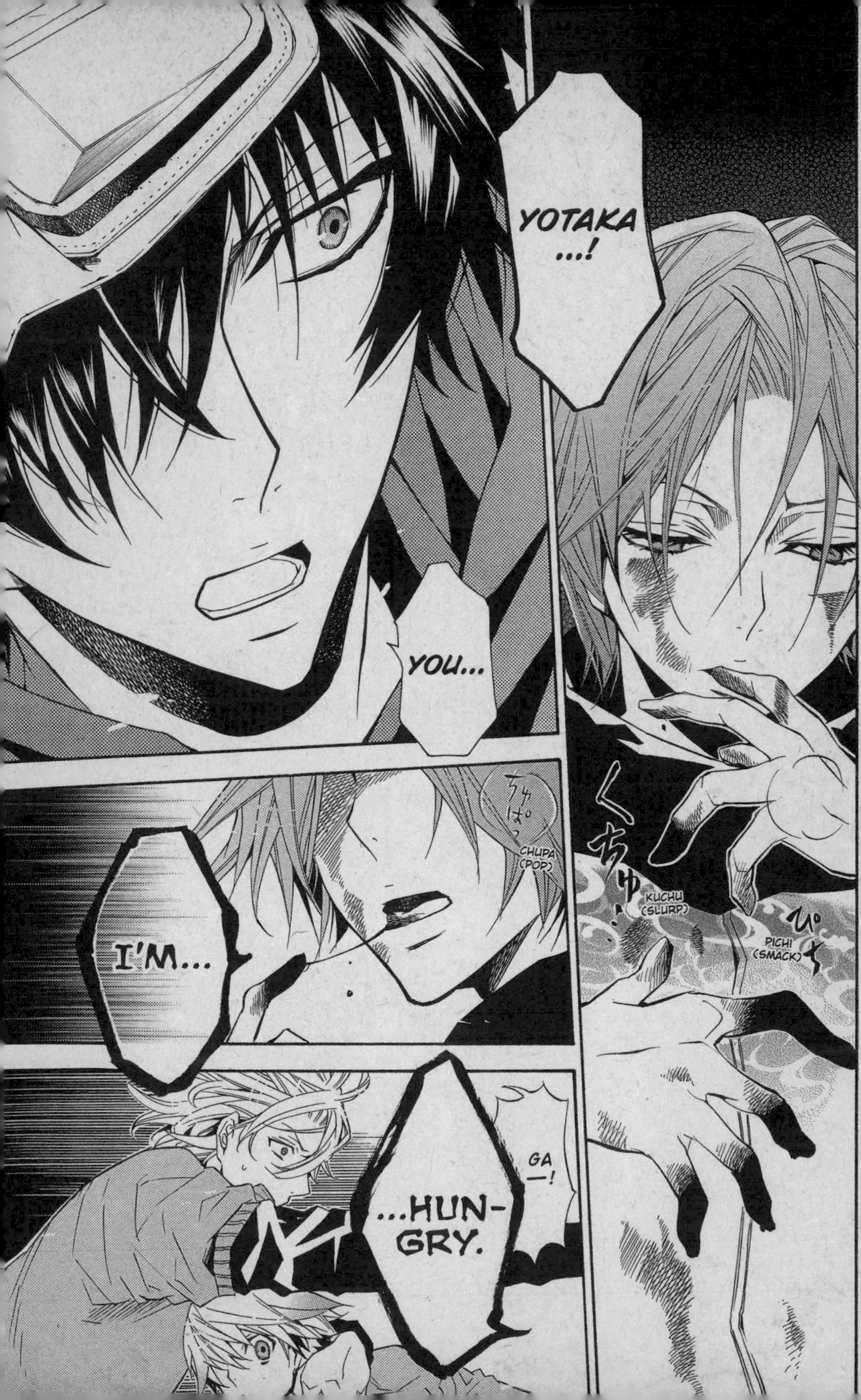

YOTAKA ...!
YOU...
くちゅ
KUCHU (SLURP)
ぴち
PICHI (SMACK)
ちゅぱっ
CHUPA (POP)
I'M...
GA—!
...HUN-GRY.

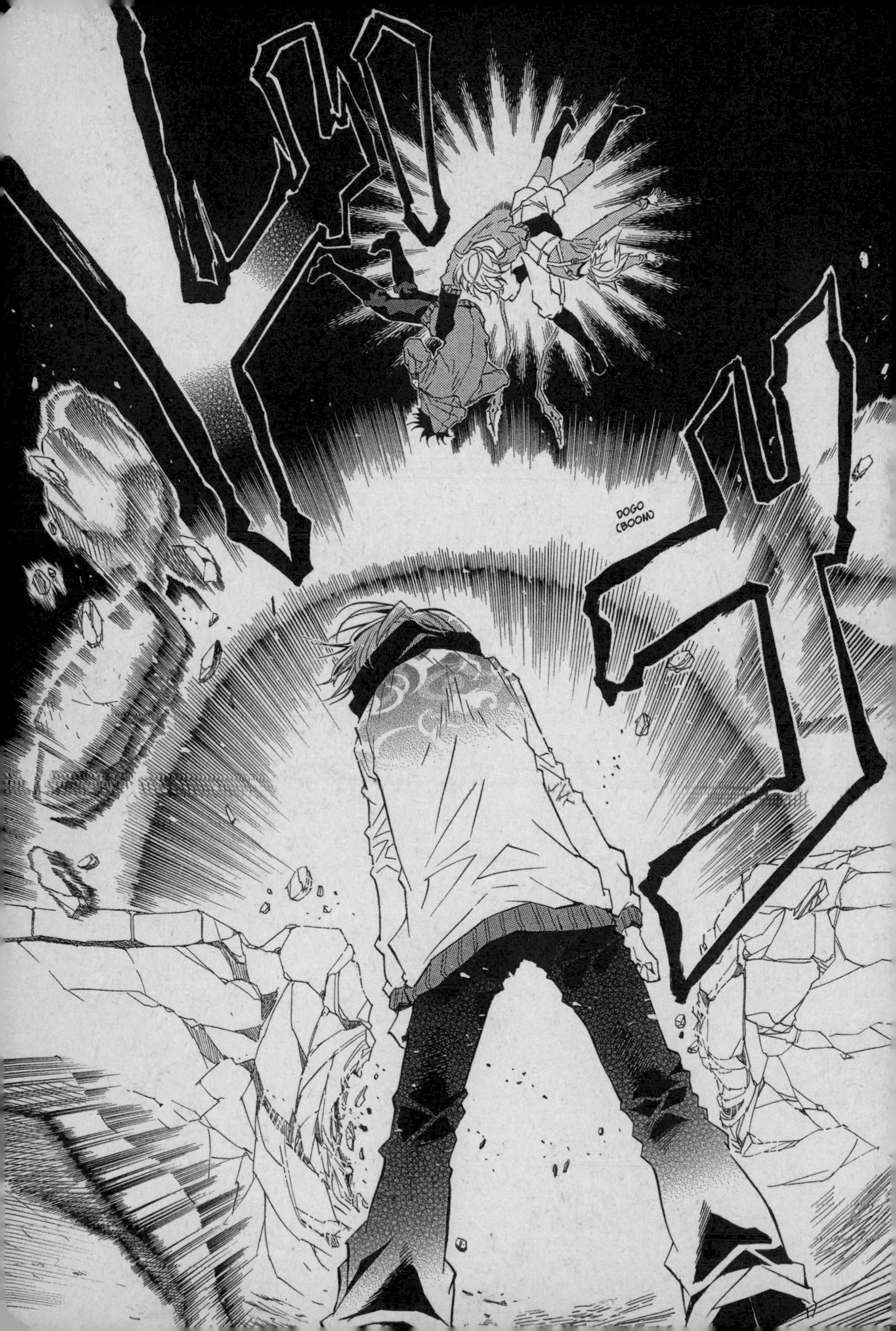
DOGO (BOOM)

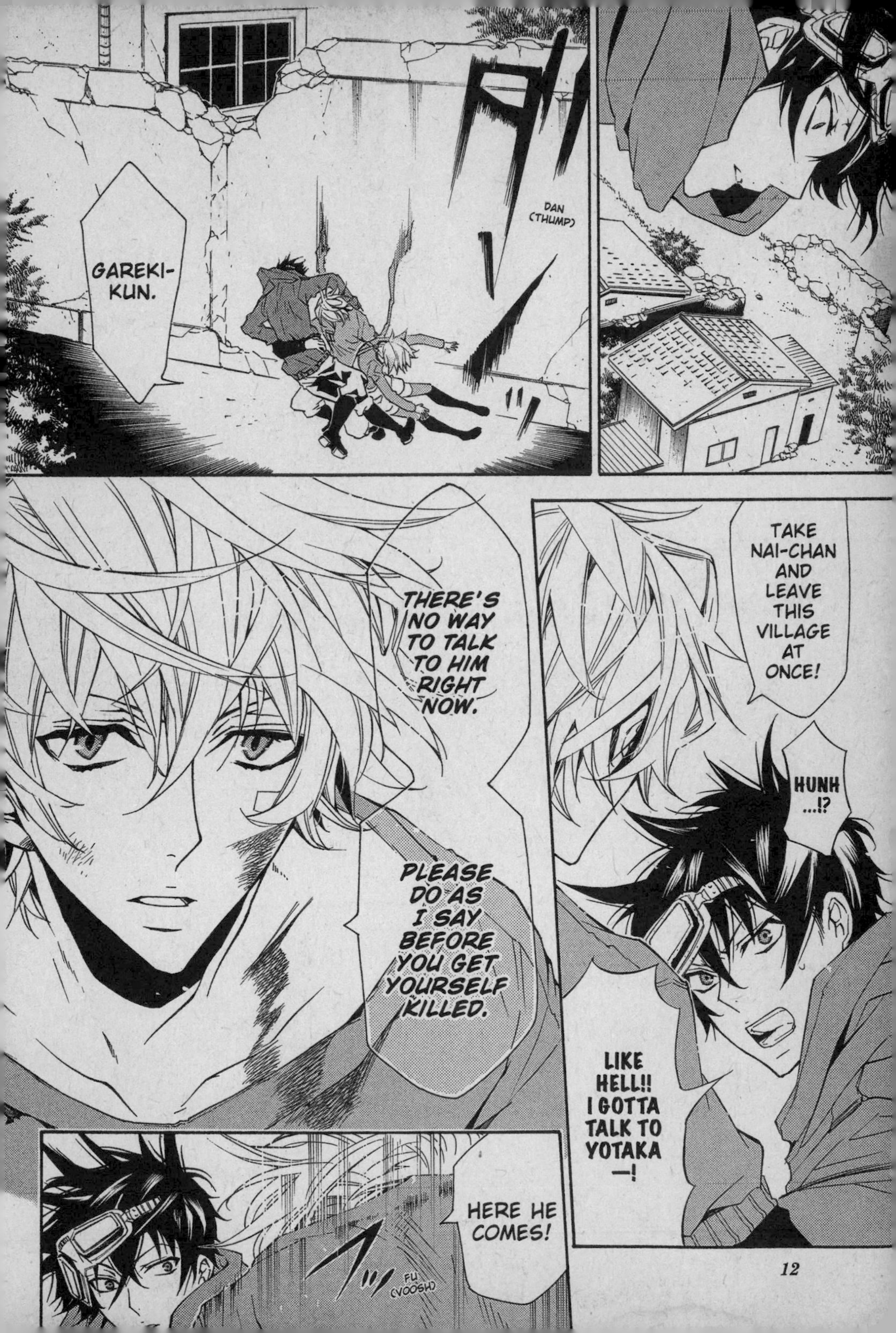
DAN (THUMP)
GAREKI-KUN.
TAKE NAI-CHAN AND LEAVE THIS VILLAGE AT ONCE!
HUNH ...!?
LIKE HELL!! I GOTTA TALK TO YOTAKA —!
THERE'S NO WAY TO TALK TO HIM RIGHT NOW.
PLEASE DO AS I SAY BEFORE YOU GET YOURSELF KILLED.
HERE HE COMES!
FU (VOOSH)

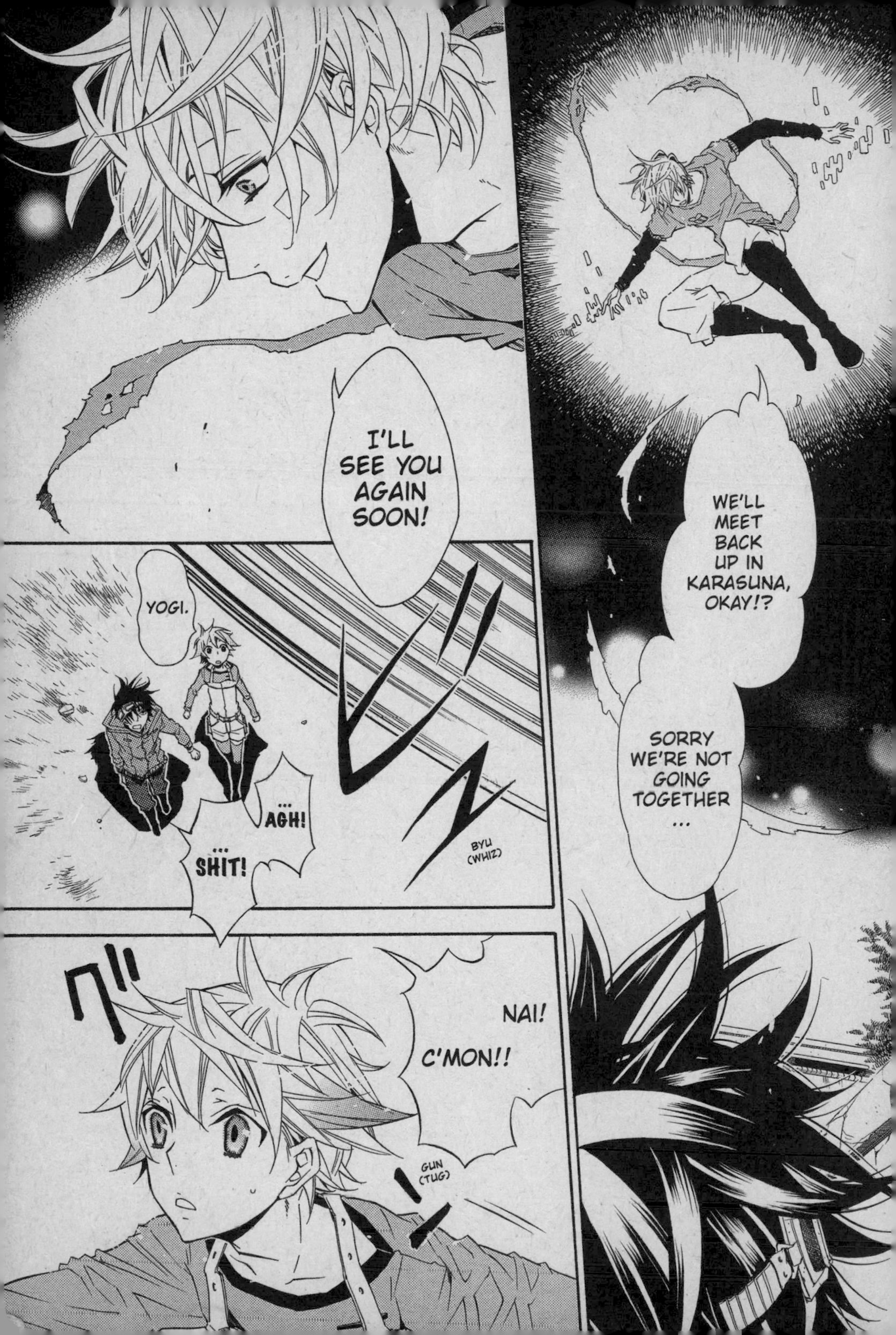
WE'LL MEET BACK UP IN KARASUNA, OKAY!?
SORRY WE'RE NOT GOING TOGETHER ...
I'LL SEE YOU AGAIN SOON!
YOGI.
... AGH!
... SHIT!
BYU (WHIZ)
NAI!
C'MON!!
GUN (TUG)

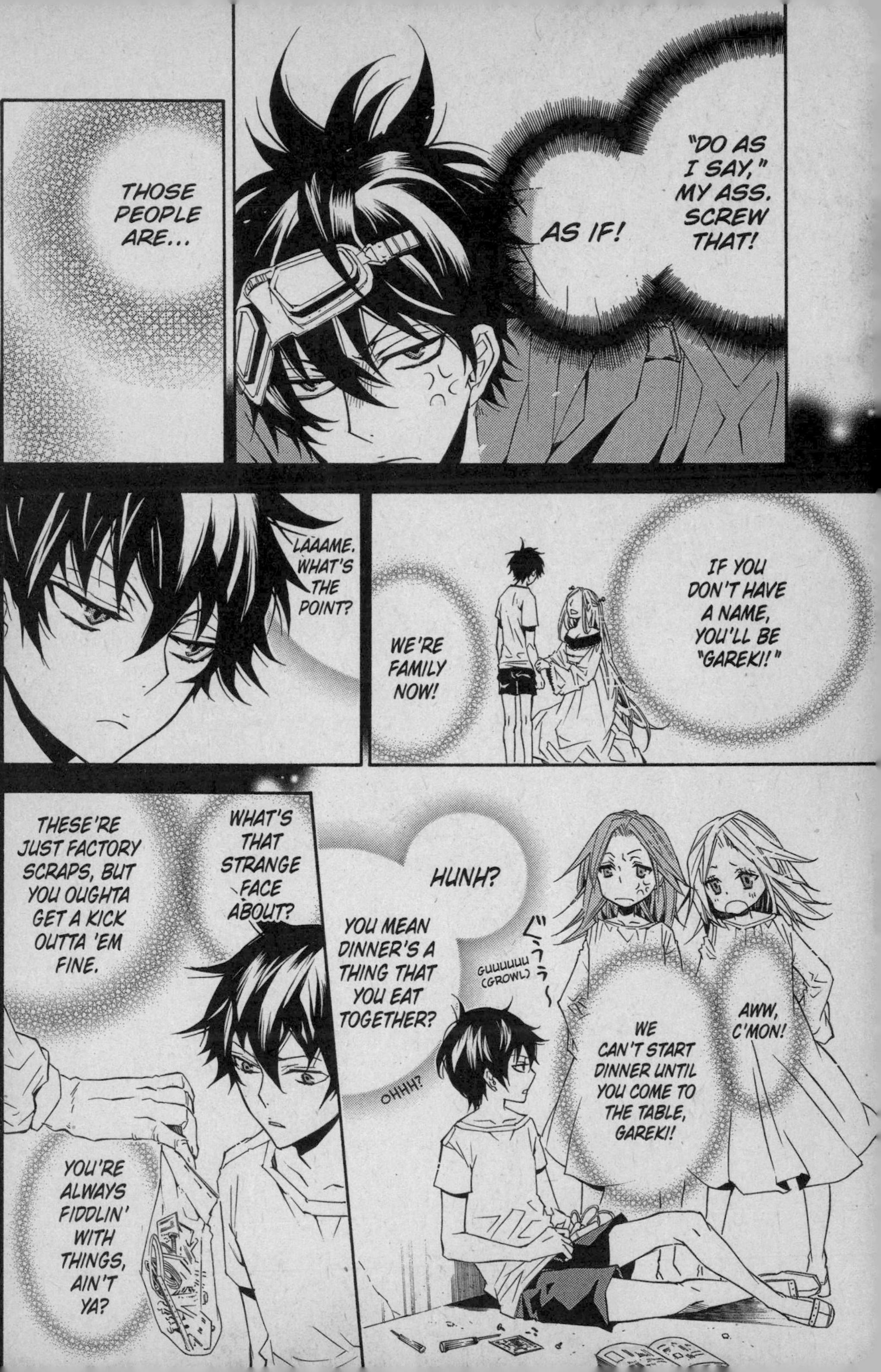
"DO AS I SAY," MY ASS. SCREW THAT!
AS IF!
THOSE PEOPLE ARE...
IF YOU DON'T HAVE A NAME, YOU'LL BE "GAREKI!"
WE'RE FAMILY NOW!
LAAAME. WHAT'S THE POINT?
AWW, C'MON!
WE CAN'T START DINNER UNTIL YOU COME TO THE TABLE, GAREKI!
GUUUUUU (GROWL)
HUNH?
YOU MEAN DINNER'S A THING THAT YOU EAT TOGETHER?
OHHH?
WHAT'S THAT STRANGE FACE ABOUT?
THESE'RE JUST FACTORY SCRAPS, BUT YOU OUGHTA GET A KICK OUTTA 'EM FINE.
YOU'RE ALWAYS FIDDLIN' WITH THINGS, AIN'T YA?

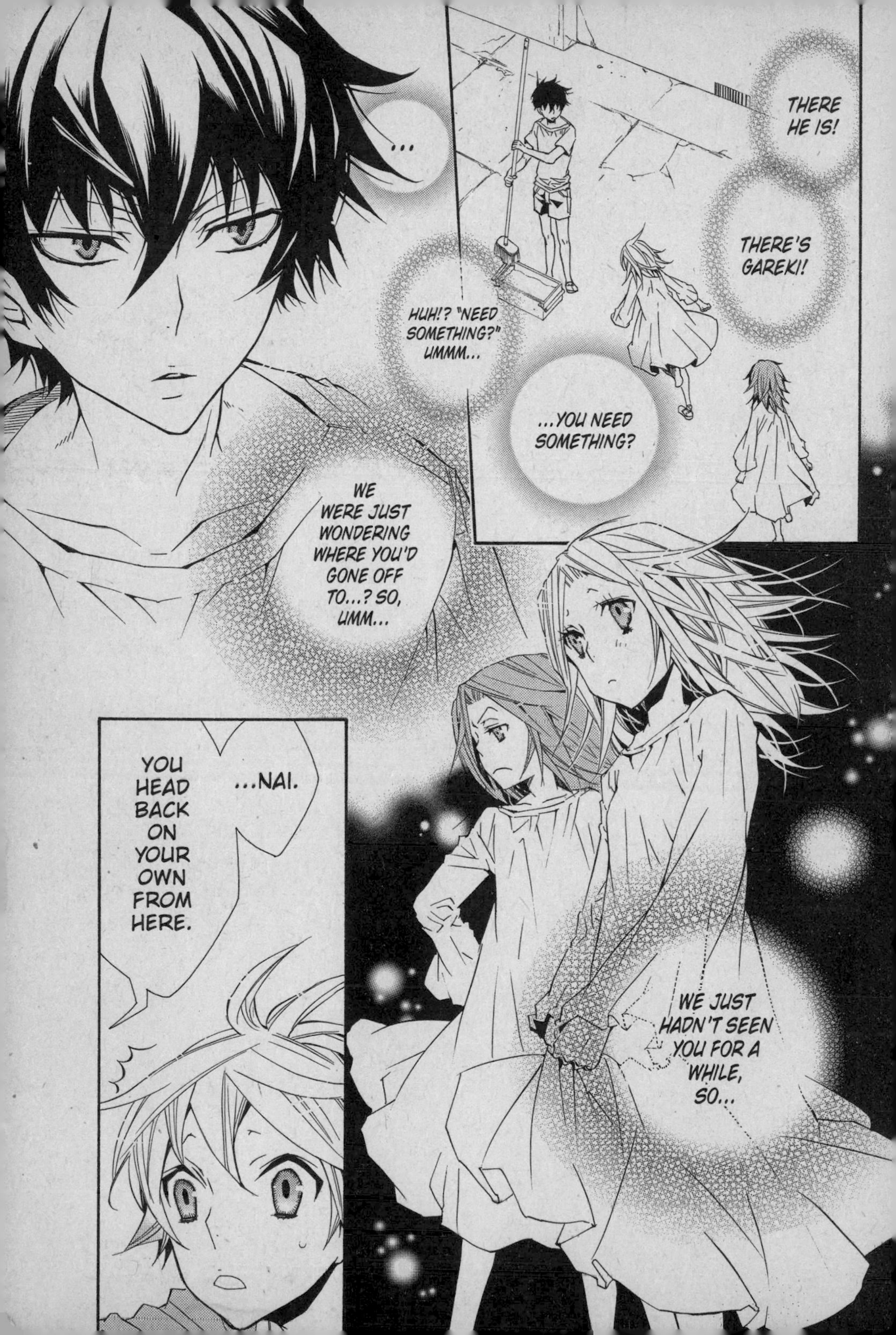
THERE HE IS!
THERE'S GAREKI!
...YOU NEED SOMETHING?
HUH!? "NEED SOMETHING?" UMMM...
...
WE WERE JUST WONDERING WHERE YOU'D GONE OFF TO...? SO, UMM...
WE JUST HADN'T SEEN YOU FOR A WHILE, SO...
...NAI.
YOU HEAD BACK ON YOUR OWN FROM HERE.

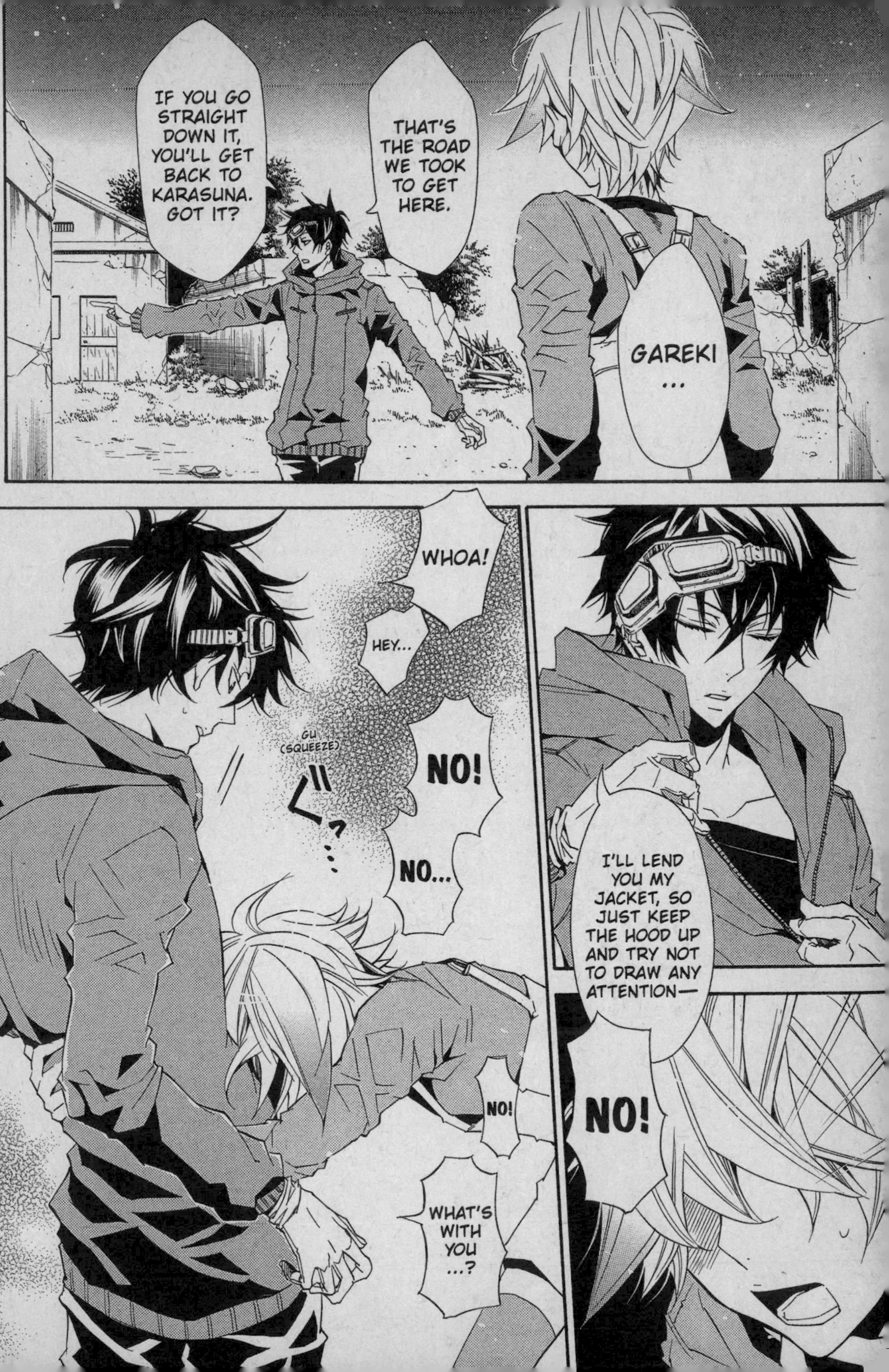
GAREKI ...
THAT'S THE ROAD WE TOOK TO GET HERE.
IF YOU GO STRAIGHT DOWN IT, YOU'LL GET BACK TO KARASUNA. GOT IT?
I'LL LEND YOU MY JACKET, SO JUST KEEP THE HOOD UP AND TRY NOT TO DRAW ANY ATTENTION—
NO!
WHOA!
HEY...
GU (SQUEEZE)
NO!
NO...
NO!
WHAT'S WITH YOU ...?

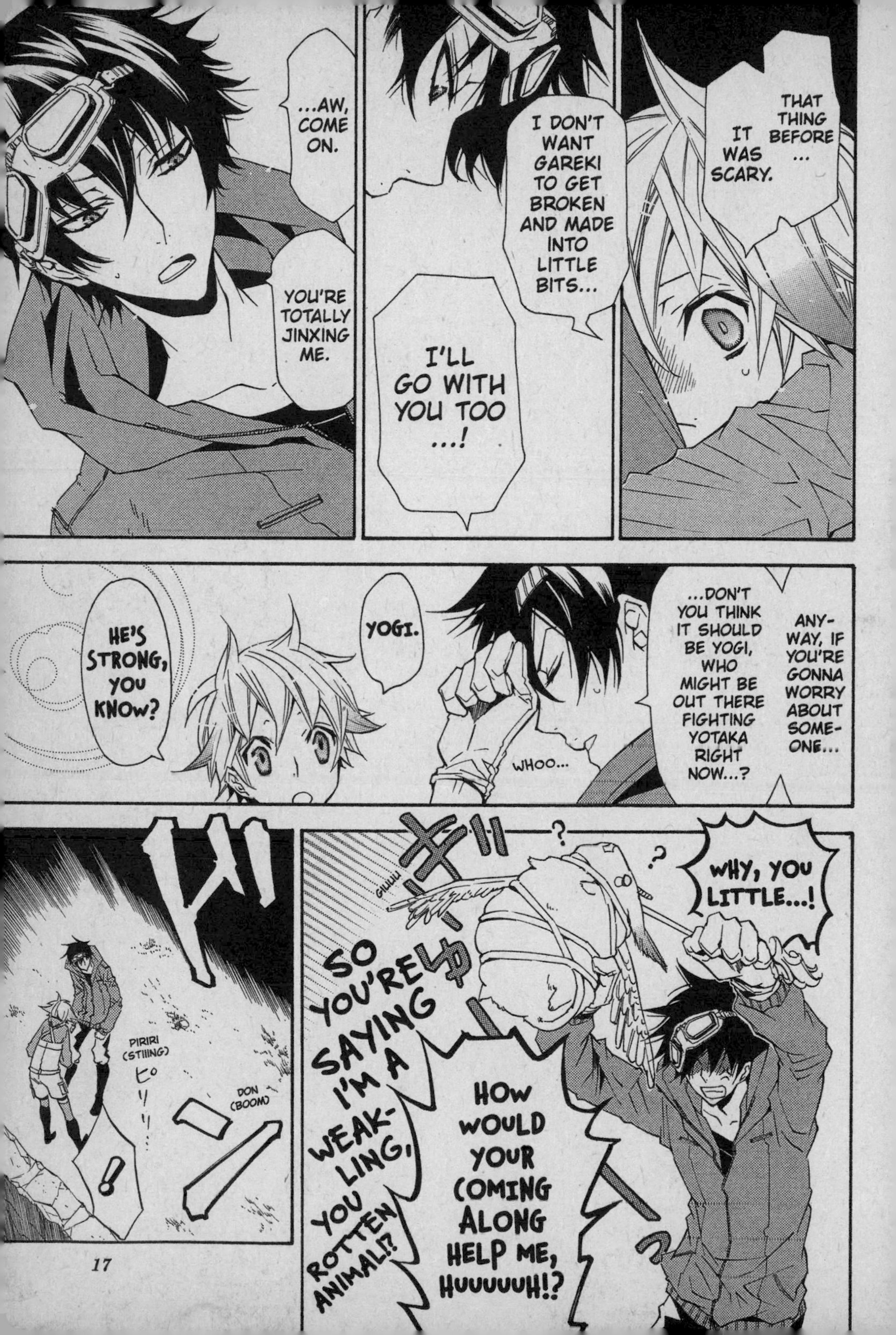
THAT THING BEFORE...
IT WAS SCARY.
I DON'T WANT GAREKI TO GET BROKEN AND MADE INTO LITTLE BITS...
I'LL GO WITH YOU TOO...!
...AW, COME ON.
YOU'RE TOTALLY JINXING ME.
ANY-WAY, IF YOU'RE GONNA WORRY ABOUT SOME-ONE...
...DON'T YOU THINK IT SHOULD BE YOGI, WHO MIGHT BE OUT THERE FIGHTING YOTAKA RIGHT NOW...?
WHOO...
YOGI.
HE'S STRONG, YOU KNOW?
WHY, YOU LITTLE...!
?
?
GIUUU
HOW WOULD YOUR COMING ALONG HELP ME, HUUUUUH!?
SO YOU'RE SAYING I'M A WEAK-LING, YOU ROTTEN ANIMAL!?
PIRIRI (STIIING)
DON (BOOM)
!

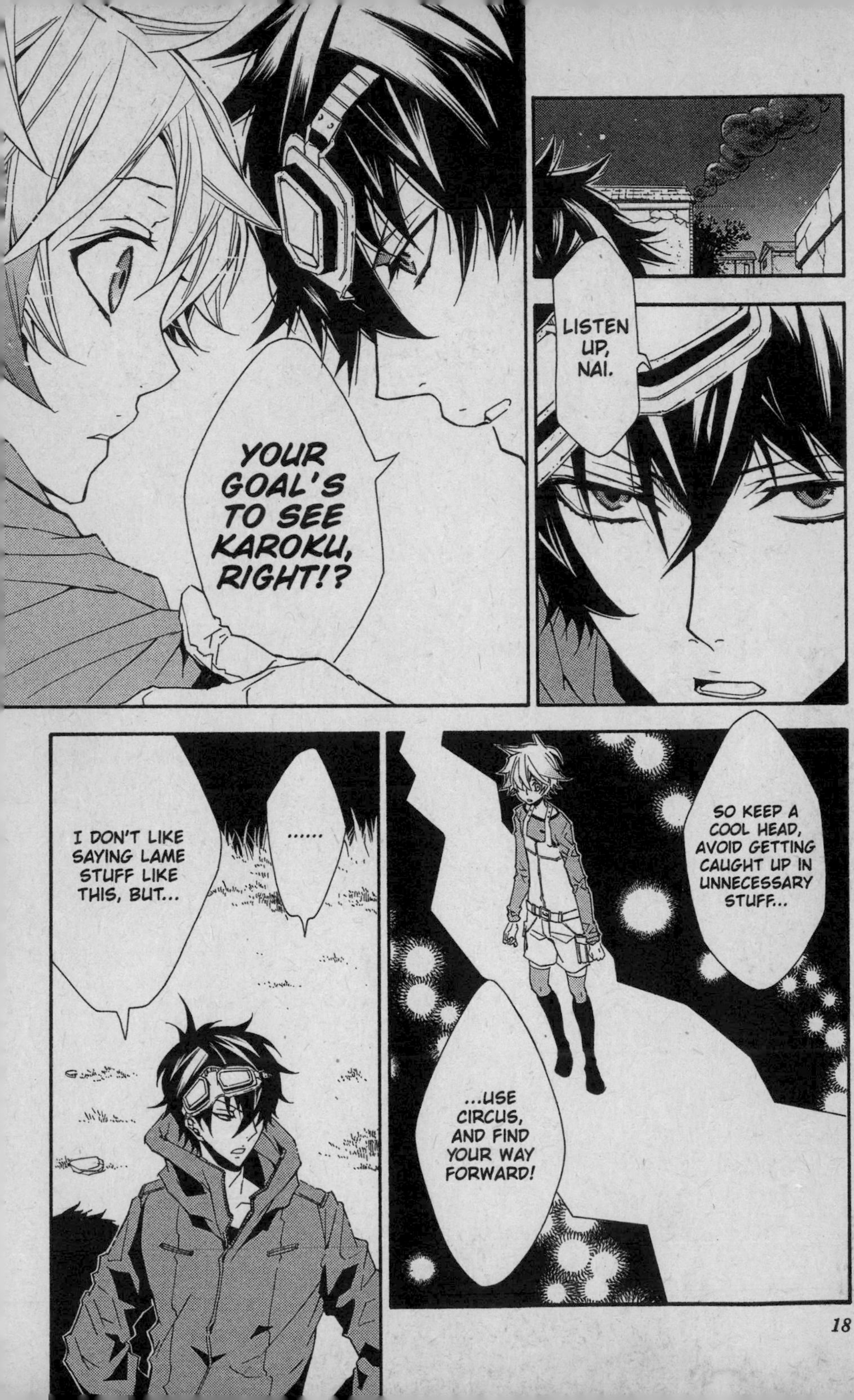
LISTEN UP, NAI.
YOUR GOAL'S TO SEE KAROKU, RIGHT!?
SO KEEP A COOL HEAD, AVOID GETTING CAUGHT UP IN UNNECESSARY STUFF...
...USE CIRCUS, AND FIND YOUR WAY FORWARD!
......
I DON'T LIKE SAYING LAME STUFF LIKE THIS, BUT...

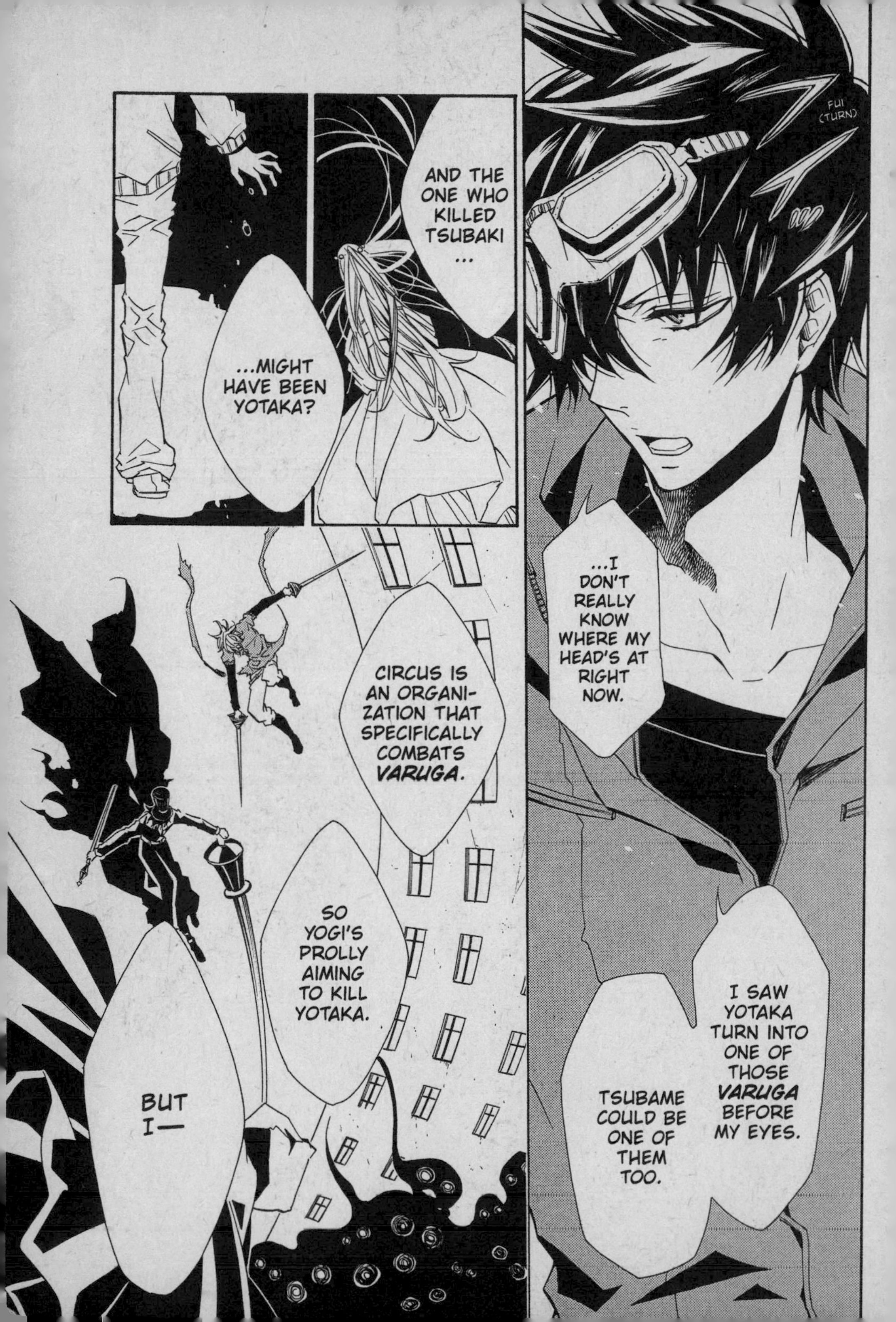
FUI (TURN)
...I DON'T REALLY KNOW WHERE MY HEAD'S AT RIGHT NOW.
I SAW YOTAKA TURN INTO ONE OF THOSE *VARUGA* BEFORE MY EYES.
TSUBAME COULD BE ONE OF THEM TOO.
AND THE ONE WHO KILLED TSUBAKI ...
...MIGHT HAVE BEEN YOTAKA?
CIRCUS IS AN ORGANIZATION THAT SPECIFICALLY COMBATS *VARUGA*.
SO YOGI'S PROLLY AIMING TO KILL YOTAKA.
BUT I—

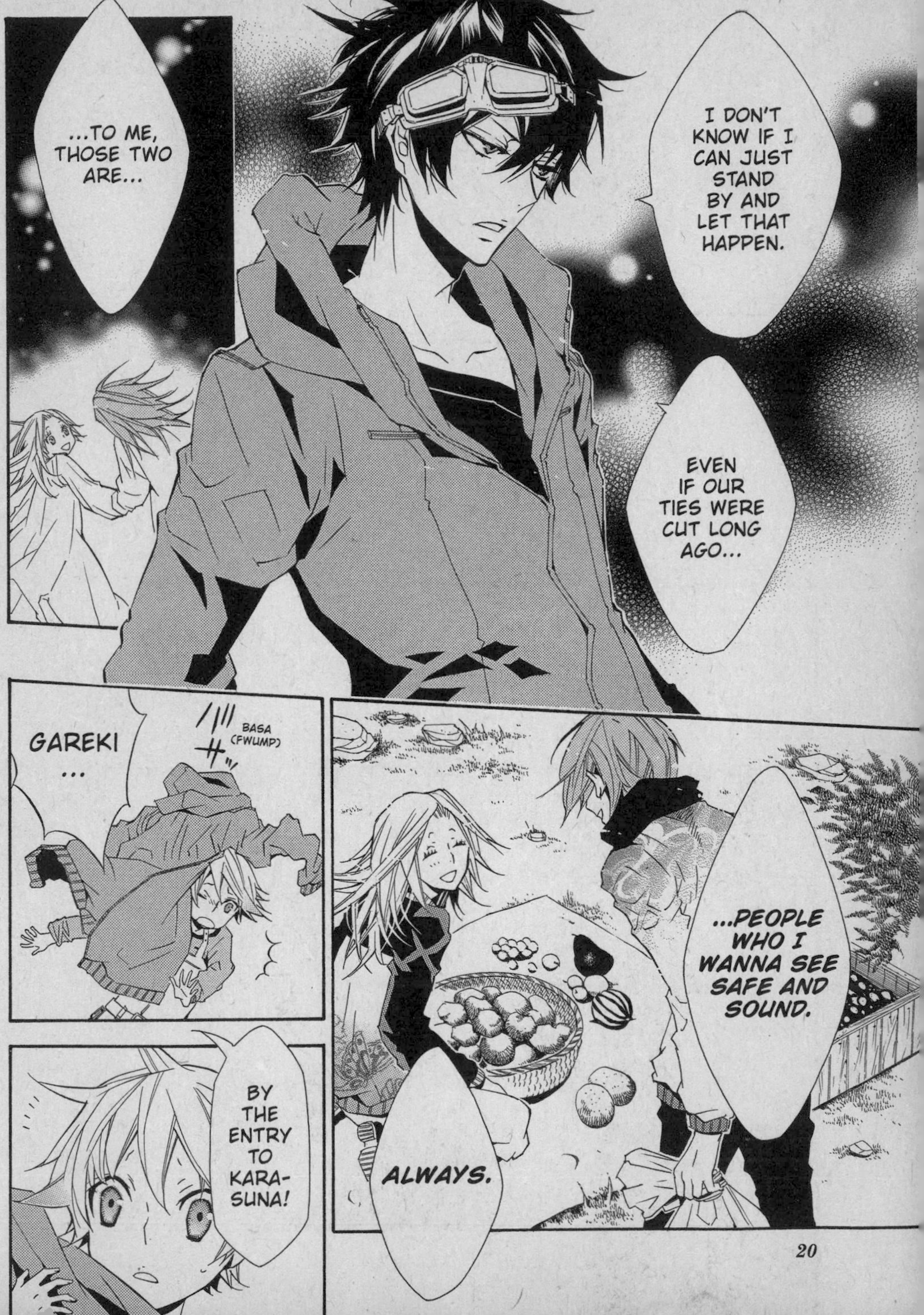
I DON'T KNOW IF I CAN JUST STAND BY AND LET THAT HAPPEN.
EVEN IF OUR TIES WERE CUT LONG AGO...
...TO ME, THOSE TWO ARE...
...PEOPLE WHO I WANNA SEE SAFE AND SOUND.
ALWAYS.
GAREKI ...
BASA (FWUMP)
BY THE ENTRY TO KARA-SUNA!

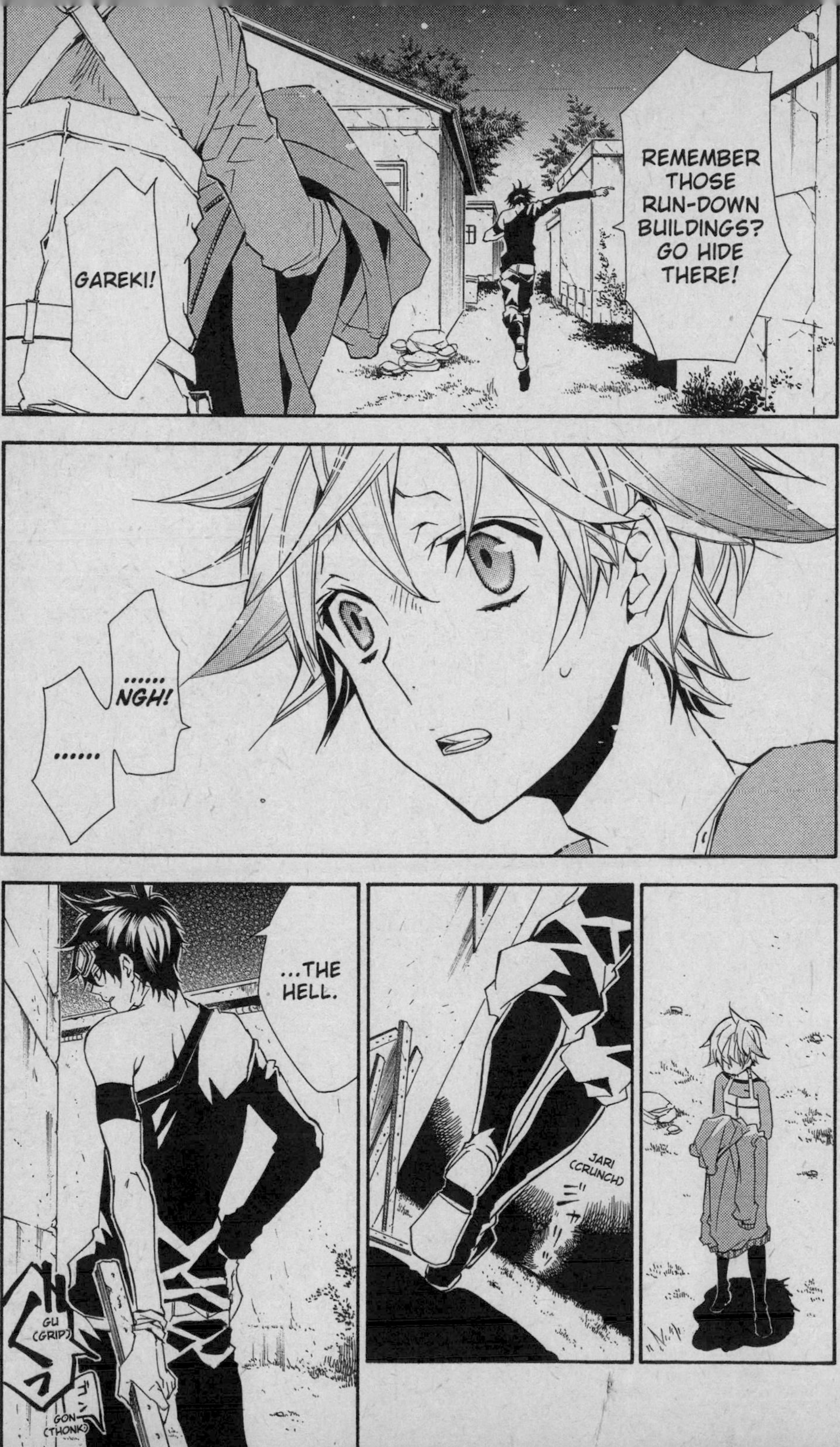
REMEMBER THOSE RUN-DOWN BUILDINGS? GO HIDE THERE!
GAREKI!
...... NGH!
......
JARI (CRUNCH)
...THE HELL.
GU (GRIP)
GON (THONK)

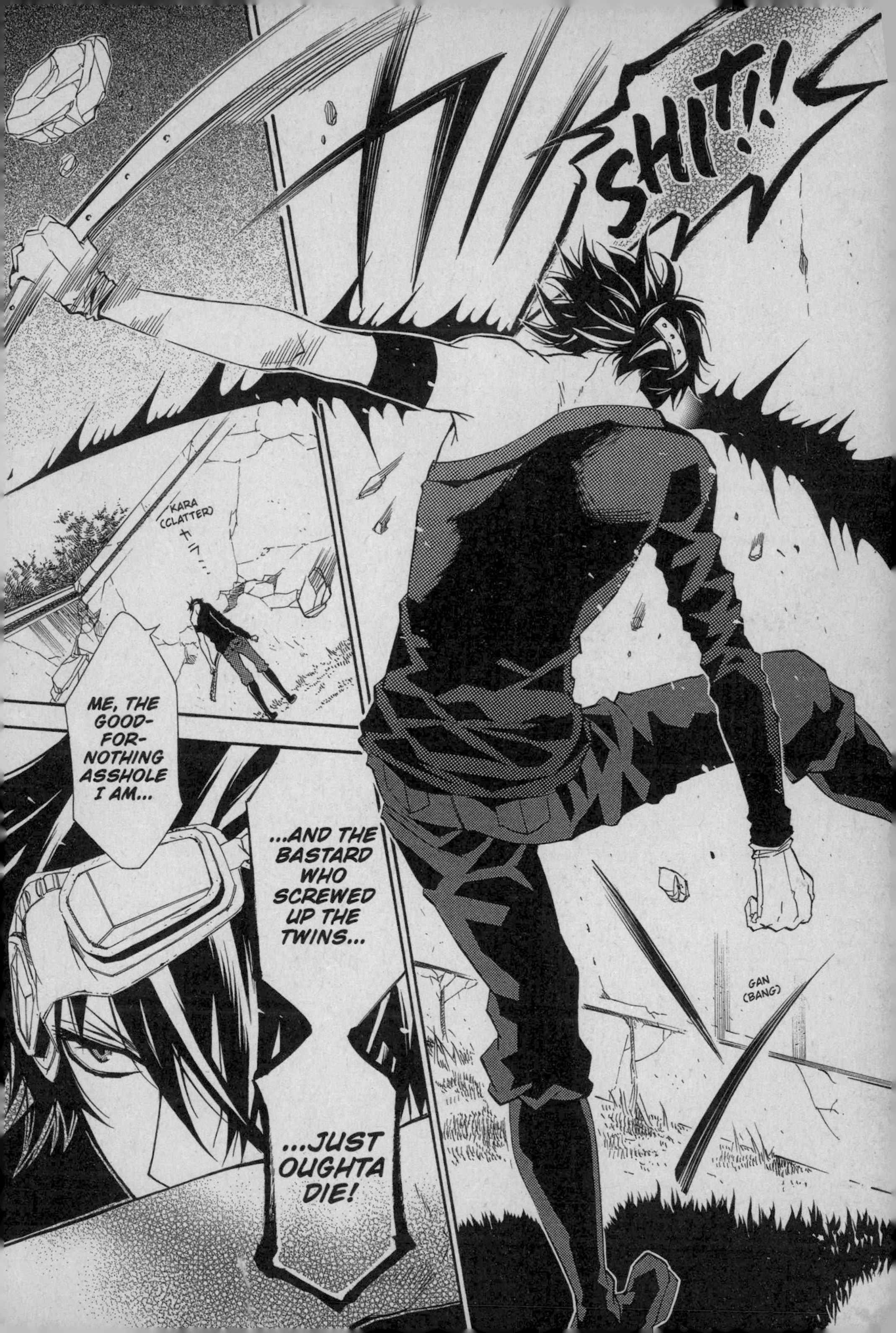
SHIT!!
GAN (BANG)
KARA (CLATTER)
ME, THE GOOD-FOR-NOTHING ASSHOLE I AM...
...AND THE BASTARD WHO SCREWED UP THE TWINS...
...JUST OUGHTA DIE!

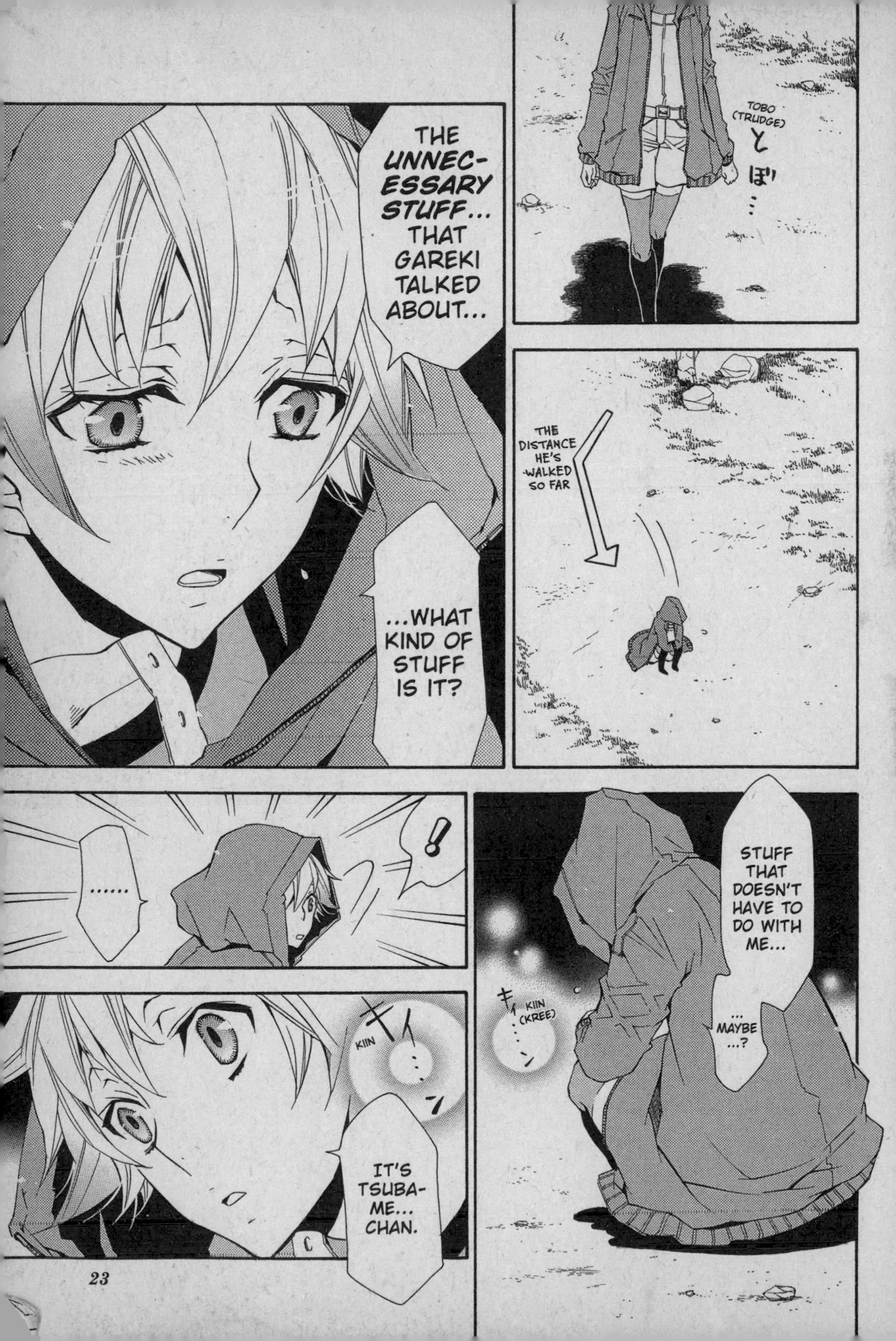

TOBO (TRUDGE)
とぼ…
THE DISTANCE HE'S WALKED SO FAR
THE UNNECESSARY STUFF... THAT GAREKI TALKED ABOUT...
...WHAT KIND OF STUFF IS IT?
STUFF THAT DOESN'T HAVE TO DO WITH ME...
...MAYBE...?
キィ…ン
KIIN (KREE)
!
......
キィ…ン
KIIN
IT'S TSUBAME... CHAN.

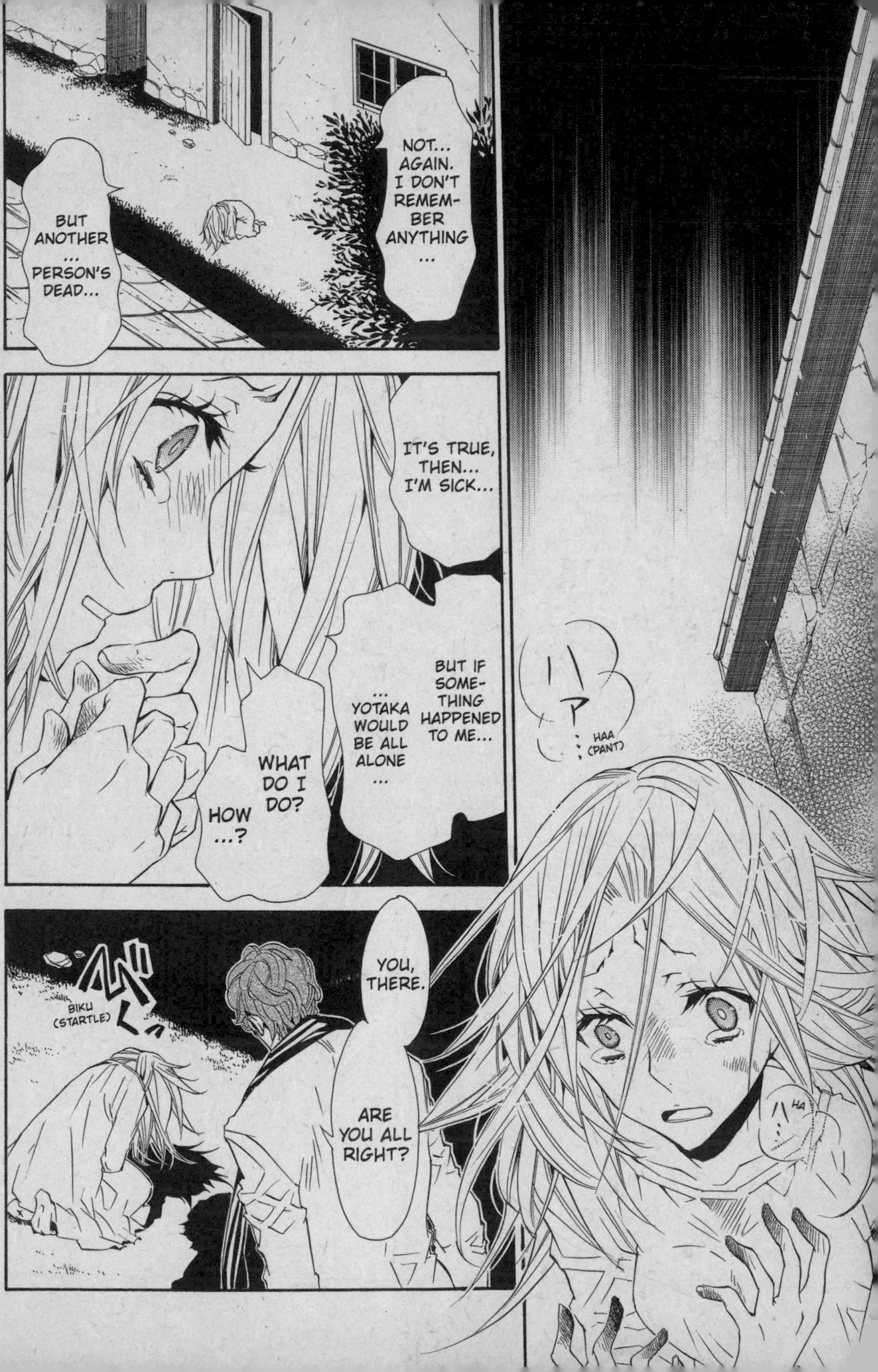
HAA (PANT)
HA
NOT... AGAIN. I DON'T REMEMBER ANYTHING...
BUT ANOTHER... PERSON'S DEAD...
IT'S TRUE, THEN... I'M SICK...
BUT IF SOMETHING HAPPENED TO ME...
...YOTAKA WOULD BE ALL ALONE...
WHAT DO I DO?
HOW...?
BIKU (STARTLE)
YOU, THERE.
ARE YOU ALL RIGHT?

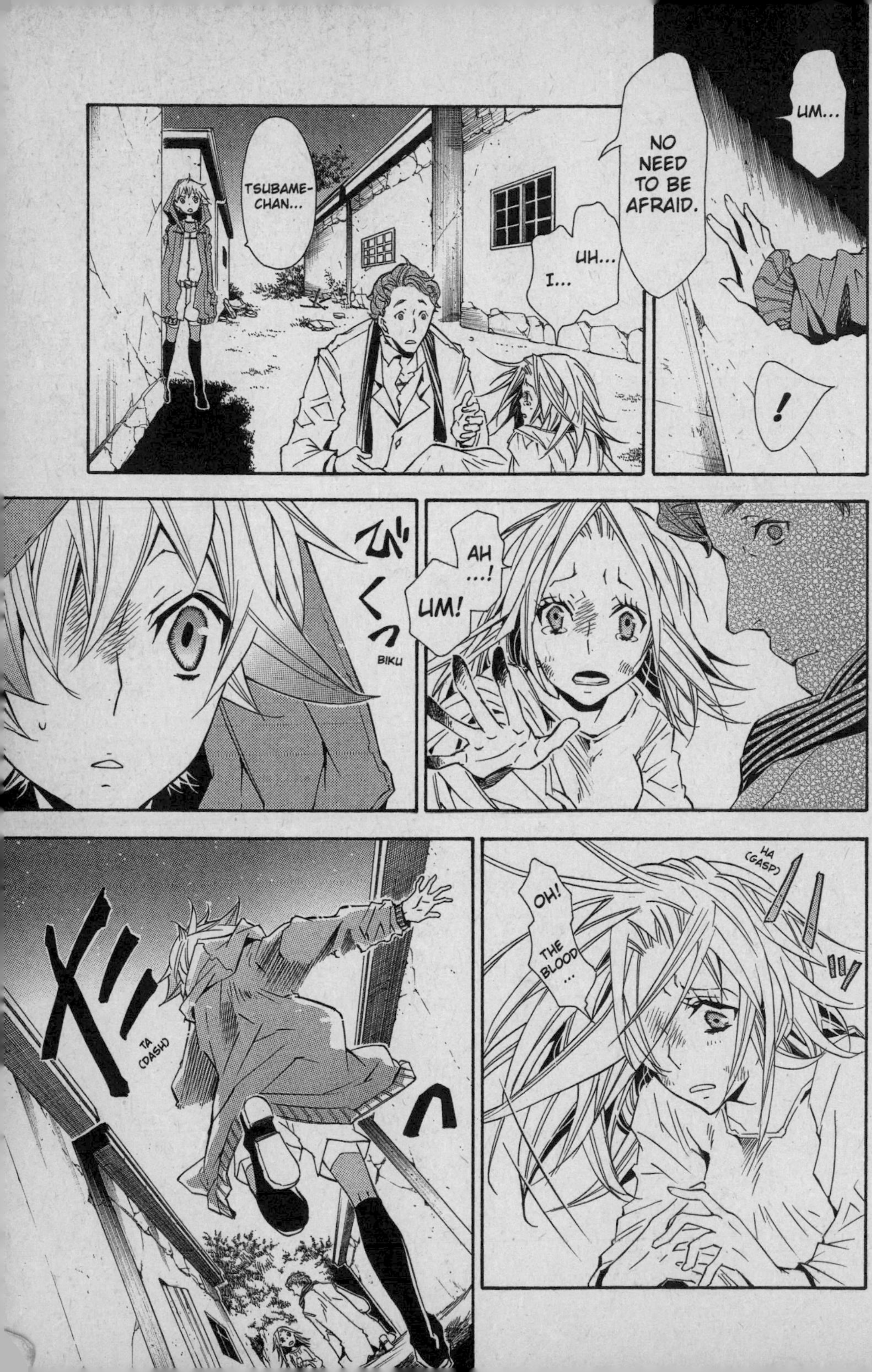
UM...
!
NO NEED TO BE AFRAID.
UH... I...
TSUBAME-CHAN...
AH ...!
UM!
びくっ
BIKU
HA (GASP)
OH! THE BLOOD ...
TA (DASH)

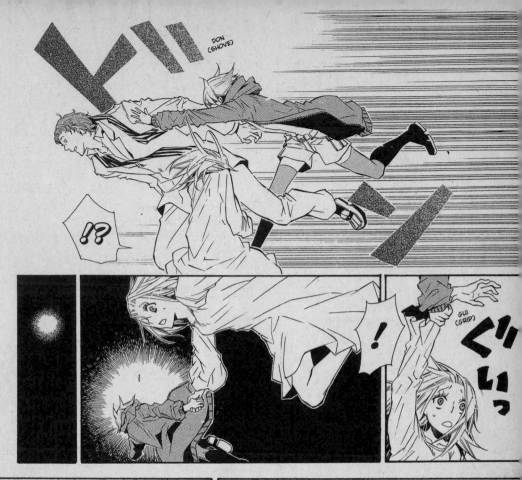

DON
(SHOVE)

!?

!

GUI
(GRIP)

THAT PERSON...

...WAS SCARY...

WH-WHY...?

I... DON'T KNOW...

HAA

HAA (PANT)

HAA

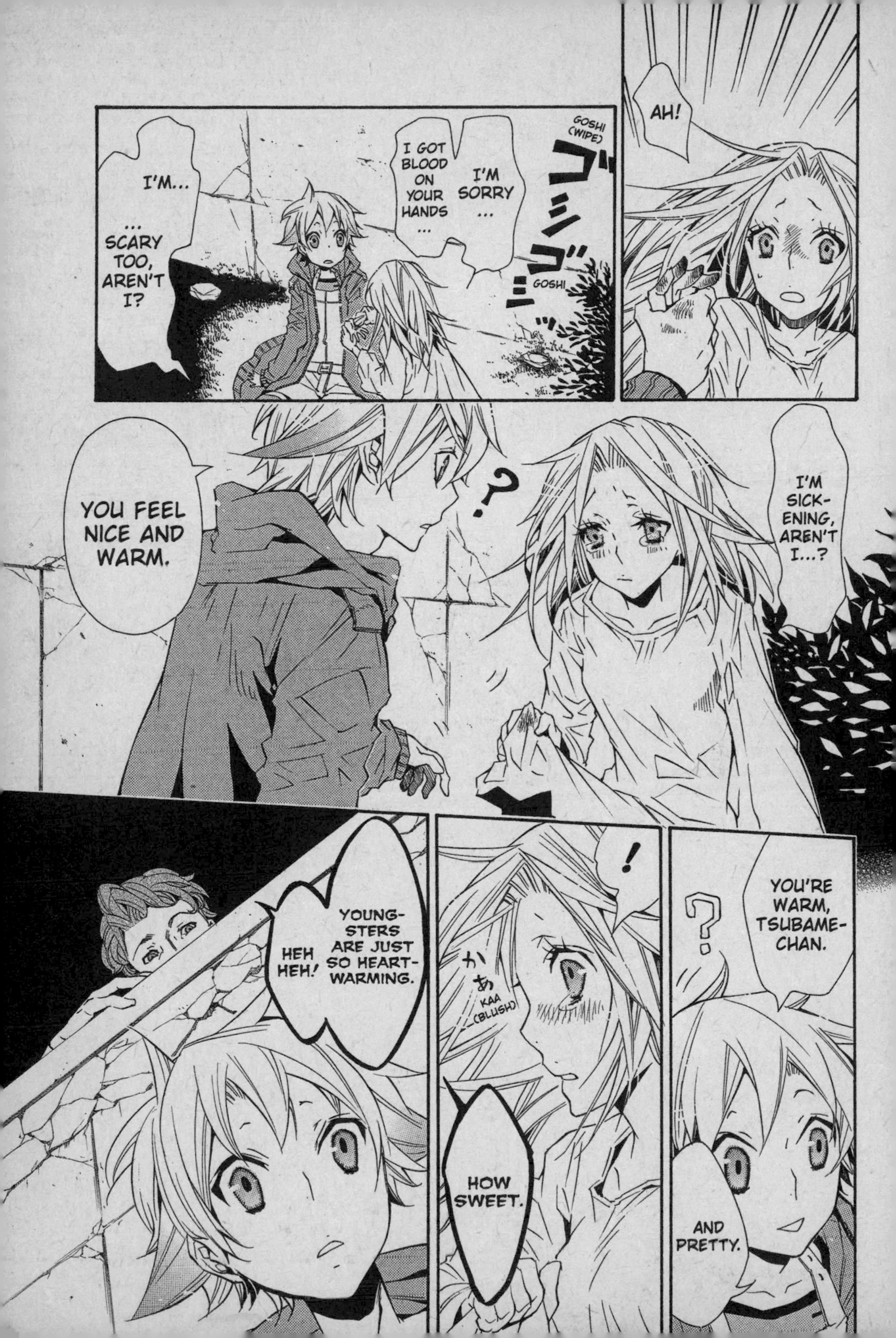
AH!
GOSHI (WIPE)
ゴシゴシ
GOSHI
I'M SORRY ...
I GOT BLOOD ON YOUR HANDS ...
I'M...
... SCARY TOO, AREN'T I?
I'M SICK-ENING, AREN'T I...?
?
YOU FEEL NICE AND WARM.
?
YOU'RE WARM, TSUBAME-CHAN.
AND PRETTY.
!
かあ
KAA (BLUSH)
HOW SWEET.
YOUNG-STERS ARE JUST SO HEART-WARMING.
HEH HEH!

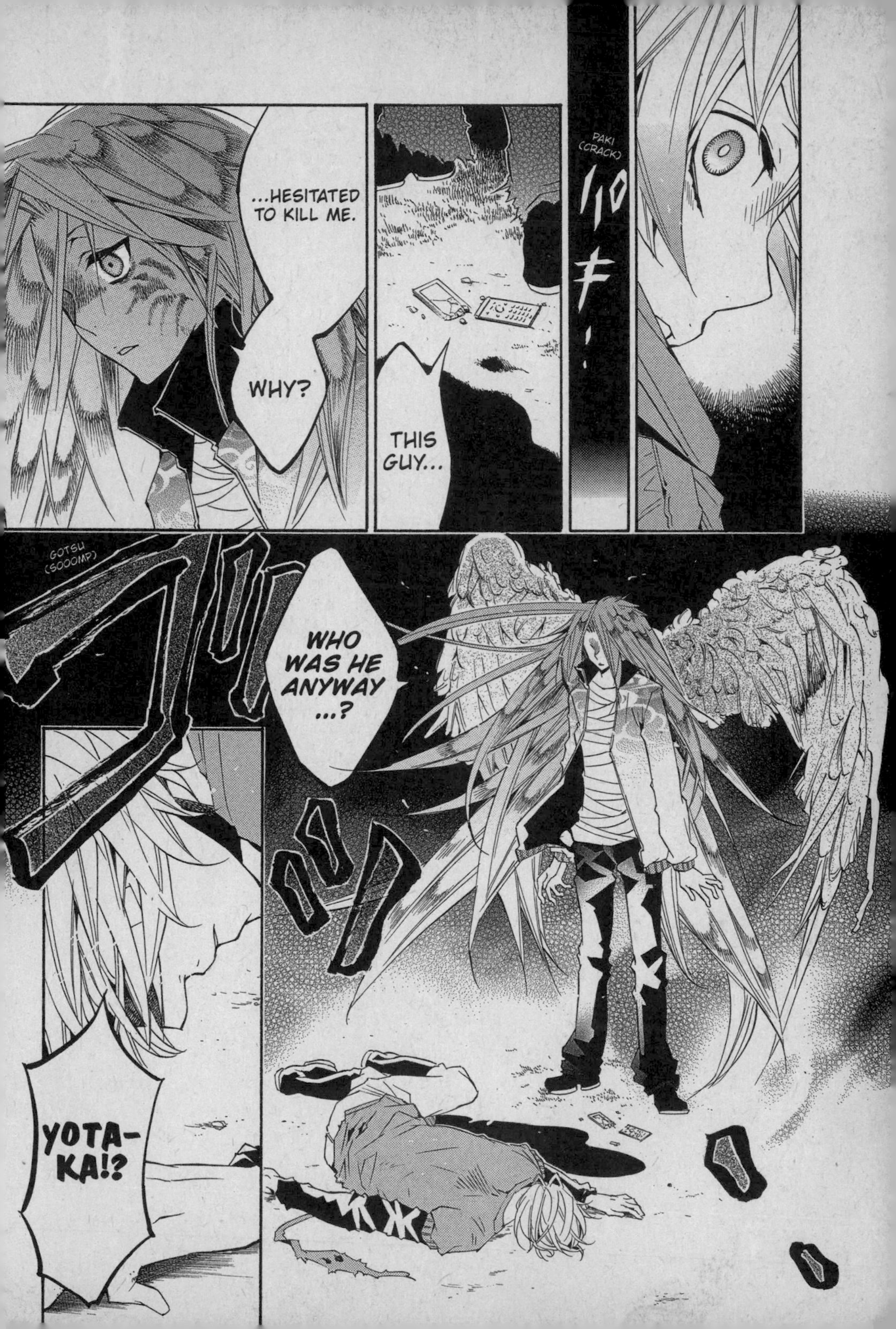
PAKI (CRACK)
THIS GUY...
...HESITATED TO KILL ME.
WHY?
GOTSU (SOOOMP)
WHO WAS HE ANYWAY ...?
YOTA-KA!?

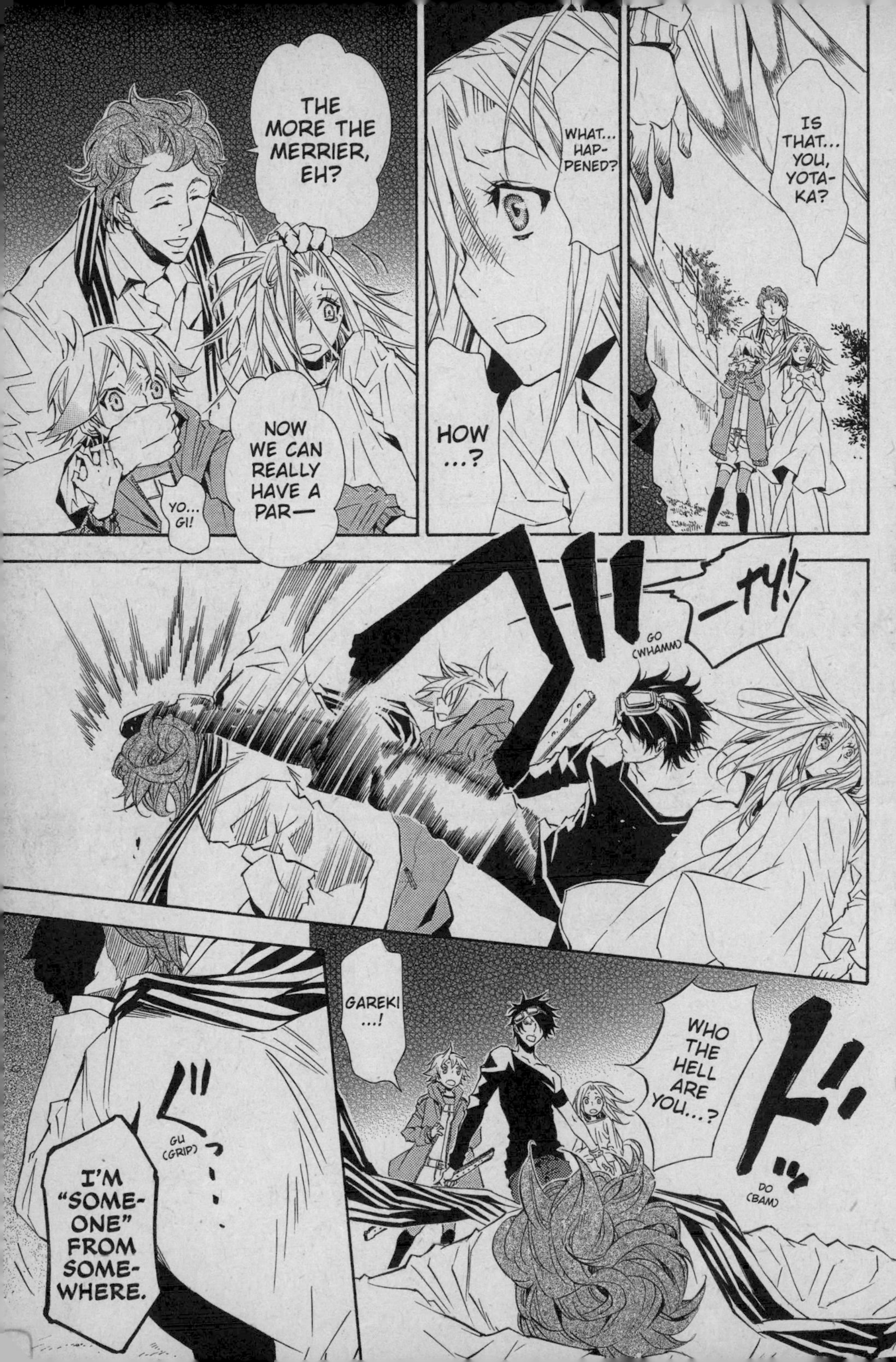
IS THAT... YOU, YOTAKA?
WHAT... HAP-PENED?
HOW ...?
THE MORE THE MERRIER, EH?
NOW WE CAN REALLY HAVE A PAR—
YO... GI!
—TY!
GO (WHAMM)
WHO THE HELL ARE YOU...?
GAREKI ...!
DO (BAM)
GU (GRIP)
I'M "SOME-ONE" FROM SOME-WHERE.

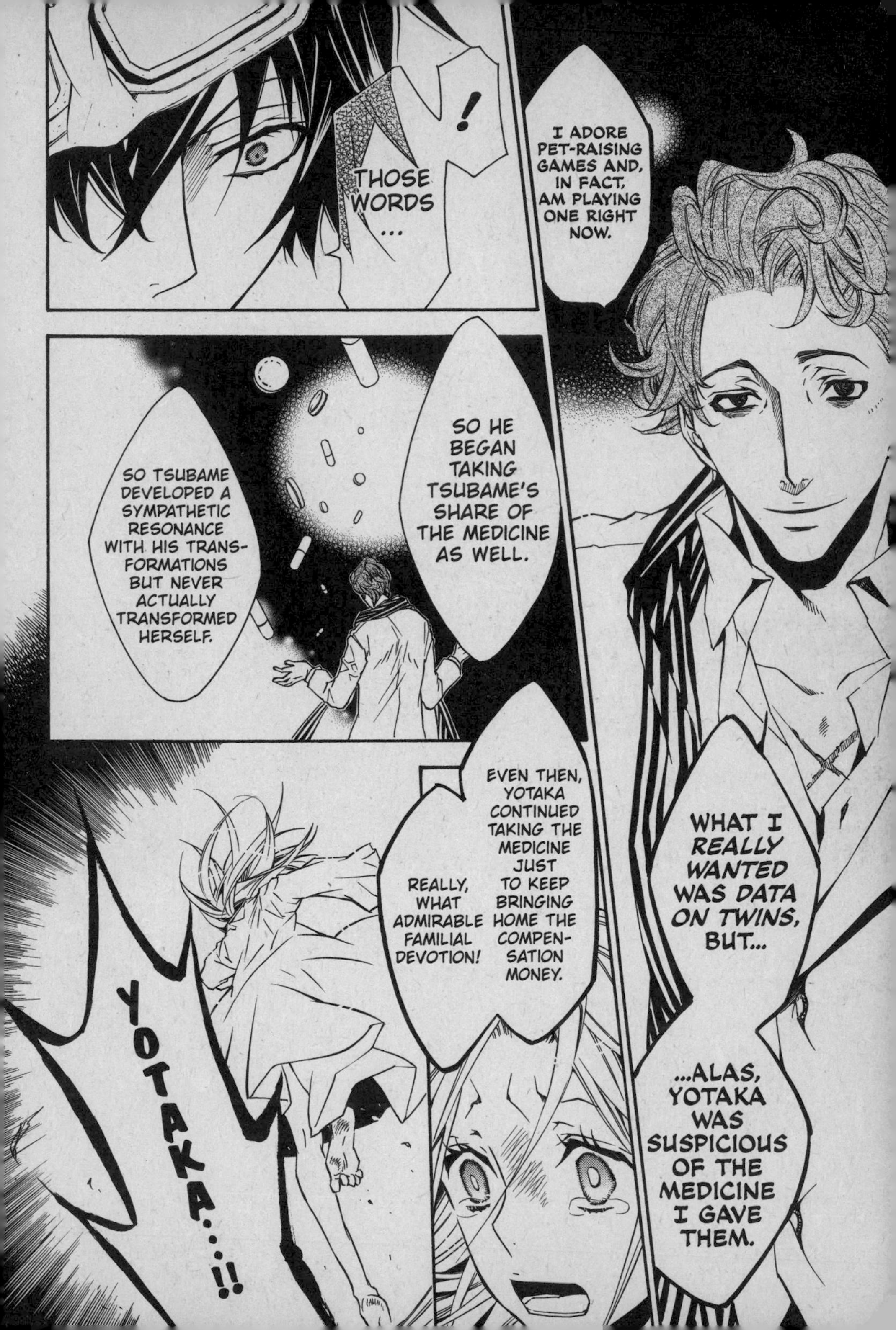
I ADORE PET-RAISING GAMES AND, IN FACT, AM PLAYING ONE RIGHT NOW.
WHAT I *REALLY WANTED* WAS *DATA ON TWINS*, BUT...
...ALAS, YOTAKA WAS SUSPICIOUS OF THE MEDICINE I GAVE THEM.
!
THOSE WORDS ...
SO HE BEGAN TAKING TSUBAME'S SHARE OF THE MEDICINE AS WELL.
SO TSUBAME DEVELOPED A SYMPATHETIC RESONANCE WITH HIS TRANS-FORMATIONS BUT NEVER ACTUALLY TRANSFORMED HERSELF.
EVEN THEN, YOTAKA CONTINUED TAKING THE MEDICINE JUST TO KEEP BRINGING HOME THE COMPEN-SATION MONEY.
REALLY, WHAT ADMIRABLE FAMILIAL DEVOTION!
YOTAKA...!!

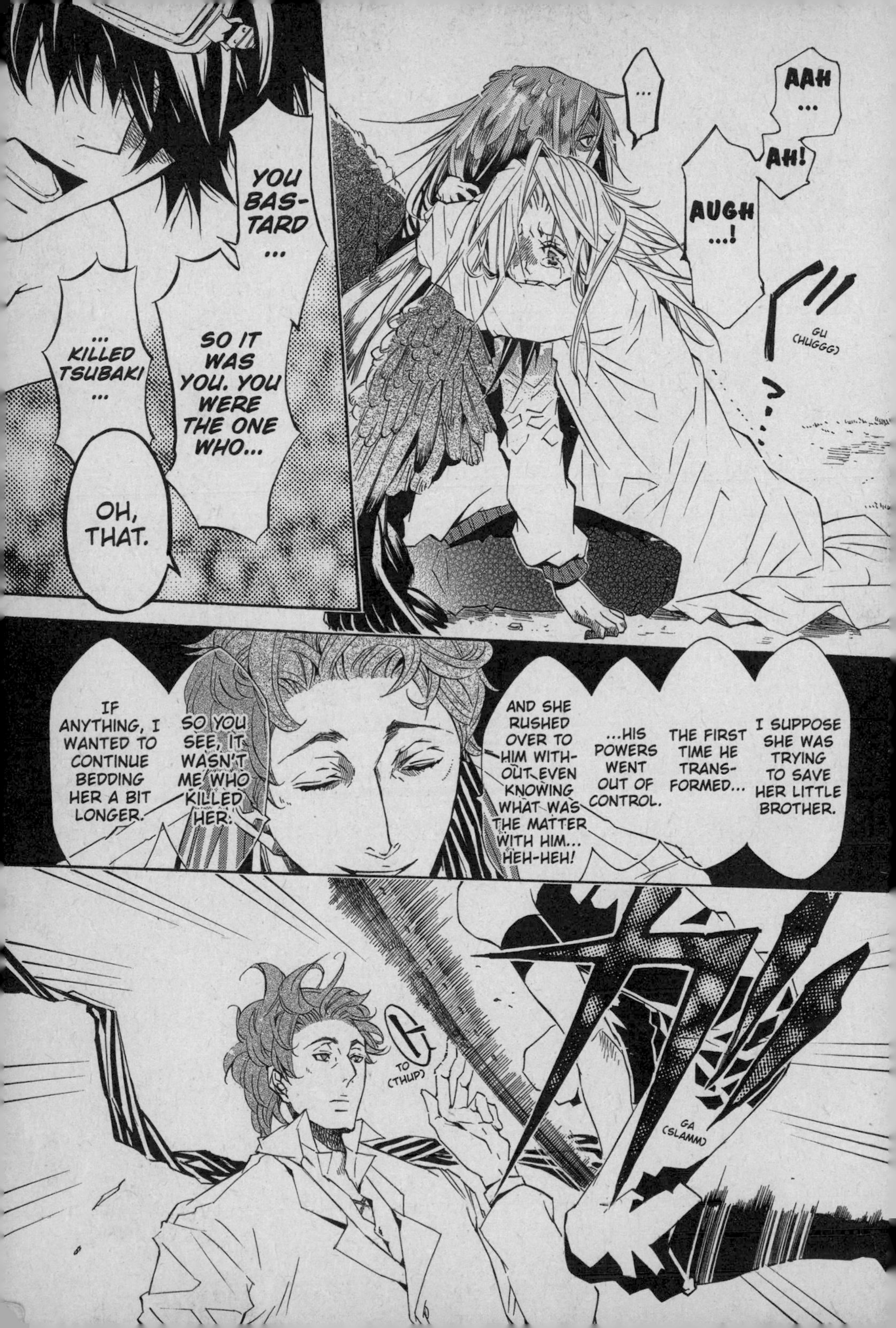
AAH ... AH!
AUGH ...!
...
GU (HUGGG)
YOU BAS-TARD ...
SO IT WAS YOU. YOU WERE THE ONE WHO...
... KILLED TSUBAKI ...
OH, THAT.
I SUPPOSE SHE WAS TRYING TO SAVE HER LITTLE BROTHER.
THE FIRST TIME HE TRANS-FORMED...
...HIS POWERS WENT OUT OF CONTROL.
AND SHE RUSHED OVER TO HIM WITH-OUT EVEN KNOWING WHAT WAS THE MATTER WITH HIM... HEH-HEH!
SO YOU SEE, IT WASN'T ME WHO KILLED HER.
IF ANYTHING, I WANTED TO CONTINUE BEDDING HER A BIT LONGER.
GA (SLAMM)
TO (THUP)

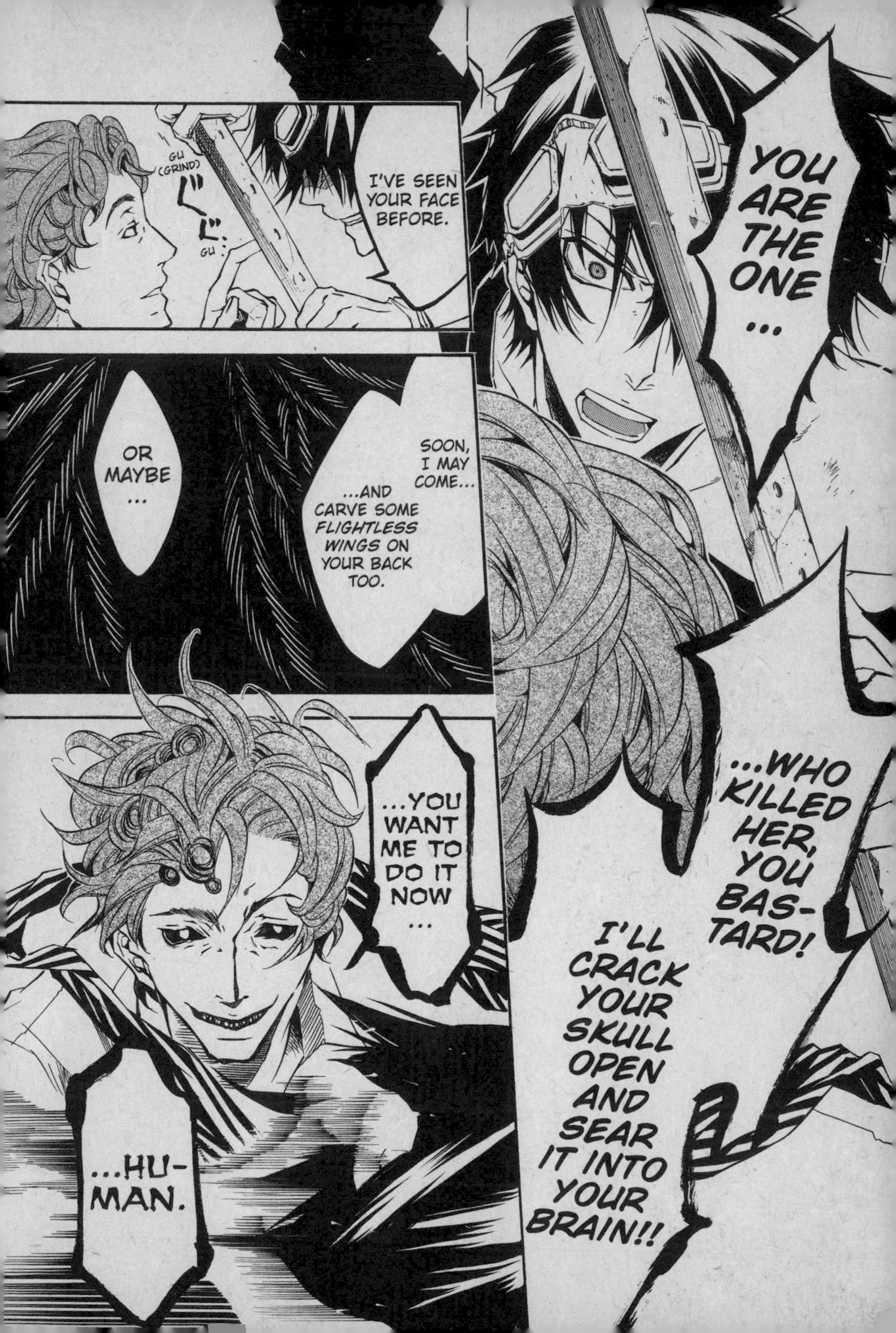
YOU ARE THE ONE ...
...WHO KILLED HER, YOU BASTARD!
I'LL CRACK YOUR SKULL OPEN AND SEAR IT INTO YOUR BRAIN!!
I'VE SEEN YOUR FACE BEFORE.
GU (GRIND)
GU
SOON, I MAY COME...
...AND CARVE SOME FLIGHTLESS WINGS ON YOUR BACK TOO.
OR MAYBE ...
...YOU WANT ME TO DO IT NOW ...
...HU-MAN.

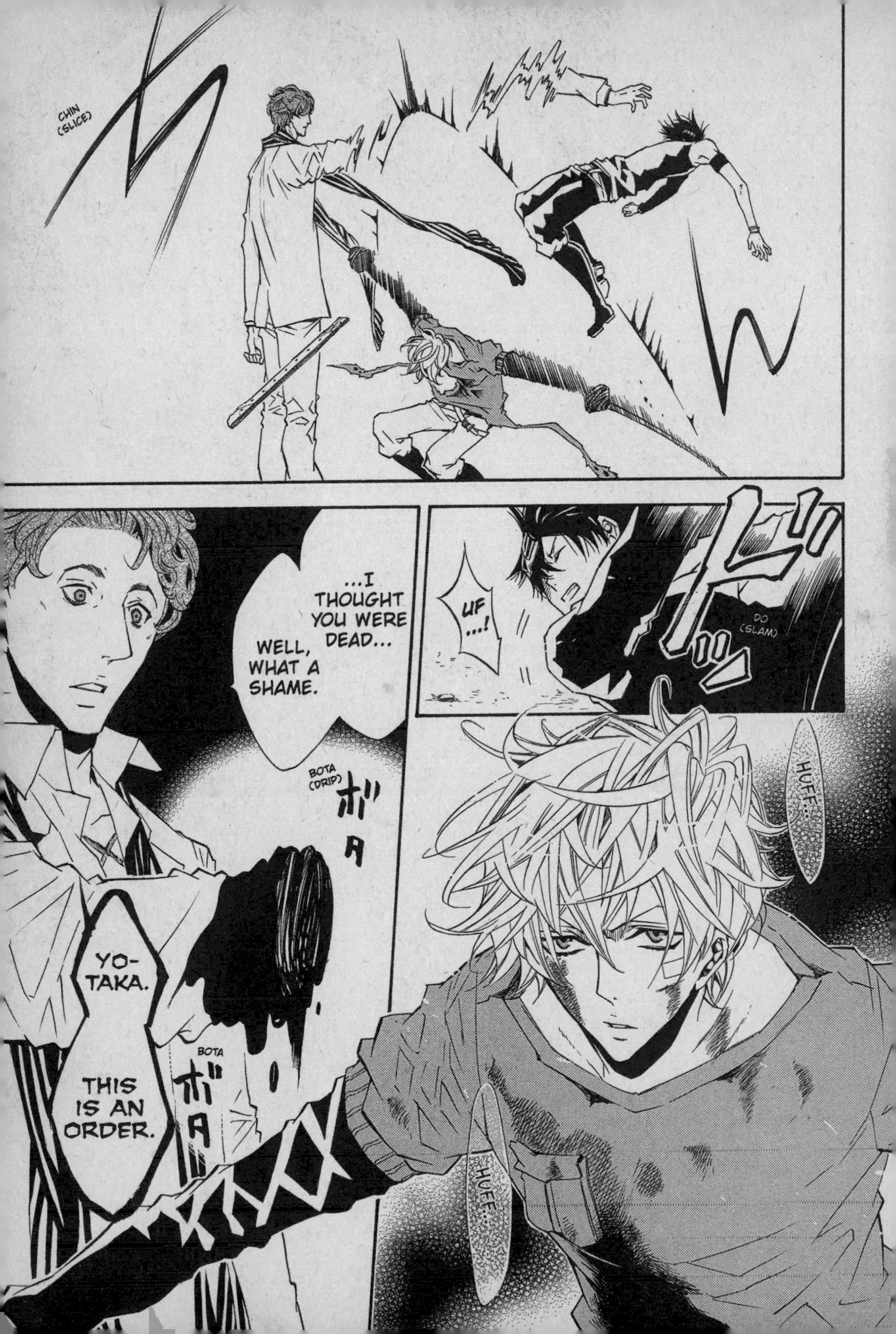
CHIN (SLICE)
UF ...!
DO (SLAM)
...I THOUGHT YOU WERE DEAD...
WELL, WHAT A SHAME.
HUFF...
BOTA (DRIP)
ボタ
YO-TAKA.
THIS IS AN ORDER.
BOTA
ボタ
HUFF...

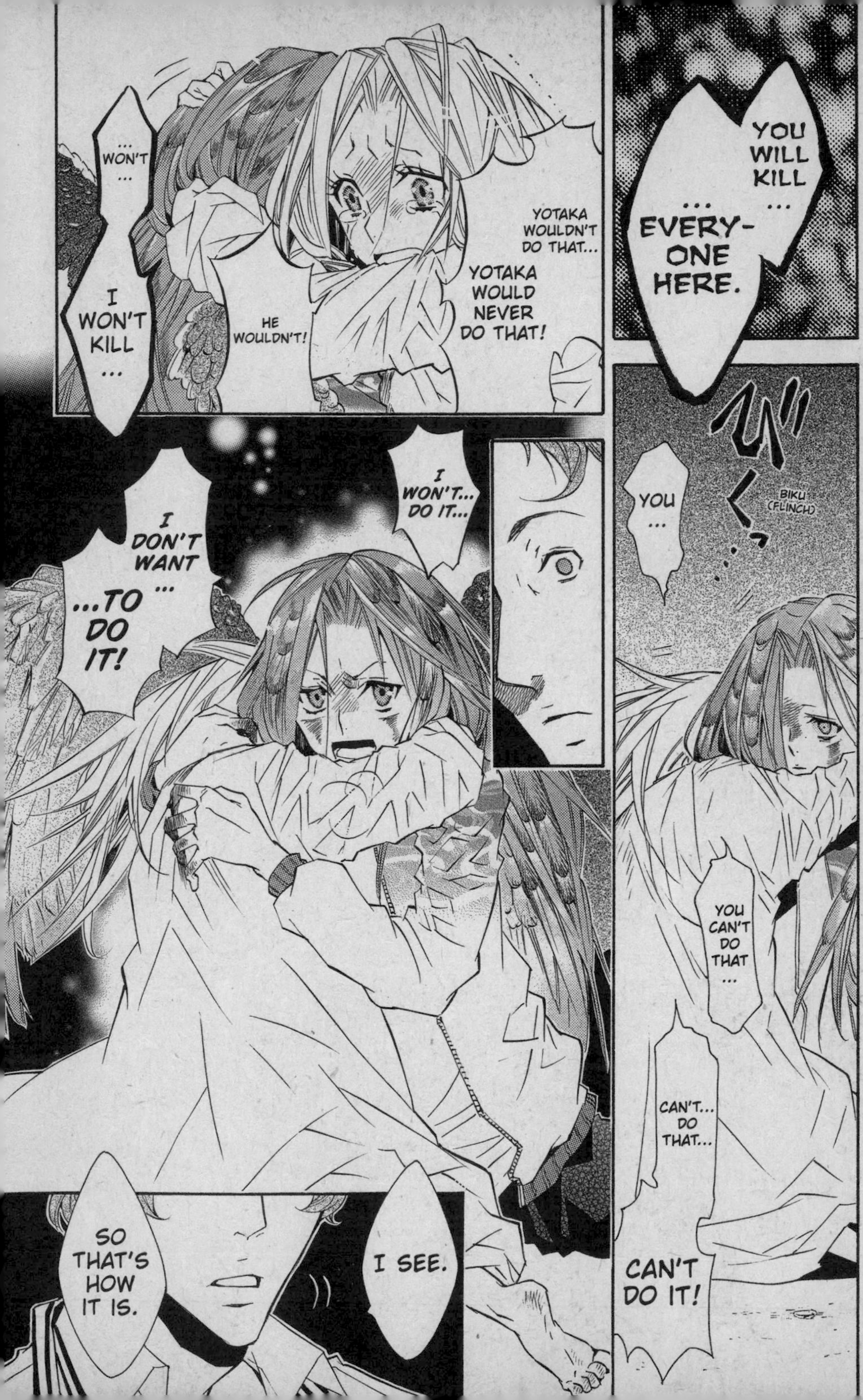
YOU WILL KILL ... EVERY-ONE HERE.
YOTAKA WOULDN'T DO THAT...
YOTAKA WOULD NEVER DO THAT!
HE WOULDN'T!
... WON'T ...
I WON'T KILL ...
YOU ...
BIKU (FLINCH)
YOU CAN'T DO THAT ...
CAN'T... DO THAT...
CAN'T DO IT!
I WON'T... DO IT...
I DON'T WANT ... ...TO DO IT!
I SEE.
SO THAT'S HOW IT IS.

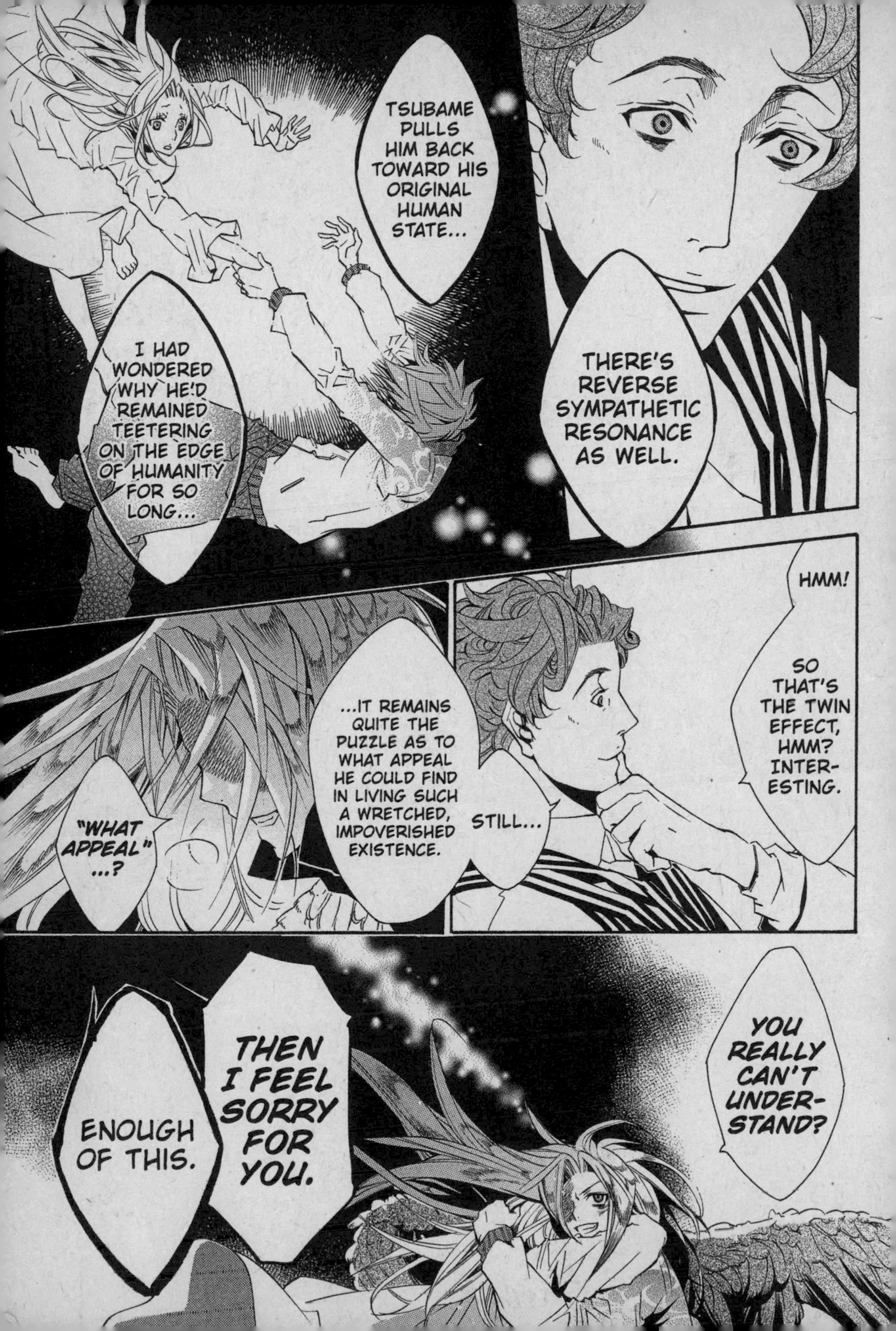
THERE'S REVERSE SYMPATHETIC RESONANCE AS WELL.
TSUBAME PULLS HIM BACK TOWARD HIS ORIGINAL HUMAN STATE...
I HAD WONDERED WHY HE'D REMAINED TEETERING ON THE EDGE OF HUMANITY FOR SO LONG...
HMM!
SO THAT'S THE TWIN EFFECT, HMM? INTER-ESTING.
STILL...
...IT REMAINS QUITE THE PUZZLE AS TO WHAT APPEAL HE COULD FIND IN LIVING SUCH A WRETCHED, IMPOVERISHED EXISTENCE.
"WHAT APPEAL" ...?
YOU REALLY CAN'T UNDER-STAND?
THEN I FEEL SORRY FOR YOU.
ENOUGH OF THIS.

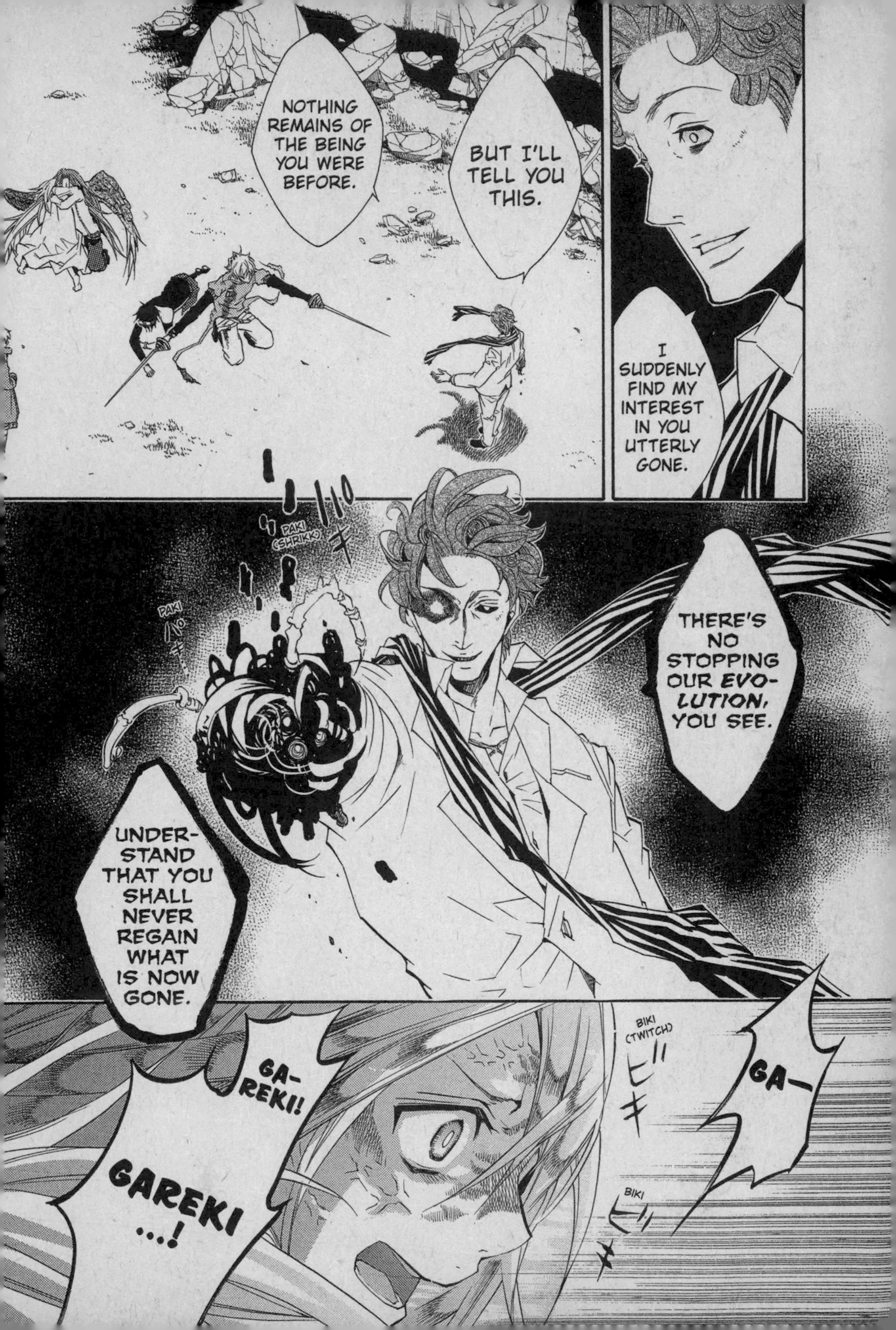

NOTHING REMAINS OF THE BEING YOU WERE BEFORE.
BUT I'LL TELL YOU THIS.
I SUDDENLY FIND MY INTEREST IN YOU UTTERLY GONE.
PAKI (SHRIKK)
PAKI
THERE'S NO STOPPING OUR *EVOLUTION*, YOU SEE.
UNDERSTAND THAT YOU SHALL NEVER REGAIN WHAT IS NOW GONE.
BIKI (TWITCH)
GA—
GA-REKI!
GAREKI ...!
BIKI

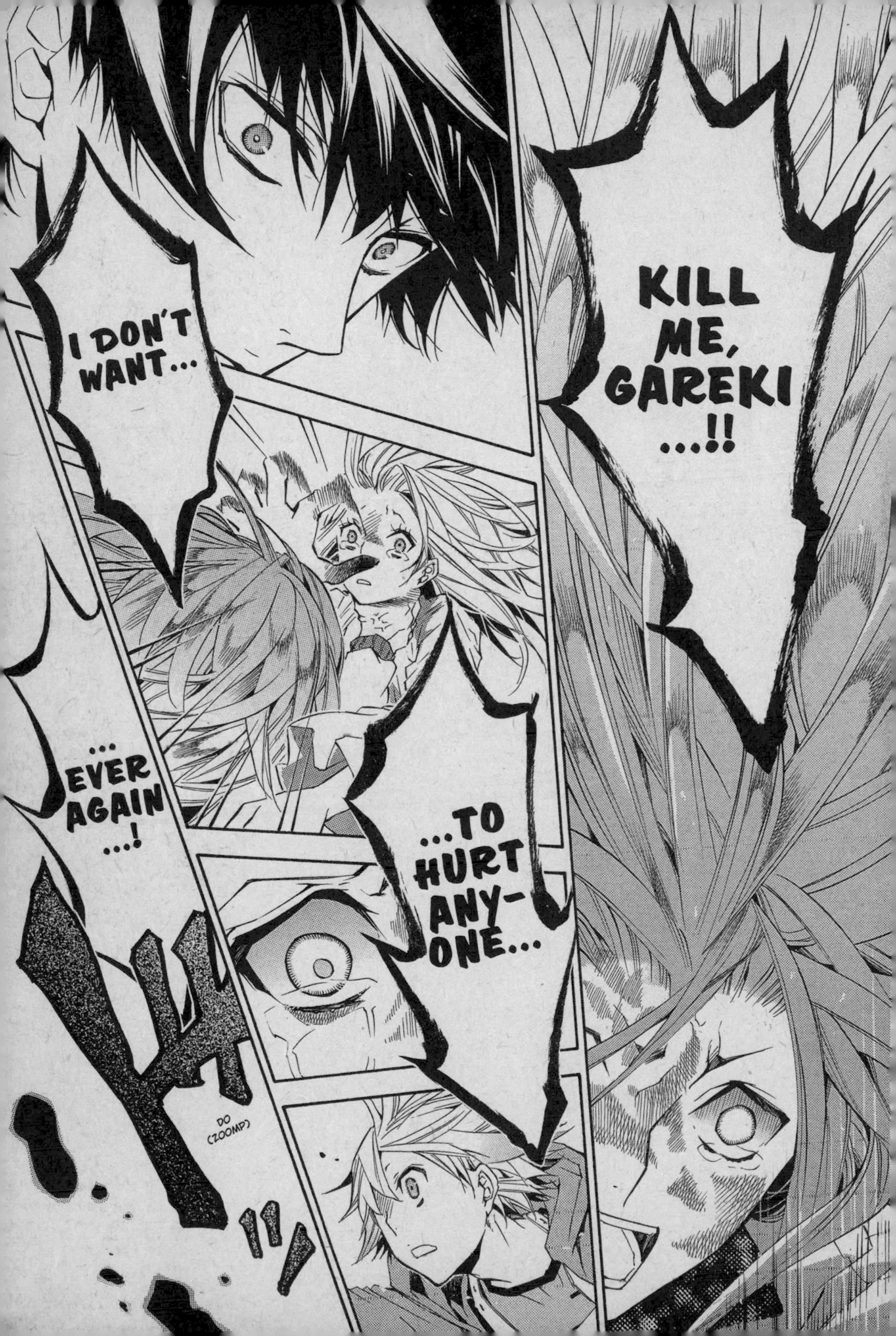
KILL ME, GAREKI ...!!
I DON'T WANT...
...TO HURT ANY-ONE...
...EVER AGAIN ...!
DO (ZOOMP)

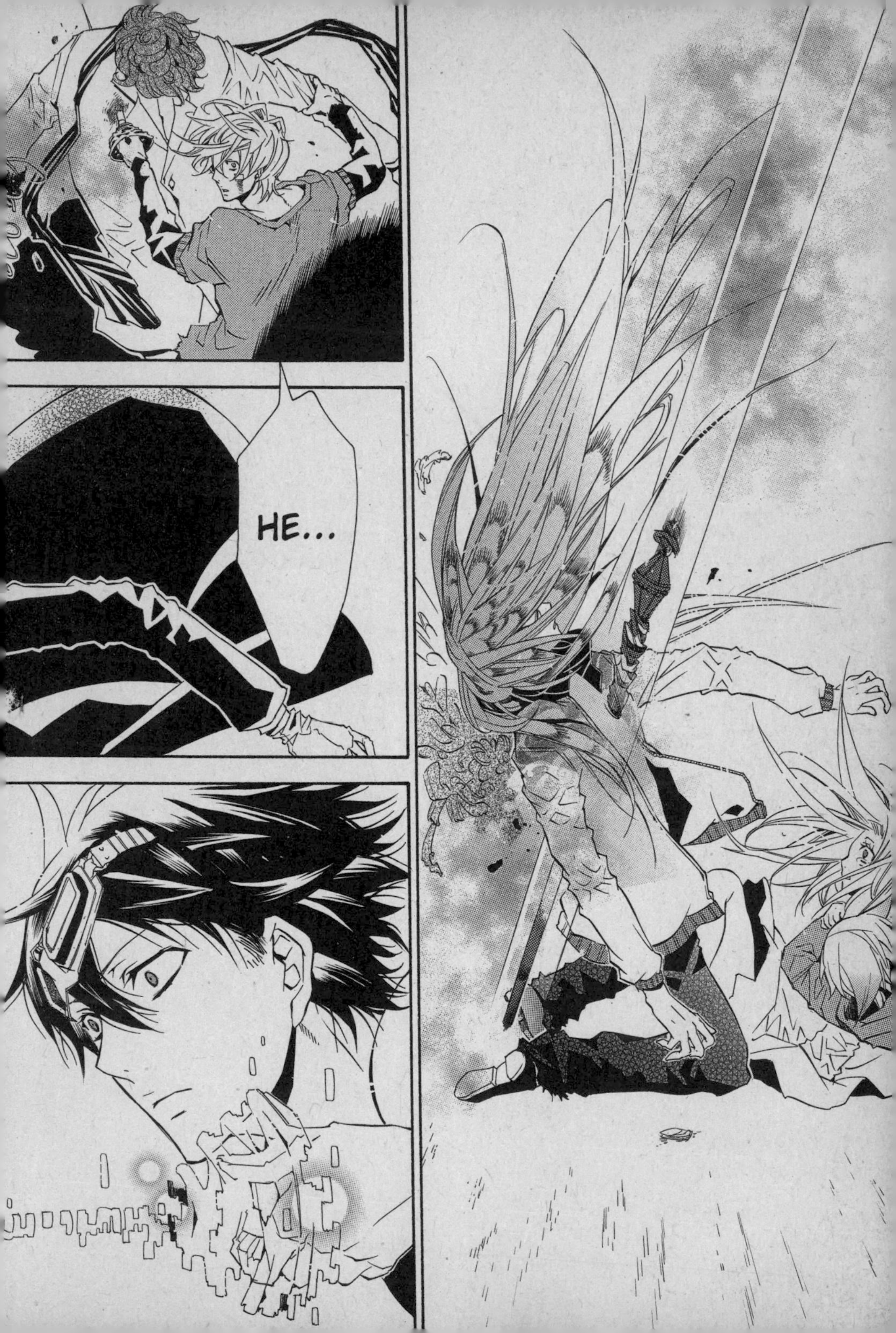
HE...

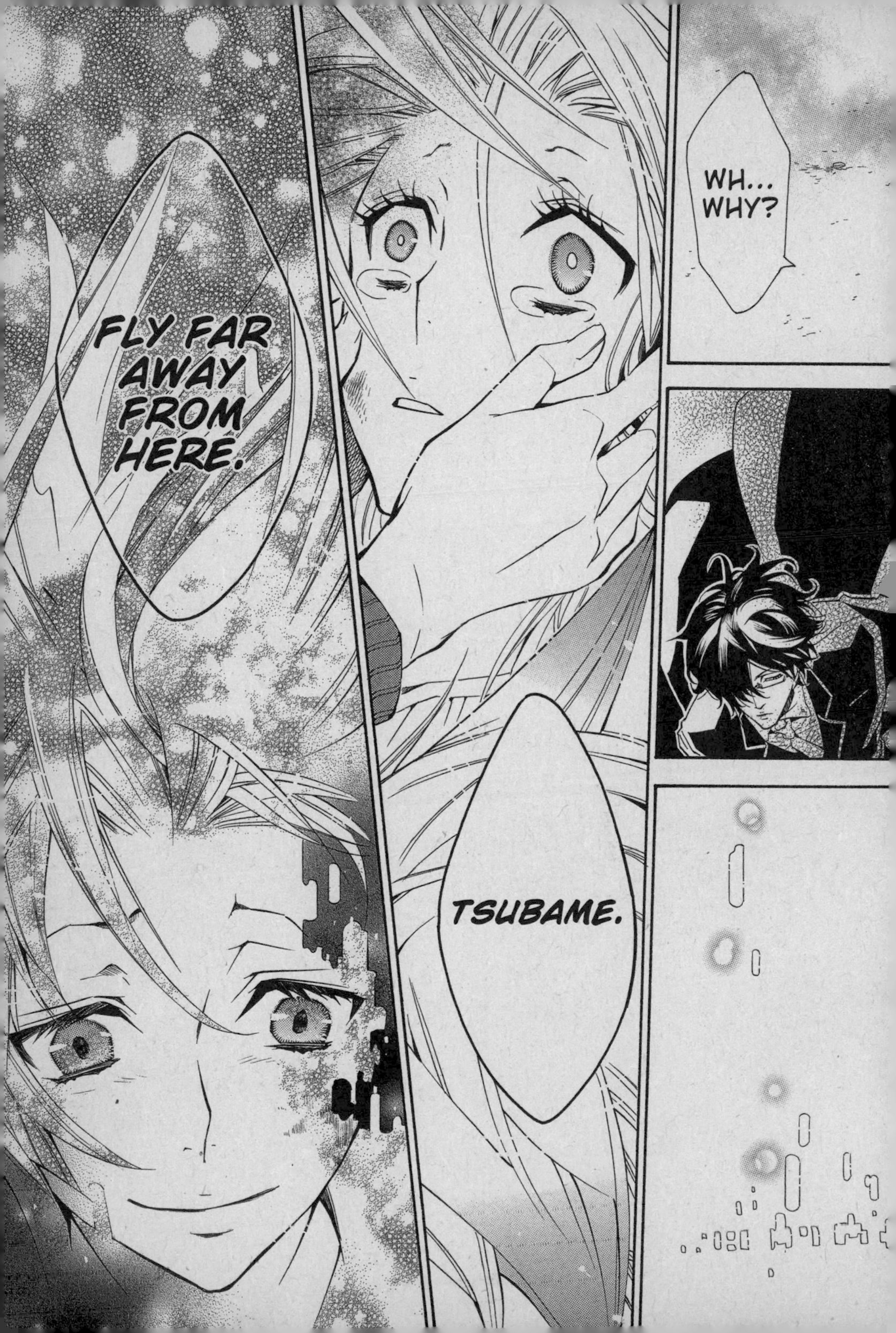
WH... WHY?
TSUBAME.
FLY FAR AWAY FROM HERE.

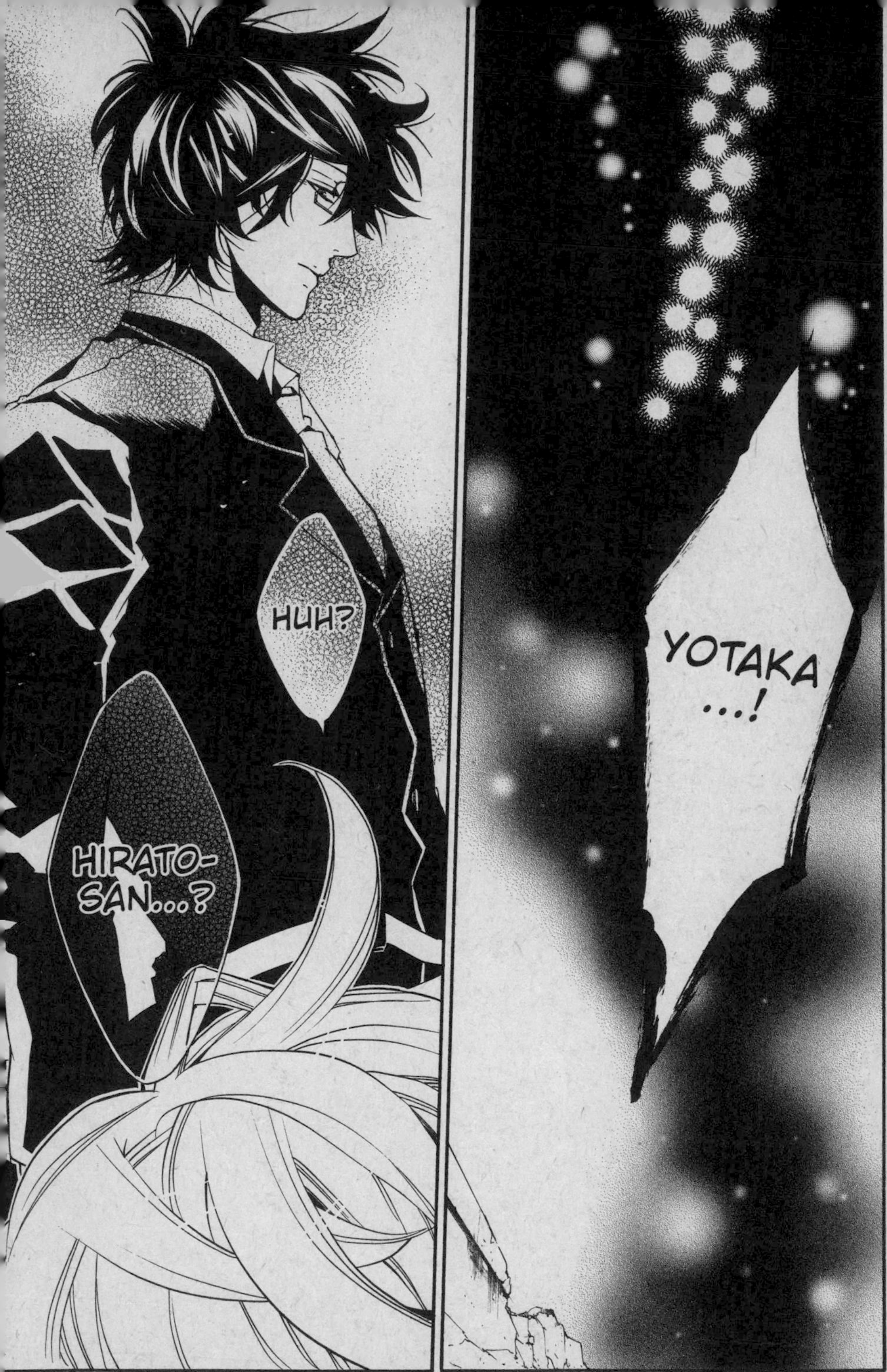
YOTAKA ...!
HUH?
HIRATO-SAN...?

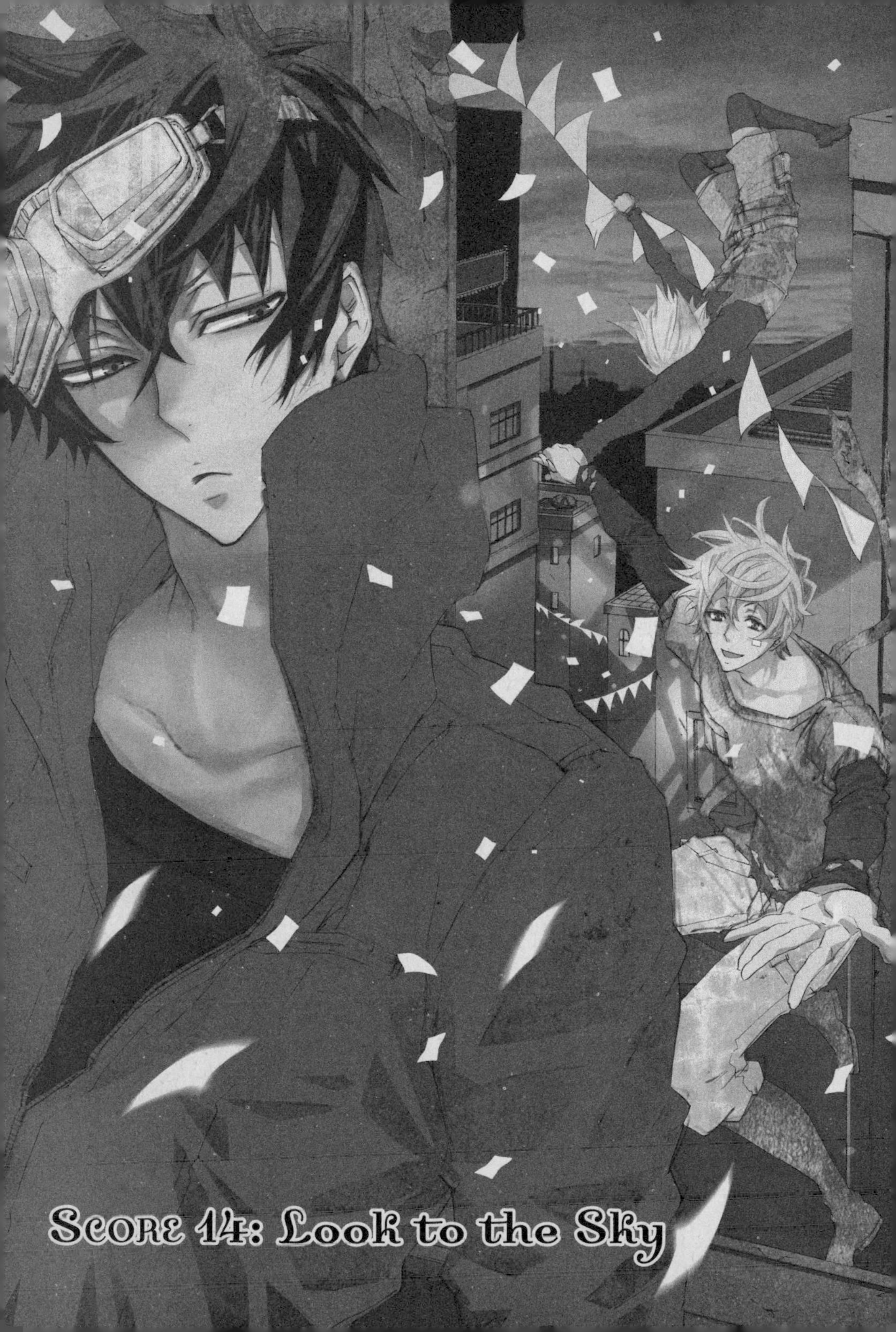
Score 14: Look to the Sky

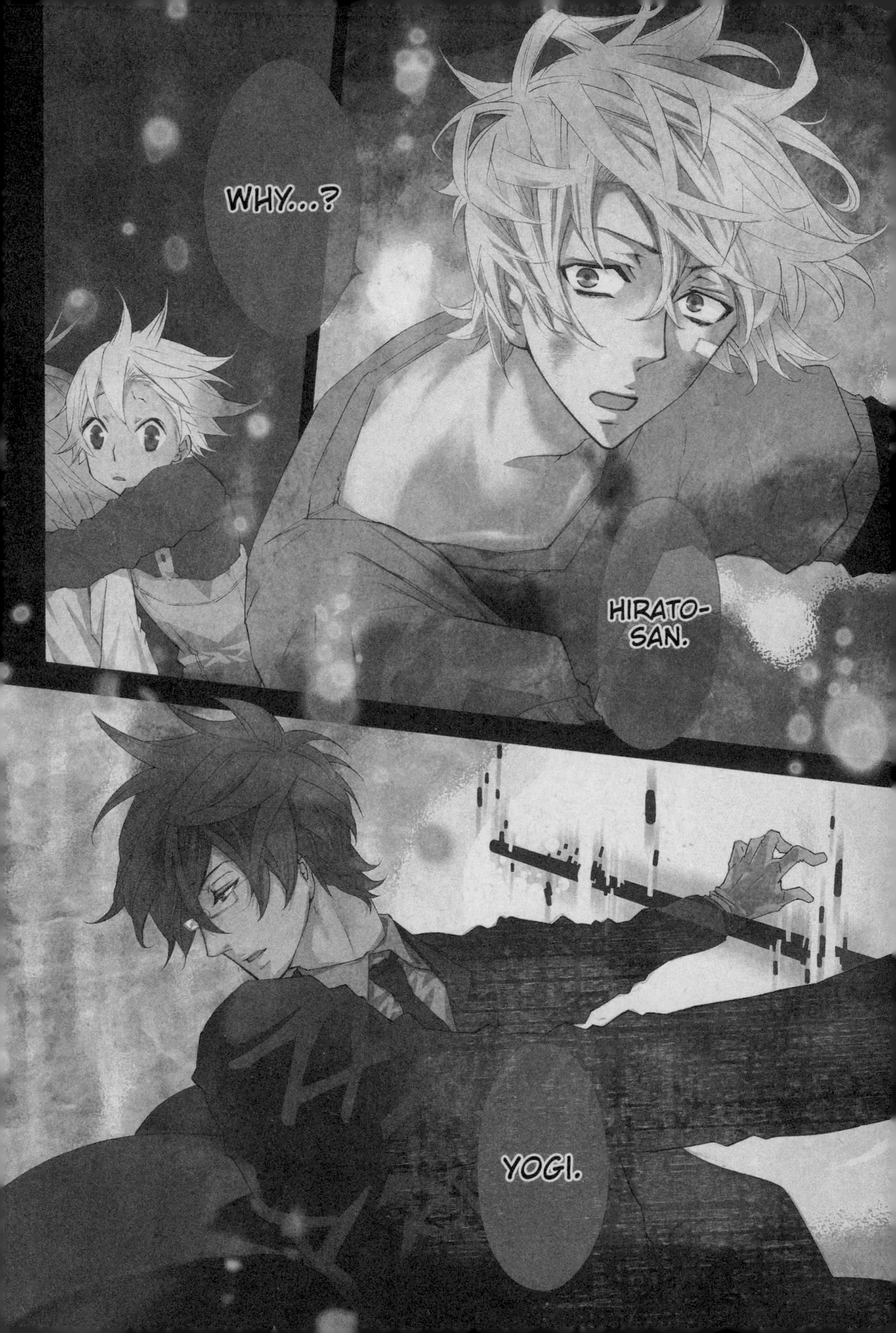
WHY...?
HIRATO-SAN.
YOGI.

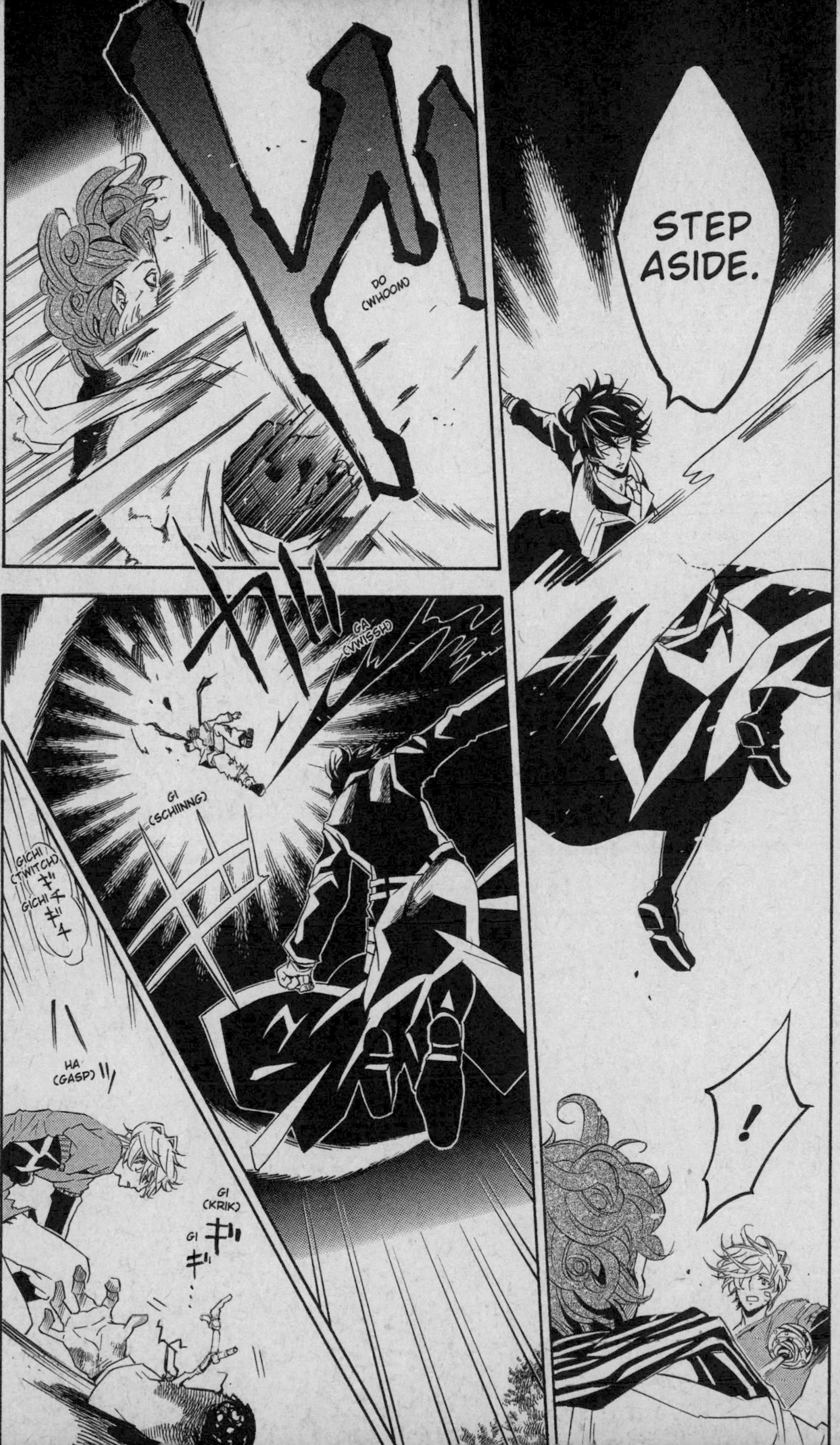
STEP ASIDE.
DO (WHOOM)
GA (VWISSH)
GI (SCHIINNG)
GICHI (TWITCH) GICHI
ギチギチ
HA (GASP)
GI (KRIK) GI
ギギ…
!

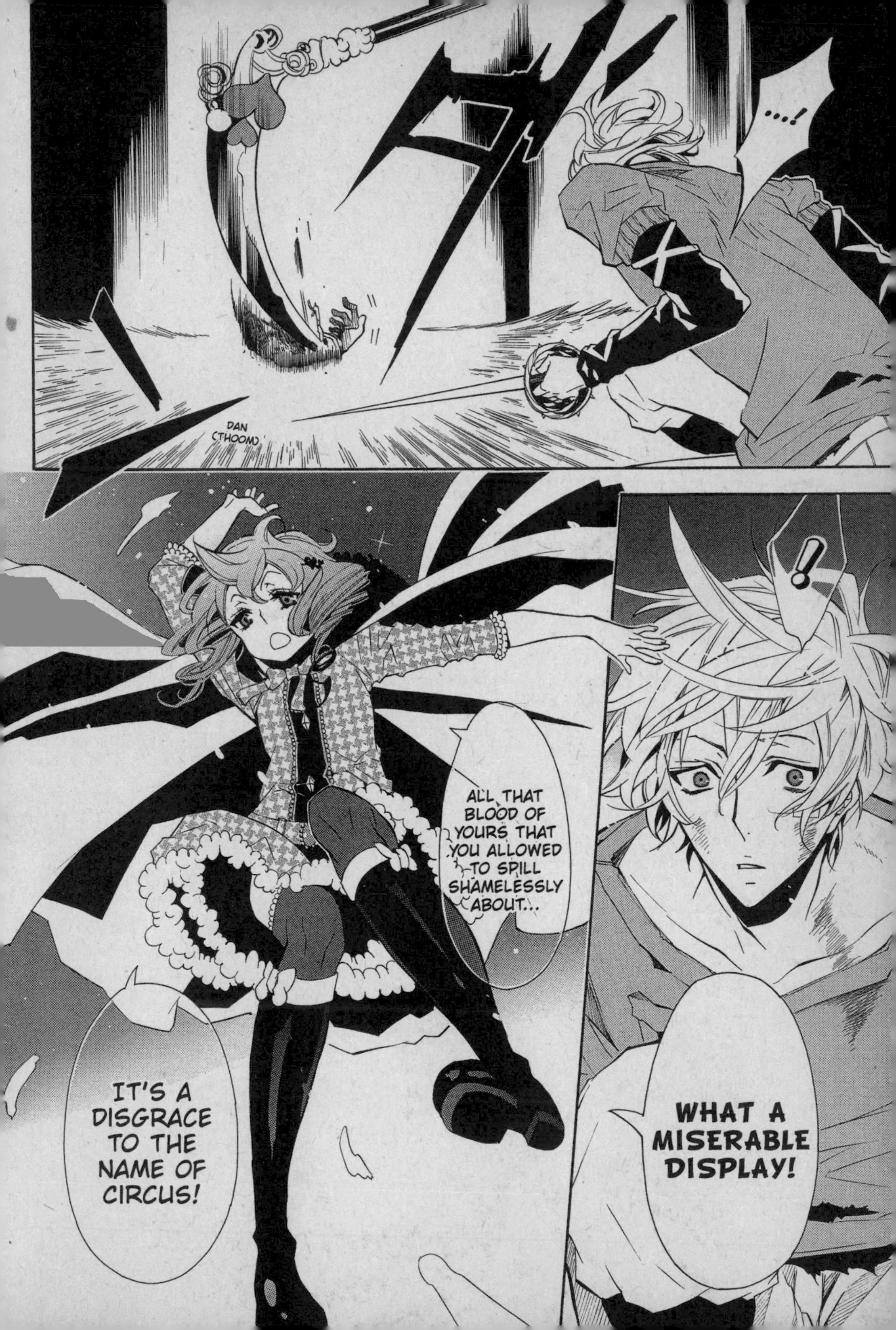
...!
DAN
(THOOM)
!
WHAT A MISERABLE DISPLAY!
ALL THAT BLOOD OF YOURS THAT YOU ALLOWED TO SPILL SHAMELESSLY ABOUT...
IT'S A DISGRACE TO THE NAME OF CIRCUS!

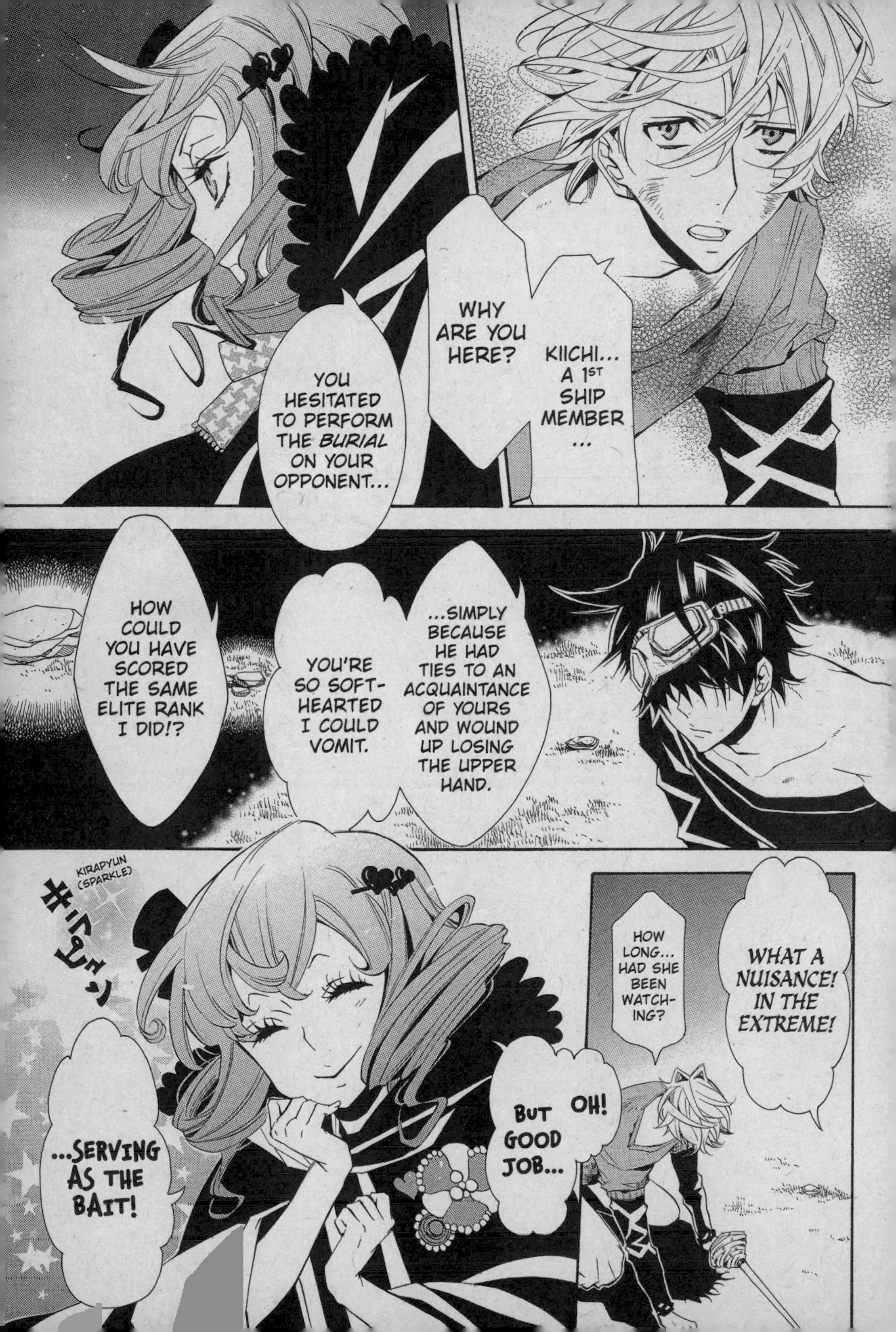
KIICHI... A 1ST SHIP MEMBER...
WHY ARE YOU HERE?
YOU HESITATED TO PERFORM THE *BURIAL* ON YOUR OPPONENT...
...SIMPLY BECAUSE HE HAD TIES TO AN ACQUAINTANCE OF YOURS AND WOUND UP LOSING THE UPPER HAND.
YOU'RE SO SOFT-HEARTED I COULD VOMIT.
HOW COULD YOU HAVE SCORED THE SAME ELITE RANK I DID!?
WHAT A NUISANCE! IN THE EXTREME!
HOW LONG... HAD SHE BEEN WATCHING?
OH!
BUT GOOD JOB...
...SERVING AS THE BAIT!
KIRAPYUN (SPARKLE)

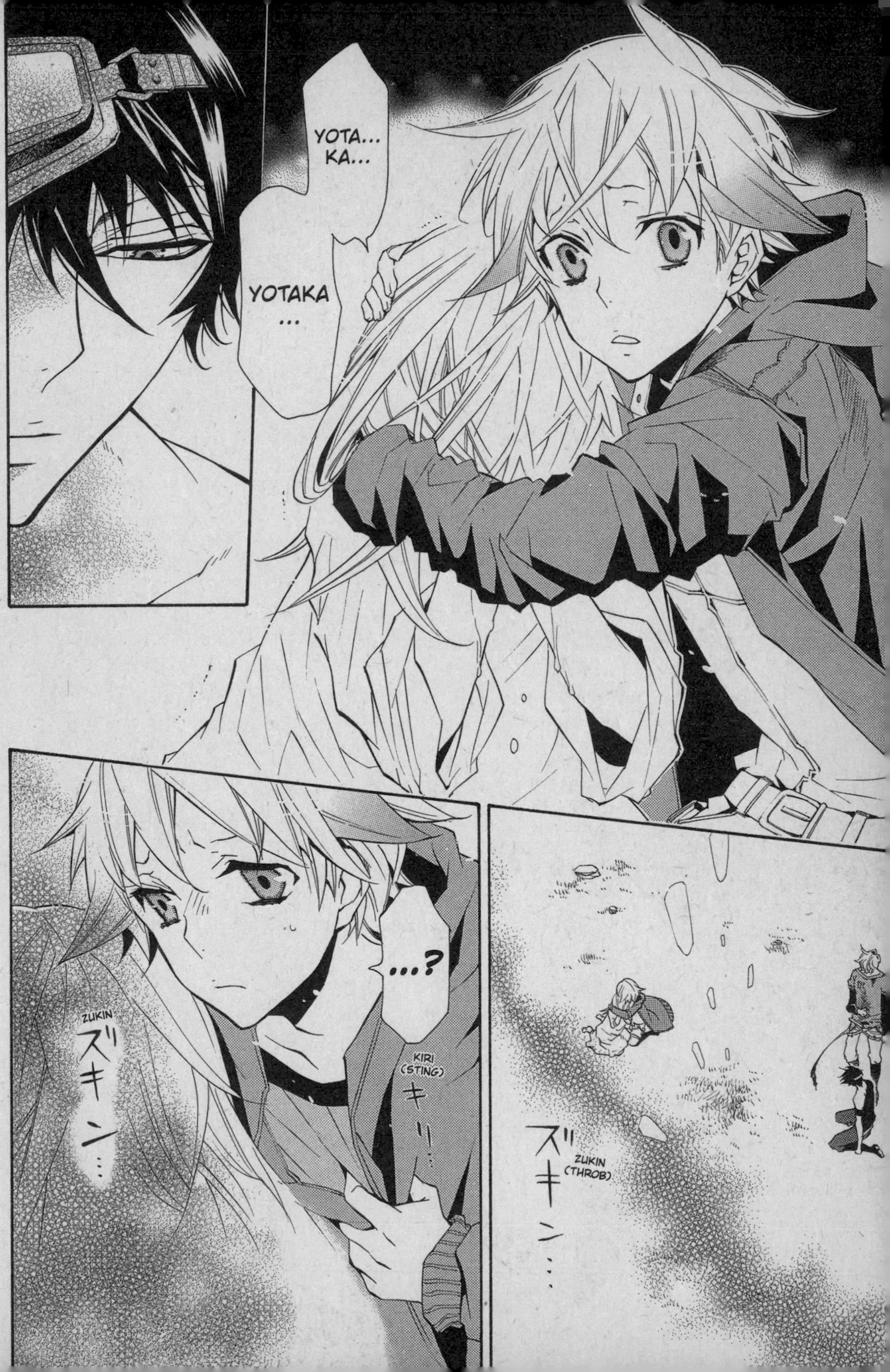
YOTA... KA...
YOTAKA ...
ズキン…
ZUKIN (THROB)
...?
KIRI (STING)
キーン
ZUKIN
ズキン…

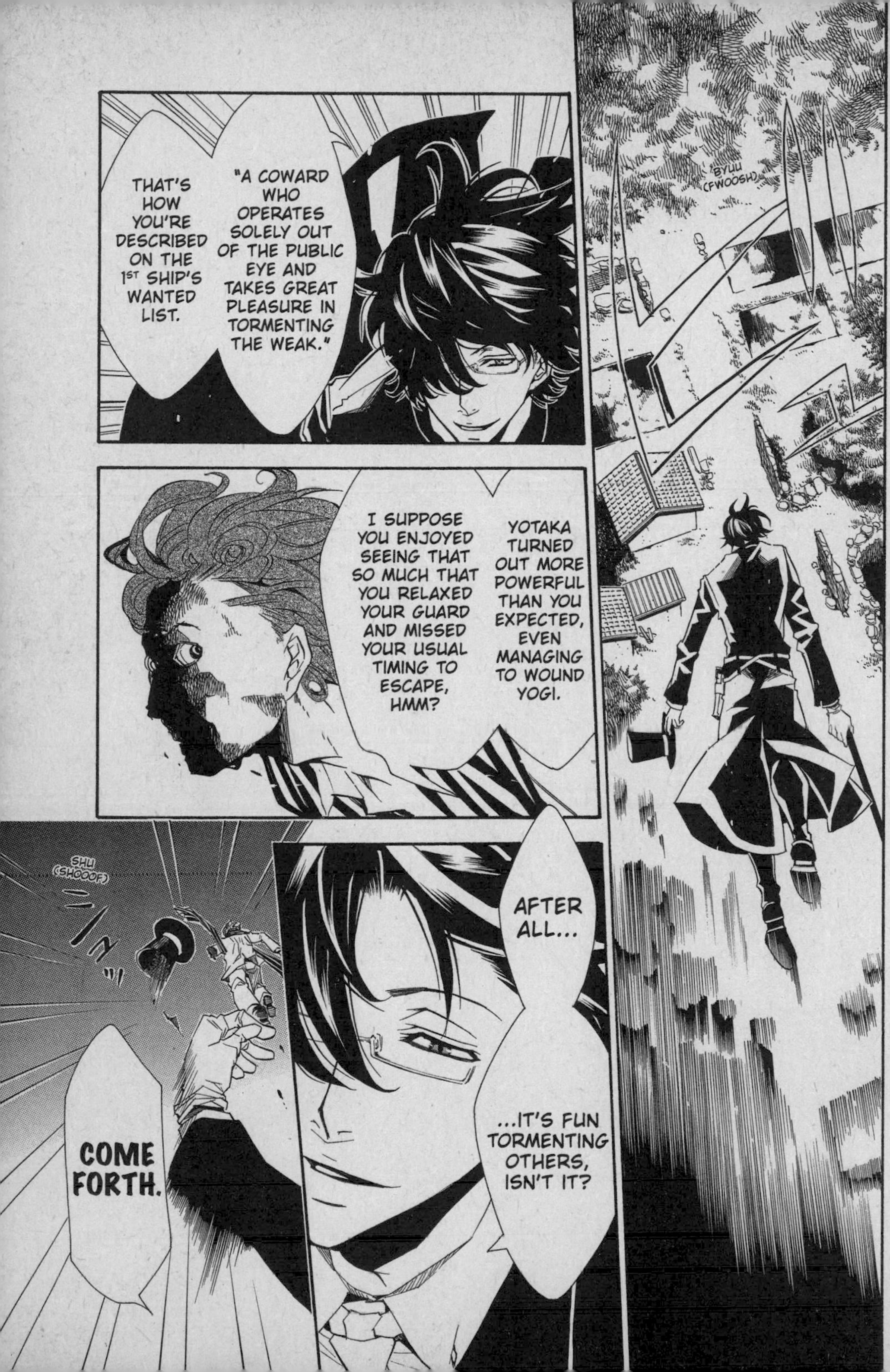
BYUU (FWOOSH)
"A COWARD WHO OPERATES SOLELY OUT OF THE PUBLIC EYE AND TAKES GREAT PLEASURE IN TORMENTING THE WEAK."
THAT'S HOW YOU'RE DESCRIBED ON THE 1ST SHIP'S WANTED LIST.
YOTAKA TURNED OUT MORE POWERFUL THAN YOU EXPECTED, EVEN MANAGING TO WOUND YOGI.
I SUPPOSE YOU ENJOYED SEEING THAT SO MUCH THAT YOU RELAXED YOUR GUARD AND MISSED YOUR USUAL TIMING TO ESCAPE, HMM?
AFTER ALL...
...IT'S FUN TORMENTING OTHERS, ISN'T IT?
SHU (SHOOOF)
COME FORTH.

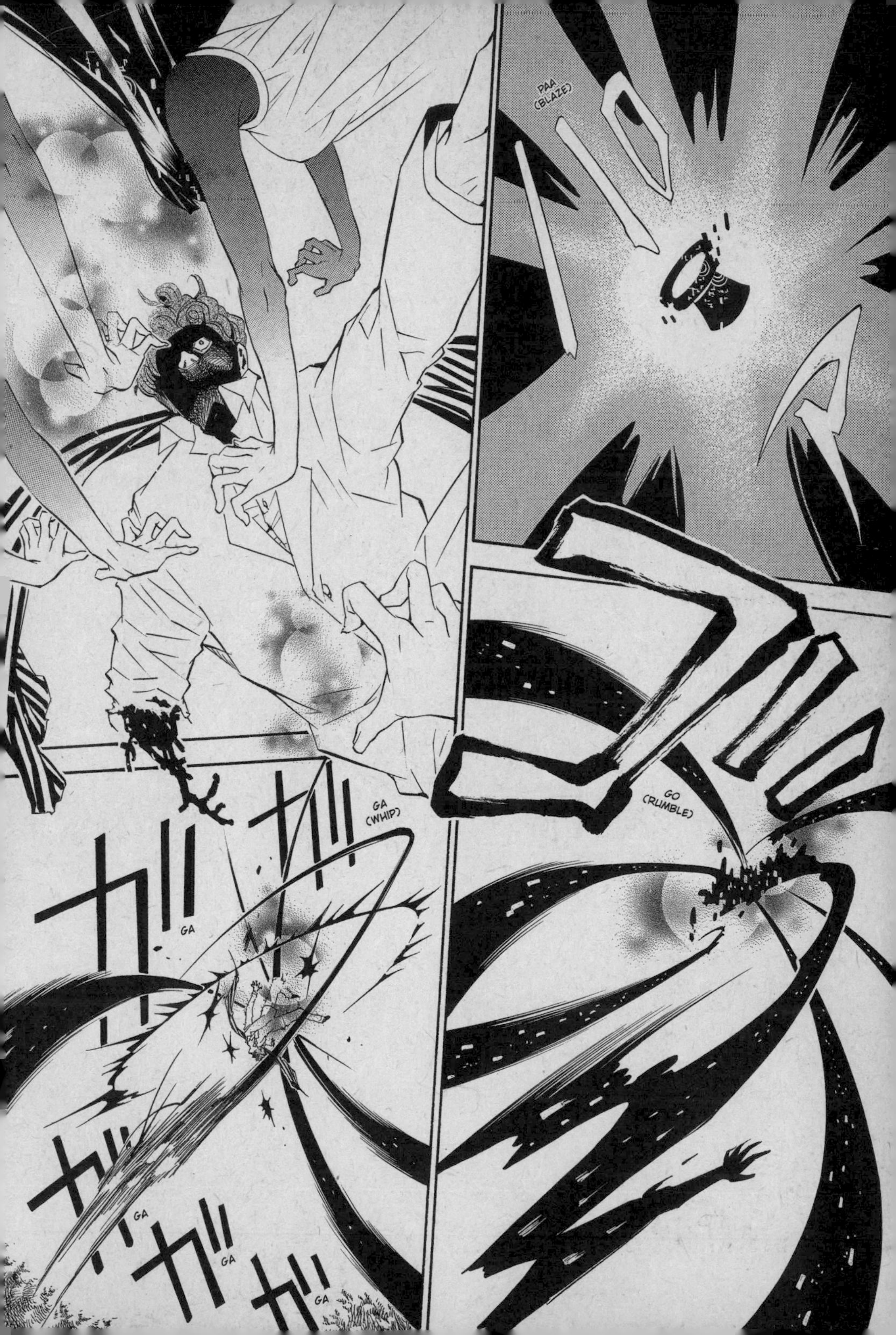
PAA
(BLAZE)
GO
(RUMBLE)
GA
(WHIP)
GA
GA
GA
GA

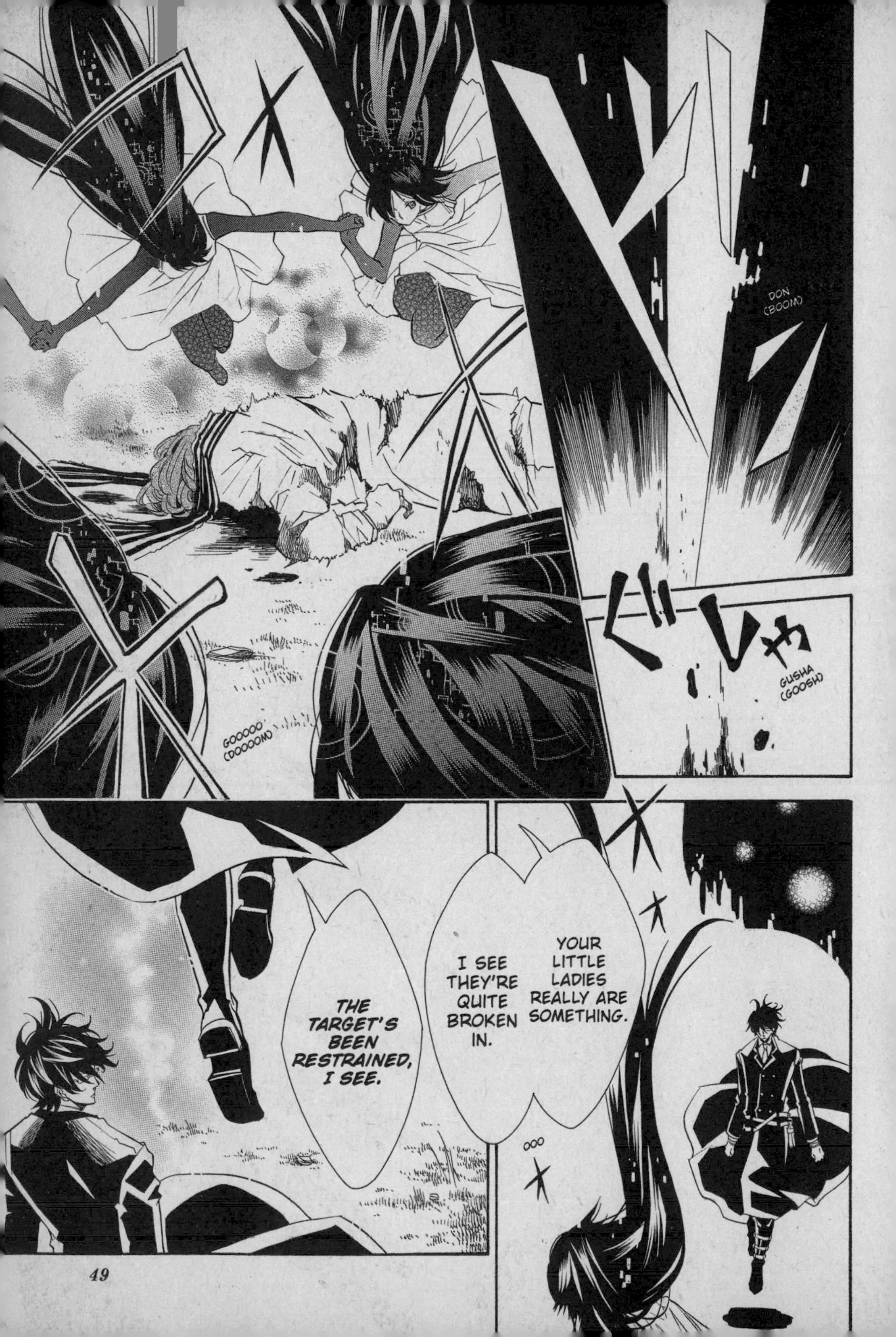
DON (BOOM)
ぐしゃ
GUSHA (GOOSH)
GOOOOO (DOOOOM)
YOUR LITTLE LADIES REALLY ARE SOMETHING.
I SEE THEY'RE QUITE BROKEN IN.
ooo
THE TARGET'S BEEN RESTRAINED, I SEE.

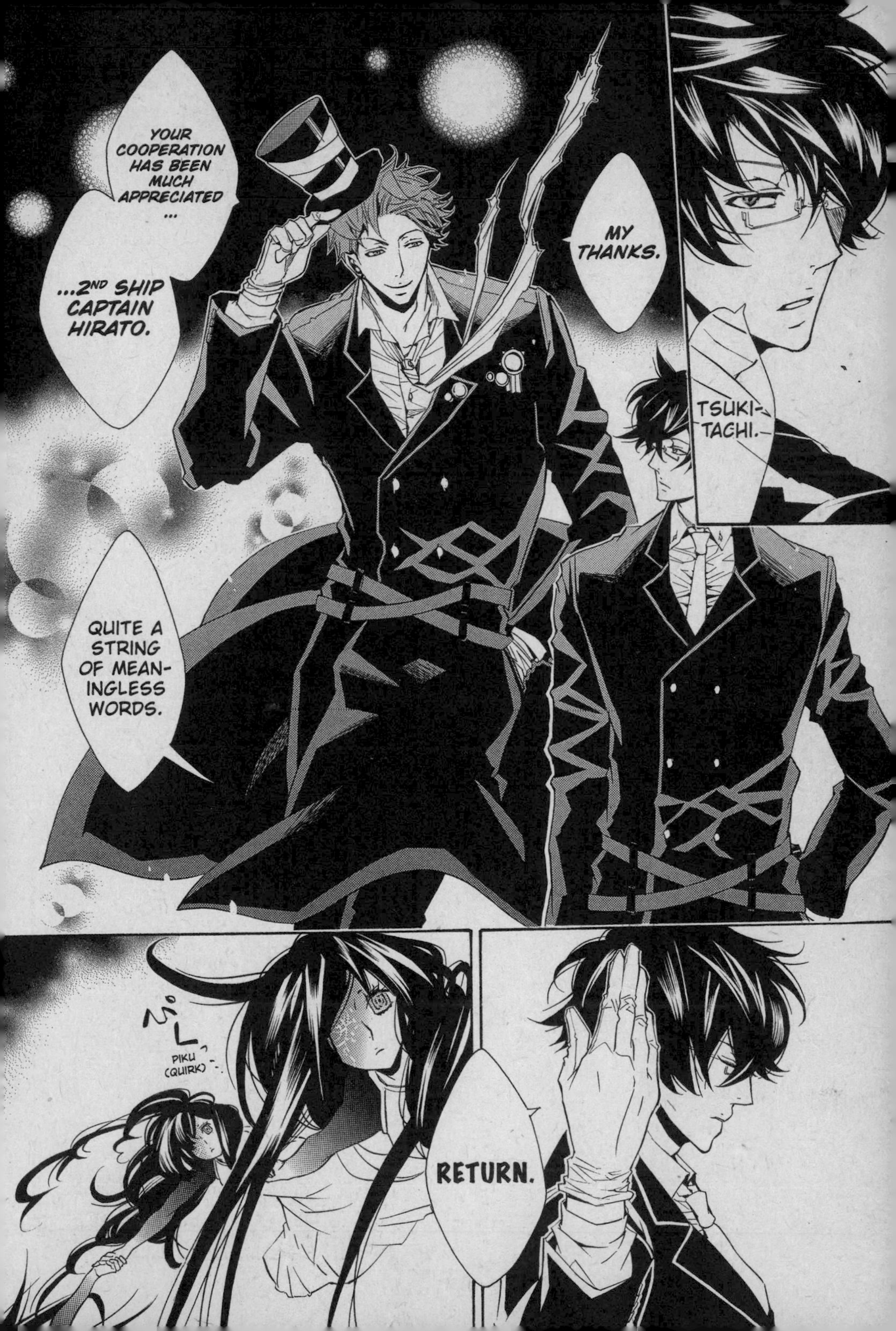
YOUR COOPERATION HAS BEEN MUCH APPRECIATED ...
...2ND SHIP CAPTAIN HIRATO.
MY THANKS.
TSUKI-TACHI.
QUITE A STRING OF MEAN-INGLESS WORDS.
RETURN.
PIKU (QUIRK)

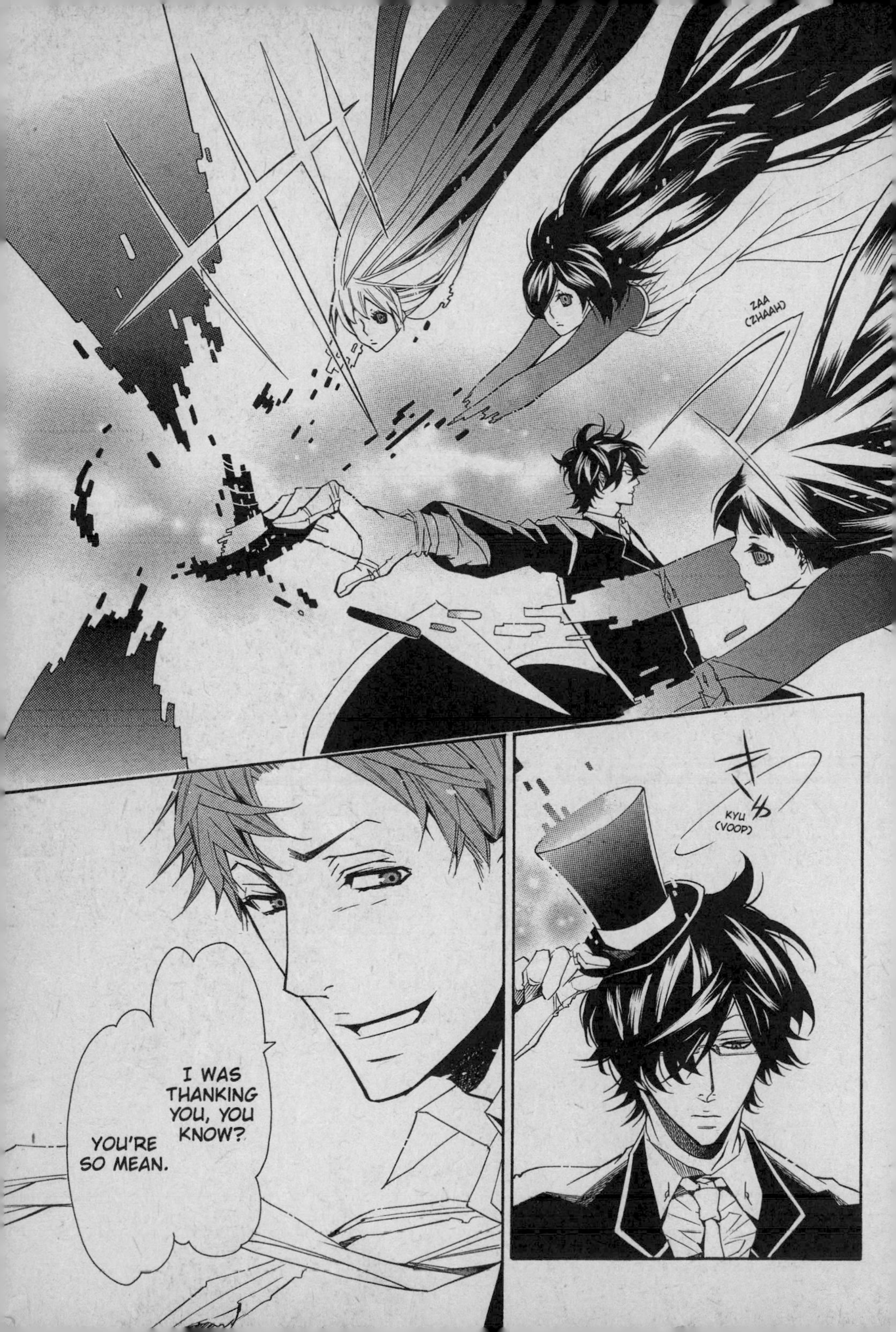
ZAA (ZHAAH)
KYU (VOOP)
I WAS THANKING YOU, YOU KNOW?
YOU'RE SO MEAN.

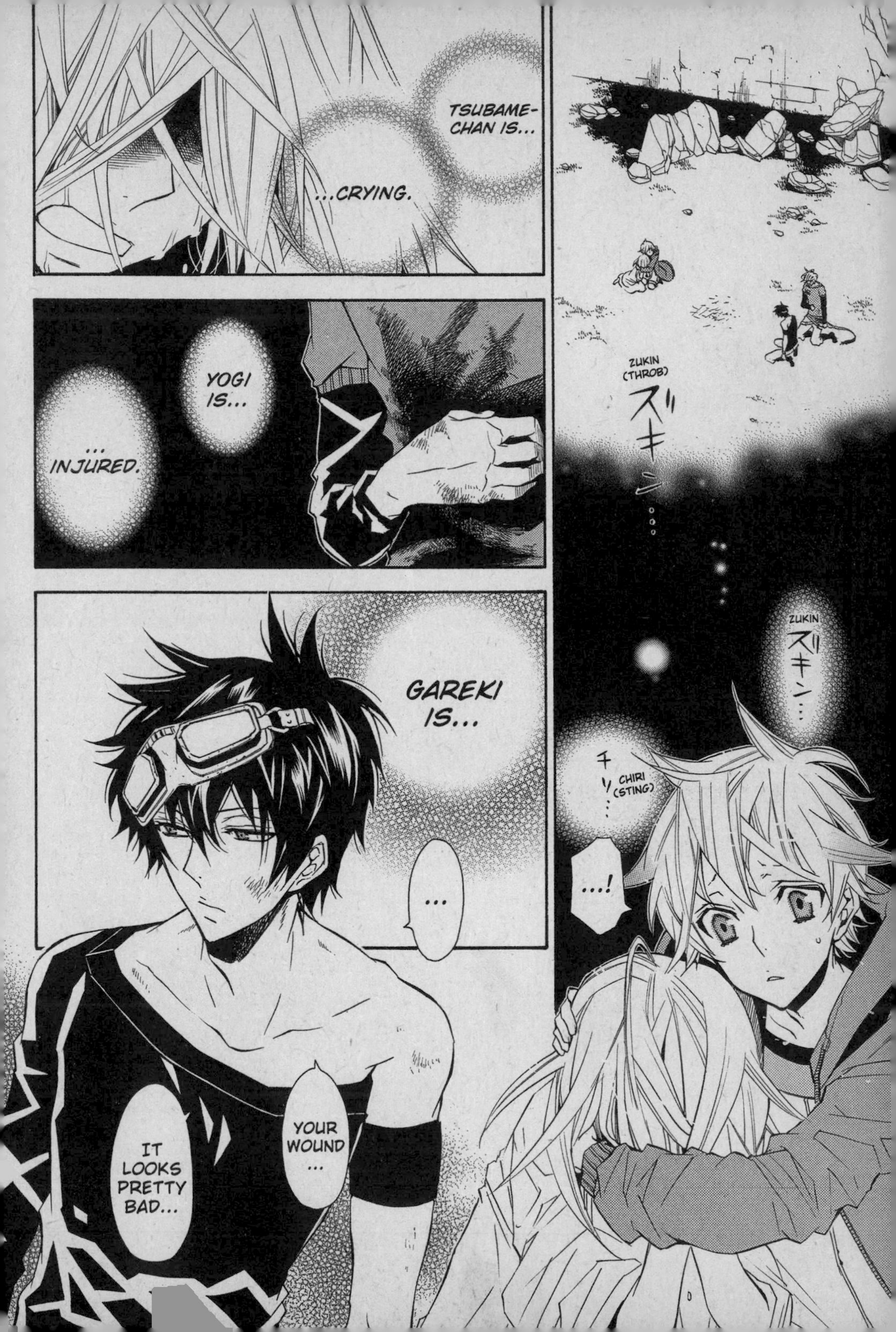
ZUKIN (THROB)
ズキン…
ZUKIN
ズキン…
チリ…
CHIRI (STING)
...!
TSUBAME-CHAN IS...
...CRYING.
YOGI IS...
... INJURED.
GAREKI IS...
...
YOUR WOUND...
IT LOOKS PRETTY BAD...

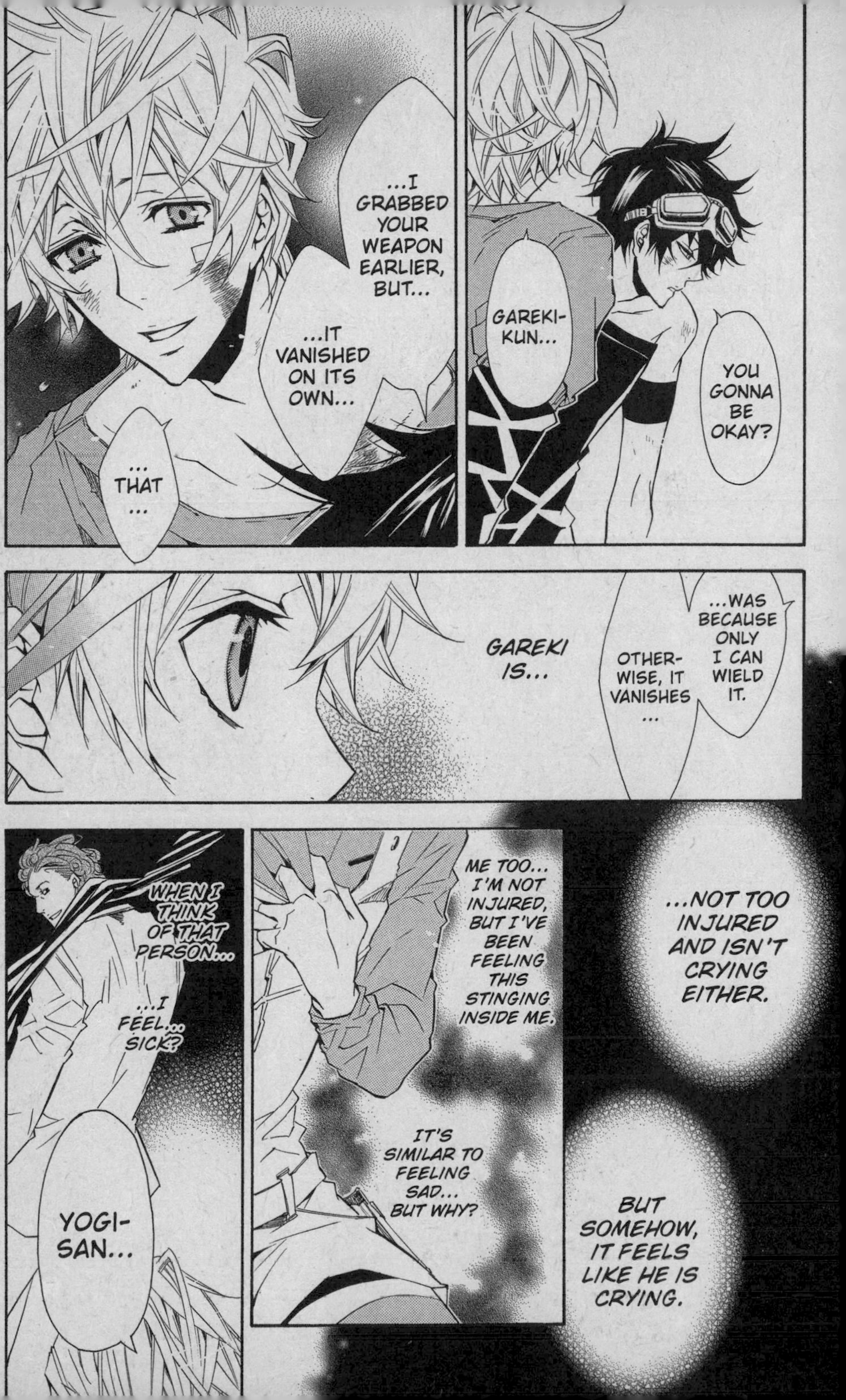
YOU GONNA BE OKAY?
GAREKI-KUN...
...I GRABBED YOUR WEAPON EARLIER, BUT...
...IT VANISHED ON ITS OWN...
...THAT...
...WAS BECAUSE ONLY I CAN WIELD IT.
OTHER-WISE, IT VANISHES...
GAREKI IS...
...NOT TOO INJURED AND ISN'T CRYING EITHER.
BUT SOMEHOW, IT FEELS LIKE HE IS CRYING.
ME TOO... I'M NOT INJURED, BUT I'VE BEEN FEELING THIS STINGING INSIDE ME.
IT'S SIMILAR TO FEELING SAD... BUT WHY?
WHEN I THINK OF THAT PERSON...
...I FEEL... SICK?
YOGI-SAN...

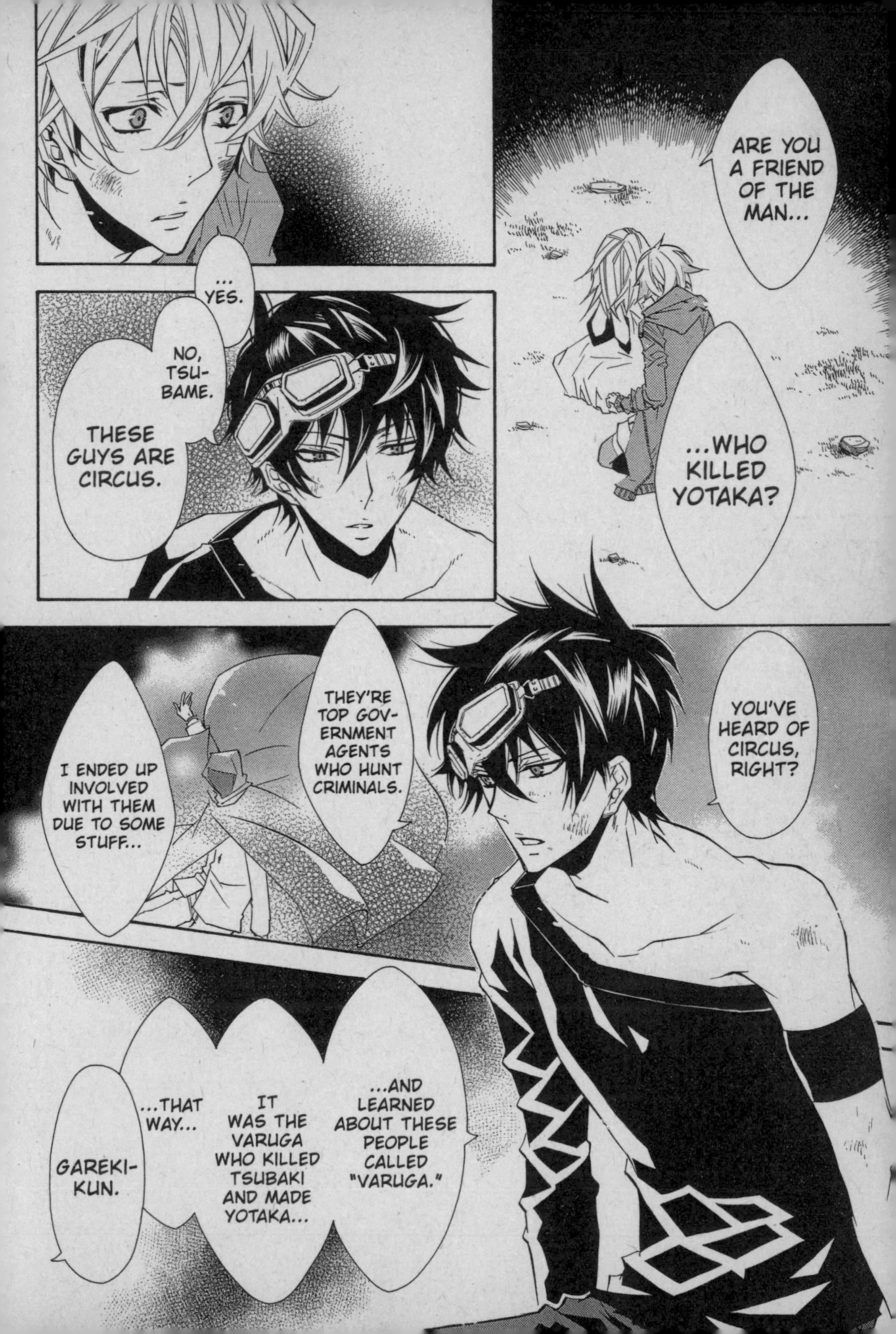
ARE YOU A FRIEND OF THE MAN...
...WHO KILLED YOTAKA?
...YES.
NO, TSUBAME.
THESE GUYS ARE CIRCUS.
YOU'VE HEARD OF CIRCUS, RIGHT?
THEY'RE TOP GOVERNMENT AGENTS WHO HUNT CRIMINALS.
I ENDED UP INVOLVED WITH THEM DUE TO SOME STUFF...
...AND LEARNED ABOUT THESE PEOPLE CALLED "VARUGA."
IT WAS THE VARUGA WHO KILLED TSUBAKI AND MADE YOTAKA...
...THAT WAY...
GAREKI-KUN.

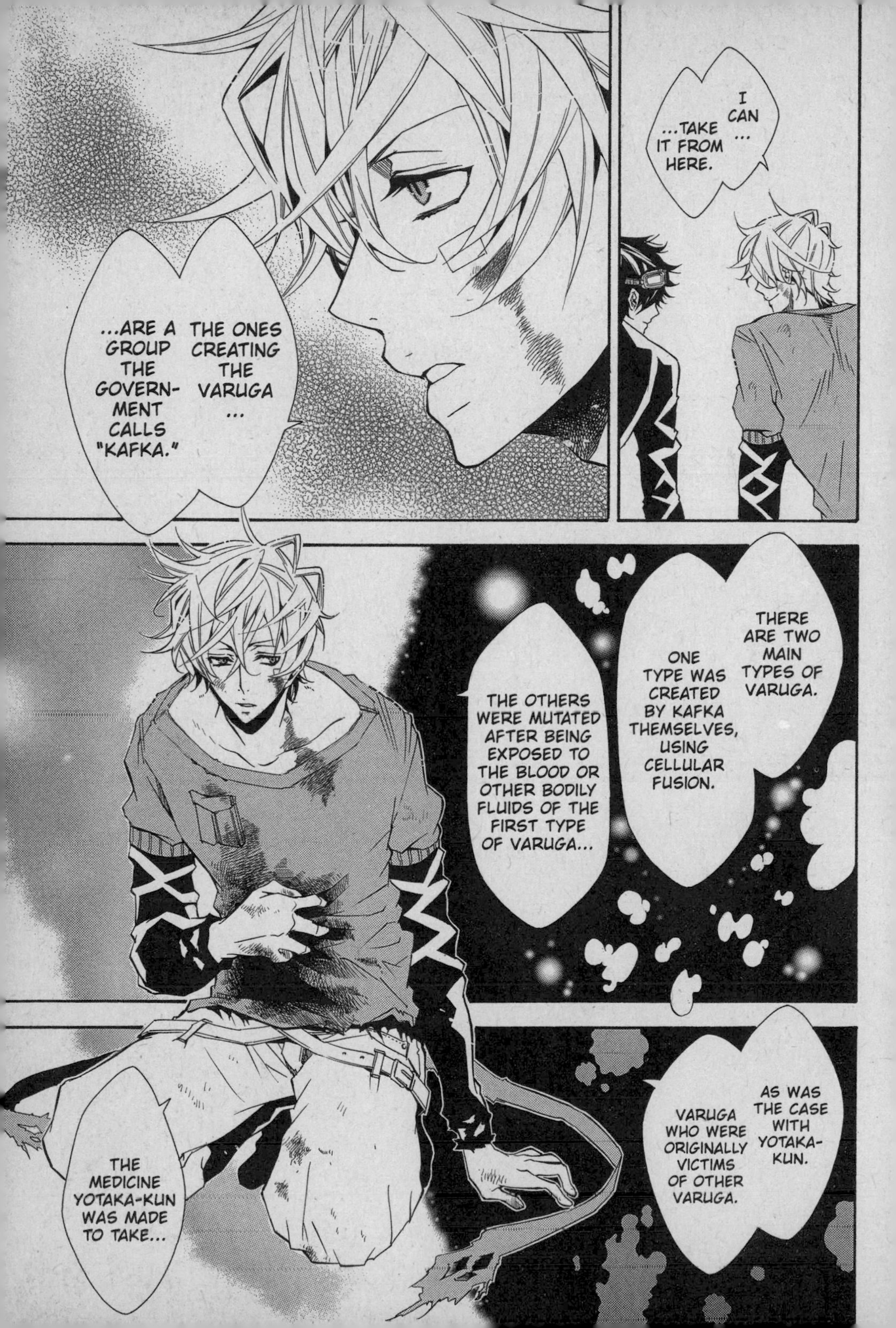
I CAN ...
...TAKE IT FROM HERE.
THE ONES CREATING THE VARUGA ...
...ARE A GROUP THE GOVERNMENT CALLS "KAFKA."
THERE ARE TWO MAIN TYPES OF VARUGA.
ONE TYPE WAS CREATED BY KAFKA THEMSELVES, USING CELLULAR FUSION.
THE OTHERS WERE MUTATED AFTER BEING EXPOSED TO THE BLOOD OR OTHER BODILY FLUIDS OF THE FIRST TYPE OF VARUGA...
AS WAS THE CASE WITH YOTAKA-KUN.
VARUGA WHO WERE ORIGINALLY VICTIMS OF OTHER VARUGA.
THE MEDICINE YOTAKA-KUN WAS MADE TO TAKE...

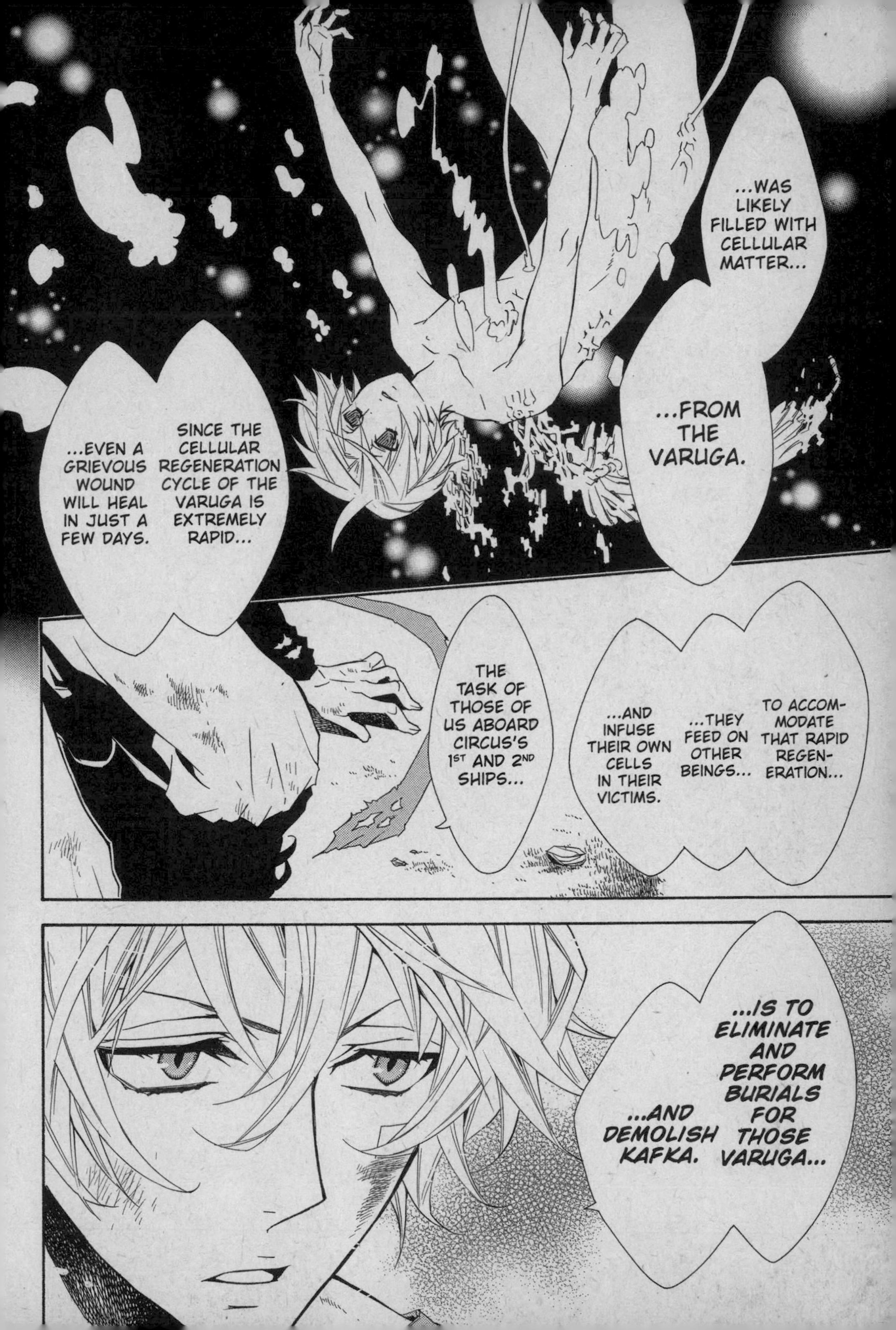
...WAS LIKELY FILLED WITH CELLULAR MATTER...
...FROM THE VARUGA.
SINCE THE CELLULAR REGENERATION CYCLE OF THE VARUGA IS EXTREMELY RAPID...
...EVEN A GRIEVOUS WOUND WILL HEAL IN JUST A FEW DAYS.
TO ACCOM-MODATE THAT RAPID REGEN-ERATION...
...THEY FEED ON OTHER BEINGS...
...AND INFUSE THEIR OWN CELLS IN THEIR VICTIMS.
THE TASK OF THOSE OF US ABOARD CIRCUS'S 1ST AND 2ND SHIPS...
...IS TO ELIMINATE AND PERFORM BURIALS FOR THOSE VARUGA...
...AND DEMOLISH KAFKA.

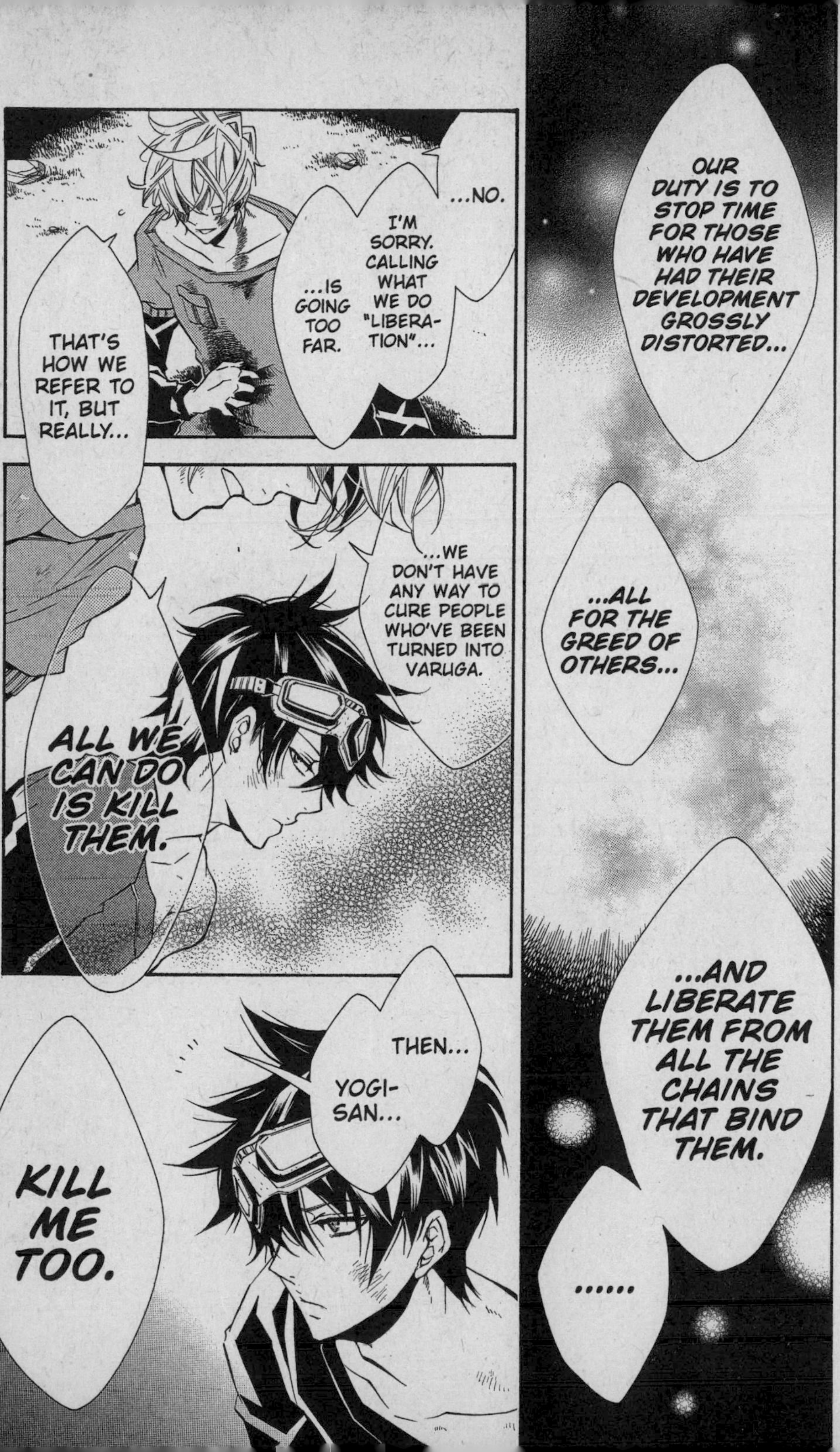
OUR DUTY IS TO STOP TIME FOR THOSE WHO HAVE HAD THEIR DEVELOPMENT GROSSLY DISTORTED...
...ALL FOR THE GREED OF OTHERS...
...AND LIBERATE THEM FROM ALL THE CHAINS THAT BIND THEM.
......
...NO.
I'M SORRY. CALLING WHAT WE DO "LIBERATION"...
...IS GOING TOO FAR.
THAT'S HOW WE REFER TO IT, BUT REALLY...
...WE DON'T HAVE ANY WAY TO CURE PEOPLE WHO'VE BEEN TURNED INTO VARUGA.
ALL WE CAN DO IS KILL THEM.
THEN...
YOGI-SAN...
KILL ME TOO.

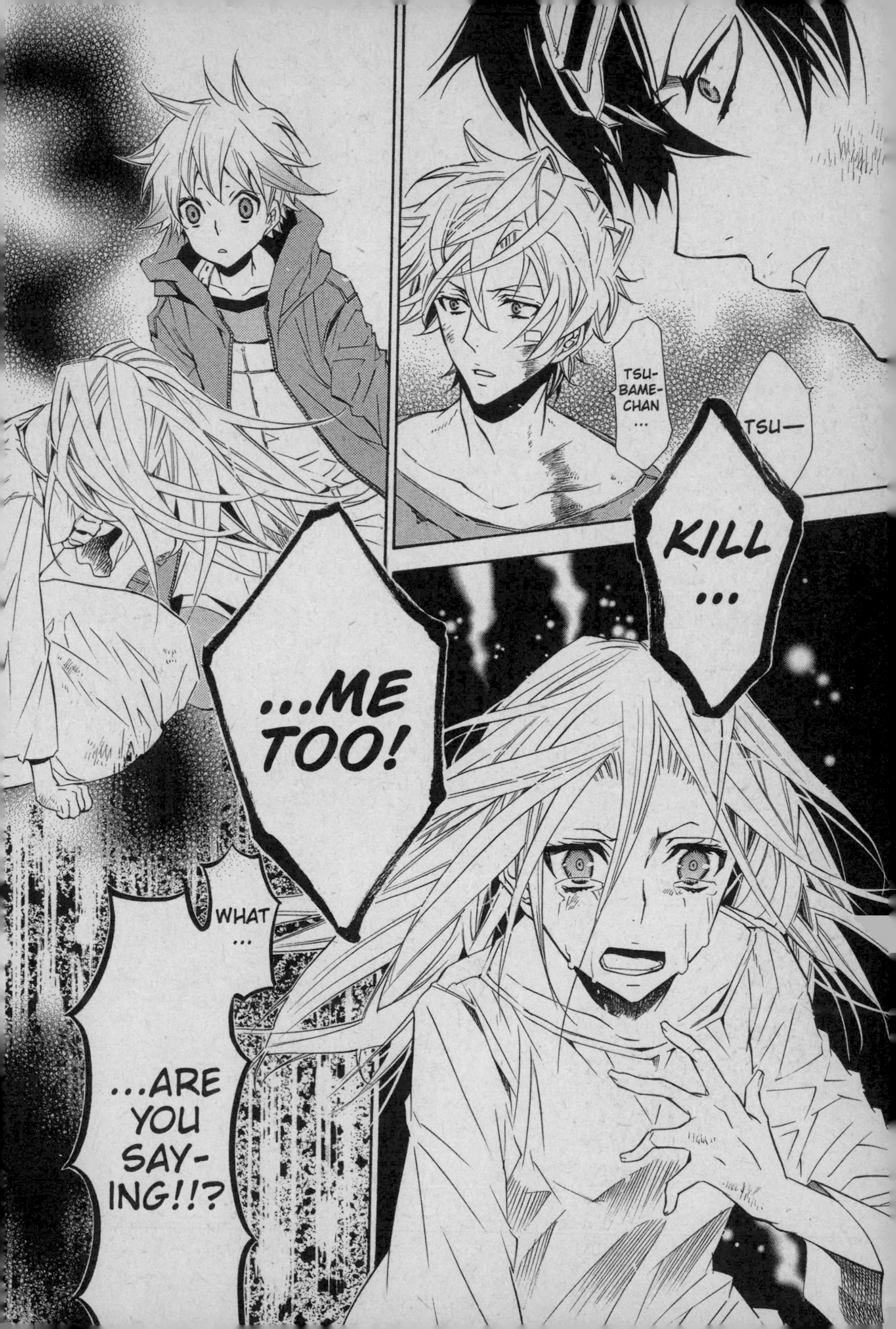
TSU—
TSU-BAME-CHAN...
KILL...
...ME TOO!
WHAT...
...ARE YOU SAYING!!?

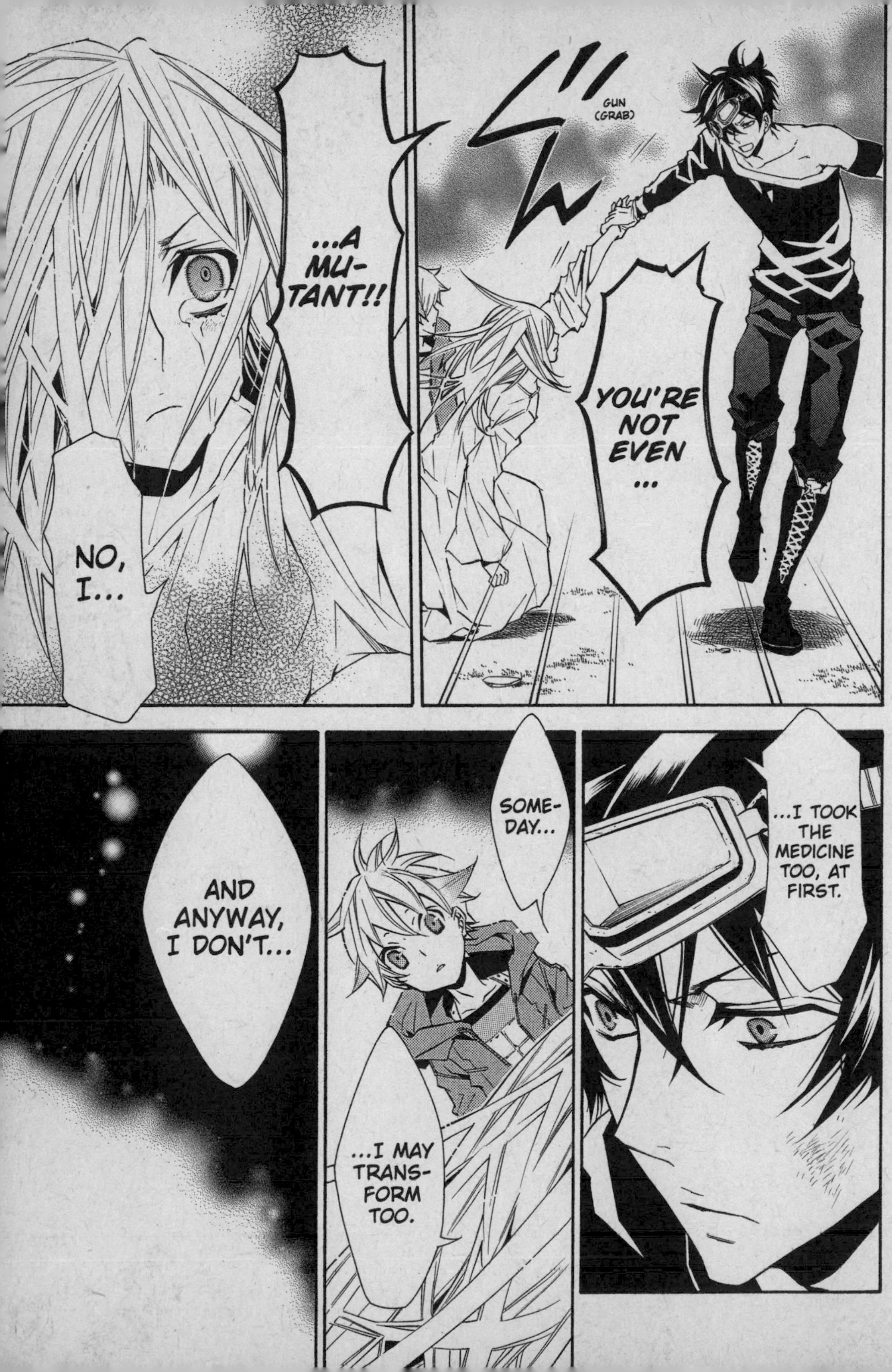
GUN (GRAB)
YOU'RE NOT EVEN ...
...A MU-TANT!!
NO, I...
...I TOOK THE MEDICINE TOO, AT FIRST.
SOME-DAY...
...I MAY TRANS-FORM TOO.
AND ANYWAY, I DON'T...

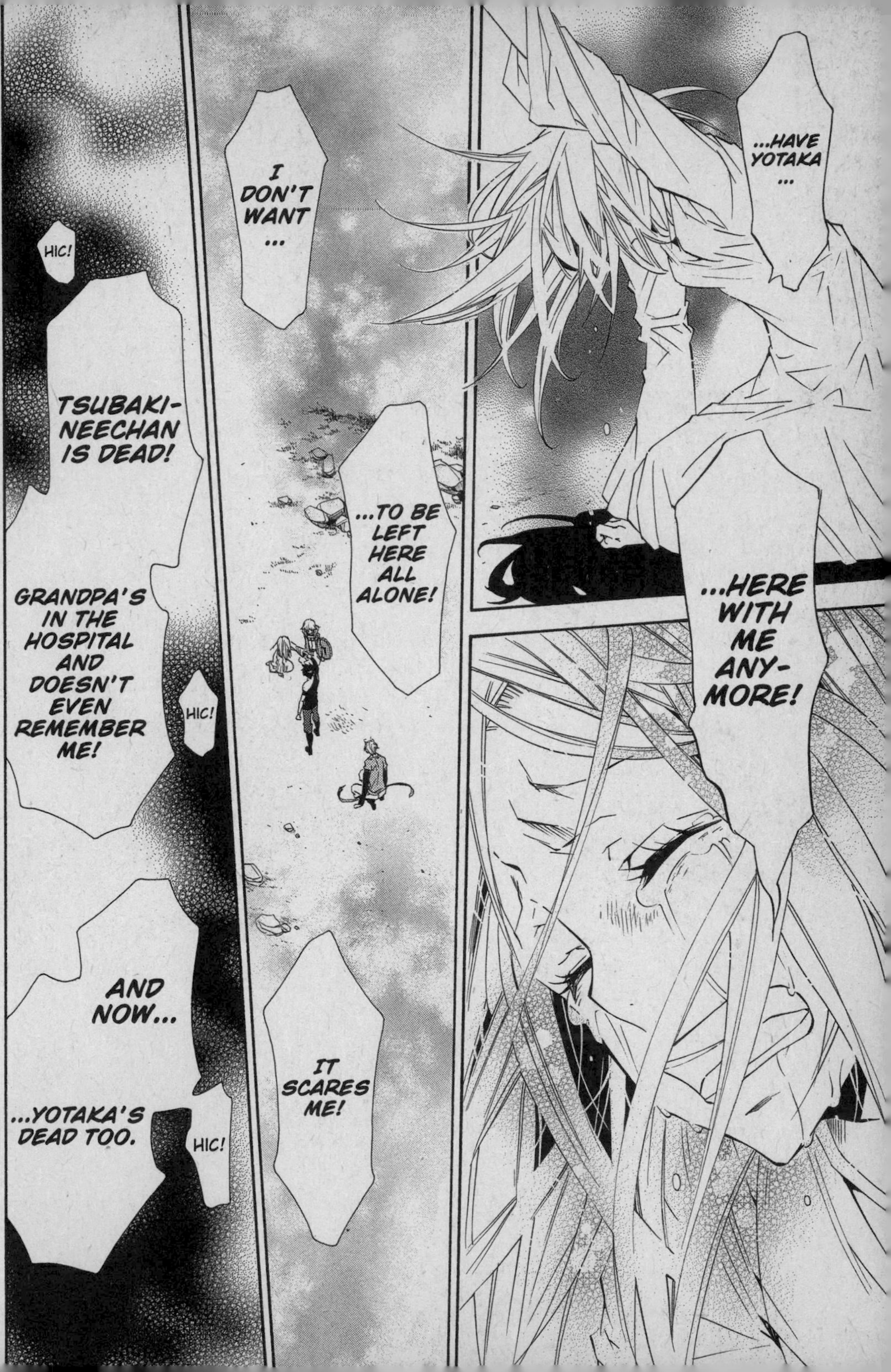
...HAVE YOTAKA ...
...HERE WITH ME ANYMORE!
I DON'T WANT ...
...TO BE LEFT HERE ALL ALONE!
IT SCARES ME!
HIC!
TSUBAKI-NEECHAN IS DEAD!
GRANDPA'S IN THE HOSPITAL AND DOESN'T EVEN REMEMBER ME!
HIC!
AND NOW...
...YOTAKA'S DEAD TOO.
HIC!

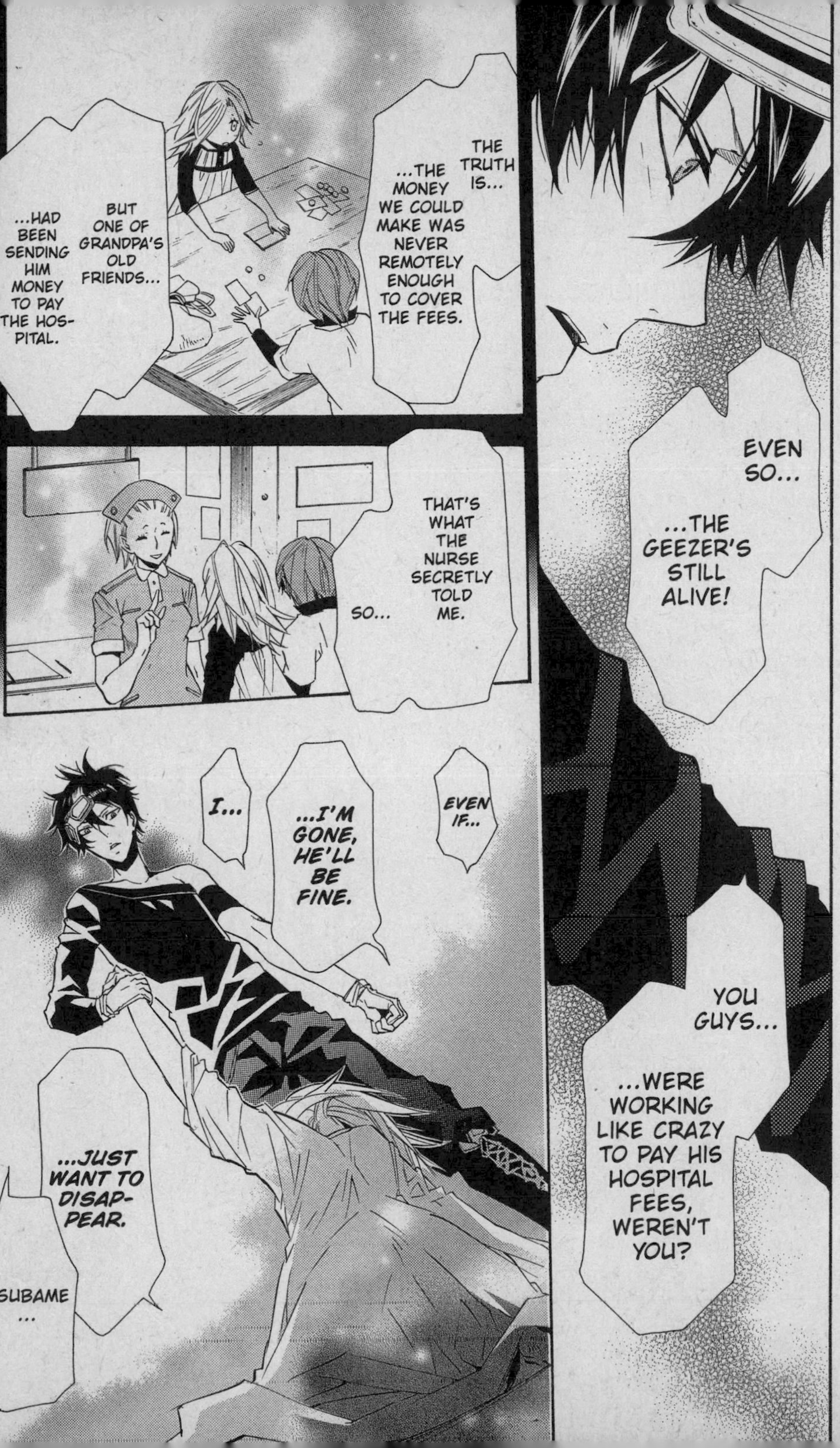
EVEN SO...
...THE GEEZER'S STILL ALIVE!
YOU GUYS...
...WERE WORKING LIKE CRAZY TO PAY HIS HOSPITAL FEES, WEREN'T YOU?
THE TRUTH IS...
...THE MONEY WE COULD MAKE WAS NEVER REMOTELY ENOUGH TO COVER THE FEES.
BUT ONE OF GRANDPA'S OLD FRIENDS...
...HAD BEEN SENDING HIM MONEY TO PAY THE HOSPITAL.
THAT'S WHAT THE NURSE SECRETLY TOLD ME.
SO...
EVEN IF...
...I'M GONE, HE'LL BE FINE.
I...
...JUST WANT TO DISAPPEAR.
TSUBAME...

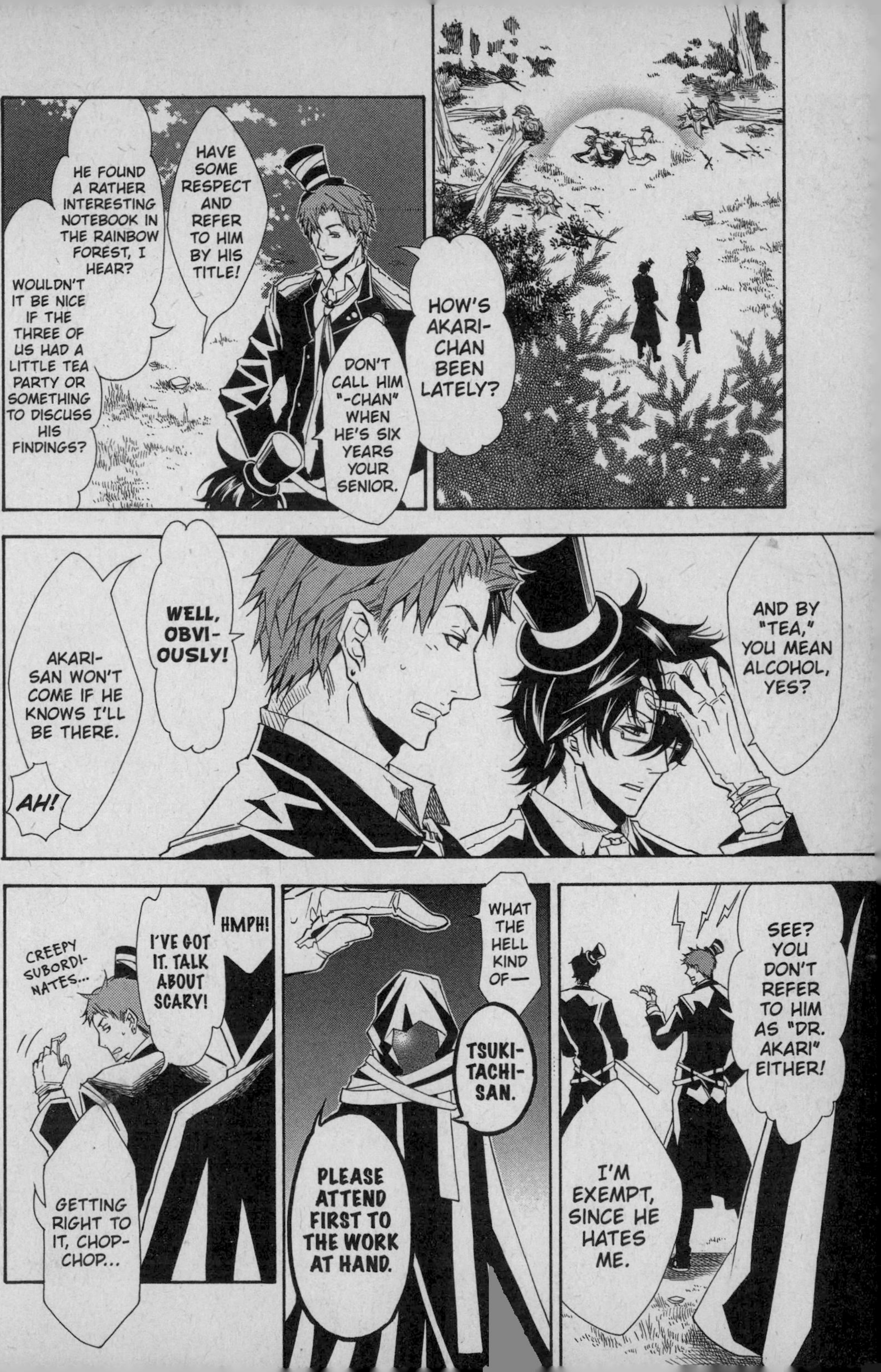
HOW'S AKARI-CHAN BEEN LATELY?
DON'T CALL HIM "-CHAN" WHEN HE'S SIX YEARS YOUR SENIOR.
HAVE SOME RESPECT AND REFER TO HIM BY HIS TITLE!
HE FOUND A RATHER INTERESTING NOTEBOOK IN THE RAINBOW FOREST, I HEAR?
WOULDN'T IT BE NICE IF THE THREE OF US HAD A LITTLE TEA PARTY OR SOMETHING TO DISCUSS HIS FINDINGS?
AND BY "TEA," YOU MEAN ALCOHOL, YES?
WELL, OBVIOUSLY!
AKARI-SAN WON'T COME IF HE KNOWS I'LL BE THERE.
AH!
SEE? YOU DON'T REFER TO HIM AS "DR. AKARI" EITHER!
I'M EXEMPT, SINCE HE HATES ME.
WHAT THE HELL KIND OF—
TSUKITACHI-SAN.
PLEASE ATTEND FIRST TO THE WORK AT HAND.
HMPH!
I'VE GOT IT. TALK ABOUT SCARY!
CREEPY SUBORDINATES...
GETTING RIGHT TO IT, CHOP-CHOP...

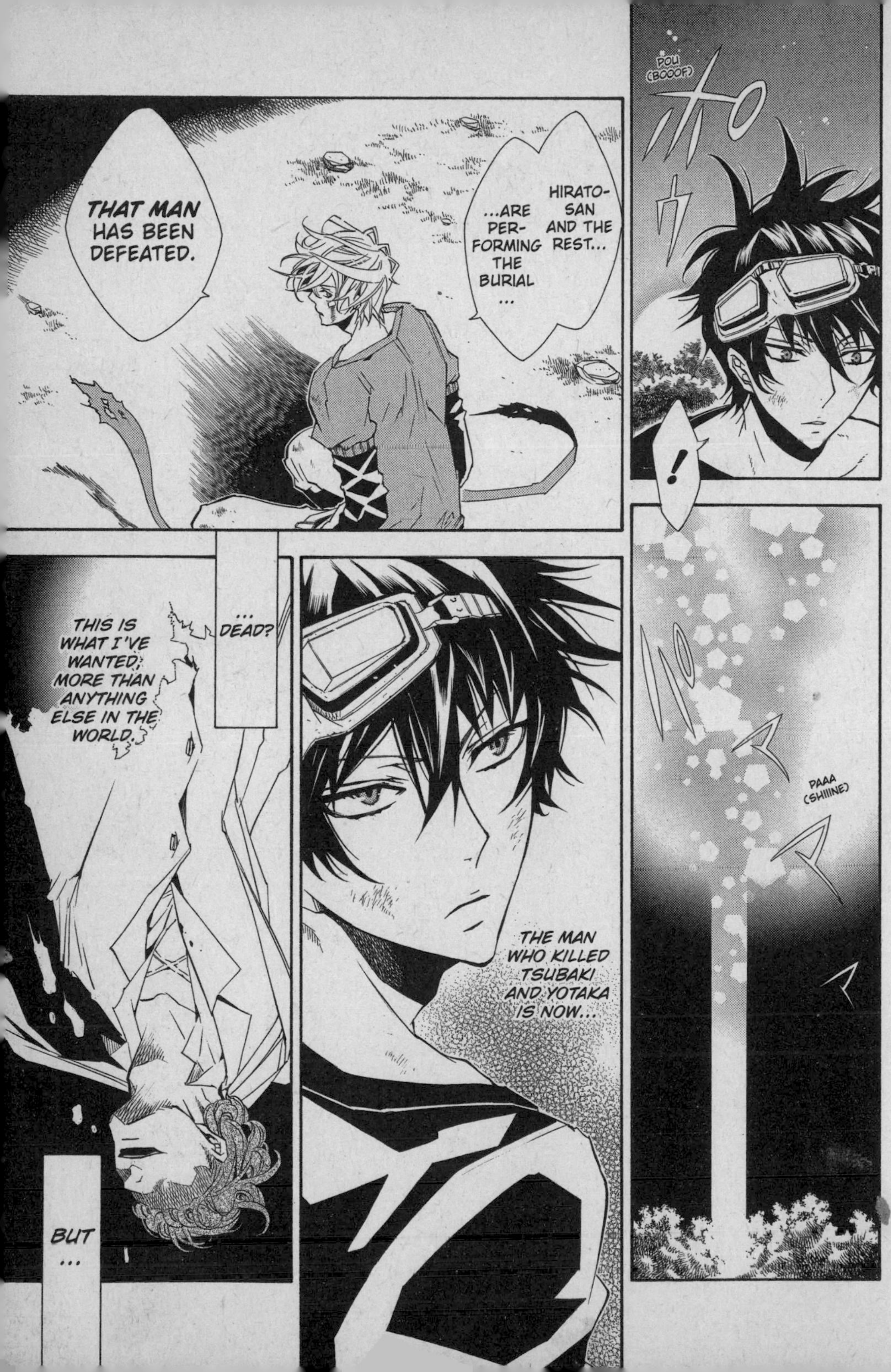
POU (BOOOF)
!
PAAA (SHIIINE)
HIRATO-SAN AND THE REST...
...ARE PERFORMING THE BURIAL...
THAT MAN HAS BEEN DEFEATED.
THE MAN WHO KILLED TSUBAKI AND YOTAKA IS NOW...
...DEAD?
THIS IS WHAT I'VE WANTED, MORE THAN ANYTHING ELSE IN THE WORLD.
BUT...

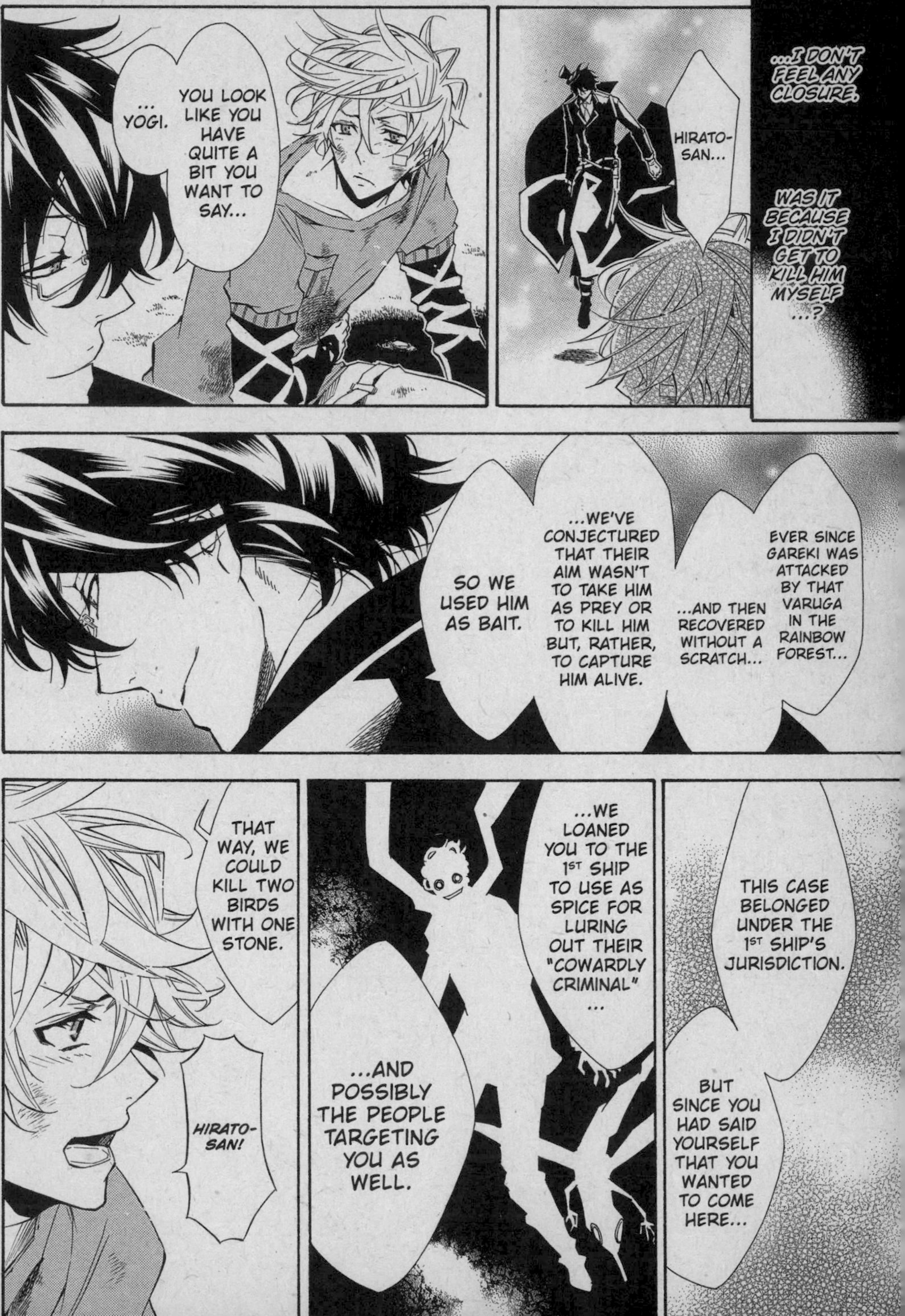

...I DON'T FEEL ANY CLOSURE.
WAS IT BECAUSE I DIDN'T GET TO KILL HIM MYSELF...?
HIRATO-SAN...
...YOGI. YOU LOOK LIKE YOU HAVE QUITE A BIT YOU WANT TO SAY...
EVER SINCE GAREKI WAS ATTACKED BY THAT VARUGA IN THE RAINBOW FOREST...
...AND THEN RECOVERED WITHOUT A SCRATCH...
...WE'VE CONJECTURED THAT THEIR AIM WASN'T TO TAKE HIM AS PREY OR TO KILL HIM BUT, RATHER, TO CAPTURE HIM ALIVE.
SO WE USED HIM AS BAIT.
THIS CASE BELONGED UNDER THE 1ST SHIP'S JURISDICTION.
BUT SINCE YOU HAD SAID YOURSELF THAT YOU WANTED TO COME HERE...
...WE LOANED YOU TO THE 1ST SHIP TO USE AS SPICE FOR LURING OUT THEIR "COWARDLY CRIMINAL"...
...AND POSSIBLY THE PEOPLE TARGETING YOU AS WELL.
THAT WAY, WE COULD KILL TWO BIRDS WITH ONE STONE.
HIRATO-SAN!

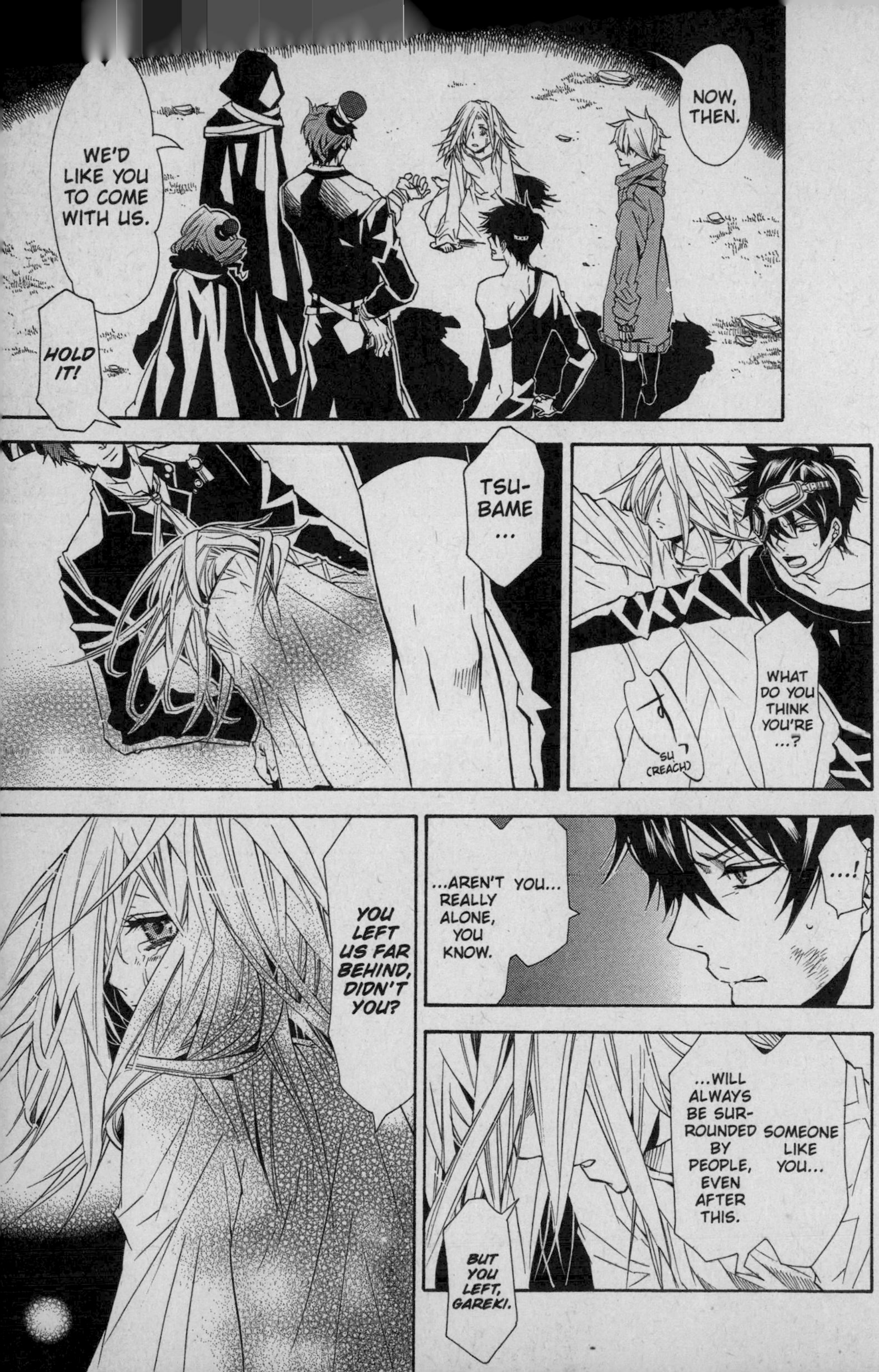
NOW, THEN.
WE'D LIKE YOU TO COME WITH US.
HOLD IT!
WHAT DO YOU THINK YOU'RE ...?
SU (REACH)
TSU-BAME ...
...!
...AREN'T YOU... REALLY ALONE, YOU KNOW.
SOMEONE LIKE YOU...
...WILL ALWAYS BE SUR-ROUNDED BY PEOPLE, EVEN AFTER THIS.
BUT YOU LEFT, GAREKI.
YOU LEFT US FAR BEHIND, DIDN'T YOU?

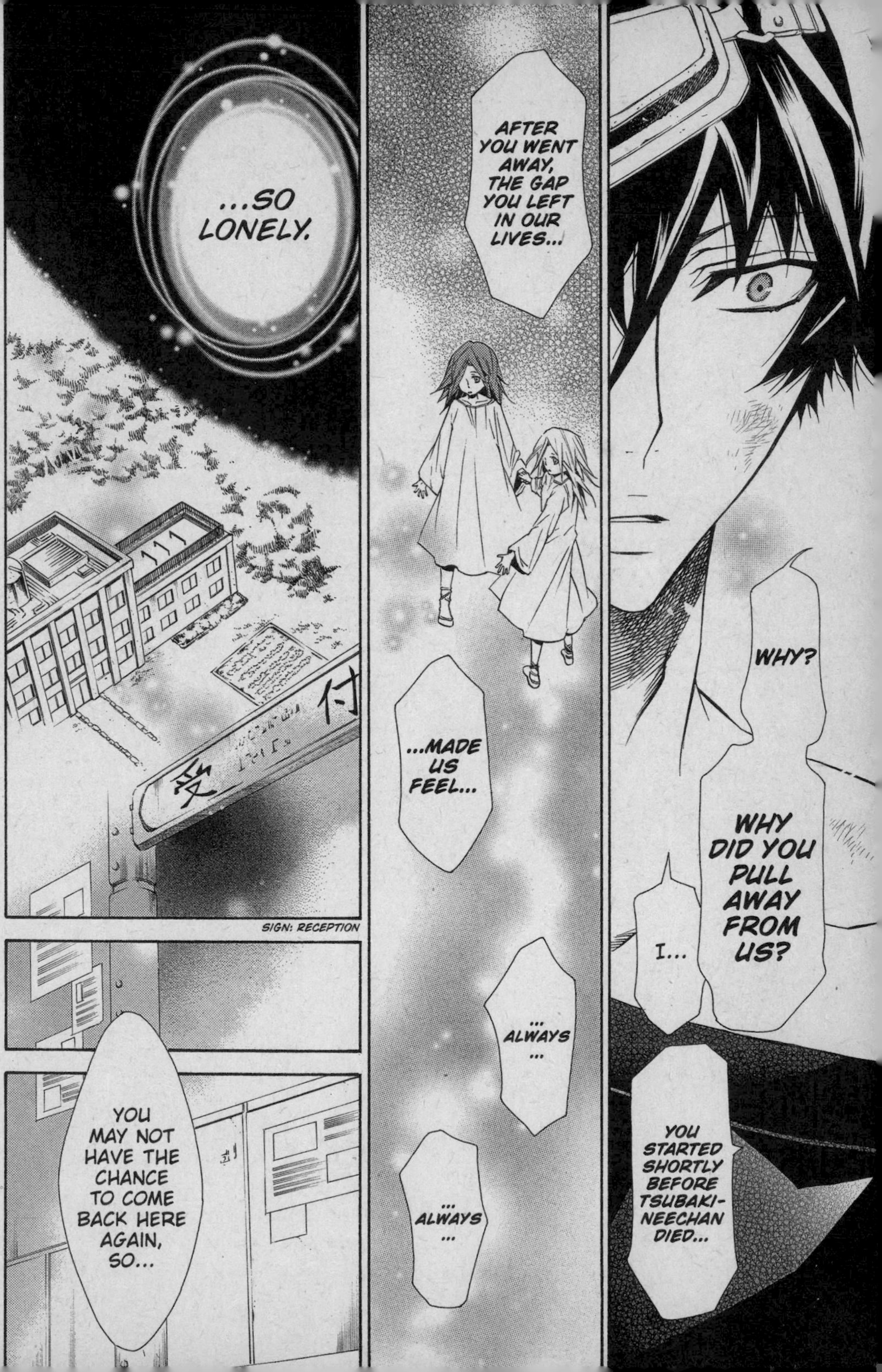
WHY?
WHY DID YOU PULL AWAY FROM US?
I...
YOU STARTED SHORTLY BEFORE TSUBAKI-NEECHAN DIED...
AFTER YOU WENT AWAY, THE GAP YOU LEFT IN OUR LIVES...
...MADE US FEEL...
... ALWAYS ...
... ALWAYS ...
...SO LONELY.
SIGN: RECEPTION
YOU MAY NOT HAVE THE CHANCE TO COME BACK HERE AGAIN, SO...

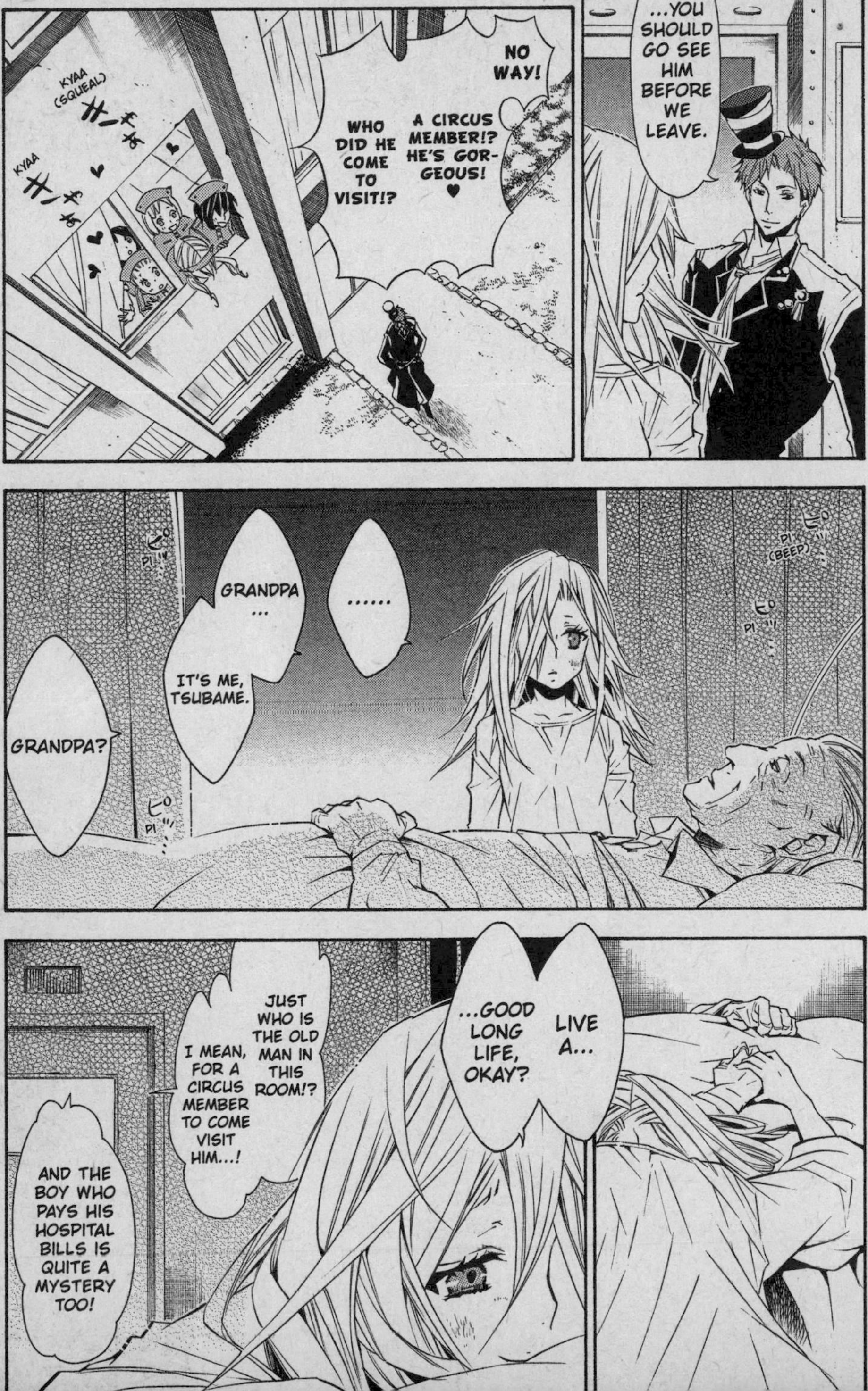
...YOU SHOULD GO SEE HIM BEFORE WE LEAVE.
NO WAY!
A CIRCUS MEMBER!? HE'S GORGEOUS! ♥
WHO DID HE COME TO VISIT!?
KYAA (SQUEAL)
KYAA
PI (BEEP)
PI
......
GRANDPA ...
IT'S ME, TSUBAME.
GRANDPA?
PI
LIVE A...
...GOOD LONG LIFE, OKAY?
JUST WHO IS THE OLD MAN IN THIS ROOM!?
I MEAN, FOR A CIRCUS MEMBER TO COME VISIT HIM...!
AND THE BOY WHO PAYS HIS HOSPITAL BILLS IS QUITE A MYSTERY TOO!

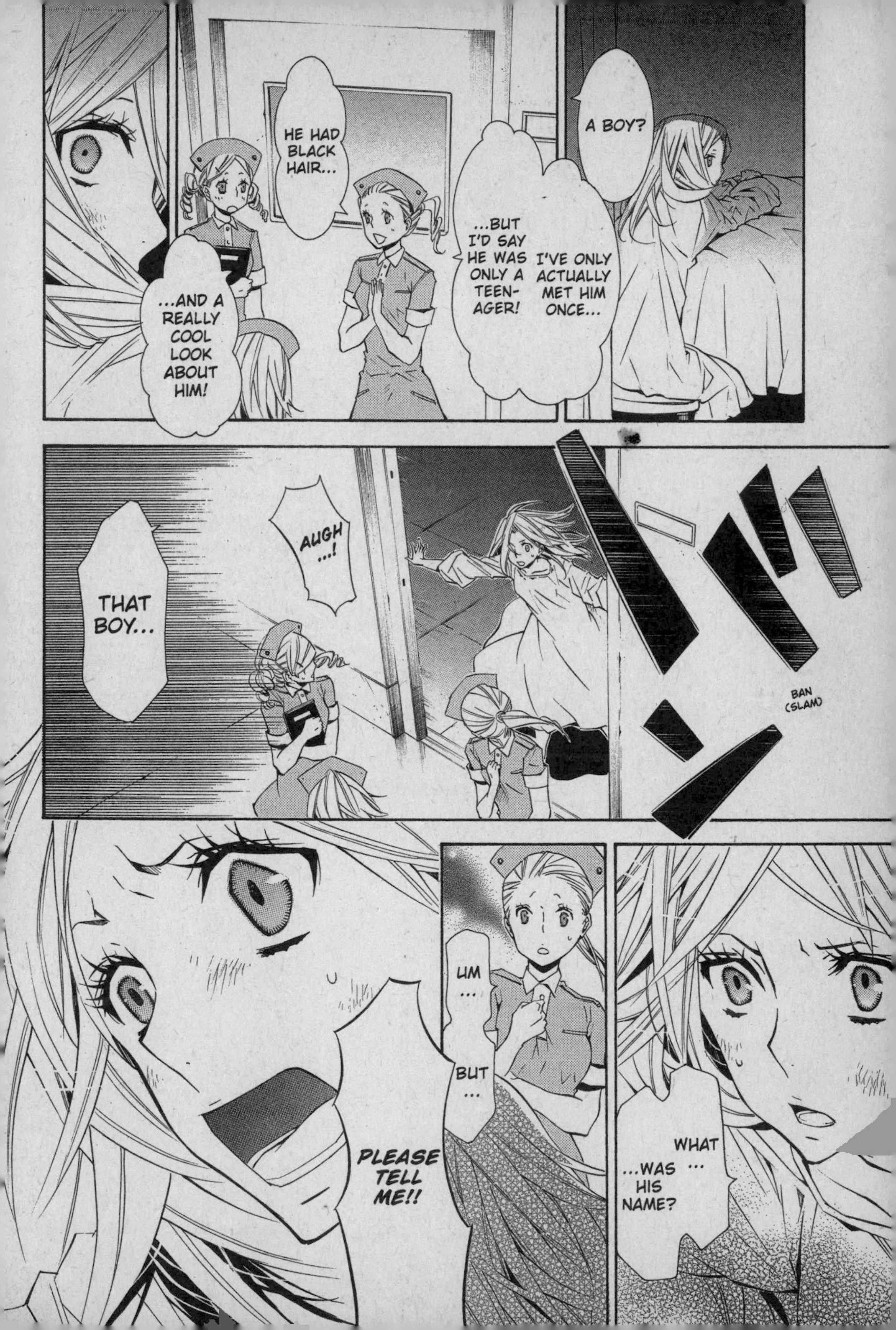
A BOY?
I'VE ONLY ACTUALLY MET HIM ONCE...
...BUT I'D SAY HE WAS ONLY A TEEN-AGER!
HE HAD BLACK HAIR...
...AND A REALLY COOL LOOK ABOUT HIM!
BAN (SLAM)
AUGH ...!
THAT BOY...
WHAT ...
...WAS HIS NAME?
UM ...
BUT ...
PLEASE TELL ME!!

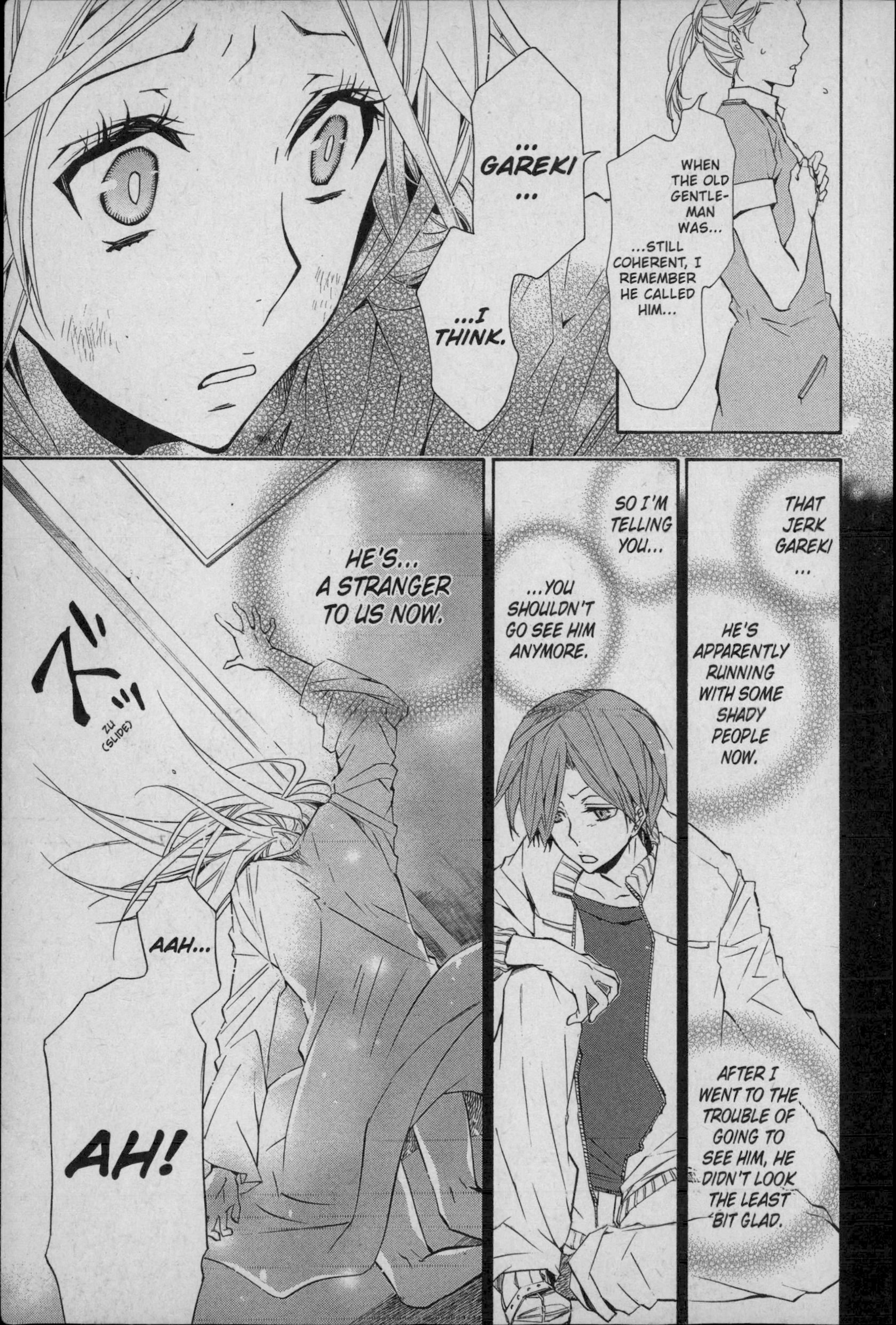
WHEN THE OLD GENTLEMAN WAS...
...STILL COHERENT, I REMEMBER HE CALLED HIM...
...GAREKI...
...I THINK.
THAT JERK GAREKI...
HE'S APPARENTLY RUNNING WITH SOME SHADY PEOPLE NOW.
AFTER I WENT TO THE TROUBLE OF GOING TO SEE HIM, HE DIDN'T LOOK THE LEAST BIT GLAD.
SO I'M TELLING YOU...
...YOU SHOULDN'T GO SEE HIM ANYMORE.
HE'S... A STRANGER TO US NOW.
ズッ
ZU (SLIDE)
AAH...
AH!

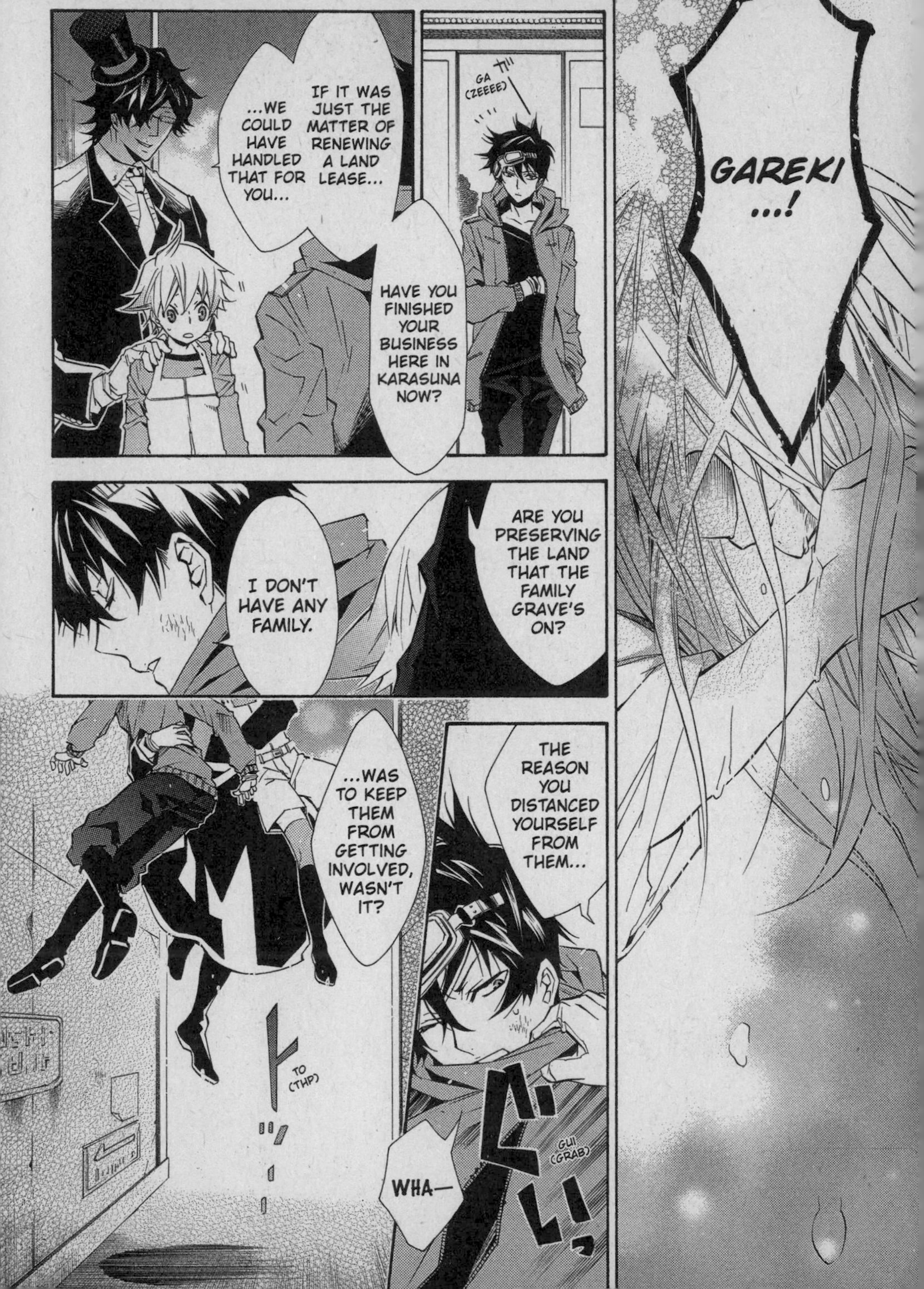
GAREKI...!
GA (ZEEEE)
IF IT WAS JUST THE MATTER OF RENEWING A LAND LEASE...
...WE COULD HAVE HANDLED THAT FOR YOU...
HAVE YOU FINISHED YOUR BUSINESS HERE IN KARASUNA NOW?
ARE YOU PRESERVING THE LAND THAT THE FAMILY GRAVE'S ON?
I DON'T HAVE ANY FAMILY.
THE REASON YOU DISTANCED YOURSELF FROM THEM...
...WAS TO KEEP THEM FROM GETTING INVOLVED, WASN'T IT?
GUI (GRAB)
WHA—
TO (THP)

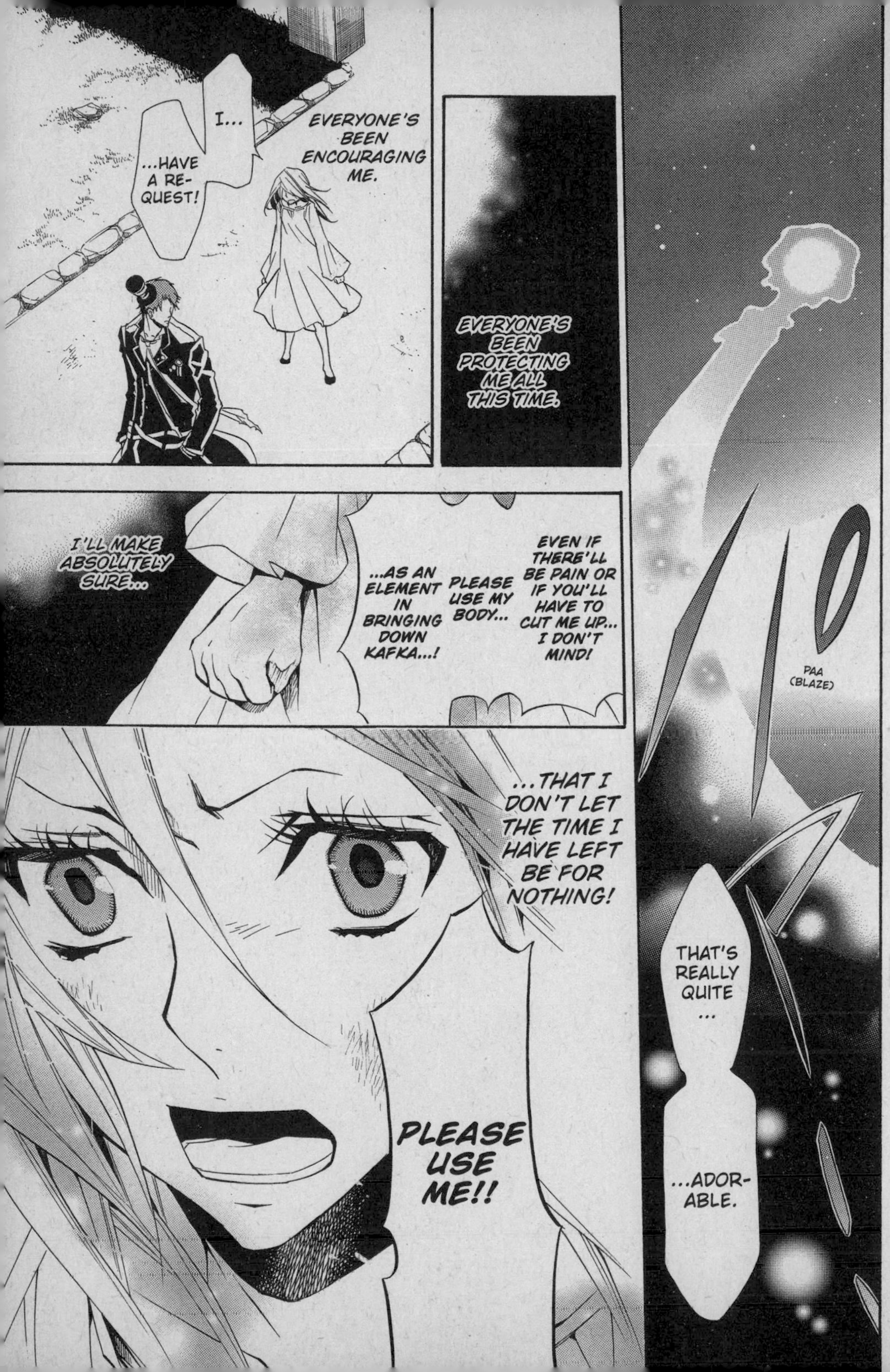

PAA (BLAZE)
THAT'S REALLY QUITE ...
...ADORABLE.
EVERYONE'S BEEN PROTECTING ME ALL THIS TIME.
EVERYONE'S BEEN ENCOURAGING ME.
I...
...HAVE A REQUEST!
EVEN IF THERE'LL BE PAIN OR IF YOU'LL HAVE TO CUT ME UP... I DON'T MIND!
PLEASE USE MY BODY...
...AS AN ELEMENT IN BRINGING DOWN KAFKA...!
I'LL MAKE ABSOLUTELY SURE...
...THAT I DON'T LET THE TIME I HAVE LEFT BE FOR NOTHING!
PLEASE USE ME!!

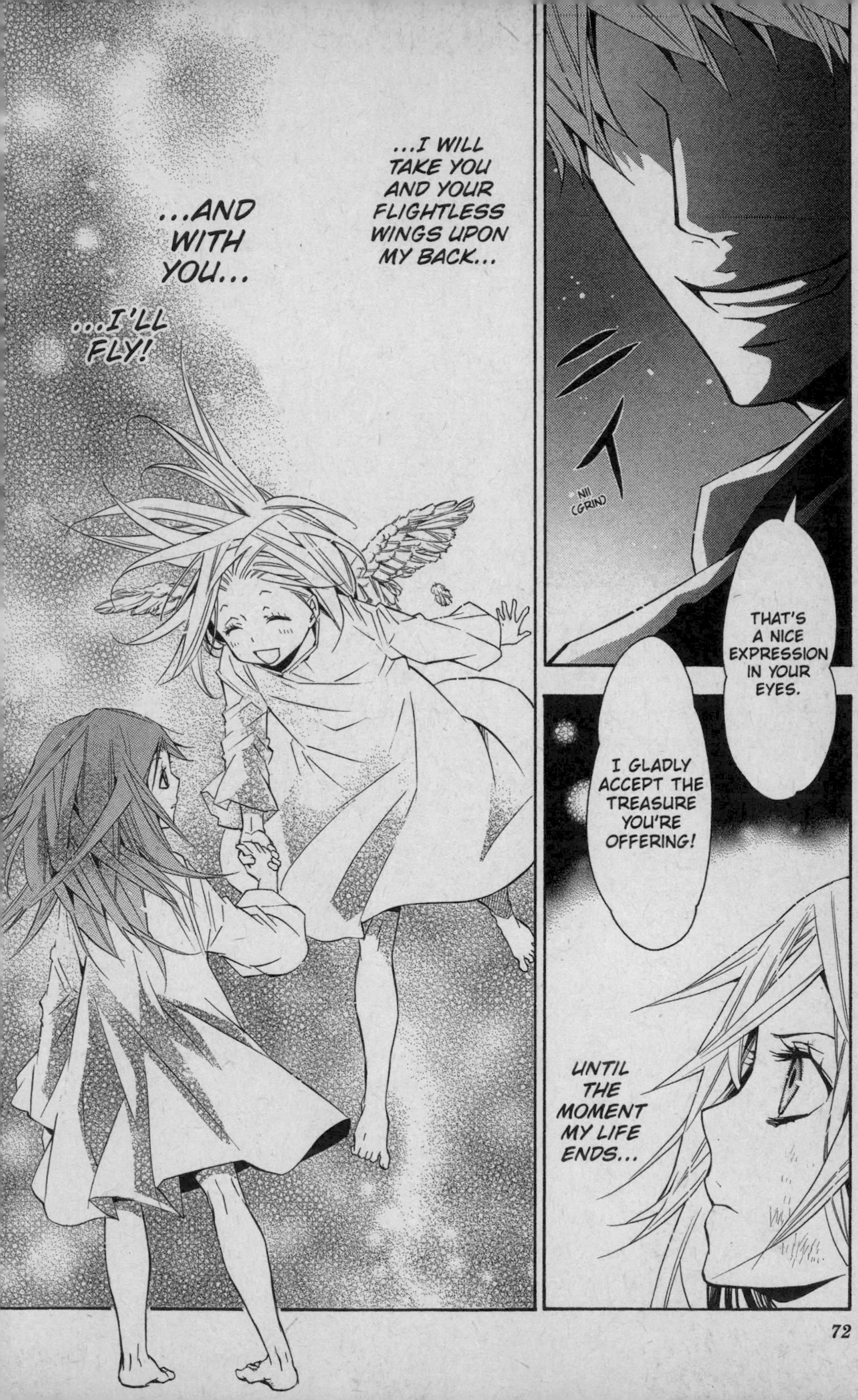
NII (GRIN)
THAT'S A NICE EXPRESSION IN YOUR EYES.
I GLADLY ACCEPT THE TREASURE YOU'RE OFFERING!
UNTIL THE MOMENT MY LIFE ENDS...
...I WILL TAKE YOU AND YOUR FLIGHTLESS WINGS UPON MY BACK...
...AND WITH YOU...
...I'LL FLY!

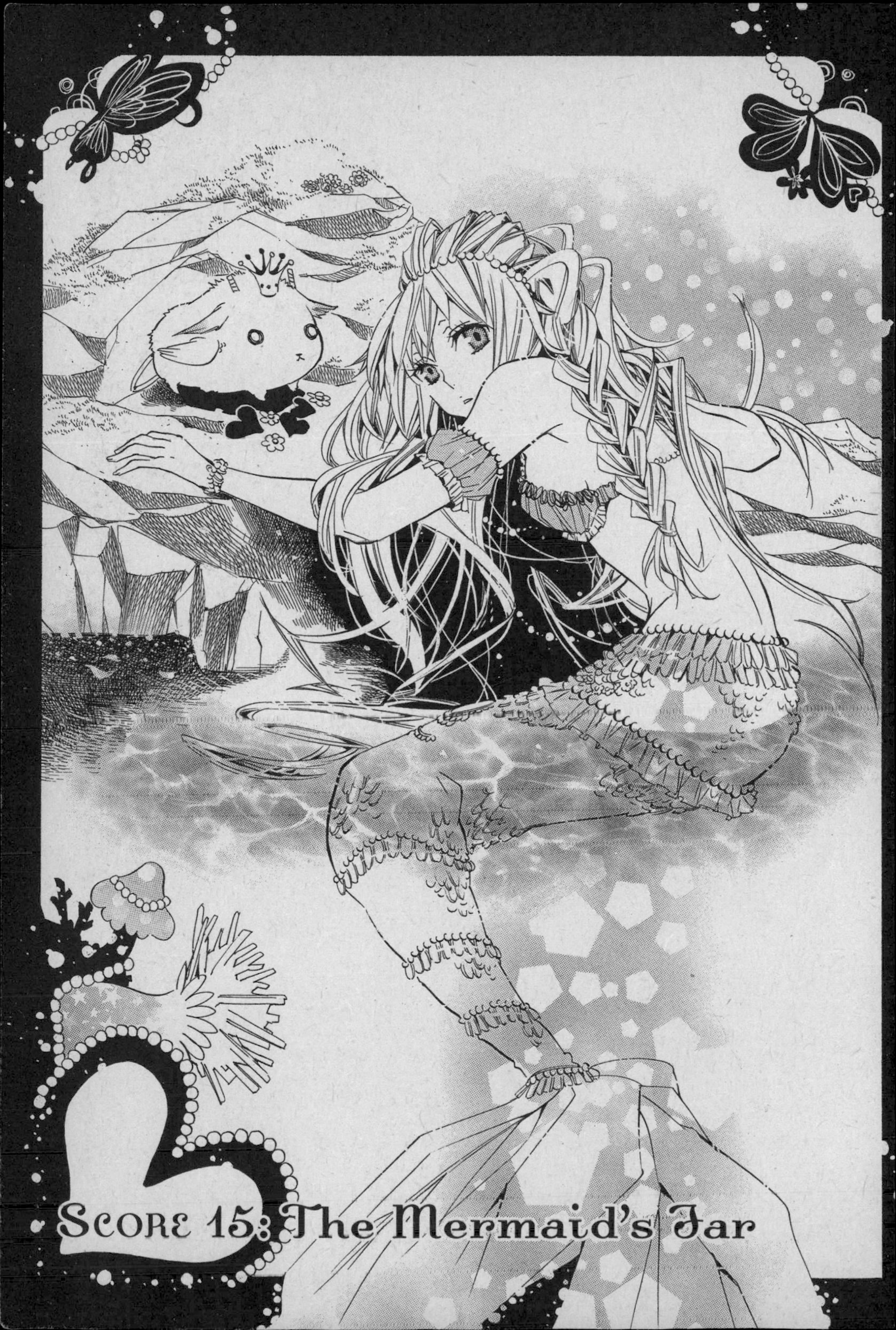
Score 15: The Mermaid's Jar

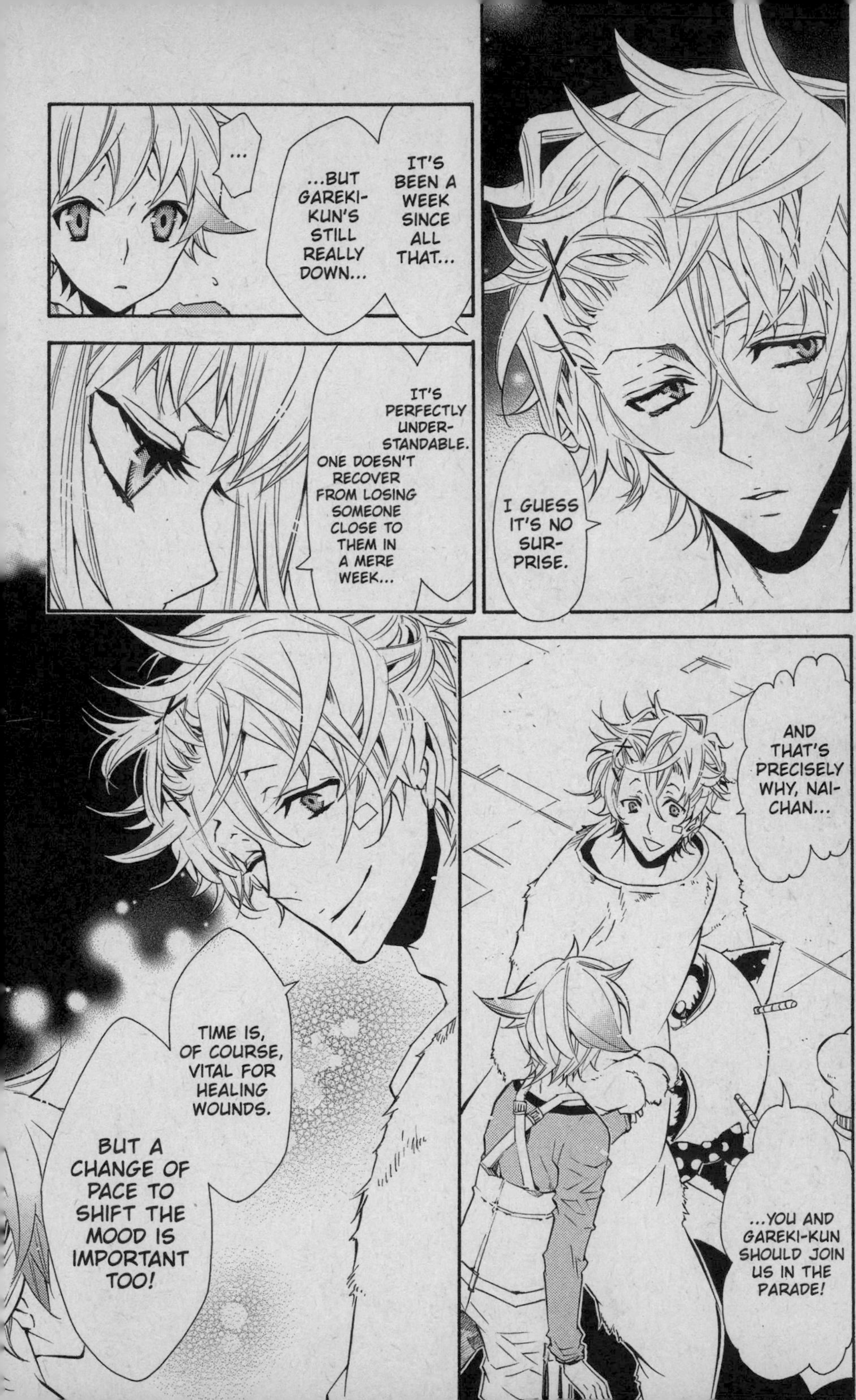
I GUESS IT'S NO SUR-PRISE.
...
IT'S BEEN A WEEK SINCE ALL THAT...
...BUT GAREKI-KUN'S STILL REALLY DOWN...
IT'S PERFECTLY UNDER-STANDABLE. ONE DOESN'T RECOVER FROM LOSING SOMEONE CLOSE TO THEM IN A MERE WEEK...
AND THAT'S PRECISELY WHY, NAI-CHAN...
...YOU AND GAREKI-KUN SHOULD JOIN US IN THE PARADE!
TIME IS, OF COURSE, VITAL FOR HEALING WOUNDS.
BUT A CHANGE OF PACE TO SHIFT THE MOOD IS IMPORTANT TOO!

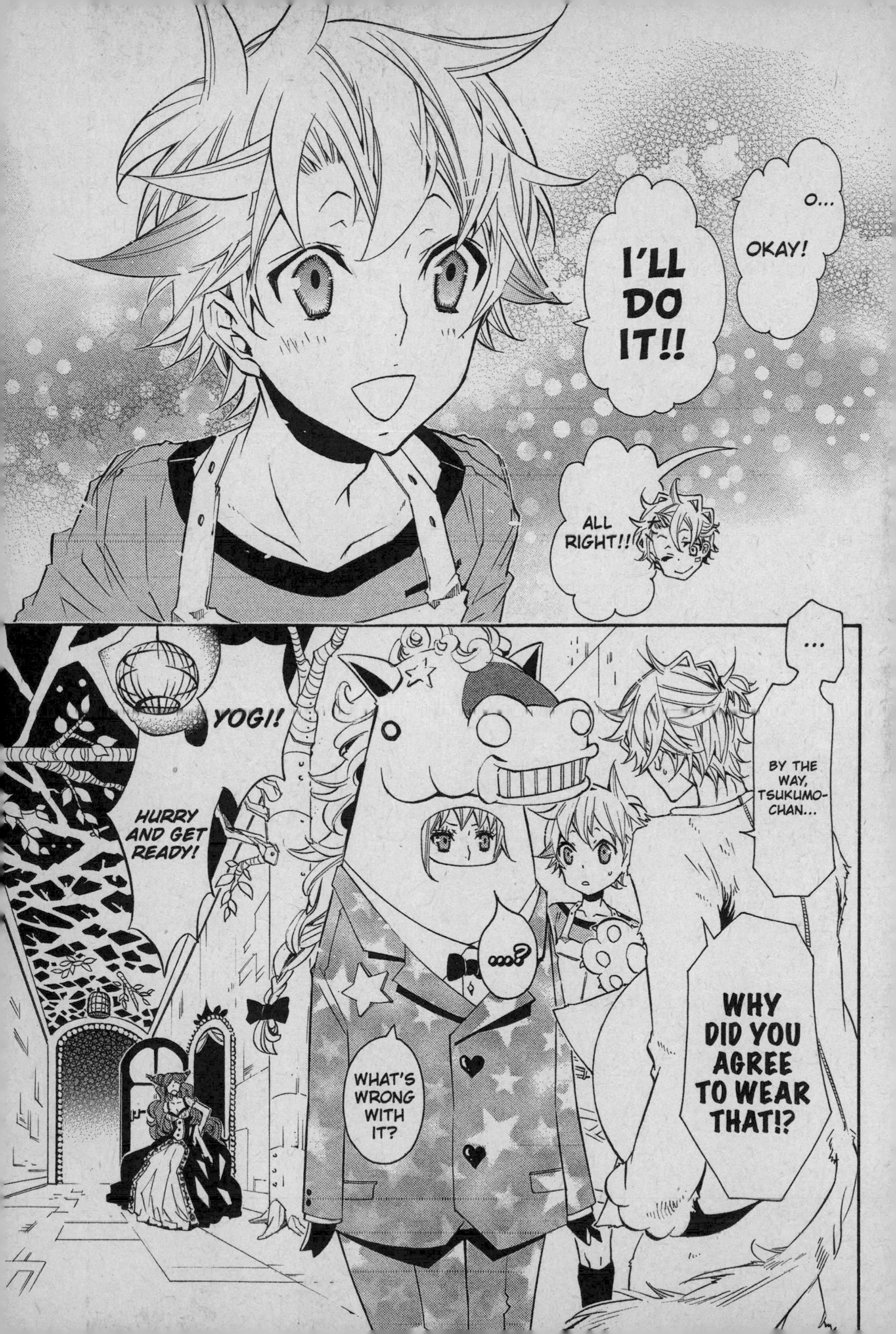
O... OKAY!
I'LL DO IT!!
ALL RIGHT!!
...
BY THE WAY, TSUKUMO-CHAN...
WHY DID YOU AGREE TO WEAR THAT!?
...?
WHAT'S WRONG WITH IT?
YOGI!
HURRY AND GET READY!

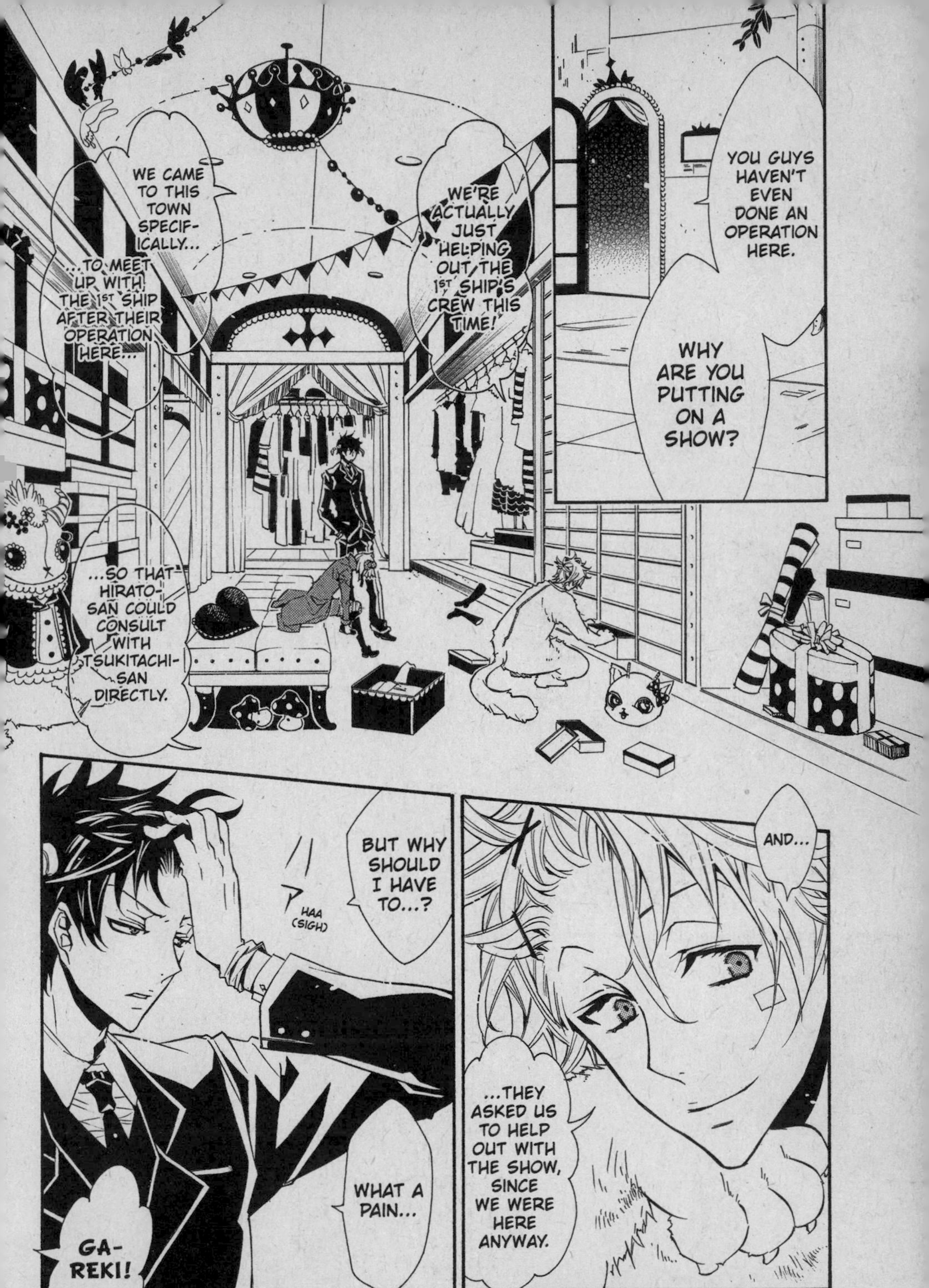
YOU GUYS HAVEN'T EVEN DONE AN OPERATION HERE.
WHY ARE YOU PUTTING ON A SHOW?
WE'RE ACTUALLY JUST HELPING OUT THE 1ST SHIP'S CREW THIS TIME!
WE CAME TO THIS TOWN SPECIFICALLY...
...TO MEET UP WITH THE 1ST SHIP AFTER THEIR OPERATION HERE...
...SO THAT HIRATO-SAN COULD CONSULT WITH TSUKITACHI-SAN DIRECTLY.
AND...
...THEY ASKED US TO HELP OUT WITH THE SHOW, SINCE WE WERE HERE ANYWAY.
BUT WHY SHOULD I HAVE TO...?
HAA (SIGH)
WHAT A PAIN...
GA-REKI!

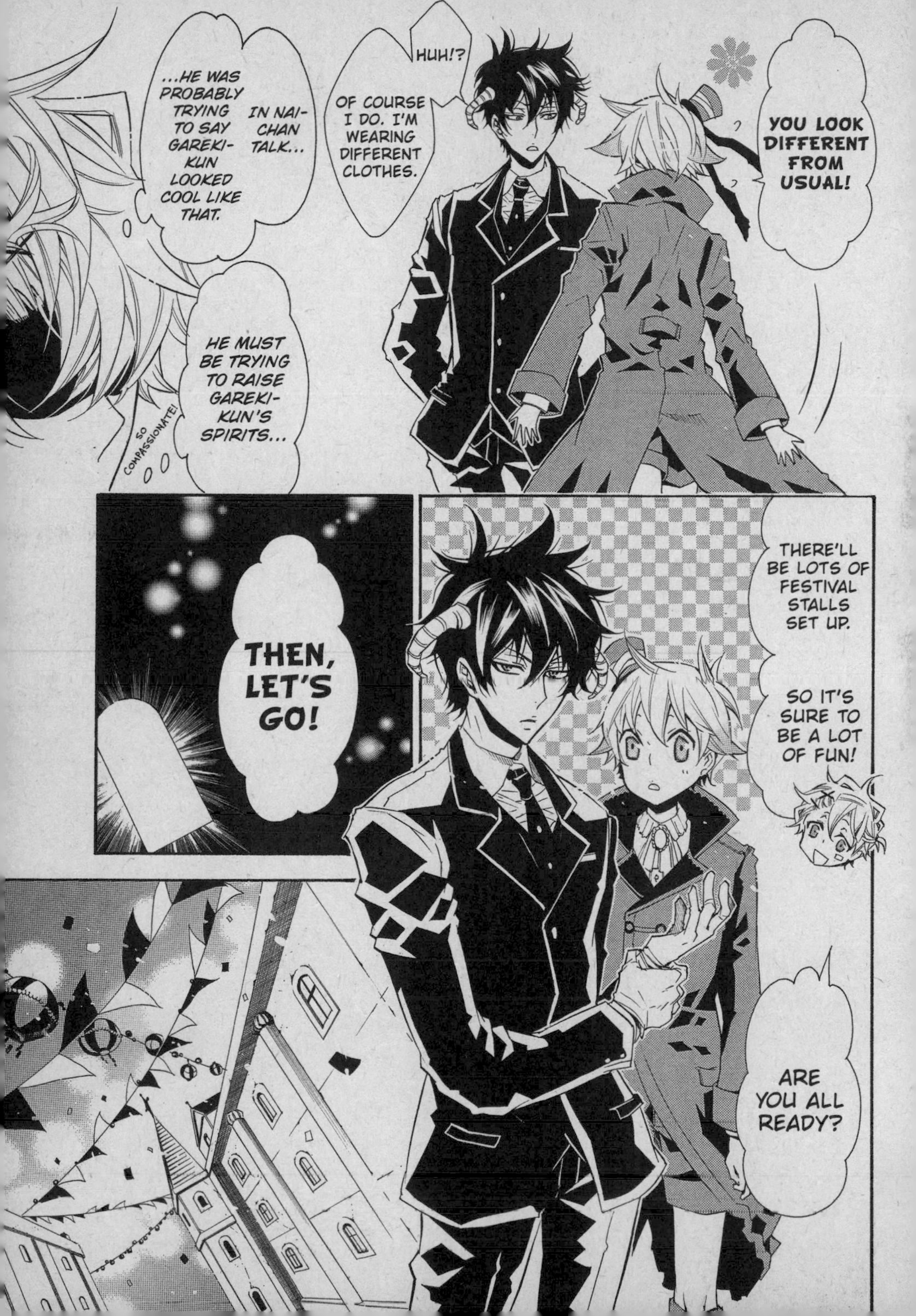
YOU LOOK DIFFERENT FROM USUAL!
HUH!?
OF COURSE I DO. I'M WEARING DIFFERENT CLOTHES.
IN NAI-CHAN TALK...
...HE WAS PROBABLY TRYING TO SAY GAREKI-KUN LOOKED COOL LIKE THAT.
HE MUST BE TRYING TO RAISE GAREKI-KUN'S SPIRITS...
SO COMPASSIONATE!
THERE'LL BE LOTS OF FESTIVAL STALLS SET UP.
SO IT'S SURE TO BE A LOT OF FUN!
ARE YOU ALL READY?
THEN, LET'S GO!

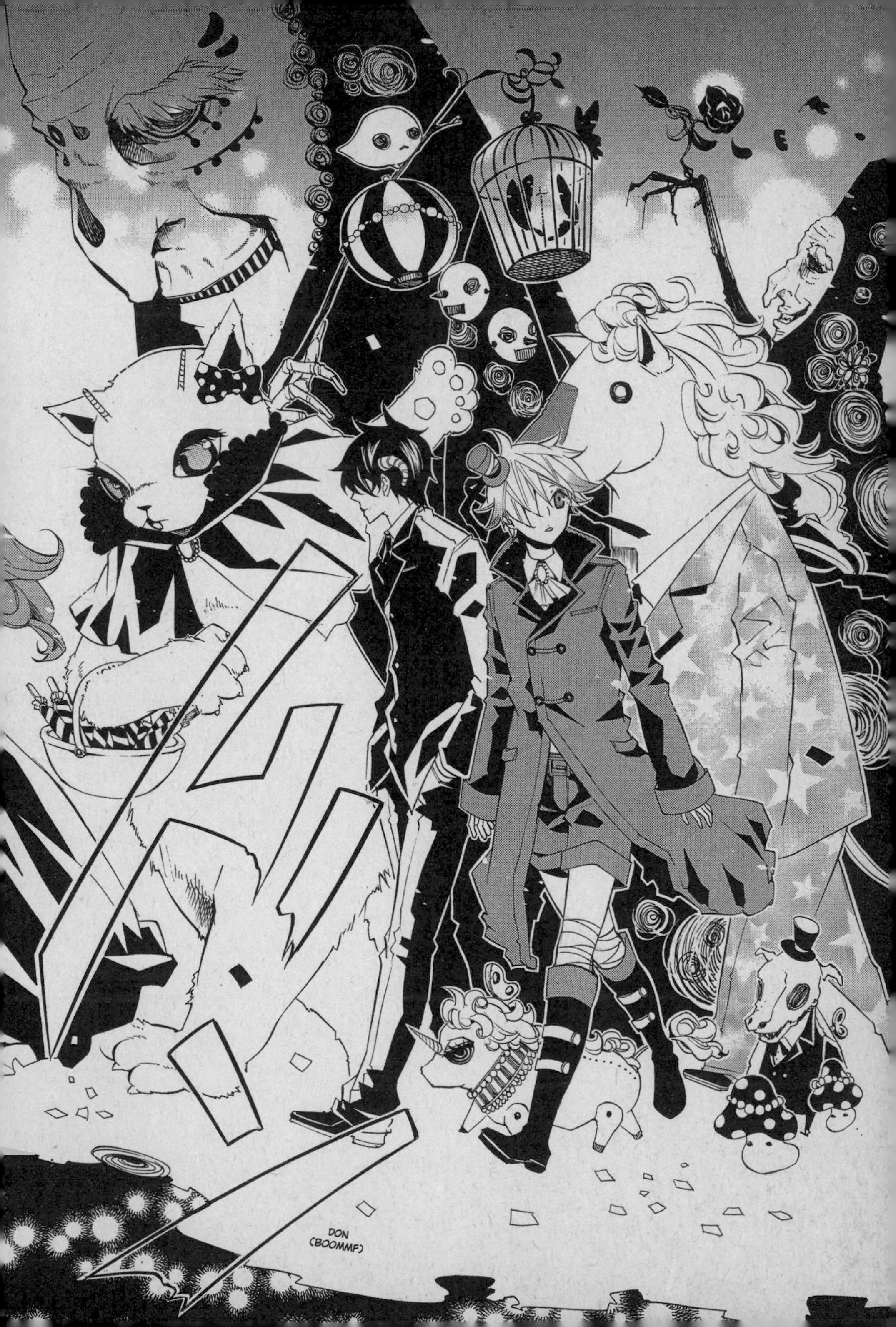
DON
(BOOMMF)

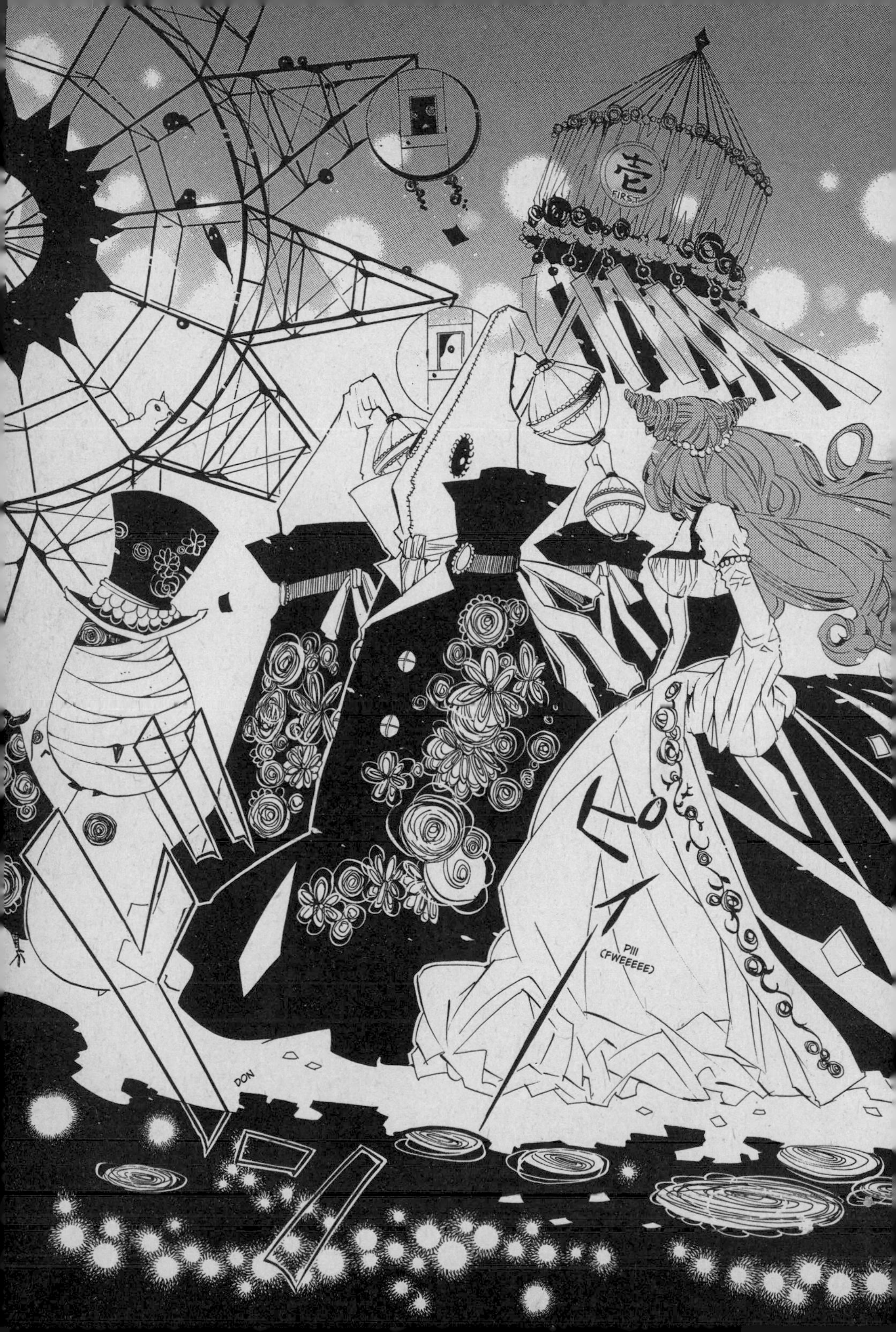
壱
FIRST
PIII
(FWEEEEE)
DON

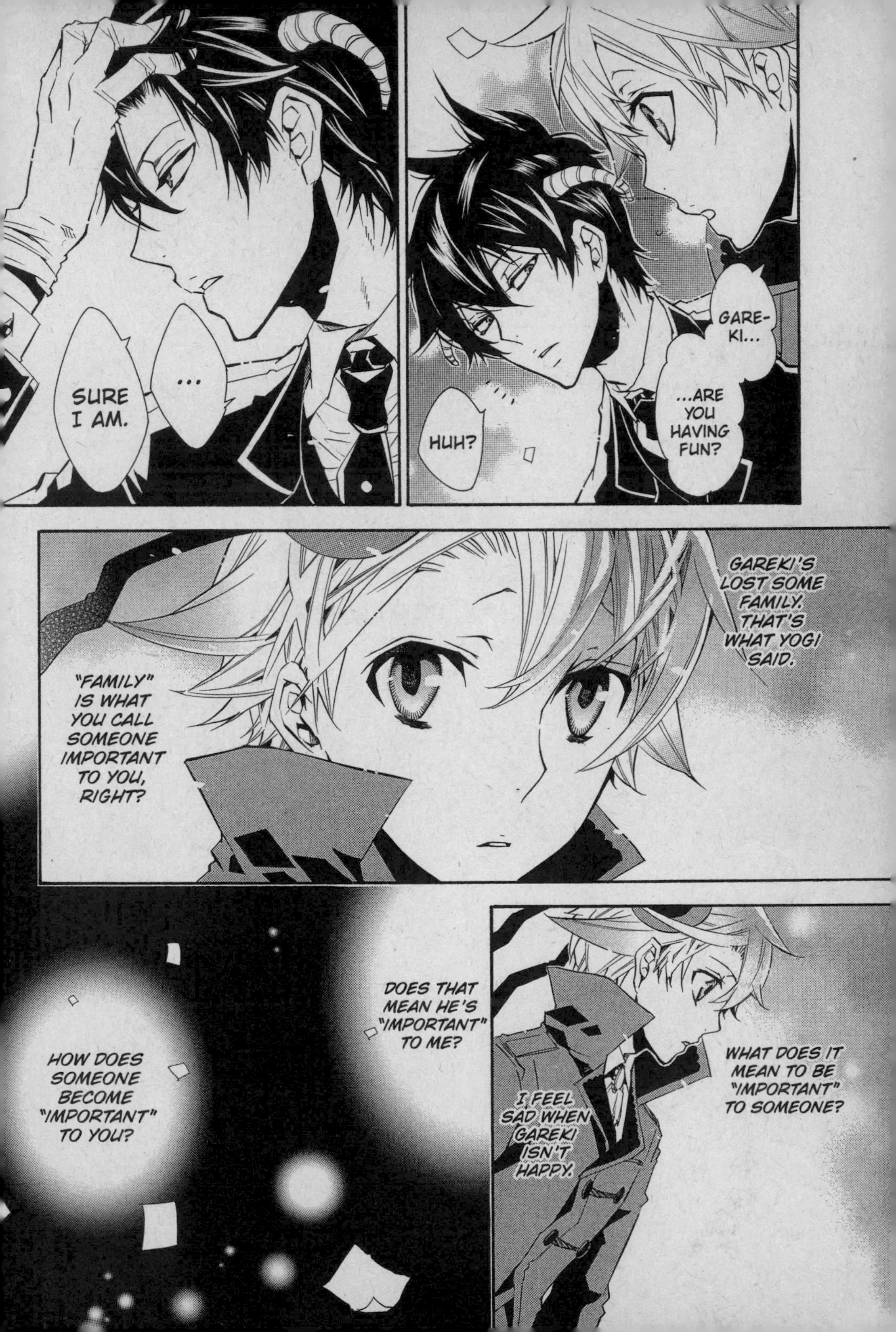
GAREKI...
...ARE YOU HAVING FUN?
HUH?
...
SURE I AM.
GAREKI'S LOST SOME FAMILY. THAT'S WHAT YOGI SAID.
"FAMILY" IS WHAT YOU CALL SOMEONE IMPORTANT TO YOU, RIGHT?
WHAT DOES IT MEAN TO BE "IMPORTANT" TO SOMEONE?
I FEEL SAD WHEN GAREKI ISN'T HAPPY.
DOES THAT MEAN HE'S "IMPORTANT" TO ME?
HOW DOES SOMEONE BECOME "IMPORTANT" TO YOU?

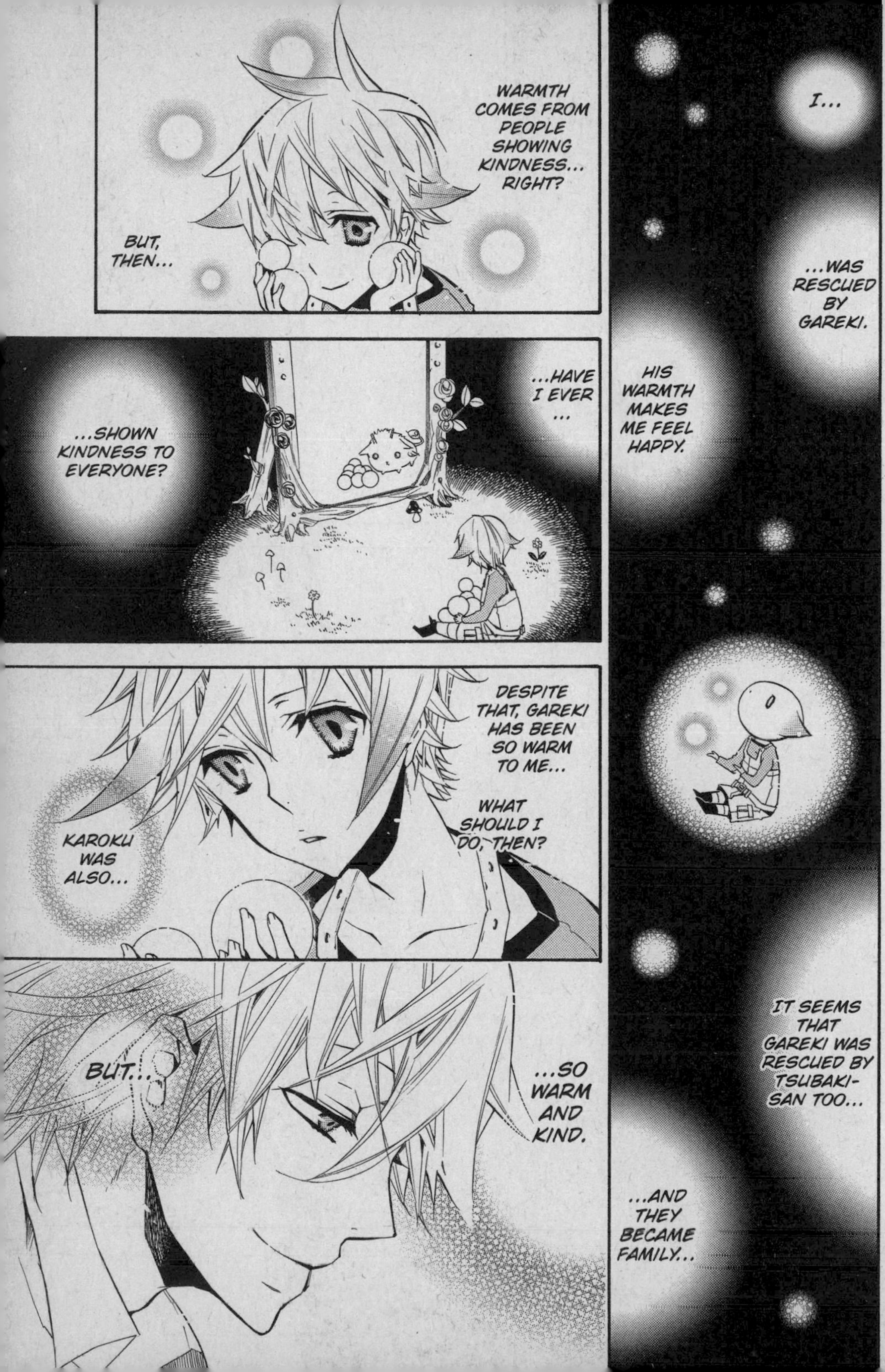
I...
...WAS RESCUED BY GAREKI.
HIS WARMTH MAKES ME FEEL HAPPY.
IT SEEMS THAT GAREKI WAS RESCUED BY TSUBAKI-SAN TOO...
...AND THEY BECAME FAMILY...
WARMTH COMES FROM PEOPLE SHOWING KINDNESS... RIGHT?
BUT, THEN...
...HAVE I EVER ...
...SHOWN KINDNESS TO EVERYONE?
DESPITE THAT, GAREKI HAS BEEN SO WARM TO ME...
WHAT SHOULD I DO, THEN?
KAROKU WAS ALSO...
...SO WARM AND KIND.
BUT...

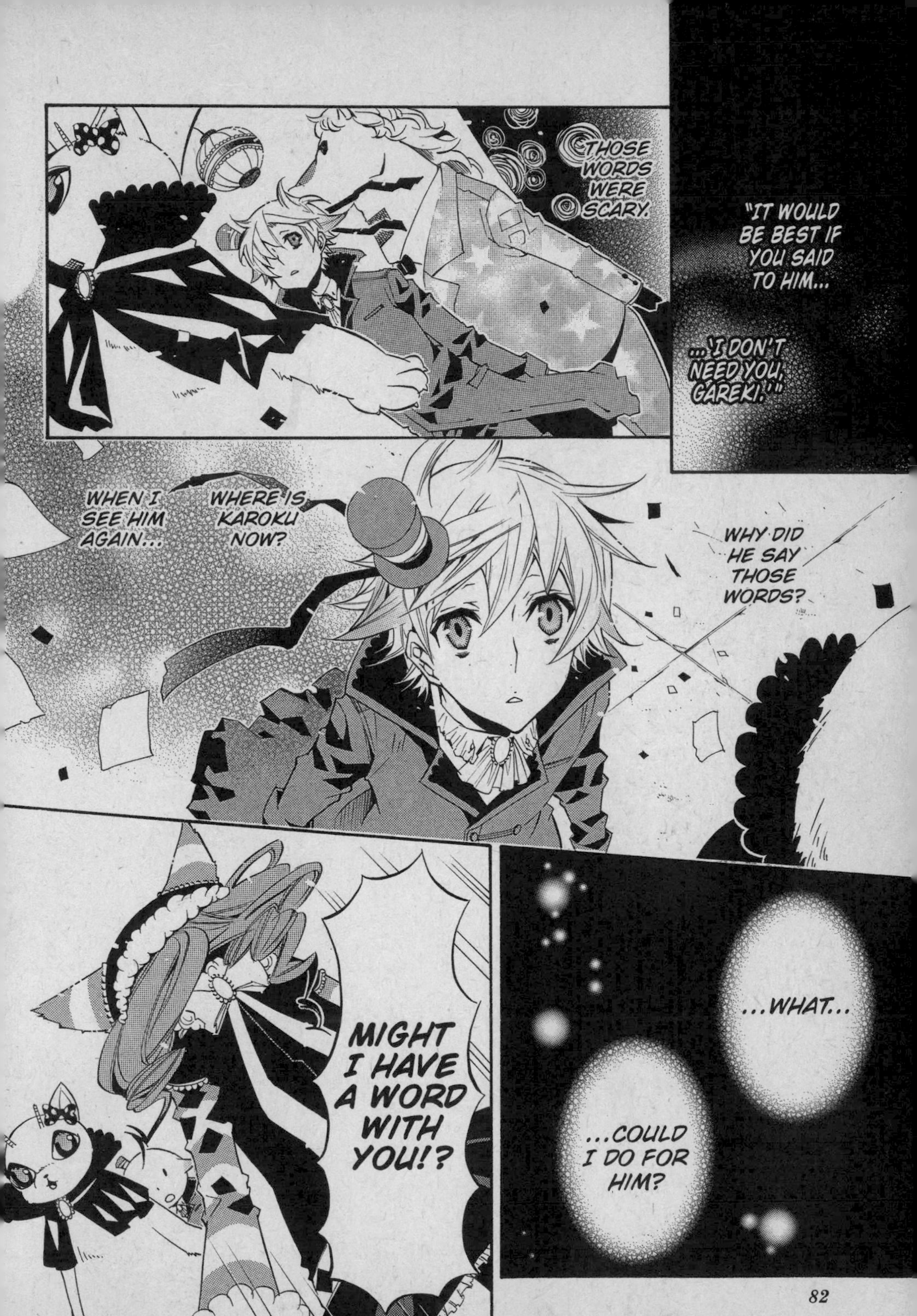
"IT WOULD BE BEST IF YOU SAID TO HIM...
...'I DON'T NEED YOU, GAREKI.'"
THOSE WORDS WERE SCARY.
WHY DID HE SAY THOSE WORDS?
WHERE IS KAROKU NOW?
WHEN I SEE HIM AGAIN...
...WHAT...
...COULD I DO FOR HIM?
MIGHT I HAVE A WORD WITH YOU!?

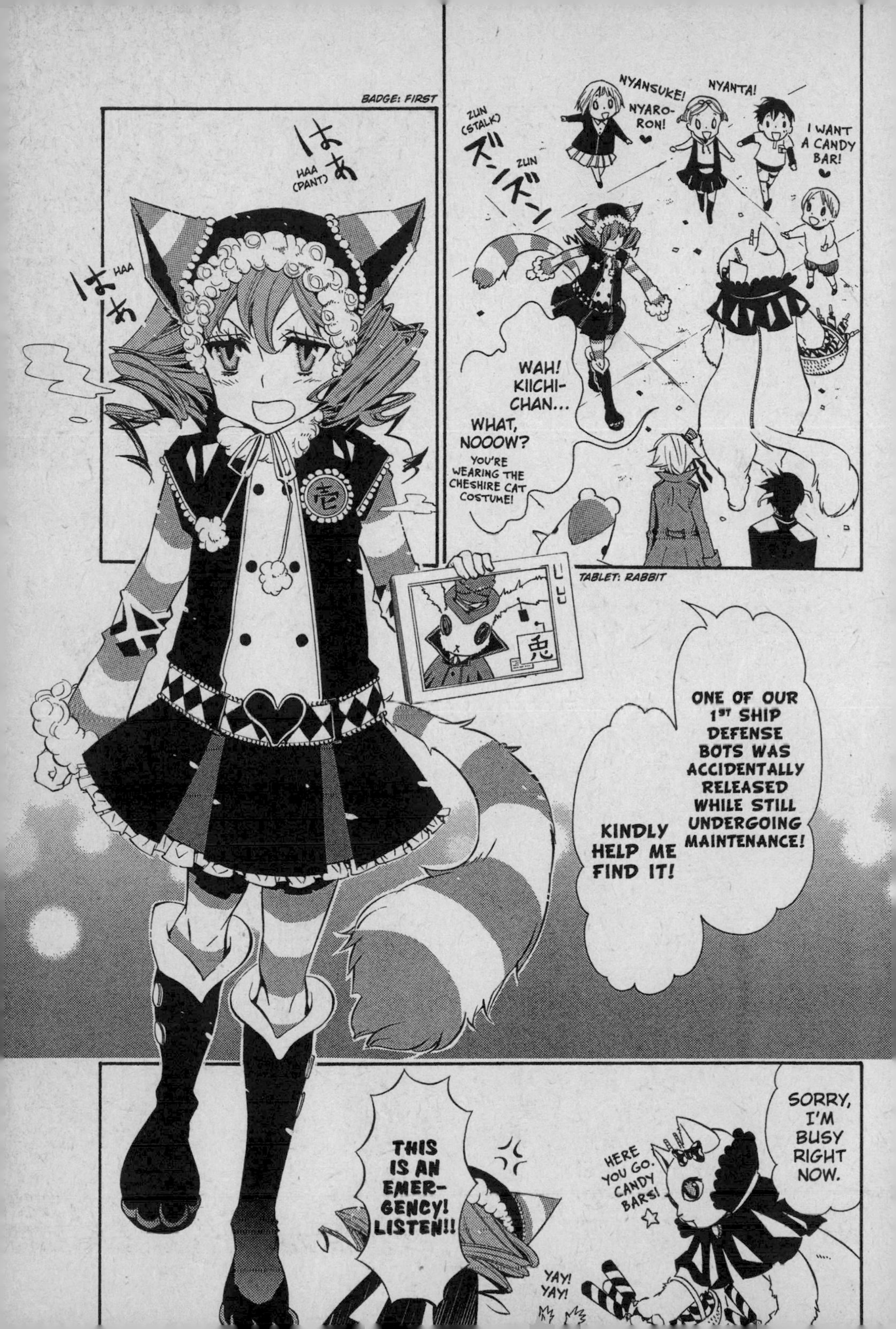

I WANT A CANDY BAR!
NYANTA!
NYARO-RON!
NYANSUKE!
ズーンズーン
ZUN (STALK)
ZUN
WAH! KIICHI-CHAN...
WHAT, NOOOW?
YOU'RE WEARING THE CHESHIRE CAT COSTUME!
BADGE: FIRST
はあ
HAA (PANT)
はあ
HAA
TABLET: RABBIT
ONE OF OUR 1ST SHIP DEFENSE BOTS WAS ACCIDENTALLY RELEASED WHILE STILL UNDERGOING MAINTENANCE!
KINDLY HELP ME FIND IT!
SORRY, I'M BUSY RIGHT NOW.
HERE YOU GO. CANDY BARS!
YAY! YAY!
THIS IS AN EMERGENCY! LISTEN!!

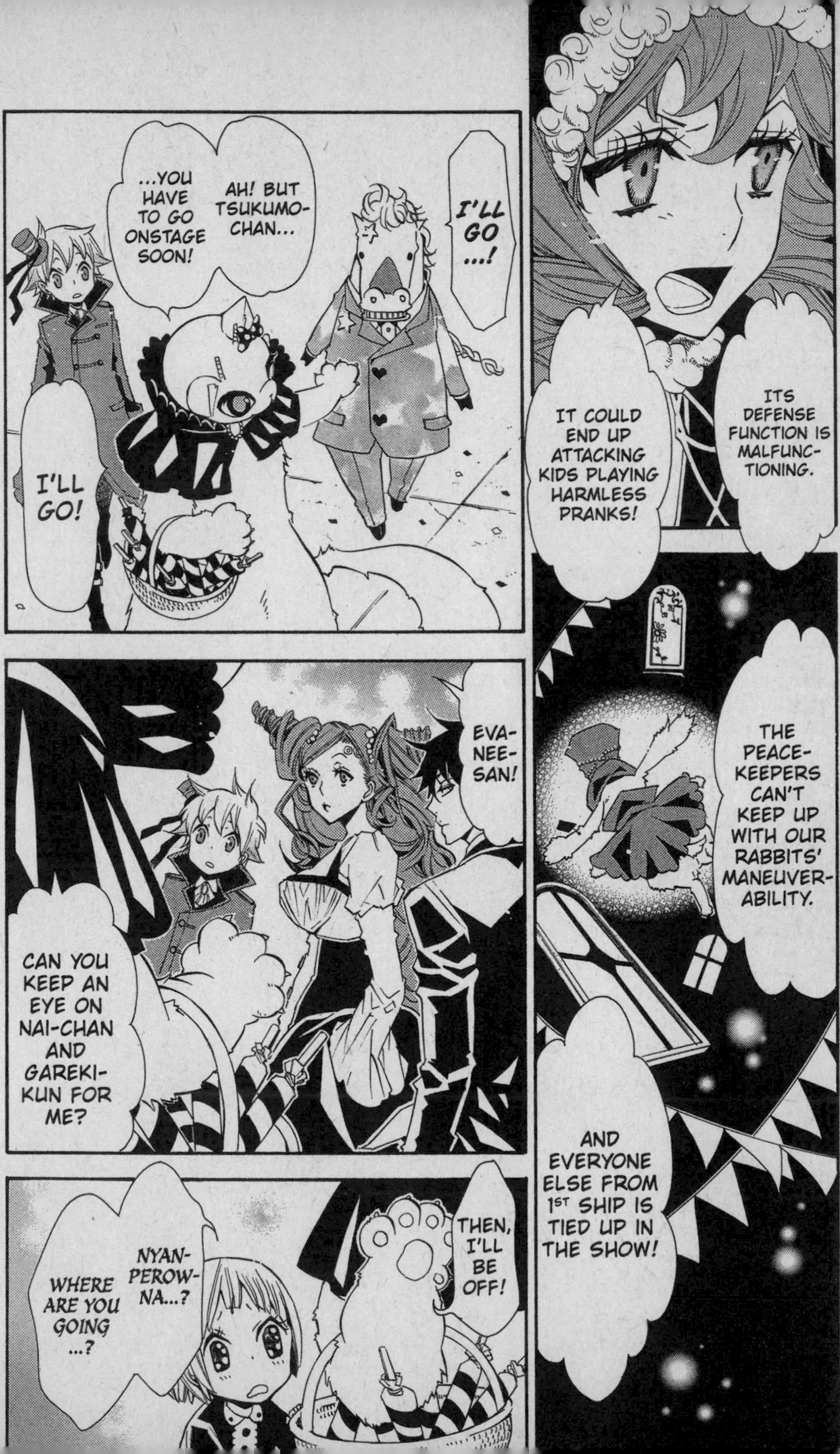
ITS DEFENSE FUNCTION IS MALFUNCTIONING.
IT COULD END UP ATTACKING KIDS PLAYING HARMLESS PRANKS!
THE PEACEKEEPERS CAN'T KEEP UP WITH OUR RABBITS' MANEUVERABILITY.
AND EVERYONE ELSE FROM 1ST SHIP IS TIED UP IN THE SHOW!
I'LL GO ...!
AH! BUT TSUKUMO-CHAN...
...YOU HAVE TO GO ONSTAGE SOON!
I'LL GO!
EVA-NEE-SAN!
CAN YOU KEEP AN EYE ON NAI-CHAN AND GAREKI-KUN FOR ME?
THEN, I'LL BE OFF!
NYAN-PEROWNA...?
WHERE ARE YOU GOING ...?

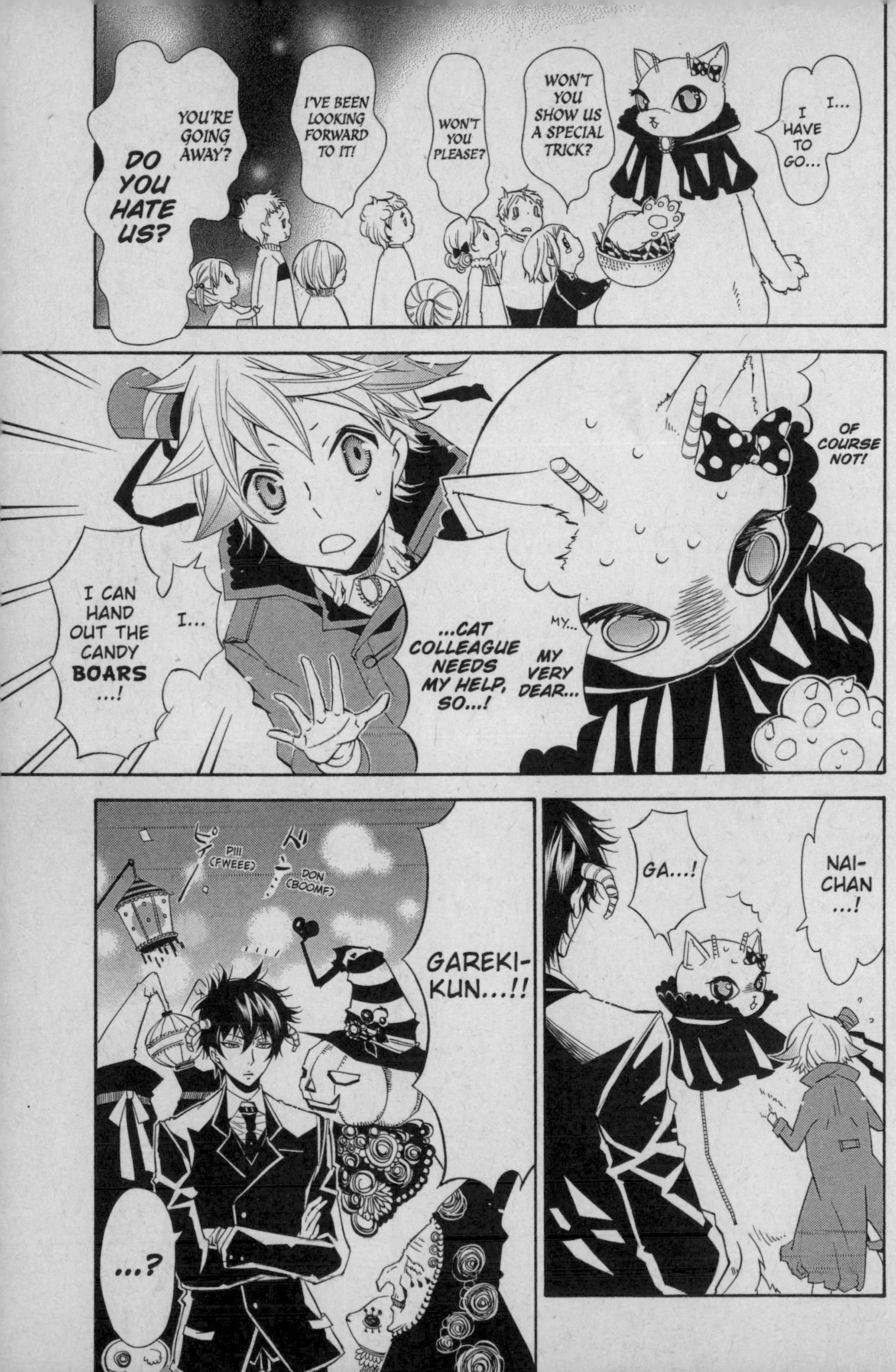
I... I HAVE TO GO...
WON'T YOU SHOW US A SPECIAL TRICK?
WON'T YOU PLEASE?
I'VE BEEN LOOKING FORWARD TO IT!
YOU'RE GOING AWAY?
DO YOU HATE US?
OF COURSE NOT!
MY...
MY VERY DEAR...
...CAT COLLEAGUE NEEDS MY HELP, SO...!
I...
I CAN HAND OUT THE CANDY BOARS ...!
NAI-CHAN ...!
GA...!
GAREKI-KUN...!!
DON (BOOMF)
PIII (FWEEE)
...?

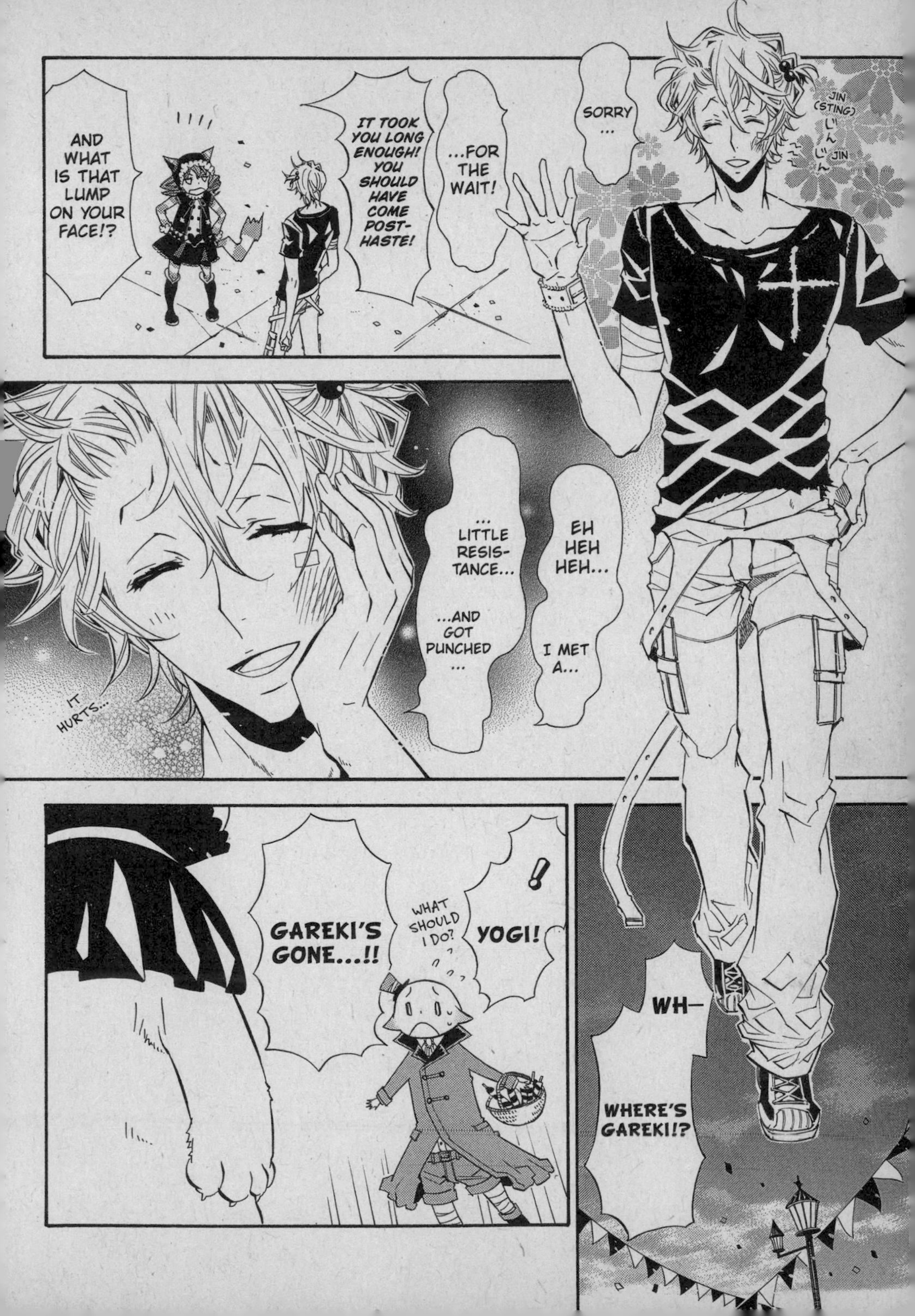
SORRY...
JIN (STING) じんじん JIN
...FOR THE WAIT!
IT TOOK YOU LONG ENOUGH! YOU SHOULD HAVE COME POST-HASTE!
AND WHAT IS THAT LUMP ON YOUR FACE!?
EH HEH HEH...
I MET A...
...LITTLE RESIS-TANCE...
...AND GOT PUNCHED...
IT HURTS...
WH—
WHERE'S GAREKI!?
YOGI!
WHAT SHOULD I DO?
GAREKI'S GONE...!!

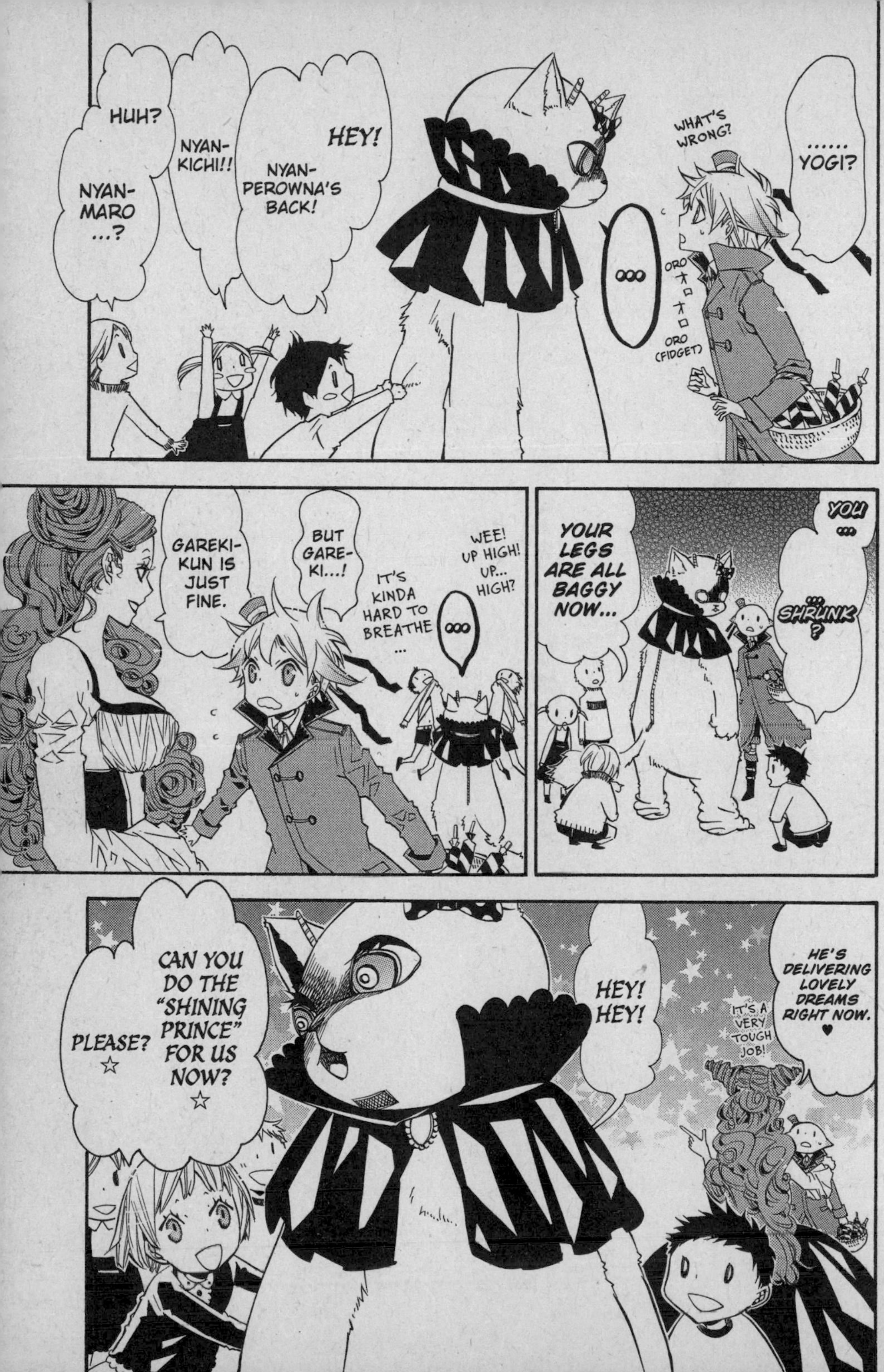

......YOGI?
WHAT'S WRONG?
ORO オロ オロ ORO (FIDGET)
...
HEY! NYAN-PEROWNA'S BACK!
NYAN-KICHI!!
HUH? NYAN-MARO ...?
YOU ... ...SHRUNK?
YOUR LEGS ARE ALL BAGGY NOW...
WEE! UP HIGH! UP... HIGH?
...
IT'S KINDA HARD TO BREATHE ...
BUT GAREKI...!
GAREKI-KUN IS JUST FINE.
HE'S DELIVERING LOVELY DREAMS RIGHT NOW. ♥
IT'S A VERY TOUGH JOB!
HEY! HEY!
CAN YOU DO THE "SHINING PRINCE" FOR US NOW? ☆
PLEASE? ☆

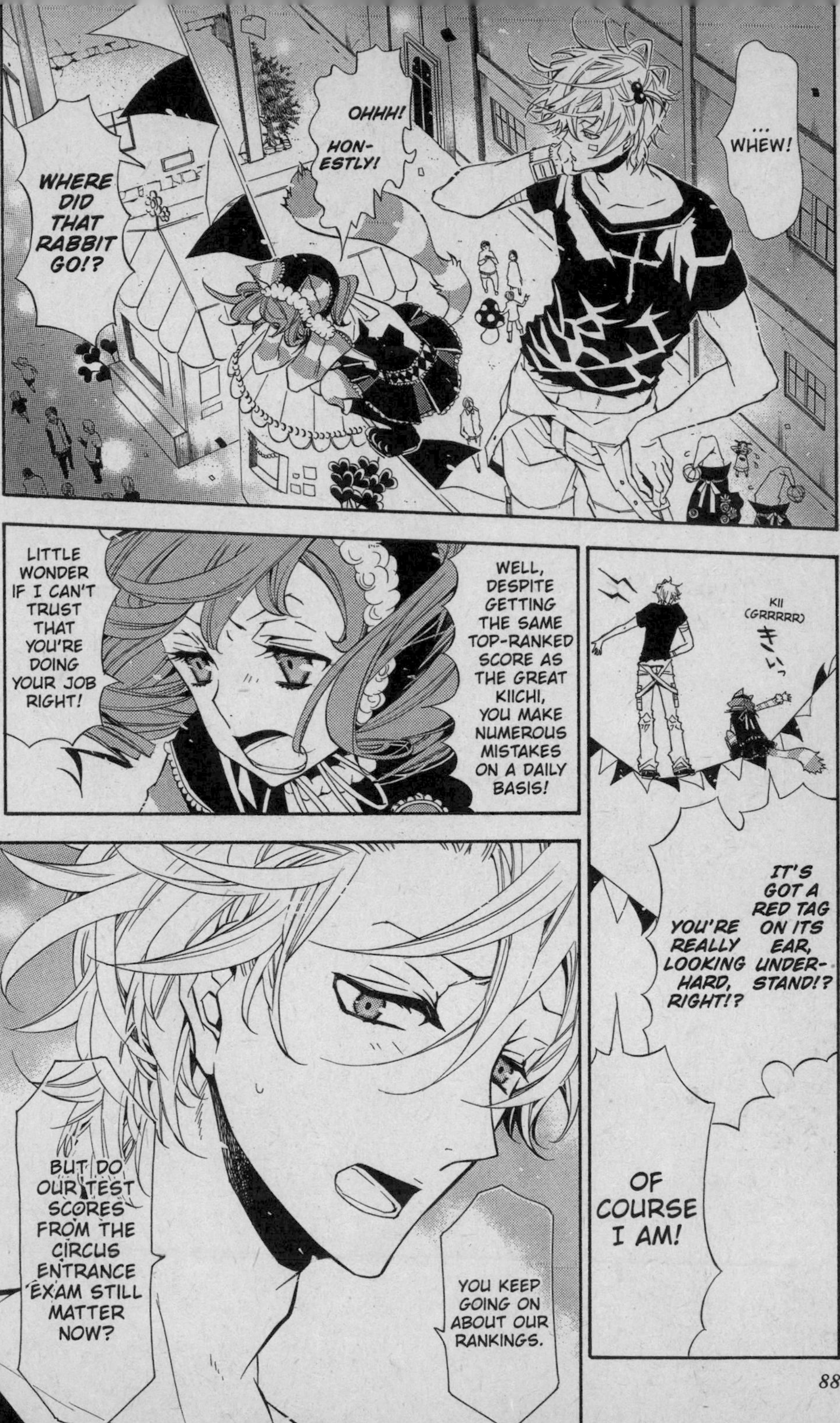

... WHEW!
OHHH! HONESTLY!
WHERE DID THAT RABBIT GO!?
KII (GRRRRR)
きぃっ
WELL, DESPITE GETTING THE SAME TOP-RANKED SCORE AS THE GREAT KIICHI, YOU MAKE NUMEROUS MISTAKES ON A DAILY BASIS!
LITTLE WONDER IF I CAN'T TRUST THAT YOU'RE DOING YOUR JOB RIGHT!
IT'S GOT A RED TAG ON ITS EAR, UNDERSTAND!?
YOU'RE REALLY LOOKING HARD, RIGHT!?
OF COURSE I AM!
YOU KEEP GOING ON ABOUT OUR RANKINGS.
BUT DO OUR TEST SCORES FROM THE CIRCUS ENTRANCE EXAM STILL MATTER NOW?

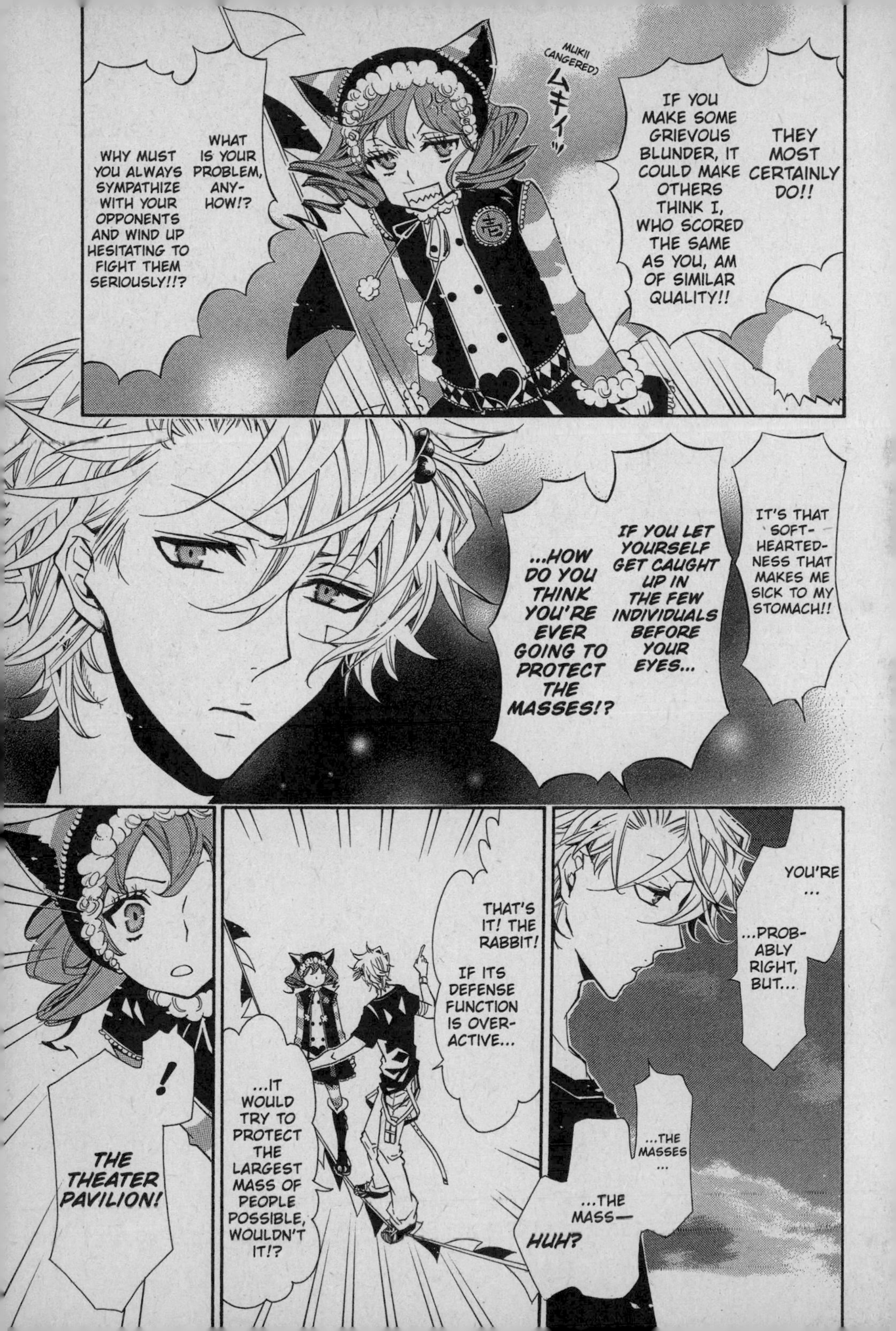
THEY MOST CERTAINLY DO!!
IF YOU MAKE SOME GRIEVOUS BLUNDER, IT COULD MAKE OTHERS THINK I, WHO SCORED THE SAME AS YOU, AM OF SIMILAR QUALITY!!
MUKII (ANGERED)
ムキィッ
WHAT IS YOUR PROBLEM, ANYHOW!?
WHY MUST YOU ALWAYS SYMPATHIZE WITH YOUR OPPONENTS AND WIND UP HESITATING TO FIGHT THEM SERIOUSLY!!?
IT'S THAT SOFT-HEARTEDNESS THAT MAKES ME SICK TO MY STOMACH!!
IF YOU LET YOURSELF GET CAUGHT UP IN THE FEW INDIVIDUALS BEFORE YOUR EYES...
...HOW DO YOU THINK YOU'RE EVER GOING TO PROTECT THE MASSES!?
YOU'RE ...
...PROBABLY RIGHT, BUT...
...THE MASSES ...
...THE MASS—
HUH?
THAT'S IT! THE RABBIT!
IF ITS DEFENSE FUNCTION IS OVERACTIVE...
...IT WOULD TRY TO PROTECT THE LARGEST MASS OF PEOPLE POSSIBLE, WOULDN'T IT!?
!
THE THEATER PAVILION!

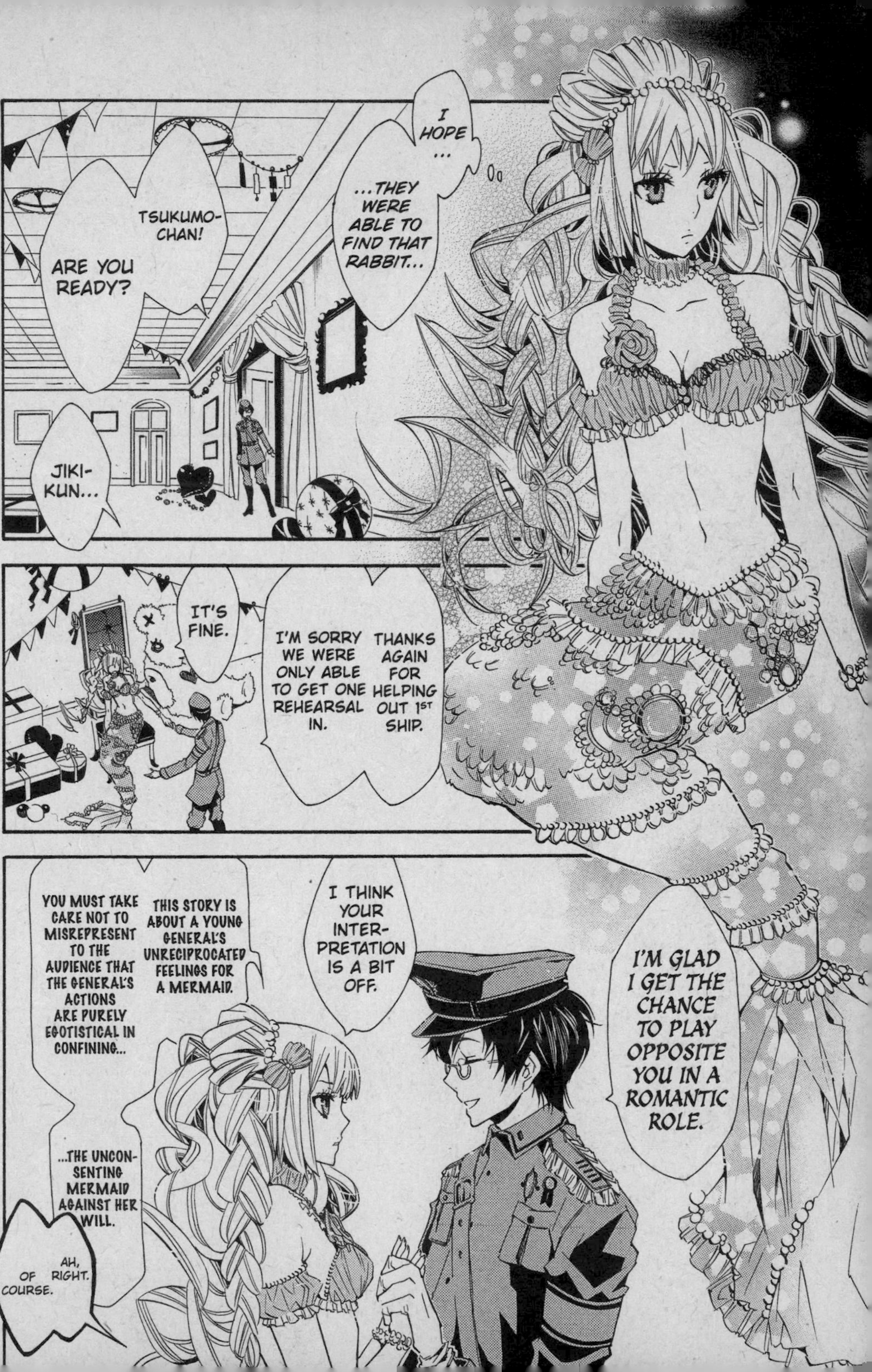
I HOPE...
...THEY WERE ABLE TO FIND THAT RABBIT...
TSUKUMO-CHAN!
ARE YOU READY?
JIKI-KUN...
THANKS AGAIN FOR HELPING OUT 1ST SHIP.
I'M SORRY WE WERE ONLY ABLE TO GET ONE REHEARSAL IN.
IT'S FINE.
I'M GLAD I GET THE CHANCE TO PLAY OPPOSITE YOU IN A ROMANTIC ROLE.
I THINK YOUR INTER-PRETATION IS A BIT OFF.
THIS STORY IS ABOUT A YOUNG GENERAL'S UNRECIPROCATED FEELINGS FOR A MERMAID.
YOU MUST TAKE CARE NOT TO MISREPRESENT TO THE AUDIENCE THAT THE GENERAL'S ACTIONS ARE PURELY EGOTISTICAL IN CONFINING...
...THE UNCON-SENTING MERMAID AGAINST HER WILL.
AH, RIGHT. OF COURSE.

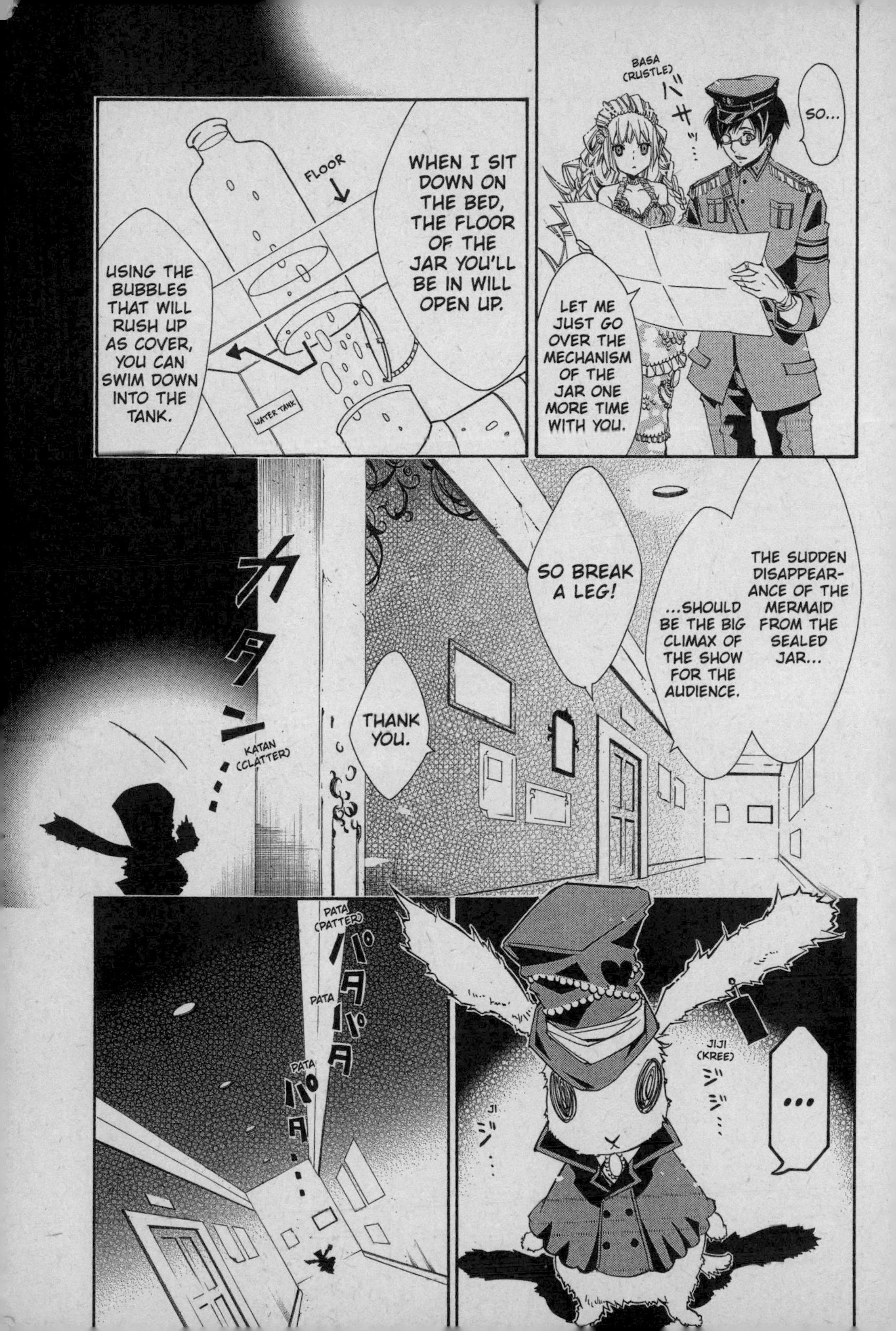
SO...
BASA (RUSTLE)
バサッ...
LET ME JUST GO OVER THE MECHANISM OF THE JAR ONE MORE TIME WITH YOU.
WHEN I SIT DOWN ON THE BED, THE FLOOR OF THE JAR YOU'LL BE IN WILL OPEN UP.
FLOOR
USING THE BUBBLES THAT WILL RUSH UP AS COVER, YOU CAN SWIM DOWN INTO THE TANK.
WATER TANK
THE SUDDEN DISAPPEARANCE OF THE MERMAID FROM THE SEALED JAR...
...SHOULD BE THE BIG CLIMAX OF THE SHOW FOR THE AUDIENCE.
SO BREAK A LEG!
THANK YOU.
カタン...
KATAN (CLATTER)
...
JIJI (KREE)
ジジ...
JI
ジ...
PATA (PATTER)
PATA
PATA
パタパタパタ...

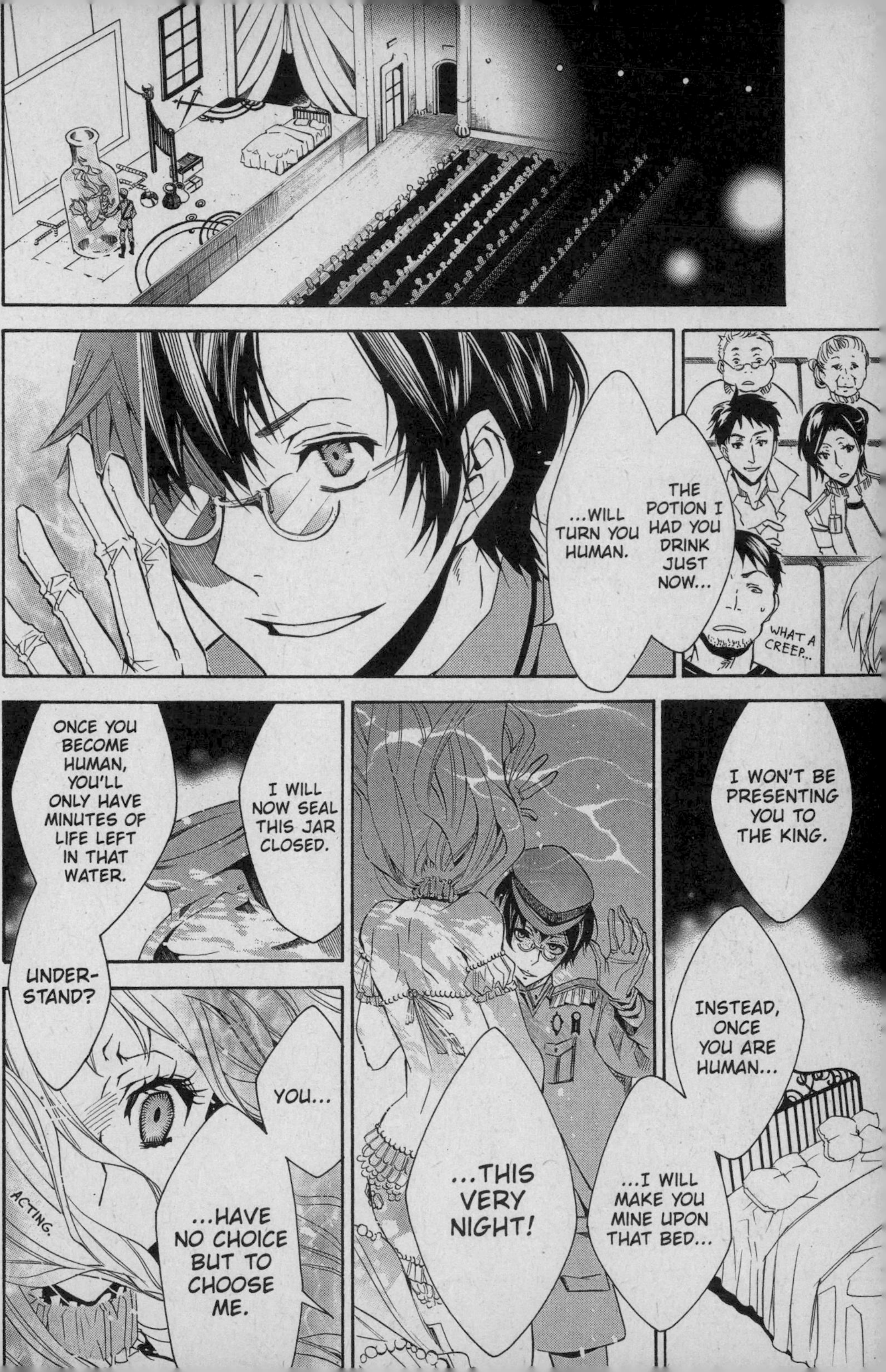
THE POTION I HAD YOU DRINK JUST NOW...
...WILL TURN YOU HUMAN.
WHAT A CREEP...
I WON'T BE PRESENTING YOU TO THE KING.
INSTEAD, ONCE YOU ARE HUMAN...
...I WILL MAKE YOU MINE UPON THAT BED...
...THIS VERY NIGHT!
I WILL NOW SEAL THIS JAR CLOSED.
ONCE YOU BECOME HUMAN, YOU'LL ONLY HAVE MINUTES OF LIFE LEFT IN THAT WATER.
UNDER-STAND?
YOU...
...HAVE NO CHOICE BUT TO CHOOSE ME.
ACTING.

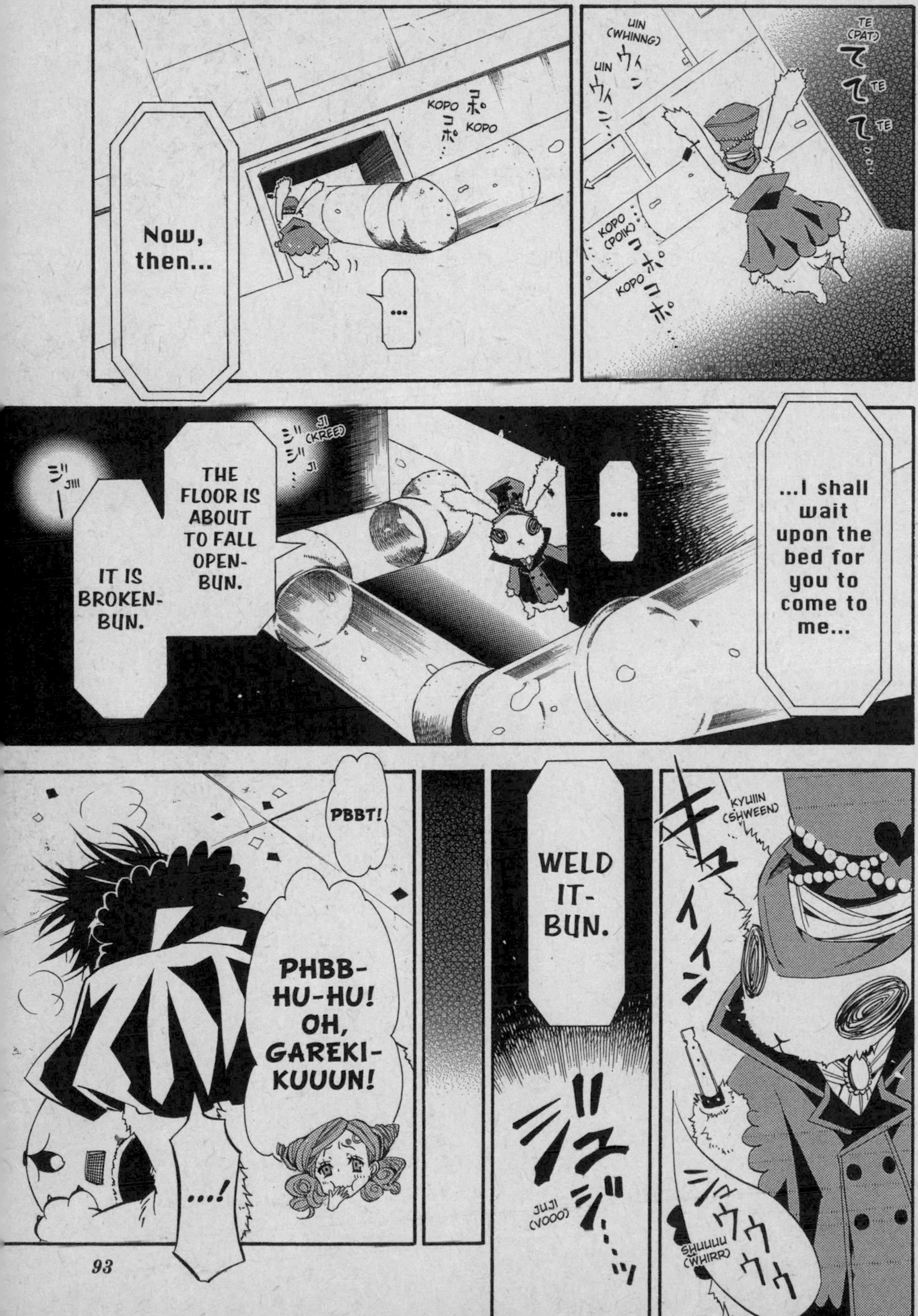
TE (PAT)
てて TE
て TE
UIN (WHINNG) ウィン
UIN ウィン
KOPO (POIK) コポ
KOPO コポ
KOPO コポ
KOPO コポ...
Now, then...
...
...I shall wait upon the bed for you to come to me...
...
JI (KREE) ジ
JI ジ
THE FLOOR IS ABOUT TO FALL OPEN-BUN.
IT IS BROKEN-BUN.
ジー JIII
KYUIIN (SHWEEN) キュイイン
SHUUUUU (WHIRR) シュウウウウ
WELD IT-BUN.
JUJI (VOOO) ジュジ...ッ
PBBT!
PHBB-HU-HU! OH, GAREKI-KUUUN!
...!

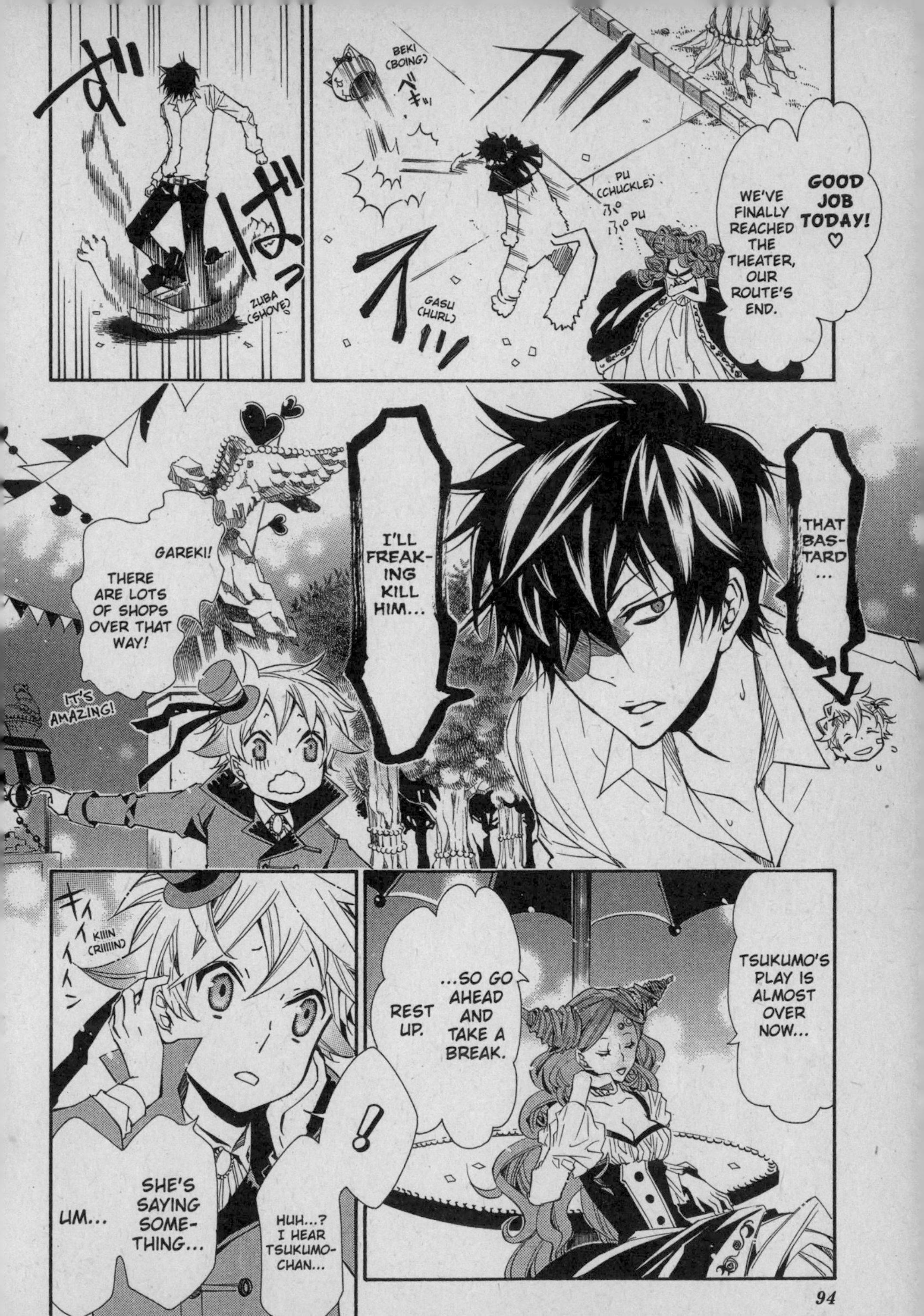
GOOD JOB TODAY! ♡
WE'VE FINALLY REACHED THE THEATER, OUR ROUTE'S END.
PU (CHUCKLE) PU PU
BEKI (BOING)
GASU (HURL)
ZUBA (SHOVE)
THAT BASTARD...
I'LL FREAKING KILL HIM...
GAREKI!
THERE ARE LOTS OF SHOPS OVER THAT WAY!
IT'S AMAZING!
TSUKUMO'S PLAY IS ALMOST OVER NOW...
...SO GO AHEAD AND TAKE A BREAK.
REST UP.
KIIIN (CRIIIIND)
!
HUH...? I HEAR TSUKUMO-CHAN...
SHE'S SAYING SOMETHING...
UM...

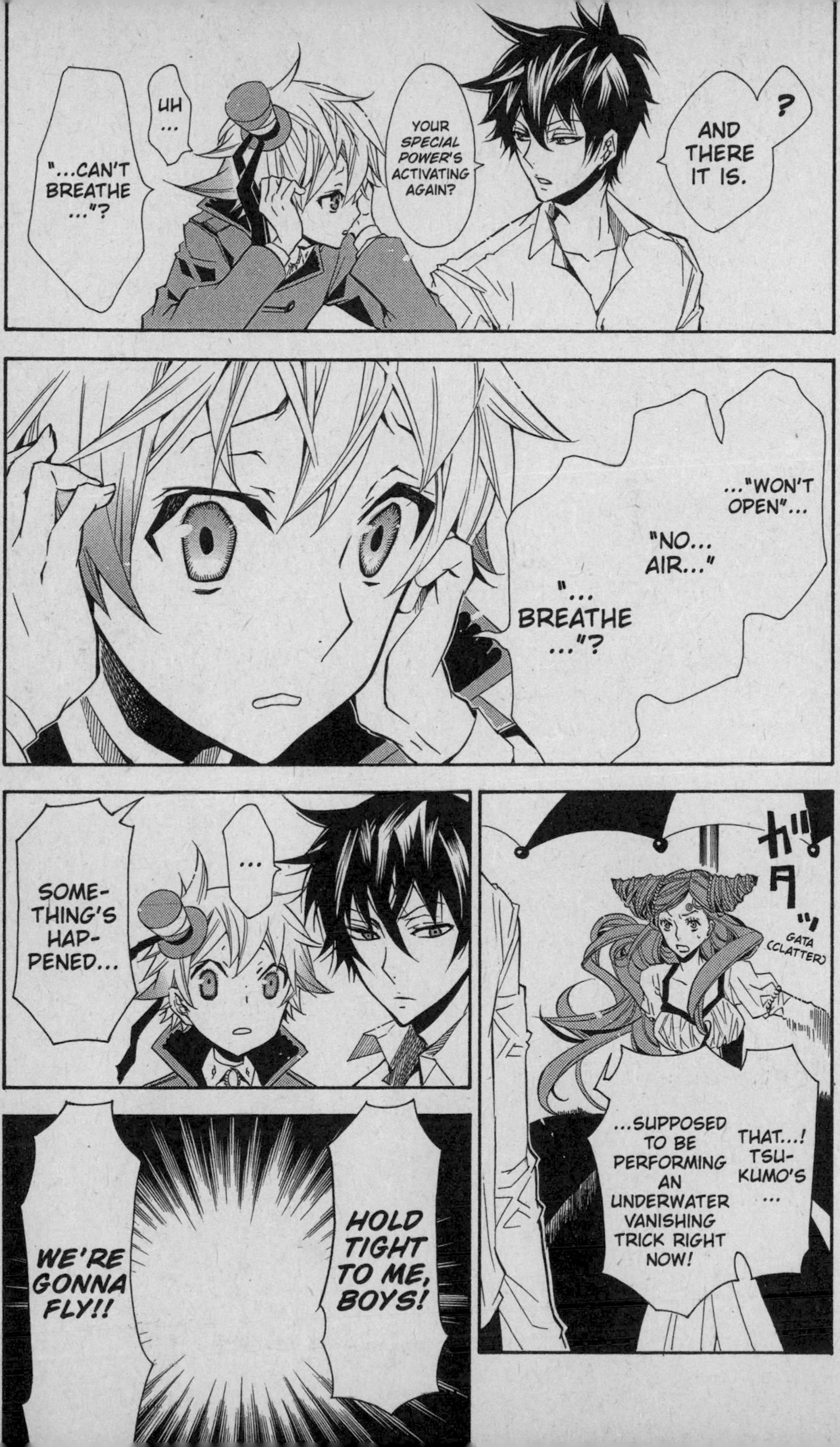
?
AND THERE IT IS.
YOUR SPECIAL POWER'S ACTIVATING AGAIN?
UH ...
"...CAN'T BREATHE ..."?
..."WON'T OPEN"...
"NO... AIR..."
"... BREATHE ..."?
ガタッ
GATA (CLATTER)
THAT...! TSU-KUMO'S ...
...SUPPOSED TO BE PERFORMING AN UNDERWATER VANISHING TRICK RIGHT NOW!
...
SOME-THING'S HAP-PENED...
HOLD TIGHT TO ME, BOYS!
WE'RE GONNA FLY!!

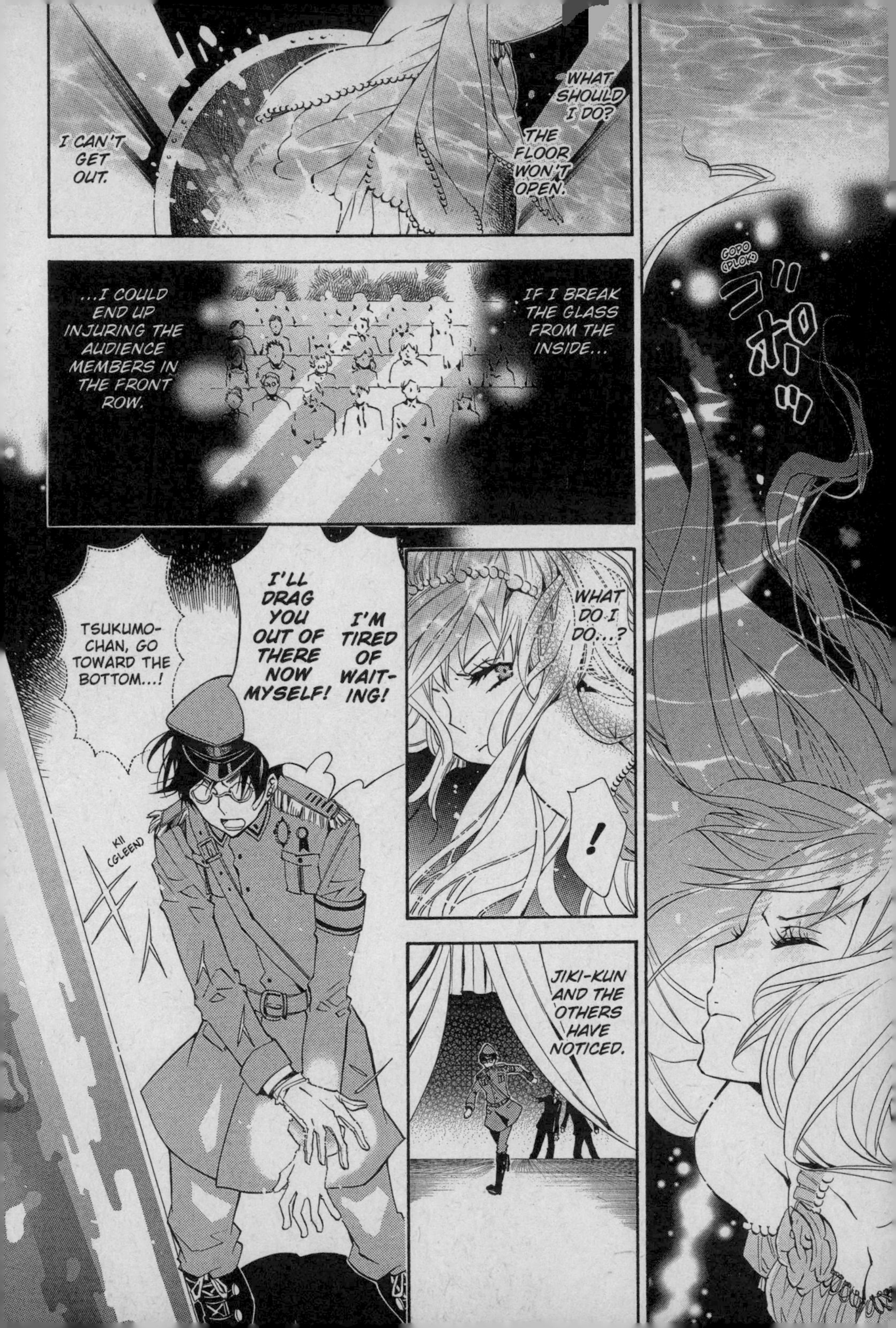
GOPO (PLOK)
ゴポッ
WHAT SHOULD I DO?
THE FLOOR WON'T OPEN.
I CAN'T GET OUT.
IF I BREAK THE GLASS FROM THE INSIDE...
...I COULD END UP INJURING THE AUDIENCE MEMBERS IN THE FRONT ROW.
WHAT DO I DO...?
!
JIKI-KUN AND THE OTHERS HAVE NOTICED.
I'M TIRED OF WAITING!
I'LL DRAG YOU OUT OF THERE NOW MYSELF!
TSUKUMO-CHAN, GO TOWARD THE BOTTOM...!
KII (GLEEN)

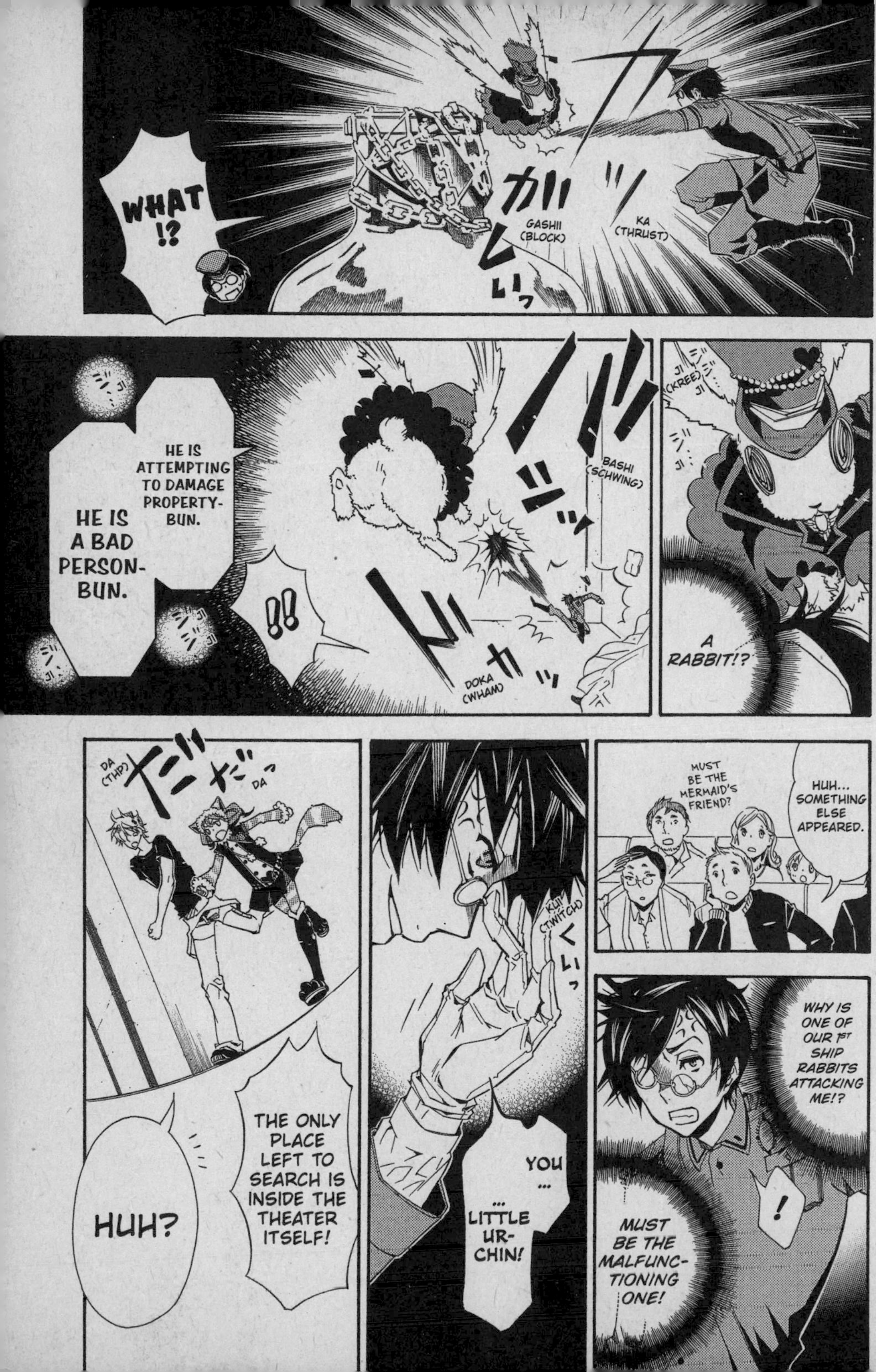
KA (THRUST)
GASHII (BLOCK)
WHAT!?
JI (KREE) JI
JI
A RABBIT!?
BASHI (SCHWING)
!!
DOKA (WHAM)
HE IS ATTEMPTING TO DAMAGE PROPERTY-BUN.
HE IS A BAD PERSON-BUN.
JI
JI
HUH... SOMETHING ELSE APPEARED.
MUST BE THE MERMAID'S FRIEND?
WHY IS ONE OF OUR 1ST SHIP RABBITS ATTACKING ME!?
!
MUST BE THE MALFUNCTIONING ONE!
KUI (TWITCH)
YOU ...
... LITTLE UR-CHIN!
DA (THP) DA
THE ONLY PLACE LEFT TO SEARCH IS INSIDE THE THEATER ITSELF!
HUH?

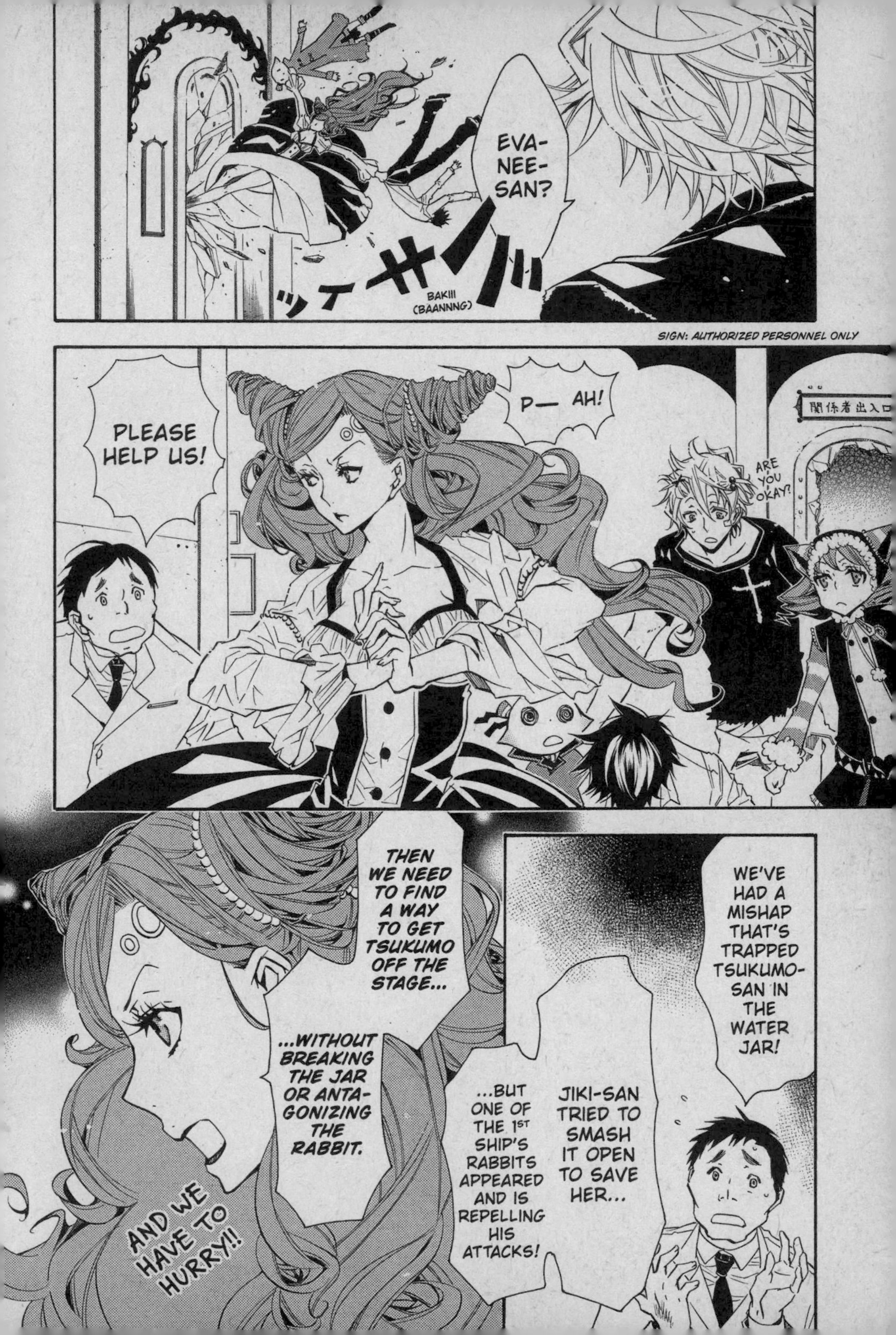
EVA-NEE-SAN?
BAKIII (BAANNNG)
SIGN: AUTHORIZED PERSONNEL ONLY
関係者出入口
ARE YOU OKAY?
P— AH!
PLEASE HELP US!
WE'VE HAD A MISHAP THAT'S TRAPPED TSUKUMO-SAN IN THE WATER JAR!
JIKI-SAN TRIED TO SMASH IT OPEN TO SAVE HER...
...BUT ONE OF THE 1ST SHIP'S RABBITS APPEARED AND IS REPELLING HIS ATTACKS!
THEN WE NEED TO FIND A WAY TO GET TSUKUMO OFF THE STAGE...
...WITHOUT BREAKING THE JAR OR ANTAGONIZING THE RABBIT.
AND WE HAVE TO HURRY!!

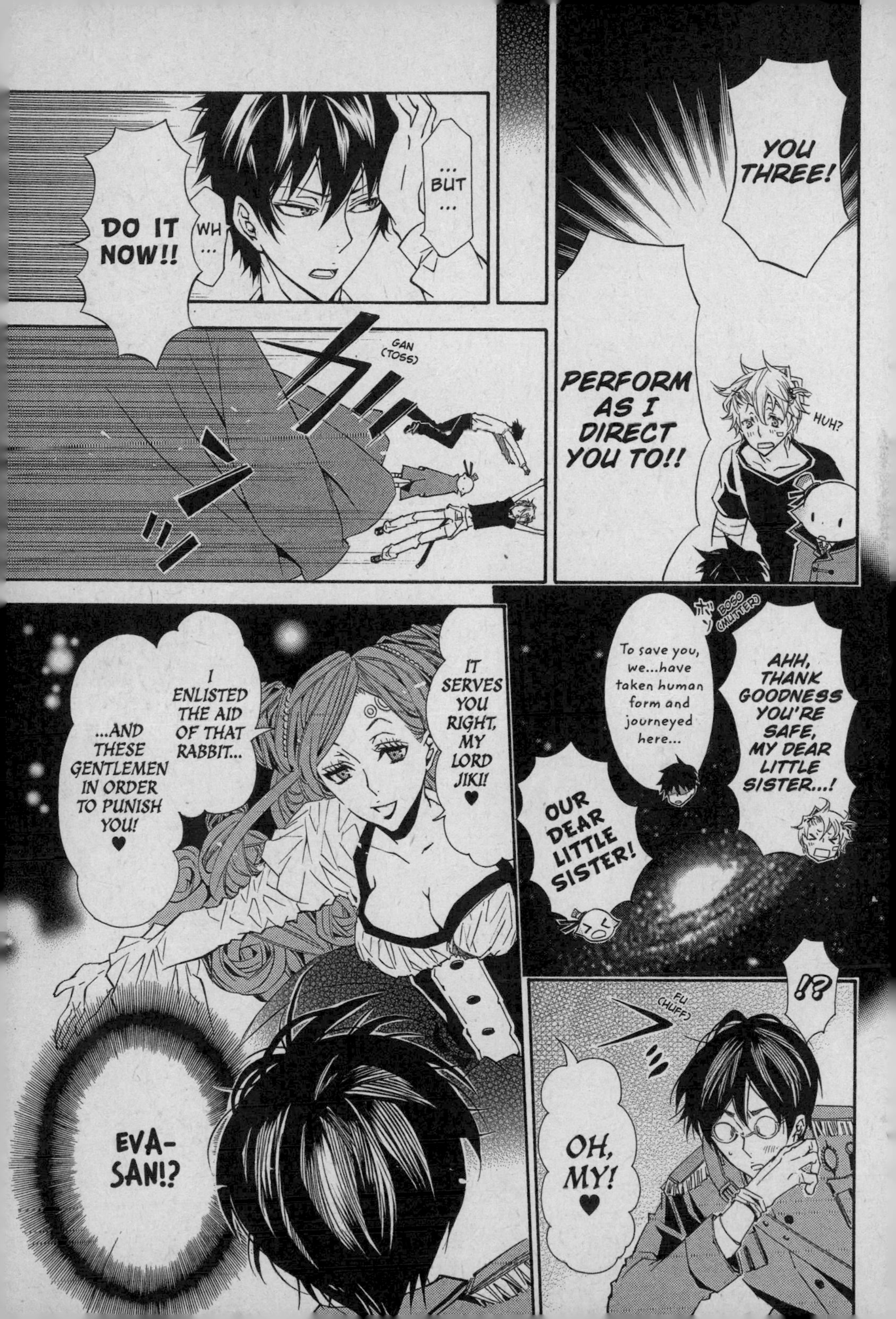
YOU THREE!
PERFORM AS I DIRECT YOU TO!!
HUH?
...BUT...
WH...
DO IT NOW!!
GAN (TOSS)
BOGO (MUTTER)
AHH, THANK GOODNESS YOU'RE SAFE, MY DEAR LITTLE SISTER...!
To save you, we...have taken human form and journeyed here...
OUR DEAR LITTLE SISTER!
IT SERVES YOU RIGHT, MY LORD JIKI! ♥
I ENLISTED THE AID OF THAT RABBIT...
...AND THESE GENTLEMEN IN ORDER TO PUNISH YOU! ♥
!?
FU (HUFF)
OH, MY! ♥
EVA-SAN!?

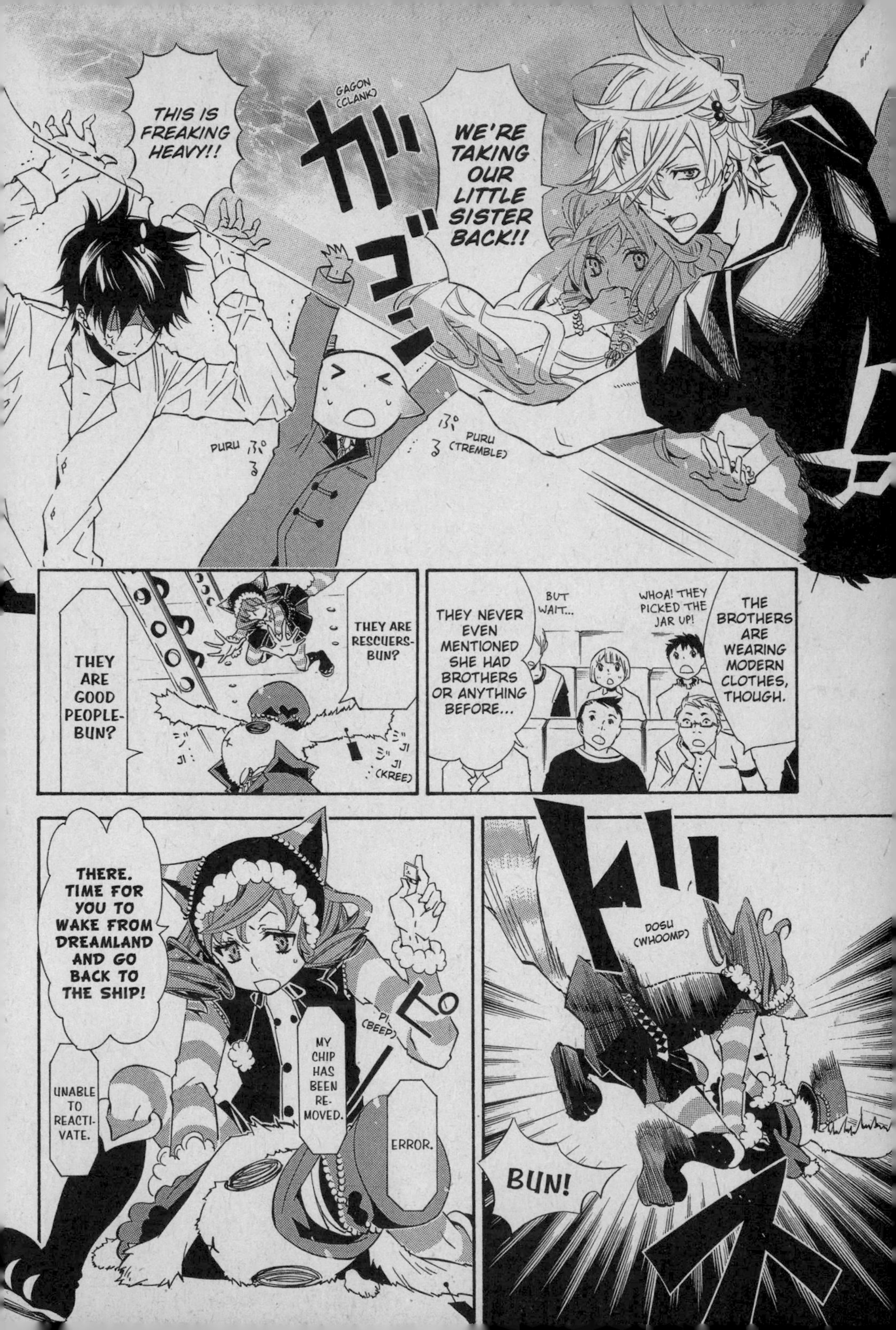
WE'RE TAKING OUR LITTLE SISTER BACK!!
GAGON (CLANK)
THIS IS FREAKING HEAVY!!
PURU (TREMBLE)
PURU
THE BROTHERS ARE WEARING MODERN CLOTHES, THOUGH.
WHOA! THEY PICKED THE JAR UP!
BUT WAIT...
THEY NEVER EVEN MENTIONED SHE HAD BROTHERS OR ANYTHING BEFORE...
THEY ARE RESCUERS-BUN?
THEY ARE GOOD PEOPLE-BUN?
JI JI (KREE)
JI
DOSU (WHOOMP)
BUN!
THERE. TIME FOR YOU TO WAKE FROM DREAMLAND AND GO BACK TO THE SHIP!
PI (BEEP)
ERROR.
MY CHIP HAS BEEN RE-MOVED.
UNABLE TO REACTI-VATE.

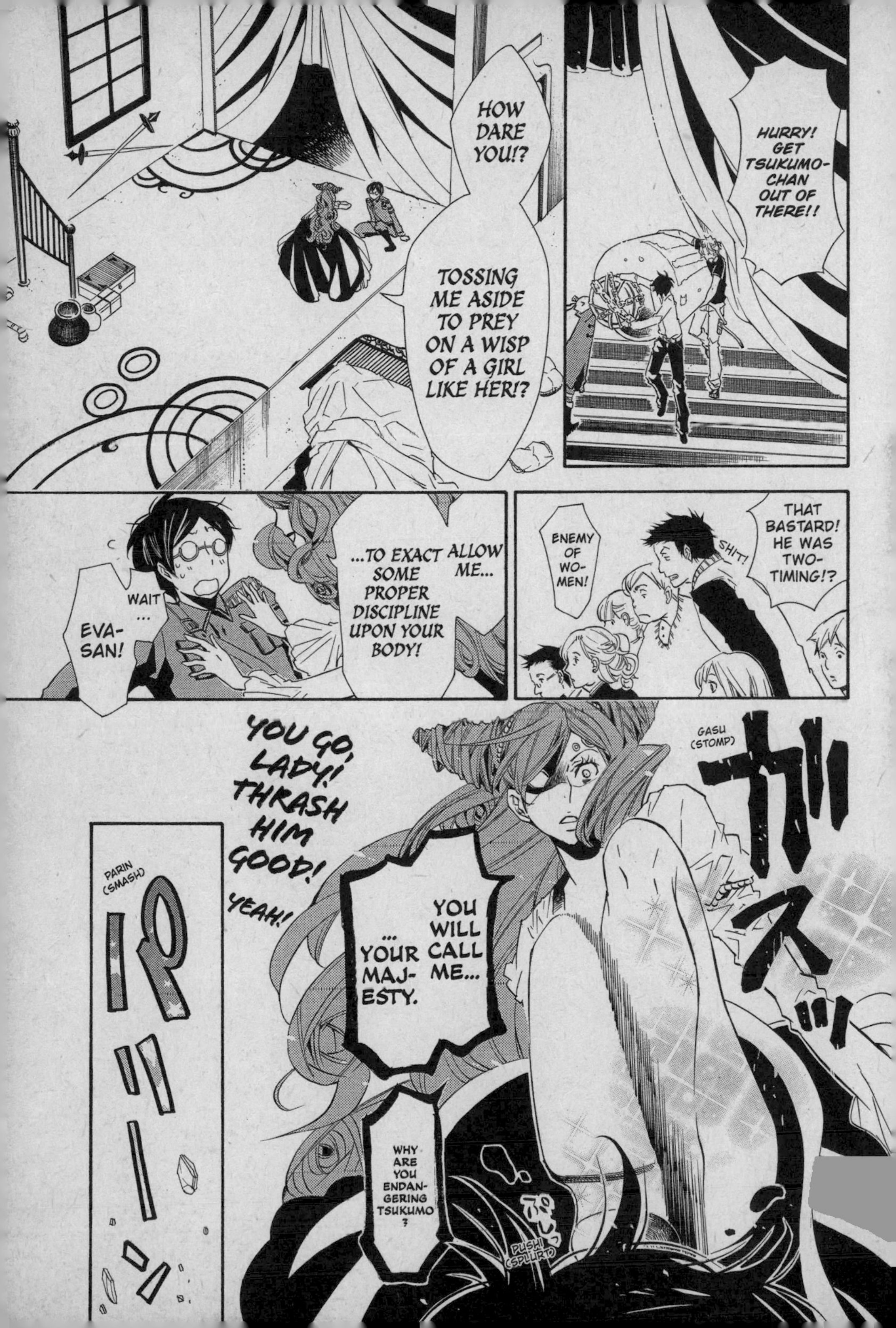
HURRY! GET TSUKUMO-CHAN OUT OF THERE!!
HOW DARE YOU!?
TOSSING ME ASIDE TO PREY ON A WISP OF A GIRL LIKE HER!?
THAT BASTARD! HE WAS TWO-TIMING!?
SHIT!
ENEMY OF WO-MEN!
ALLOW ME...
...TO EXACT SOME PROPER DISCIPLINE UPON YOUR BODY!
WAIT... EVA-SAN!
GASU (STOMP)
ガスッ
YOU GO, LADY! THRASH HIM GOOD!
YEAH!
YOU WILL CALL ME...
...YOUR MAJ-ESTY.
PARIN (SMASH)
パリーン
WHY ARE YOU ENDANGERING TSUKUMO?
PUSHI (SPLURT)

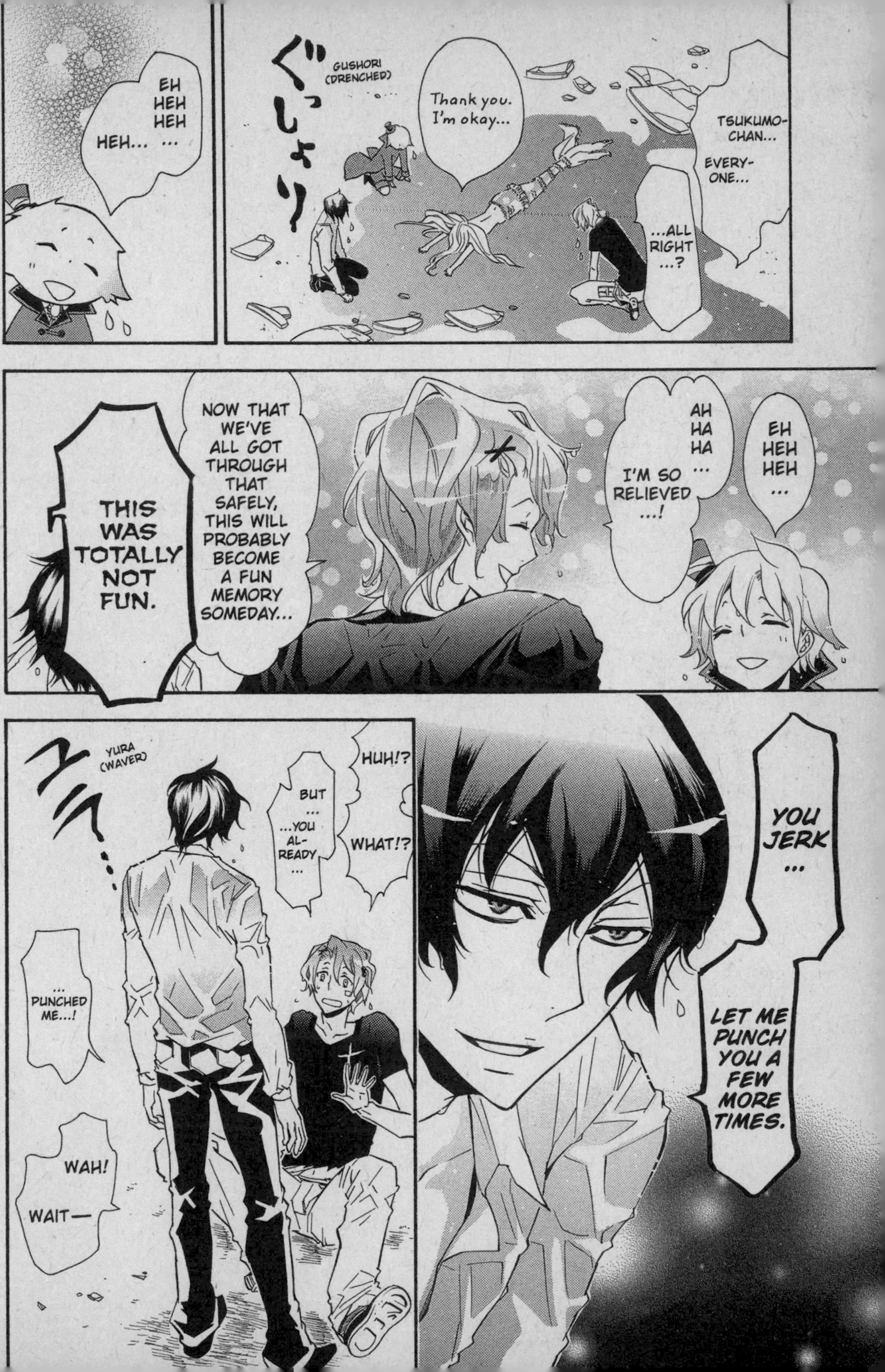
TSUKUMO-CHAN... EVERY-ONE...
...ALL RIGHT ...?
Thank you. I'm okay...
GUSHORI (DRENCHED)
ぐっしょり
EH HEH HEH HEH... ...
EH HEH HEH ...
AH HA HA ... I'M SO RELIEVED ...!
NOW THAT WE'VE ALL GOT THROUGH THAT SAFELY, THIS WILL PROBABLY BECOME A FUN MEMORY SOMEDAY...
THIS WAS TOTALLY NOT FUN.
YOU JERK ...
LET ME PUNCH YOU A FEW MORE TIMES.
HUH!?
WHAT!?
BUT ... ...YOU AL-READY ...
... PUNCHED ME...!
YURA (WAVER)
ゆら...
WAH! WAIT—

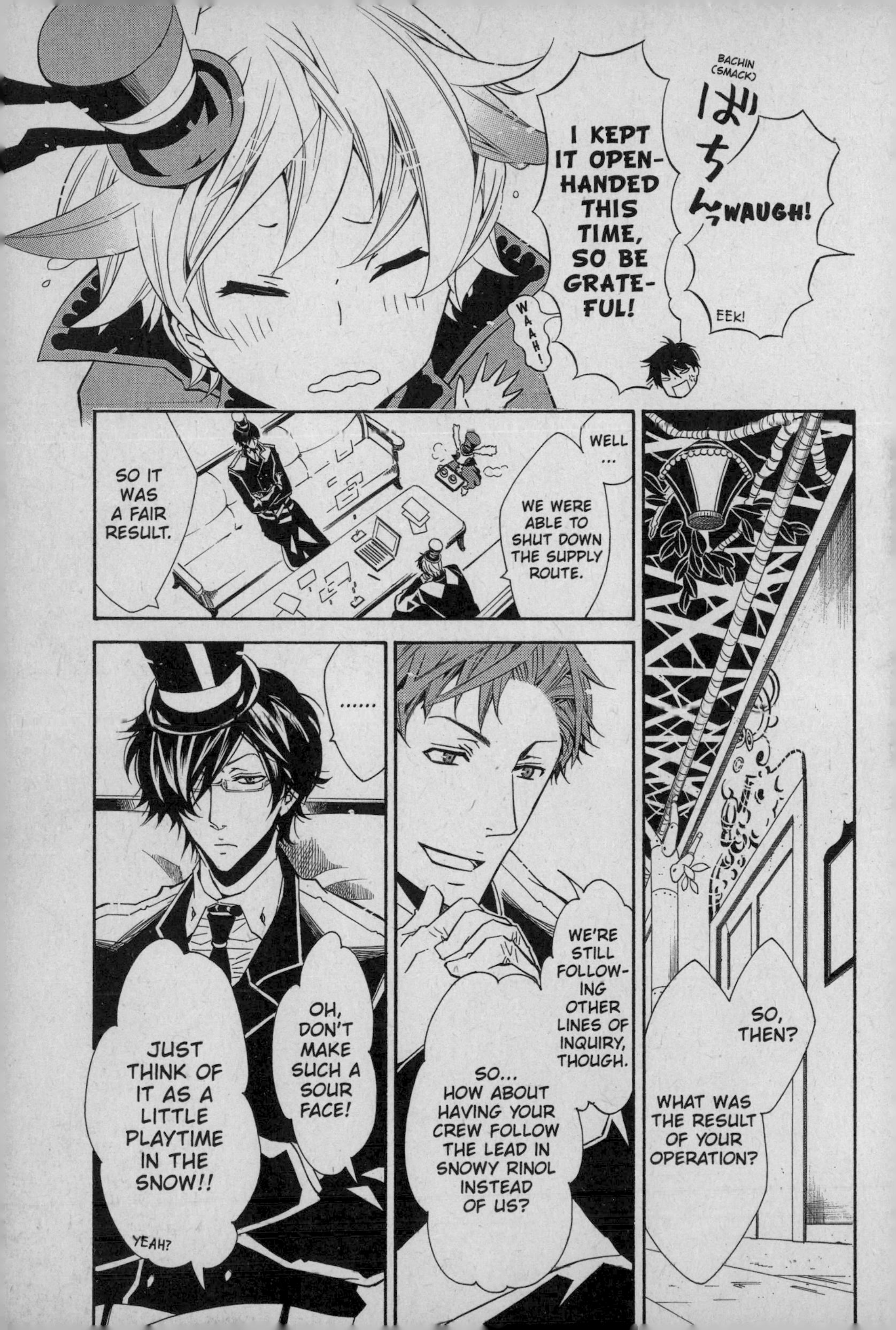
BACHIN (SMACK)
ぱちんっ
WAUGH!
EEK!
I KEPT IT OPEN-HANDED THIS TIME, SO BE GRATEFUL!
WAAH!
SO, THEN?
WHAT WAS THE RESULT OF YOUR OPERATION?
WELL ...
WE WERE ABLE TO SHUT DOWN THE SUPPLY ROUTE.
SO IT WAS A FAIR RESULT.
WE'RE STILL FOLLOWING OTHER LINES OF INQUIRY, THOUGH.
SO... HOW ABOUT HAVING YOUR CREW FOLLOW THE LEAD IN SNOWY RINOL INSTEAD OF US?
......
OH, DON'T MAKE SUCH A SOUR FACE!
JUST THINK OF IT AS A LITTLE PLAYTIME IN THE SNOW!!
YEAH?

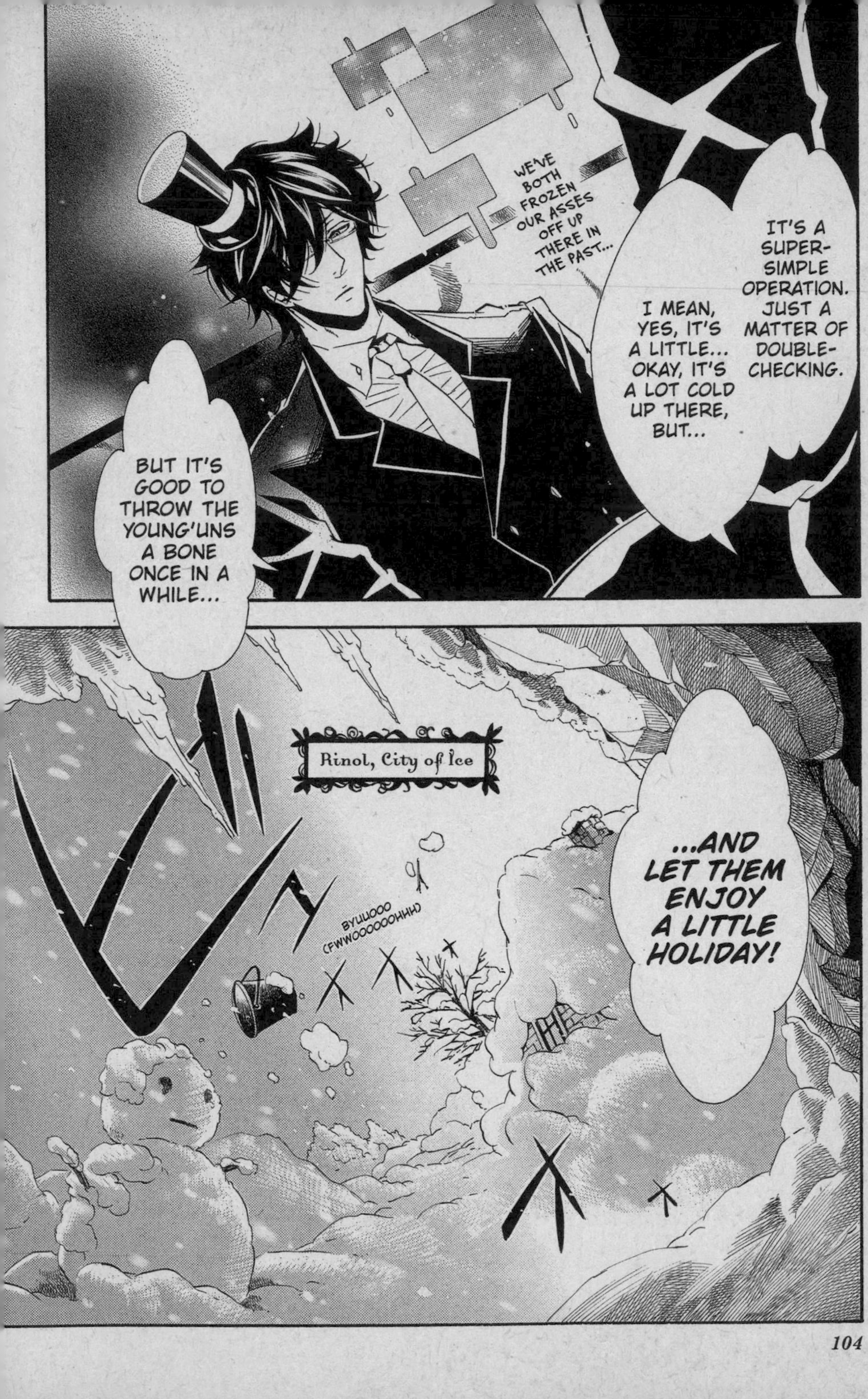
IT'S A SUPER-SIMPLE OPERATION. JUST A MATTER OF DOUBLE-CHECKING.
I MEAN, YES, IT'S A LITTLE... OKAY, IT'S A LOT COLD UP THERE, BUT...
WE'VE BOTH FROZEN OUR ASSES OFF UP THERE IN THE PAST...
BUT IT'S GOOD TO THROW THE YOUNG'UNS A BONE ONCE IN A WHILE...
...AND LET THEM ENJOY A LITTLE HOLIDAY!
Rinol, City of Ice
BYUUOOO (FWWOOOOOOHHH)

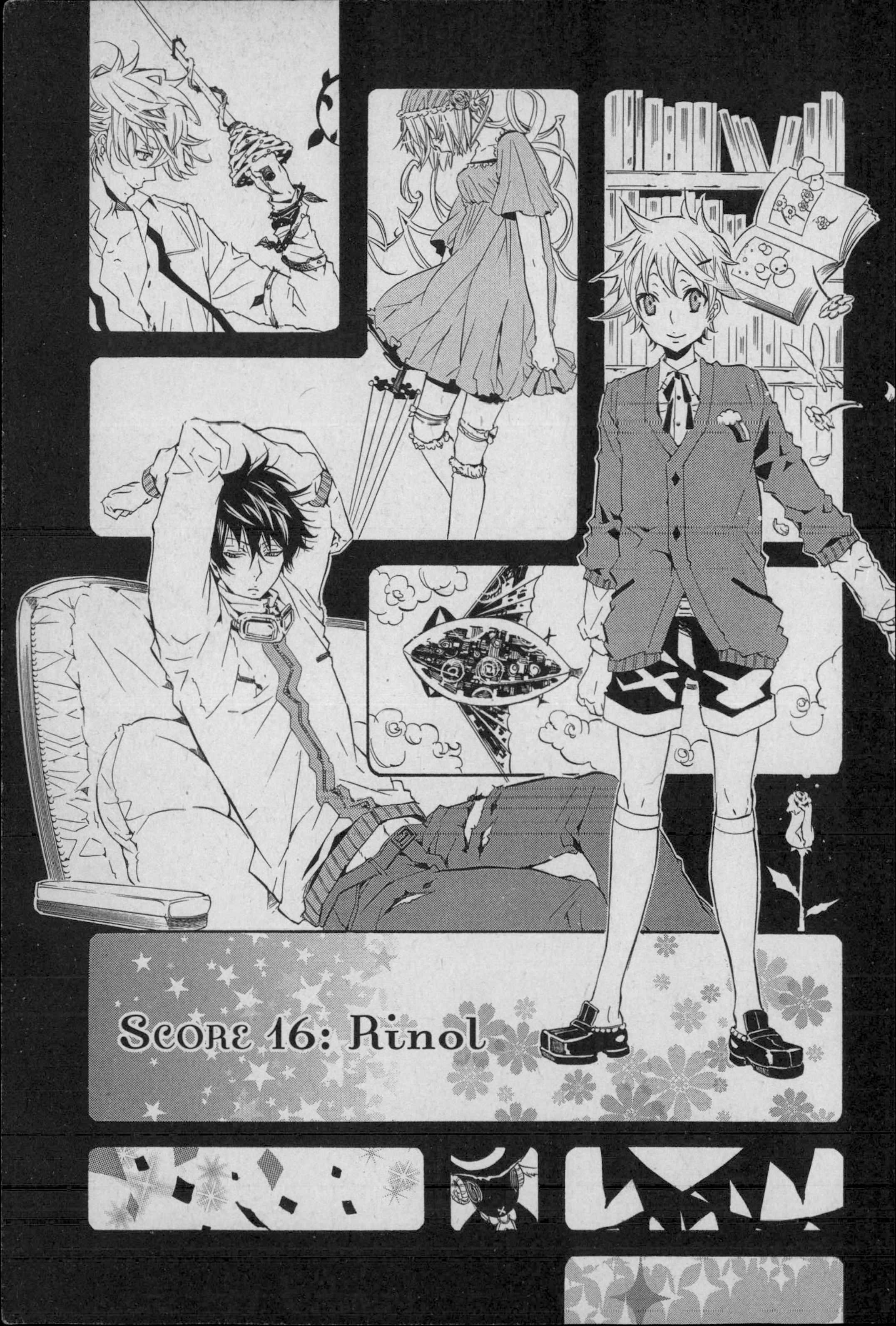
Score 16: Rinol

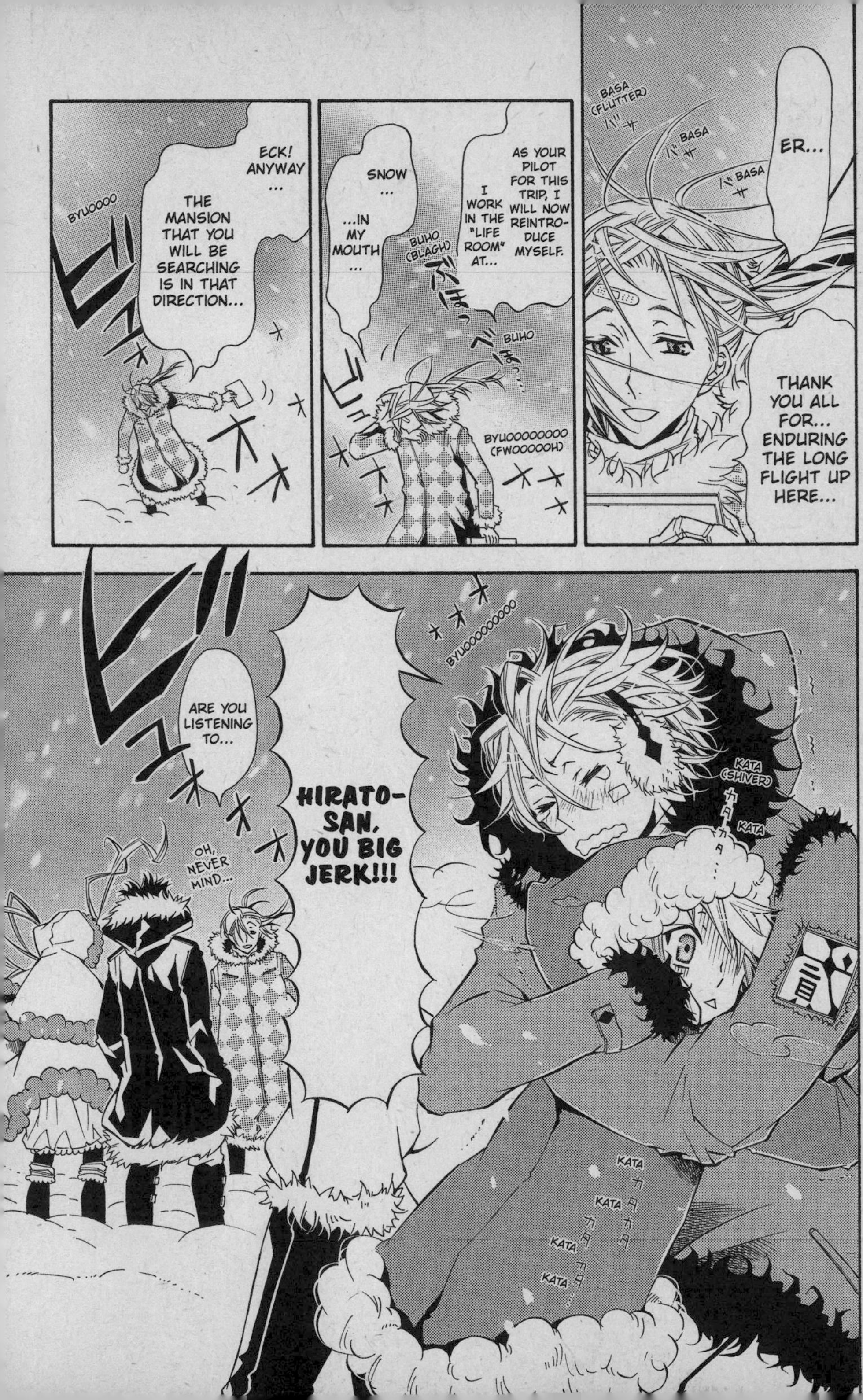

ER...
BASA (FLUTTER)
BASA
BASA
THANK YOU ALL FOR... ENDURING THE LONG FLIGHT UP HERE...
AS YOUR PILOT FOR THIS TRIP, I WILL NOW REINTRO-DUCE MYSELF.
I WORK IN THE "LIFE ROOM" AT...
SNOW...
...IN MY MOUTH...
BUHO (BLAGH)
BUHO
BYUOOOOOOOO (FWOOOOOH)
ECK! ANYWAY...
THE MANSION THAT YOU WILL BE SEARCHING IS IN THAT DIRECTION...
BYUOOOO
BYUOOOOOOOOO
ARE YOU LISTENING TO...
HIRATO-SAN, YOU BIG JERK!!!
KATA (SHIVER)
KATA
OH, NEVER MIND...
KATA
KATA
KATA
KATA

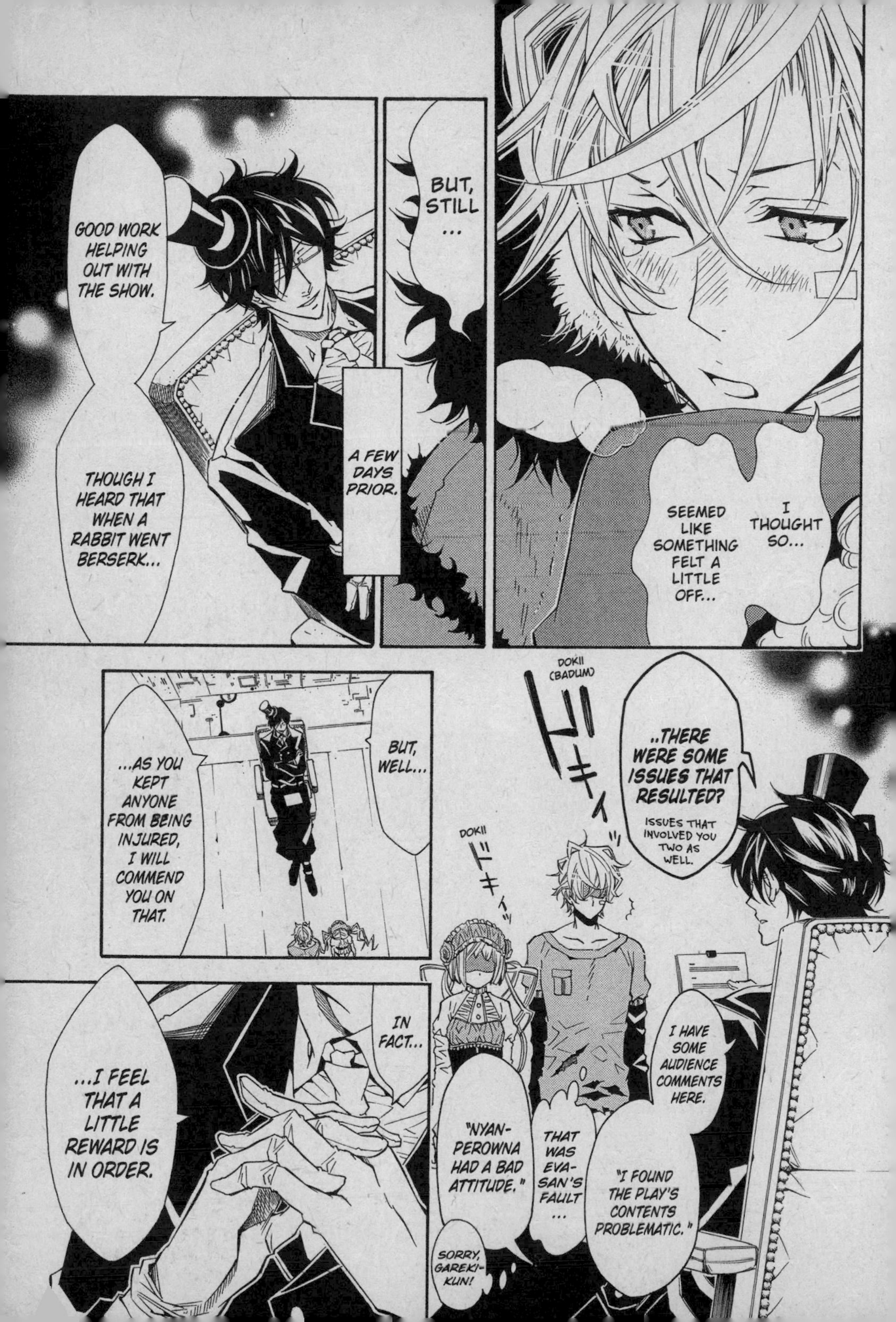
I THOUGHT SO...
SEEMED LIKE SOMETHING FELT A LITTLE OFF...
BUT, STILL...
A FEW DAYS PRIOR.
GOOD WORK HELPING OUT WITH THE SHOW.
THOUGH I HEARD THAT WHEN A RABBIT WENT BERSERK...
DOKII (BADUM)
..THERE WERE SOME ISSUES THAT RESULTED?
ISSUES THAT INVOLVED YOU TWO AS WELL.
DOKII
I HAVE SOME AUDIENCE COMMENTS HERE.
"I FOUND THE PLAY'S CONTENTS PROBLEMATIC."
THAT WAS EVA-SAN'S FAULT...
"NYAN-PEROWNA HAD A BAD ATTITUDE."
SORRY, GAREKI-KUN!
BUT, WELL...
...AS YOU KEPT ANYONE FROM BEING INJURED, I WILL COMMEND YOU ON THAT.
IN FACT...
...I FEEL THAT A LITTLE REWARD IS IN ORDER.

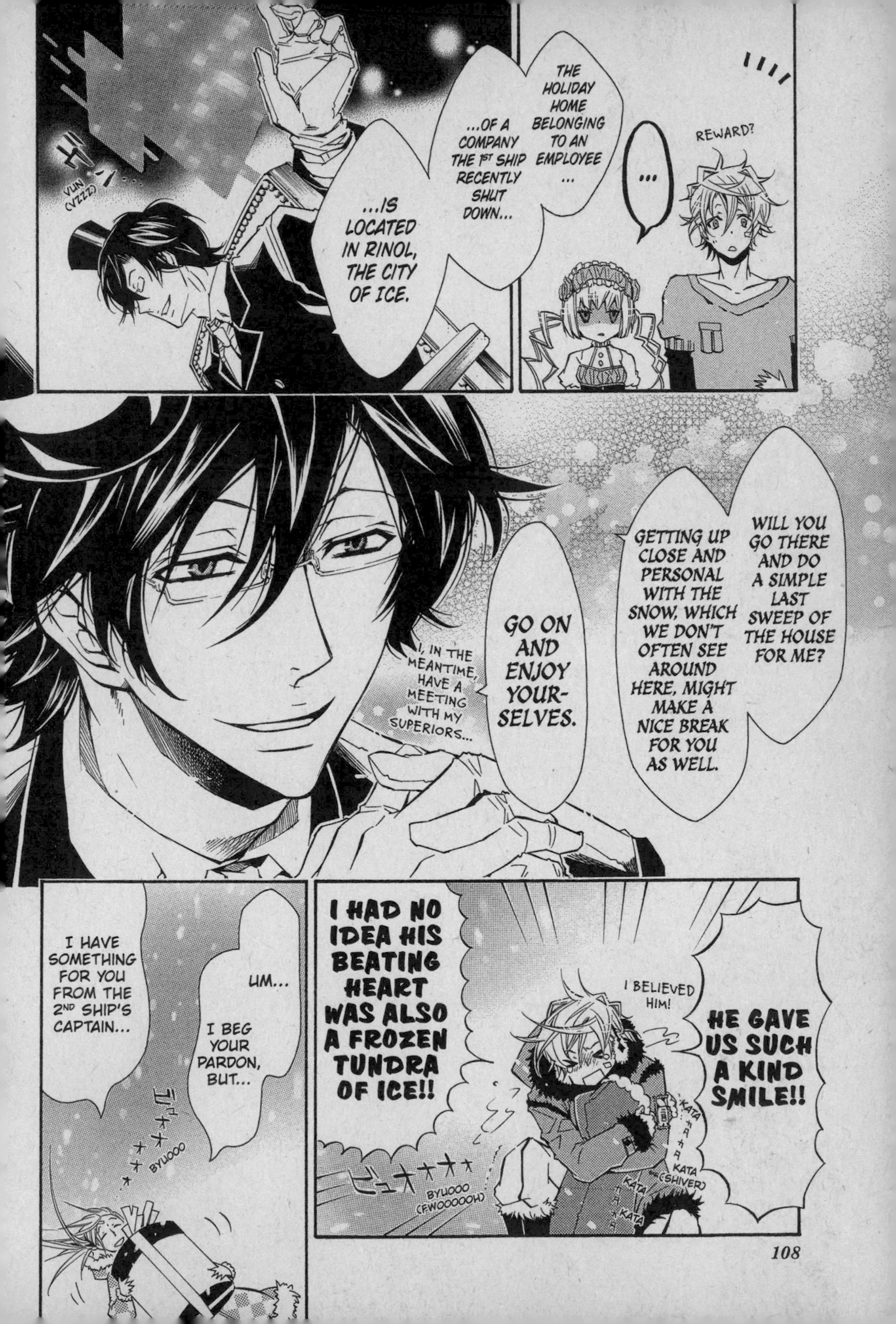

REWARD?
...
THE HOLIDAY HOME BELONGING TO AN EMPLOYEE ...
...OF A COMPANY THE 1ST SHIP RECENTLY SHUT DOWN...
...IS LOCATED IN RINOL, THE CITY OF ICE.
VUN (VZZZ)
WILL YOU GO THERE AND DO A SIMPLE LAST SWEEP OF THE HOUSE FOR ME?
GETTING UP CLOSE AND PERSONAL WITH THE SNOW, WHICH WE DON'T OFTEN SEE AROUND HERE, MIGHT MAKE A NICE BREAK FOR YOU AS WELL.
GO ON AND ENJOY YOURSELVES.
I, IN THE MEANTIME, HAVE A MEETING WITH MY SUPERIORS...
HE GAVE US SUCH A KIND SMILE!!
I BELIEVED HIM!
I HAD NO IDEA HIS BEATING HEART WAS ALSO A FROZEN TUNDRA OF ICE!!
KATA KATA (SHIVER)
KATA KATA
BYUOOO (FWOOOOOH)
UM...
I BEG YOUR PARDON, BUT...
I HAVE SOMETHING FOR YOU FROM THE 2ND SHIP'S CAPTAIN...
BYUOOO

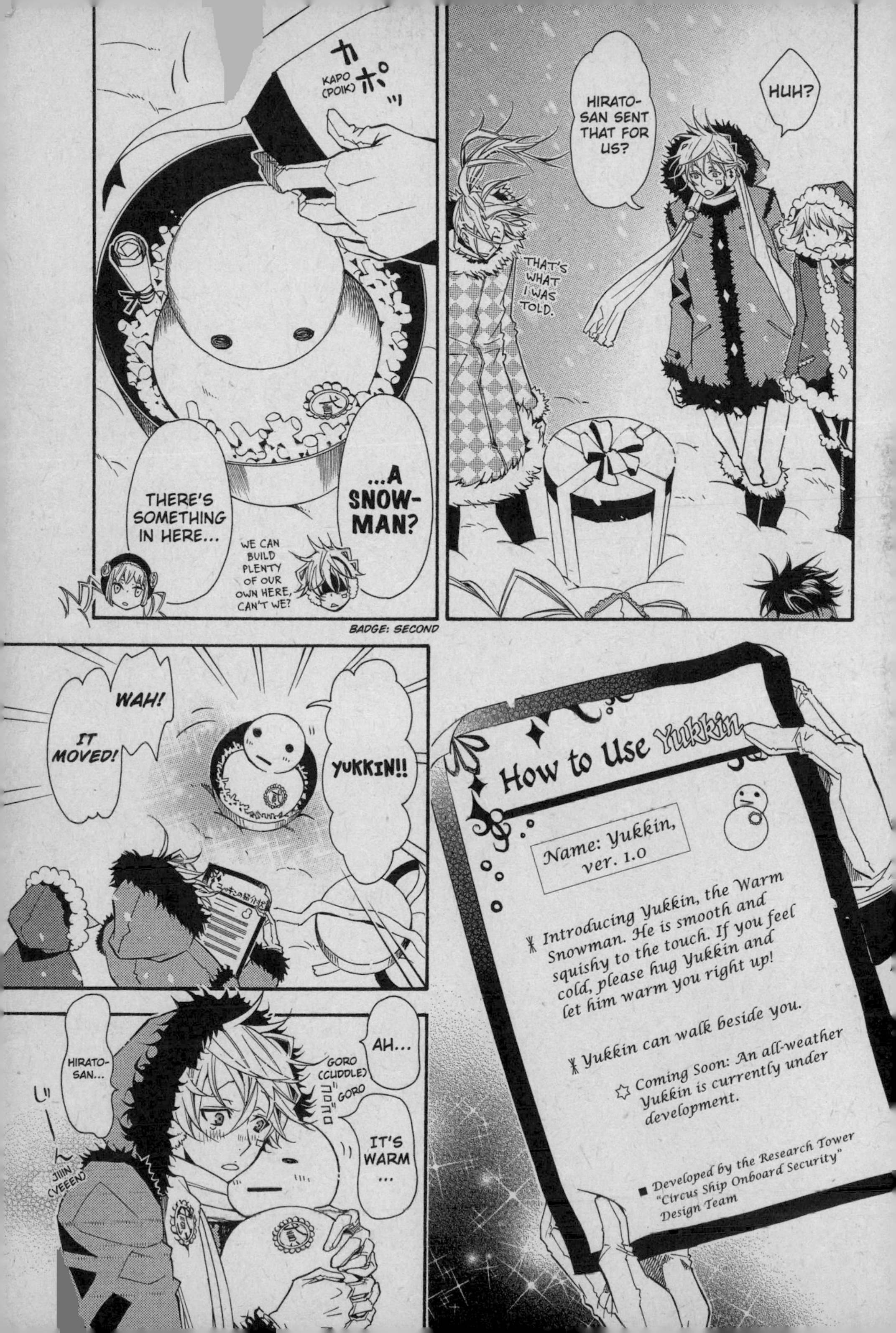
HUH?
HIRATO-SAN SENT THAT FOR US?
THAT'S WHAT I WAS TOLD.
カポッ
KAPO (POIK)
...A SNOWMAN?
THERE'S SOMETHING IN HERE...
WE CAN BUILD PLENTY OF OUR OWN HERE, CAN'T WE?
BADGE: SECOND
How to Use Yukkin
Name: Yukkin, ver. 1.0
Introducing Yukkin, the Warm Snowman. He is smooth and squishy to the touch. If you feel cold, please hug Yukkin and let him warm you right up!
Yukkin can walk beside you.
Coming Soon: An all-weather Yukkin is currently under development.
■ Developed by the Research Tower "Circus Ship Onboard Security" Design Team
YUKKIN!!
WAH!
IT MOVED!
AH...
GORO (CUDDLE) GORO
IT'S WARM...
HIRATO-SAN...
JIIIN (VEEEEN)

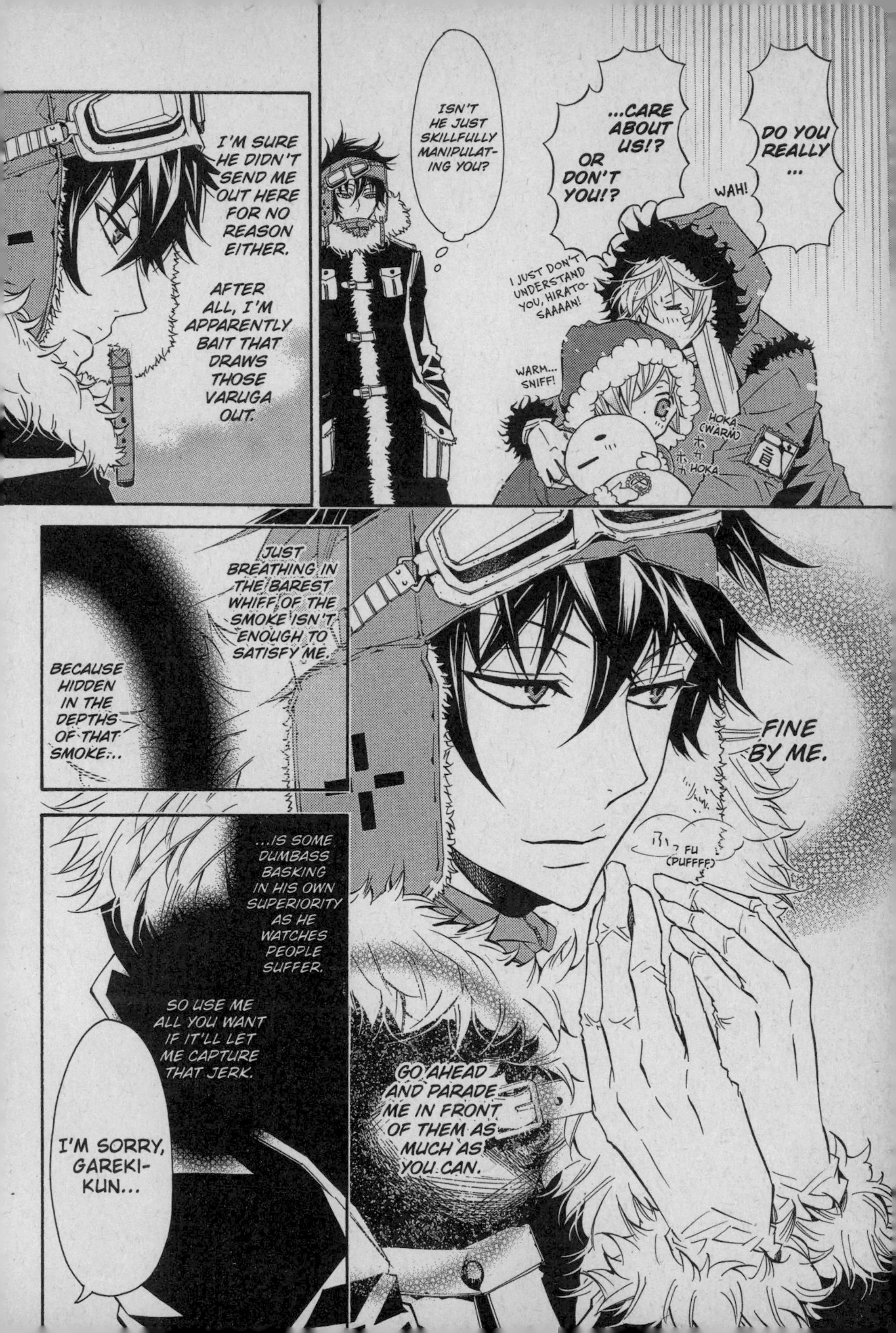
DO YOU REALLY...
...CARE ABOUT US!? OR DON'T YOU!?
WAH!
I JUST DON'T UNDERSTAND YOU, HIRATO-SAAAAN!
WARM... SNIFF!
HOKA (WARM) HOKA
ISN'T HE JUST SKILLFULLY MANIPULATING YOU?
I'M SURE HE DIDN'T SEND ME OUT HERE FOR NO REASON EITHER.
AFTER ALL, I'M APPARENTLY BAIT THAT DRAWS THOSE VARUGA OUT.
FINE BY ME.
FU (PUFFFF)
GO AHEAD AND PARADE ME IN FRONT OF THEM AS MUCH AS YOU CAN.
JUST BREATHING IN THE BAREST WHIFF OF THE SMOKE ISN'T ENOUGH TO SATISFY ME.
BECAUSE HIDDEN IN THE DEPTHS OF THAT SMOKE...
...IS SOME DUMBASS BASKING IN HIS OWN SUPERIORITY AS HE WATCHES PEOPLE SUFFER.
SO USE ME ALL YOU WANT IF IT'LL LET ME CAPTURE THAT JERK.
I'M SORRY, GAREKI-KUN...

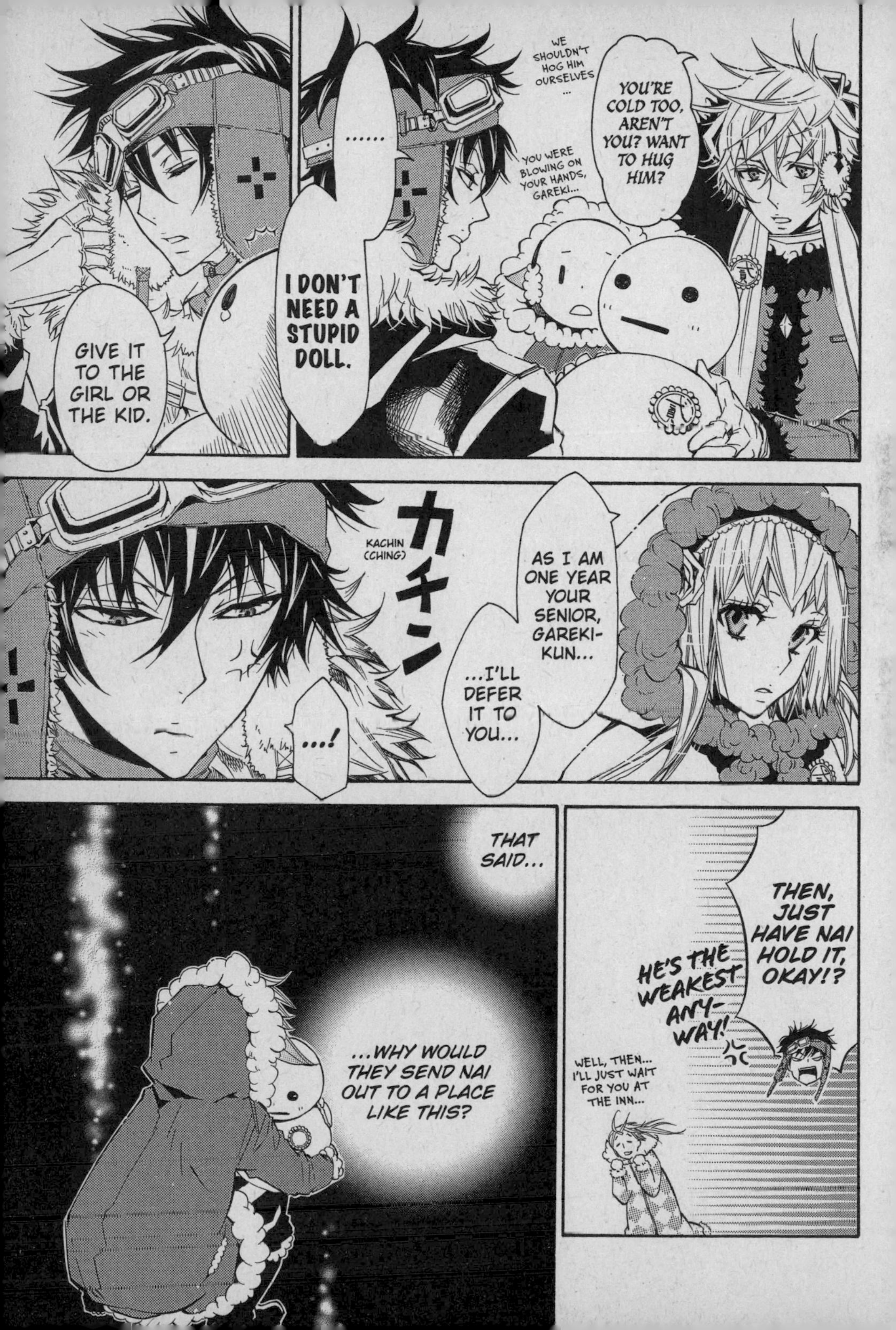
YOU'RE COLD TOO, AREN'T YOU? WANT TO HUG HIM?
WE SHOULDN'T HOG HIM OURSELVES...
YOU WERE BLOWING ON YOUR HANDS, GAREKI...
......
I DON'T NEED A STUPID DOLL.
GIVE IT TO THE GIRL OR THE KID.
AS I AM ONE YEAR YOUR SENIOR, GAREKI-KUN...
...I'LL DEFER IT TO YOU...
カチン
KACHIN (CHING)
...!
THEN, JUST HAVE NAI HOLD IT, OKAY!?
HE'S THE WEAKEST ANY-WAY!
WELL, THEN... I'LL JUST WAIT FOR YOU AT THE INN...
THAT SAID...
...WHY WOULD THEY SEND NAI OUT TO A PLACE LIKE THIS?

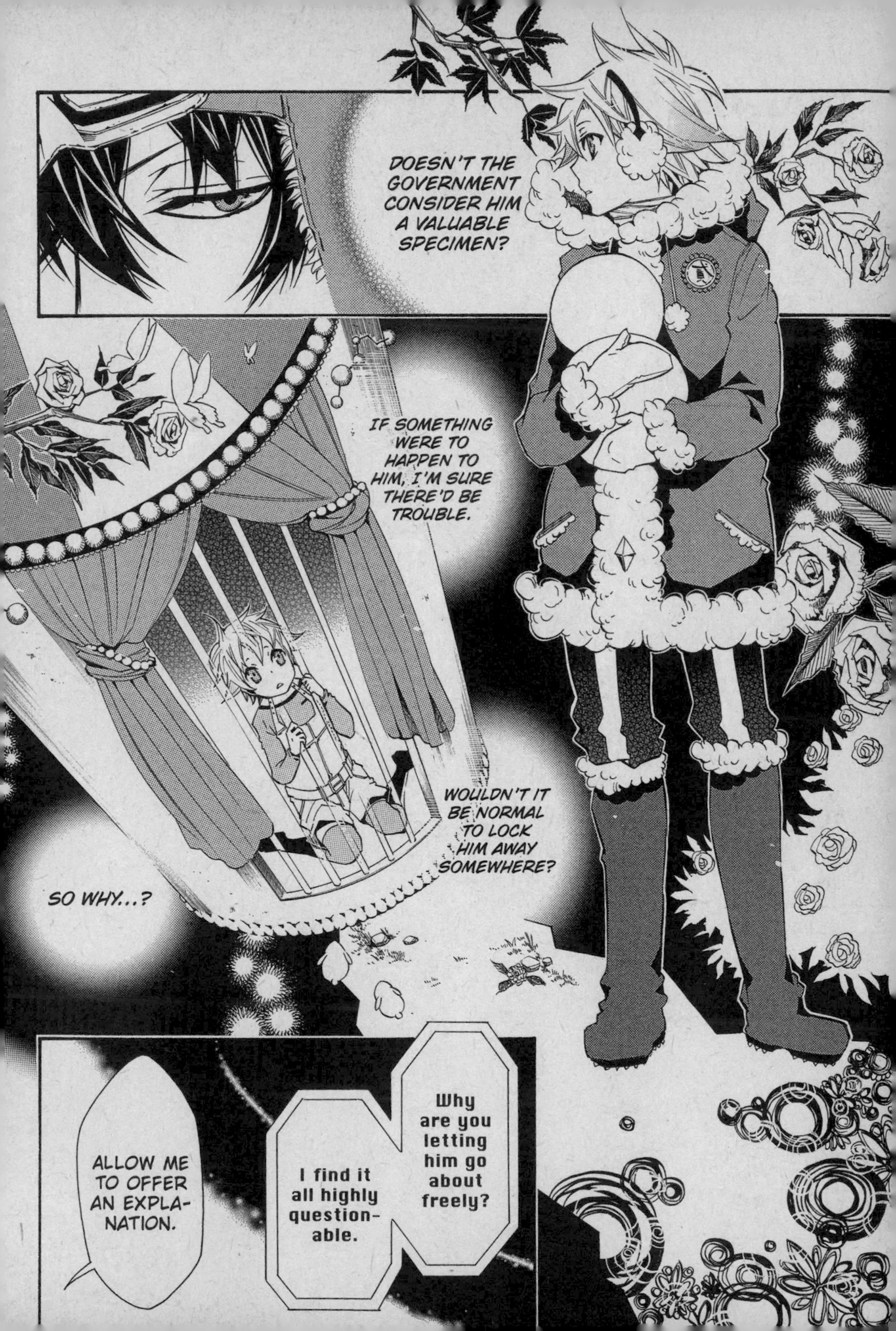
DOESN'T THE GOVERNMENT CONSIDER HIM A VALUABLE SPECIMEN?
IF SOMETHING WERE TO HAPPEN TO HIM, I'M SURE THERE'D BE TROUBLE.
WOULDN'T IT BE NORMAL TO LOCK HIM AWAY SOMEWHERE?
SO WHY...?
Why are you letting him go about freely?
I find it all highly question-able.
ALLOW ME TO OFFER AN EXPLA-NATION.

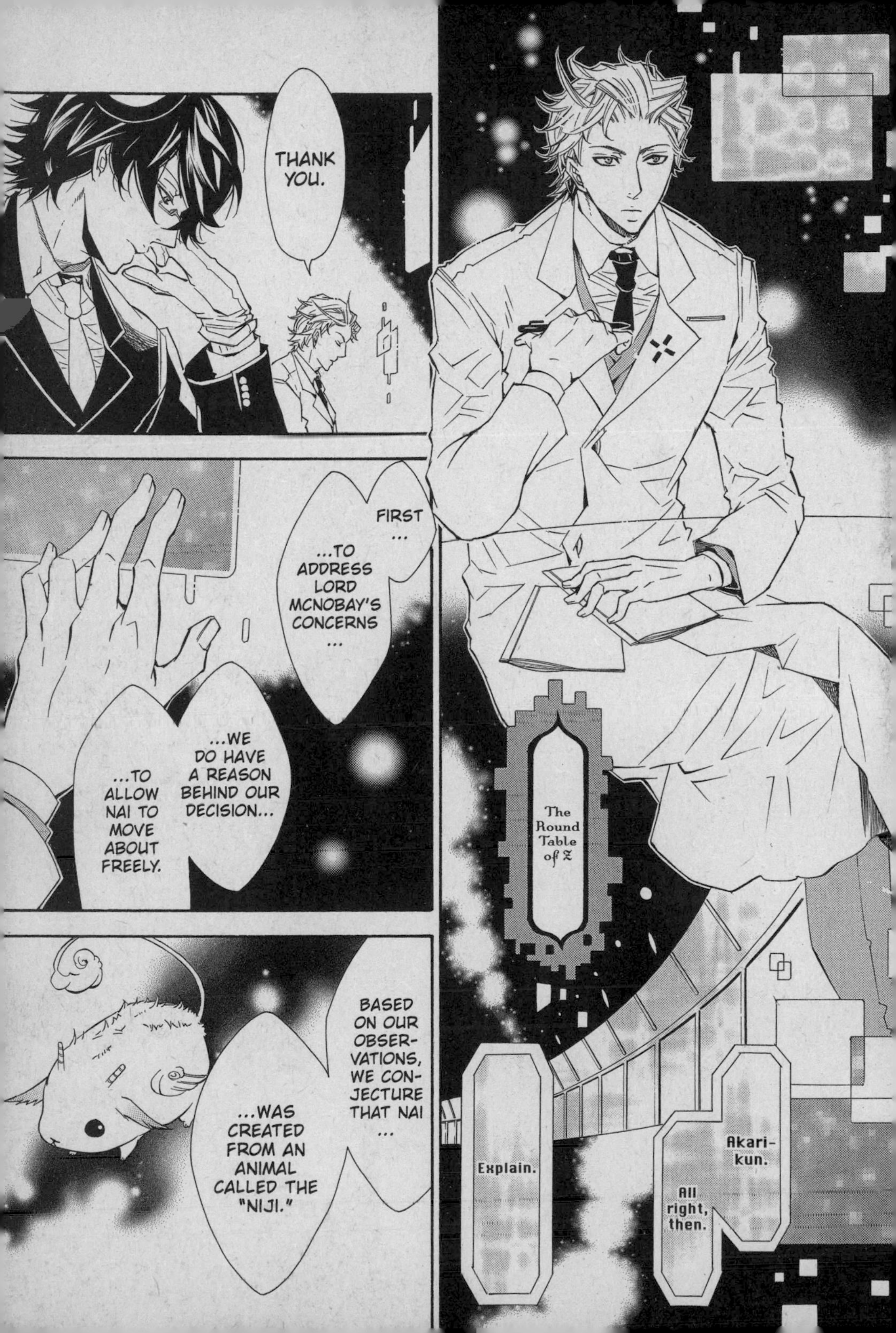
The Round Table of Z
Akari-kun.
Explain.
All right, then.
THANK YOU.
FIRST ...
...TO ADDRESS LORD MCNOBAY'S CONCERNS ...
...WE DO HAVE A REASON BEHIND OUR DECISION...
...TO ALLOW NAI TO MOVE ABOUT FREELY.
BASED ON OUR OBSER-VATIONS, WE CON-JECTURE THAT NAI ...
...WAS CREATED FROM AN ANIMAL CALLED THE "NIJI."

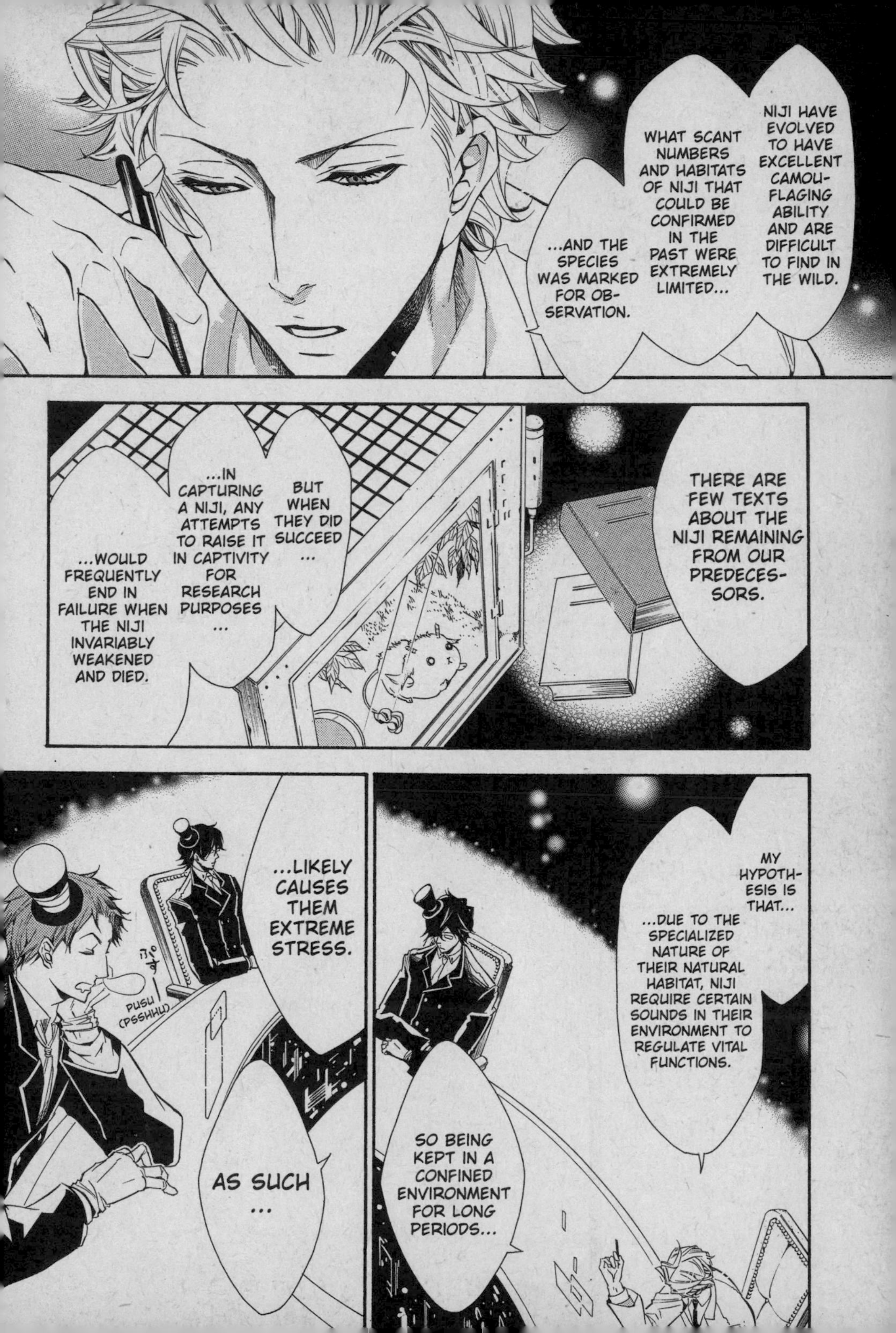
NIJI HAVE EVOLVED TO HAVE EXCELLENT CAMOUFLAGING ABILITY AND ARE DIFFICULT TO FIND IN THE WILD.
WHAT SCANT NUMBERS AND HABITATS OF NIJI THAT COULD BE CONFIRMED IN THE PAST WERE EXTREMELY LIMITED...
...AND THE SPECIES WAS MARKED FOR OBSERVATION.
THERE ARE FEW TEXTS ABOUT THE NIJI REMAINING FROM OUR PREDECESSORS.
BUT WHEN THEY DID SUCCEED ...
...IN CAPTURING A NIJI, ANY ATTEMPTS TO RAISE IT IN CAPTIVITY FOR RESEARCH PURPOSES ...
...WOULD FREQUENTLY END IN FAILURE WHEN THE NIJI INVARIABLY WEAKENED AND DIED.
MY HYPOTHESIS IS THAT...
...DUE TO THE SPECIALIZED NATURE OF THEIR NATURAL HABITAT, NIJI REQUIRE CERTAIN SOUNDS IN THEIR ENVIRONMENT TO REGULATE VITAL FUNCTIONS.
SO BEING KEPT IN A CONFINED ENVIRONMENT FOR LONG PERIODS...
...LIKELY CAUSES THEM EXTREME STRESS.
ぷす
PUSU (PSSHHH)
AS SUCH ...

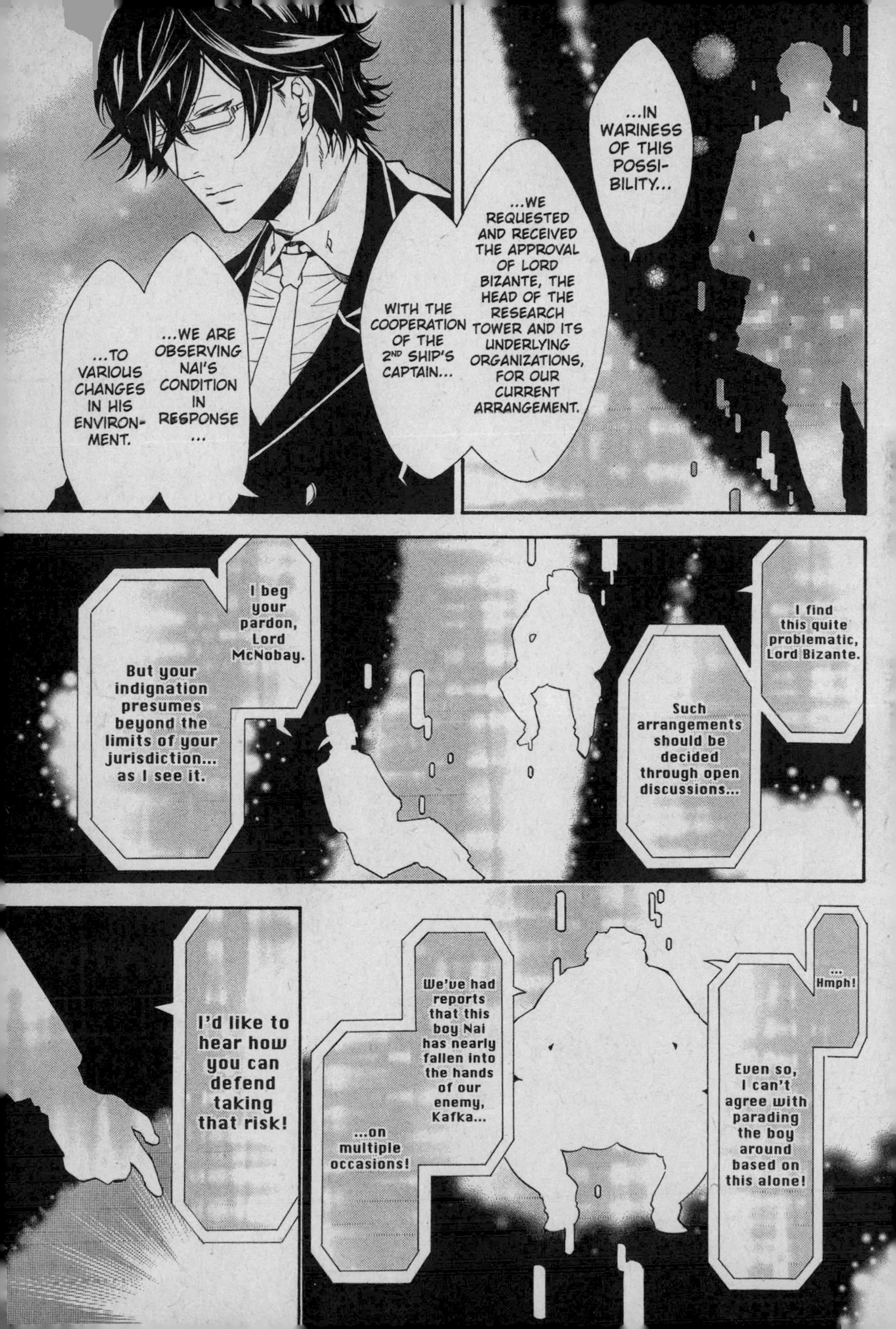
...IN WARINESS OF THIS POSSIBILITY...
...WE REQUESTED AND RECEIVED THE APPROVAL OF LORD BIZANTE, THE HEAD OF THE RESEARCH TOWER AND ITS UNDERLYING ORGANIZATIONS, FOR OUR CURRENT ARRANGEMENT.
WITH THE COOPERATION OF THE 2ND SHIP'S CAPTAIN...
...WE ARE OBSERVING NAI'S CONDITION IN RESPONSE...
...TO VARIOUS CHANGES IN HIS ENVIRONMENT.
I find this quite problematic, Lord Bizante.
Such arrangements should be decided through open discussions...
I beg your pardon, Lord McNobay.
But your indignation presumes beyond the limits of your jurisdiction... as I see it.
...Hmph!
Even so, I can't agree with parading the boy around based on this alone!
We've had reports that this boy Nai has nearly fallen into the hands of our enemy, Kafka...
...on multiple occasions!
I'd like to hear how you can defend taking that risk!

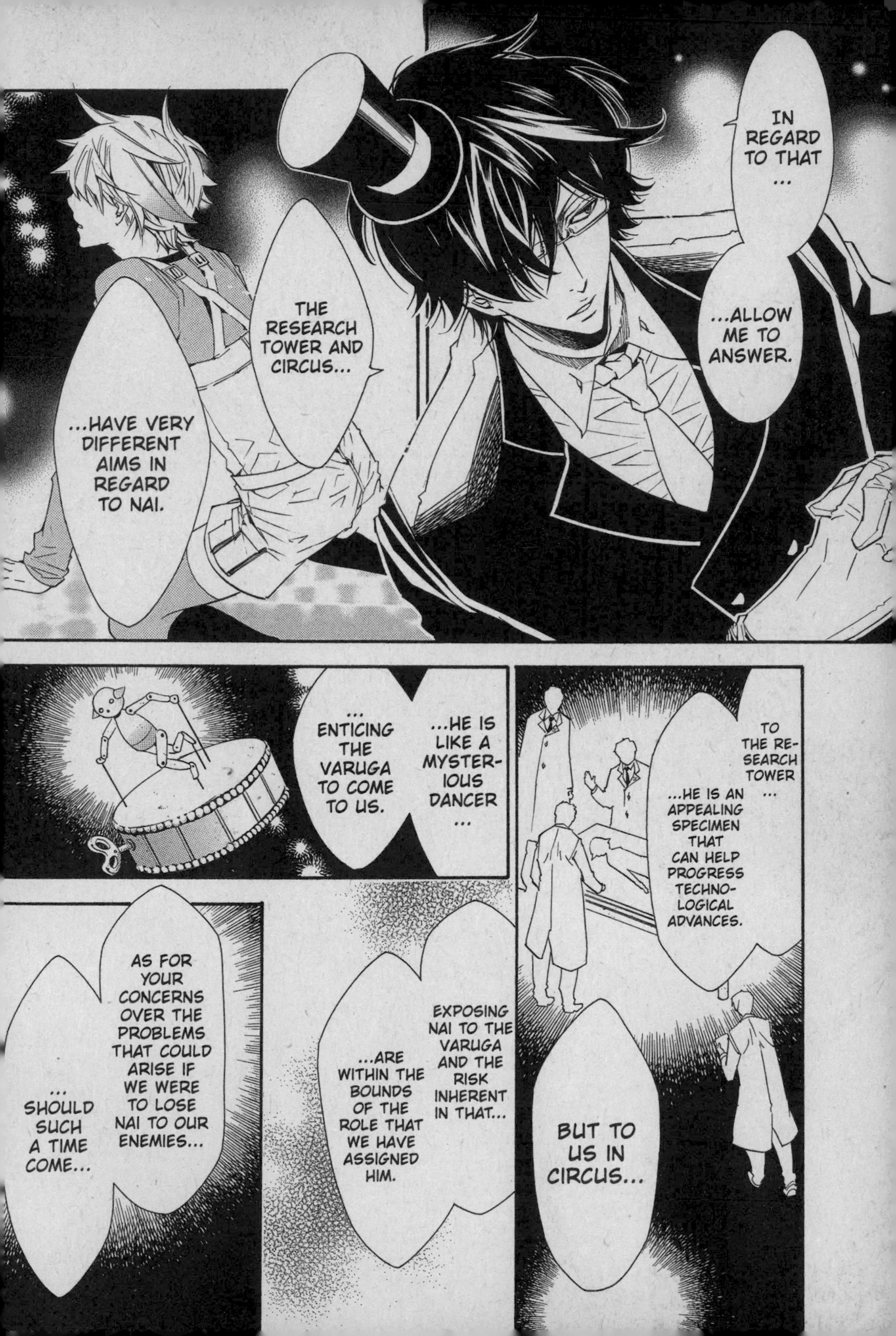
IN REGARD TO THAT ...
...ALLOW ME TO ANSWER.
THE RESEARCH TOWER AND CIRCUS...
...HAVE VERY DIFFERENT AIMS IN REGARD TO NAI.
TO THE RE-SEARCH TOWER ...
...HE IS AN APPEALING SPECIMEN THAT CAN HELP PROGRESS TECHNO-LOGICAL ADVANCES.
BUT TO US IN CIRCUS...
...HE IS LIKE A MYSTER-IOUS DANCER ...
... ENTICING THE VARUGA TO COME TO US.
EXPOSING NAI TO THE VARUGA AND THE RISK INHERENT IN THAT...
...ARE WITHIN THE BOUNDS OF THE ROLE THAT WE HAVE ASSIGNED HIM.
AS FOR YOUR CONCERNS OVER THE PROBLEMS THAT COULD ARISE IF WE WERE TO LOSE NAI TO OUR ENEMIES...
... SHOULD SUCH A TIME COME...

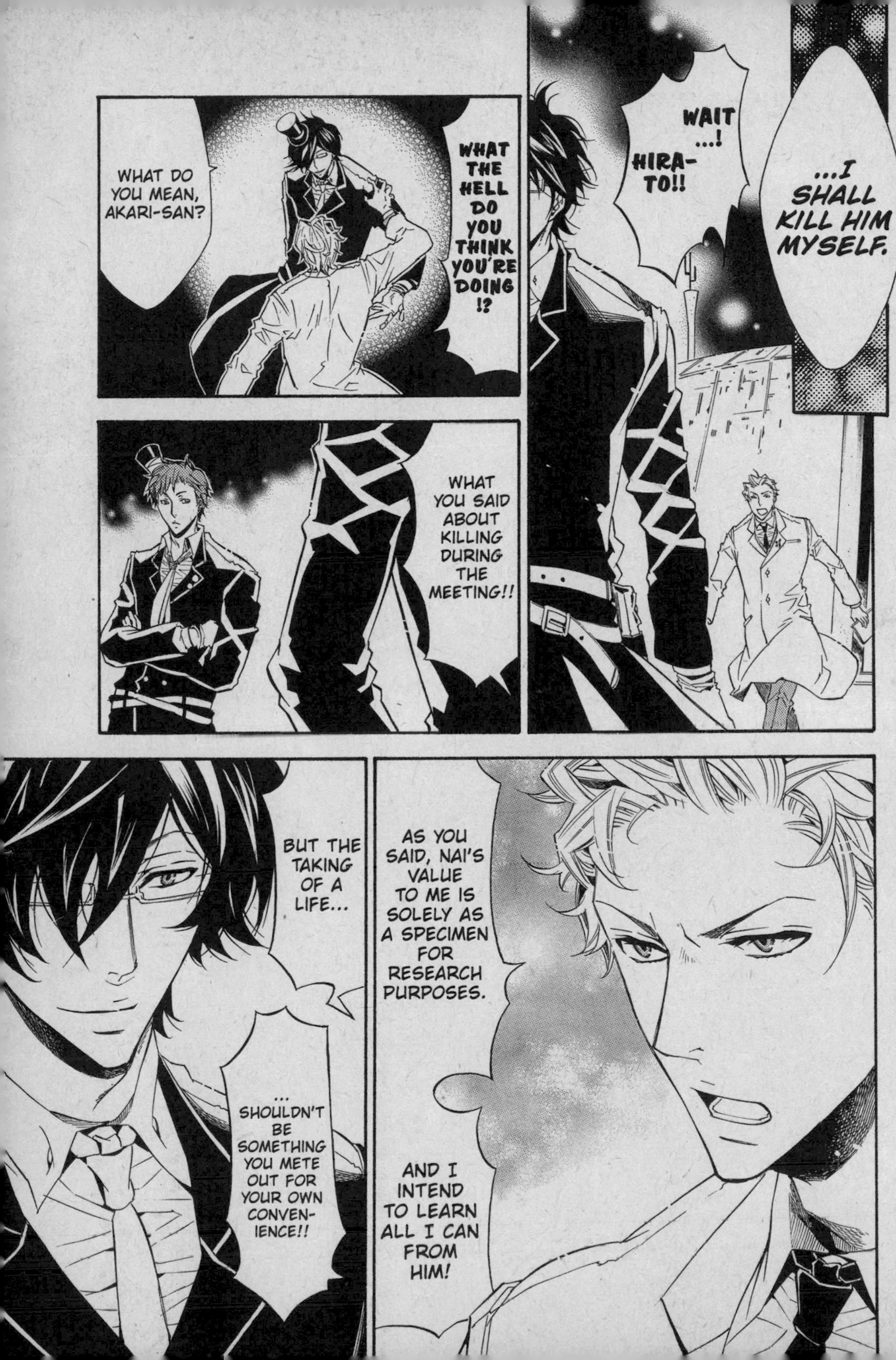
...I SHALL KILL HIM MYSELF.
WAIT ...! HIRA-TO!!
WHAT THE HELL DO YOU THINK YOU'RE DOING !?
WHAT DO YOU MEAN, AKARI-SAN?
WHAT YOU SAID ABOUT KILLING DURING THE MEETING!!
AS YOU SAID, NAI'S VALUE TO ME IS SOLELY AS A SPECIMEN FOR RESEARCH PURPOSES.
AND I INTEND TO LEARN ALL I CAN FROM HIM!
BUT THE TAKING OF A LIFE...
... SHOULDN'T BE SOMETHING YOU METE OUT FOR YOUR OWN CONVEN-IENCE!!

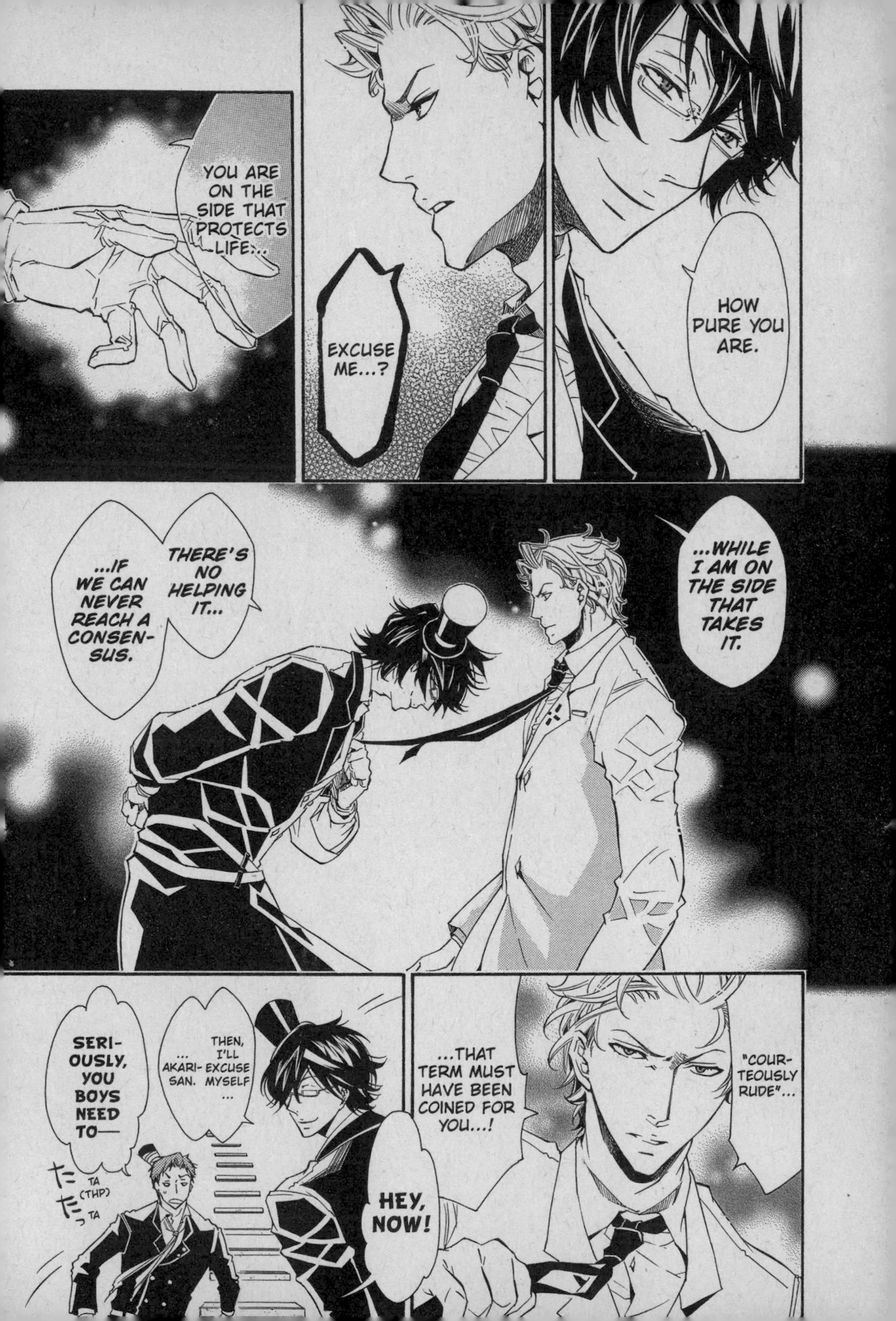
HOW PURE YOU ARE.
EXCUSE ME...?
YOU ARE ON THE SIDE THAT PROTECTS LIFE...
...WHILE I AM ON THE SIDE THAT TAKES IT.
THERE'S NO HELPING IT...
...IF WE CAN NEVER REACH A CONSENSUS.
"COURTEOUSLY RUDE"...
...THAT TERM MUST HAVE BEEN COINED FOR YOU...!
THEN, I'LL EXCUSE MYSELF...
...AKARI-SAN.
SERIOUSLY, YOU BOYS NEED TO—
HEY, NOW!
たたっ TA (THP) TA

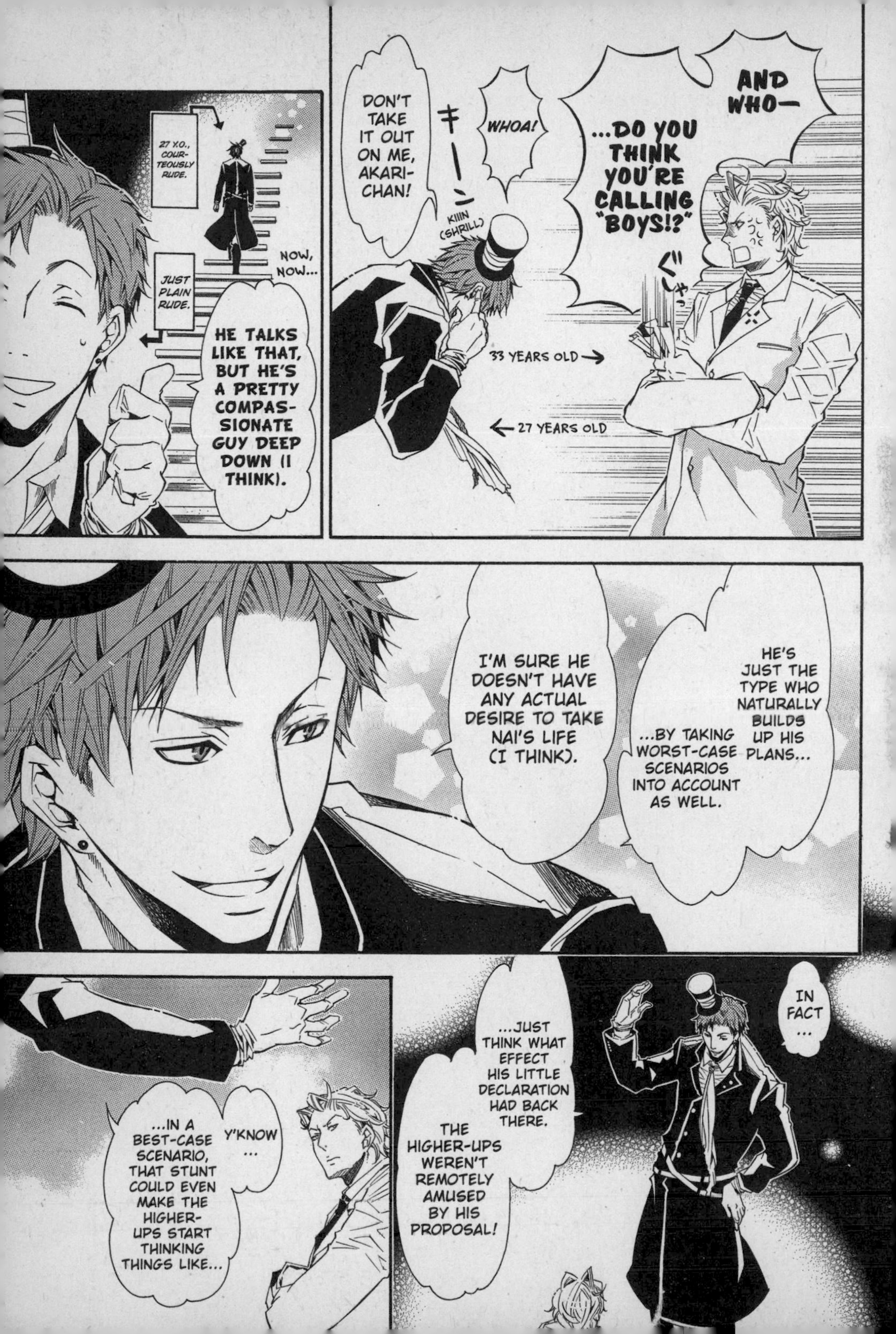
AND WHO—
...DO YOU THINK YOU'RE CALLING "BOYS!?"
ぐしゃ
33 YEARS OLD →
WHOA!
キーン
KIIN (SHRILL)
DON'T TAKE IT OUT ON ME, AKARI-CHAN!
← 27 YEARS OLD
NOW, NOW...
27 Y.O., COURTEOUSLY RUDE.
JUST PLAIN RUDE.
HE TALKS LIKE THAT, BUT HE'S A PRETTY COMPASSIONATE GUY DEEP DOWN (I THINK).
HE'S JUST THE TYPE WHO NATURALLY BUILDS UP HIS PLANS...
...BY TAKING WORST-CASE SCENARIOS INTO ACCOUNT AS WELL.
I'M SURE HE DOESN'T HAVE ANY ACTUAL DESIRE TO TAKE NAI'S LIFE (I THINK).
IN FACT...
...JUST THINK WHAT EFFECT HIS LITTLE DECLARATION HAD BACK THERE.
THE HIGHER-UPS WEREN'T REMOTELY AMUSED BY HIS PROPOSAL!
Y'KNOW...
...IN A BEST-CASE SCENARIO, THAT STUNT COULD EVEN MAKE THE HIGHER-UPS START THINKING THINGS LIKE...

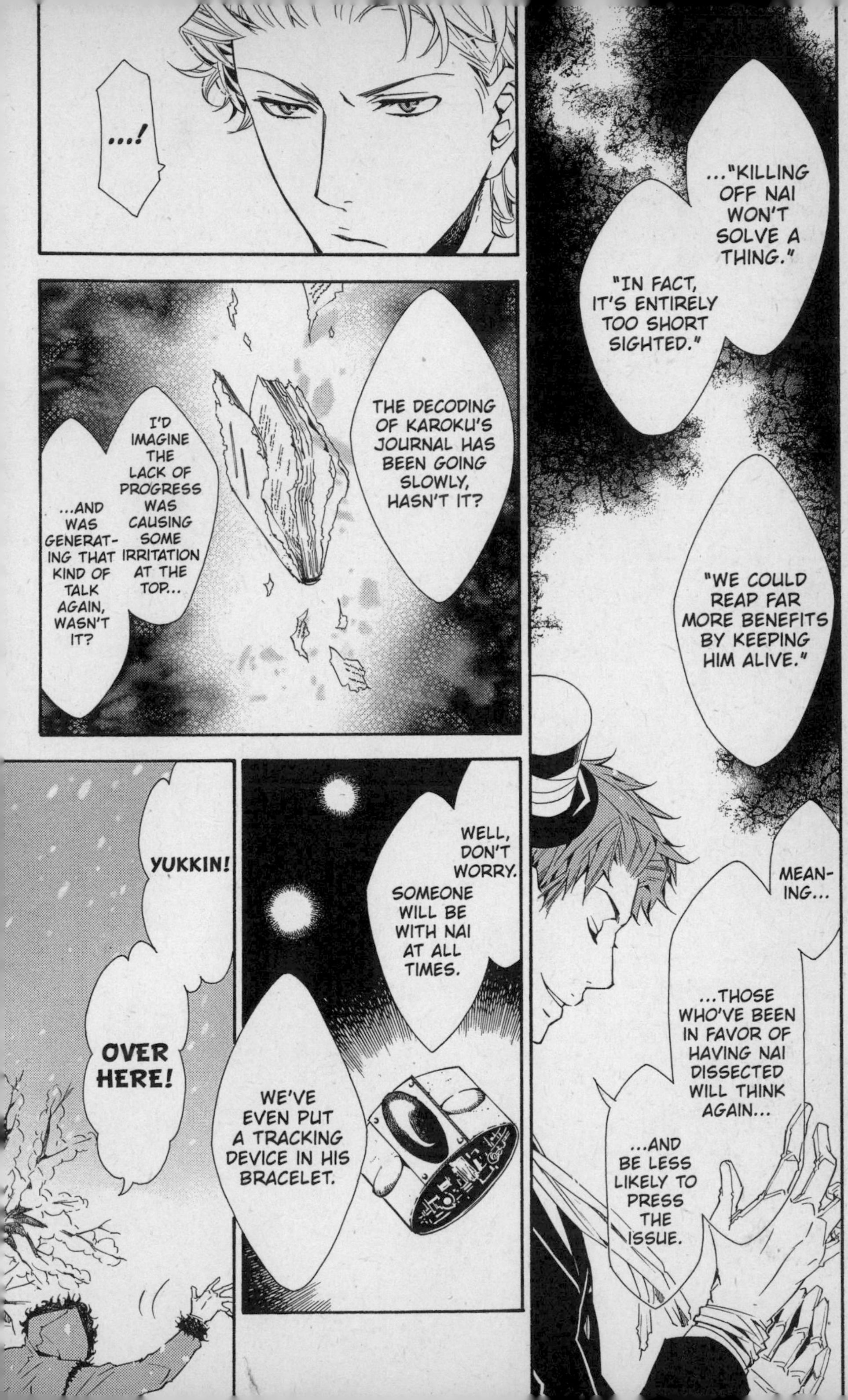
..."KILLING OFF NAI WON'T SOLVE A THING."
"IN FACT, IT'S ENTIRELY TOO SHORT SIGHTED."
"WE COULD REAP FAR MORE BENEFITS BY KEEPING HIM ALIVE."
MEAN-ING...
...THOSE WHO'VE BEEN IN FAVOR OF HAVING NAI DISSECTED WILL THINK AGAIN...
...AND BE LESS LIKELY TO PRESS THE ISSUE.
...!
THE DECODING OF KAROKU'S JOURNAL HAS BEEN GOING SLOWLY, HASN'T IT?
I'D IMAGINE THE LACK OF PROGRESS WAS CAUSING SOME IRRITATION AT THE TOP...
...AND WAS GENERAT-ING THAT KIND OF TALK AGAIN, WASN'T IT?
WELL, DON'T WORRY.
SOMEONE WILL BE WITH NAI AT ALL TIMES.
WE'VE EVEN PUT A TRACKING DEVICE IN HIS BRACELET.
YUKKIN!
OVER HERE!

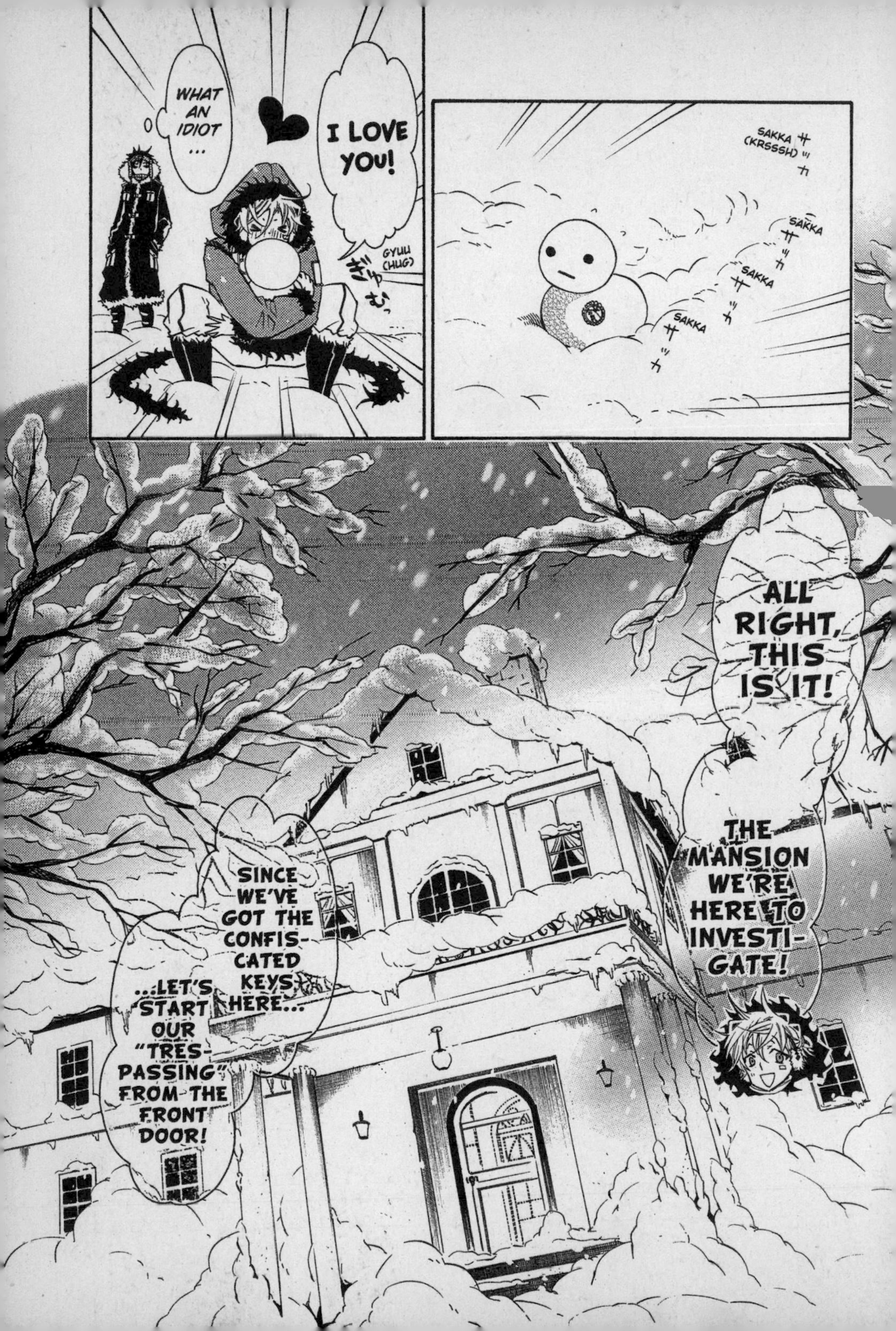
SAKKA (KRSSSH)
SAKKA
SAKKA
SAKKA
I LOVE YOU!
GYUU (HUG)
WHAT AN IDIOT...
ALL RIGHT, THIS IS IT!
THE MANSION WE'RE HERE TO INVESTIGATE!
SINCE WE'VE GOT THE CONFISCATED KEYS HERE...
...LET'S START OUR "TRESPASSING" FROM THE FRONT DOOR!

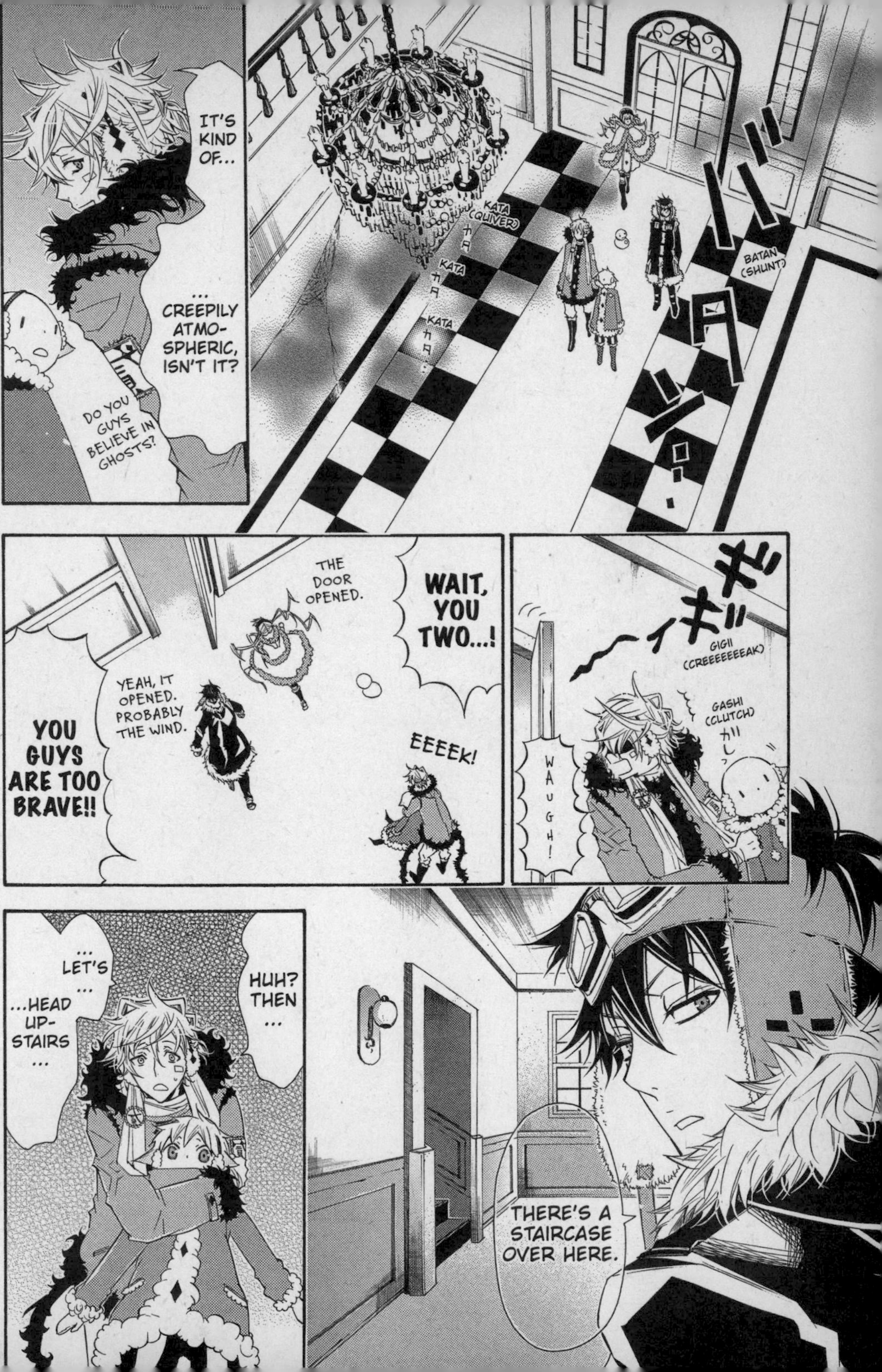
BATAN (SHUNT)
KATA (QUIVER)
KATA
KATA
IT'S KIND OF...
...CREEPILY ATMO-SPHERIC, ISN'T IT?
DO YOU GUYS BELIEVE IN GHOSTS?
GIGII (CREEEEEEEAK)
GASHI (CLUTCH)
WAUGH!
WAIT, YOU TWO...!
THE DOOR OPENED.
EEEEK!
YEAH, IT OPENED. PROBABLY THE WIND.
YOU GUYS ARE TOO BRAVE!!
THERE'S A STAIRCASE OVER HERE.
HUH? THEN...
...LET'S...
...HEAD UP-STAIRS...

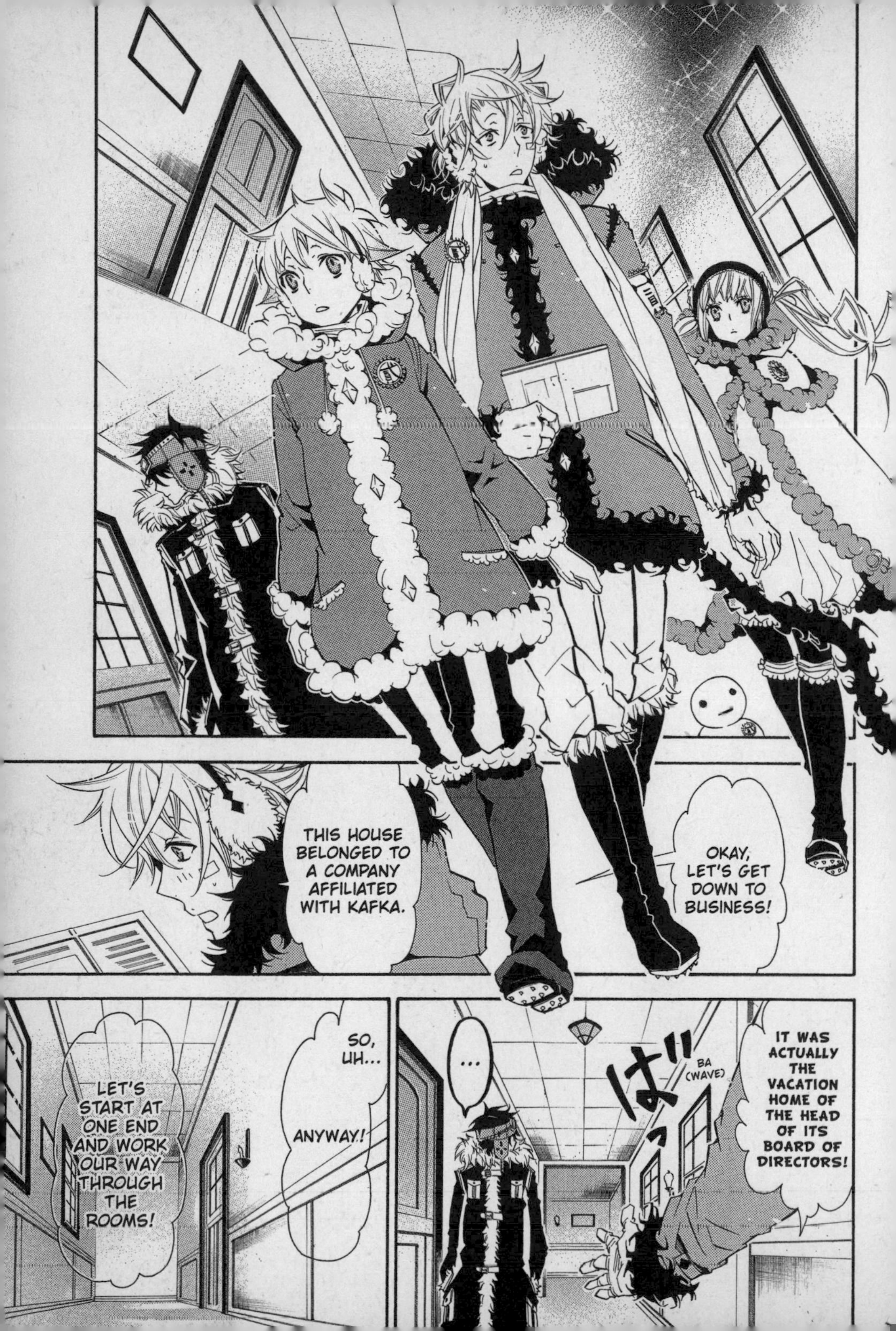
OKAY, LET'S GET DOWN TO BUSINESS!
THIS HOUSE BELONGED TO A COMPANY AFFILIATED WITH KAFKA.
IT WAS ACTUALLY THE VACATION HOME OF THE HEAD OF ITS BOARD OF DIRECTORS!
BA (WAVE)
...
SO, UH...
ANYWAY!
LET'S START AT ONE END AND WORK OUR WAY THROUGH THE ROOMS!

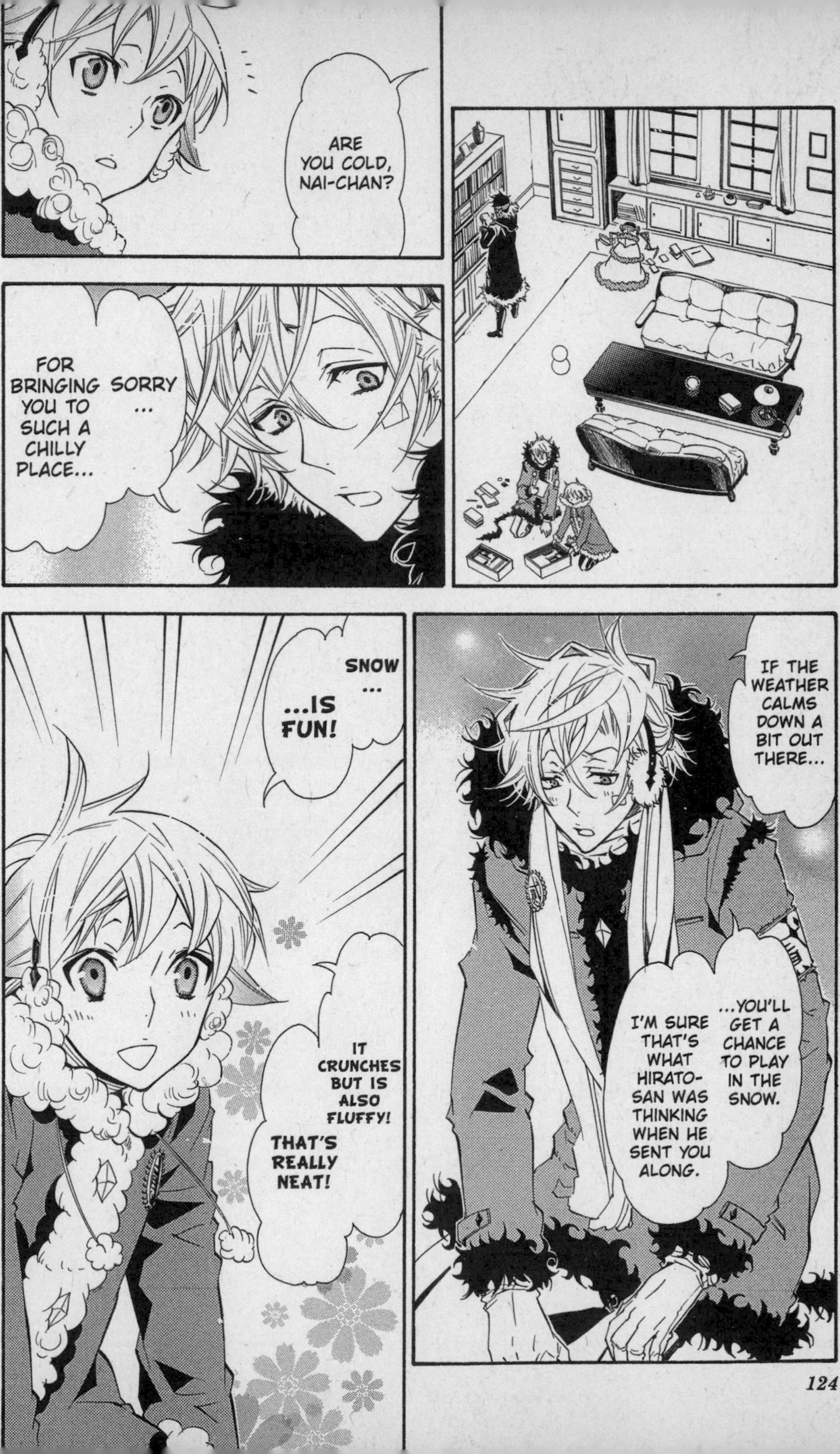
ARE YOU COLD, NAI-CHAN?
SORRY...
FOR BRINGING YOU TO SUCH A CHILLY PLACE...
IF THE WEATHER CALMS DOWN A BIT OUT THERE...
...YOU'LL GET A CHANCE TO PLAY IN THE SNOW.
I'M SURE THAT'S WHAT HIRATO-SAN WAS THINKING WHEN HE SENT YOU ALONG.
SNOW...
...IS FUN!
IT CRUNCHES BUT IS ALSO FLUFFY!
THAT'S REALLY NEAT!

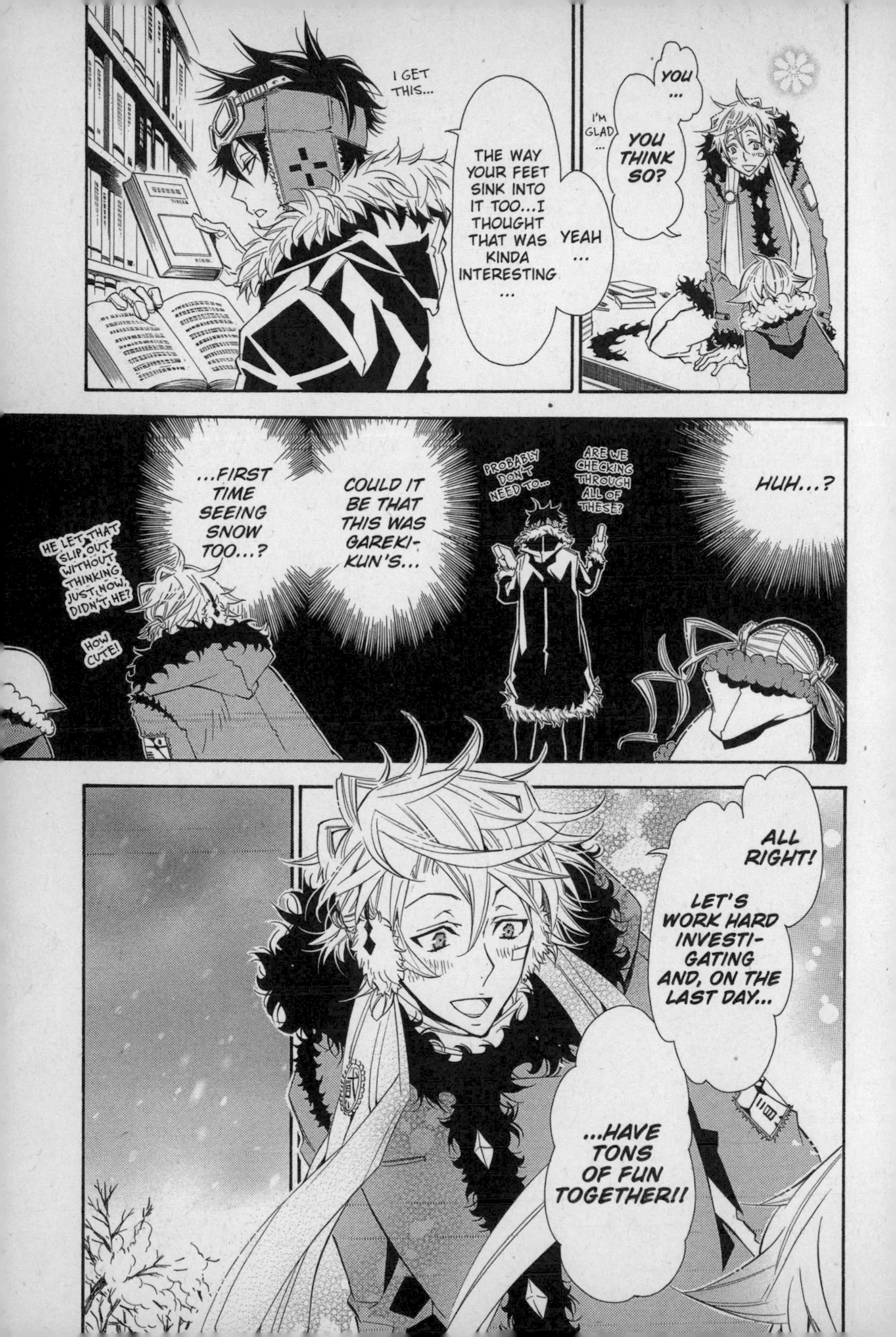
YOU... YOU THINK SO?
I'M GLAD...
I GET THIS...
THE WAY YOUR FEET SINK INTO IT TOO...I THOUGHT THAT WAS KINDA INTERESTING...
YEAH...
HUH...?
ARE WE CHECKING THROUGH ALL OF THESE?
PROBABLY DON'T NEED TO...
COULD IT BE THAT THIS WAS GAREKI-KUN'S...
...FIRST TIME SEEING SNOW TOO...?
HE LET THAT SLIP OUT WITHOUT THINKING JUST NOW, DIDN'T HE?
HOW CUTE!
ALL RIGHT!
LET'S WORK HARD INVESTI-GATING AND, ON THE LAST DAY...
...HAVE TONS OF FUN TOGETHER!!

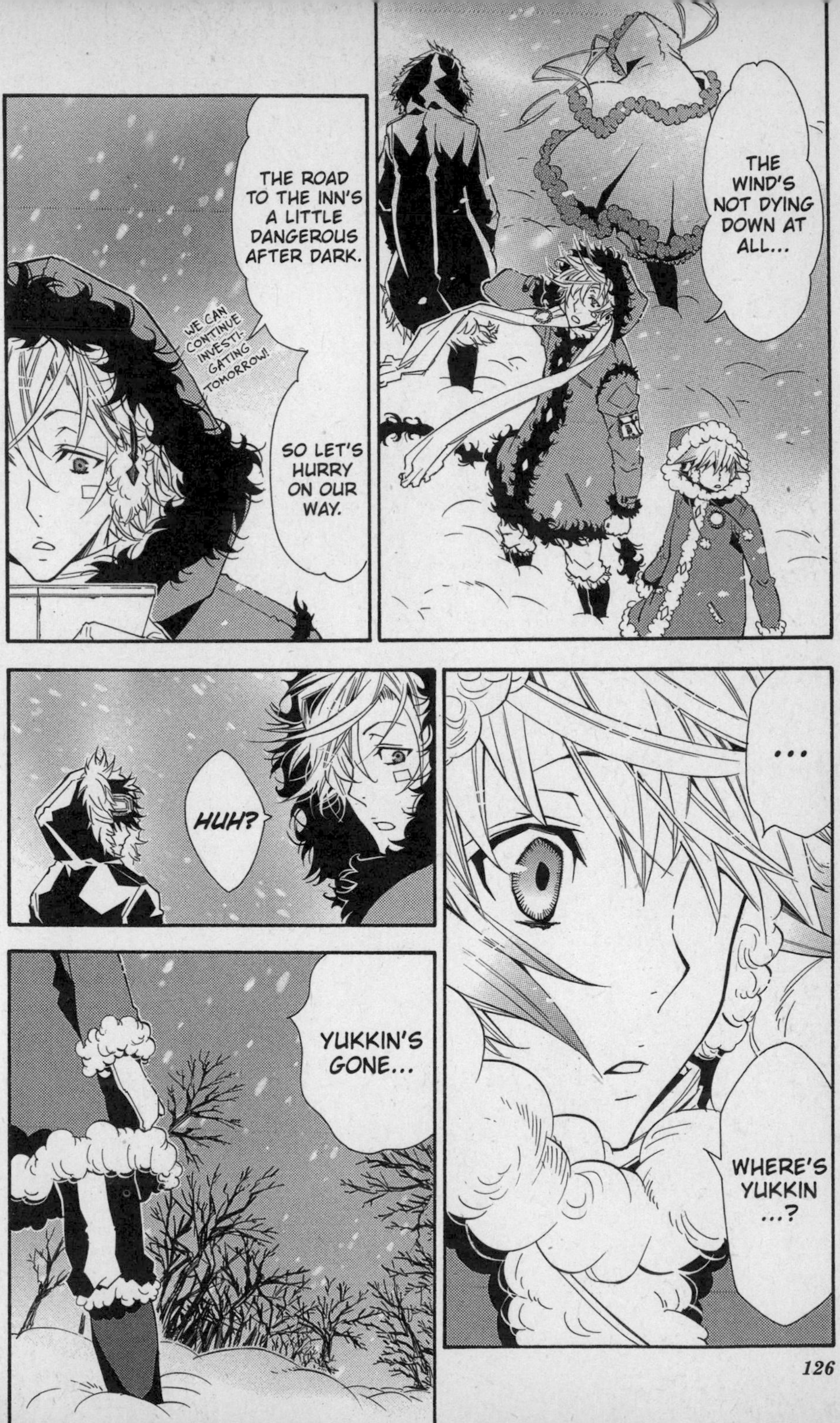
THE WIND'S NOT DYING DOWN AT ALL...
THE ROAD TO THE INN'S A LITTLE DANGEROUS AFTER DARK.
WE CAN CONTINUE INVESTIGATING TOMORROW!
SO LET'S HURRY ON OUR WAY.
...
WHERE'S YUKKIN ...?
HUH?
YUKKIN'S GONE...

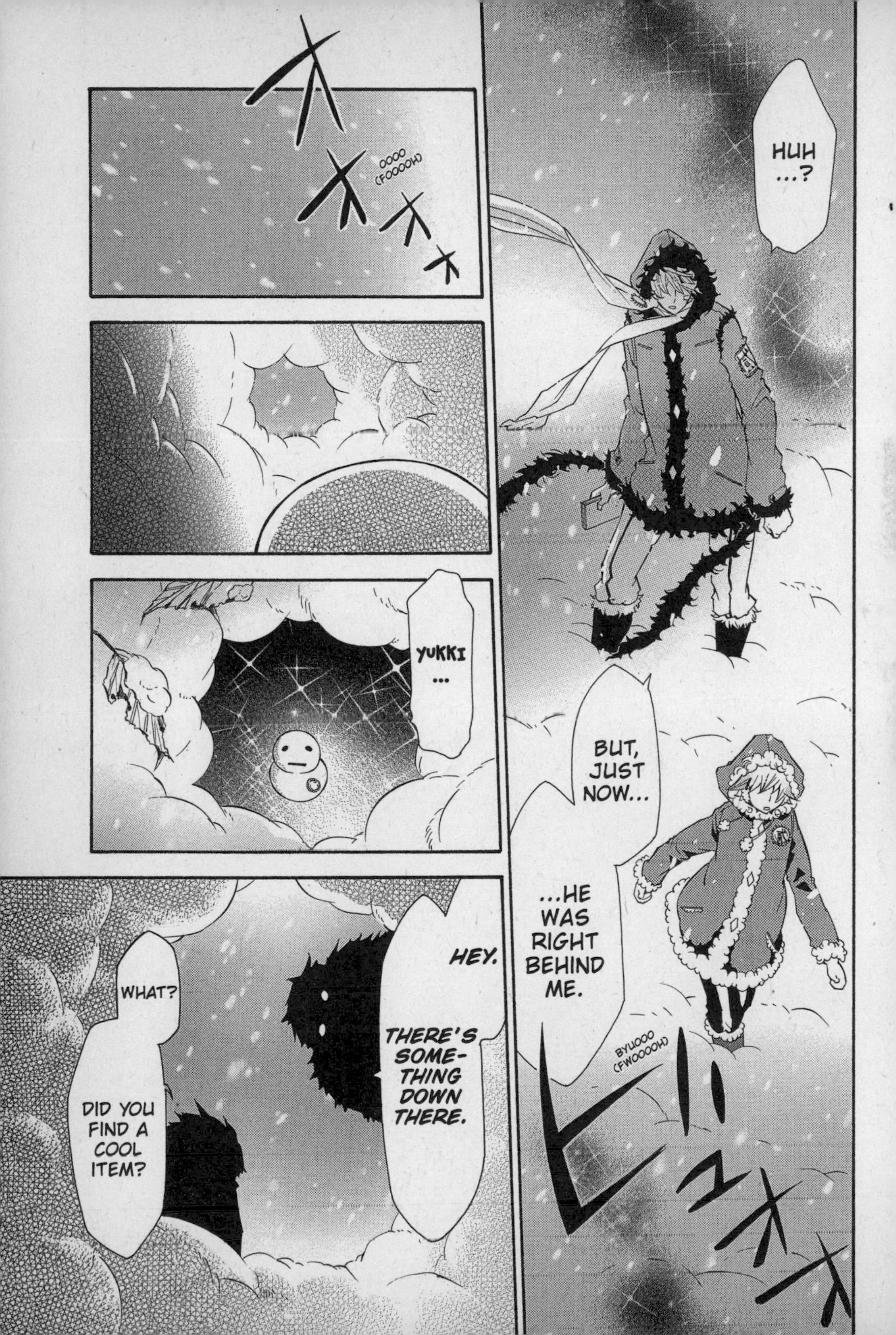
HUH...?
BUT, JUST NOW...
...HE WAS RIGHT BEHIND ME.
BYUOOO (FWOOOOH)
OOOO (FOOOOH)
YUKKI...
HEY.
THERE'S SOME-THING DOWN THERE.
WHAT?
DID YOU FIND A COOL ITEM?

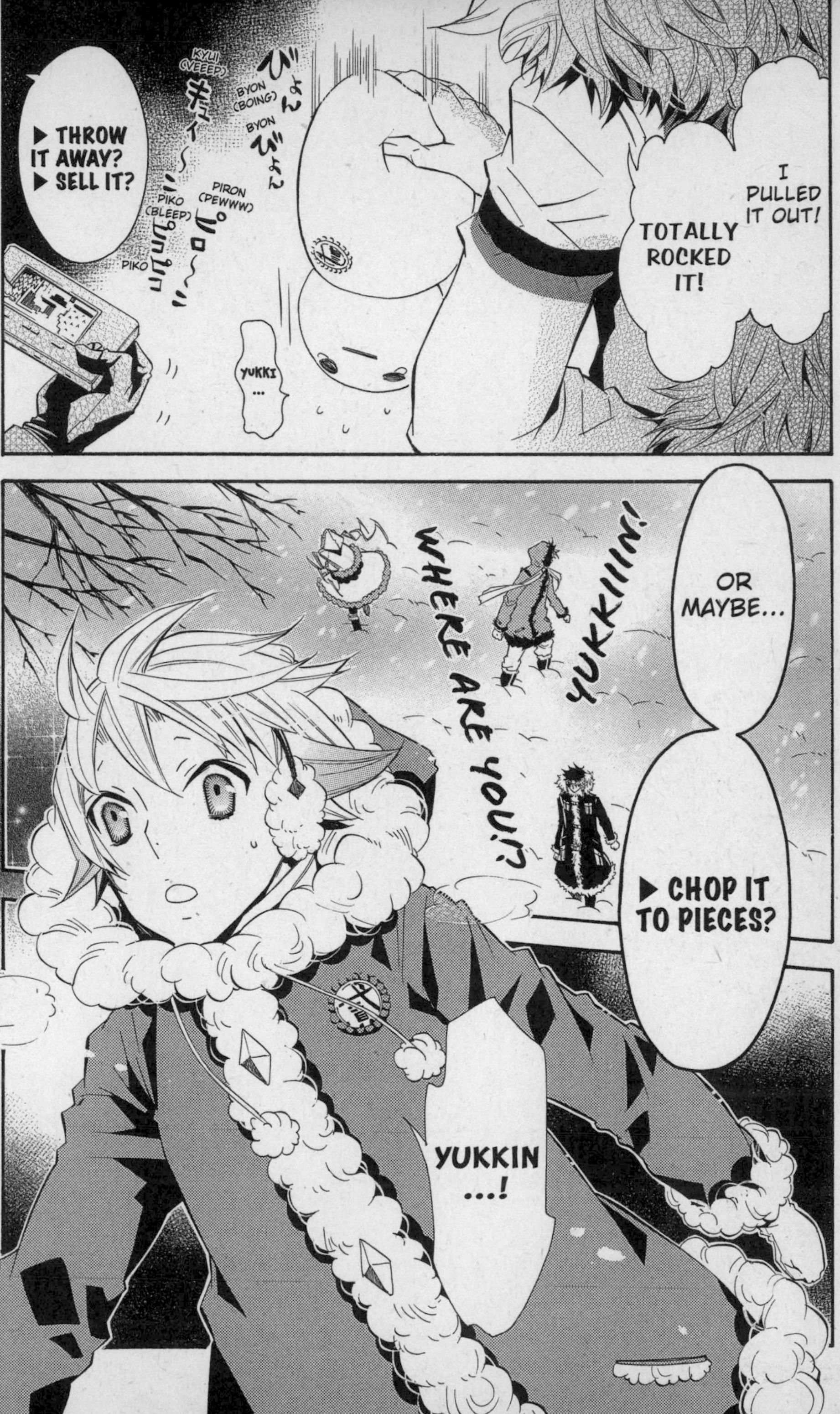

I PULLED IT OUT!
TOTALLY ROCKED IT!
BYON (BOING) BYON
KYUI (VEEEP)
PIRON (PEWWW)
PIKO (BLEEP) PIKO
▶ THROW IT AWAY? ▶ SELL IT?
YUKKI ...
OR MAYBE...
▶ CHOP IT TO PIECES?
YUKKIIIN!
WHERE ARE YOU!?
YUKKIN ...!

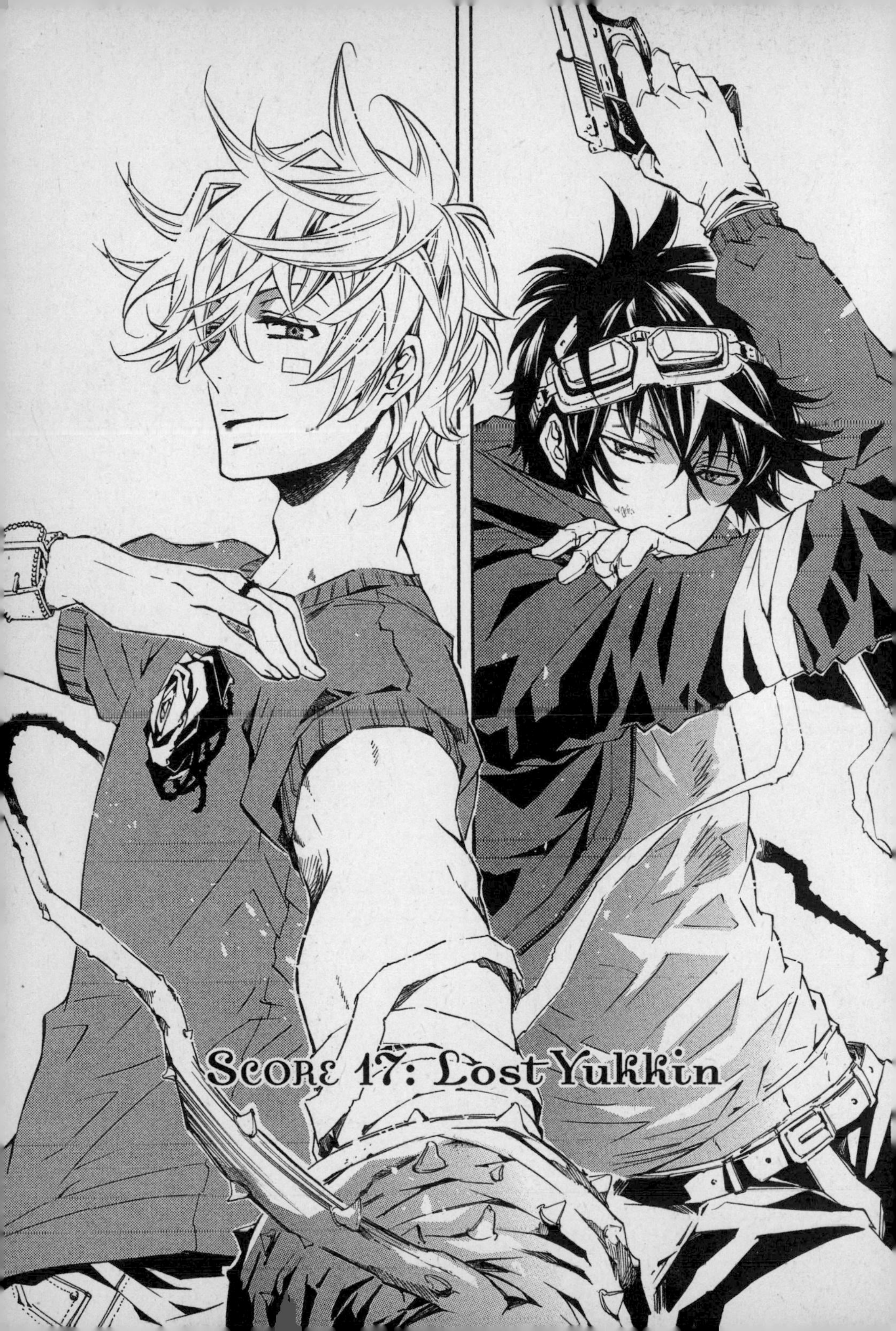
Score 17: Lost Yukkin

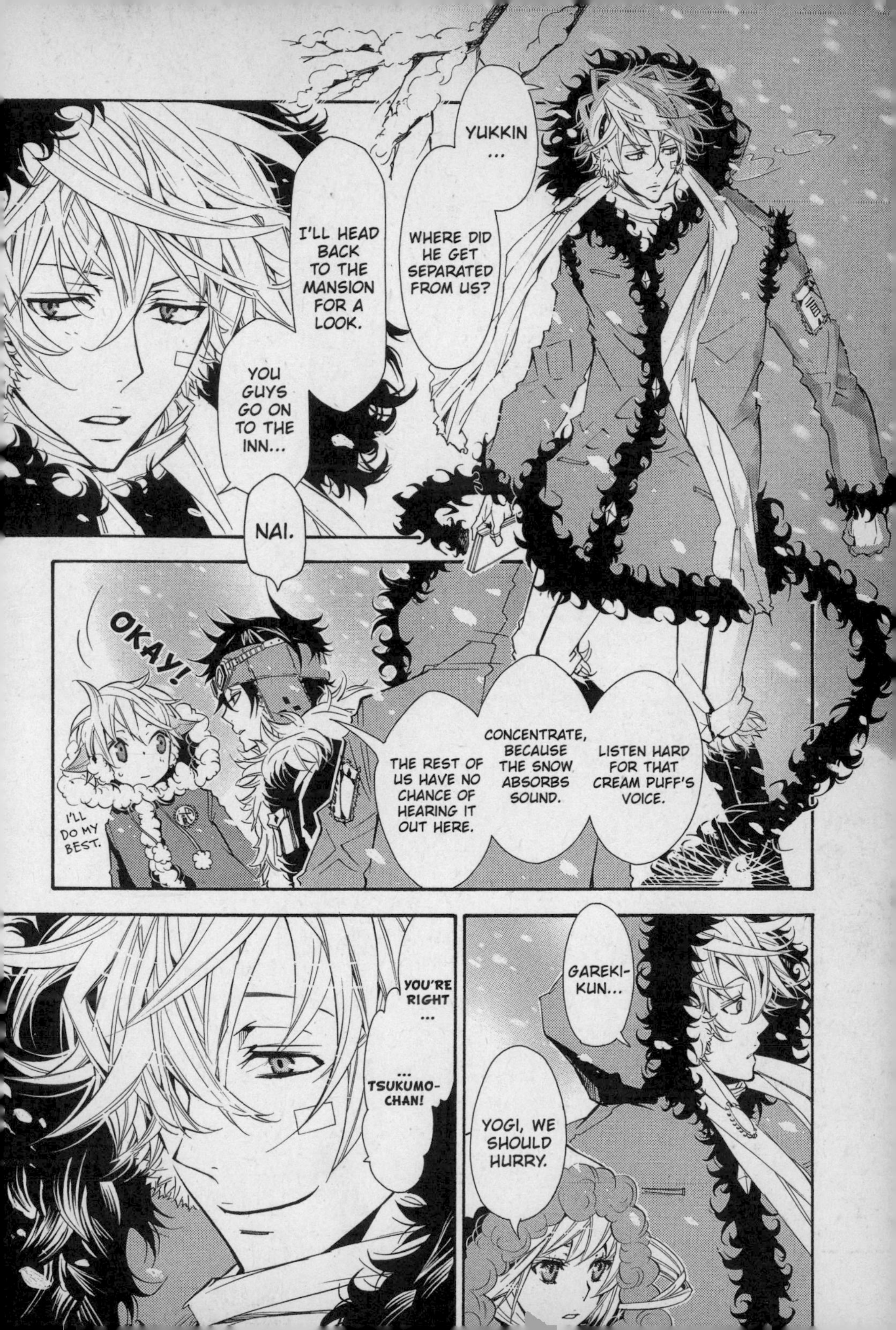
YUKKIN ...
WHERE DID HE GET SEPARATED FROM US?
I'LL HEAD BACK TO THE MANSION FOR A LOOK.
YOU GUYS GO ON TO THE INN...
NAI.
LISTEN HARD FOR THAT CREAM PUFF'S VOICE.
CONCENTRATE, BECAUSE THE SNOW ABSORBS SOUND.
THE REST OF US HAVE NO CHANCE OF HEARING IT OUT HERE.
OKAY!
I'LL DO MY BEST.
GAREKI-KUN...
YOGI, WE SHOULD HURRY.
YOU'RE RIGHT ...
... TSUKUMO-CHAN!

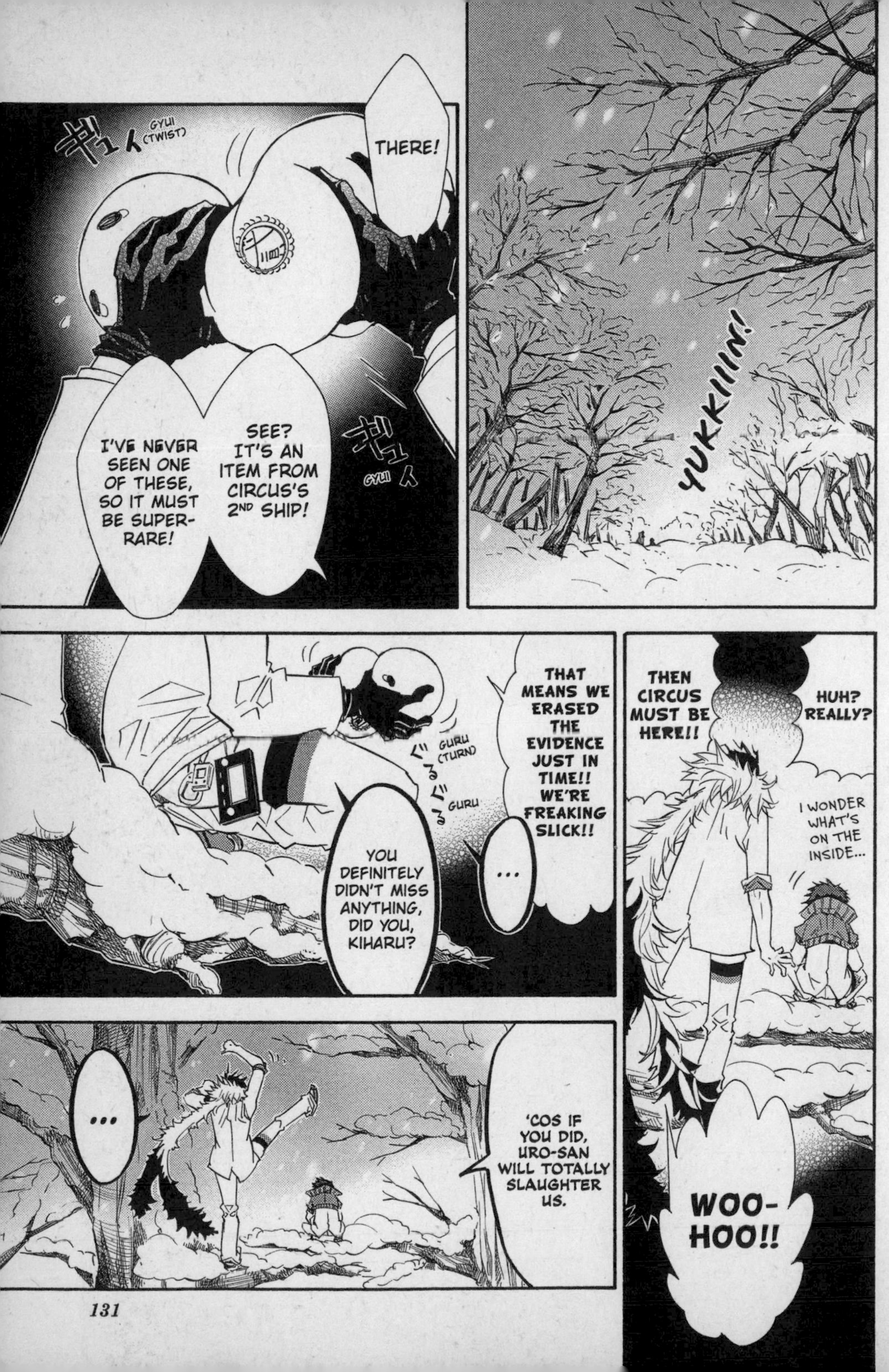
YUKKIIIN!
GYUI (TWIST)
THERE!
SEE? IT'S AN ITEM FROM CIRCUS'S 2ND SHIP!
GYUI
I'VE NEVER SEEN ONE OF THESE, SO IT MUST BE SUPER-RARE!
HUH? REALLY?
THEN CIRCUS MUST BE HERE!!
I WONDER WHAT'S ON THE INSIDE...
WOO-HOO!!
THAT MEANS WE ERASED THE EVIDENCE JUST IN TIME!! WE'RE FREAKING SLICK!!
...
GURU (TURN)
GURU
YOU DEFINITELY DIDN'T MISS ANYTHING, DID YOU, KIHARU?
'COS IF YOU DID, URO-SAN WILL TOTALLY SLAUGHTER US.
...

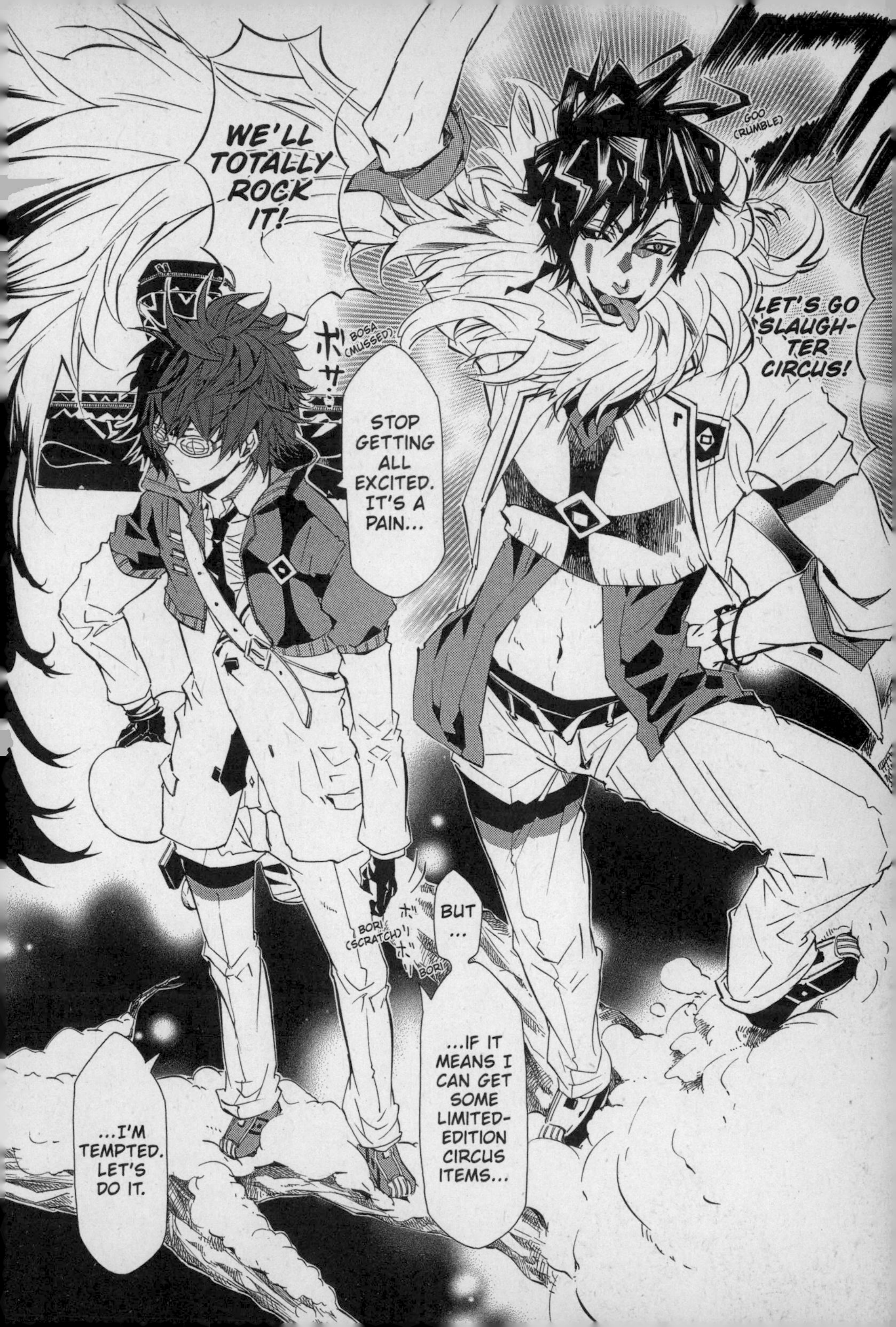
GOO (RUMBLE)
LET'S GO SLAUGHTER CIRCUS!
WE'LL TOTALLY ROCK IT!
ボサ
BOSA (MUSSED)
STOP GETTING ALL EXCITED. IT'S A PAIN...
BUT ...
ボリボリ
BORI (SCRATCH) BORI
...IF IT MEANS I CAN GET SOME LIMITED-EDITION CIRCUS ITEMS...
...I'M TEMPTED. LET'S DO IT.

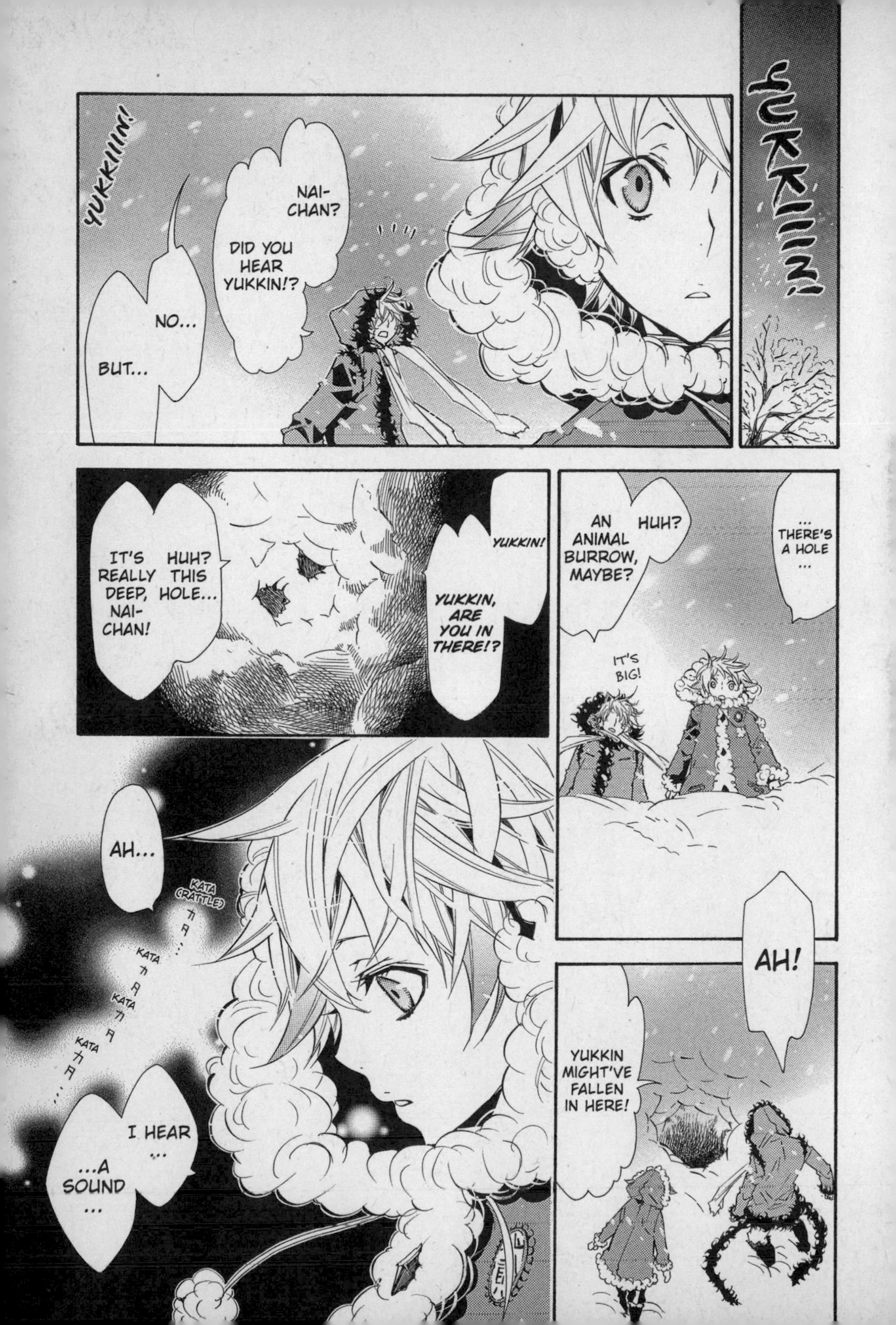
YUKKIIIIN!
NAI-CHAN? DID YOU HEAR YUKKIN!?
NO... BUT...
YUKKIIIN!
...THERE'S A HOLE...
HUH? AN ANIMAL BURROW, MAYBE?
IT'S BIG!
YUKKIN!
YUKKIN, ARE YOU IN THERE!?
HUH? THIS HOLE... IT'S REALLY DEEP, NAI-CHAN!
AH!
YUKKIN MIGHT'VE FALLEN IN HERE!
AH...
KATA (RATTLE)
KATA KATA KATA...
I HEAR... ...A SOUND...

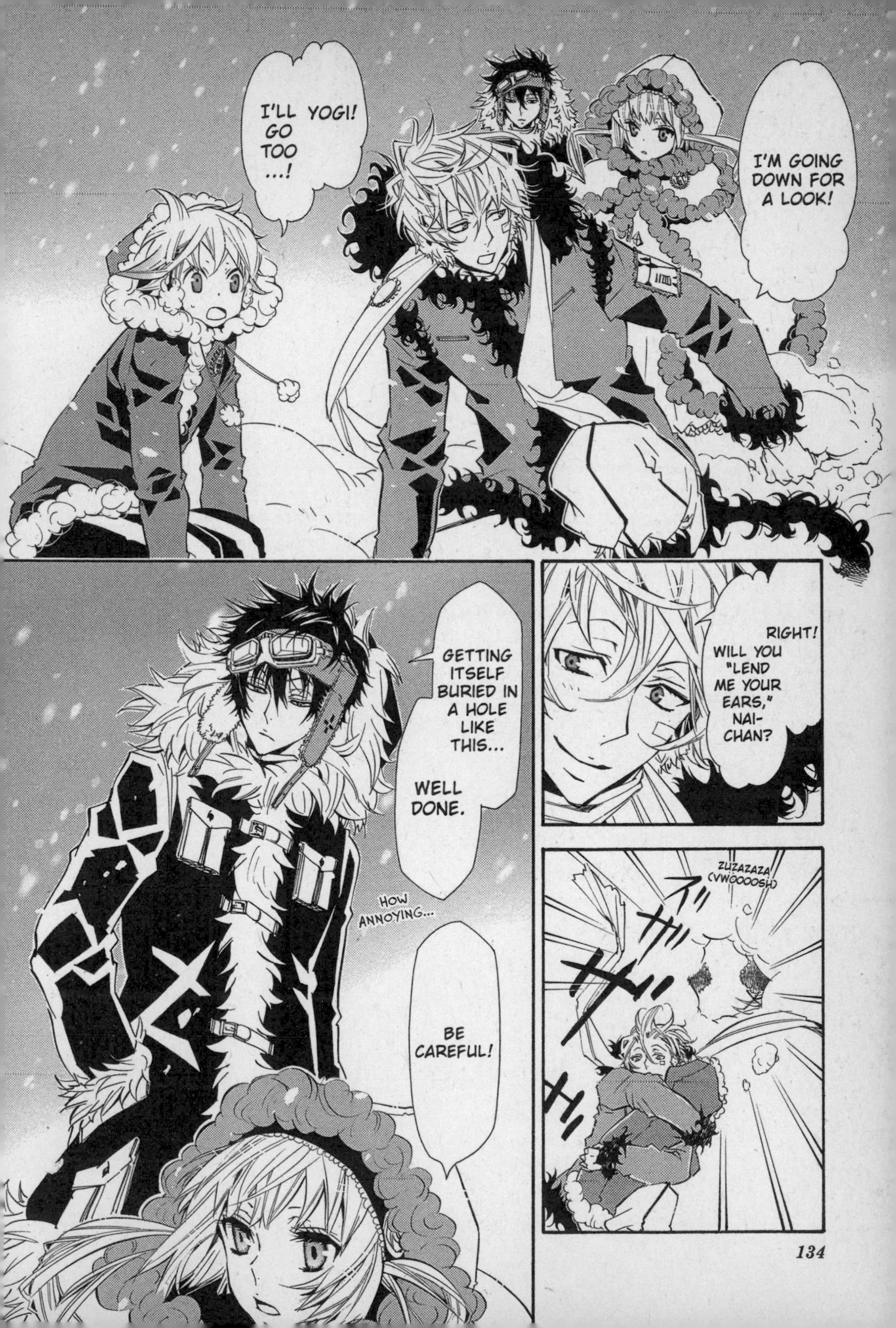
I'M GOING DOWN FOR A LOOK!
YOGI! I'LL GO TOO ...!
RIGHT! WILL YOU "LEND ME YOUR EARS," NAI-CHAN?
ZUZAZAZA (VWOOOOSH)
GETTING ITSELF BURIED IN A HOLE LIKE THIS...
WELL DONE.
HOW ANNOYING...
BE CAREFUL!

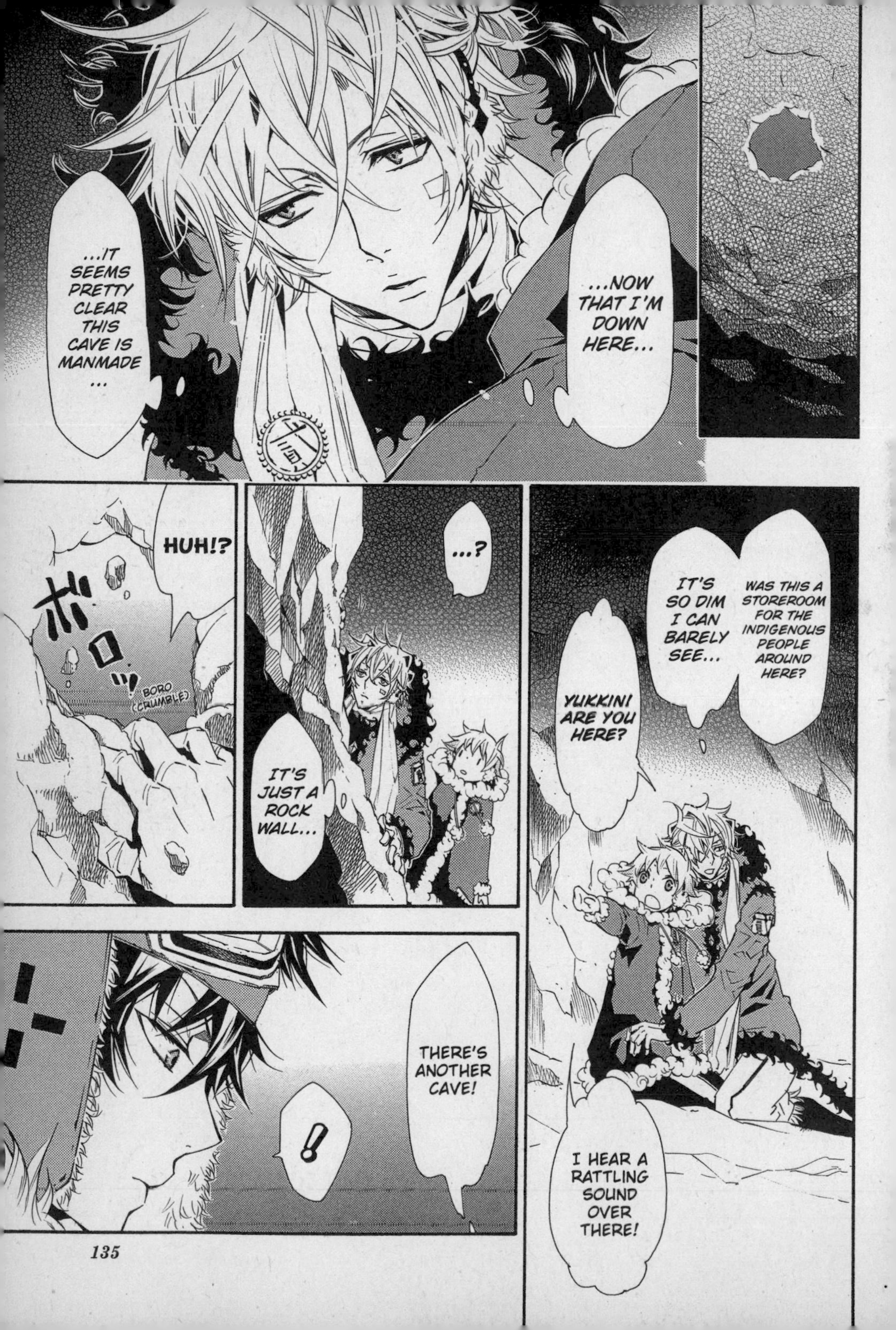
...NOW THAT I'M DOWN HERE...
...IT SEEMS PRETTY CLEAR THIS CAVE IS MANMADE...
WAS THIS A STOREROOM FOR THE INDIGENOUS PEOPLE AROUND HERE?
IT'S SO DIM I CAN BARELY SEE...
YUKKIN! ARE YOU HERE?
I HEAR A RATTLING SOUND OVER THERE!
...?
IT'S JUST A ROCK WALL...
HUH!?
ボロッ
BORO (CRUMBLE)
THERE'S ANOTHER CAVE!
!

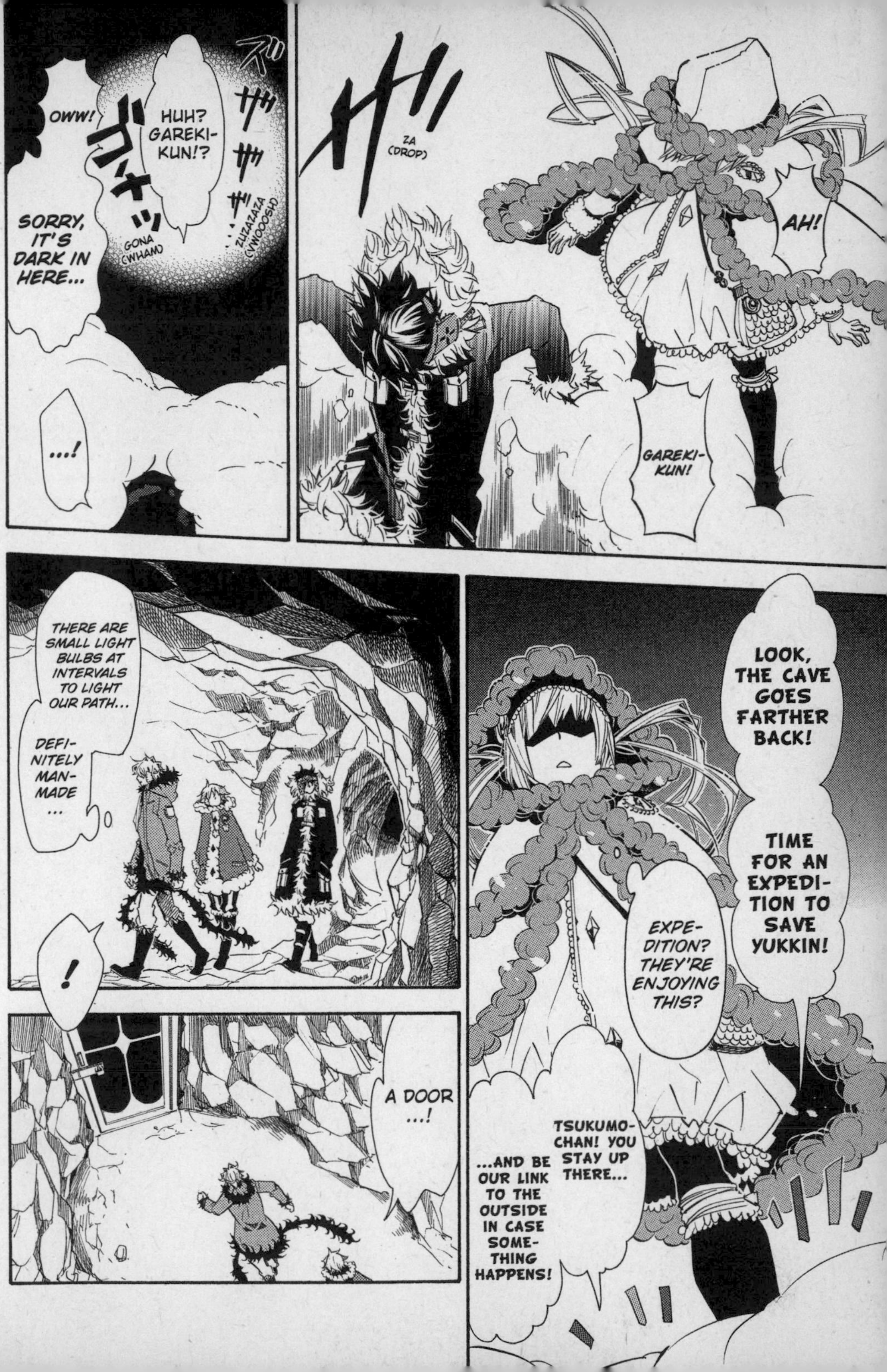
AH!
GAREKI-KUN!
ZA (DROP)
ZUZAZAZA (VWOOOSH)
HUH? GAREKI-KUN!?
GONA (WHAM)
OWW!
SORRY, IT'S DARK IN HERE...
...!
LOOK, THE CAVE GOES FARTHER BACK!
TIME FOR AN EXPEDITION TO SAVE YUKKIN!
EXPEDITION? THEY'RE ENJOYING THIS?
TSUKUMO-CHAN! YOU STAY UP THERE...
...AND BE OUR LINK TO THE OUTSIDE IN CASE SOMETHING HAPPENS!
THERE ARE SMALL LIGHT BULBS AT INTERVALS TO LIGHT OUR PATH...
DEFINITELY MAN-MADE...
!
A DOOR...!

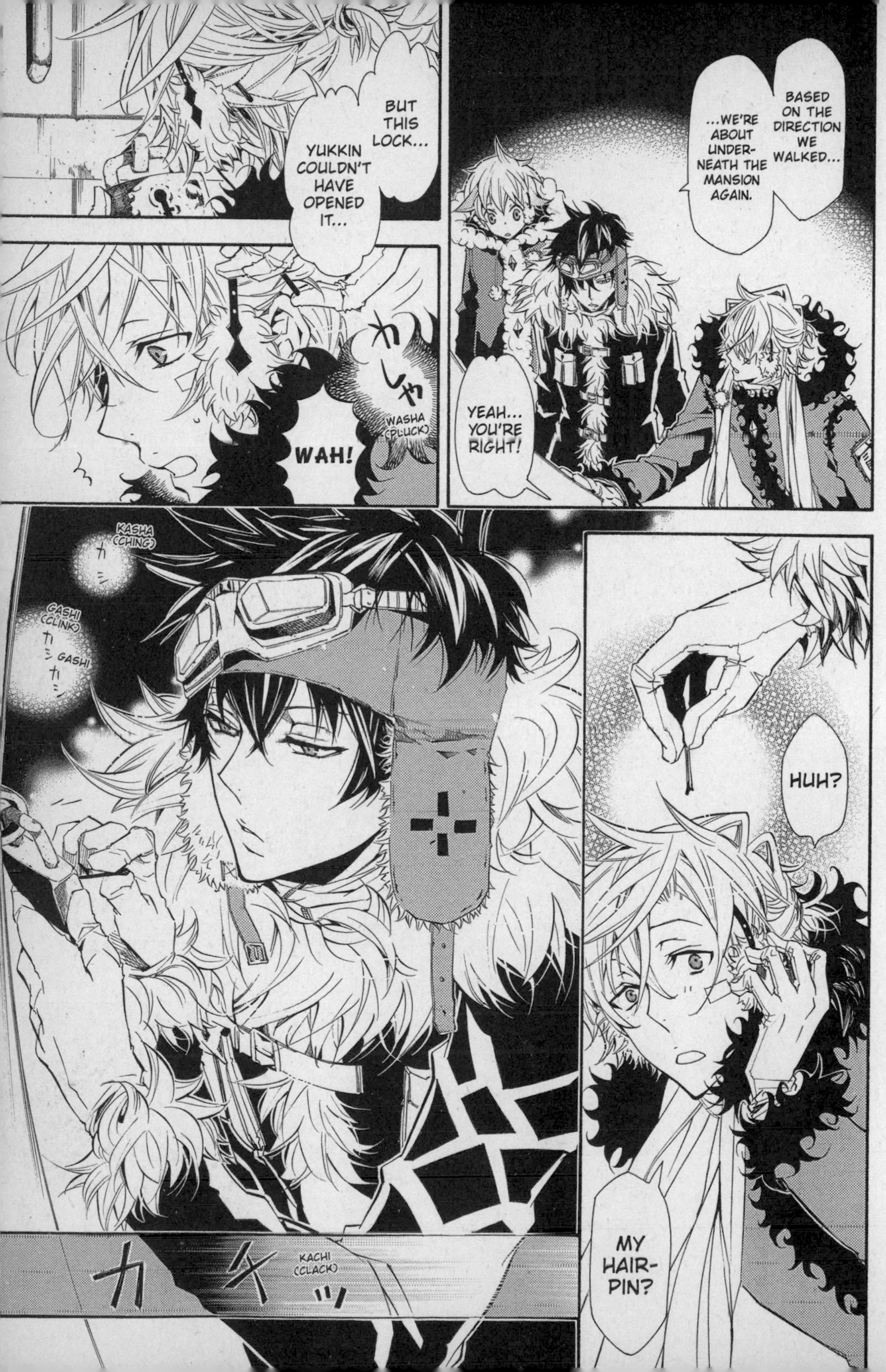
BASED ON THE DIRECTION WE WALKED...
...WE'RE ABOUT UNDER-NEATH THE MANSION AGAIN.
YEAH... YOU'RE RIGHT!
BUT THIS LOCK...
YUKKIN COULDN'T HAVE OPENED IT...
カしゃ
WASHA (PLUCK)
WAH!
HUH?
MY HAIR-PIN?
KASHA (CHING)
カシ
GASHI (CLINK)
カシ GASHI カシ
KACHI (CLACK)
カチッ

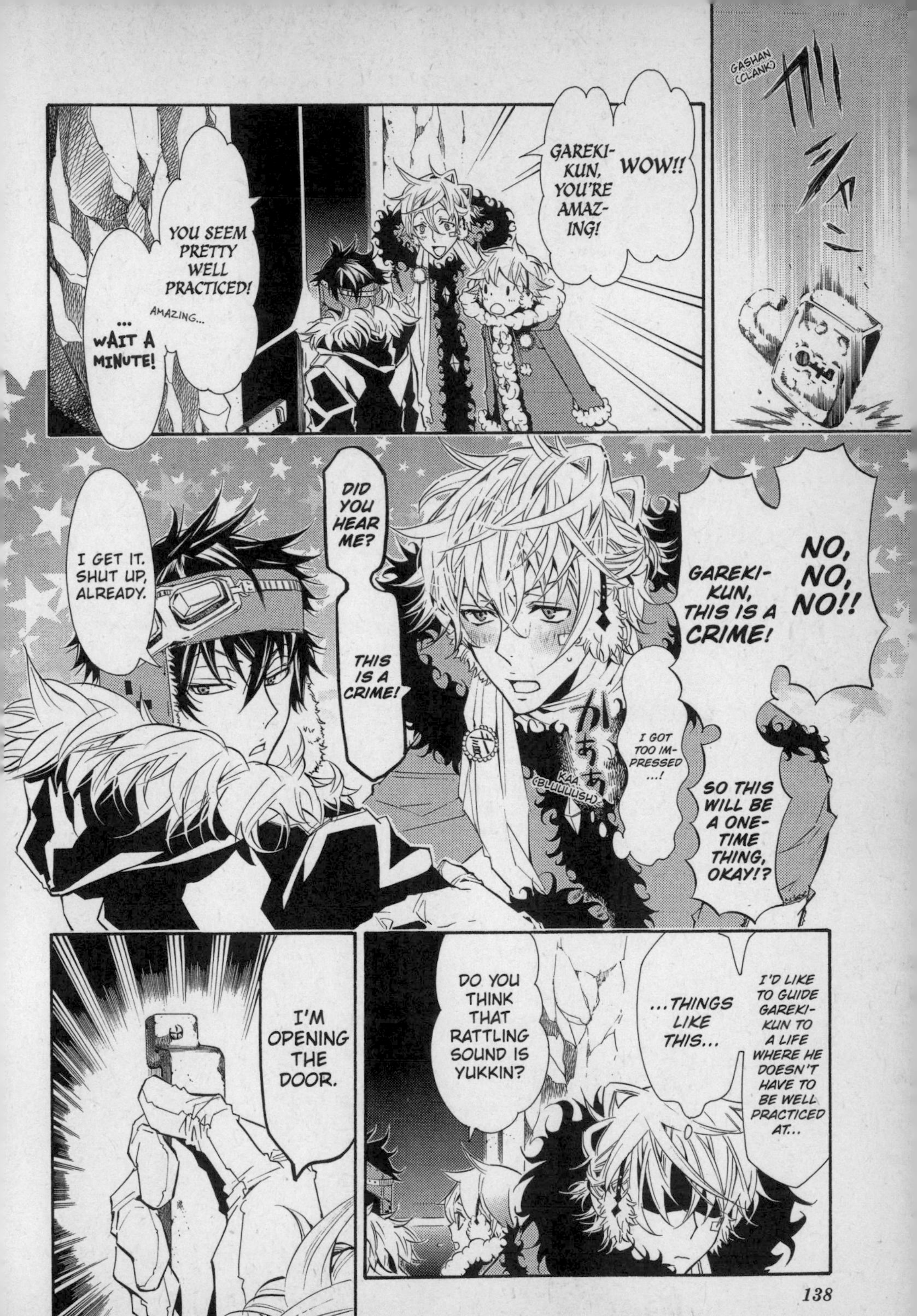
GASHAN (CLANK)
WOW!!
GAREKI-KUN, YOU'RE AMAZING!
YOU SEEM PRETTY WELL PRACTICED!
AMAZING...
... WAIT A MINUTE!
NO, NO, NO!!
GAREKI-KUN, THIS IS A CRIME!
SO THIS WILL BE A ONE-TIME THING, OKAY!?
I GOT TOO IMPRESSED ...!
KAA (BLUUUUSH)
DID YOU HEAR ME?
THIS IS A CRIME!
I GET IT. SHUT UP, ALREADY.
I'D LIKE TO GUIDE GAREKI-KUN TO A LIFE WHERE HE DOESN'T HAVE TO BE WELL PRACTICED AT...
...THINGS LIKE THIS...
DO YOU THINK THAT RATTLING SOUND IS YUKKIN?
I'M OPENING THE DOOR.

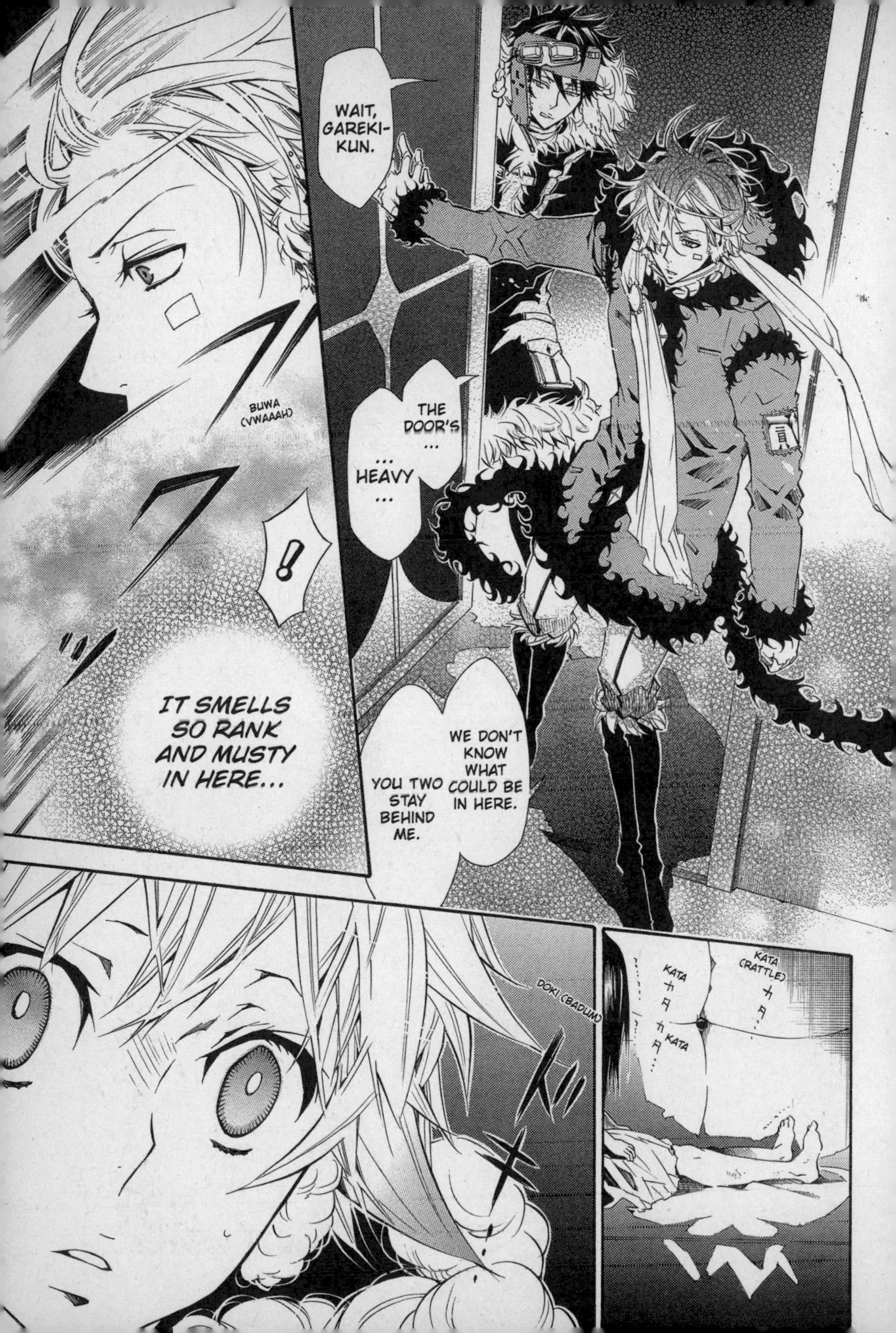
WAIT, GAREKI-KUN.
THE DOOR'S ...
... HEAVY ...
WE DON'T KNOW WHAT COULD BE IN HERE.
YOU TWO STAY BEHIND ME.
BUWA (VWAAAH)
!
IT SMELLS SO RANK AND MUSTY IN HERE...
KATA (RATTLE)
KATA
KATA
DOKI (BADUM)

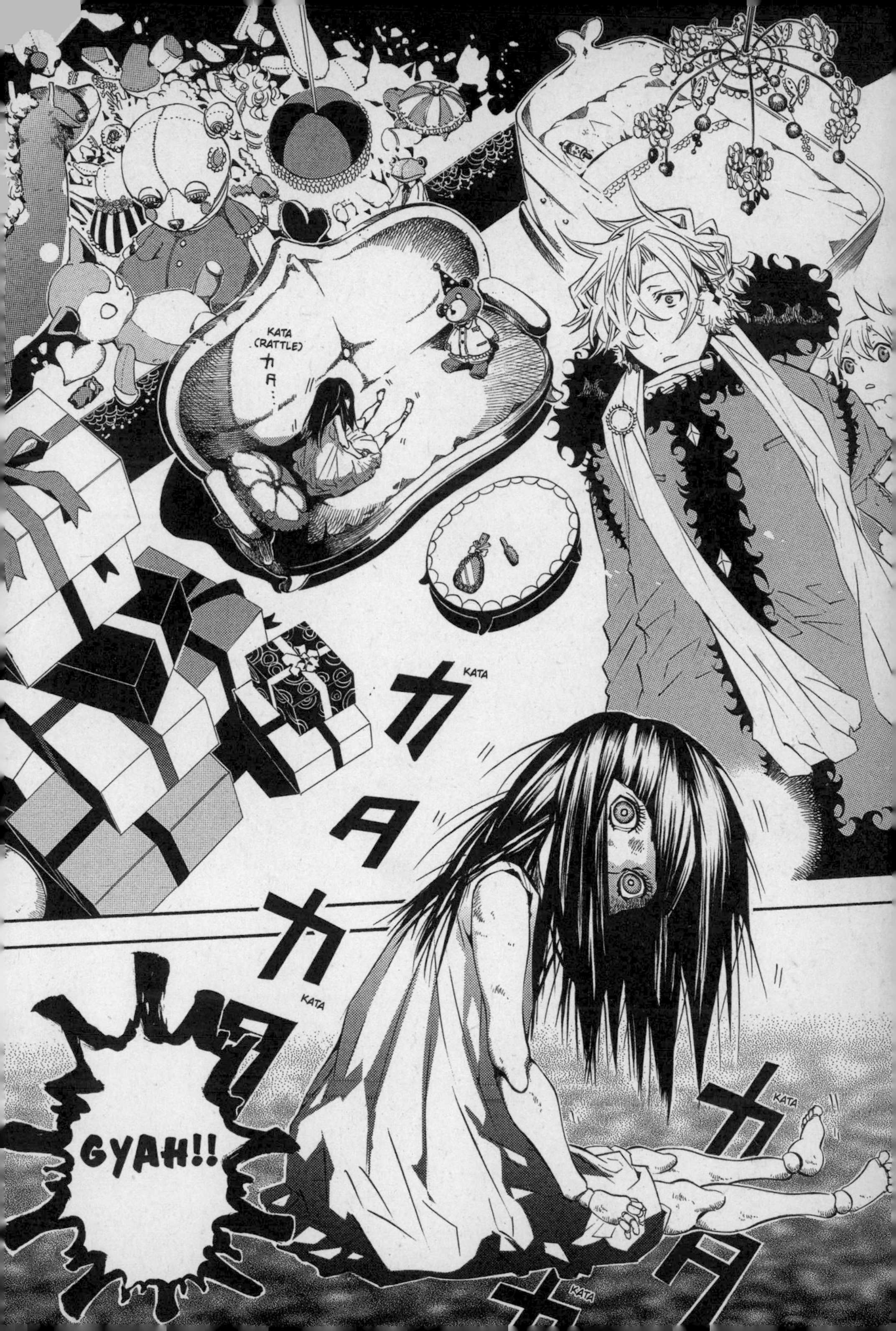
KATA (RATTLE)
カタ…
KATA
カタ
KATA
カタ
KATA
カタ
KATA
GYAH!!

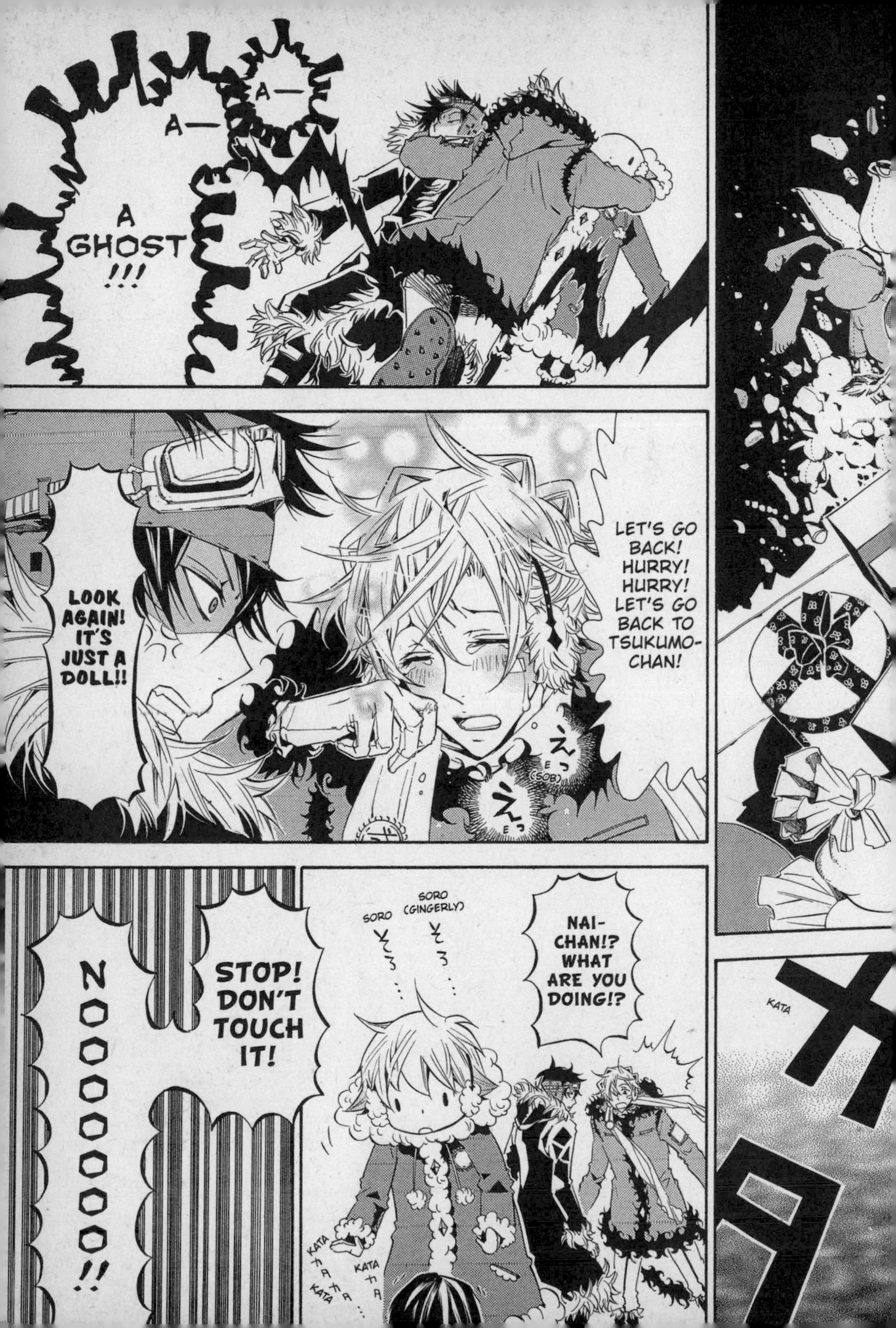
A—
A—
A GHOST!!!
LET'S GO BACK! HURRY! HURRY! LET'S GO BACK TO TSUKUMO-CHAN!
(SOB)
LOOK AGAIN! IT'S JUST A DOLL!!
KATA
NAI-CHAN!? WHAT ARE YOU DOING!?
SORO SORO (GINGERLY)
STOP! DON'T TOUCH IT!
KATA KATA KATA
NOOOOOOOO!!

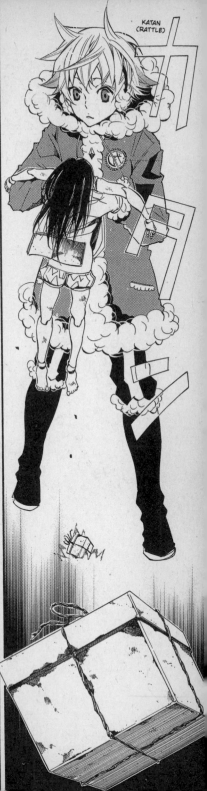

KATAN
(RATTLE)

KATA
KATA
KATA
KATA
KATA

...A BOX?

SOME-
THING'S
...

...MOVING
INSIDE
THE BOX
...?

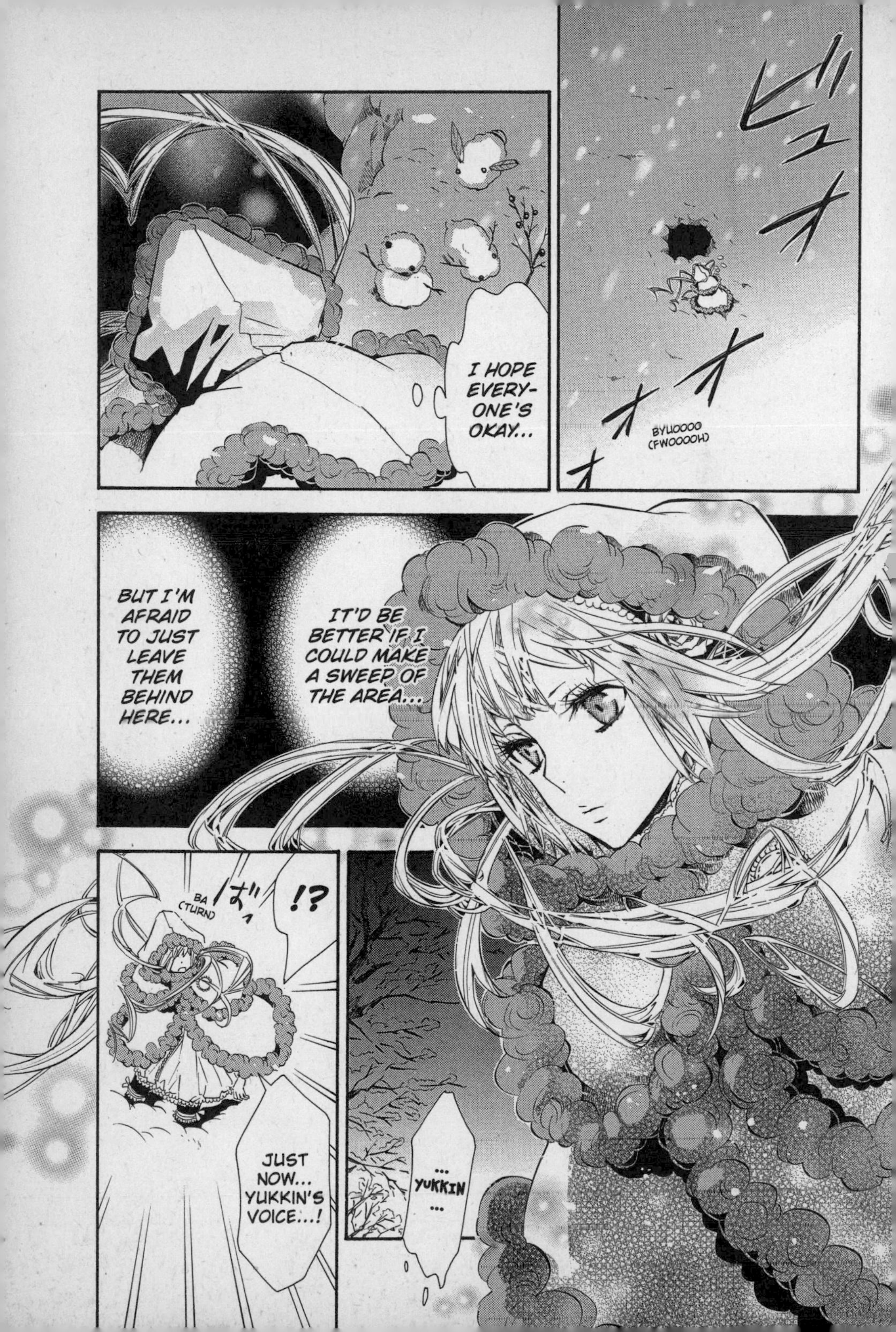
BYUOOOO (FWOOOOH)
I HOPE EVERY-ONE'S OKAY...
IT'D BE BETTER IF I COULD MAKE A SWEEP OF THE AREA...
BUT I'M AFRAID TO JUST LEAVE THEM BEHIND HERE...
...YUKKIN...
!?
BA (TURN)
JUST NOW... YUKKIN'S VOICE...!

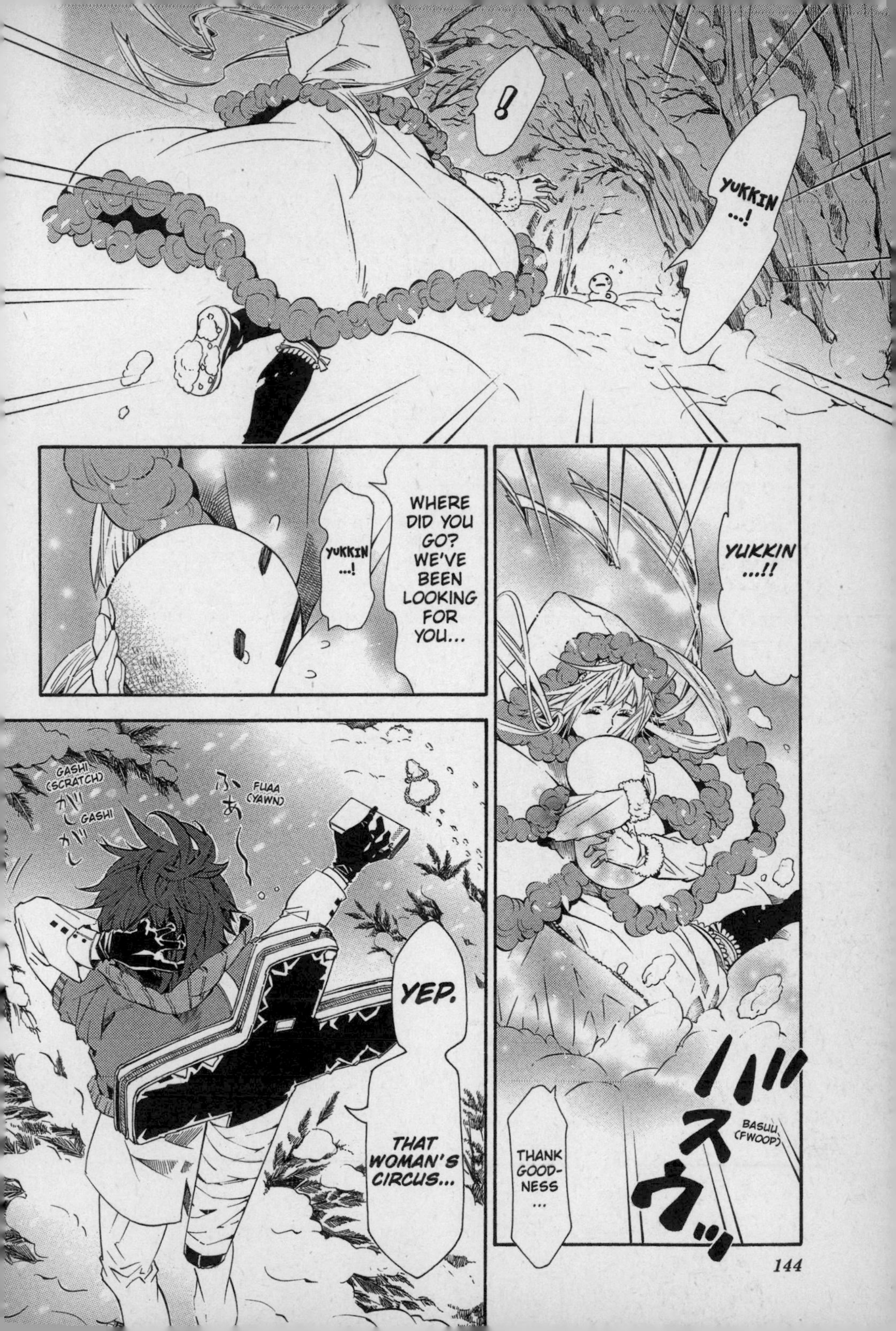

YUKKIN ...!
!
YUKKIN ...!!
バスッ
BASUU (FWOOP)
THANK GOOD-NESS ...
WHERE DID YOU GO? WE'VE BEEN LOOKING FOR YOU...
YUKKIN ...!
YEP.
THAT WOMAN'S CIRCUS...
ふあ~
FUAA (YAWN)
ガシ ガシ
GASHI (SCRATCH) GASHI

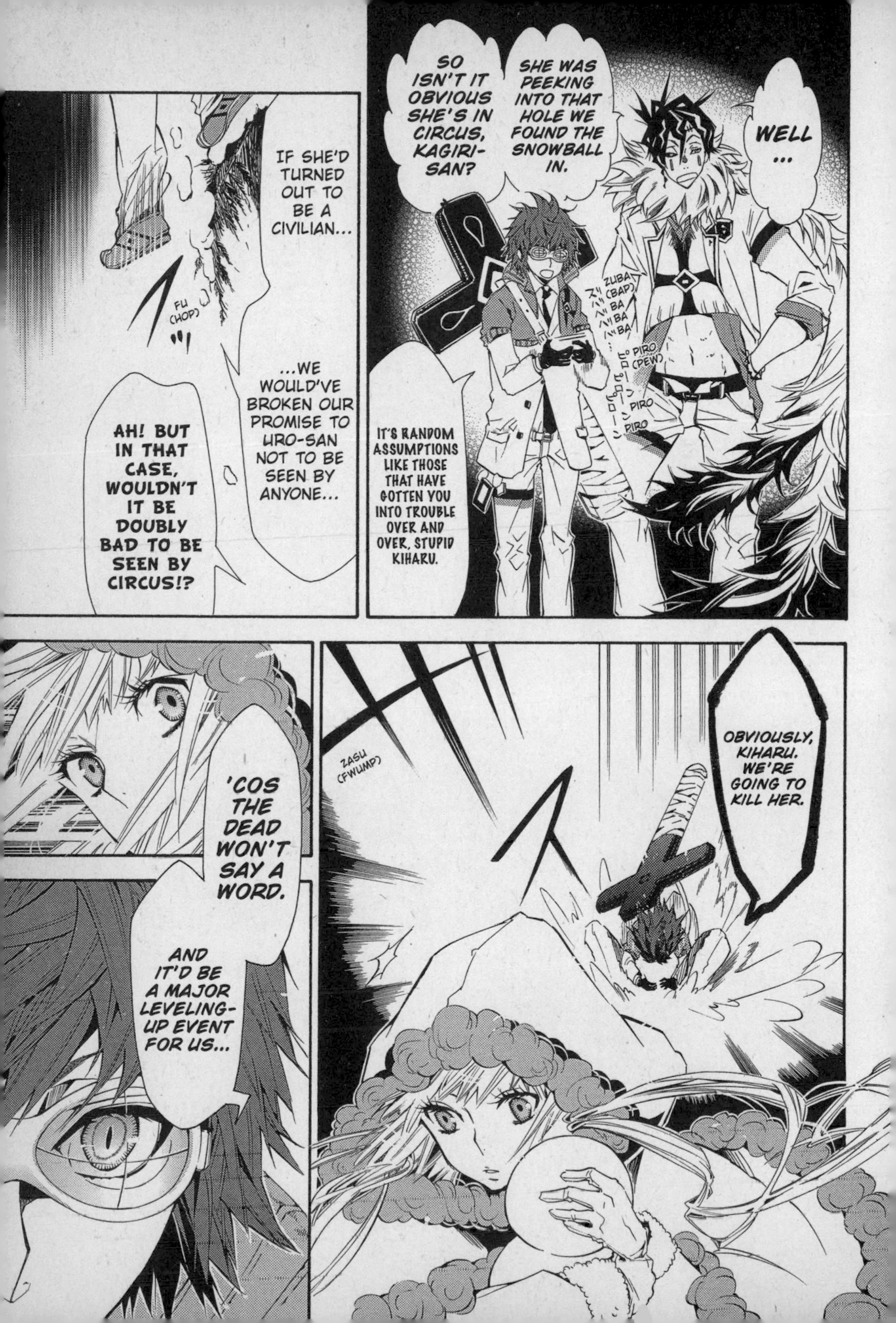
WELL...
SHE WAS PEEKING INTO THAT HOLE WE FOUND THE SNOWBALL IN.
SO ISN'T IT OBVIOUS SHE'S IN CIRCUS, KAGIRI-SAN?
ZUBA (BAP) BA BA BA
PIRO (PEW) PIRO PIRO
IT'S RANDOM ASSUMPTIONS LIKE THOSE THAT HAVE GOTTEN YOU INTO TROUBLE OVER AND OVER, STUPID KIHARU.
IF SHE'D TURNED OUT TO BE A CIVILIAN...
FU (HOP)
...WE WOULD'VE BROKEN OUR PROMISE TO URO-SAN NOT TO BE SEEN BY ANYONE...
AH! BUT IN THAT CASE, WOULDN'T IT BE DOUBLY BAD TO BE SEEN BY CIRCUS!?
OBVIOUSLY, KIHARU. WE'RE GOING TO KILL HER.
ZASU (FWUMP)
'COS THE DEAD WON'T SAY A WORD.
AND IT'D BE A MAJOR LEVELING-UP EVENT FOR US...

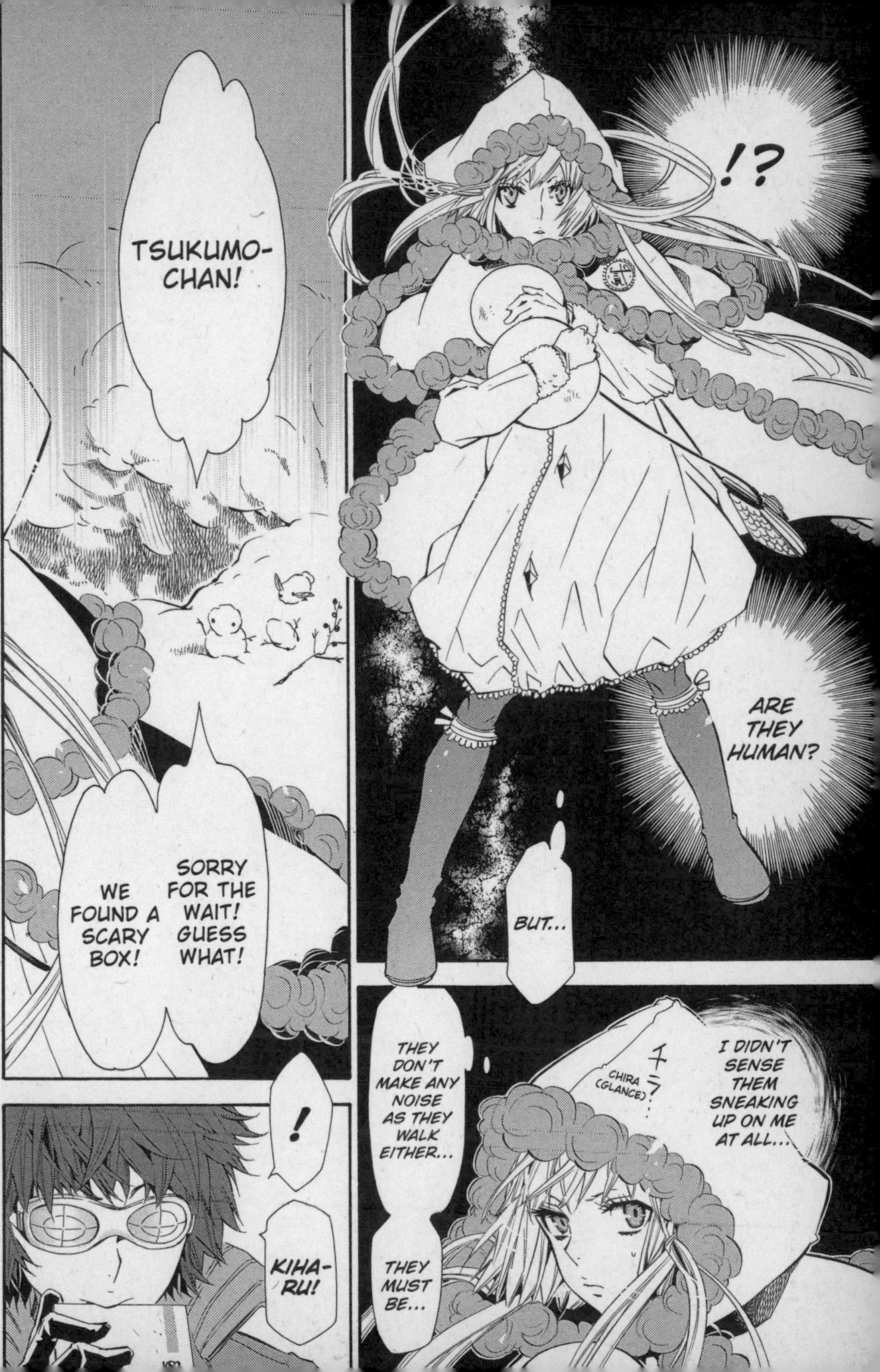
!?
ARE THEY HUMAN?
BUT...
TSUKUMO-CHAN!
SORRY FOR THE WAIT! GUESS WHAT!
WE FOUND A SCARY BOX!
I DIDN'T SENSE THEM SNEAKING UP ON ME AT ALL...
CHIRA (GLANCE)
THEY DON'T MAKE ANY NOISE AS THEY WALK EITHER...
THEY MUST BE...
!
KIHA-RU!

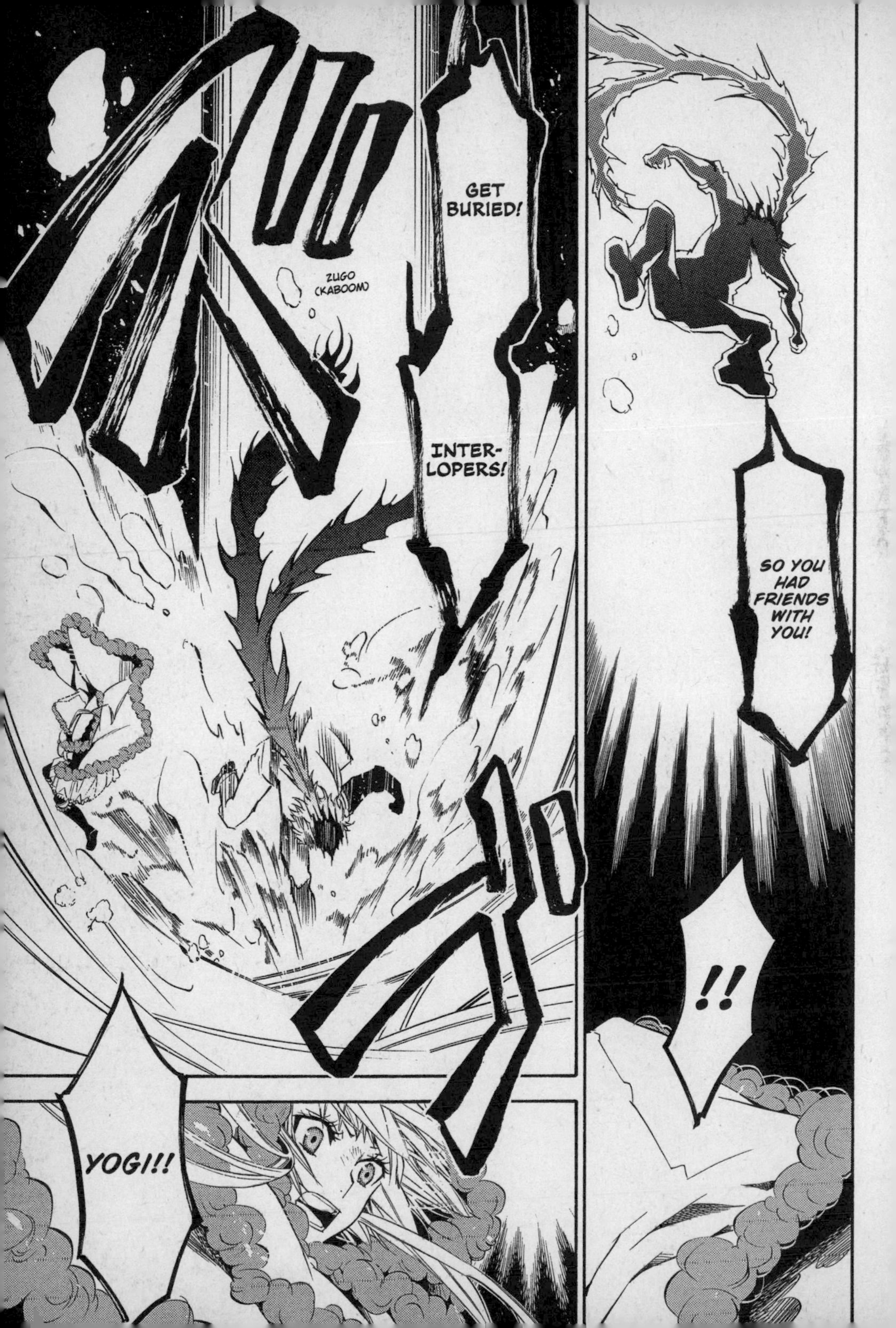
SO YOU HAD FRIENDS WITH YOU!
!!
GET BURIED!
ZUGO (KABOOM)
INTERLOPERS!
YOGI!!

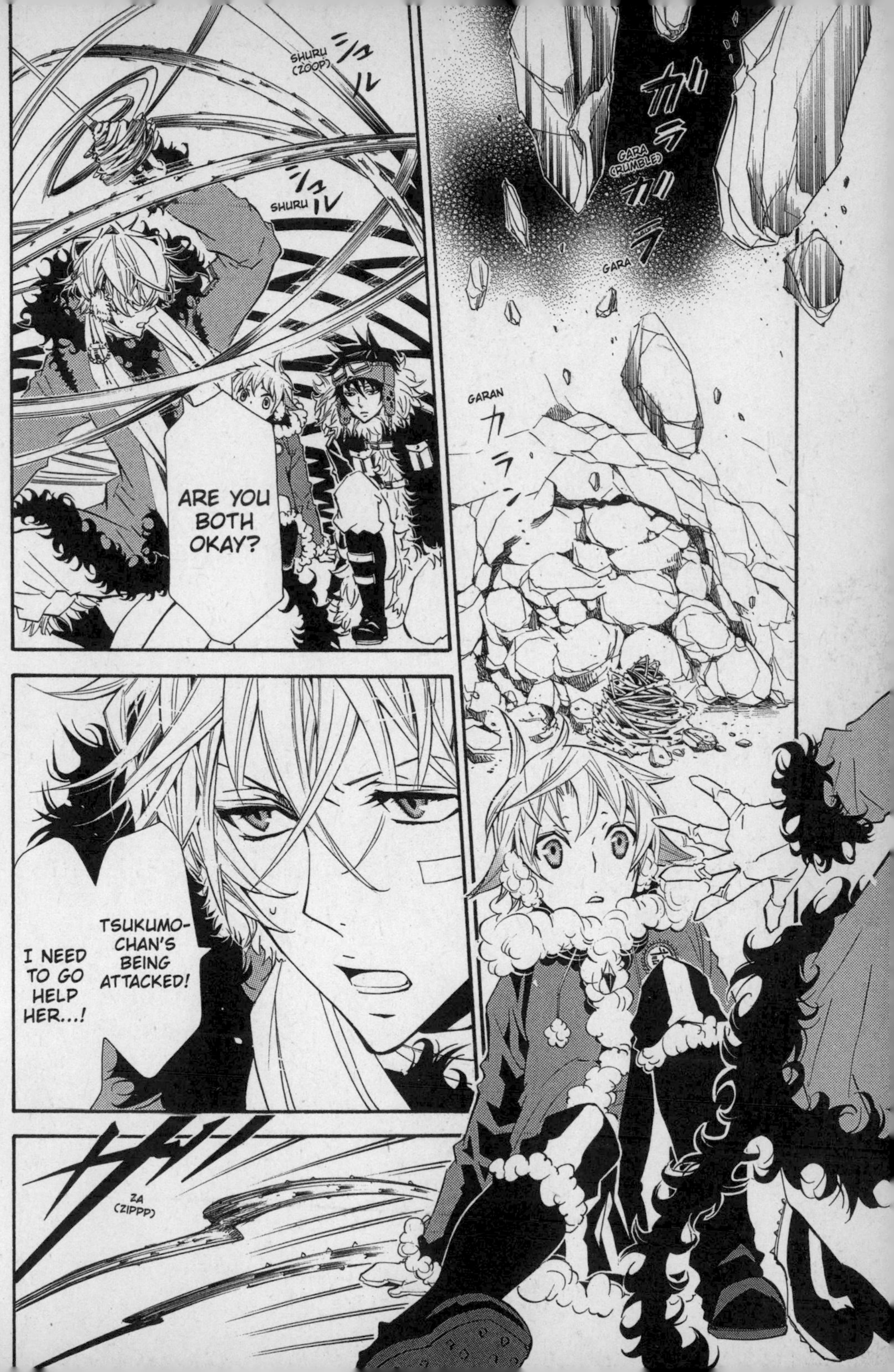
GARA (RUMBLE)
GARA
GARAN
SHURU (ZOOP)
SHURU
ARE YOU BOTH OKAY?
TSUKUMO-CHAN'S BEING ATTACKED!
I NEED TO GO HELP HER...!
ZA (ZIPPP)

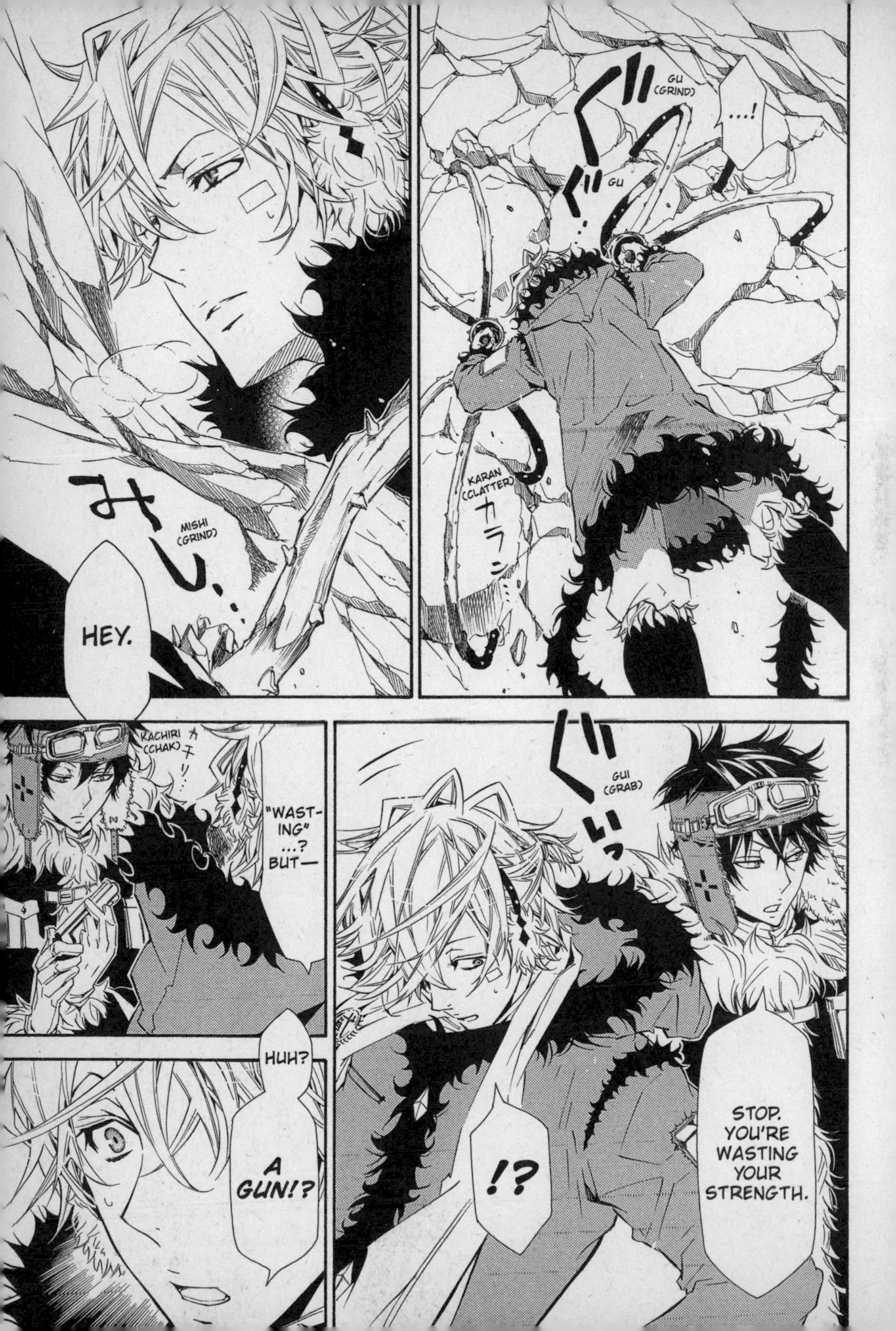

GU (GRIND)
...!
GU
KARAN (CLATTER)
カラン
MISHI (GRIND)
みし
HEY.
GUI (GRAB)
STOP. YOU'RE WASTING YOUR STRENGTH.
!?
KACHIRI (CHAK)
カチリ
"WASTING" ...? BUT—
HUH?
A GUN!?

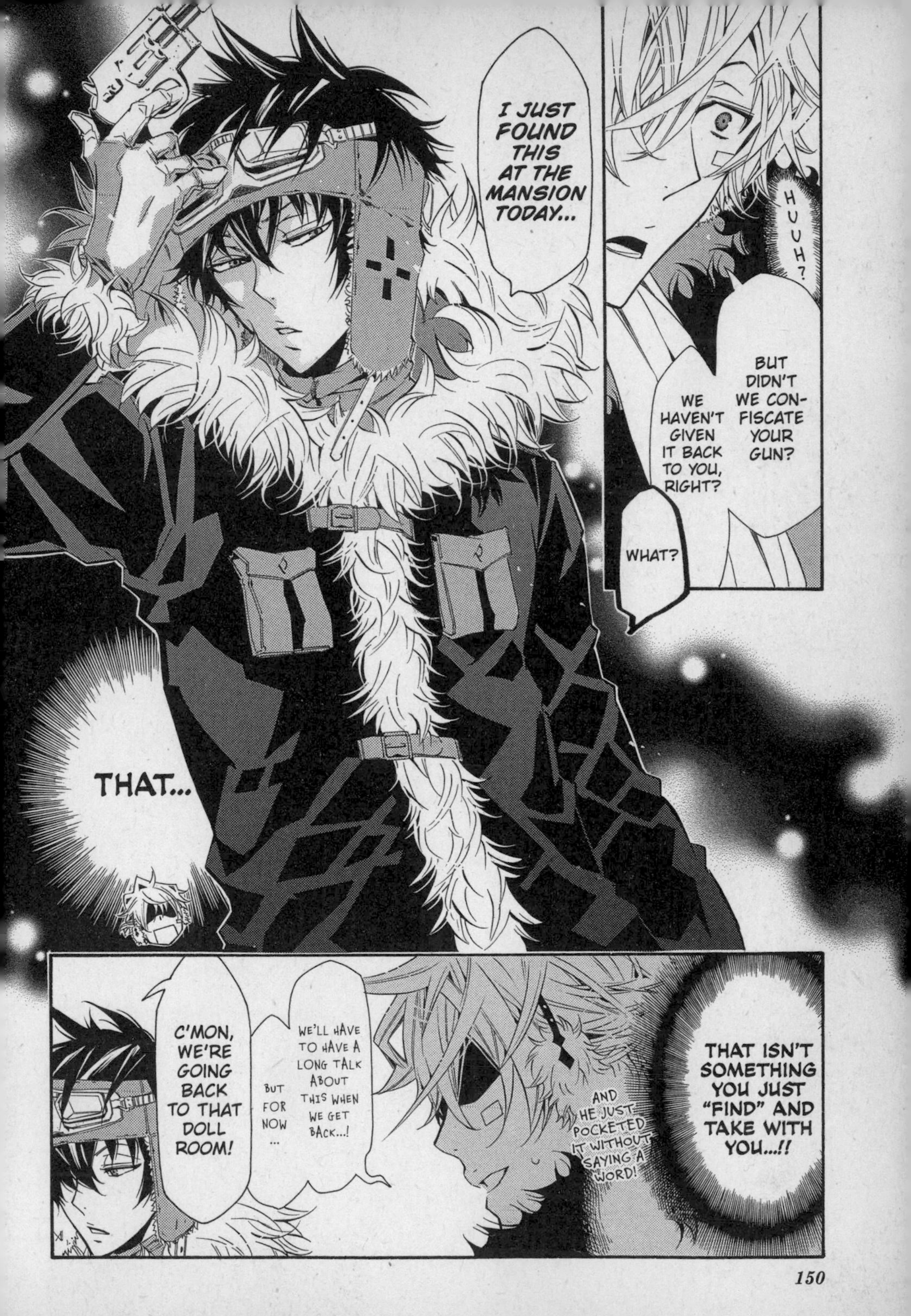
HUUH?
BUT DIDN'T WE CON-FISCATE YOUR GUN?
WE HAVEN'T GIVEN IT BACK TO YOU, RIGHT?
WHAT?
I JUST FOUND THIS AT THE MANSION TODAY...
THAT...
THAT ISN'T SOMETHING YOU JUST "FIND" AND TAKE WITH YOU...!!
AND HE JUST POCKETED IT WITHOUT SAYING A WORD!
WE'LL HAVE TO HAVE A LONG TALK ABOUT THIS WHEN WE GET BACK...!
BUT FOR NOW ...
C'MON, WE'RE GOING BACK TO THAT DOLL ROOM!

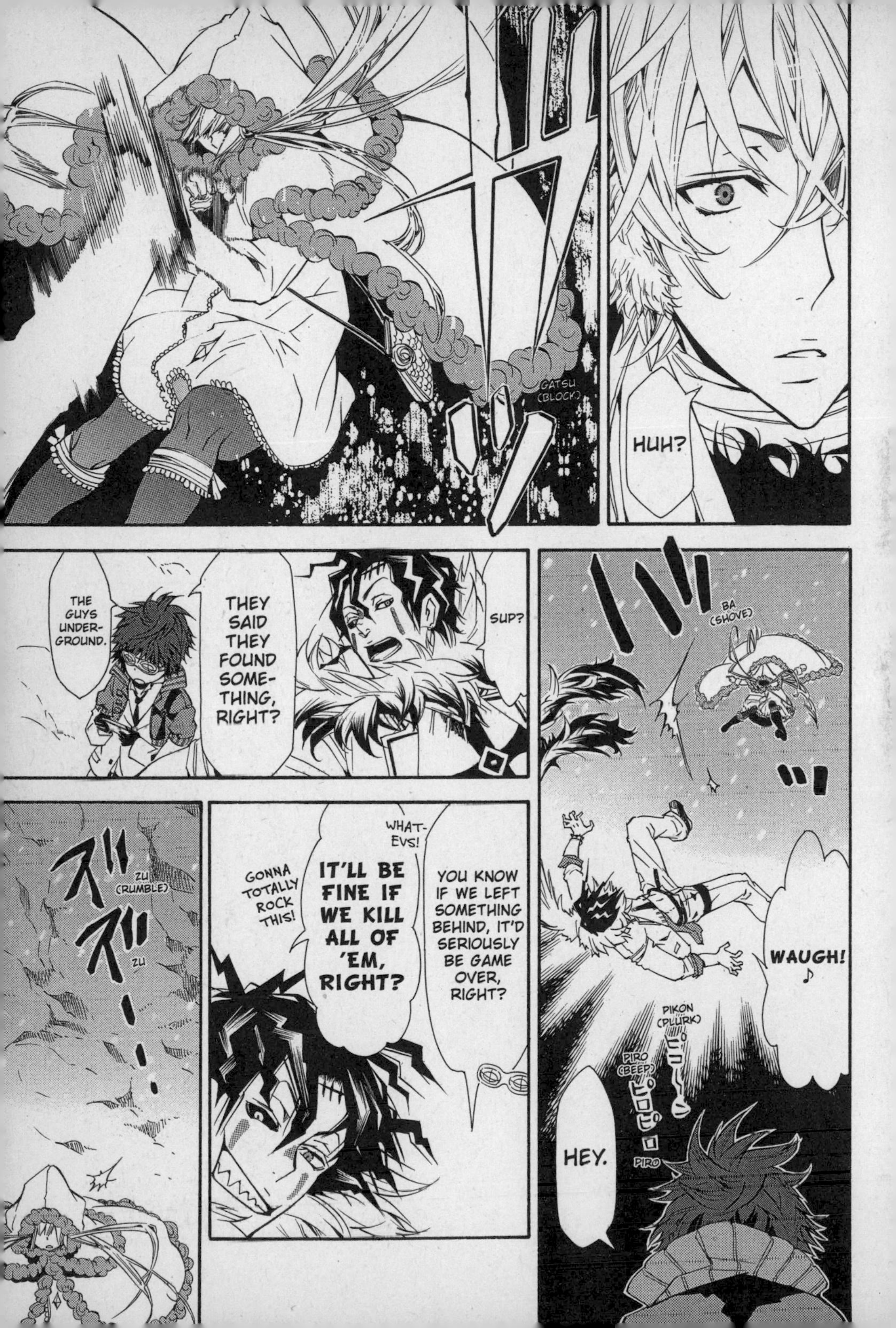
HUH?
GATSU (BLOCK)
BA (SHOVE)
WAUGH! ♪
PIKON (PLURK)
PIRO (BEEP)
PIRO
HEY.
SUP?
THEY SAID THEY FOUND SOMETHING, RIGHT?
THE GUYS UNDERGROUND.
YOU KNOW IF WE LEFT SOMETHING BEHIND, IT'D SERIOUSLY BE GAME OVER, RIGHT?
WHAT-EVS!
IT'LL BE FINE IF WE KILL ALL OF 'EM, RIGHT?
GONNA TOTALLY ROCK THIS!
ZU (RUMBLE)
ZU

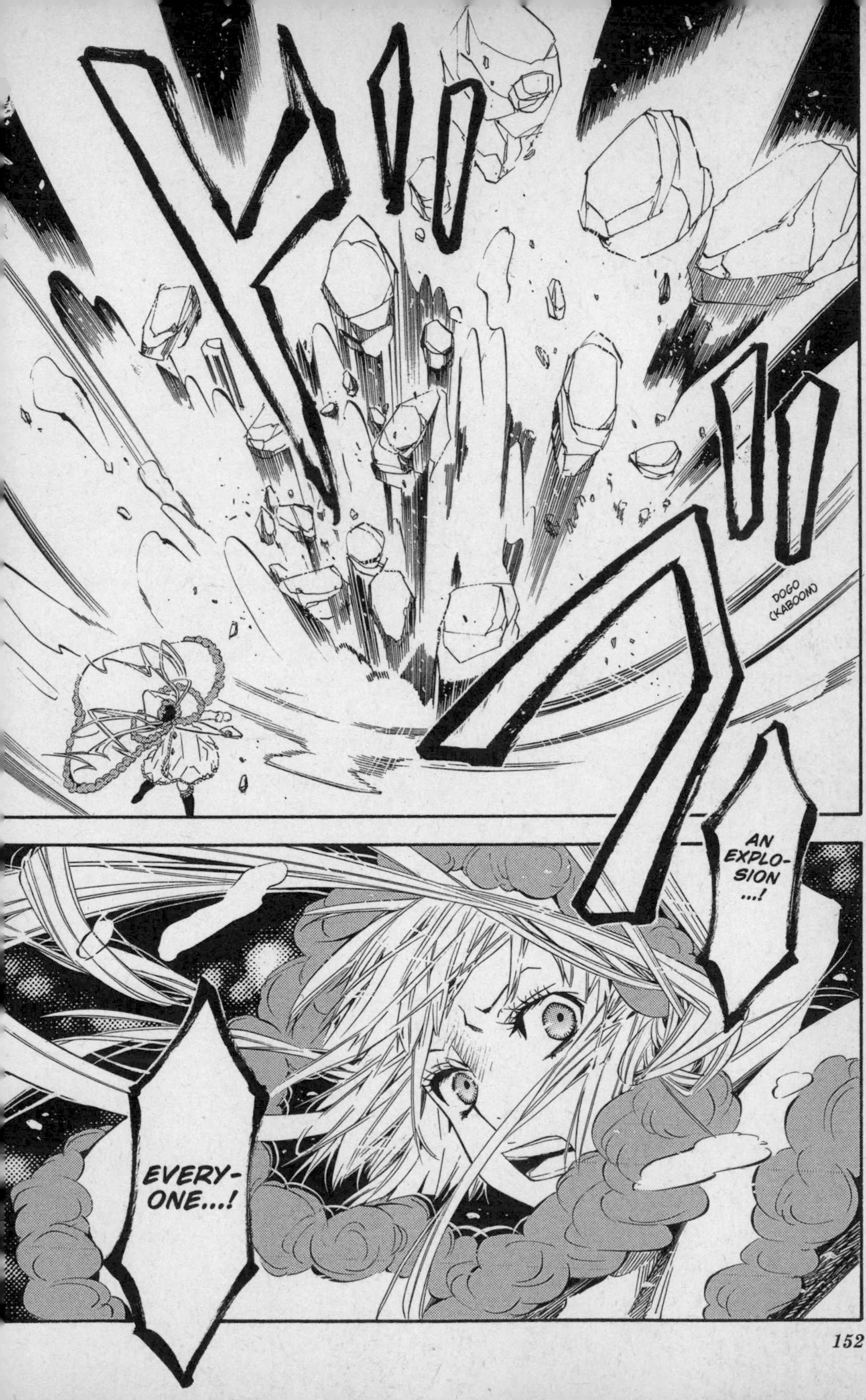
DOGO (KABOOM)
AN EXPLOSION ...!
EVERY-ONE...!

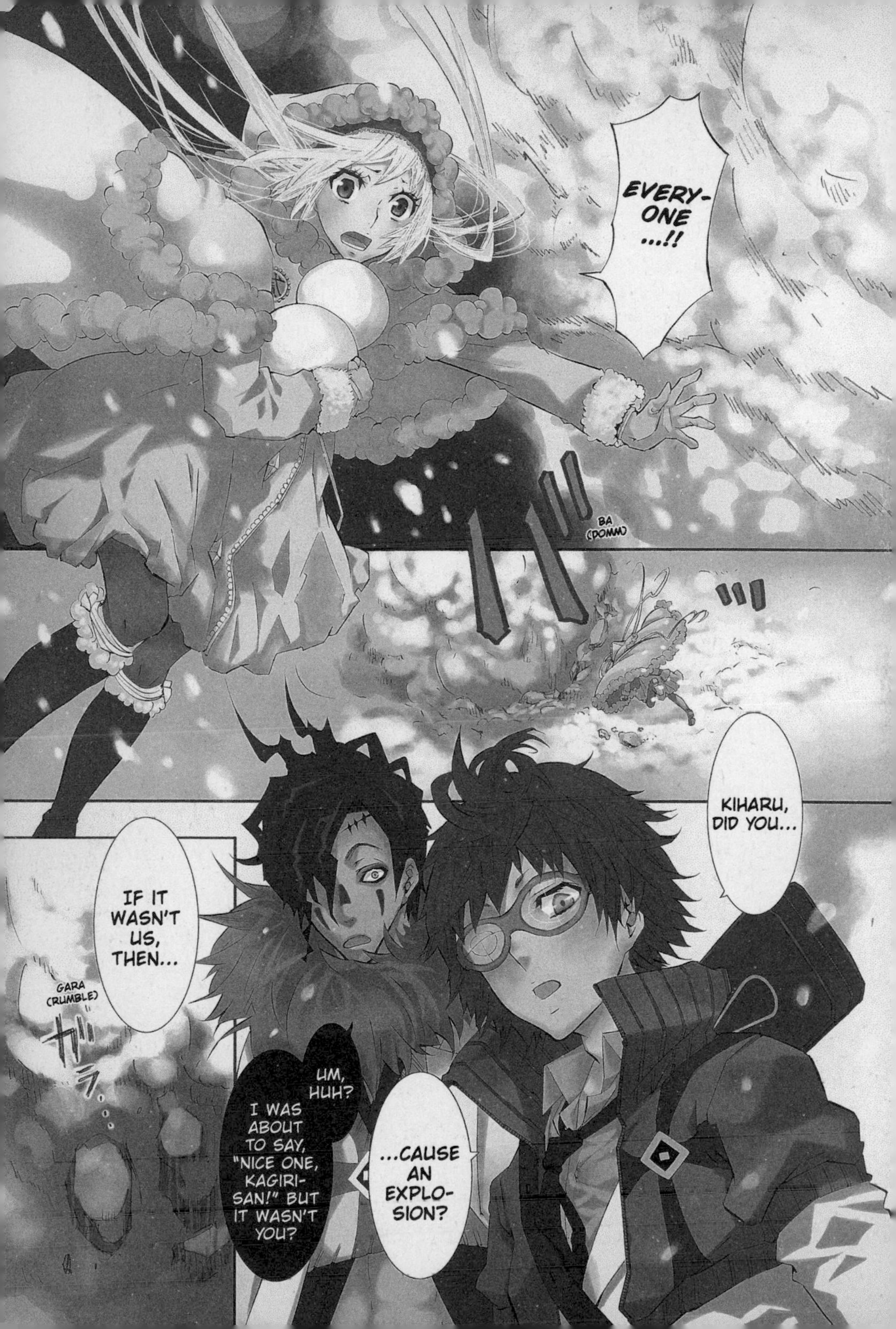
EVERY-ONE ...!!
BA (DOMM)
KIHARU, DID YOU...
...CAUSE AN EXPLOSION?
UM, HUH? I WAS ABOUT TO SAY, "NICE ONE, KAGIRI-SAN!" BUT IT WASN'T YOU?
IF IT WASN'T US, THEN...
GARA (RUMBLE)

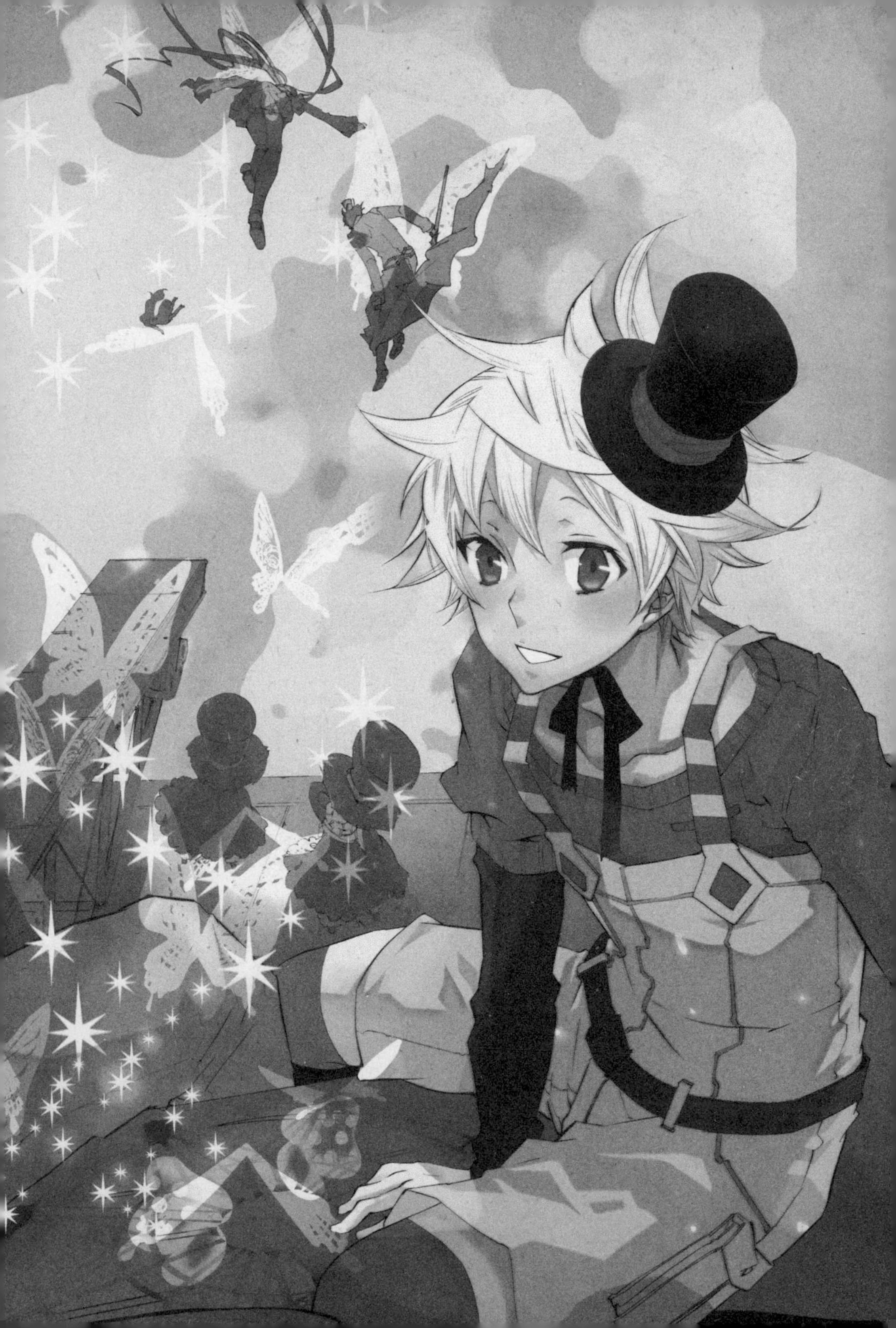

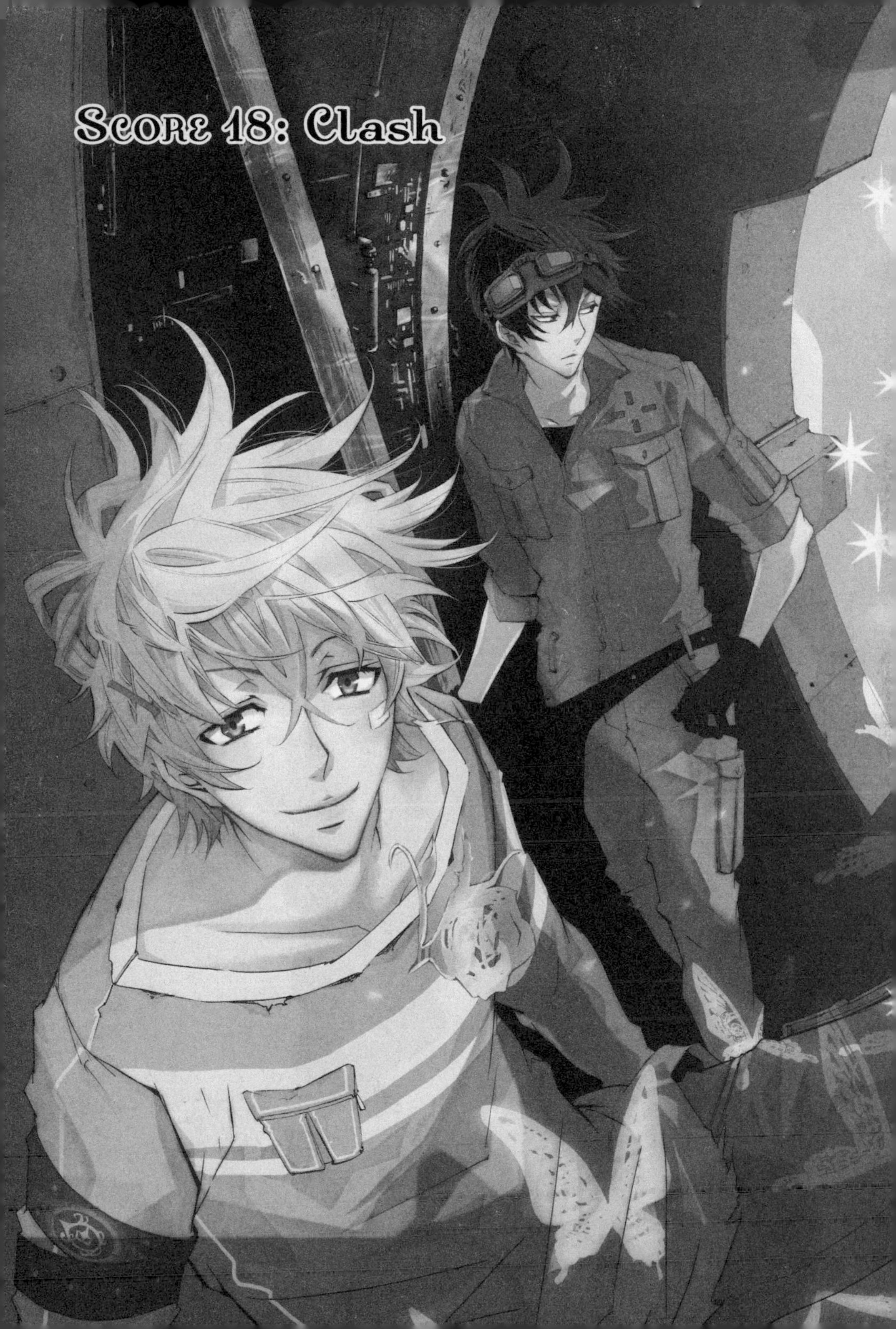
Score 18: Clash

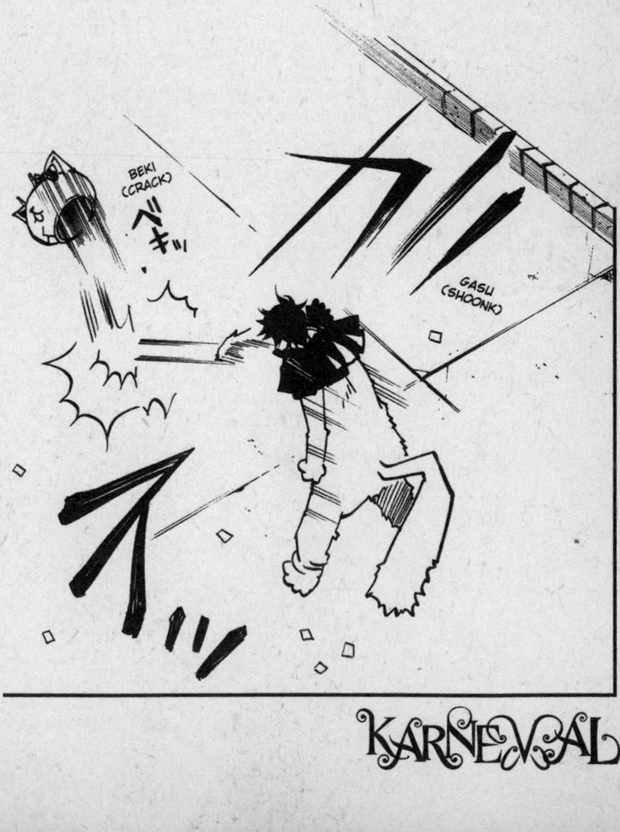
GASU (SHOONK)
BEKI (CRACK)

KARNEVAL

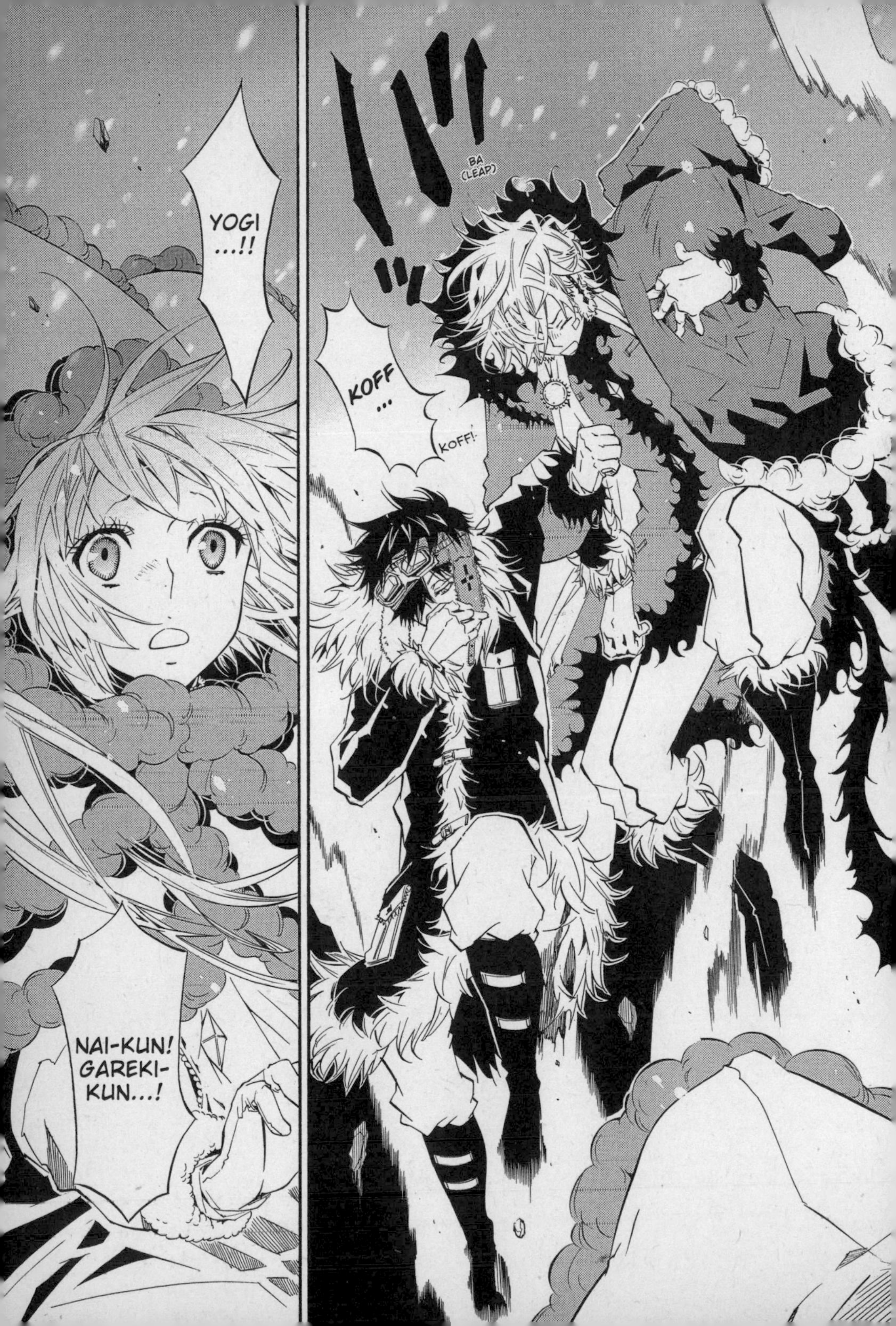
BA (LEAP)
KOFF...
KOFF!
YOGI...!!
NAI-KUN! GAREKI-KUN...!

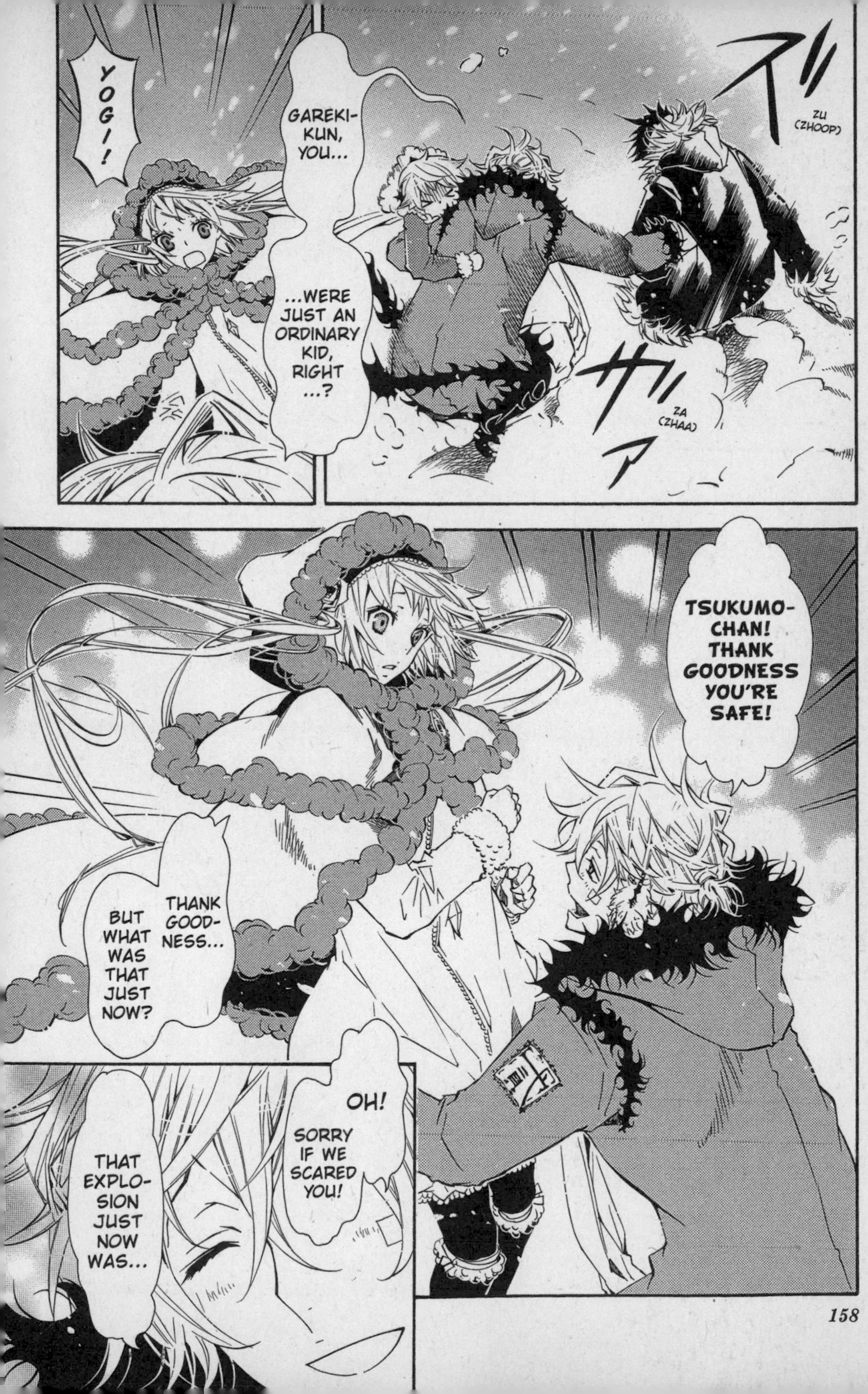
ズ
ZU (ZHOOP)
ザァ
ZA (ZHAA)
GAREKI-KUN, YOU...
...WERE JUST AN ORDINARY KID, RIGHT...?
YOGI!
TSUKUMO-CHAN! THANK GOODNESS YOU'RE SAFE!
THANK GOODNESS...
BUT WHAT WAS THAT JUST NOW?
OH!
SORRY IF WE SCARED YOU!
THAT EXPLOSION JUST NOW WAS...

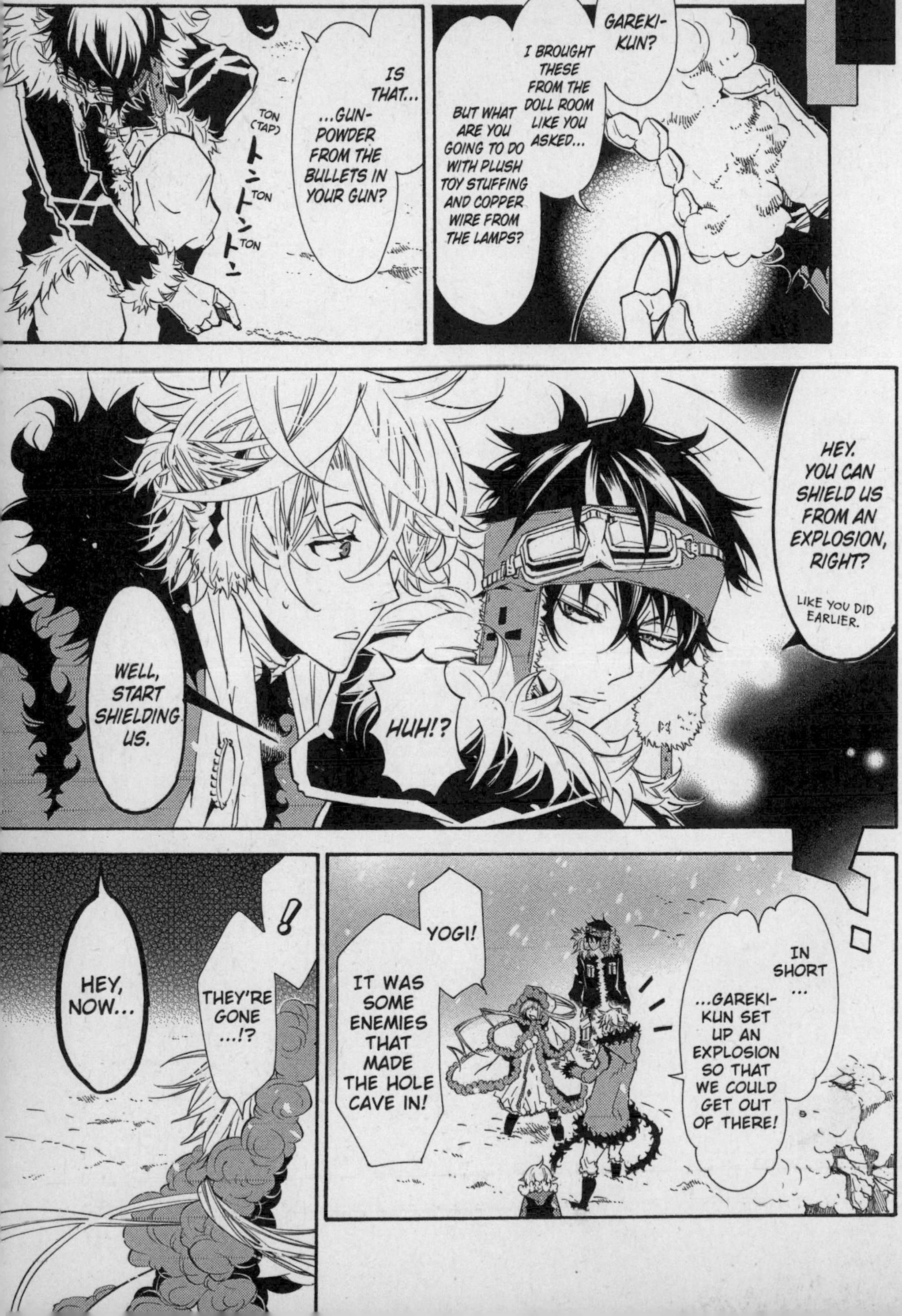
GAREKI-KUN?
I BROUGHT THESE FROM THE DOLL ROOM LIKE YOU ASKED...
BUT WHAT ARE YOU GOING TO DO WITH PLUSH TOY STUFFING AND COPPER WIRE FROM THE LAMPS?
IS THAT... ...GUN-POWDER FROM THE BULLETS IN YOUR GUN?
TON (TAP) トントントン TON TON
HEY. YOU CAN SHIELD US FROM AN EXPLOSION, RIGHT?
LIKE YOU DID EARLIER.
HUH!?
WELL, START SHIELDING US.
IN SHORT ...
...GAREKI-KUN SET UP AN EXPLOSION SO THAT WE COULD GET OUT OF THERE!
YOGI!
IT WAS SOME ENEMIES THAT MADE THE HOLE CAVE IN!
!
THEY'RE GONE ...!?
HEY, NOW...

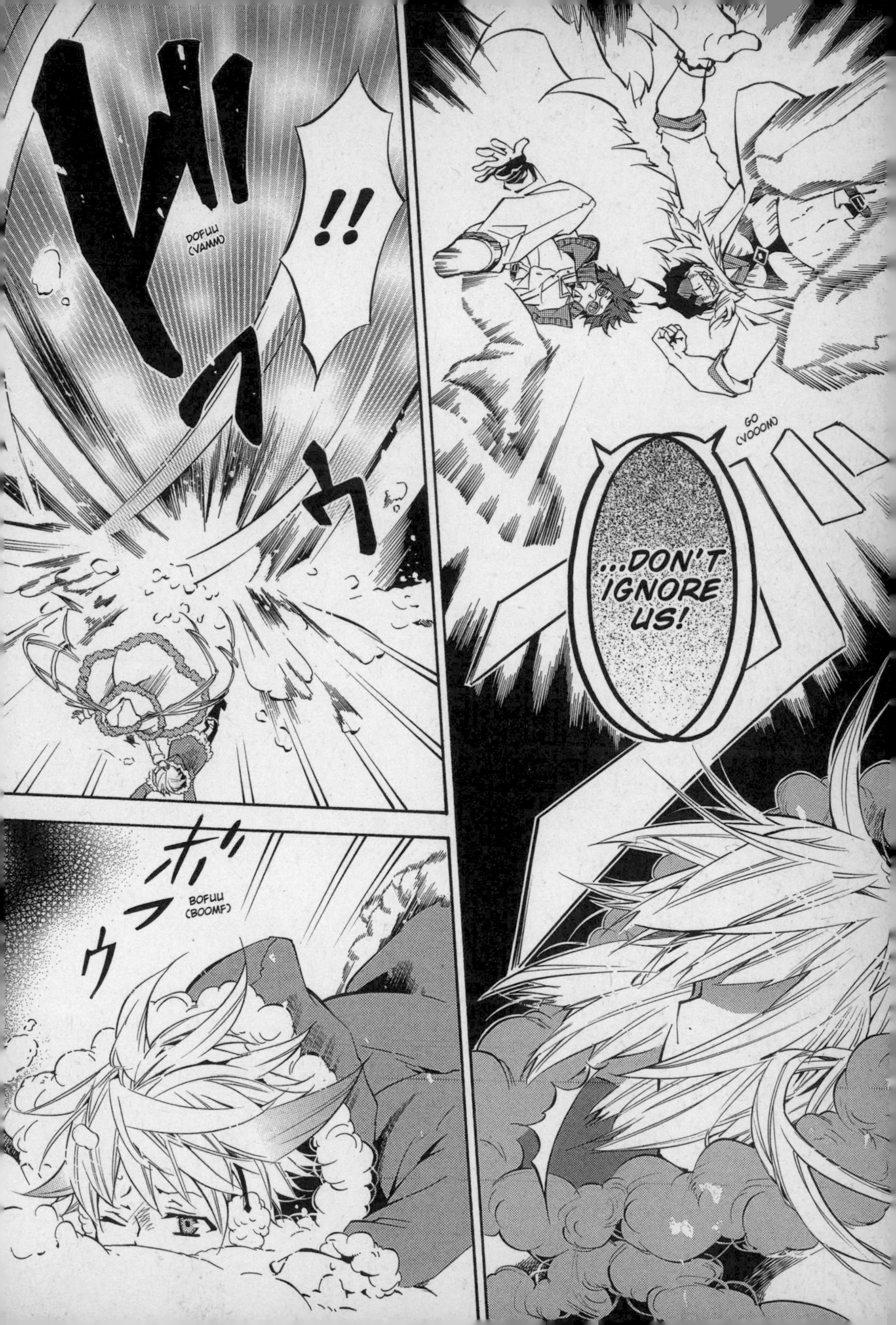
GO (VOOOM)
...DON'T IGNORE US!
DOFUU (VAMM)
!!
BOFUU (BOOMF)

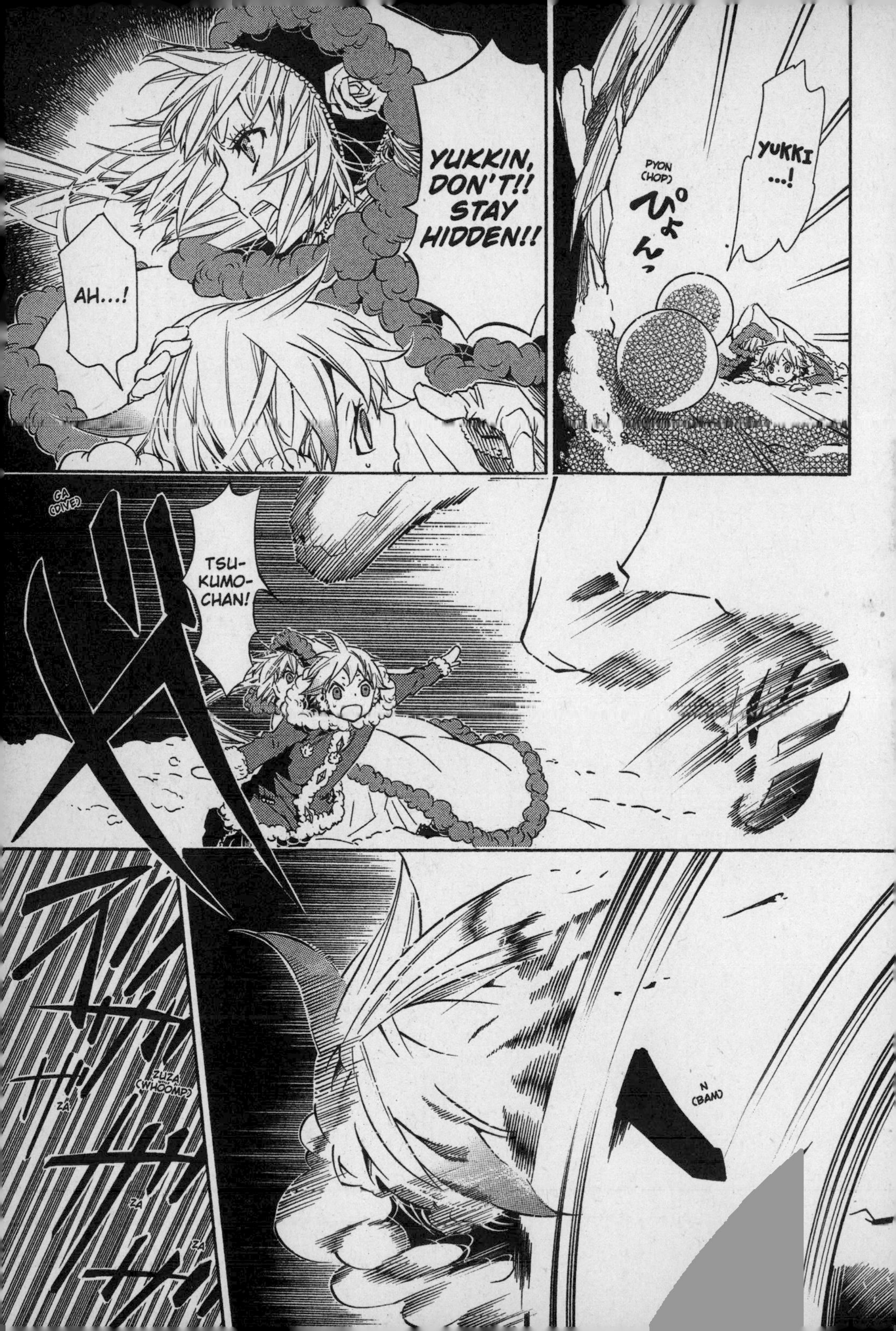
YUKKI ...!
PYON (HOP)
ぴょんっ
YUKKIN, DON'T!! STAY HIDDEN!!
AH...!
TSU-KUMO-CHAN!
GA (DIVE)
N (BAM)
ZUZA (WHOOMP)
ZA
ZA
ZA

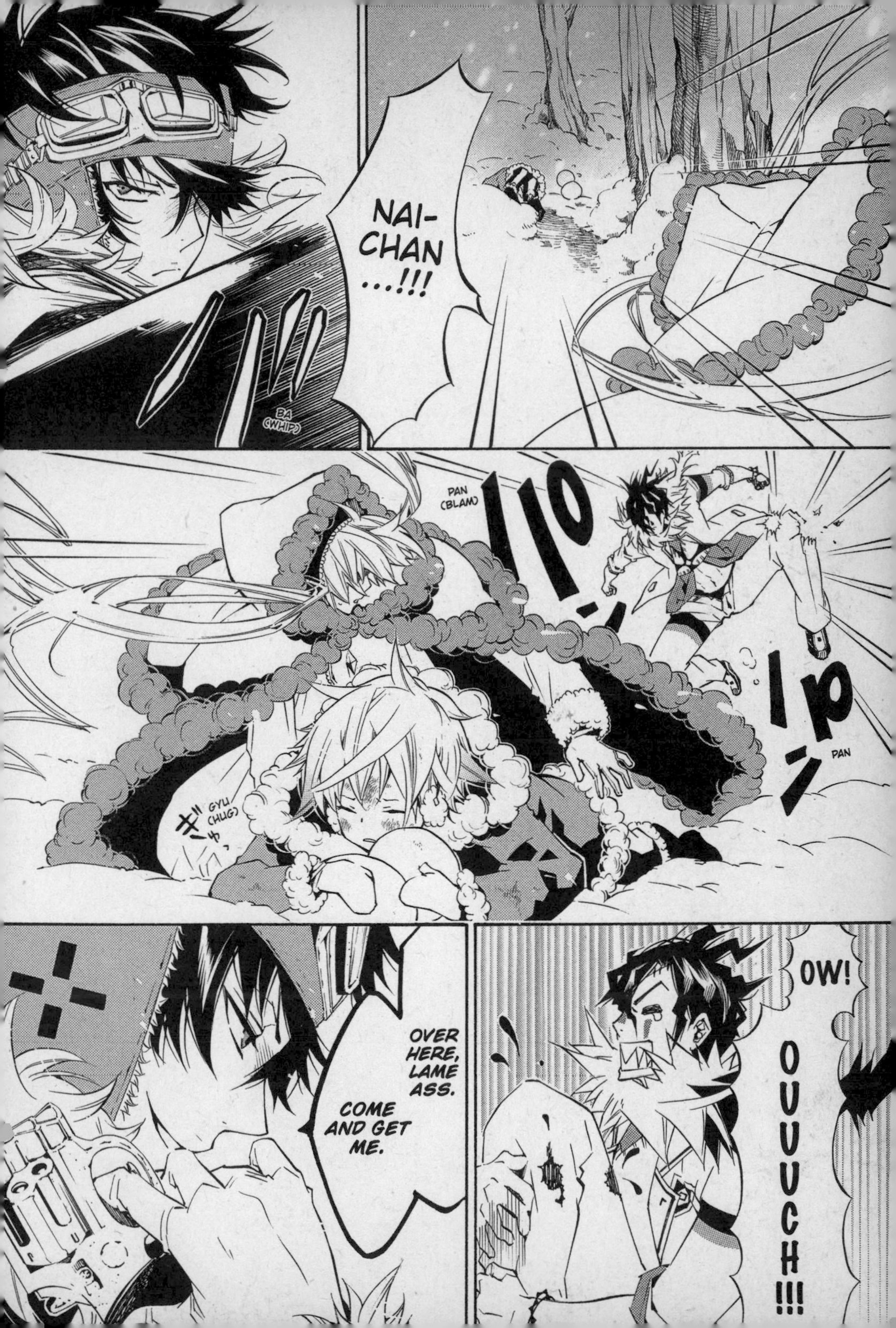
NAI-CHAN ...!!!
BA (WHIP)
PAN (BLAM)
PAN
GYU (HUG)
OW!
OUUUCH!!!
OVER HERE, LAME ASS.
COME AND GET ME.

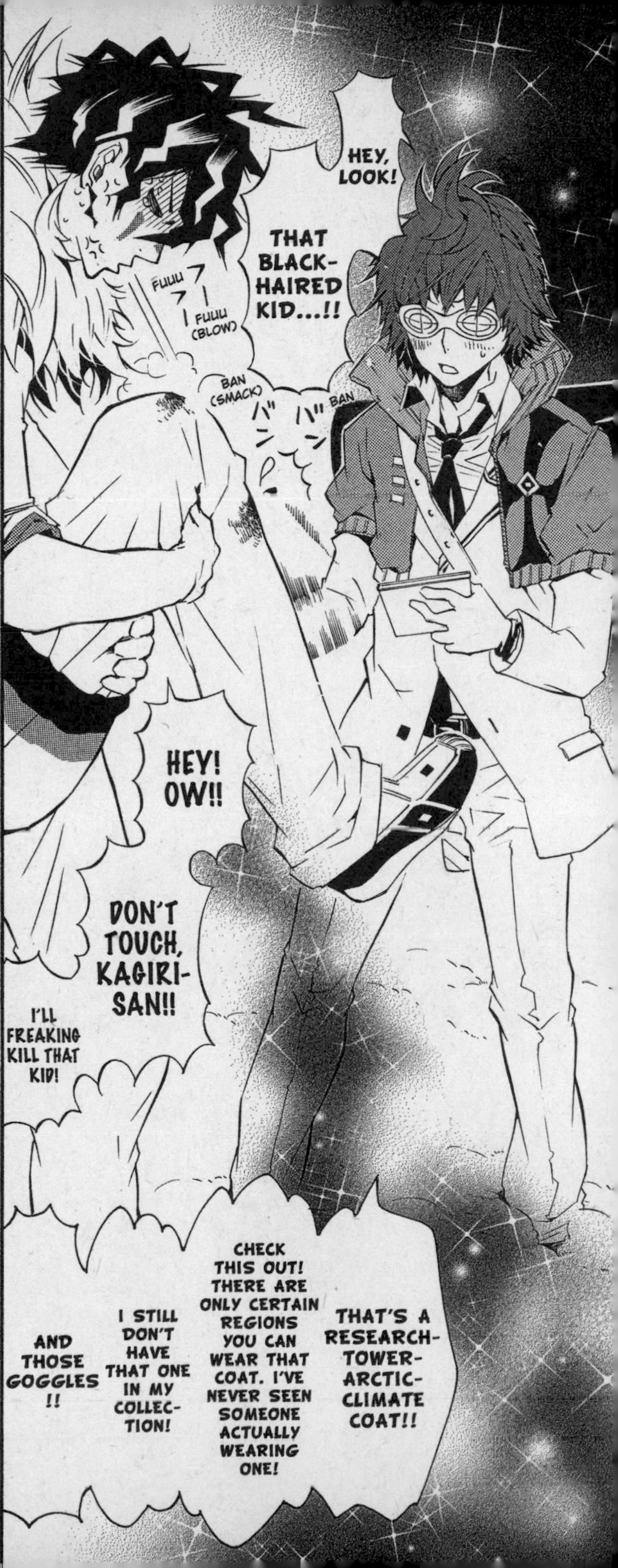
HEY, LOOK!
THAT BLACK-HAIRED KID...!!
FUUU FUUU (BLOW)
BAN (SMACK) BAN
HEY! OW!!
DON'T TOUCH, KAGIRI-SAN!!
I'LL FREAKING KILL THAT KID!
THAT'S A RESEARCH-TOWER-ARCTIC-CLIMATE COAT!!
CHECK THIS OUT! THERE ARE ONLY CERTAIN REGIONS YOU CAN WEAR THAT COAT. I'VE NEVER SEEN SOMEONE ACTUALLY WEARING ONE!
I STILL DON'T HAVE THAT ONE IN MY COLLEC-TION!
AND THOSE GOGGLES!!
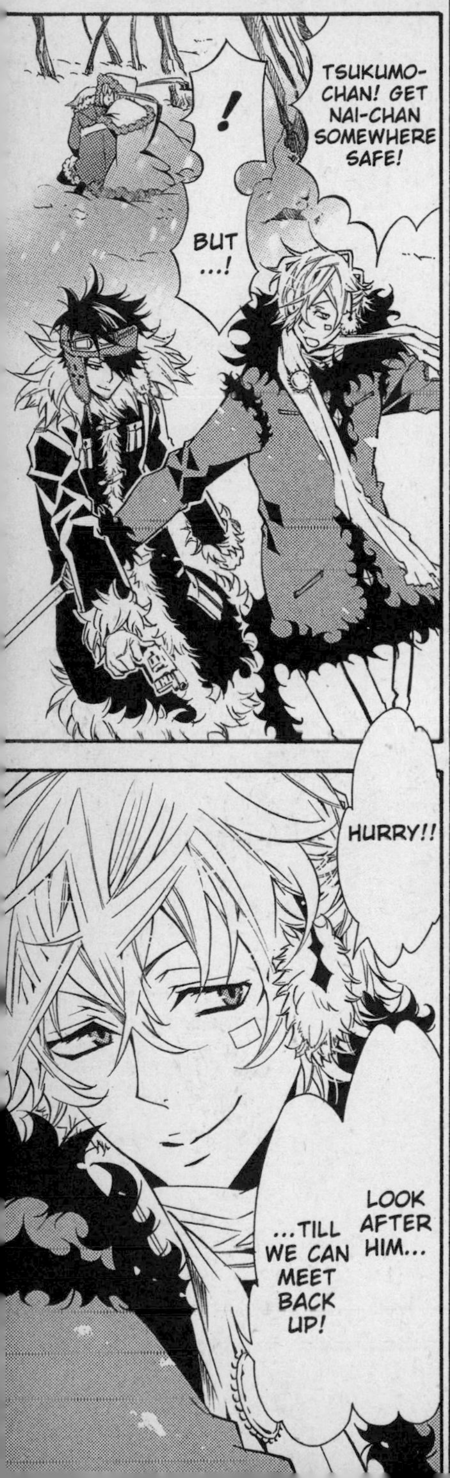
TSUKUMO-CHAN! GET NAI-CHAN SOMEWHERE SAFE!
!
BUT...!
HURRY!!
LOOK AFTER HIM...
...TILL WE CAN MEET BACK UP!

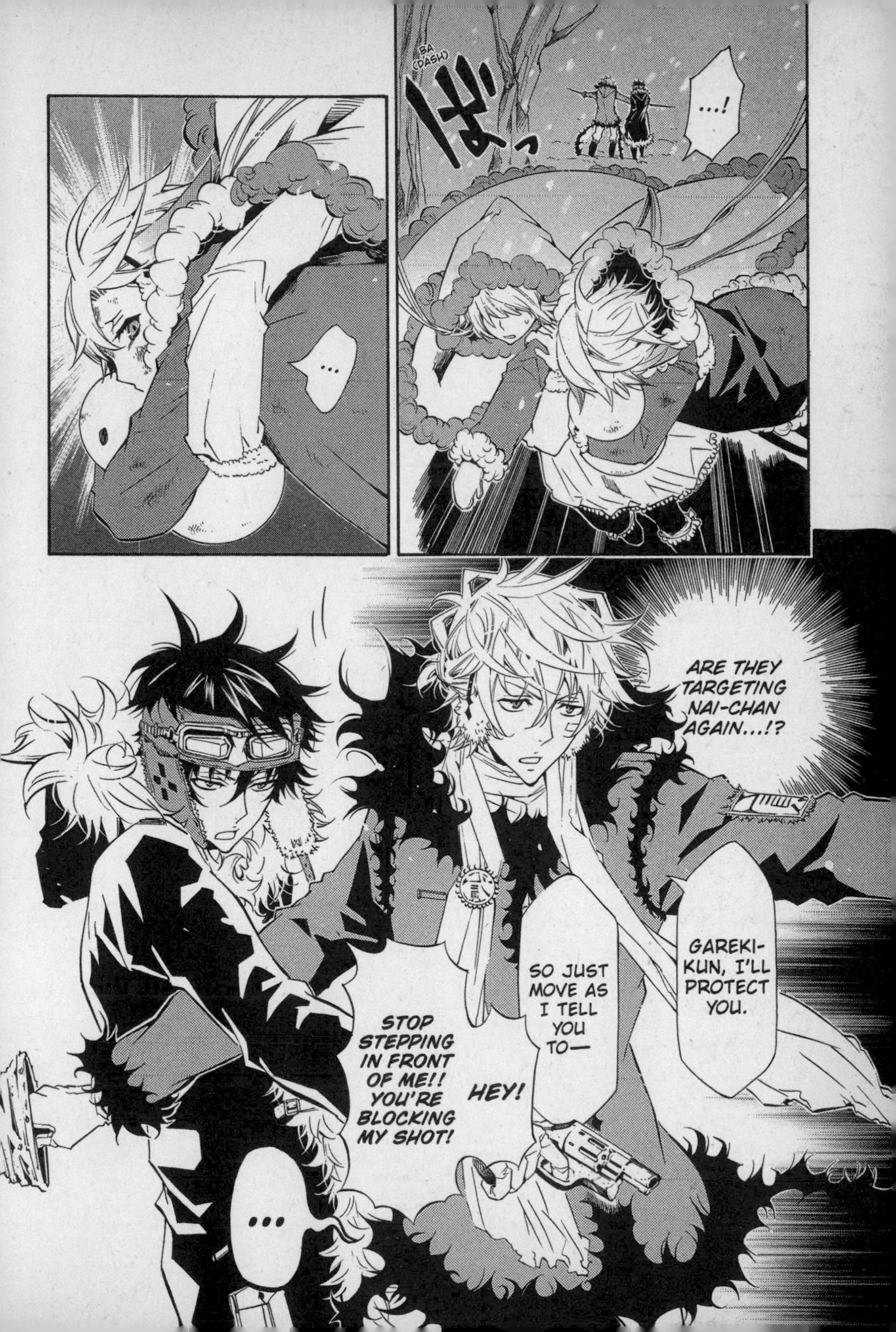
BA (DASH)
ばっ
...!
...
ARE THEY TARGETING NAI-CHAN AGAIN...!?
GAREKI-KUN, I'LL PROTECT YOU.
SO JUST MOVE AS I TELL YOU TO—
HEY!
STOP STEPPING IN FRONT OF ME!! YOU'RE BLOCKING MY SHOT!
...

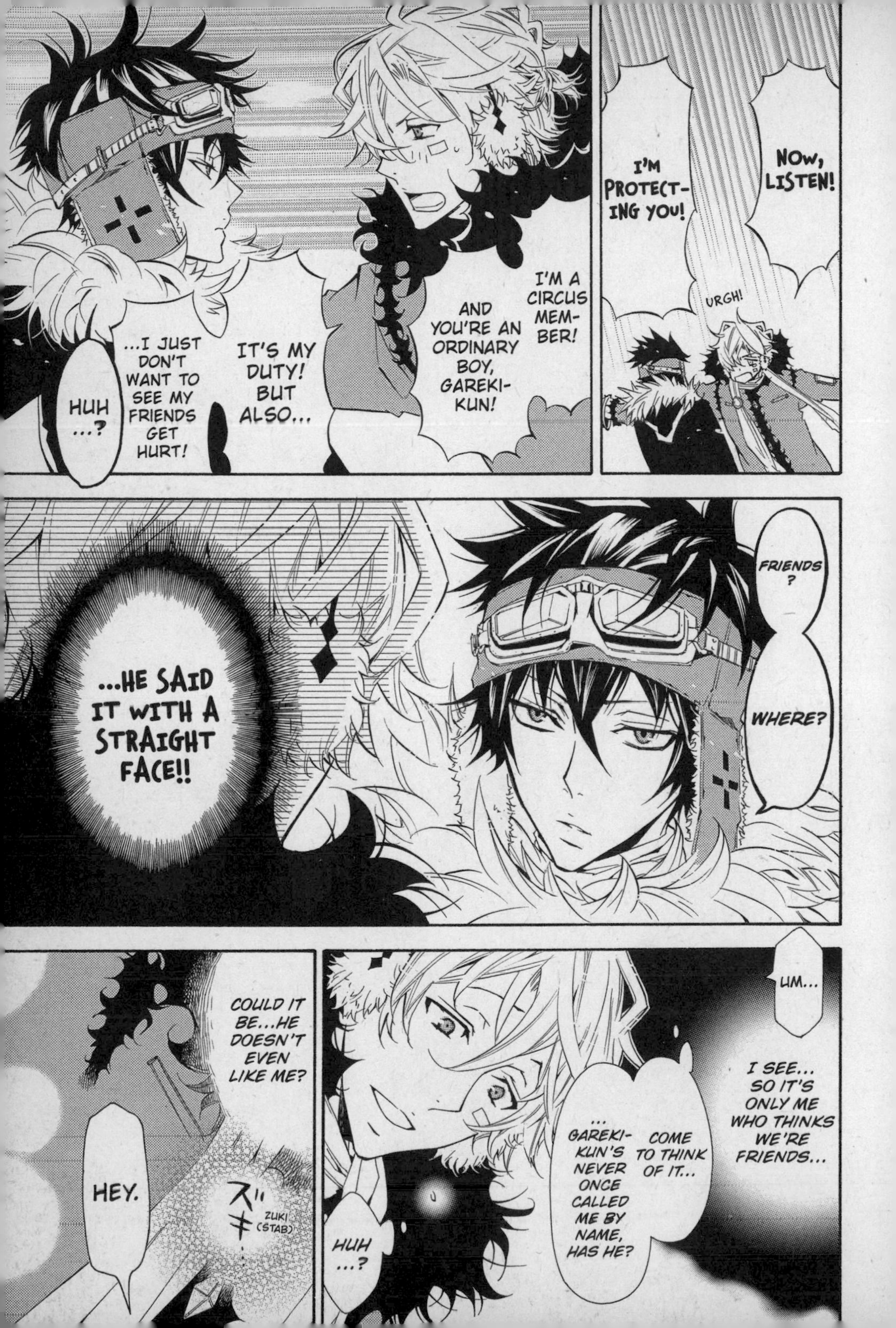

NOW, LISTEN!
I'M PROTECTING YOU!
URGH!
I'M A CIRCUS MEMBER!
AND YOU'RE AN ORDINARY BOY, GAREKI-KUN!
IT'S MY DUTY! BUT ALSO...
...I JUST DON'T WANT TO SEE MY FRIENDS GET HURT!
HUH...?
FRIENDS?
WHERE?
...HE SAID IT WITH A STRAIGHT FACE!!
UM...
I SEE... SO IT'S ONLY ME WHO THINKS WE'RE FRIENDS...
COME TO THINK OF IT...
...GAREKI-KUN'S NEVER ONCE CALLED ME BY NAME, HAS HE?
HUH...?
COULD IT BE...HE DOESN'T EVEN LIKE ME?
ズキ
ZUKI (STAB)
HEY.

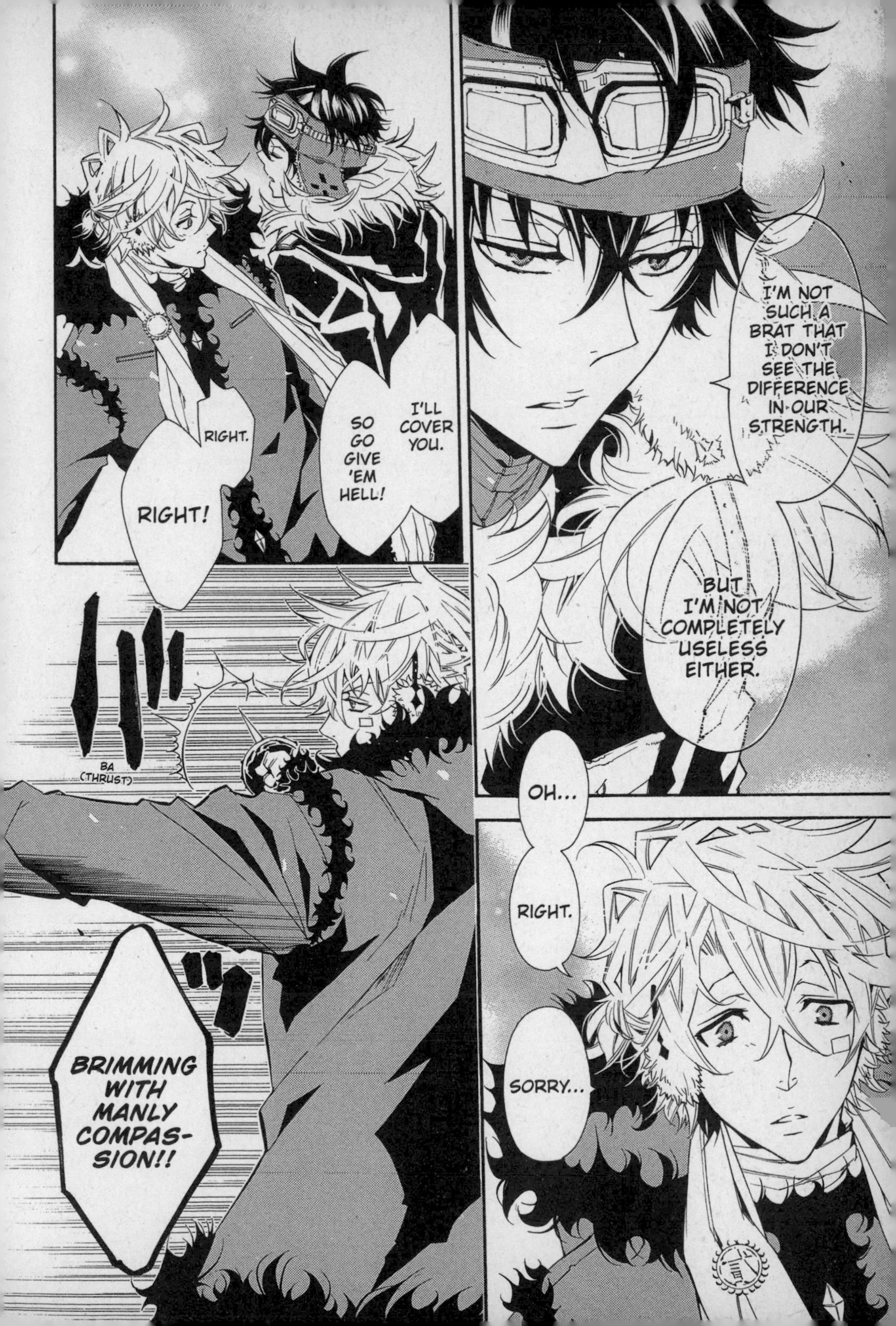

I'M NOT SUCH A BRAT THAT I DON'T SEE THE DIFFERENCE IN OUR STRENGTH.
BUT I'M NOT COMPLETELY USELESS EITHER.
I'LL COVER YOU.
SO GO GIVE 'EM HELL!
RIGHT.
RIGHT!
OH...
RIGHT.
SORRY...
BA (THRUST)
BRIMMING WITH MANLY COMPASSION!!

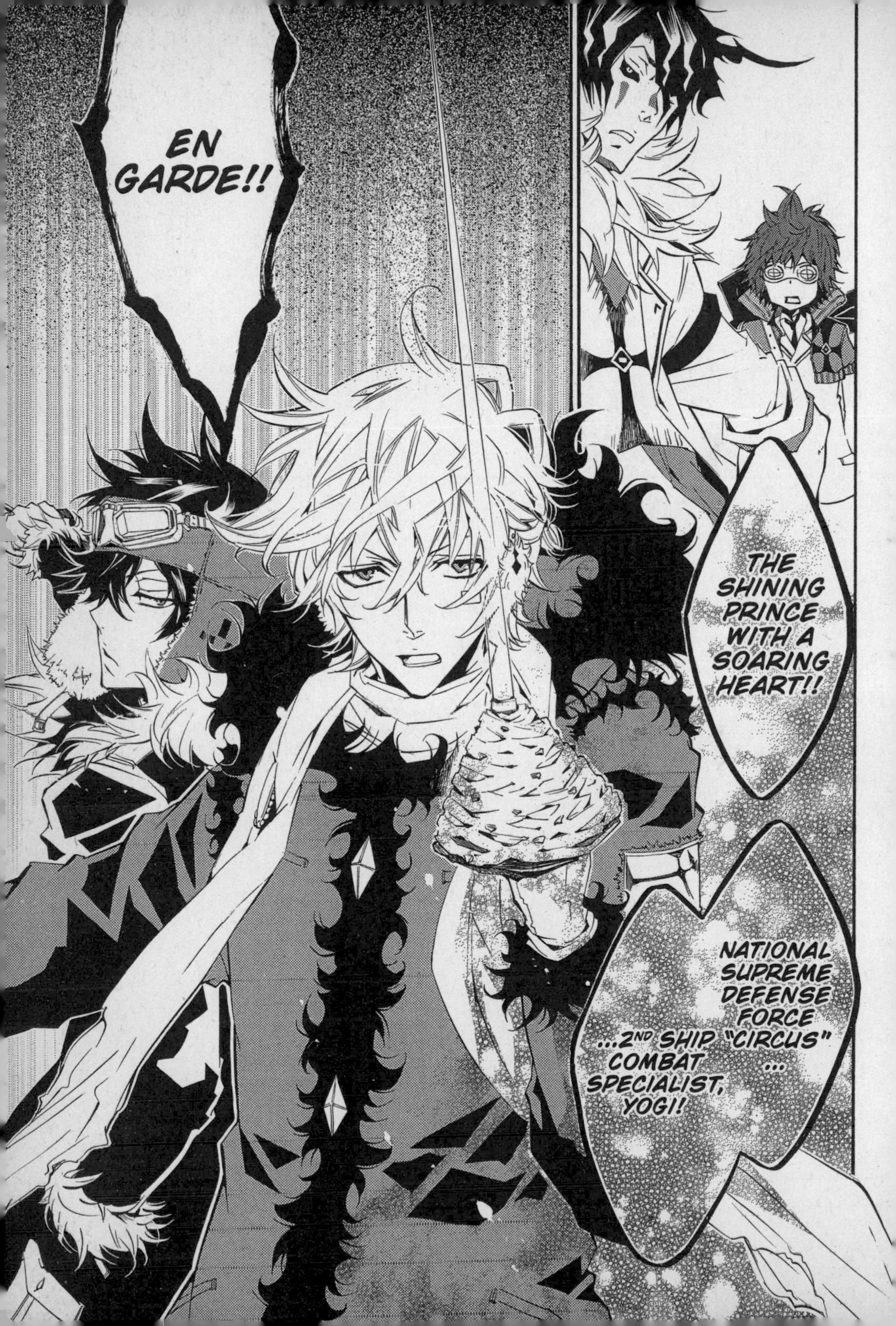
THE SHINING PRINCE WITH A SOARING HEART!!
NATIONAL SUPREME DEFENSE FORCE "CIRCUS" ...
...2ND SHIP COMBAT SPECIALIST, YOGI!
EN GARDE!!

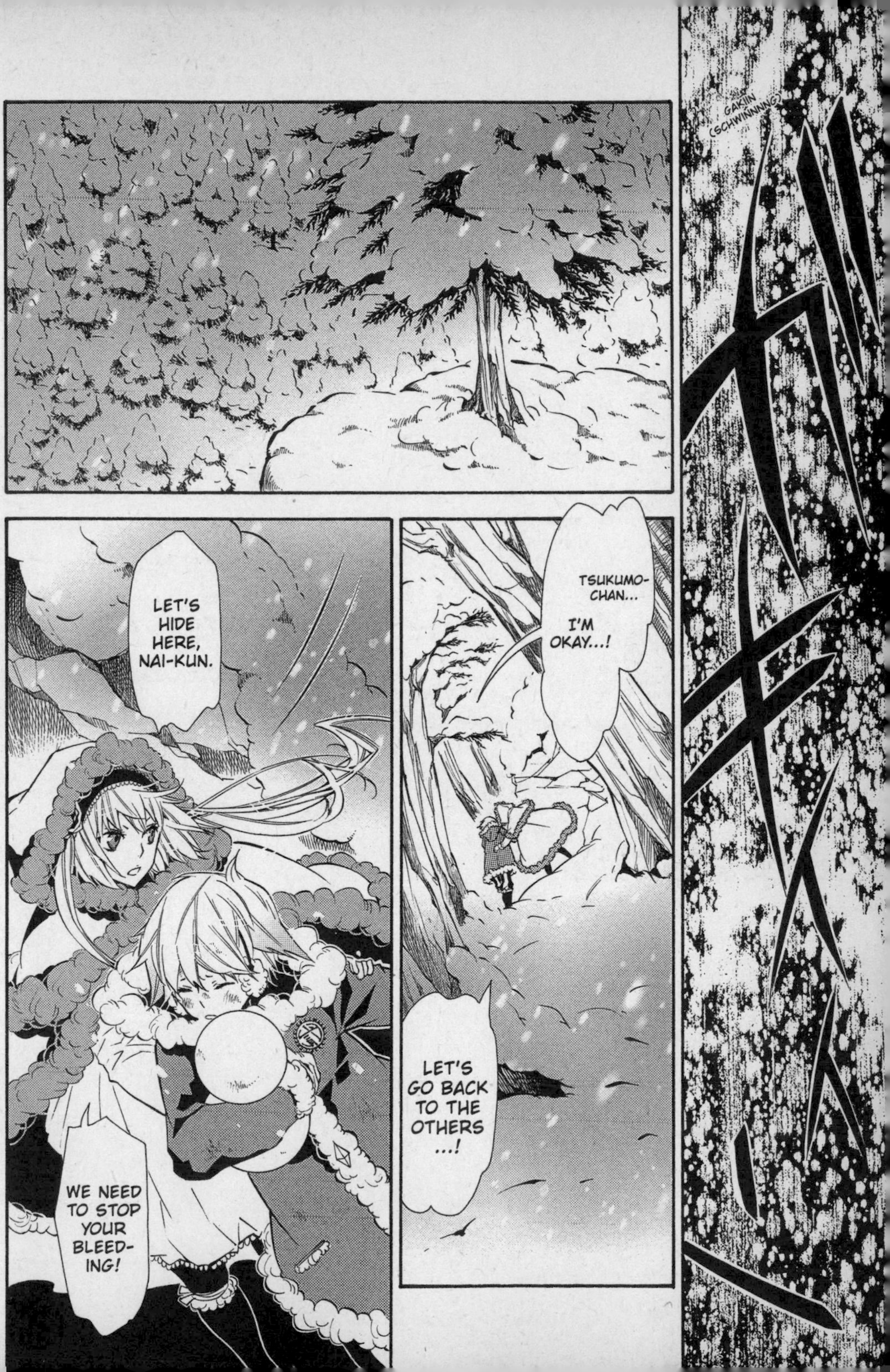
GAKIIN (SCHWIÑNNNG)
TSUKUMO-CHAN...
I'M OKAY...!
LET'S GO BACK TO THE OTHERS ...!
LET'S HIDE HERE, NAI-KUN.
WE NEED TO STOP YOUR BLEED-ING!

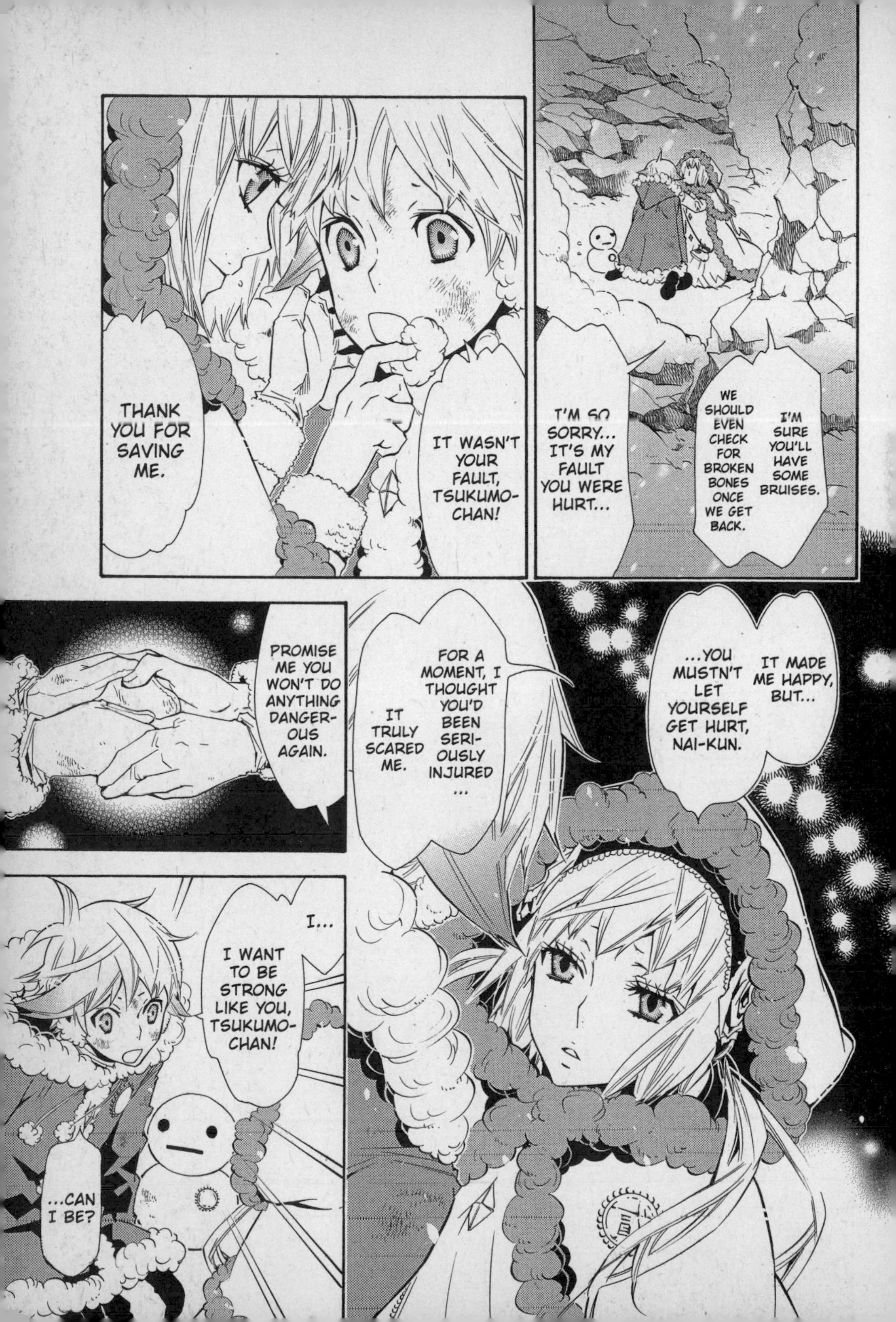
I'M SURE YOU'LL HAVE SOME BRUISES.
WE SHOULD EVEN CHECK FOR BROKEN BONES ONCE WE GET BACK.
I'M SO SORRY... IT'S MY FAULT YOU WERE HURT...
IT WASN'T YOUR FAULT, TSUKUMO-CHAN!
THANK YOU FOR SAVING ME.
IT MADE ME HAPPY, BUT...
...YOU MUSTN'T LET YOURSELF GET HURT, NAI-KUN.
FOR A MOMENT, I THOUGHT YOU'D BEEN SERIOUSLY INJURED...
IT TRULY SCARED ME.
PROMISE ME YOU WON'T DO ANYTHING DANGEROUS AGAIN.
I...
I WANT TO BE STRONG LIKE YOU, TSUKUMO-CHAN!
...CAN I BE?

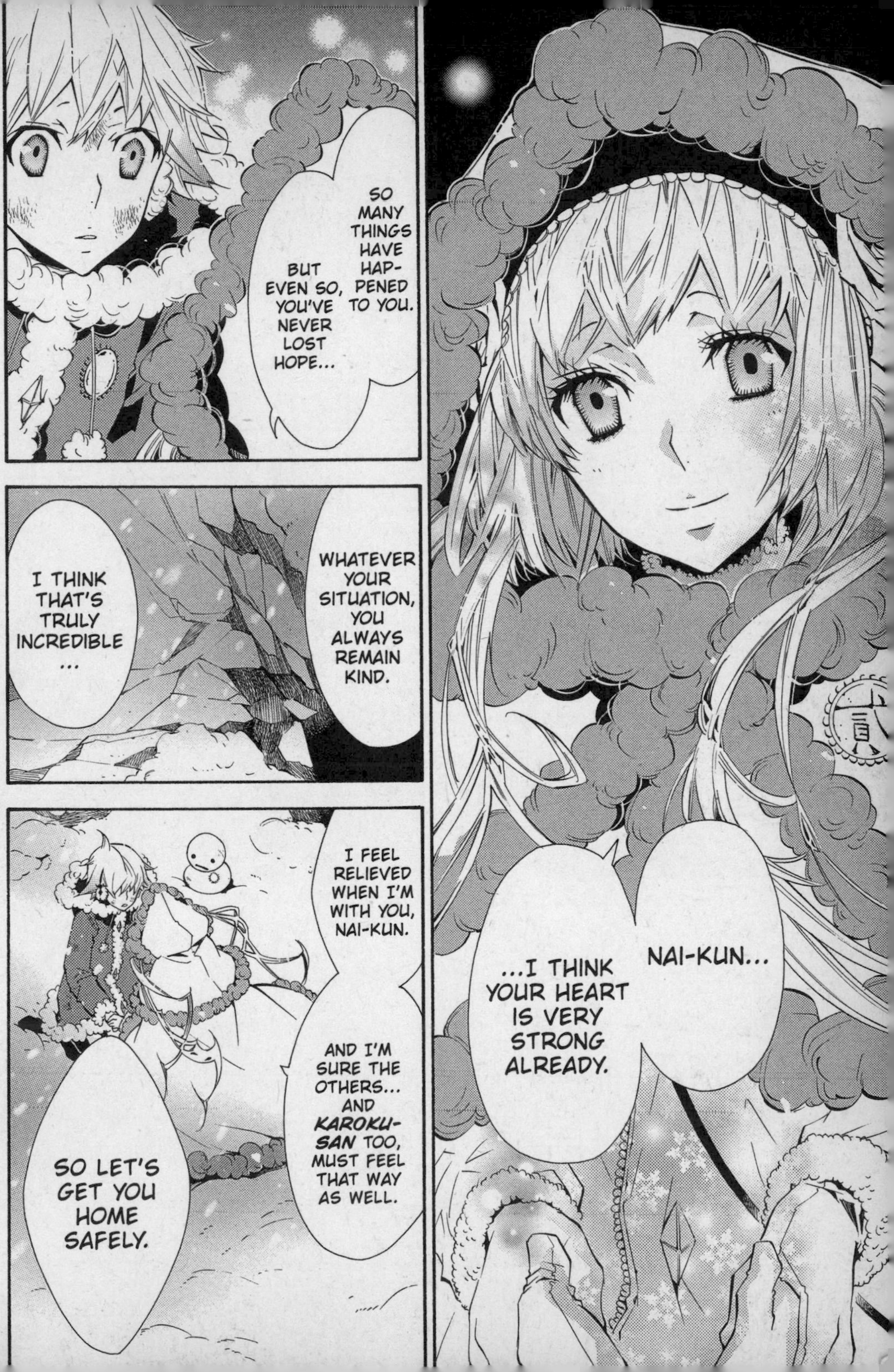
NAI-KUN...
...I THINK YOUR HEART IS VERY STRONG ALREADY.
SO MANY THINGS HAVE HAP-PENED TO YOU.
BUT EVEN SO, YOU'VE NEVER LOST HOPE...
WHATEVER YOUR SITUATION, YOU ALWAYS REMAIN KIND.
I THINK THAT'S TRULY INCREDIBLE...
I FEEL RELIEVED WHEN I'M WITH YOU, NAI-KUN.
AND I'M SURE THE OTHERS... AND KAROKU-SAN TOO, MUST FEEL THAT WAY AS WELL.
SO LET'S GET YOU HOME SAFELY.

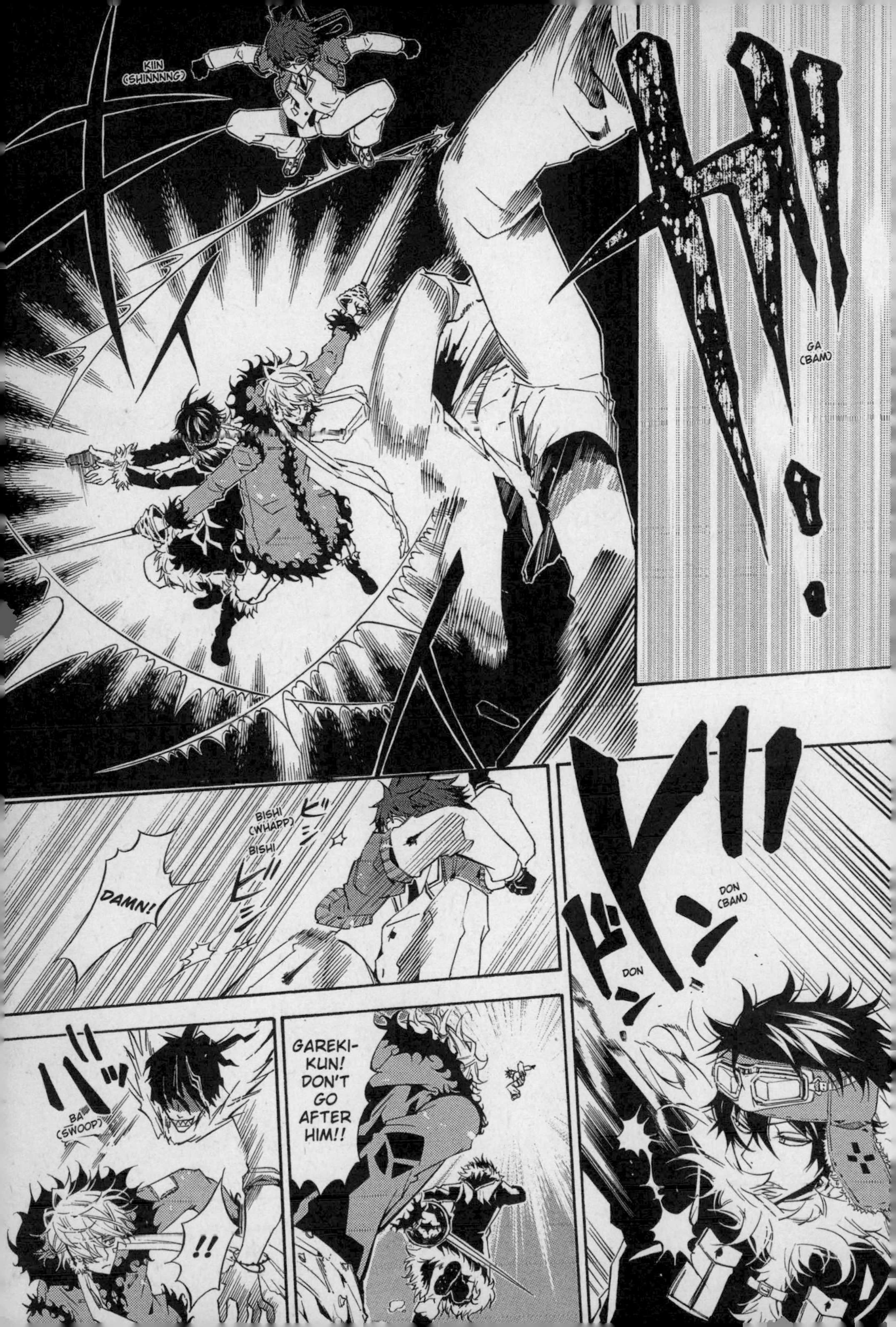
GA (BAM)
KIIN (SHINNNNG)
DON (BAM)
DON
BISHI (WHAPP)
BISHI
DAMN!
GAREKI-KUN! DON'T GO AFTER HIM!!
BA (SWOOP)
!!

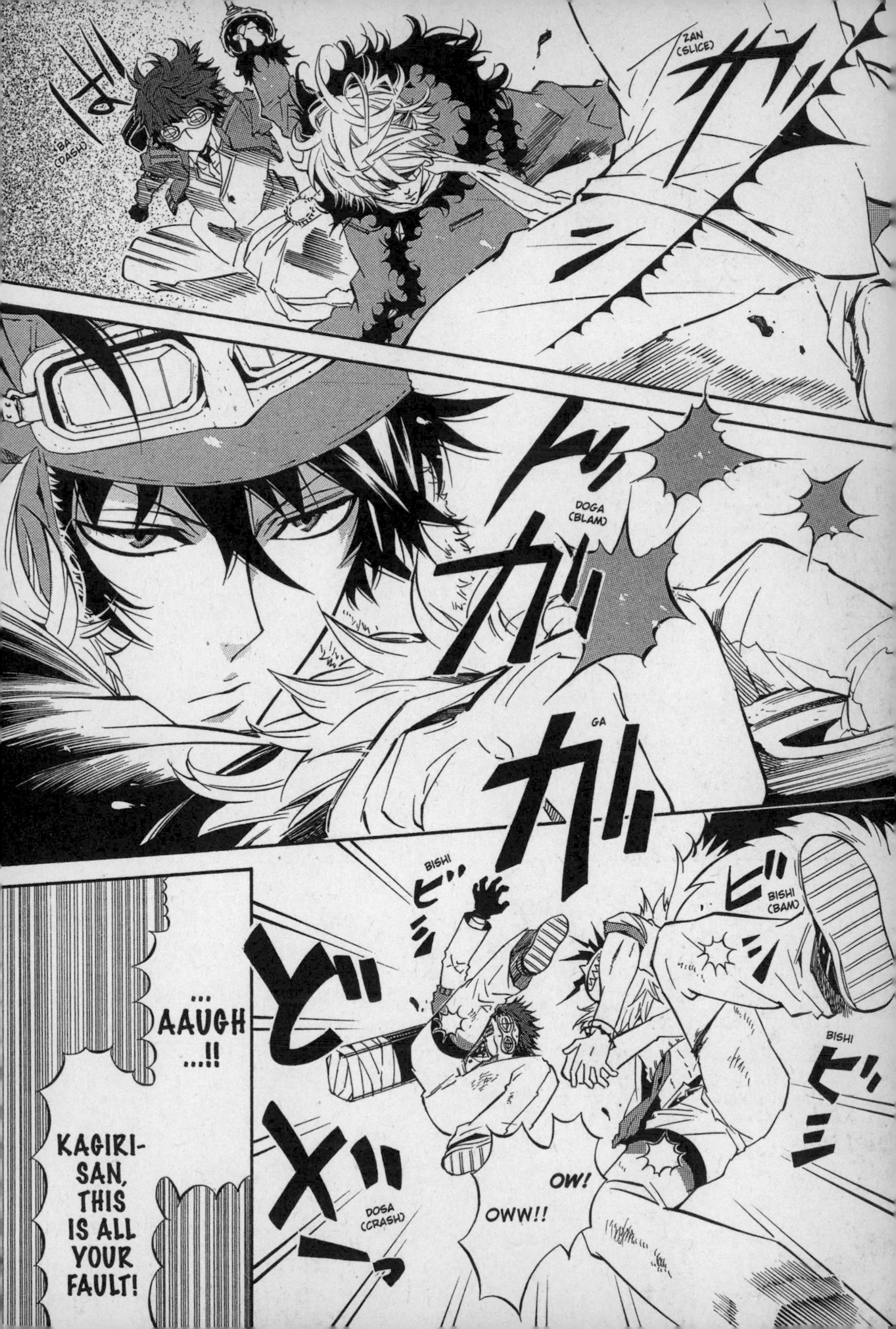
ZAN (SLICE)
BA (DASH)
DOGA (BLAM)
GA
BISHI (BAM)
BISHI
BISHI
OW!
OWW!!
DOSA (CRASH)
... AAÜGH ...!!
KAGIRI-SAN, THIS IS ALL YOUR FAULT!

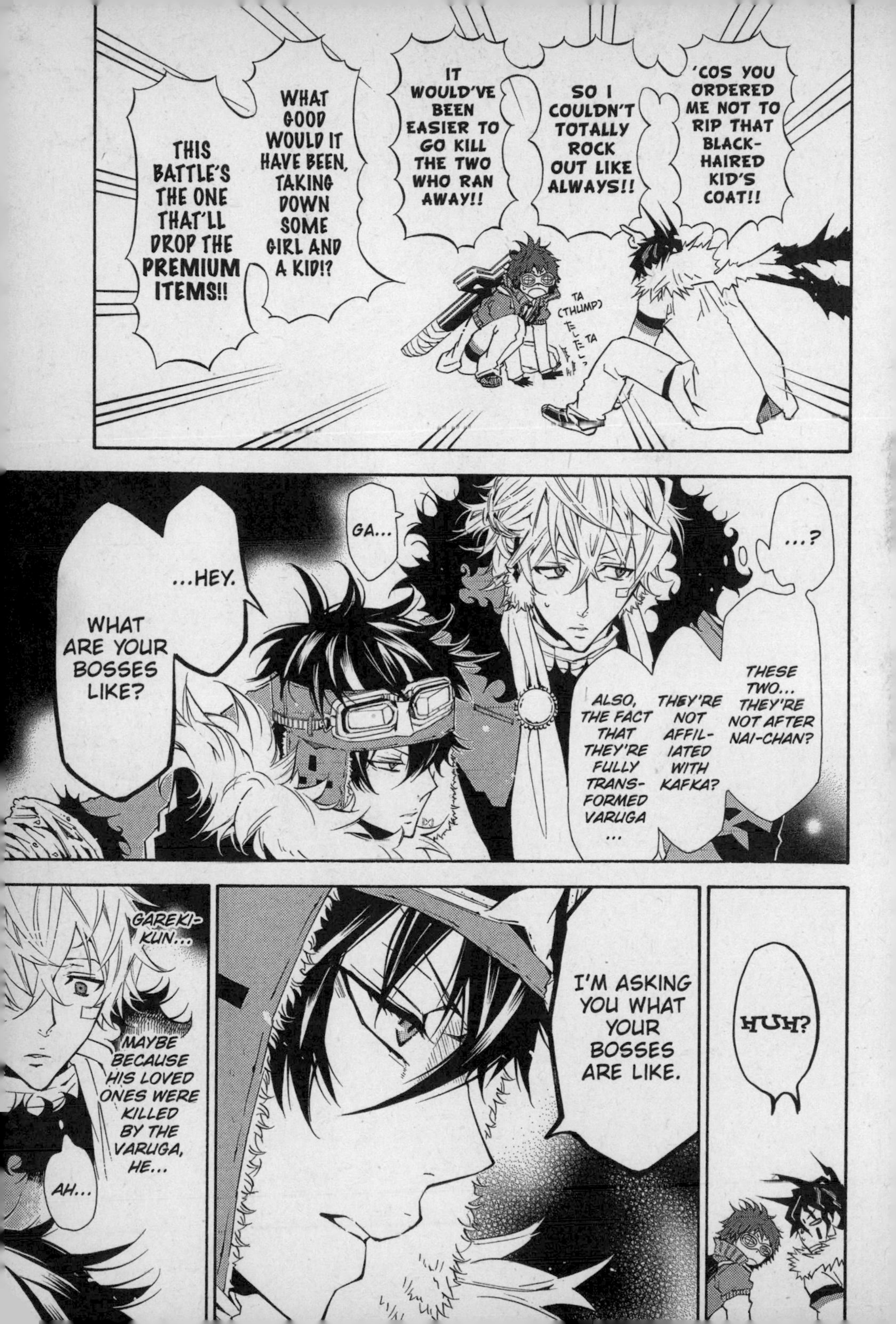
'COS YOU ORDERED ME NOT TO RIP THAT BLACK-HAIRED KID'S COAT!!
SO I COULDN'T TOTALLY ROCK OUT LIKE ALWAYS!!
IT WOULD'VE BEEN EASIER TO GO KILL THE TWO WHO RAN AWAY!!
WHAT GOOD WOULD IT HAVE BEEN, TAKING DOWN SOME GIRL AND A KID!?
THIS BATTLE'S THE ONE THAT'LL DROP THE PREMIUM ITEMS!!
TA (THUMP)
TA
...?
THESE TWO... THEY'RE NOT AFTER NAI-CHAN?
THEY'RE NOT AFFIL-IATED WITH KAFKA?
ALSO, THE FACT THAT THEY'RE FULLY TRANS-FORMED VARUGA ...
GA...
...HEY.
WHAT ARE YOUR BOSSES LIKE?
HUH?
I'M ASKING YOU WHAT YOUR BOSSES ARE LIKE.
GAREKI-KUN...
MAYBE BECAUSE HIS LOVED ONES WERE KILLED BY THE VARUGA, HE...
AH...

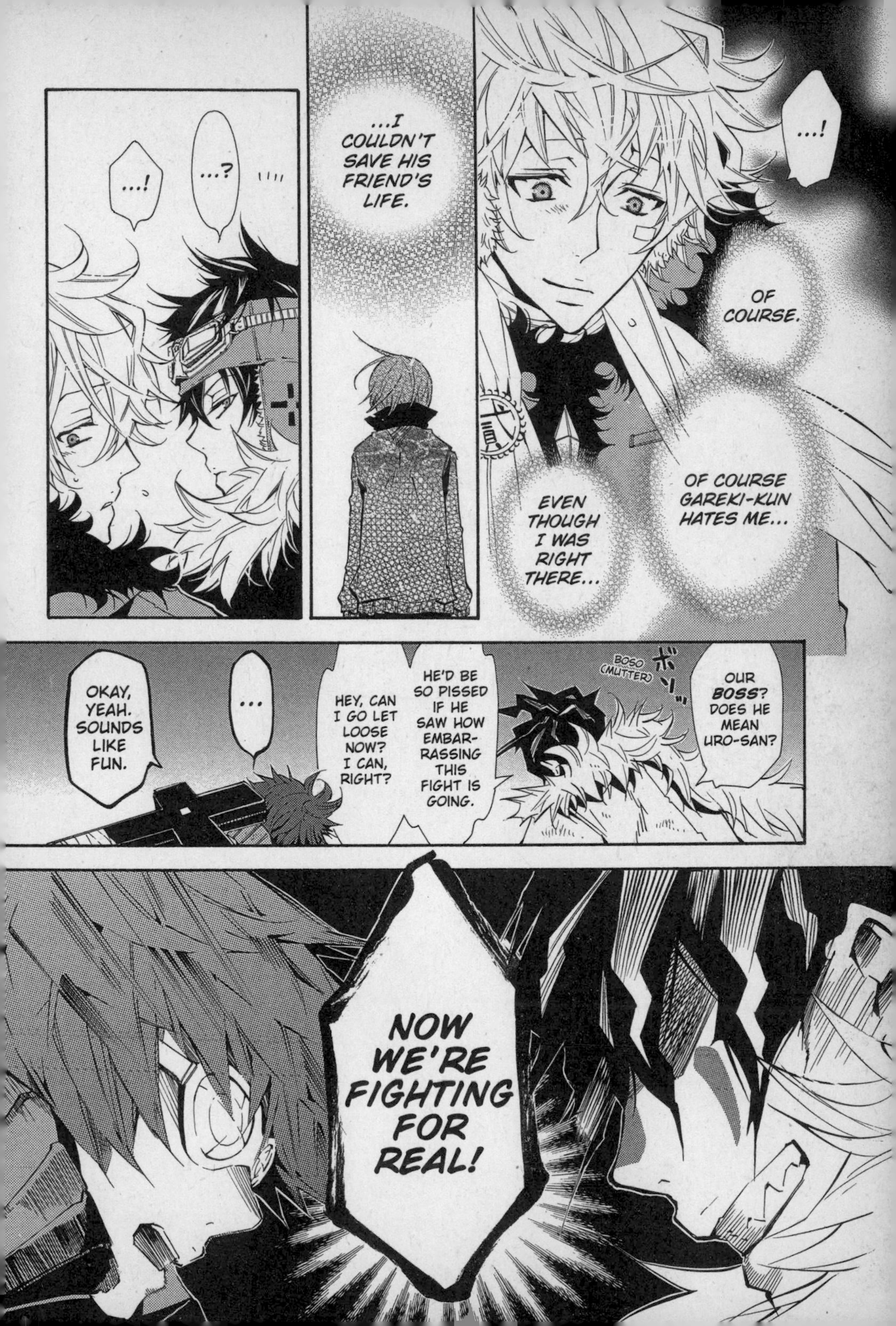
...!
OF COURSE.
OF COURSE GAREKI-KUN HATES ME...
EVEN THOUGH I WAS RIGHT THERE...
...I COULDN'T SAVE HIS FRIEND'S LIFE.
...?
...!
OUR BOSS? DOES HE MEAN URO-SAN?
BOSO (MUTTER)
HE'D BE SO PISSED IF HE SAW HOW EMBARRASSING THIS FIGHT IS GOING.
HEY, CAN I GO LET LOOSE NOW? I CAN, RIGHT?
...
OKAY, YEAH. SOUNDS LIKE FUN.
NOW WE'RE FIGHTING FOR REAL!

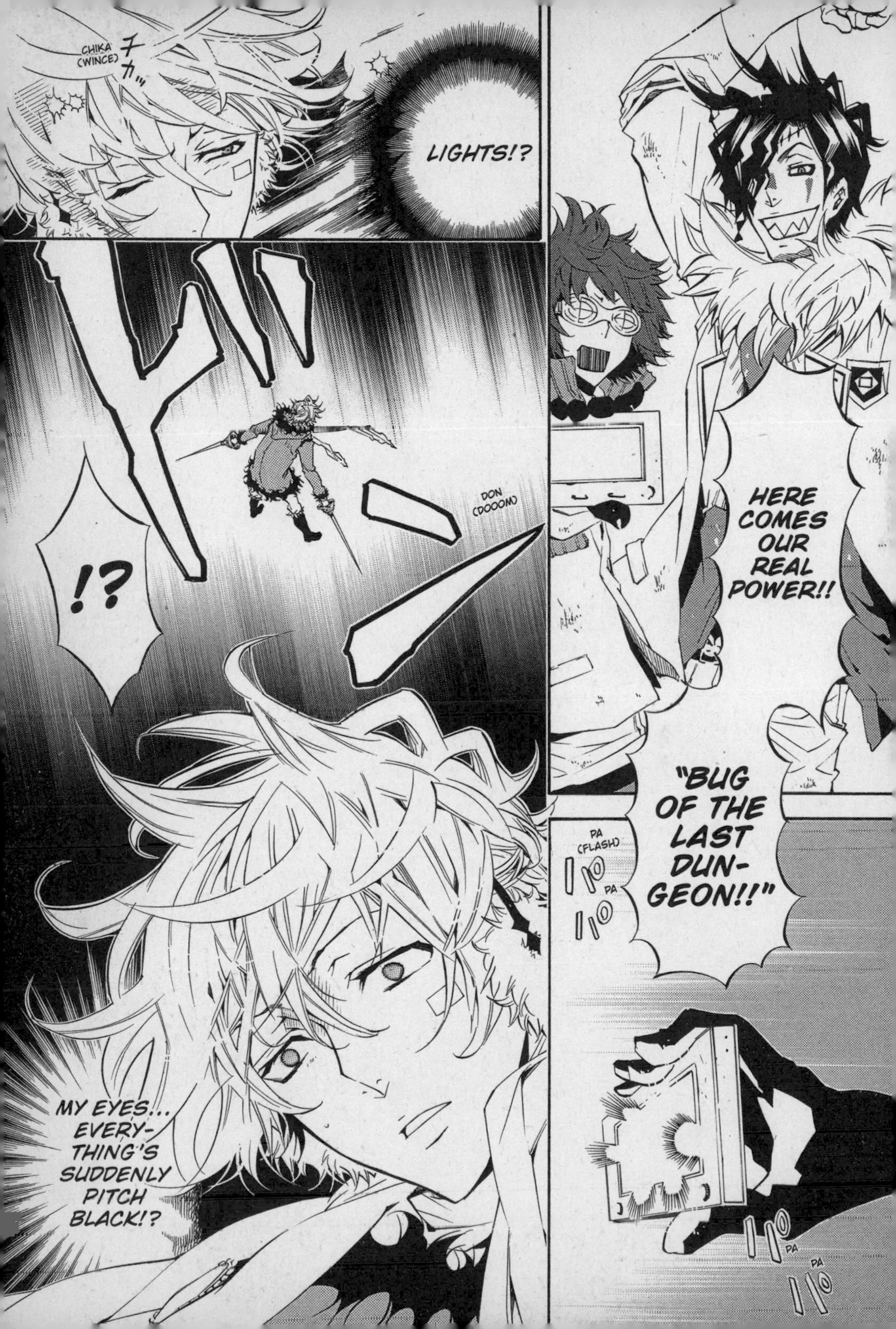
HERE COMES OUR REAL POWER!!
"BUG OF THE LAST DUNGEON!!"
PA (FLASH)
PA
PA
PA
CHIKA (WINCE)
LIGHTS!?
!?
DON (DOOOM)
MY EYES... EVERYTHING'S SUDDENLY PITCH BLACK!?

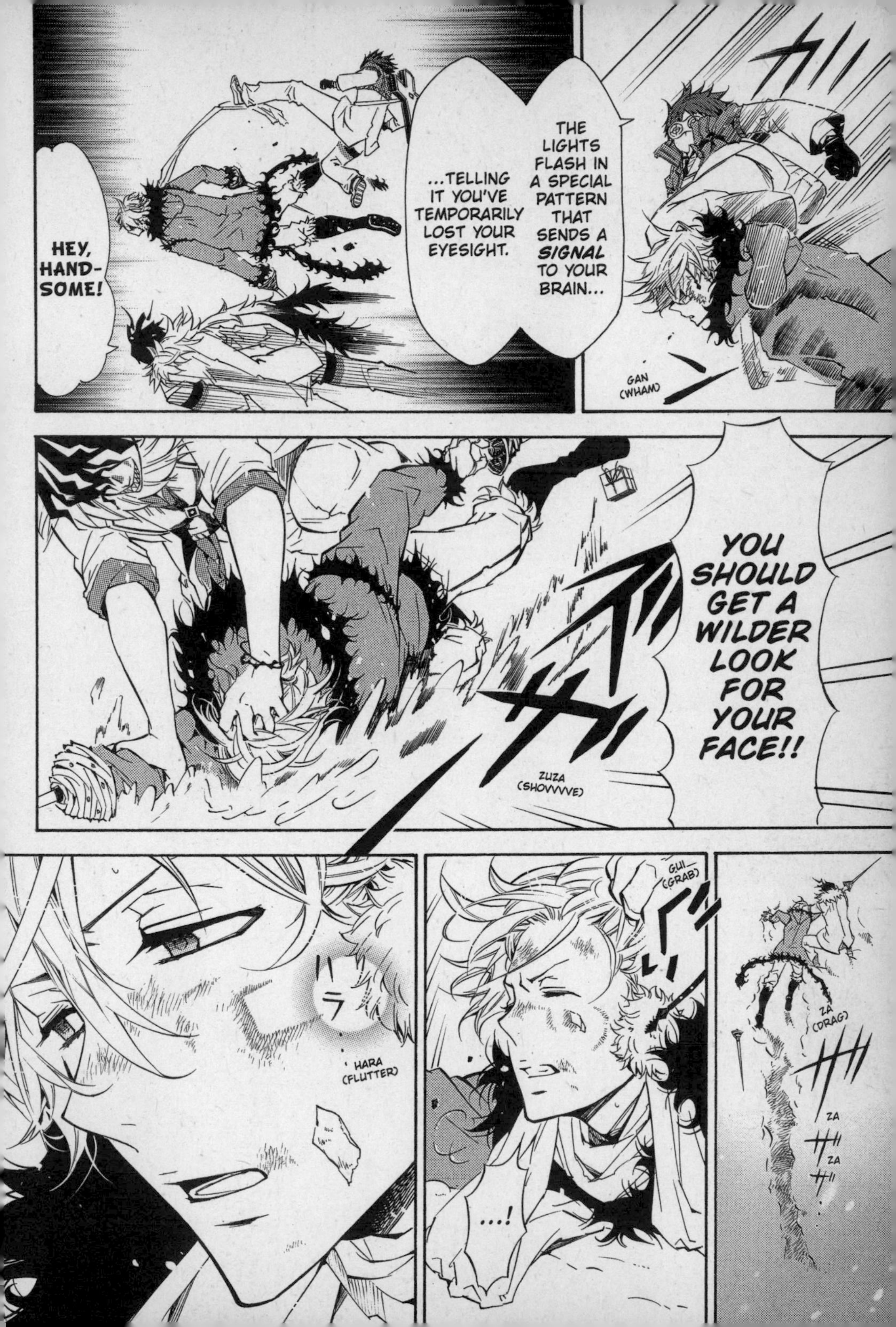
GAN (WHAM)
THE LIGHTS FLASH IN A SPECIAL PATTERN THAT SENDS A *SIGNAL* TO YOUR BRAIN...
...TELLING IT YOU'VE TEMPORARILY LOST YOUR EYESIGHT.
HEY, HAND-SOME!
YOU SHOULD GET A WILDER LOOK FOR YOUR FACE!!
ZUZA (SHOVVVVE)
ZA (DRAG)
ZA
ZA
GUI (GRAB)
...!
HARA (FLUTTER)

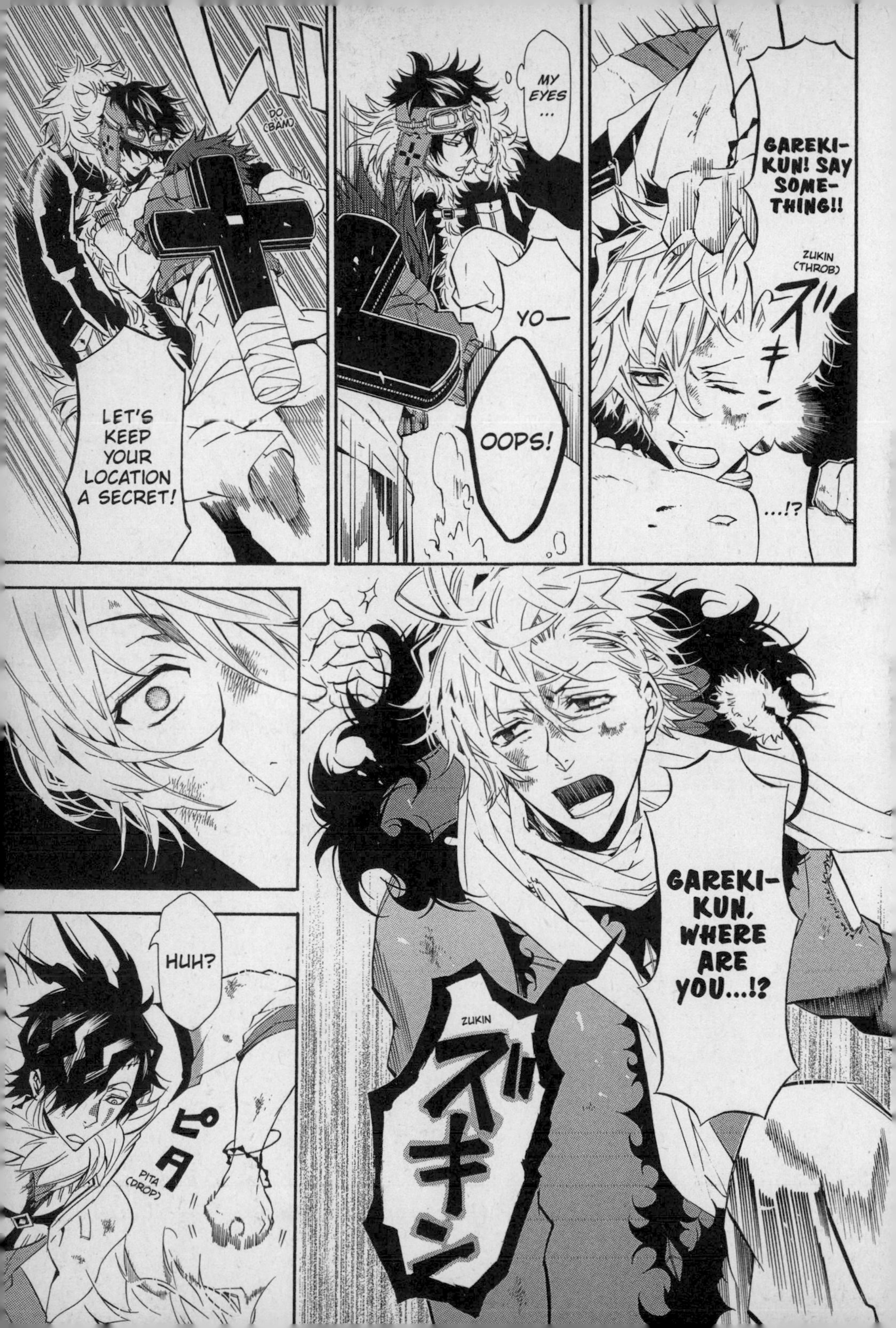
GAREKI-KUN! SAY SOMETHING!!
ZUKIN (THROB)
ズキン
...!?
MY EYES ...
YO—
OOPS!
DO (BAM)
LET'S KEEP YOUR LOCATION A SECRET!
GAREKI-KUN, WHERE ARE YOU...!?
ZUKIN
ズキン
HUH?
ピタ
PITA (DROP)

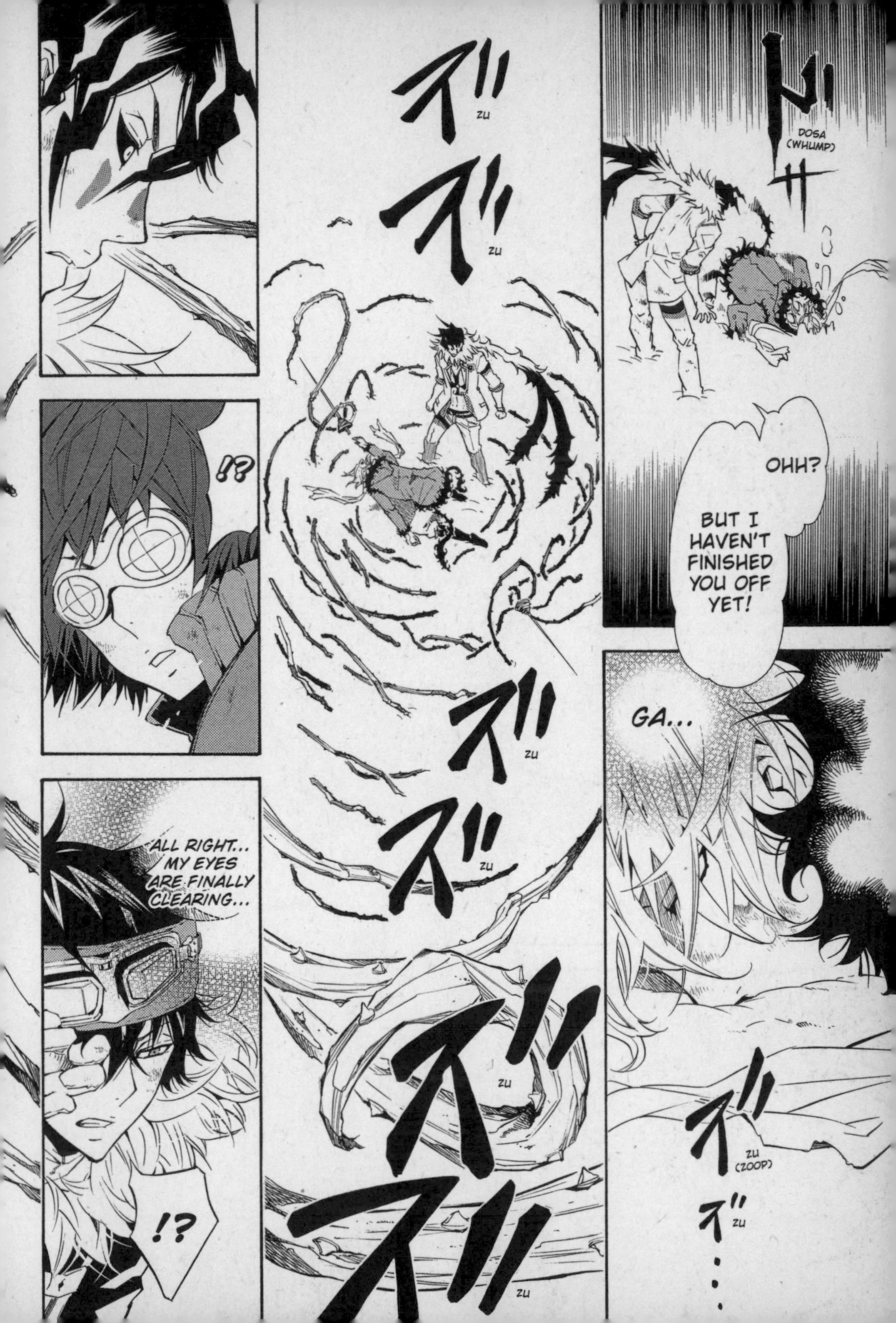
DOSA (WHUMP)
OHH?
BUT I HAVEN'T FINISHED YOU OFF YET!
GA...
ZU (ZOOP)
ZU
ZU
ZU
ZU
ZU
ZU
ZU
!?
ALL RIGHT... MY EYES ARE FINALLY CLEARING...
!?

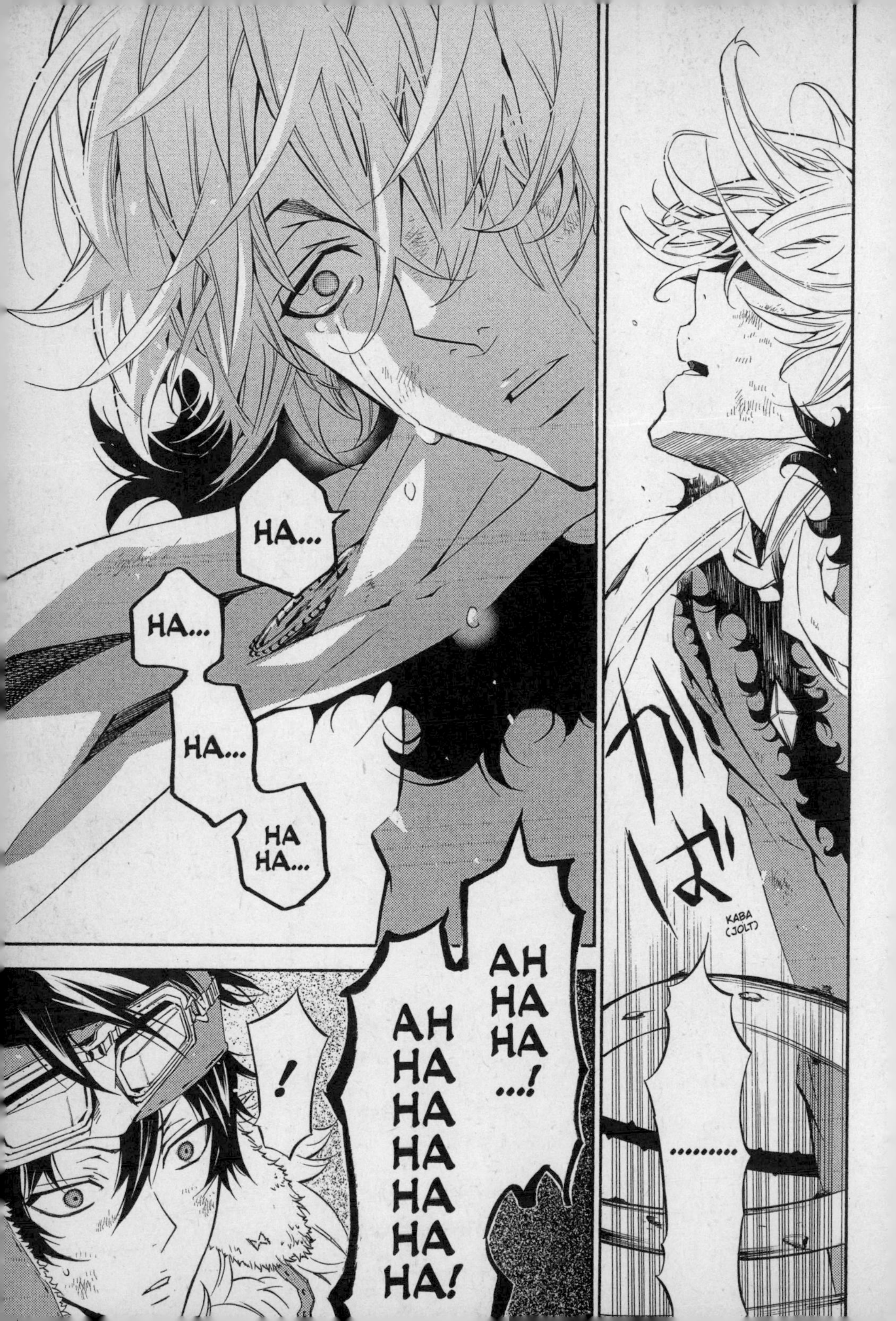
KABA (JOLT)
HA...
HA...
HA...
HA HA...
....
AH HA HA ...!
AH HA HA HA HA HA HA HA HA!
!

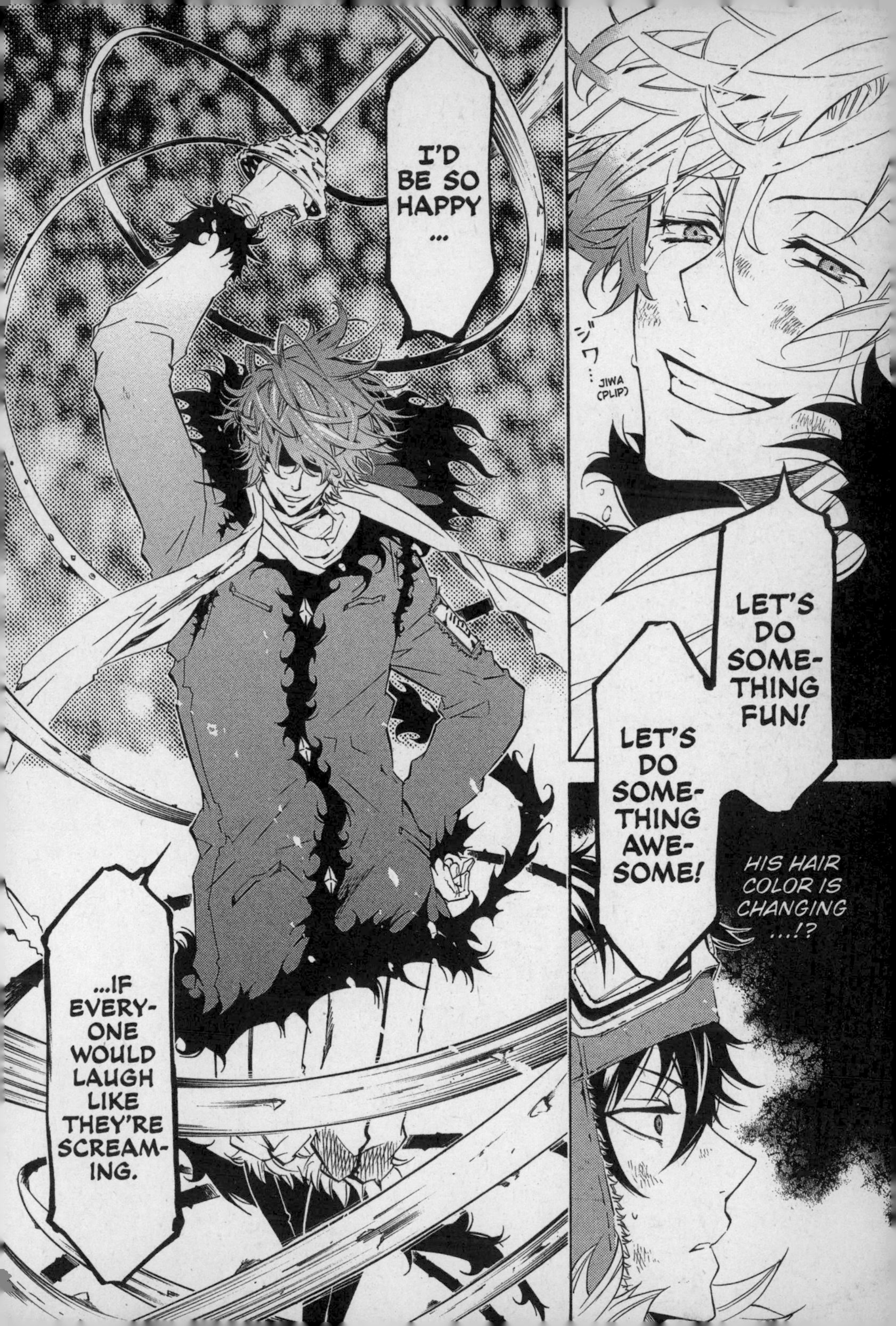
ジワ…
JIWA (PLIP)
LET'S DO SOME-THING FUN!
LET'S DO SOME-THING AWE-SOME!
HIS HAIR COLOR IS CHANGING ...!?
I'D BE SO HAPPY ...
...IF EVERY-ONE WOULD LAUGH LIKE THEY'RE SCREAM-ING.

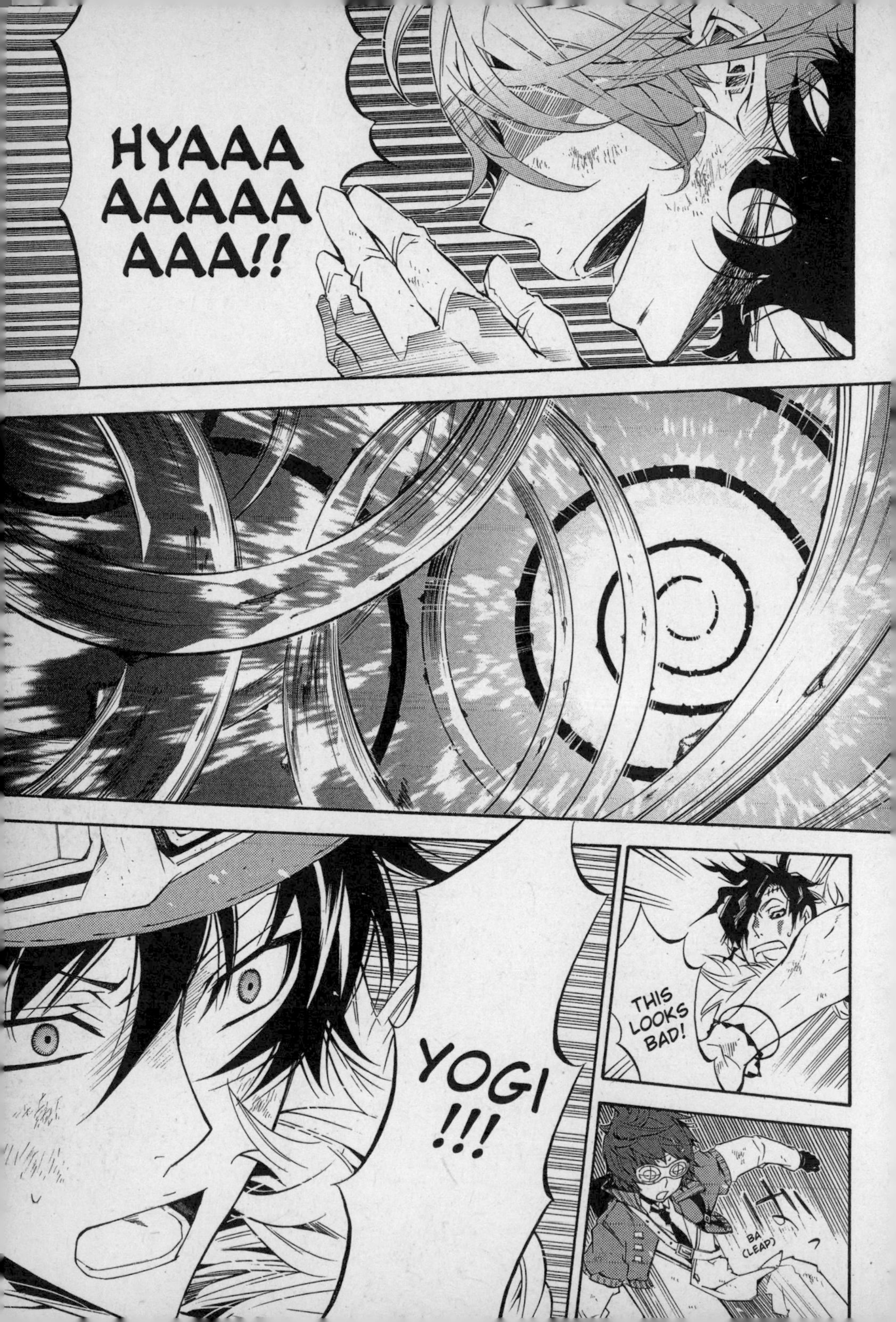
HYAAA AAAAA AAA!!
THIS LOOKS BAD!
BA (LEAP)
YOGI !!!

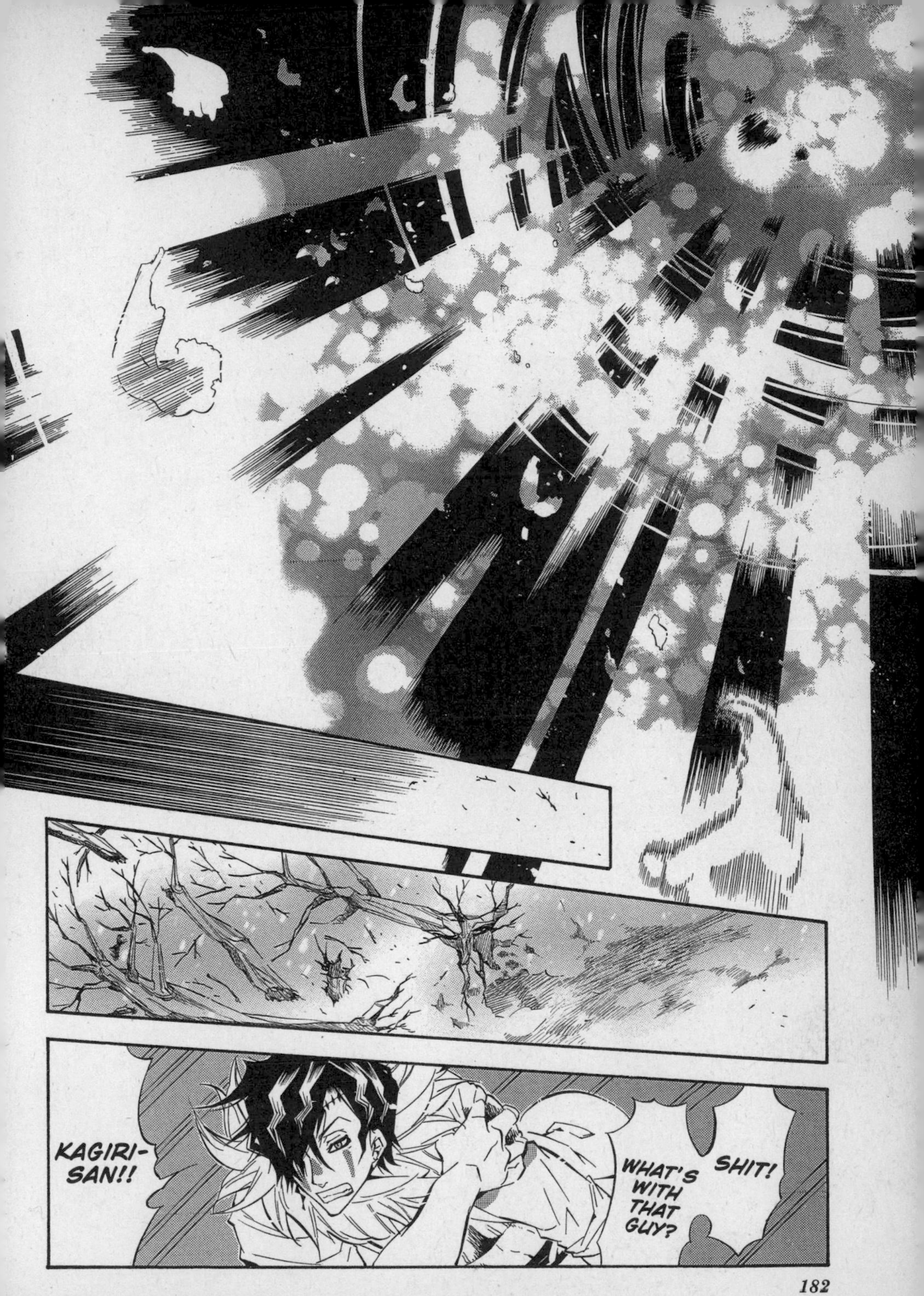
SHIT!
WHAT'S WITH THAT GUY?
KAGIRI-SAN!!

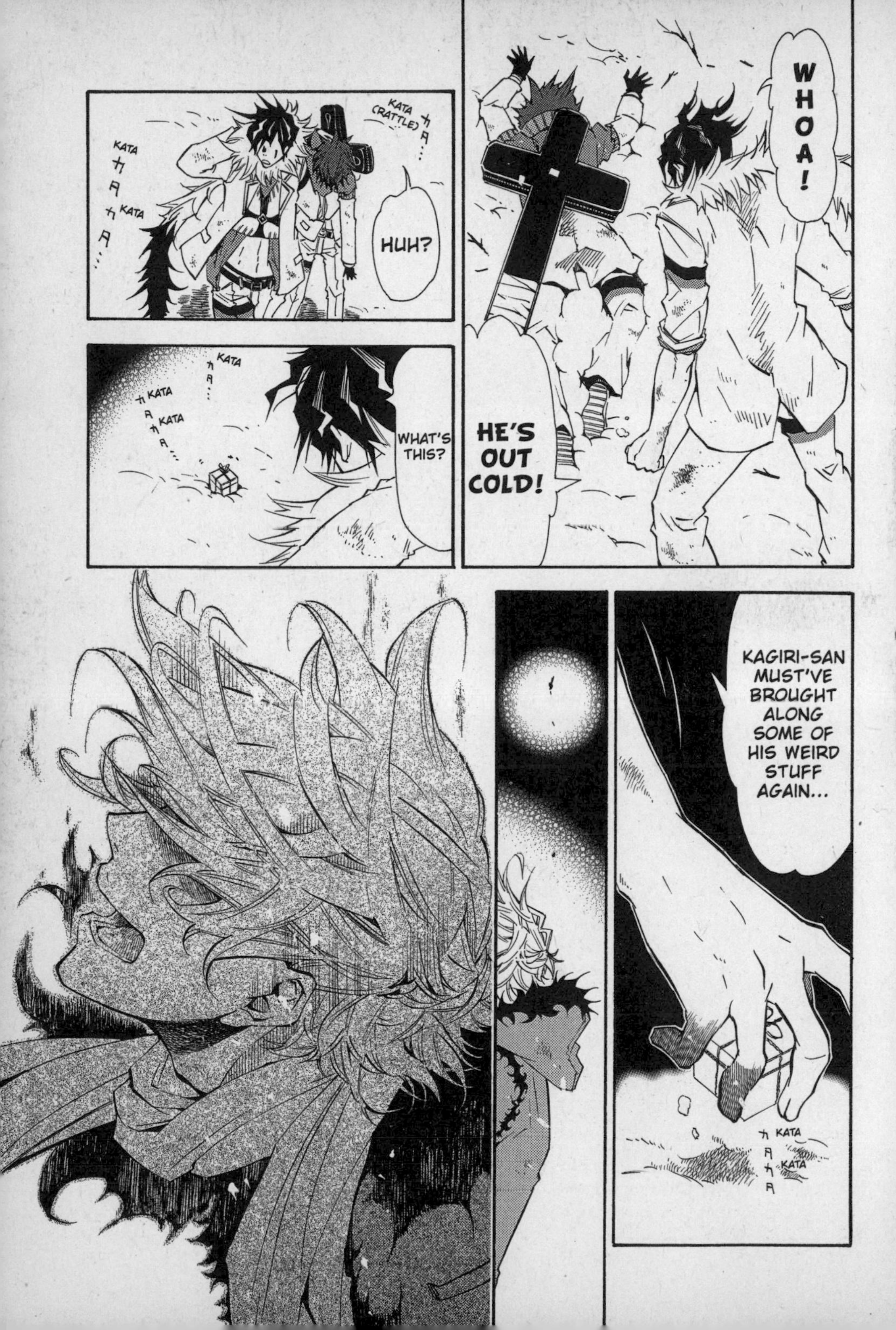
WHOA!
HE'S OUT COLD!
KATA (RATTLE)
カタ…
KATA
カタ
KATA
カタ…
HUH?
KATA
カタ…
KATA
カタ
KATA
カタ…
WHAT'S THIS?
KAGIRI-SAN MUST'VE BROUGHT ALONG SOME OF HIS WEIRD STUFF AGAIN...
KATA
カタ
KATA
カタ

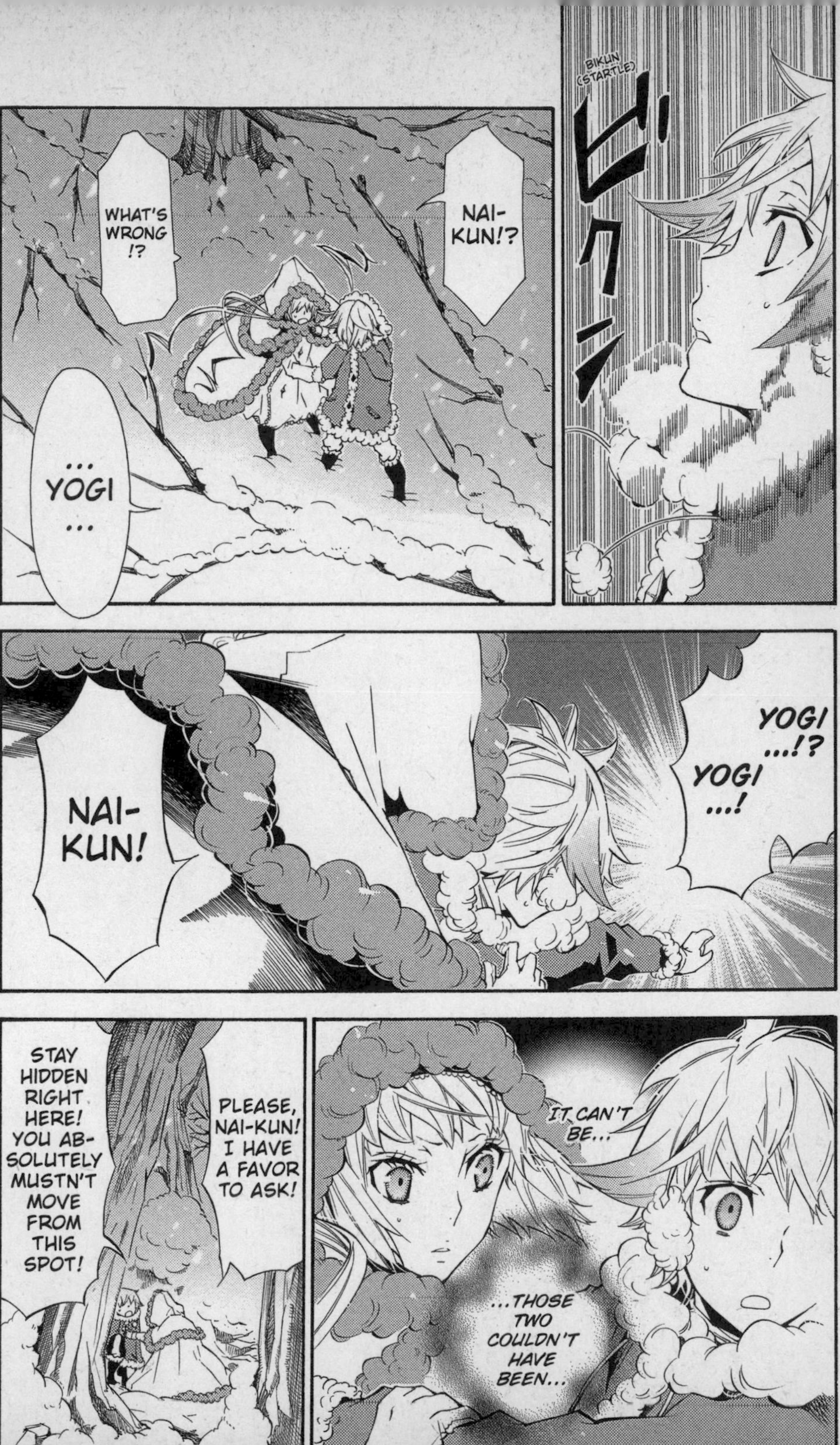
BIKUN (STARTLE)
NAI-KUN!?
WHAT'S WRONG!?
...YOGI...
YOGI...!?
YOGI...!
NAI-KUN!
IT CAN'T BE...
...THOSE TWO COULDN'T HAVE BEEN...
PLEASE, NAI-KUN! I HAVE A FAVOR TO ASK!
STAY HIDDEN RIGHT HERE! YOU ABSOLUTELY MUSTN'T MOVE FROM THIS SPOT!

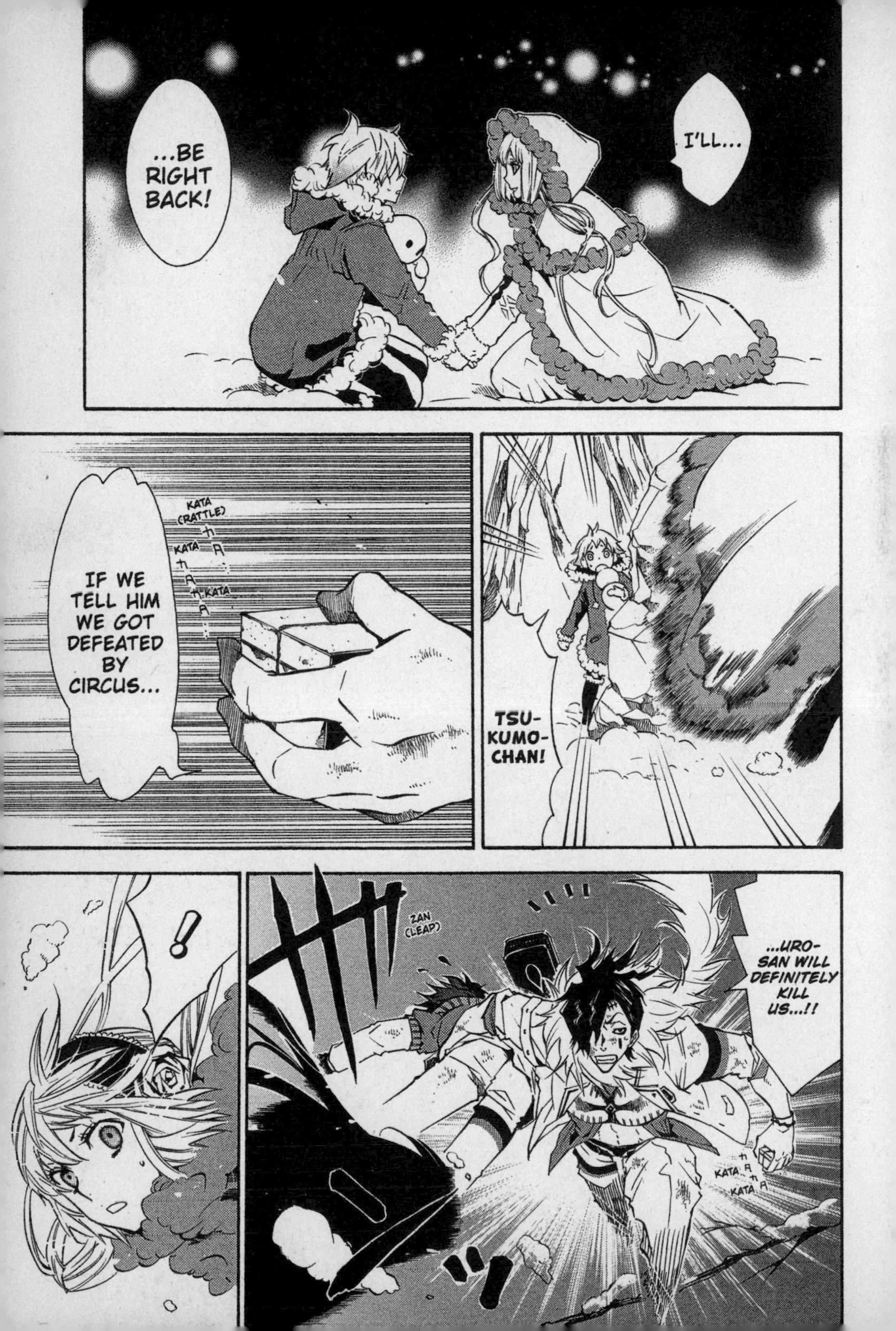
I'LL...
...BE RIGHT BACK!
TSU-KUMO-CHAN!
IF WE TELL HIM WE GOT DEFEATED BY CIRCUS...
KATA (RATTLE) KATA KATA
...URO-SAN WILL DEFINITELY KILL US...!!
ZAN (LEAP)
KATA KATA
!

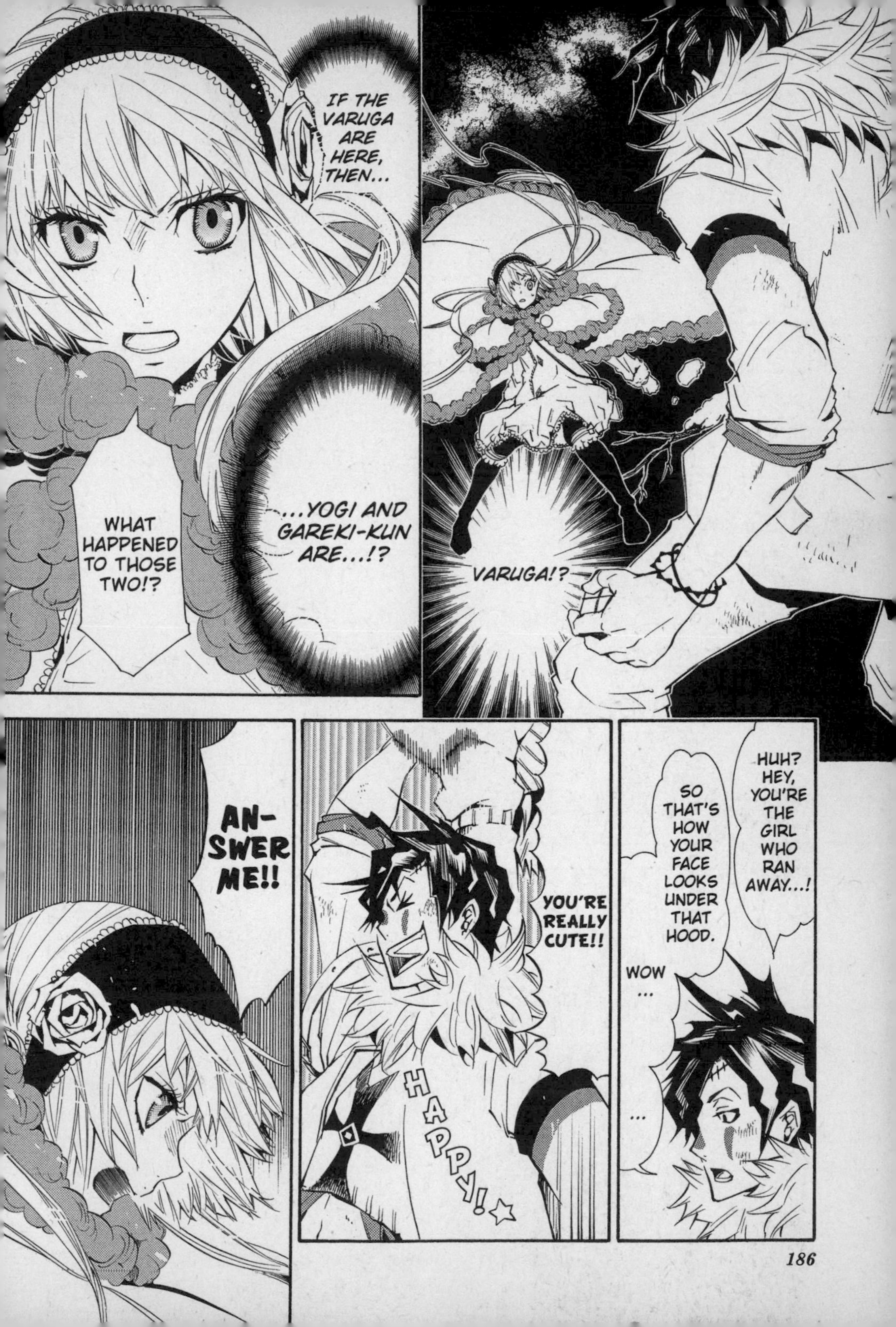
VARUGA!?
IF THE VARUGA ARE HERE, THEN...
...YOGI AND GAREKI-KUN ARE...!?
WHAT HAPPENED TO THOSE TWO!?
HUH? HEY, YOU'RE THE GIRL WHO RAN AWAY...!
SO THAT'S HOW YOUR FACE LOOKS UNDER THAT HOOD.
WOW ...
...
YOU'RE REALLY CUTE!!
HAPPY!☆
AN-SWER ME!!

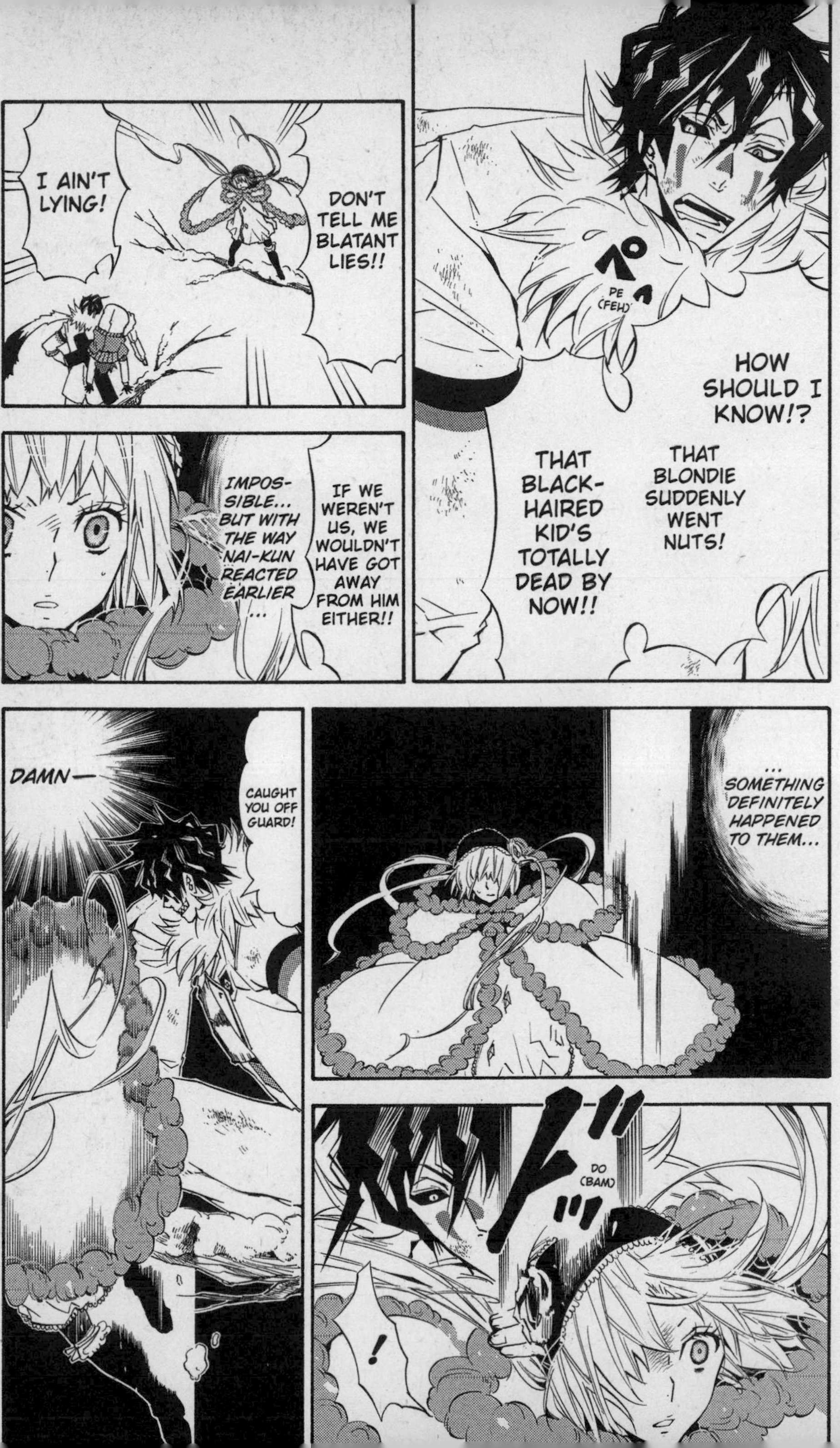
PE (FEH)
HOW SHOULD I KNOW!?
THAT BLONDIE SUDDENLY WENT NUTS!
THAT BLACK-HAIRED KID'S TOTALLY DEAD BY NOW!!
DON'T TELL ME BLATANT LIES!!
I AIN'T LYING!
IF WE WEREN'T US, WE WOULDN'T HAVE GOT AWAY FROM HIM EITHER!!
IMPOSSIBLE... BUT WITH THE WAY NAI-KUN REACTED EARLIER...
...SOMETHING DEFINITELY HAPPENED TO THEM...
DO (BAM)
!
CAUGHT YOU OFF GUARD!
DAMN—

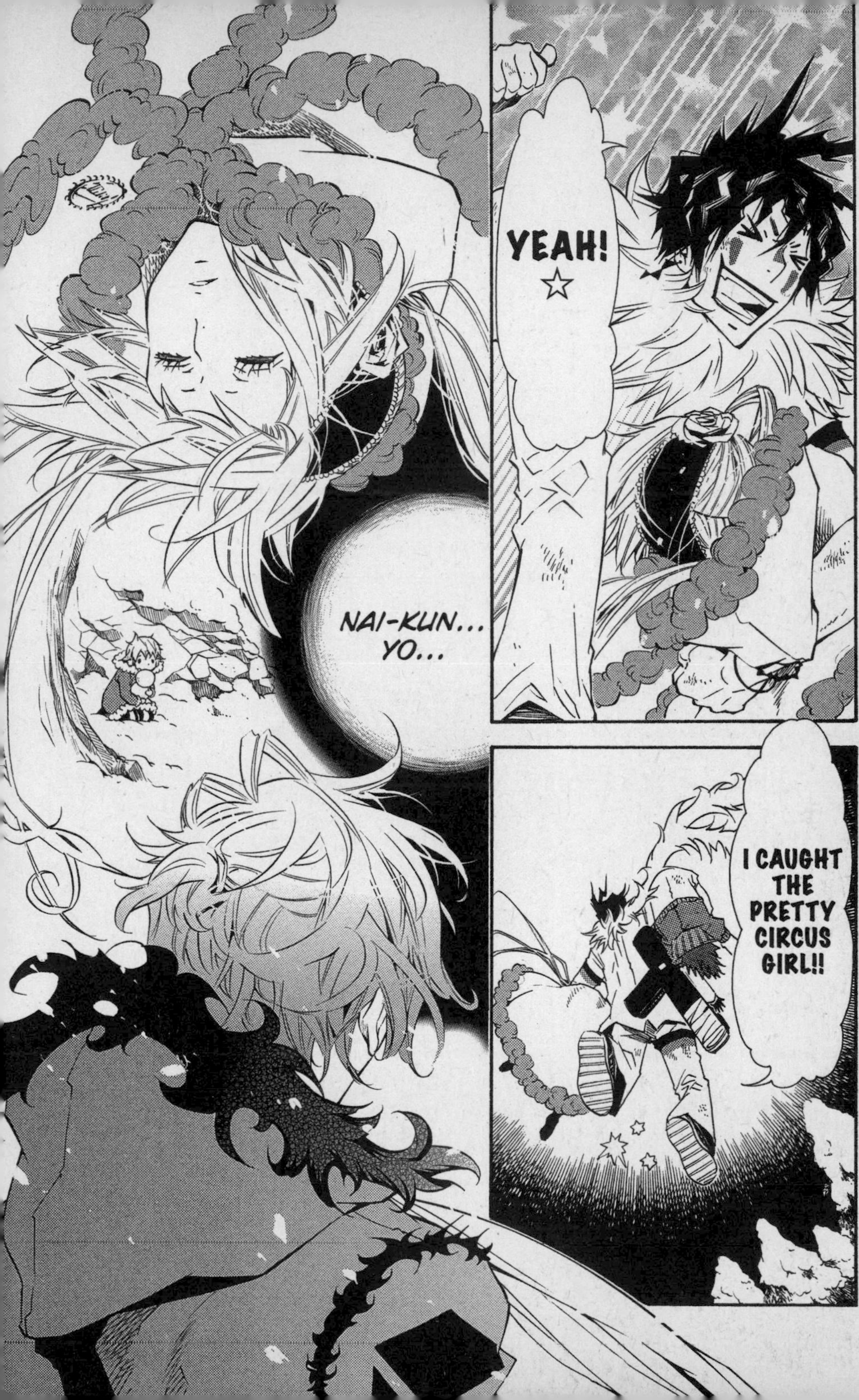
YEAH! ☆
I CAUGHT THE PRETTY CIRCUS GIRL!!
NAI-KUN... YO...

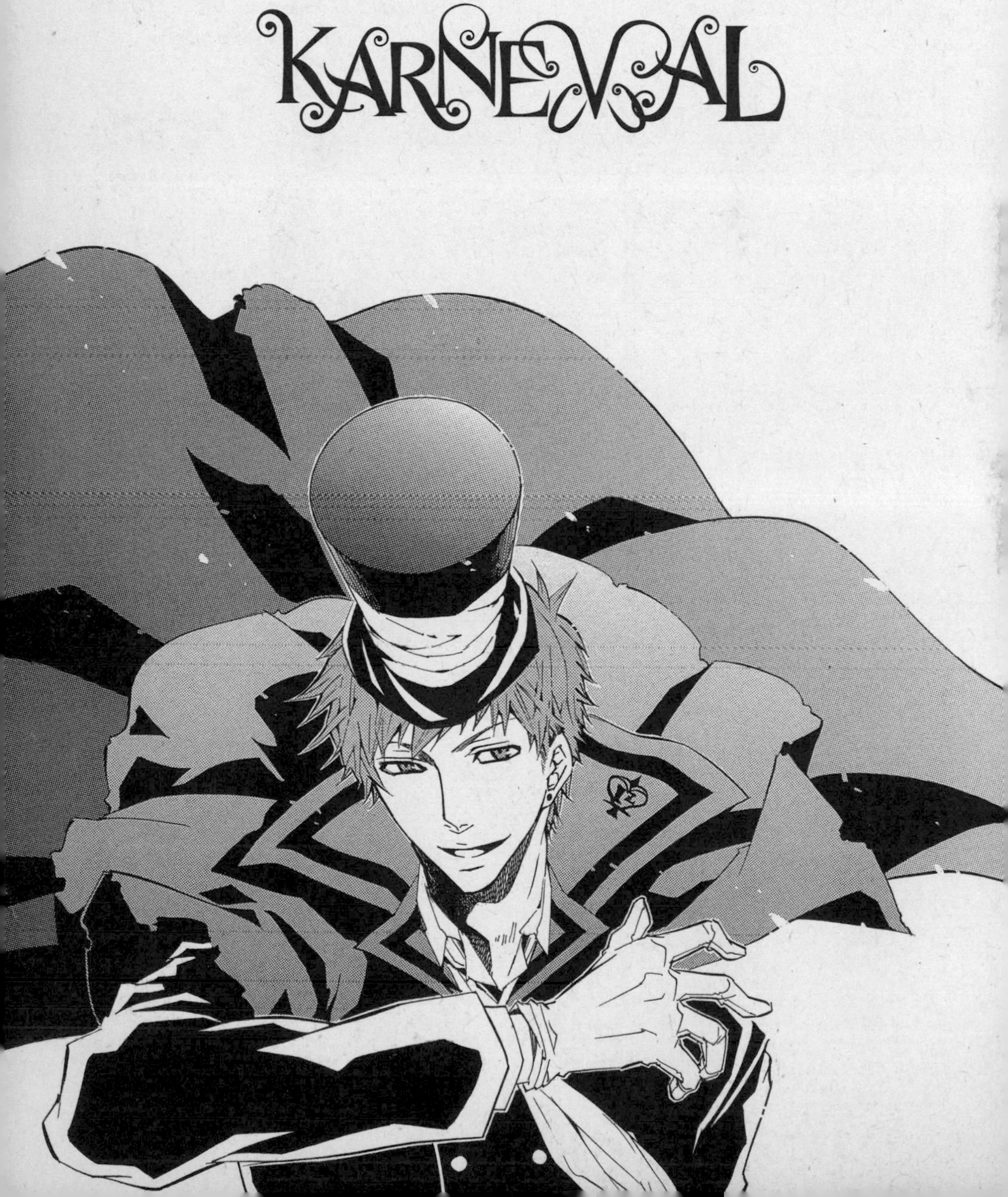
KARNEVAL

Bonus Comic 1 - The Professional

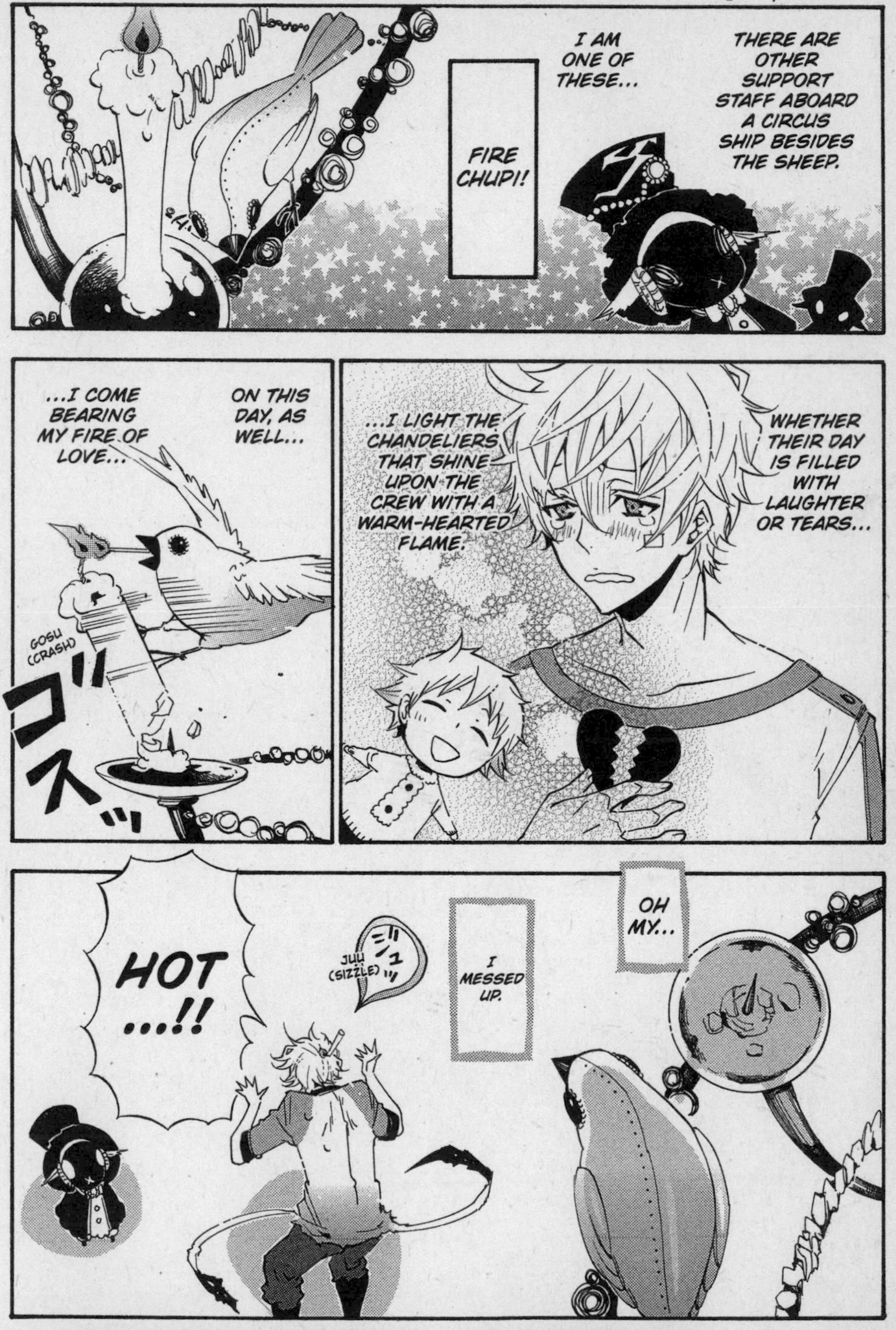
THERE ARE OTHER SUPPORT STAFF ABOARD A CIRCUS SHIP BESIDES THE SHEEP.
I AM ONE OF THESE...
FIRE CHUPI!
WHETHER THEIR DAY IS FILLED WITH LAUGHTER OR TEARS...
...I LIGHT THE CHANDELIERS THAT SHINE UPON THE CREW WITH A WARM-HEARTED FLAME.
ON THIS DAY, AS WELL...
...I COME BEARING MY FIRE OF LOVE...
GOSU (CRASH)
ゴスッ
OH MY...
I MESSED UP.
ジュ〜ッ
JUU (SIZZLE)
HOT ...!!

☆ I APPEAR SOMEWHERE IN VOLUME 1! SEE IF YOU CAN FIND ME. ☆

Bonus Comic 2 - Type ♥

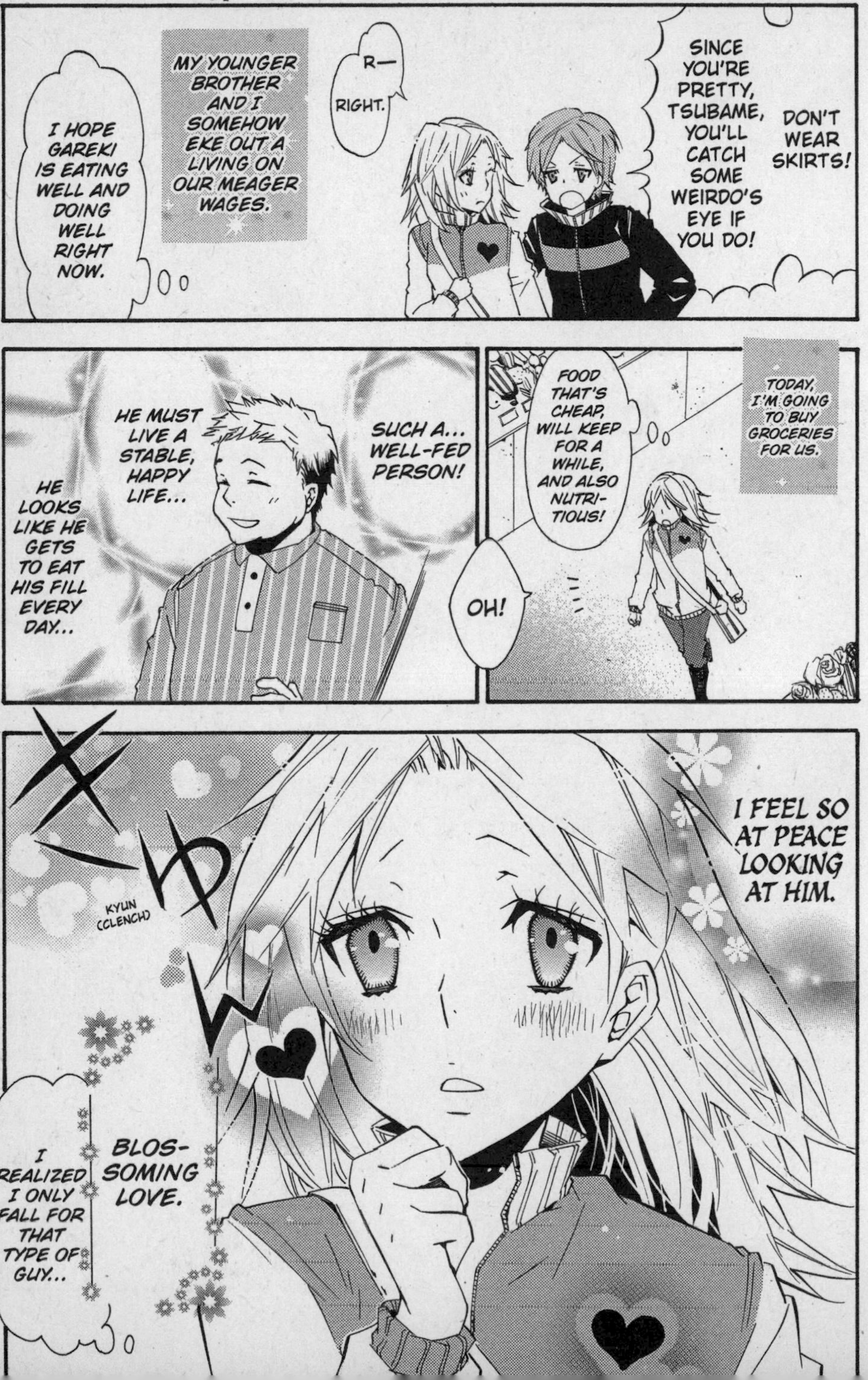
DON'T WEAR SKIRTS!
SINCE YOU'RE PRETTY, TSUBAME, YOU'LL CATCH SOME WEIRDO'S EYE IF YOU DO!
R— RIGHT.
MY YOUNGER BROTHER AND I SOMEHOW EKE OUT A LIVING ON OUR MEAGER WAGES.
I HOPE GAREKI IS EATING WELL AND DOING WELL RIGHT NOW.
TODAY, I'M GOING TO BUY GROCERIES FOR US.
FOOD THAT'S CHEAP, WILL KEEP FOR A WHILE, AND ALSO NUTRI-TIOUS!
OH!
SUCH A... WELL-FED PERSON!
HE MUST LIVE A STABLE, HAPPY LIFE...
HE LOOKS LIKE HE GETS TO EAT HIS FILL EVERY DAY...
I FEEL SO AT PEACE LOOKING AT HIM.
KYUN (CLENCH)
BLOS-SOMING LOVE.
I REALIZED I ONLY FALL FOR THAT TYPE OF GUY...

Bonus Comic 3 - Many Things I Don't Know

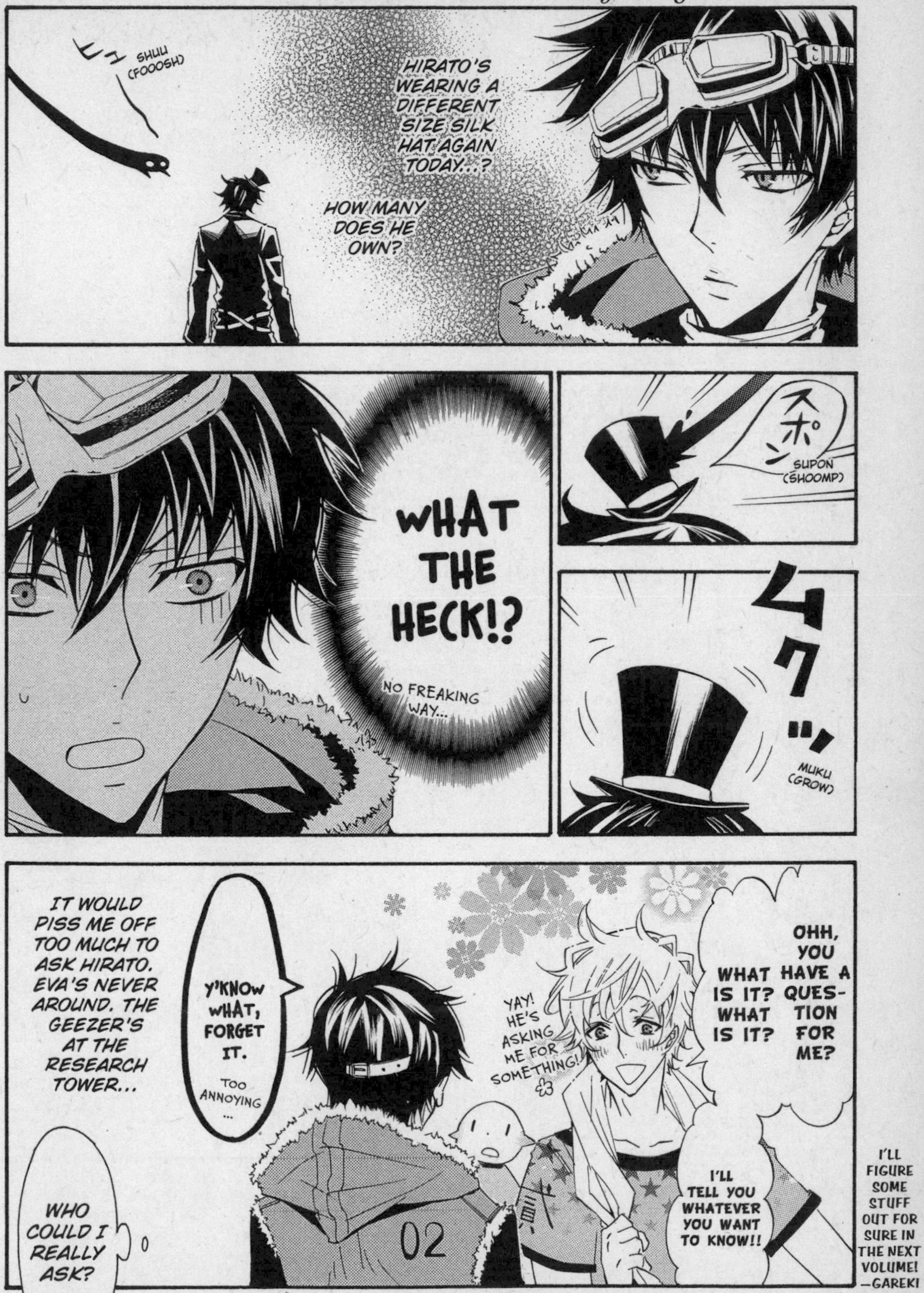

HIRATO'S WEARING A DIFFERENT SIZE SILK HAT AGAIN TODAY...?
HOW MANY DOES HE OWN?
ヒュ
SHUU (FOOOSH)
スポン
SUPON (SHOOMP)
ムクッ
MUKU (GROW)
WHAT THE HECK!?
NO FREAKING WAY...
OHH, YOU HAVE A QUESTION FOR ME?
WHAT IS IT? WHAT IS IT?
I'LL TELL YOU WHATEVER YOU WANT TO KNOW!!
YAY! HE'S ASKING ME FOR SOMETHING!
Y'KNOW WHAT, FORGET IT.
TOO ANNOYING...
IT WOULD PISS ME OFF TOO MUCH TO ASK HIRATO. EVA'S NEVER AROUND. THE GEEZER'S AT THE RESEARCH TOWER...
WHO COULD I REALLY ASK?
I'LL FIGURE SOME STUFF OUT FOR SURE IN THE NEXT VOLUME! —GAREKI

The End

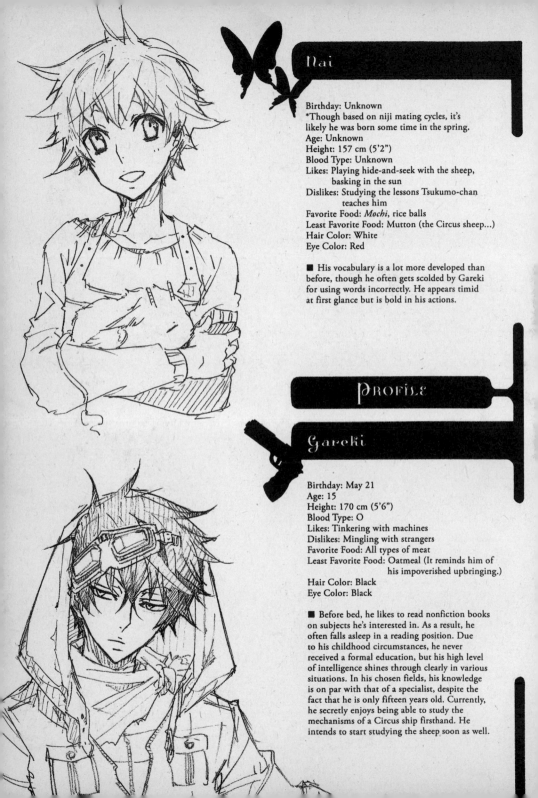

Nai

Birthday: Unknown
*Though based on niji mating cycles, it's
likely he was born some time in the spring.
Age: Unknown
Height: 157 cm (5'2")
Blood Type: Unknown
Likes: Playing hide-and-seek with the sheep,
       basking in the sun
Dislikes: Studying the lessons Tsukumo-chan
          teaches him
Favorite Food: *Mochi*, rice balls
Least Favorite Food: Mutton (the Circus sheep...)
Hair Color: White
Eye Color: Red

■ His vocabulary is a lot more developed than
before, though he often gets scolded by Gareki
for using words incorrectly. He appears timid
at first glance but is bold in his actions.

PROFILE

Gareki

Birthday: May 21
Age: 15
Height: 170 cm (5'6")
Blood Type: O
Likes: Tinkering with machines
Dislikes: Mingling with strangers
Favorite Food: All types of meat
Least Favorite Food: Oatmeal (It reminds him of
                     his impoverished upbringing.)

Hair Color: Black
Eye Color: Black

■ Before bed, he likes to read nonfiction books
on subjects he's interested in. As a result, he
often falls asleep in a reading position. Due
to his childhood circumstances, he never
received a formal education, but his high level
of intelligence shines through clearly in various
situations. In his chosen fields, his knowledge
is on par with that of a specialist, despite the
fact that he is only fifteen years old. Currently,
he secretly enjoys being able to study the
mechanisms of a Circus ship firsthand. He
intends to start studying the sheep soon as well.

Yogi

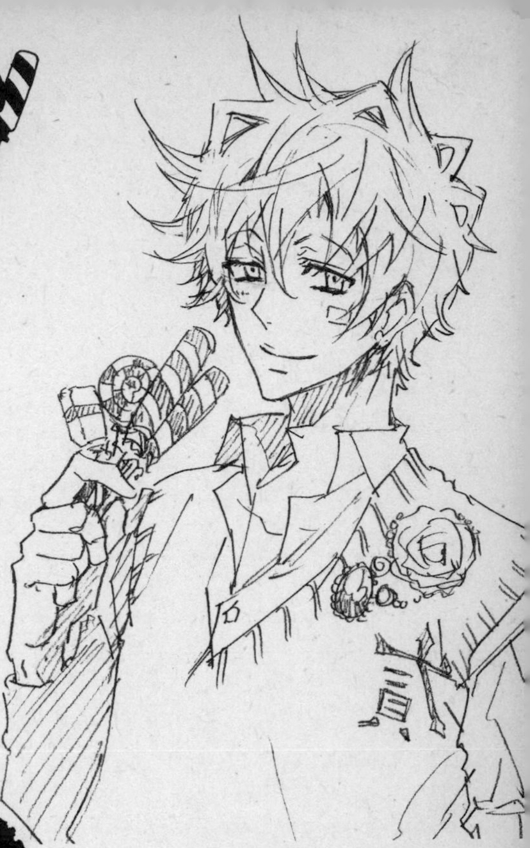

Birthday: February 11
Age: 21
Height: 181 cm (5'9")
Blood Type: B
Likes: Playing Nyanperowna
Dislikes: Battling, Dr. Akari
Favorite Food: Chocolate, candy bars
Least Favorite Food: Bell peppers, carrots
Hair Color: Golden
Eye Color: Purple

■ He wonders if it's truly acceptable for a combat specialist to work as Nyanperowna...and honestly worries about it a little. Incidentally, his bombastic self-introduction speech (the "brimming with manly compassion" one) was written by Hirato. Every candidate who hopes to become a combat specialist must submit a self-introduction, but as Yogi hadn't thought of one, he entrusted his superior Hirato with coming up with one for him. The result was Hirato writing some rather preposterous lines. However, it ended up being popular with the kids, so Yogi rather likes it now. Yogi comes from a small rural country. He apparently has a younger sister as well.

Tsukumo

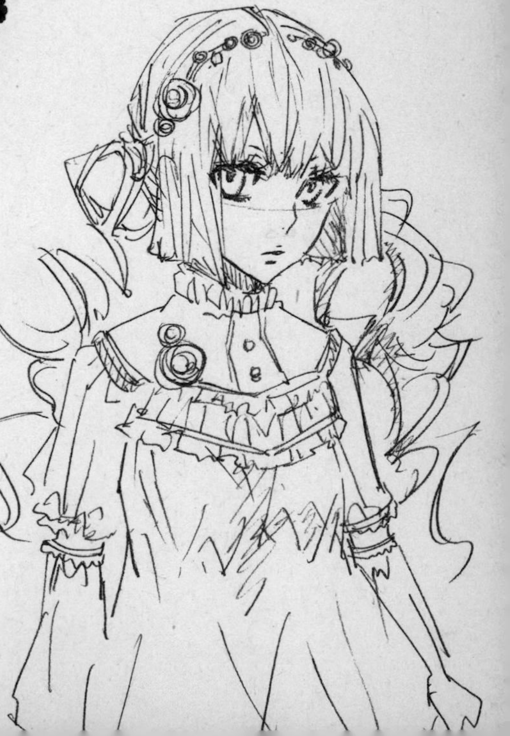

Birthday: March 2
Age: 16
Height: 159 cm (5'2")
Blood Type: A
Likes: Reading, studying
Dislikes: Cooking (though she can cook well...), sewing
Favorite Food: Fruits (except for mandoradora fruit)
Least Favorite Thing: Insects (especially hairy ones or ones with many legs)
Hair Color: Pale gold
Eye Color: Purple

■ A beautiful girl who is the acrobatic star of Circus's show. Because of her serious personality and complete lack of flirtatiousness toward men, she is doted upon by women as well as men. She hails from one of five nations that are global superpowers. She has known Hirato since childhood, well before she joined Circus. Kiichi was her junior at the prep school she attended before joining Circus. She secretly has a complex because her hands lack the deftness for skillful tasks (example: the clumsy snow bunnies she built).

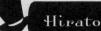

Hirato

Birthday: October 22
Age: 27
Height: 185 cm (6'1")
Blood Type: AB
Likes: Poking people (figuratively)
Dislikes: Unknown
Favorite Food: Wine, kirine fruit
Least Favorite Food: Unknown
Hair Color: Dark purple
Eye Color: Dark purple

■ 2nd Ship Captain; he rarely allows his real feelings to show on the surface. Because it is impossible to know what he is really thinking, he often gets teased by supervisors and managers at the Control Tower outside of his chain of command for looking so suspicious. However, he appears not to mind this at all. He apparently has an older brother. He is often absent from the ship, ostensibly doing work out in the field...He is the same age as the 1st Ship Captain Tsukitachi.

Akari

Birthday: December 23
Age: 33
Height: 185 cm (6'1")
Blood Type: O
Likes: Research, exploring uncharted lands, playing board games
Dislikes: People who try to use clever words to make themselves appear smarter than they are; for completely separate reasons, he also dislikes Hirato.
Favorite Food: Black tea, brown sugar coral candy
Least Favorite Food: Smoked talnero (fish)
Hair Color: Light peach and pale brown
Eye Color: Peach

■ A high-minded man with a blunt attitude; he often says indelicate things like, "What's wrong with saying it if it's true?" or "If you don't like hearing it, then fix it!" This has led to him having many enemies among the nurses, though he actually has no ill will toward anyone whatsoever. There is also a faction within the nurses that seeks to cheer on doctors like him. When his mentor, Ryoushi, was still actively practicing, Akari studied hard under his guidance and grew to display his prominent talent.

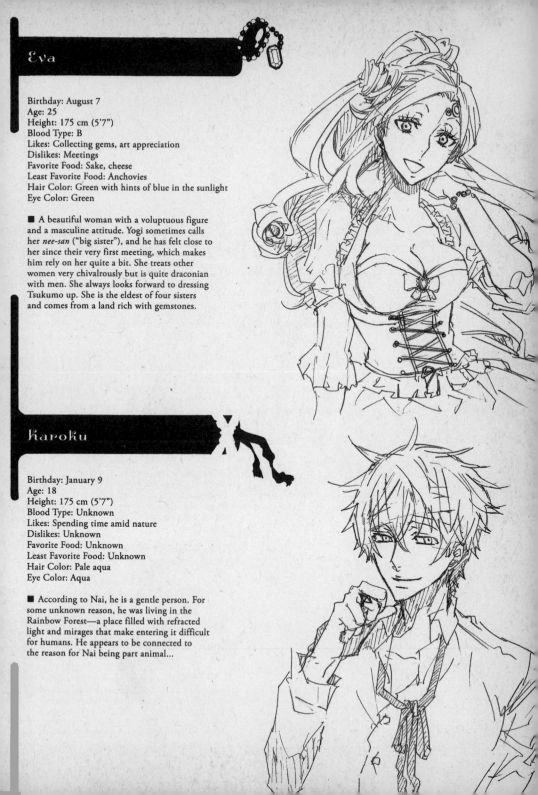

Eva

Birthday: August 7
Age: 25
Height: 175 cm (5'7")
Blood Type: B
Likes: Collecting gems, art appreciation
Dislikes: Meetings
Favorite Food: Sake, cheese
Least Favorite Food: Anchovies
Hair Color: Green with hints of blue in the sunlight
Eye Color: Green

■ A beautiful woman with a voluptuous figure and a masculine attitude. Yogi sometimes calls her *nee-san* ("big sister"), and he has felt close to her since their very first meeting, which makes him rely on her quite a bit. She treats other women very chivalrously but is quite draconian with men. She always looks forward to dressing Tsukumo up. She is the eldest of four sisters and comes from a land rich with gemstones.

Karoku

Birthday: January 9
Age: 18
Height: 175 cm (5'7")
Blood Type: Unknown
Likes: Spending time amid nature
Dislikes: Unknown
Favorite Food: Unknown
Least Favorite Food: Unknown
Hair Color: Pale aqua
Eye Color: Aqua

■ According to Nai, he is a gentle person. For some unknown reason, he was living in the Rainbow Forest—a place filled with refracted light and mirages that make entering it difficult for humans. He appears to be connected to the reason for Nai being part animal...

HI THERE. THIS IS TOUYA. THANK YOU SO MUCH FOR READING *KARNEVAL*, VOLUME 3! I'VE RECEIVED MANY LETTERS FROM READERS ASKING WHAT MEANINGS THERE ARE BEHIND THE KARNEVAL CHARACTERS' NAMES, SO I THOUGHT I'D TALK ABOUT THEM A BIT HERE. THIS IS TRUE WITH ALL THE CHARACTERS IN THE STORY, BUT I'LL COVER THE CHARACTERS WHOSE NAME READINGS I CHOSE BASED ON BOTH THEIR PERSONALITIES AND THE IMAGE OF THE VARIOUS KANJI I CHOSE FOR THEIR NAMES. THE CHARACTERS I DID THIS FOR WHO HAVE APPEARED UP THROUGH VOLUME 3 ARE:

- NAI ➔ NORMALLY READ "MU"
- GAREKI ➔ NORMALLY READ "KAREKI"
- AKARI ➔ NORMALLY READ "SHOKU"
- TSUKITACHI ➔ NORMALLY READ "SAKU"

*AS FOR THE KANJI, I CHOSE READINGS FROM OTHER KANJI WITH SIMILAR MEANINGS.

I ALSO WANTED THE NAMES OF THESE CHARACTERS FROM THE WORLD OF KARNEVAL TO HAVE A DISTINCT SORT OF SOUND, AND FOR READERS TO ENJOY THEMSELVES READING THESE NAMES. THE REST OF MY REASONING IS AS I HAVE MENTIONED ABOVE. IN GAREKI'S CASE, HE WAS COLLAPSED ON SOME RUBBLE WHEN TSUBAKI FOUND HIM. THAT'S WHY, WHEN HE TOLD TSUBAKI HE DIDN'T HAVE A NAME, HER FIRST THOUGHT WAS TO NAME HIM "GAREKI" AS IN "RUBBLE." BUT THE HARSH IMAGE DIDN'T SUIT HIS CHARACTER, AND I ALSO WANTED SOMETHING MORE GLAMOROUS FOR HIM, SO I CHANGED THE "GA" KANJI TO "FLOWER" AND NAMED HIM "FLOWER GRAVEL". IT LOOKS LIKE I'M RUNNING OUT OF SPACE TO WRITE NOW, SO I WANT TO END WITH ONE THING THAT'S BEEN ON MY MIND: THESE KANJI READINGS AND COMBINATIONS ARE ONLY VALID IN THE WORLD OF KARNEVAL. ANYWHERE ELSE, THEY WOULD BE CONSIDERED MISREADINGS. SO PLEASE BE EXTRA CAREFUL WHEN YOU'RE WRITING THESE KANJI ON TESTS, ET CETERA. SO NOW YOU DON'T HAVE TO WONDER WHY THE KANJI YOU'RE EXPECTING DON'T POP UP AUTOMATICALLY WHEN YOU'RE TYPING THEM IN THE COMPUTER, RIGHT? BUT I HOPE YOU'LL STILL BE ABLE TO ENJOY THESE NAMES GOING FORWARD!

—TOUYA

Special Thanks

- TENKO-CHAN, KAZUMI-SAN, THANK YOU FOR YOUR ASSISTANCE.
- MY EDITOR, ABE-SAN
- EVERYONE WHO'S TAKEN CARE OF ME
- ALSO JUN-SAN AND MY FAMILY

and To You

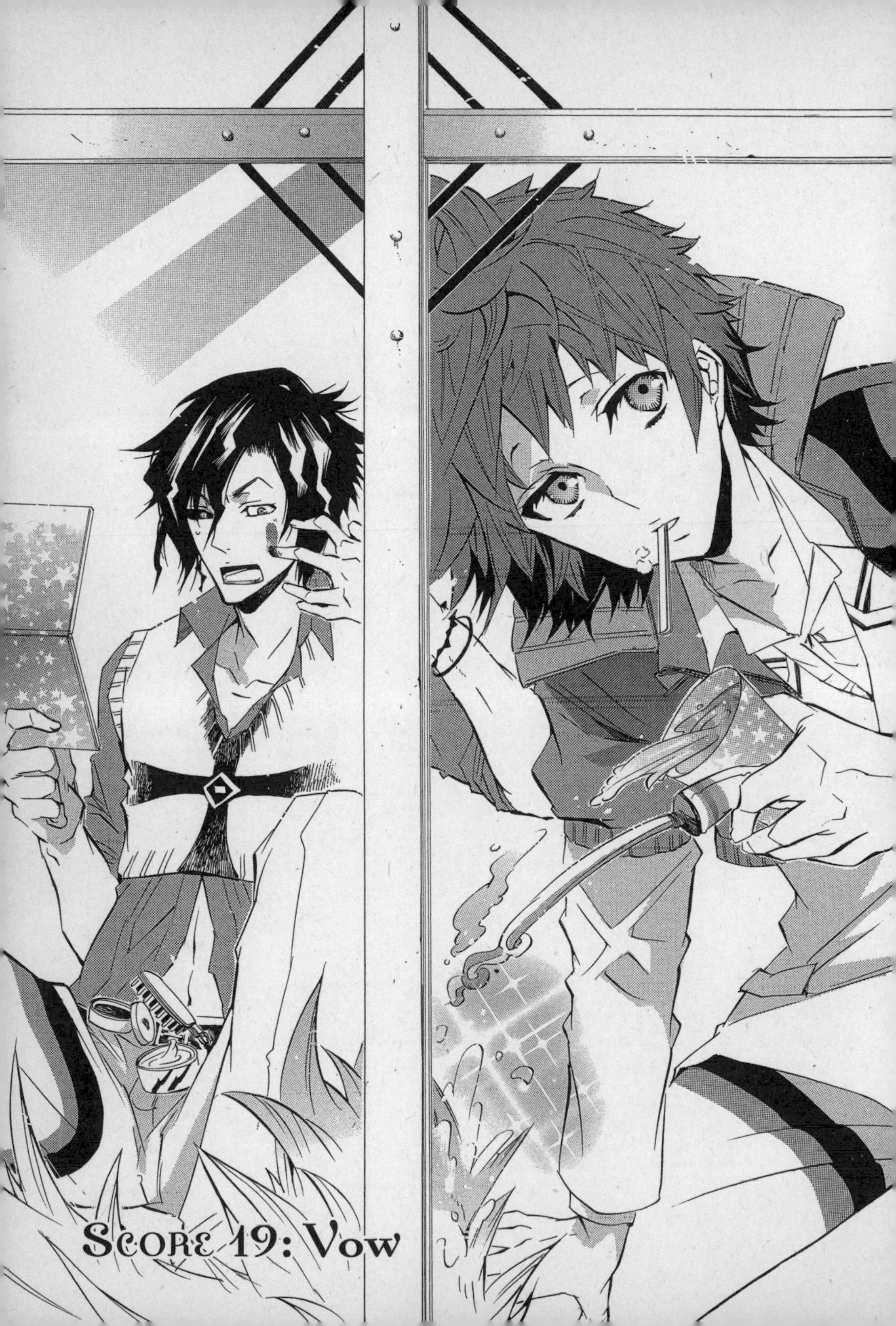
Score 19: Vow

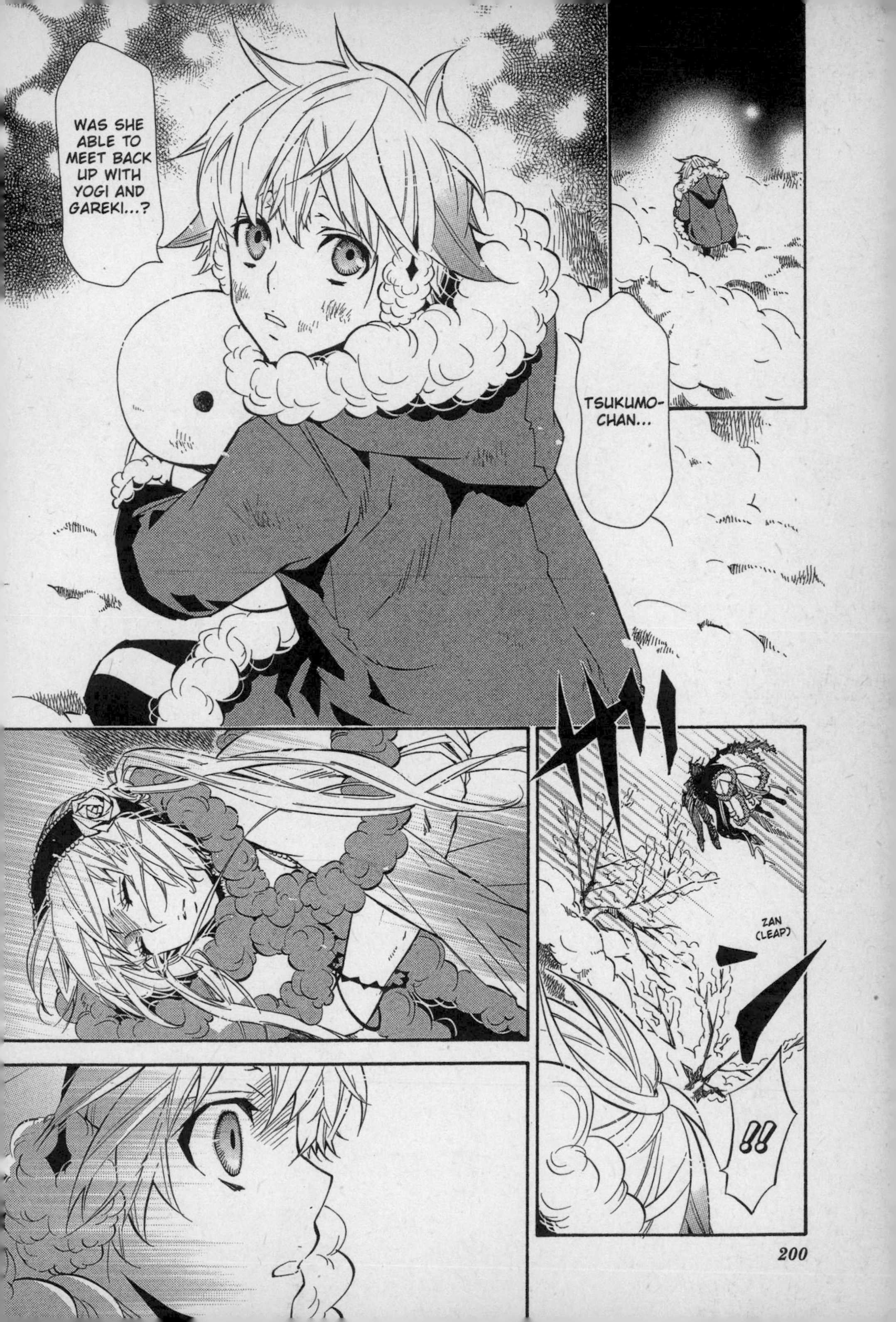
TSUKUMO-CHAN...
WAS SHE ABLE TO MEET BACK UP WITH YOGI AND GAREKI...?
ZAN (LEAP)
!!

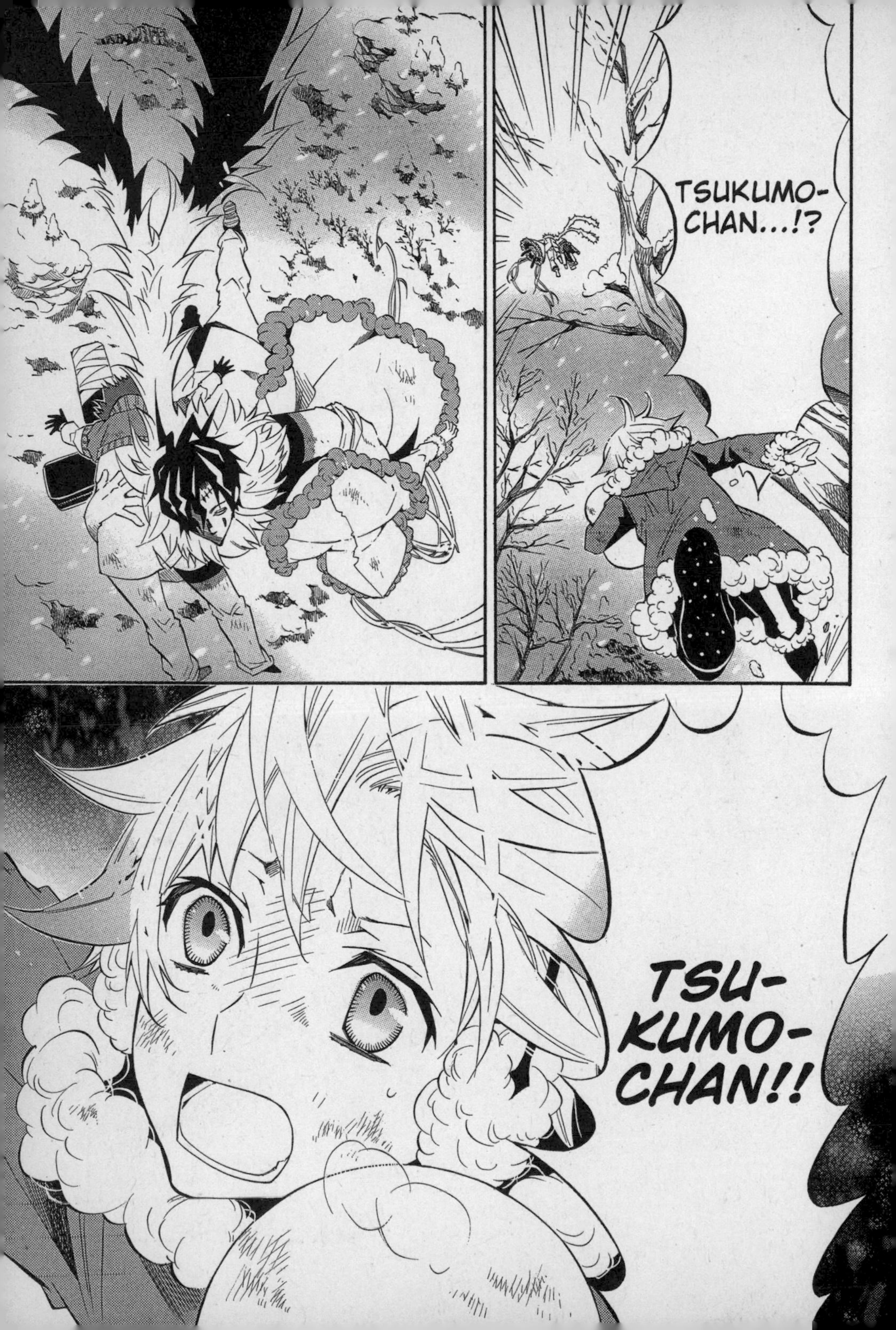
TSUKUMO-CHAN...!?
TSU-KUMO-CHAN!!

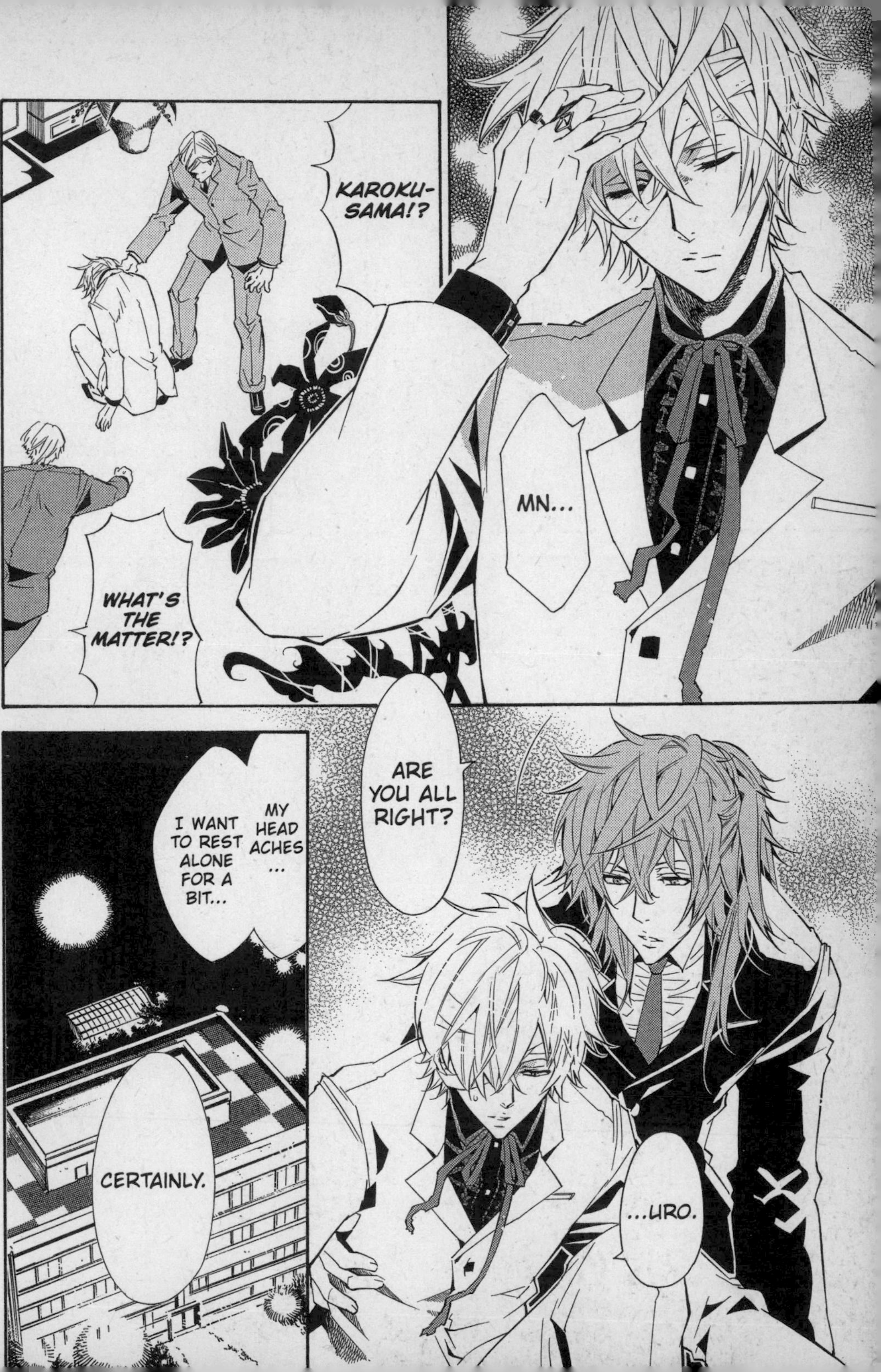
MN...
KAROKU-SAMA!?
WHAT'S THE MATTER!?
ARE YOU ALL RIGHT?
...URO.
MY HEAD ACHES...
I WANT TO REST ALONE FOR A BIT...
CERTAINLY.

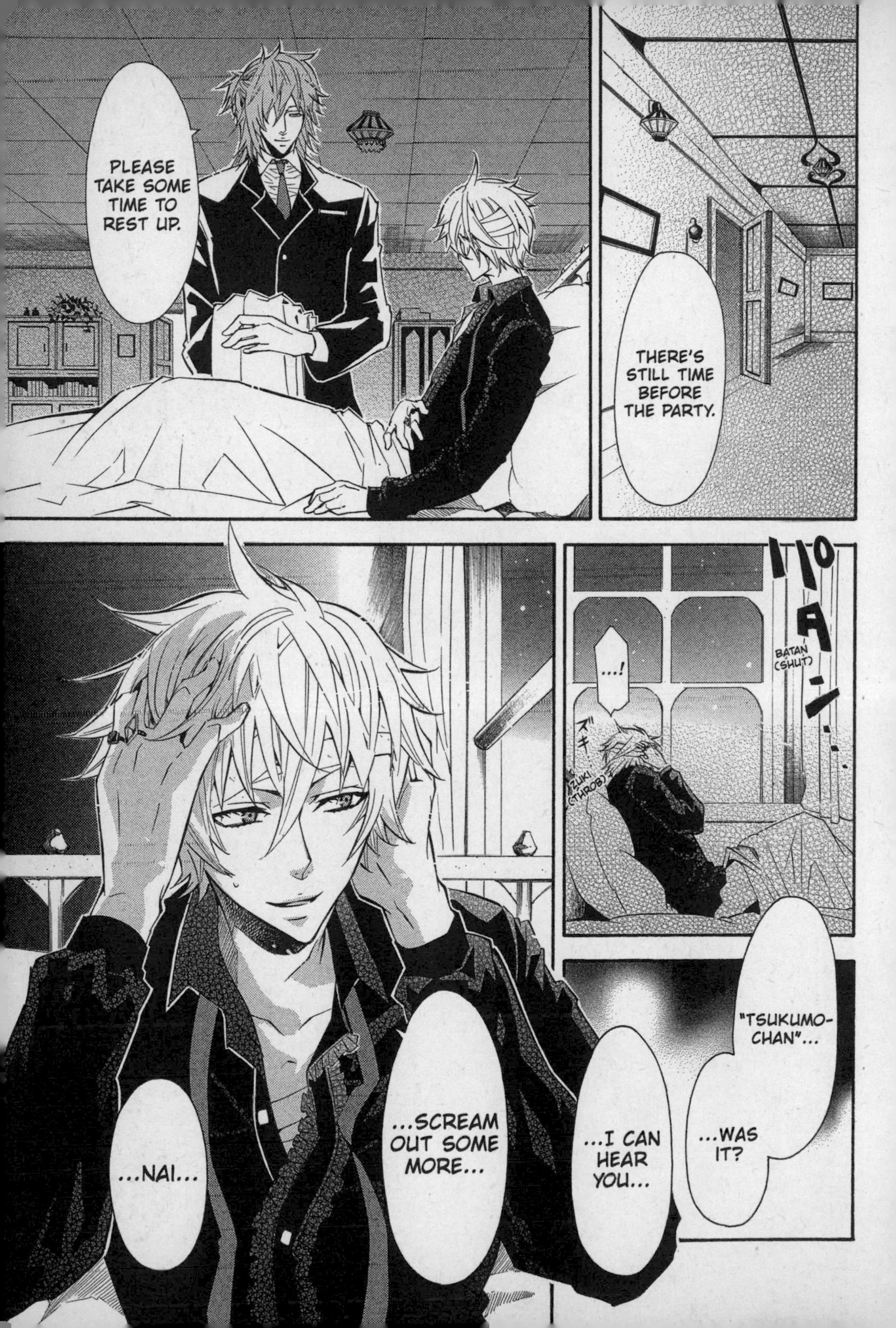
THERE'S STILL TIME BEFORE THE PARTY.
PLEASE TAKE SOME TIME TO REST UP.
BATAN (SHUT)
...!
ZUKI (THROB)
"TSUKUMO-CHAN"...
...WAS IT?
...I CAN HEAR YOU...
...SCREAM OUT SOME MORE...
...NAI...

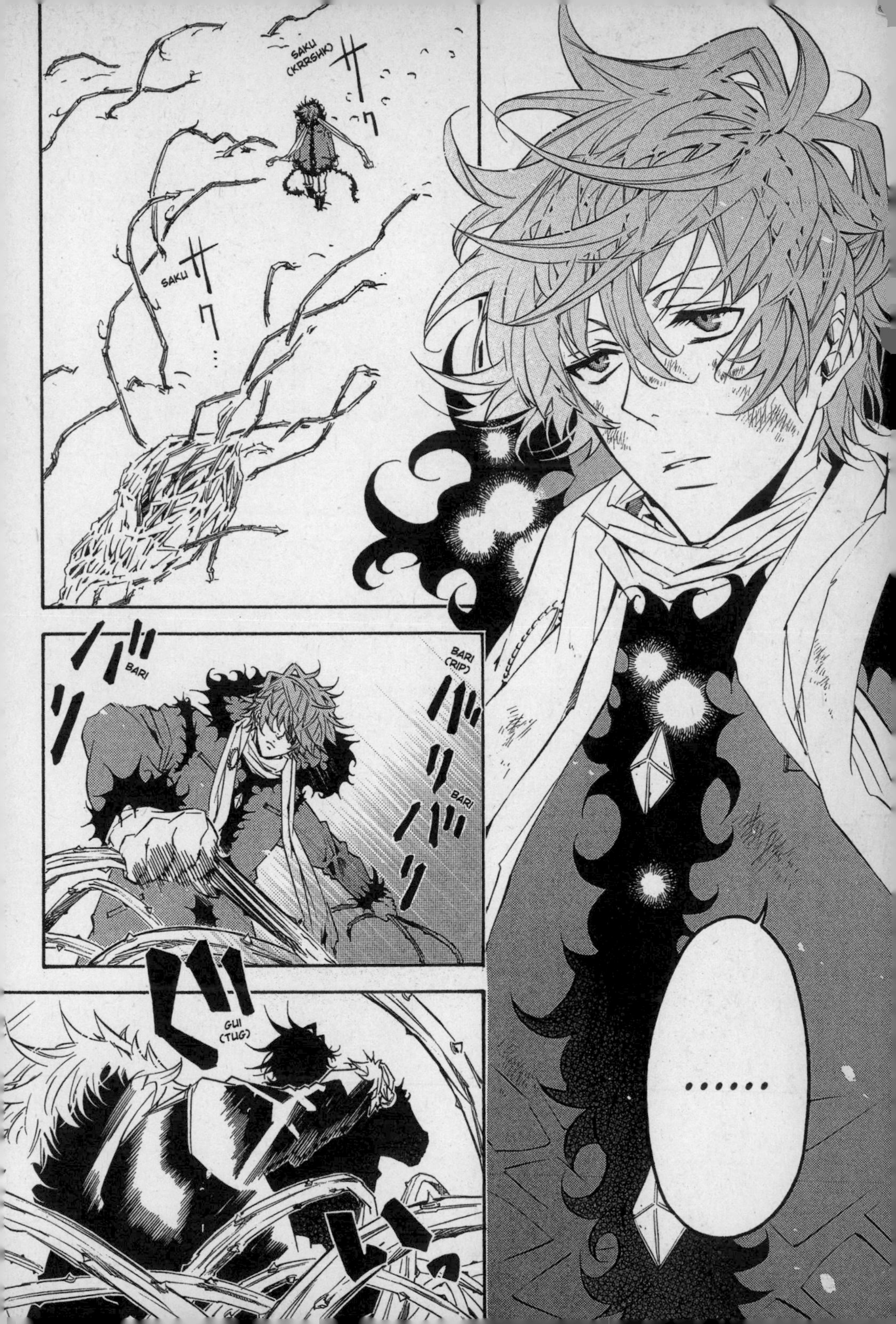

......
SAKU (KRRSHK)
SAKU
BARI (RIP)
BARI
BARI
GUI (TUG)

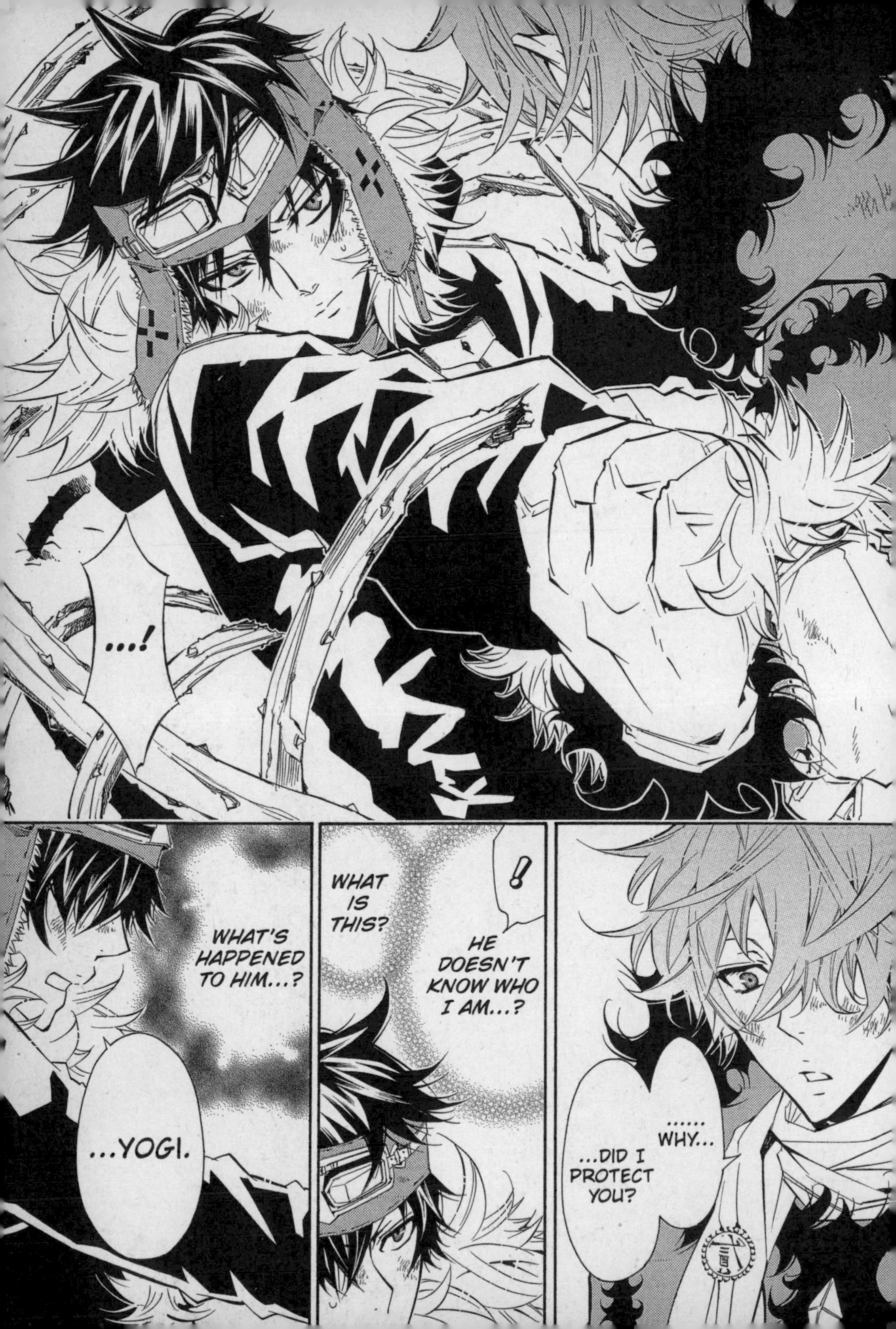
...!
...... WHY... ...DID I PROTECT YOU?
!
WHAT IS THIS?
HE DOESN'T KNOW WHO I AM...?
WHAT'S HAPPENED TO HIM...?
...YOGI.

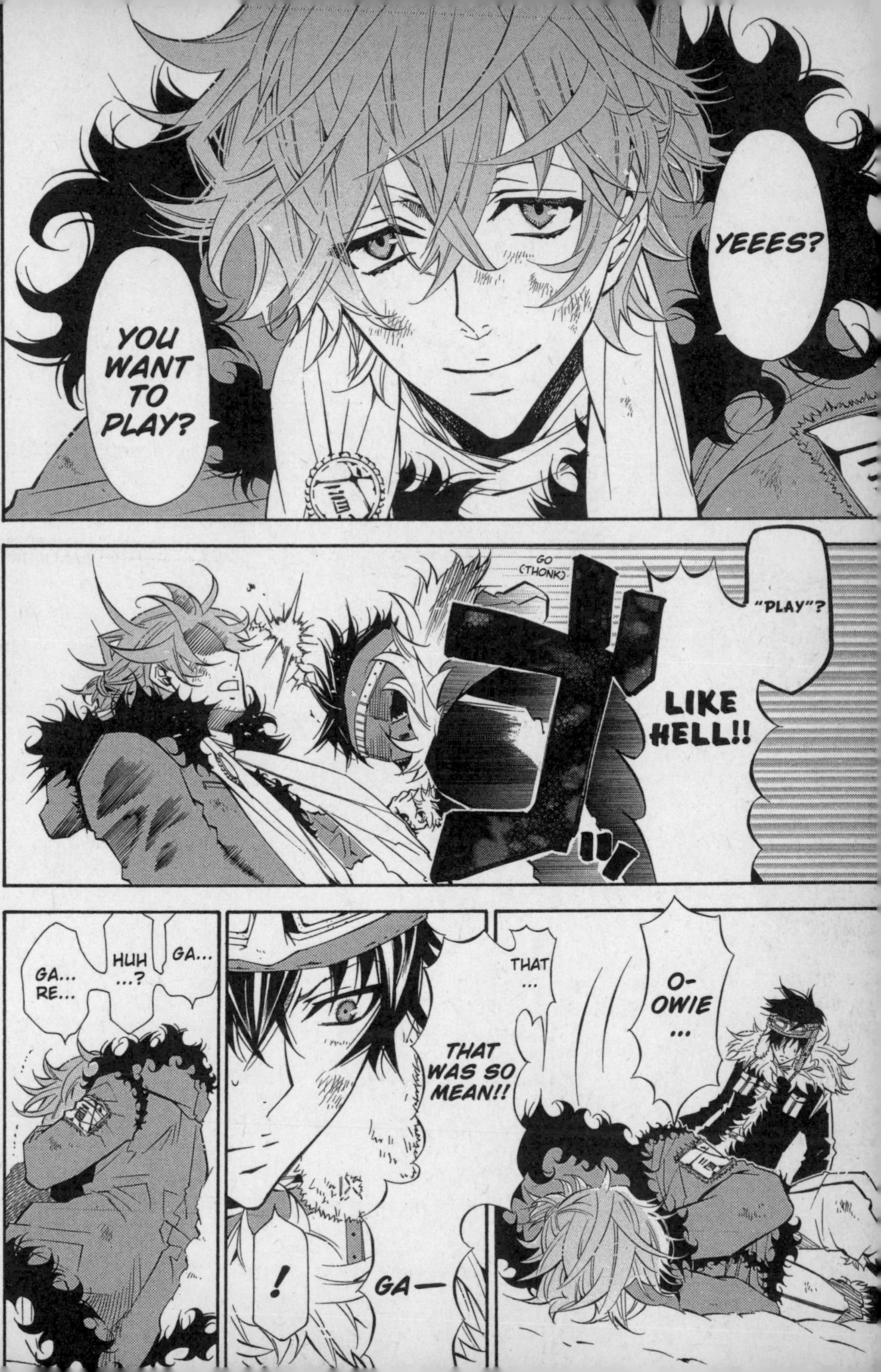
YEEES?
YOU WANT TO PLAY?
"PLAY"?
LIKE HELL!!
GO (THONK)
O-OWIE ...
THAT ...
THAT WAS SO MEAN!!
!
GA—
GA...
HUH ...?
GA... RE...

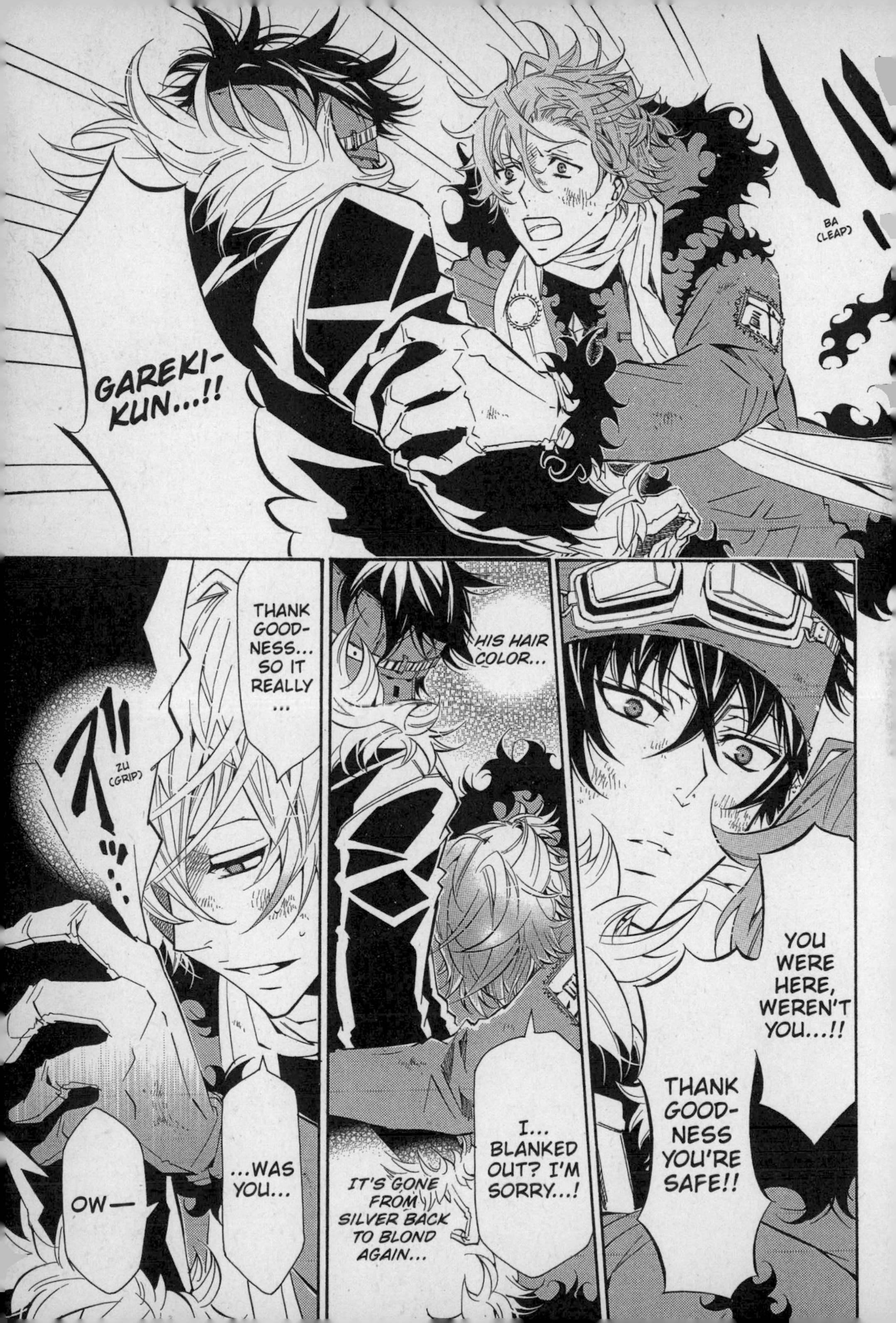
BA (LEAP)
GAREKI-KUN...!!
YOU WERE HERE, WEREN'T YOU...!!
THANK GOODNESS YOU'RE SAFE!!
HIS HAIR COLOR...
I... BLANKED OUT? I'M SORRY...!
IT'S GONE FROM SILVER BACK TO BLOND AGAIN...
THANK GOODNESS... SO IT REALLY ...
ZU (GRIP)
...WAS YOU...
OW—

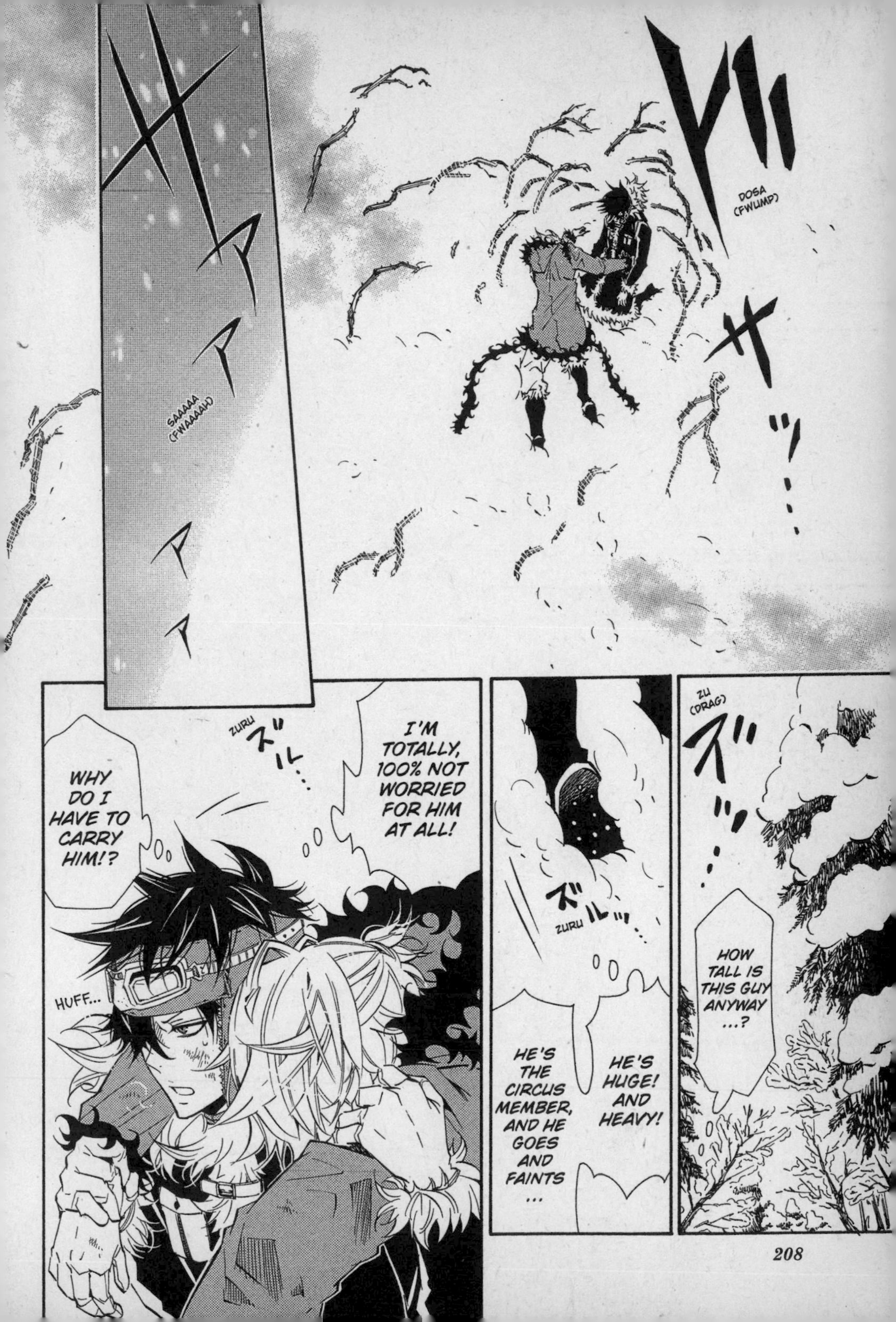
DOSA (FWUMP)
SAAAAA (FWAAAAH)
ZU (DRAG)
HOW TALL IS THIS GUY ANYWAY ...?
ZURU
HE'S HUGE! AND HEAVY!
HE'S THE CIRCUS MEMBER, AND HE GOES AND FAINTS ...
ZURU
I'M TOTALLY, 100% NOT WORRIED FOR HIM AT ALL!
WHY DO I HAVE TO CARRY HIM!?
HUFF...

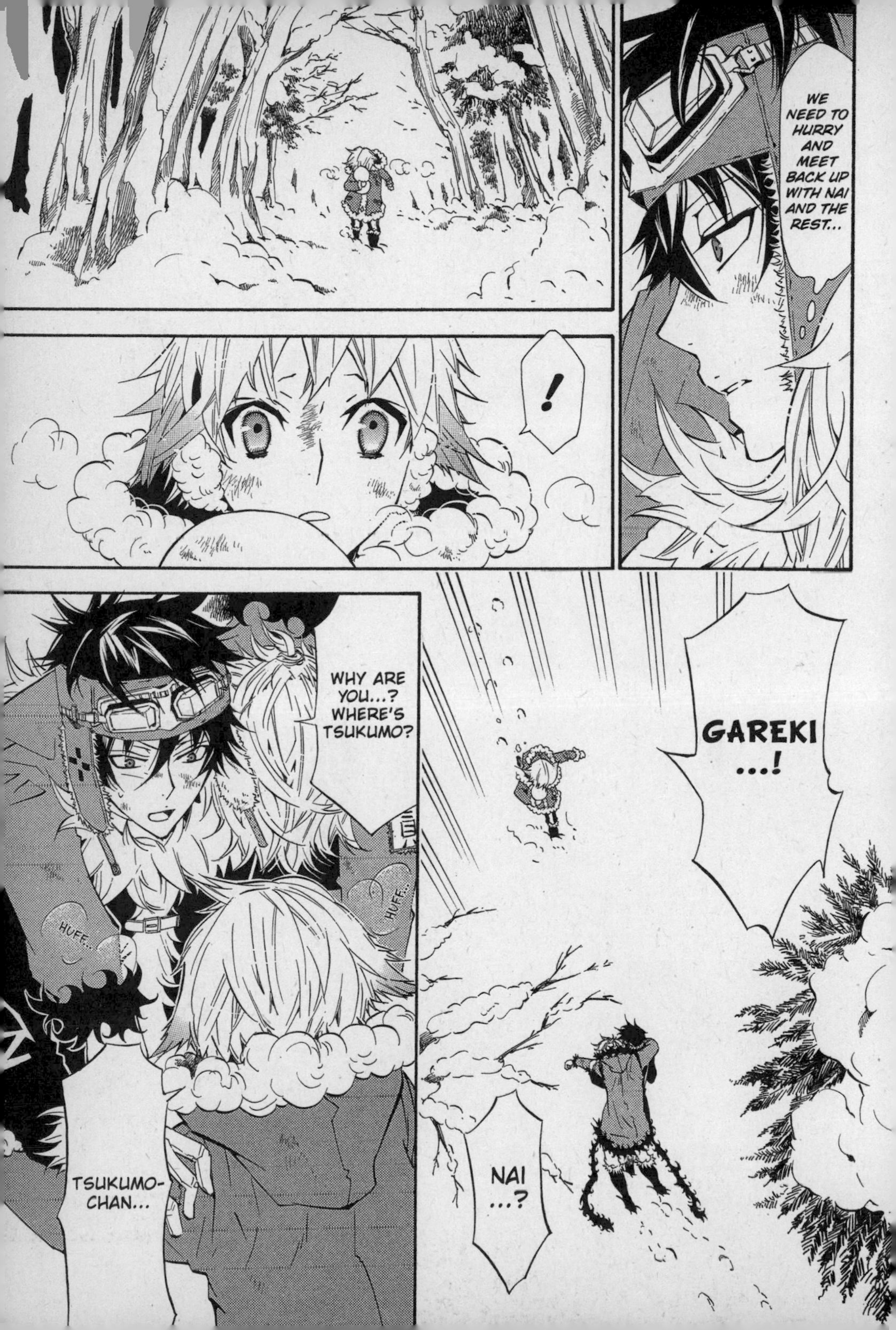
WE NEED TO HURRY AND MEET BACK UP WITH NAI AND THE REST...
!
GAREKI ...!
NAI ...?
WHY ARE YOU...? WHERE'S TSUKUMO?
HUFF...
HUFF...
TSUKUMO-CHAN...

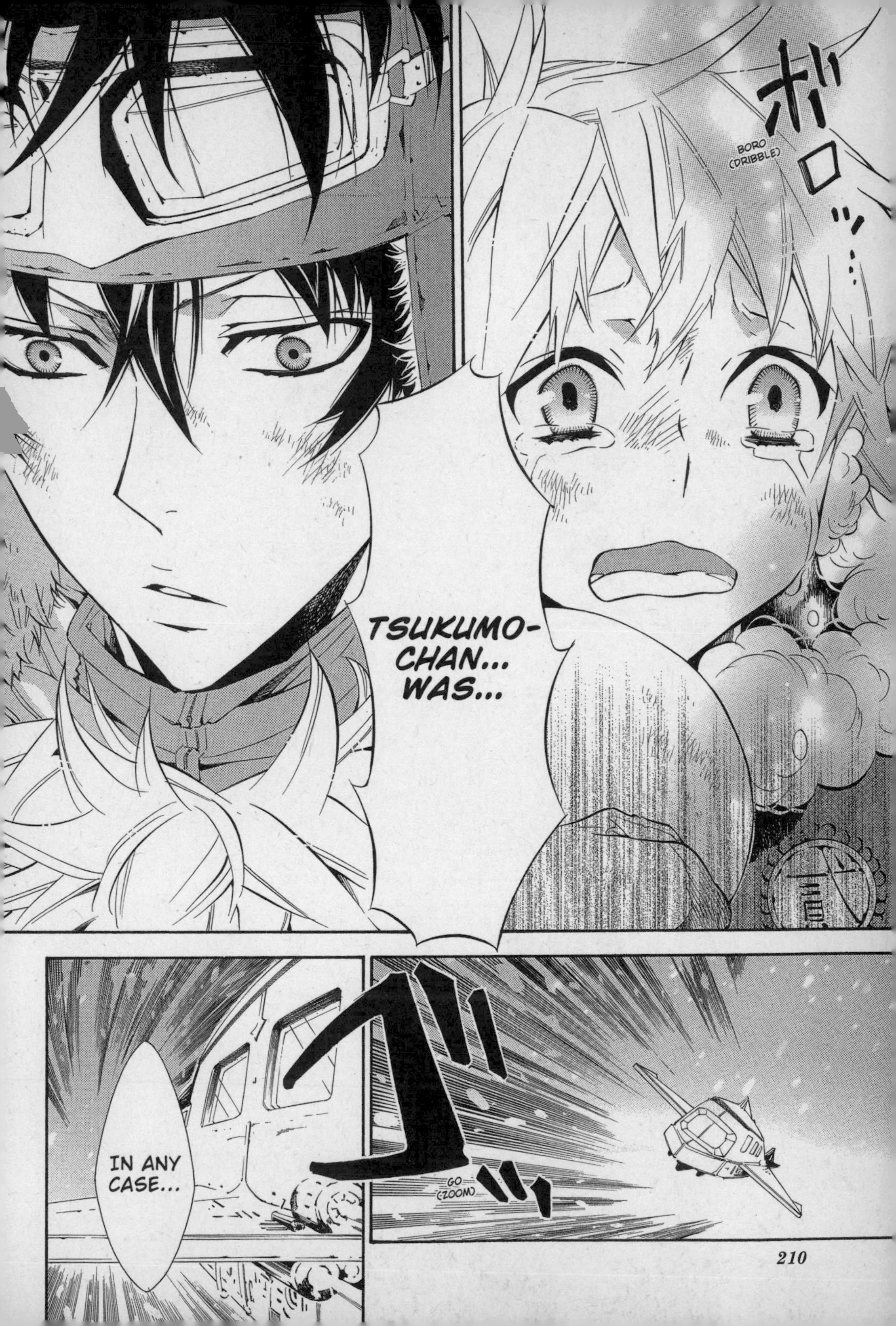
BORO (DRIBBLE)
TSUKUMO-CHAN... WAS...
GO (ZOOM)
IN ANY CASE...

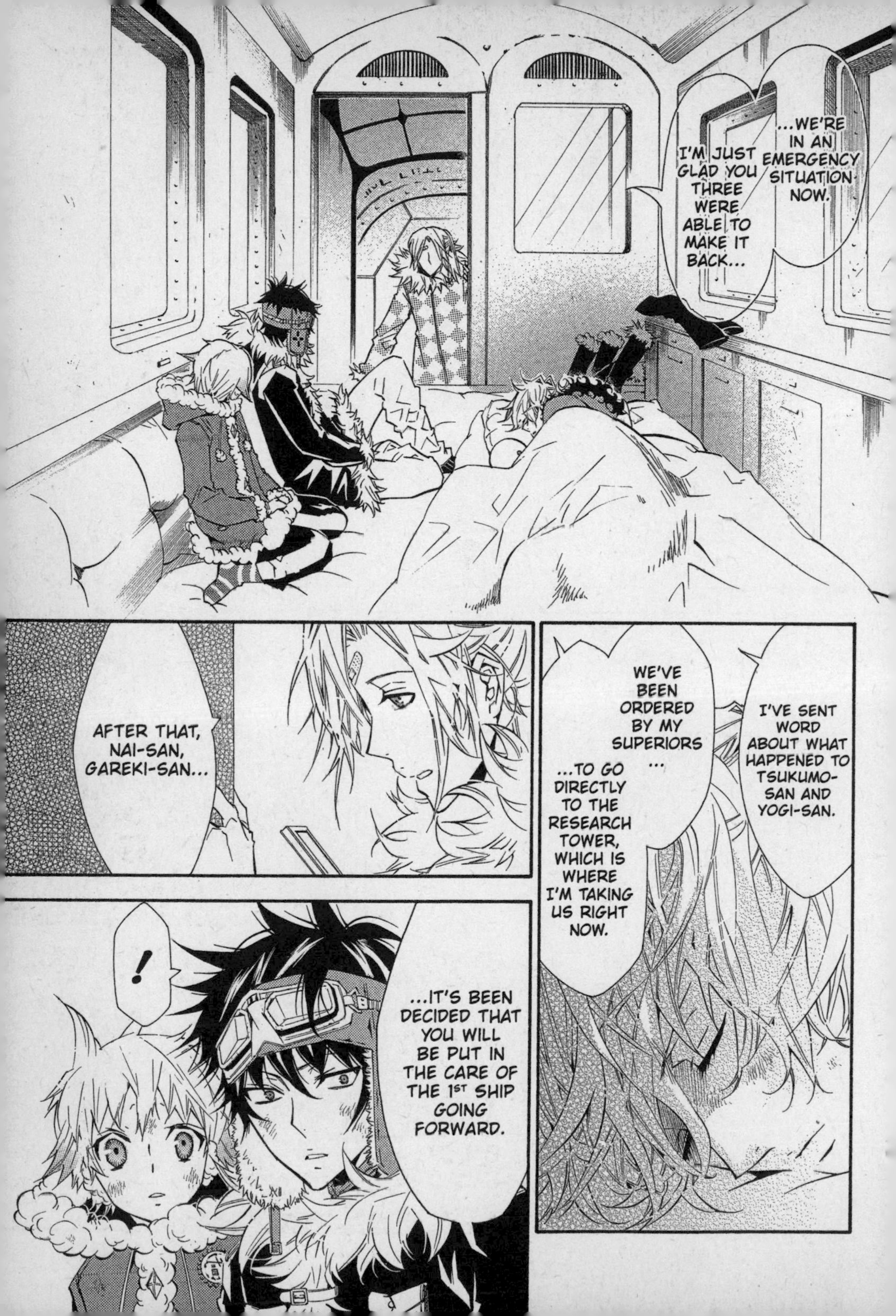
...WE'RE IN AN EMERGENCY SITUATION NOW.
I'M JUST GLAD YOU THREE WERE ABLE TO MAKE IT BACK...
I'VE SENT WORD ABOUT WHAT HAPPENED TO TSUKUMO-SAN AND YOGI-SAN.
WE'VE BEEN ORDERED BY MY SUPERIORS...
...TO GO DIRECTLY TO THE RESEARCH TOWER, WHICH IS WHERE I'M TAKING US RIGHT NOW.
AFTER THAT, NAI-SAN, GAREKI-SAN...
...IT'S BEEN DECIDED THAT YOU WILL BE PUT IN THE CARE OF THE 1ST SHIP GOING FORWARD.
!

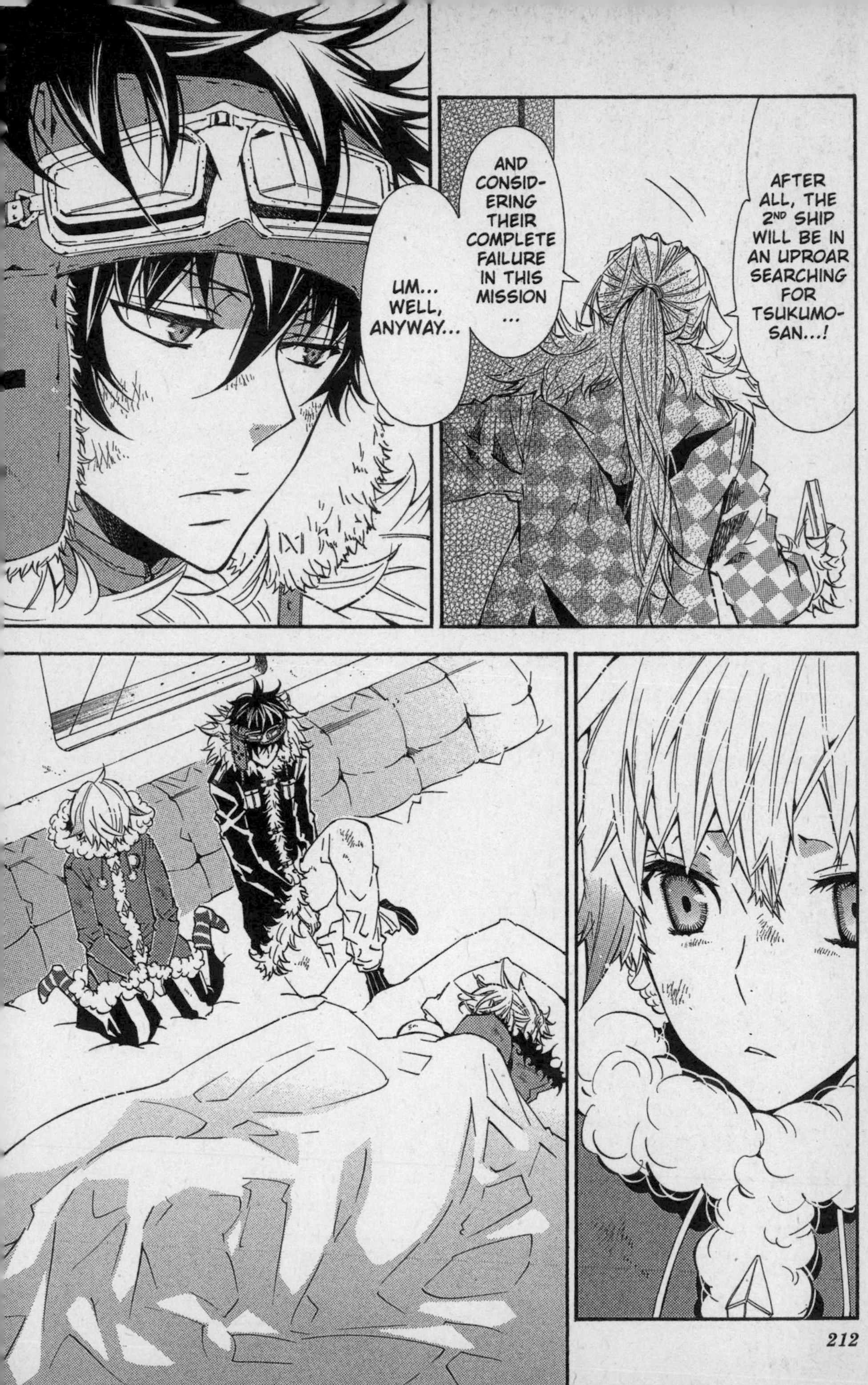
AFTER ALL, THE 2ND SHIP WILL BE IN AN UPROAR SEARCHING FOR TSUKUMO-SAN...!
AND CONSID-ERING THEIR COMPLETE FAILURE IN THIS MISSION...
UM... WELL, ANYWAY...

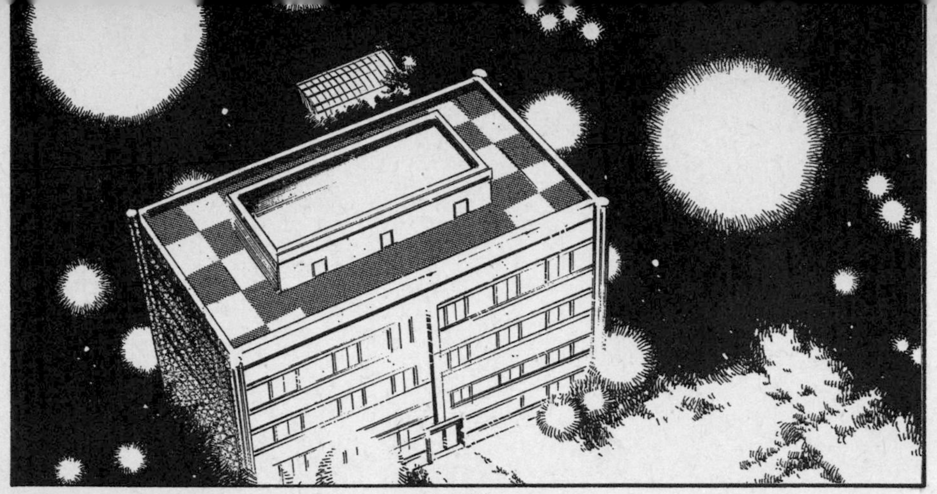
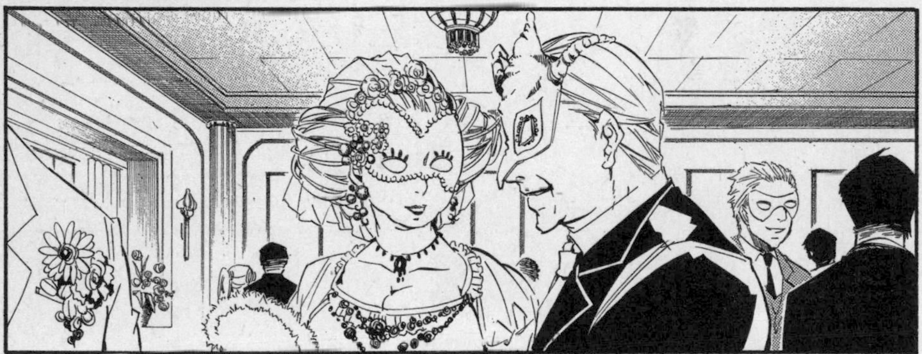
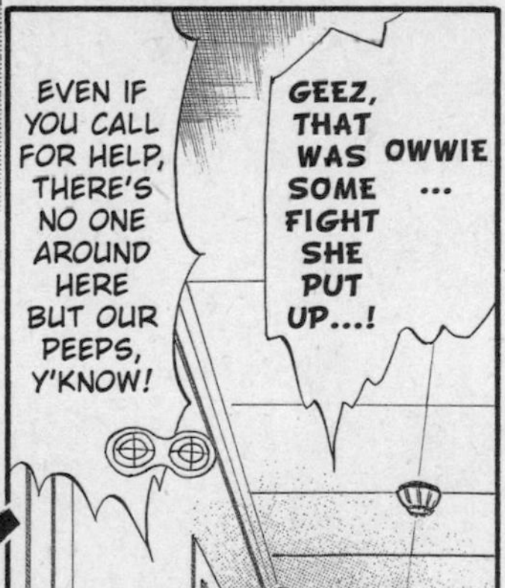
OWWIE ...
GEEZ, THAT WAS SOME FIGHT SHE PUT UP...!
EVEN IF YOU CALL FOR HELP, THERE'S NO ONE AROUND HERE BUT OUR PEEPS, Y'KNOW!
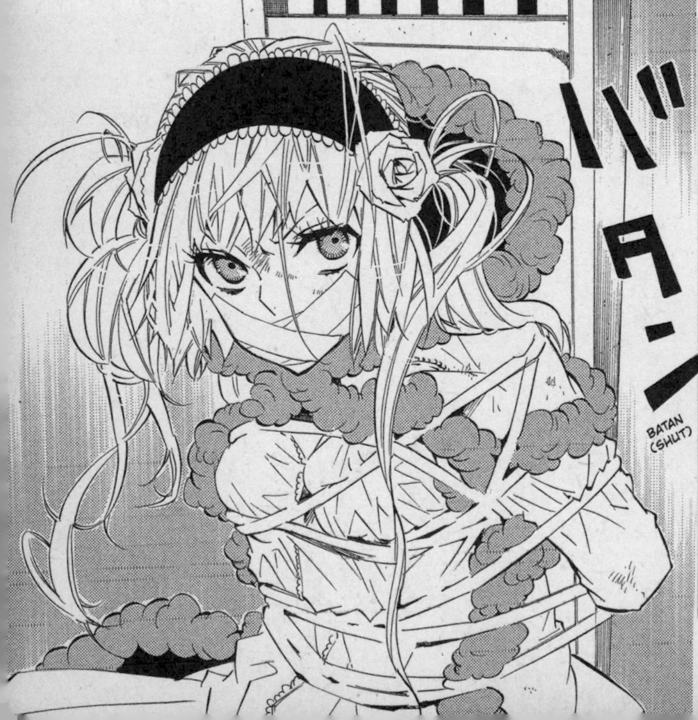
バタン
BATAN (SHUT)

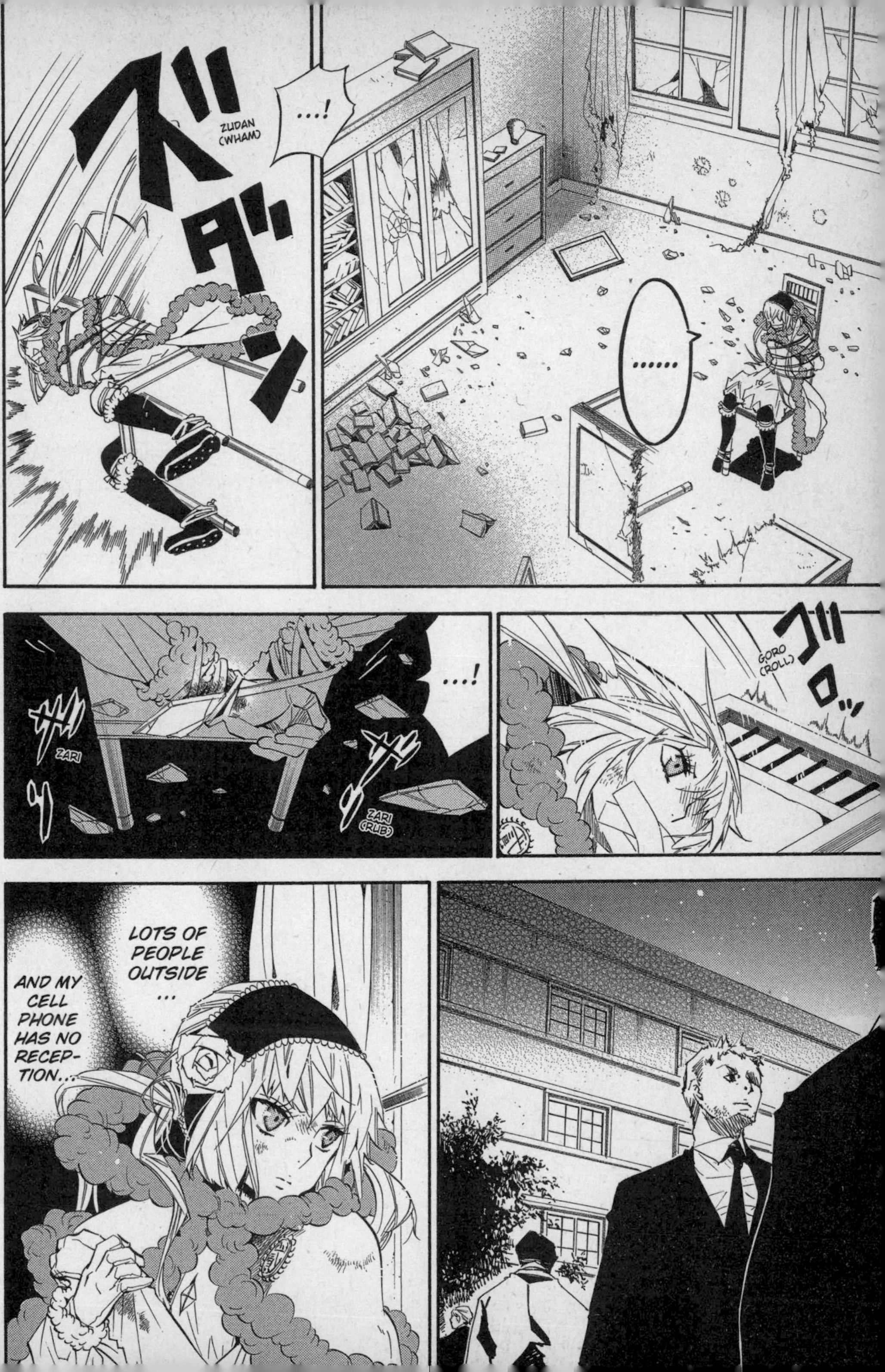
......
...!
ズダン
ZUDAN (WHAM)
ゴロッ
GORO (ROLL)
...!
ザリ
ZARI
ザリ
ZARI (RUB)
LOTS OF PEOPLE OUTSIDE ...
AND MY CELL PHONE HAS NO RECEPTION...

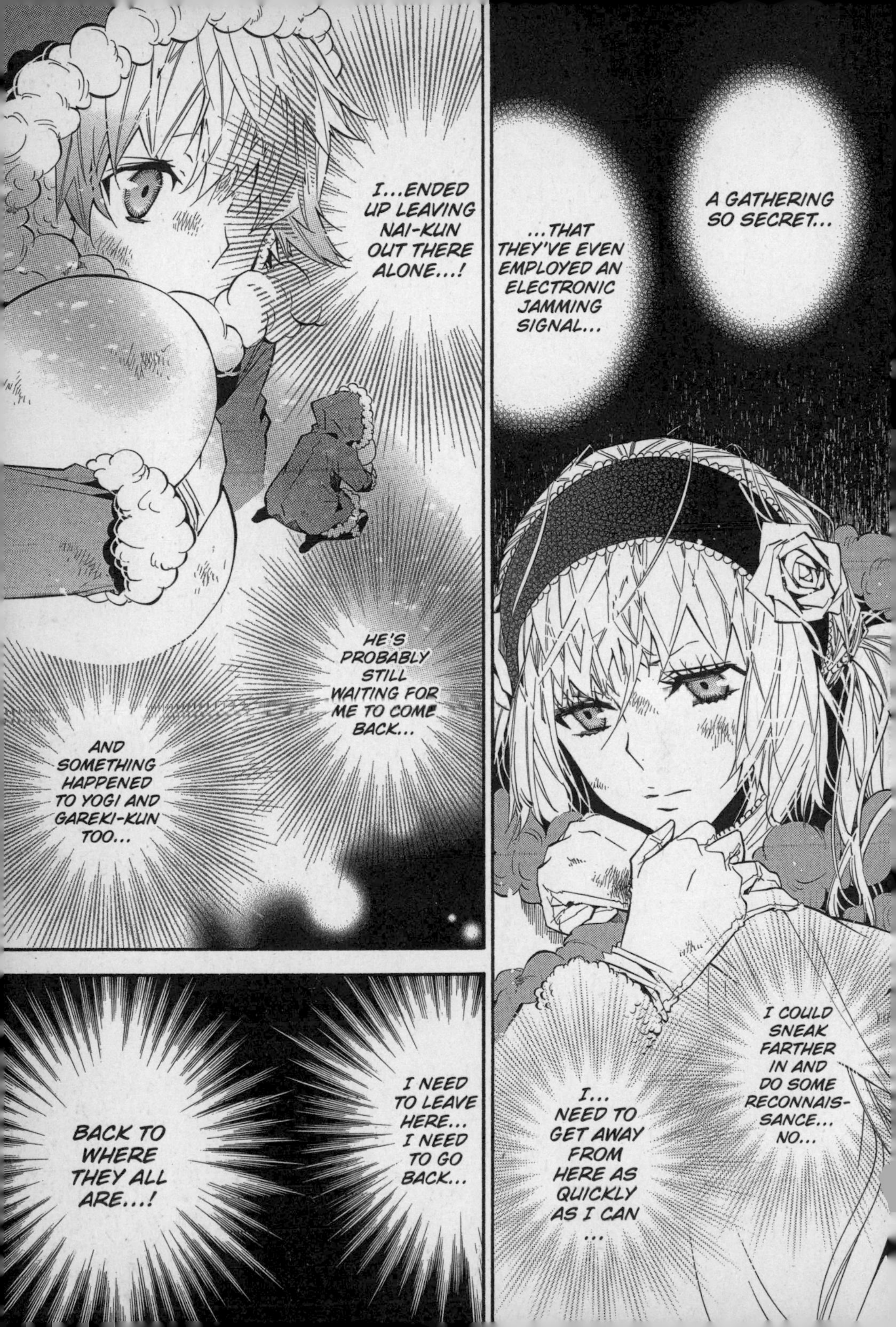
A GATHERING SO SECRET...
...THAT THEY'VE EVEN EMPLOYED AN ELECTRONIC JAMMING SIGNAL...
I COULD SNEAK FARTHER IN AND DO SOME RECONNAISSANCE... NO...
I... NEED TO GET AWAY FROM HERE AS QUICKLY AS I CAN...
I...ENDED UP LEAVING NAI-KUN OUT THERE ALONE...!
HE'S PROBABLY STILL WAITING FOR ME TO COME BACK...
AND SOMETHING HAPPENED TO YOGI AND GAREKI-KUN TOO...
I NEED TO LEAVE HERE... I NEED TO GO BACK...
BACK TO WHERE THEY ALL ARE...!

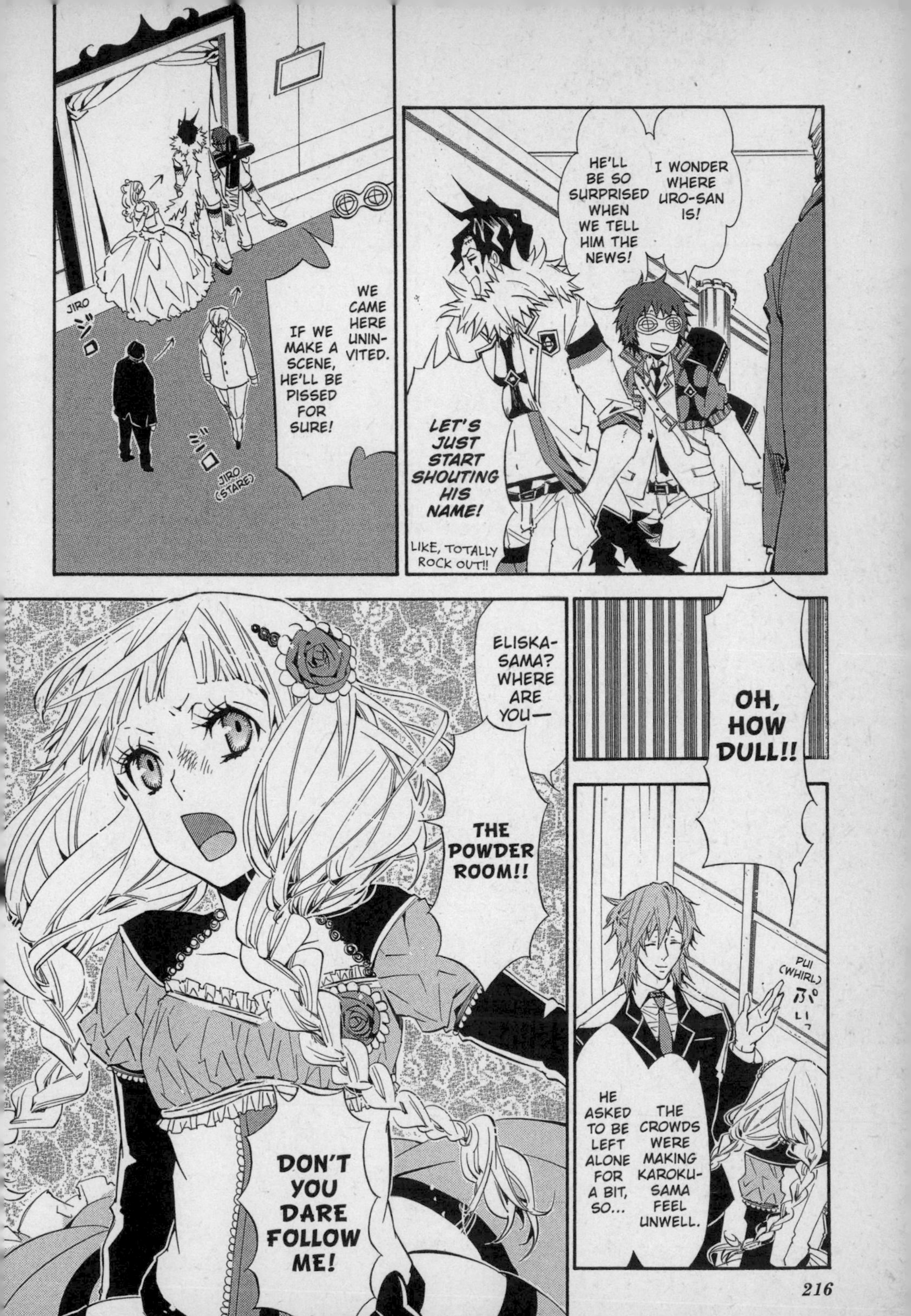
I WONDER WHERE URO-SAN IS!
HE'LL BE SO SURPRISED WHEN WE TELL HIM THE NEWS!
LET'S JUST START SHOUTING HIS NAME!
LIKE, TOTALLY ROCK OUT!!
WE CAME HERE UNINVITED.
IF WE MAKE A SCENE, HE'LL BE PISSED FOR SURE!
JIRO
JIRO (STARE)
OH, HOW DULL!!
PUI (WHIRL)
ぷいっ
THE CROWDS WERE MAKING KAROKU-SAMA FEEL UNWELL.
HE ASKED TO BE LEFT ALONE FOR A BIT, SO...
ELISKA-SAMA? WHERE ARE YOU—
THE POWDER ROOM!!
DON'T YOU DARE FOLLOW ME!

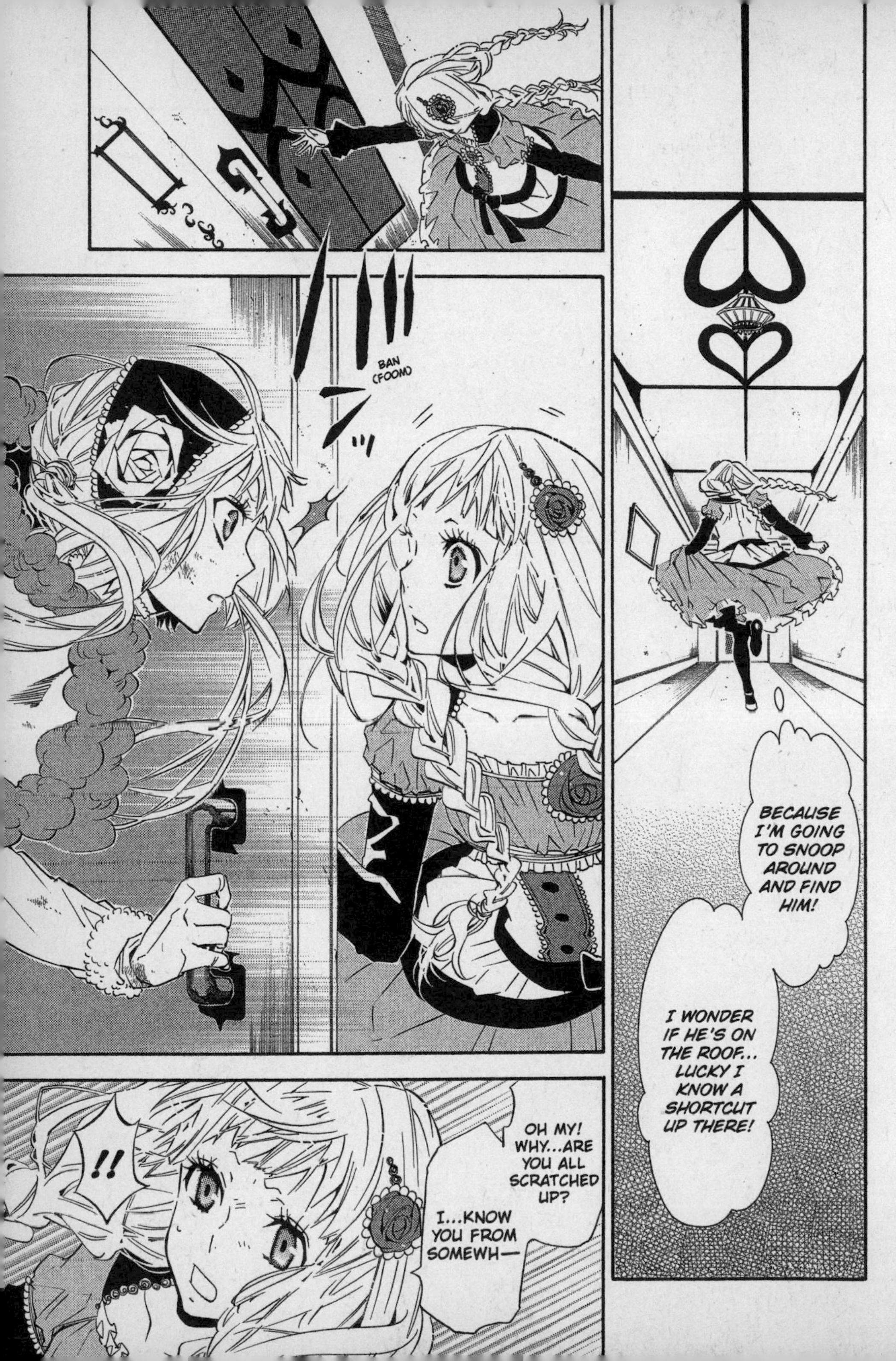
BECAUSE I'M GOING TO SNOOP AROUND AND FIND HIM!
I WONDER IF HE'S ON THE ROOF... LUCKY I KNOW A SHORTCUT UP THERE!
BAN (FOOM)
OH MY! WHY...ARE YOU ALL SCRATCHED UP?
I...KNOW YOU FROM SOMEWH—
!!

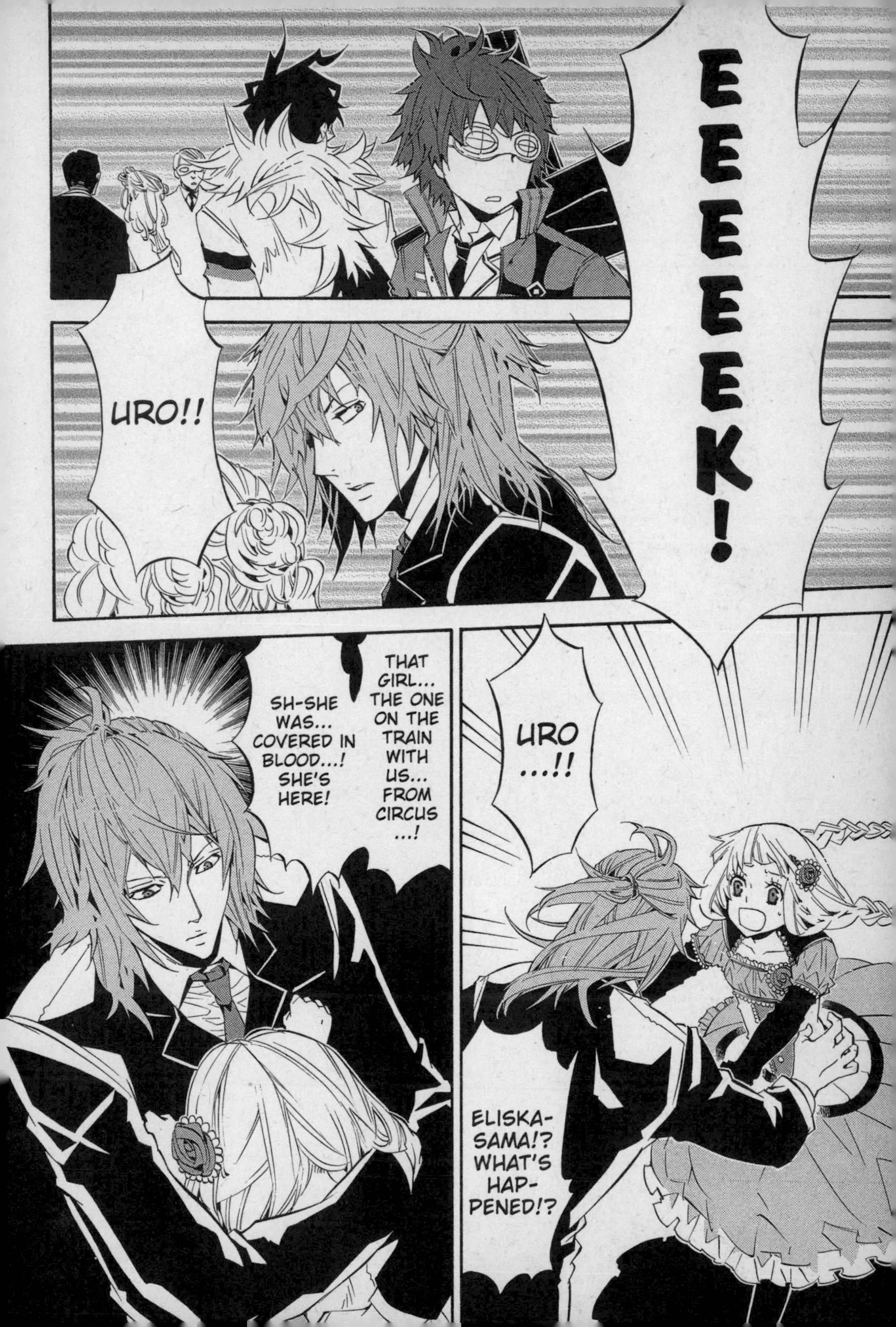
EEEEEK!
URO!!
URO...!!
ELISKA-SAMA!? WHAT'S HAPPENED!?
THAT GIRL... THE ONE ON THE TRAIN WITH US... FROM CIRCUS...!
SH-SHE WAS... COVERED IN BLOOD...! SHE'S HERE!

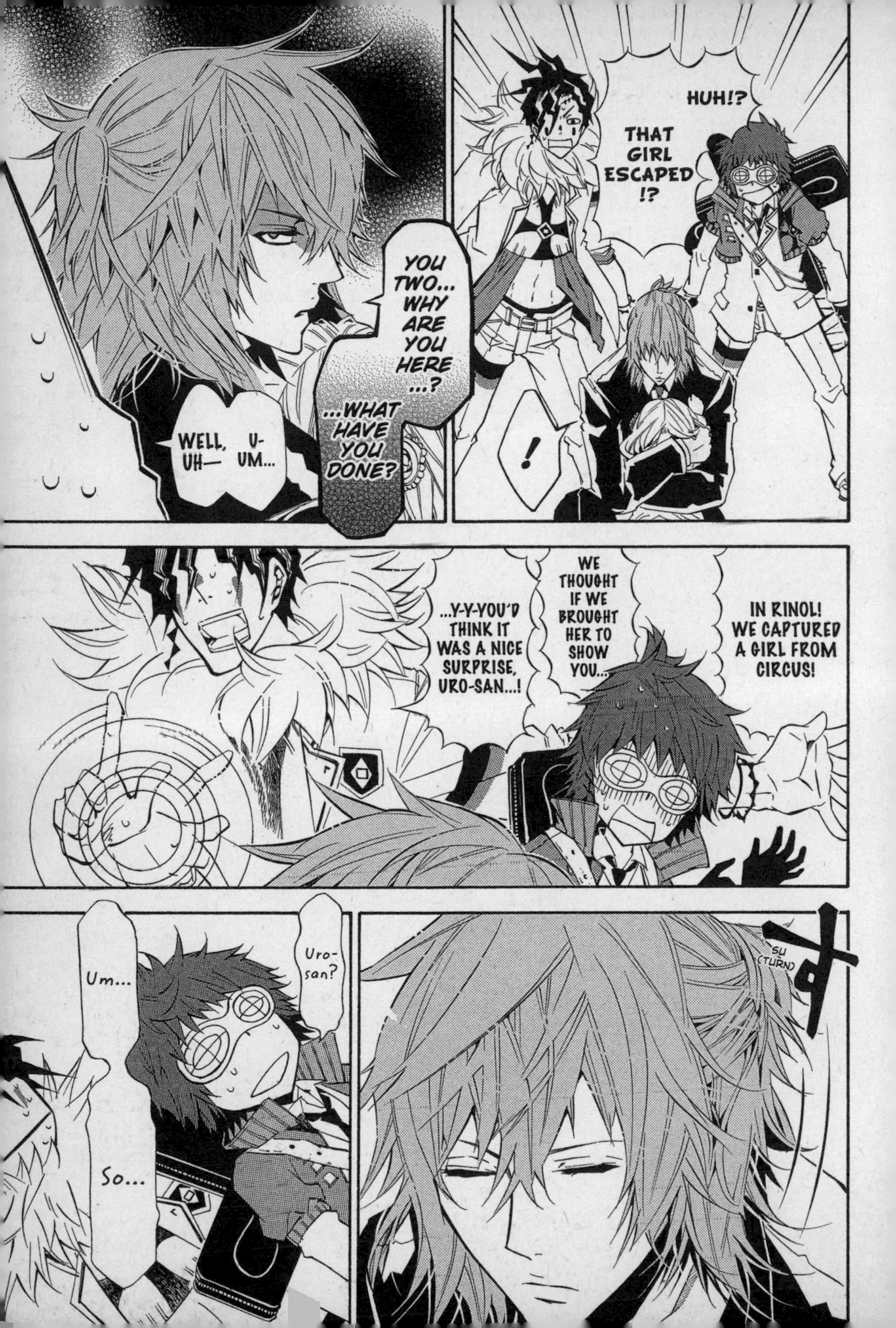
HUH!?
THAT GIRL ESCAPED!?
!
YOU TWO... WHY ARE YOU HERE...?
...WHAT HAVE YOU DONE?
WELL, UH— U-UM...
IN RINOL! WE CAPTURED A GIRL FROM CIRCUS!
WE THOUGHT IF WE BROUGHT HER TO SHOW YOU...
...Y-Y-YOU'D THINK IT WAS A NICE SURPRISE, URO-SAN...!
SU (TURN)
Uro-san?
Um...
So...

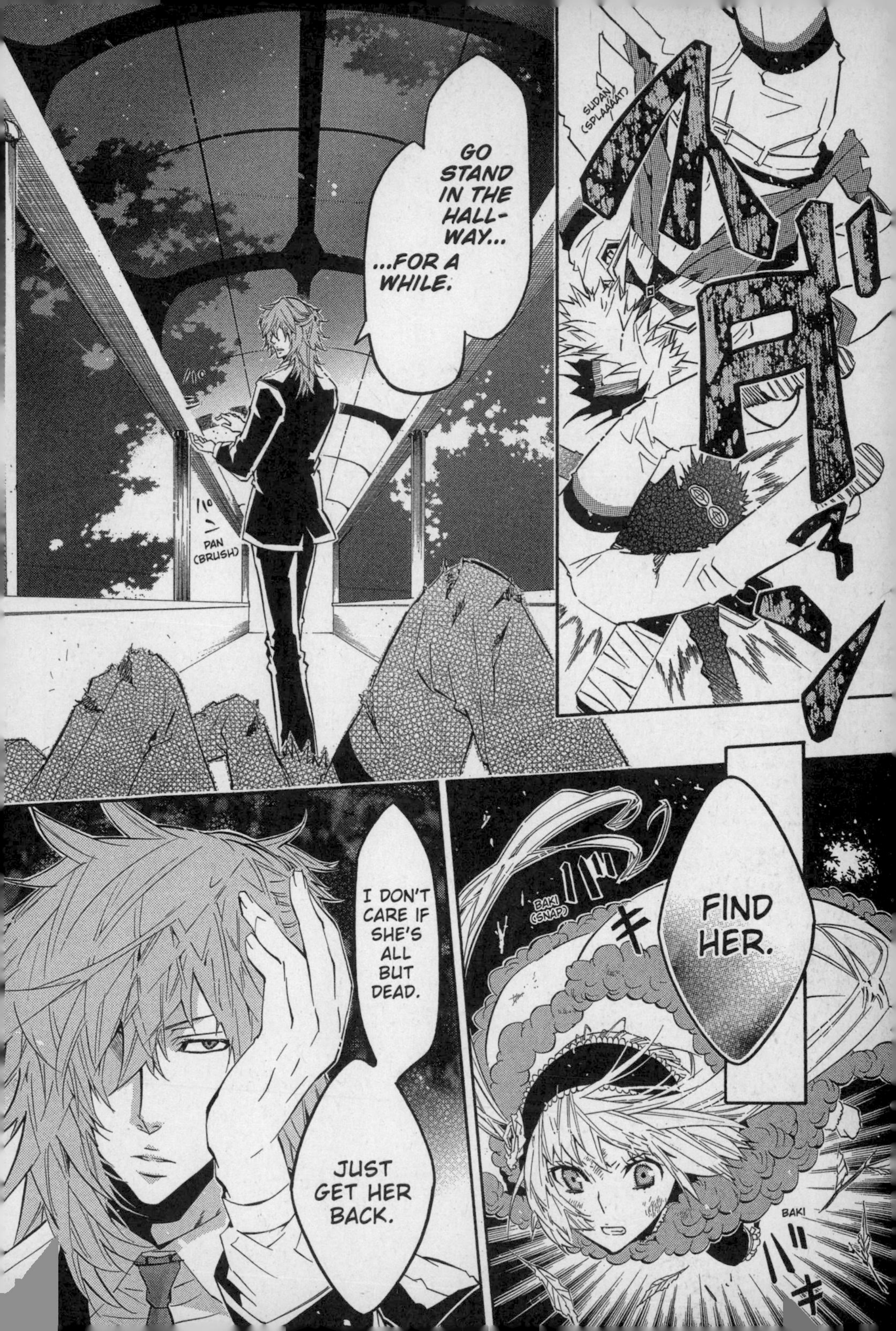
SUDAN (SPLAAAAT)
GO STAND IN THE HALL-WAY...
...FOR A WHILE.
PAN (BRUSH)
FIND HER.
BAKI (SNAP)
BAKI
I DON'T CARE IF SHE'S ALL BUT DEAD.
JUST GET HER BACK.

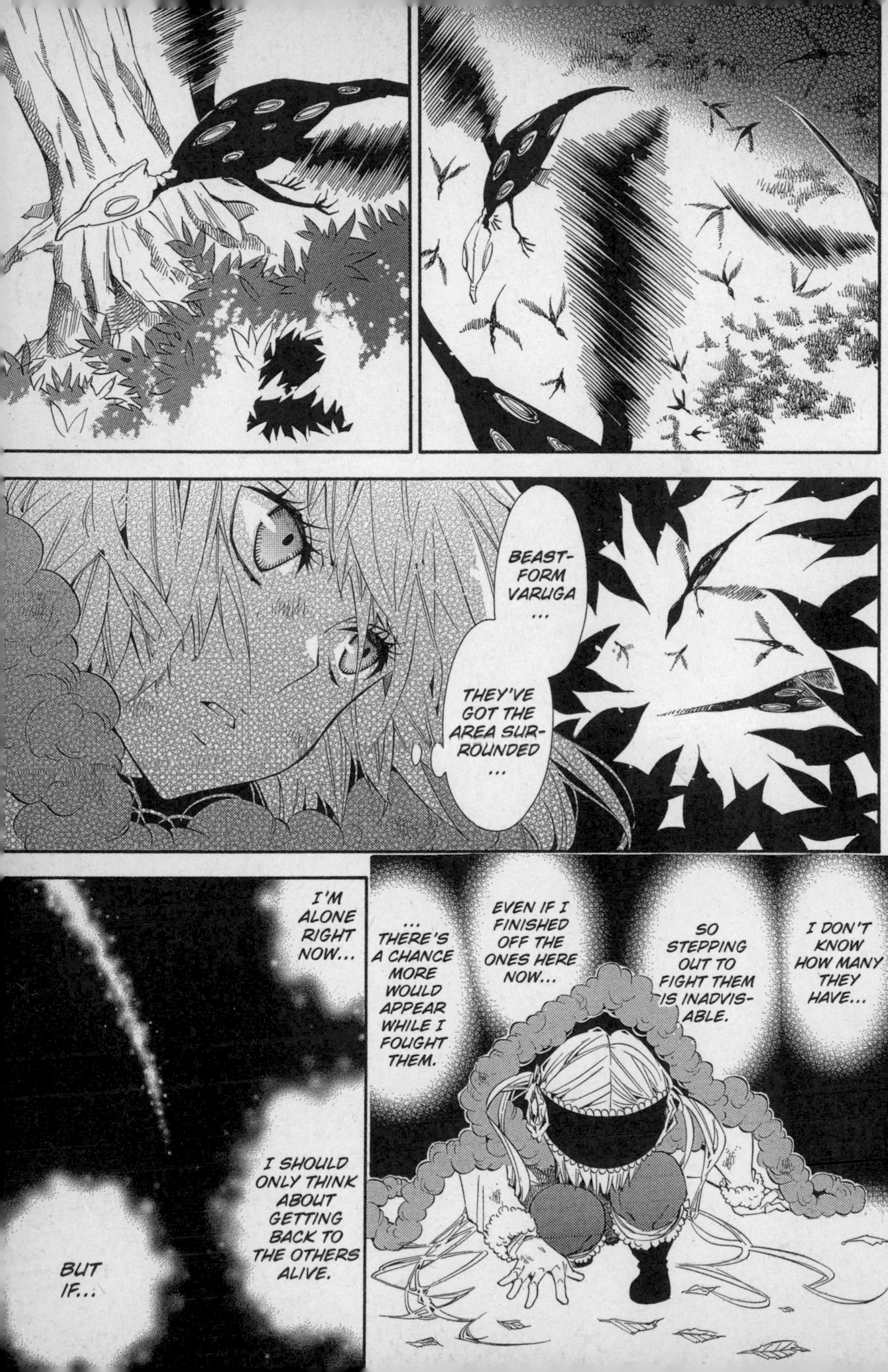
BEAST-FORM VARUGA...
THEY'VE GOT THE AREA SURROUNDED...
I DON'T KNOW HOW MANY THEY HAVE...
SO STEPPING OUT TO FIGHT THEM IS INADVISABLE.
EVEN IF I FINISHED OFF THE ONES HERE NOW...
...THERE'S A CHANCE MORE WOULD APPEAR WHILE I FOUGHT THEM.
I'M ALONE RIGHT NOW...
I SHOULD ONLY THINK ABOUT GETTING BACK TO THE OTHERS ALIVE.
BUT IF...

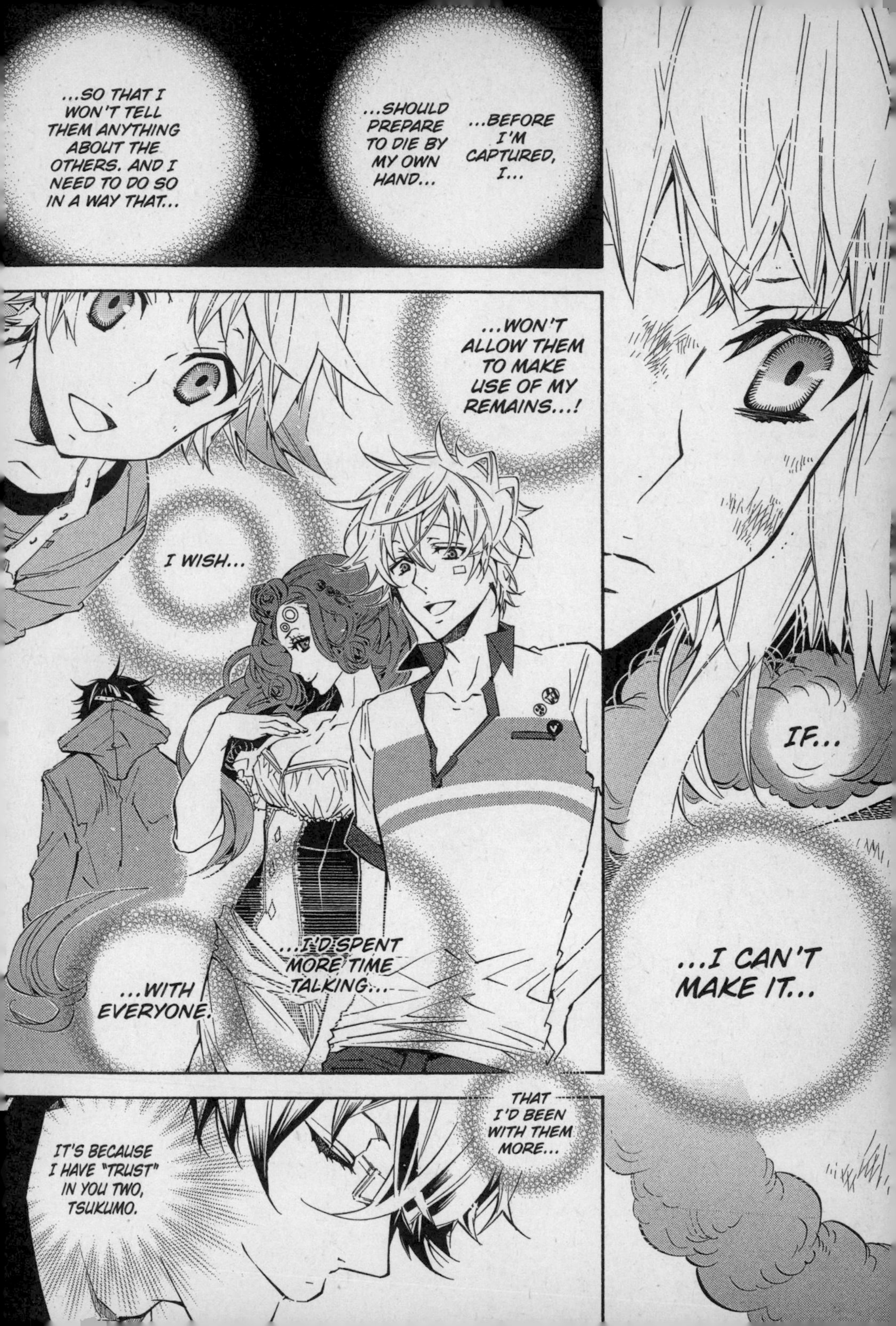
IF...
...I CAN'T MAKE IT...
...BEFORE I'M CAPTURED, I...
...SHOULD PREPARE TO DIE BY MY OWN HAND...
...SO THAT I WON'T TELL THEM ANYTHING ABOUT THE OTHERS. AND I NEED TO DO SO IN A WAY THAT...
...WON'T ALLOW THEM TO MAKE USE OF MY REMAINS...!
I WISH...
...I'D SPENT MORE TIME TALKING...
...WITH EVERYONE.
THAT I'D BEEN WITH THEM MORE...
IT'S BECAUSE I HAVE "TRUST" IN YOU TWO, TSUKUMO.

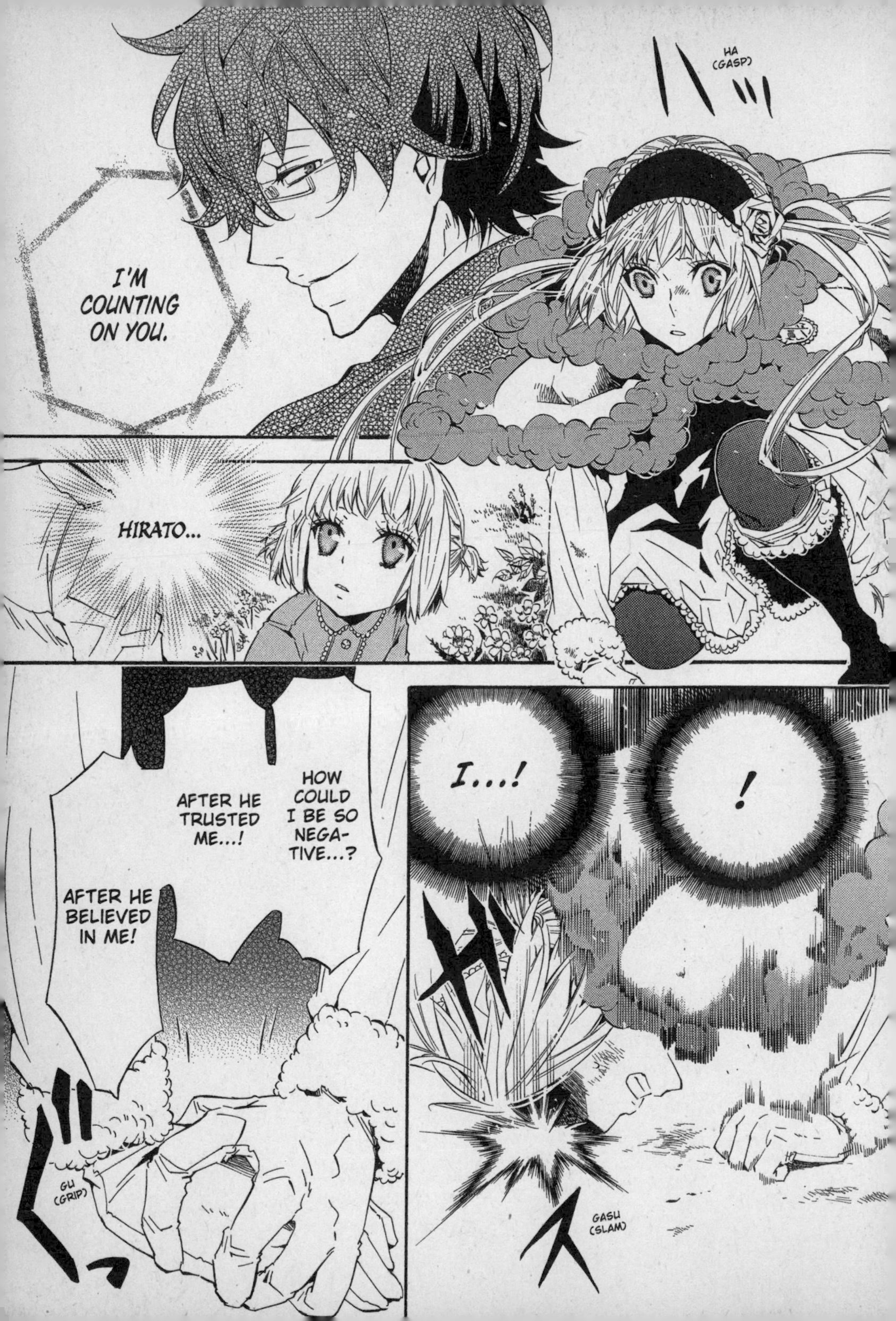

HA (GASP)
I'M COUNTING ON YOU.
HIRATO...
!
I...!
GASU (SLAM)
HOW COULD I BE SO NEGA-TIVE...?
AFTER HE TRUSTED ME...!
AFTER HE BELIEVED IN ME!
GU (GRIP)

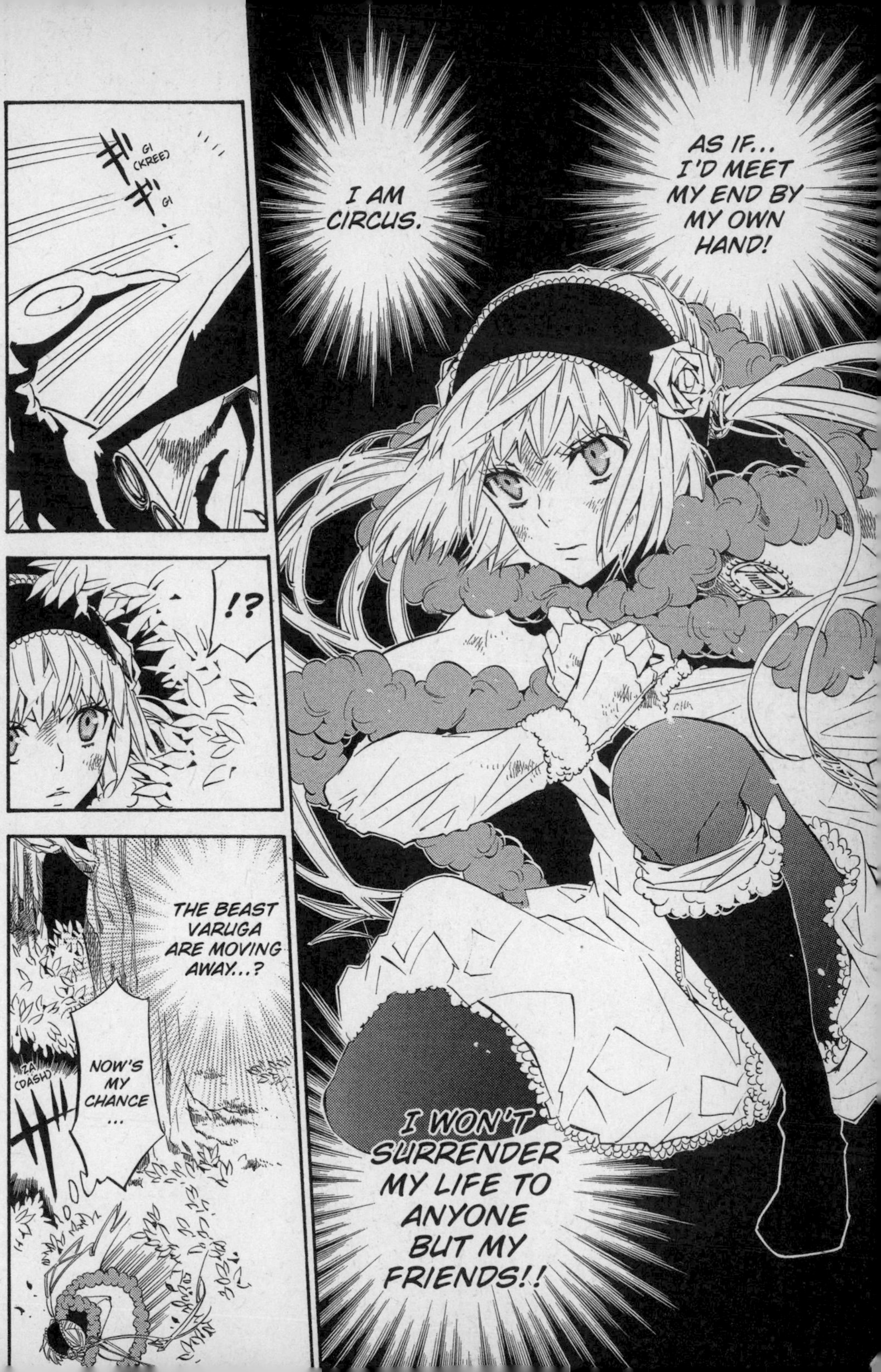
AS IF... I'D MEET MY END BY MY OWN HAND!
I AM CIRCUS.
I WON'T SURRENDER MY LIFE TO ANYONE BUT MY FRIENDS!!
GI (KREE)
GI
!?
THE BEAST VARUGA ARE MOVING AWAY...?
ZA (DASH)
NOW'S MY CHANCE...

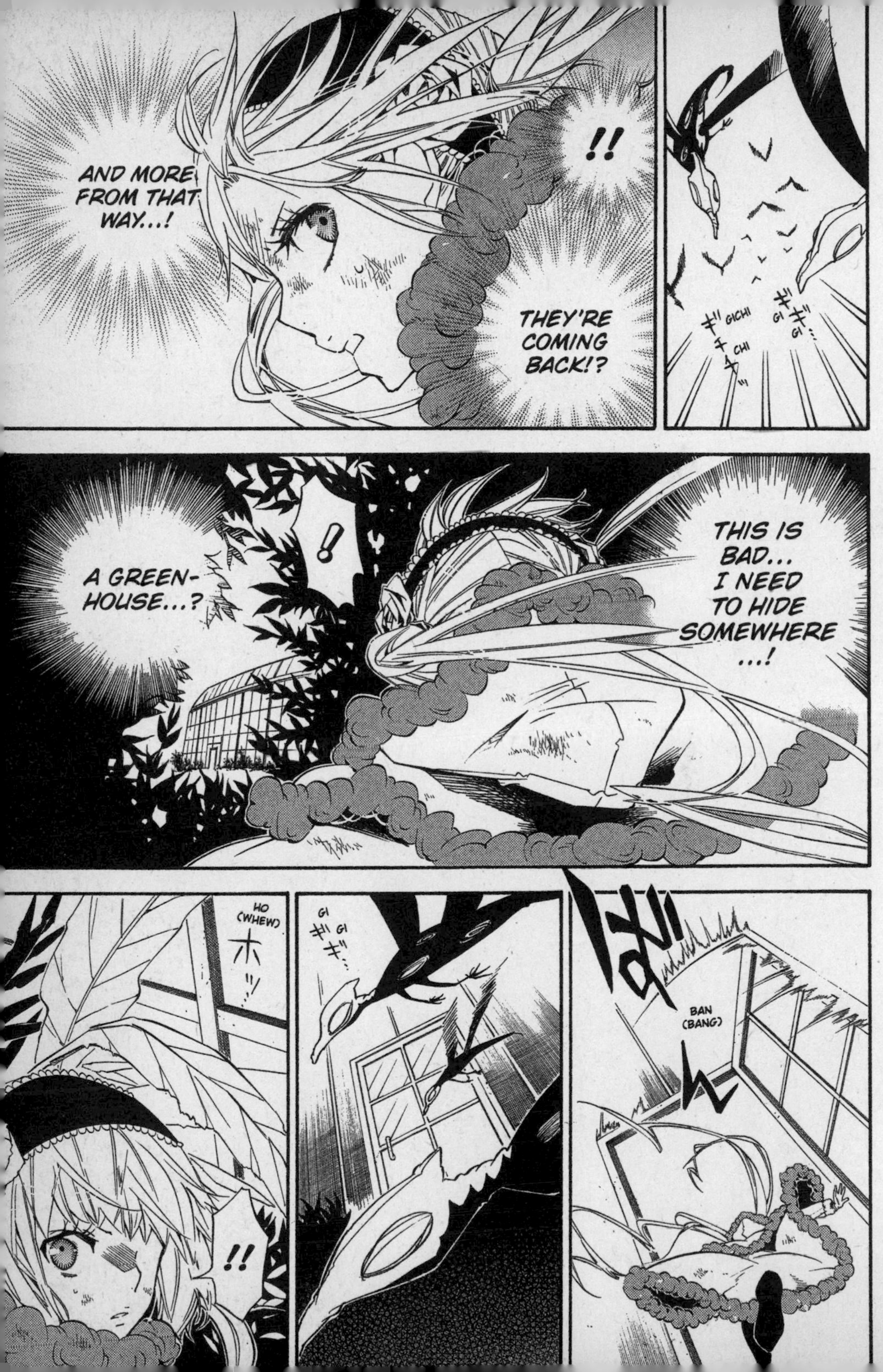
GICHI
CHI
GI
GI
!!
THEY'RE COMING BACK!?
AND MORE FROM THAT WAY...!
THIS IS BAD... I NEED TO HIDE SOMEWHERE...!
!
A GREEN-HOUSE...?
BAN (BANG)
GI
GI
HO (WHEW)
!!

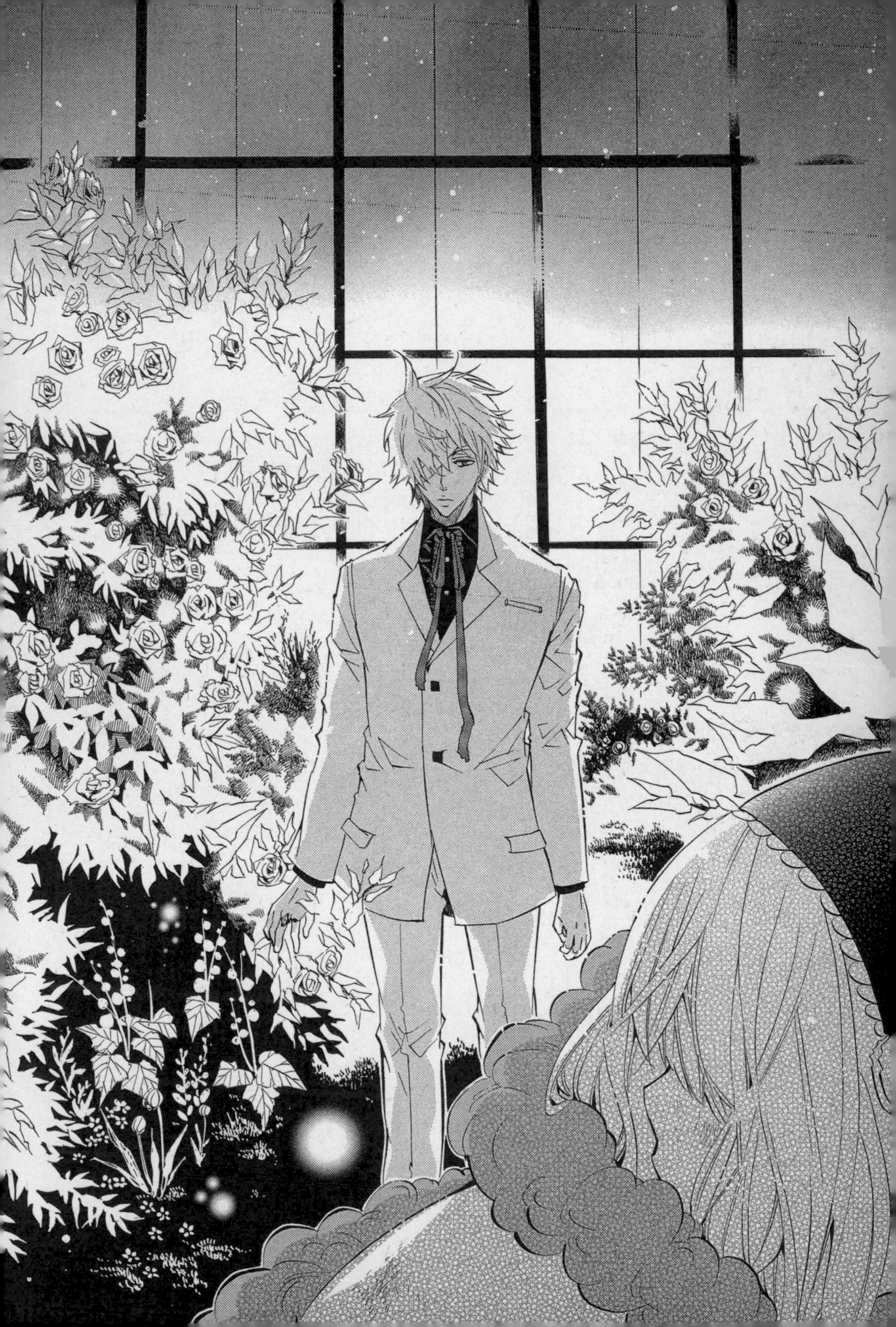

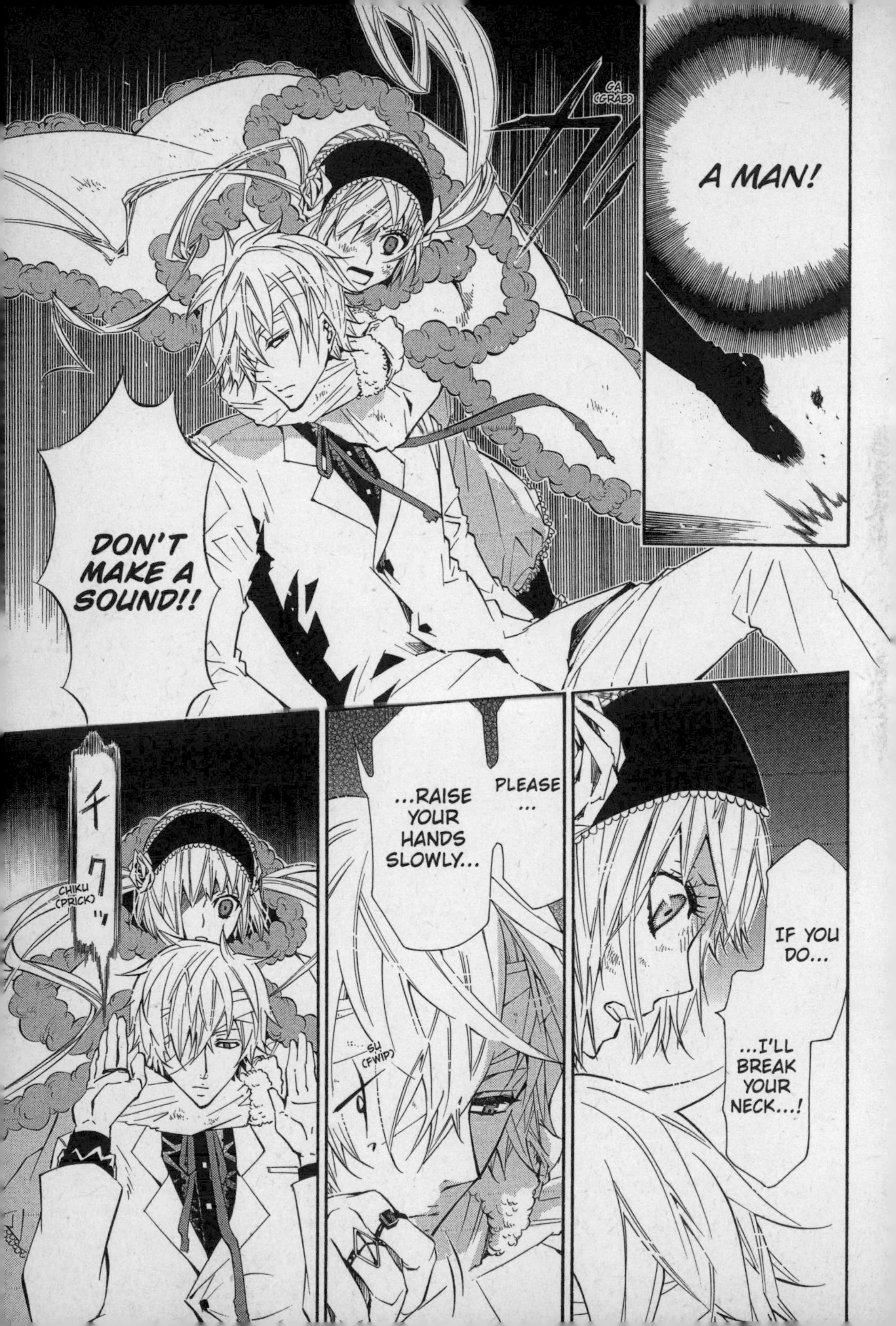
A MAN!
GA (GRAB)
DON'T MAKE A SOUND!!
IF YOU DO...
...I'LL BREAK YOUR NECK...!
PLEASE...
...RAISE YOUR HANDS SLOWLY...
SU (FWIP)
チクッ
CHIKU (PRICK)

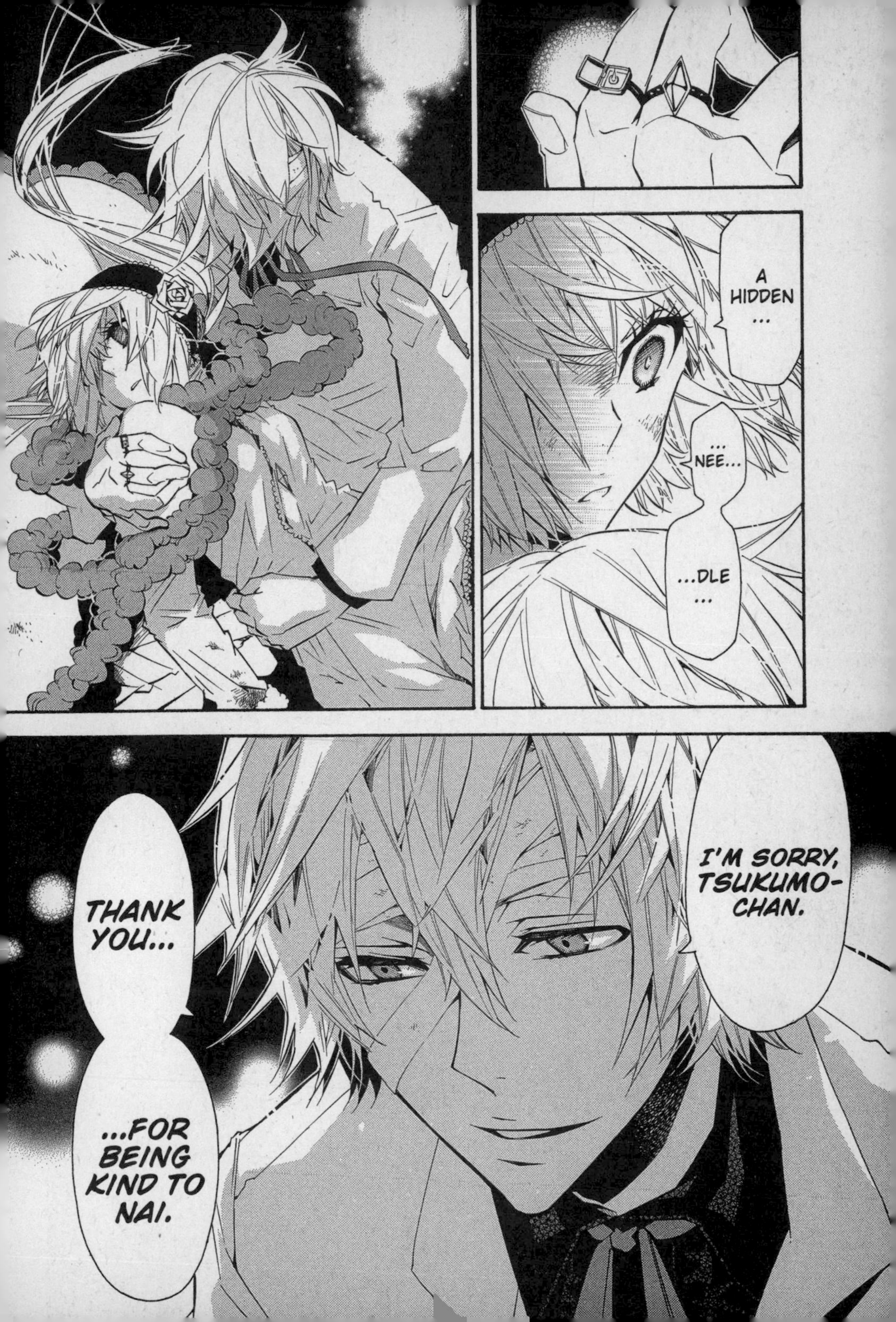
A HIDDEN ...
... NEE...
...DLE ...
I'M SORRY, TSUKUMO-CHAN.
THANK YOU...
...FOR BEING KIND TO NAI.

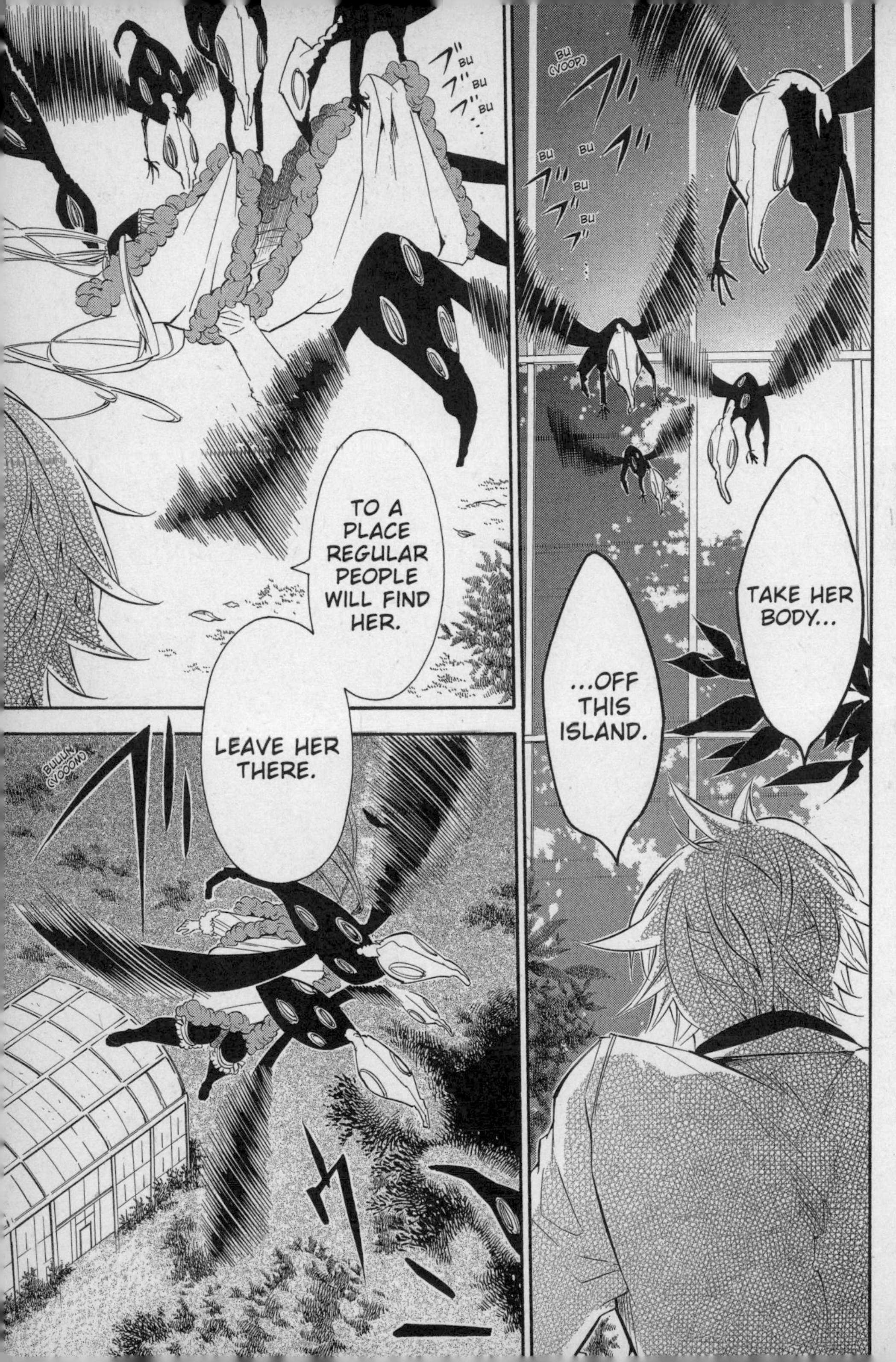
BU (VOOP)
BU
BU
BU
BU
TAKE HER BODY...
...OFF THIS ISLAND.
BU
BU
BU
TO A PLACE REGULAR PEOPLE WILL FIND HER.
LEAVE HER THERE.
BUUUN (VOOOM)

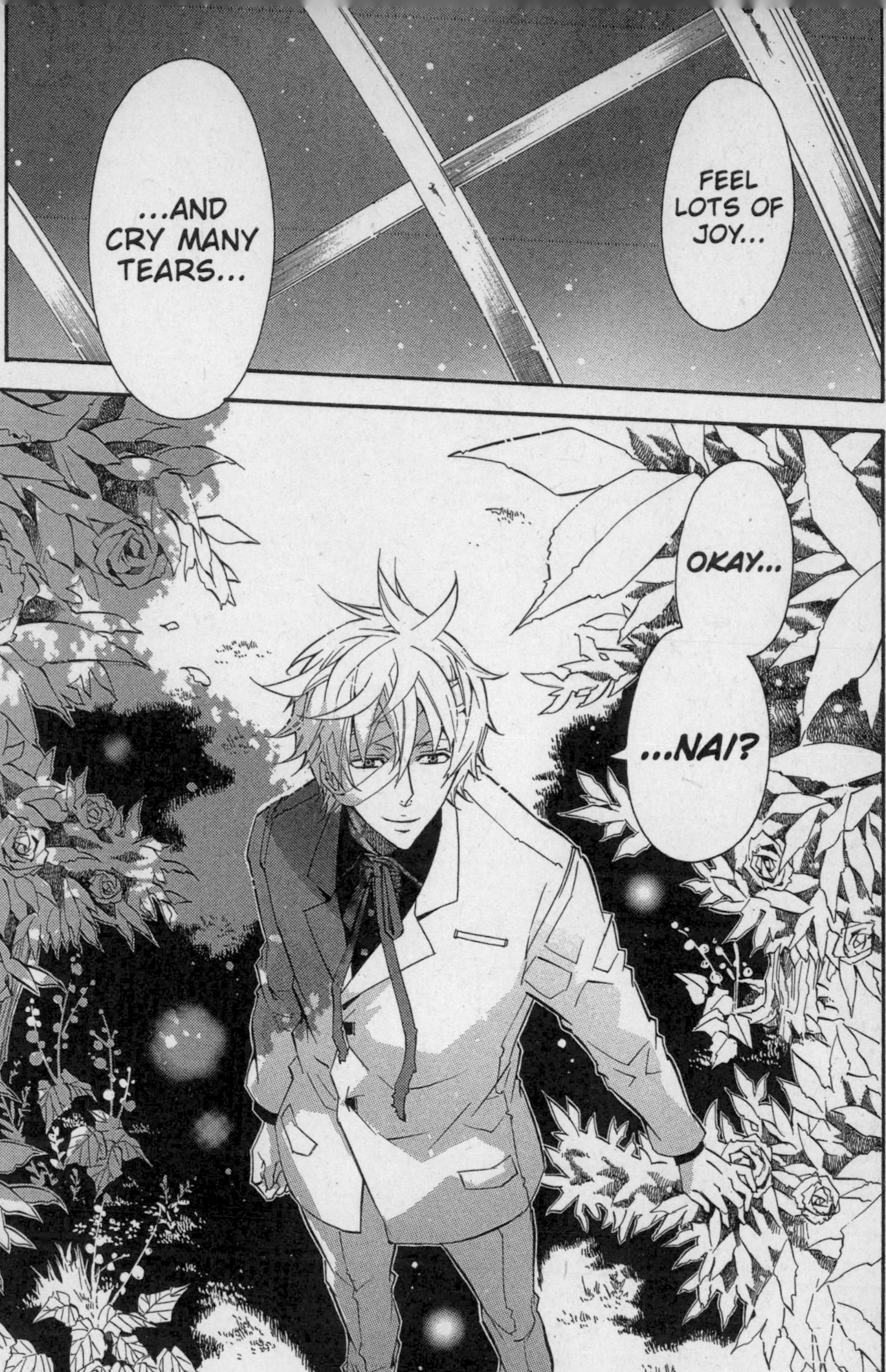
FEEL LOTS OF JOY...
...AND CRY MANY TEARS...
OKAY...
...NAI?

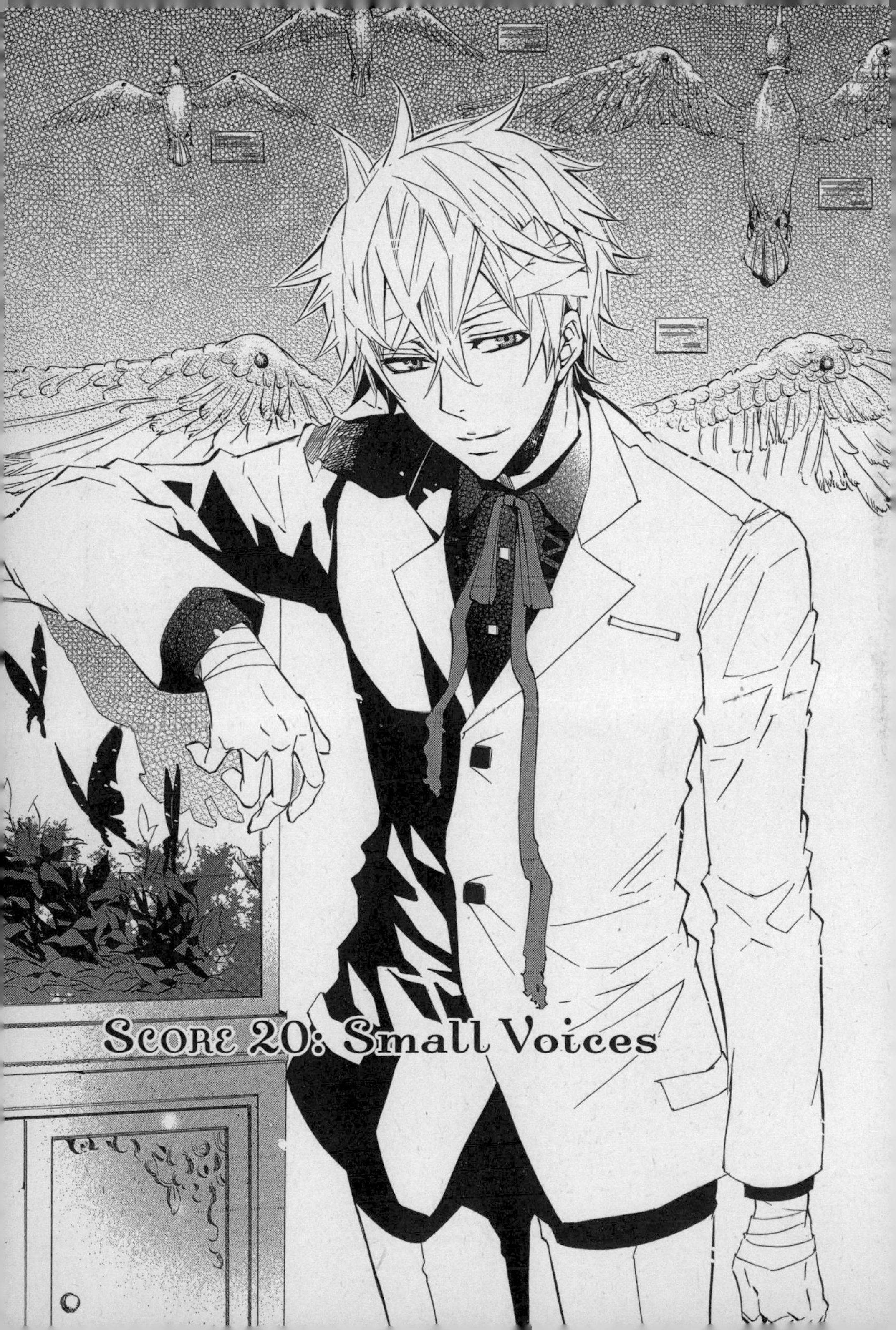
Score 20: Small Voices

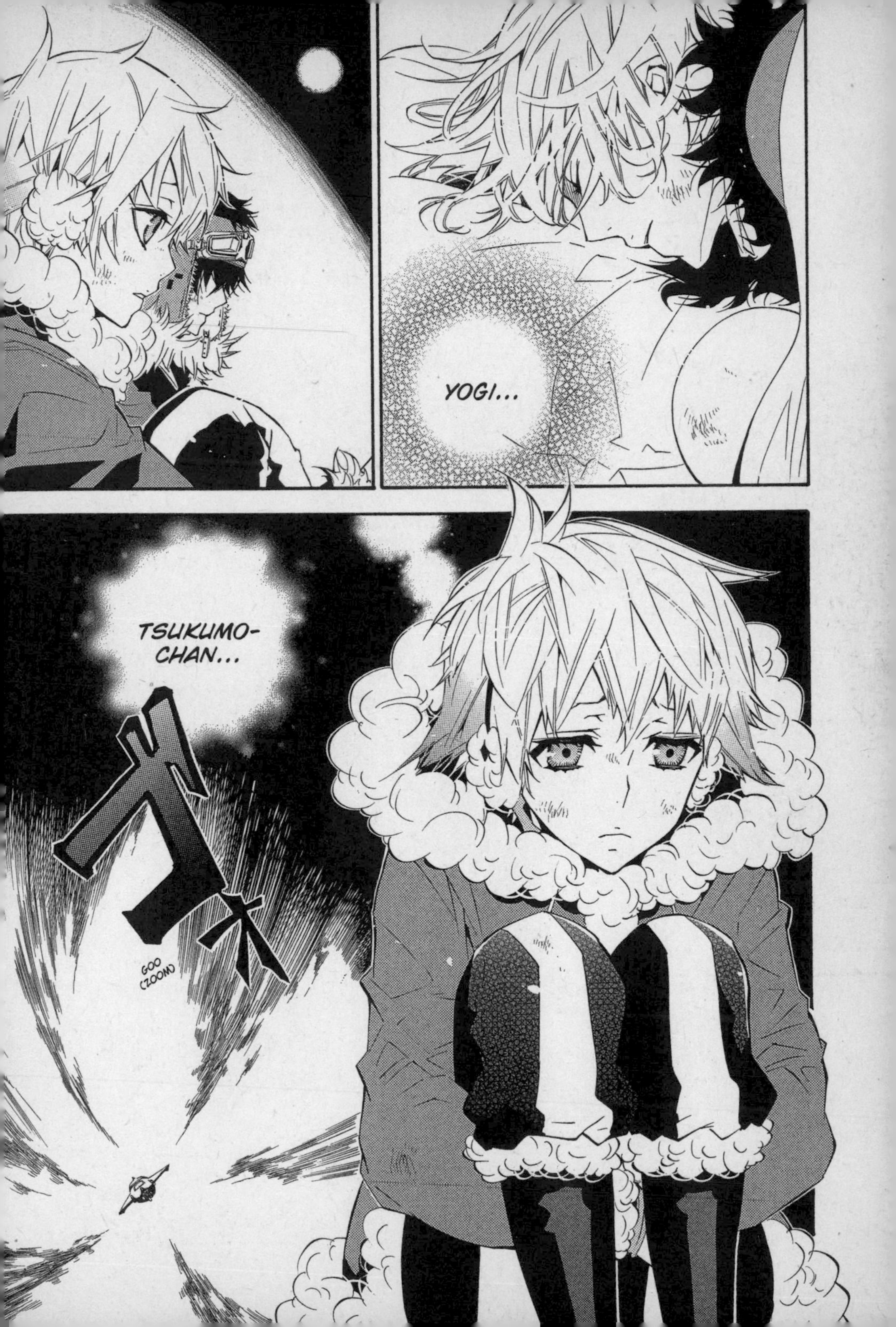
YOGI...
TSUKUMO-CHAN...
GOO (ZOOM)

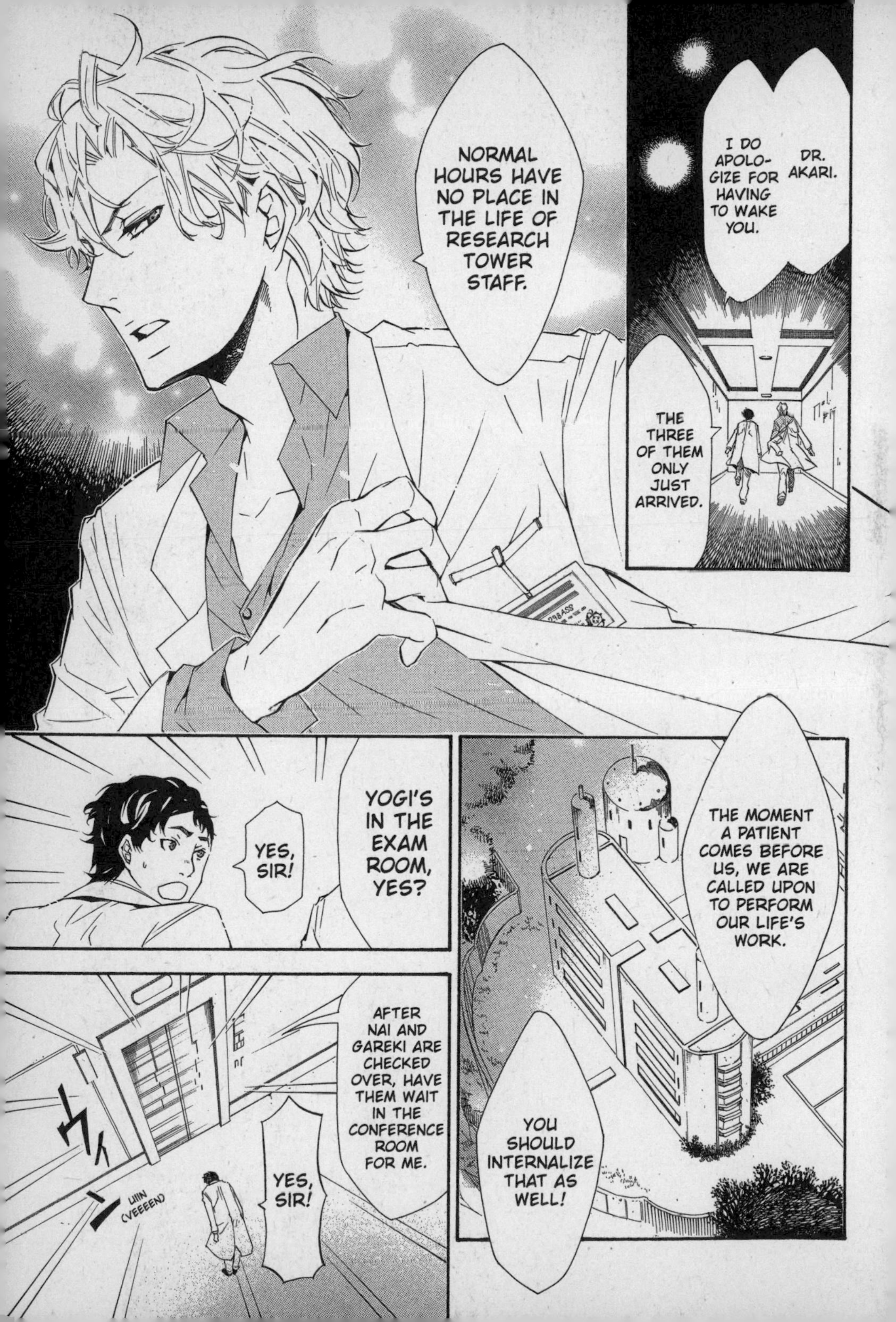
DR. AKARI.
I DO APOLOGIZE FOR HAVING TO WAKE YOU.
THE THREE OF THEM ONLY JUST ARRIVED.
NORMAL HOURS HAVE NO PLACE IN THE LIFE OF RESEARCH TOWER STAFF.
THE MOMENT A PATIENT COMES BEFORE US, WE ARE CALLED UPON TO PERFORM OUR LIFE'S WORK.
YOU SHOULD INTERNALIZE THAT AS WELL!
YOGI'S IN THE EXAM ROOM, YES?
YES, SIR!
AFTER NAI AND GAREKI ARE CHECKED OVER, HAVE THEM WAIT IN THE CONFERENCE ROOM FOR ME.
YES, SIR!
UIIN (VEEEEND)

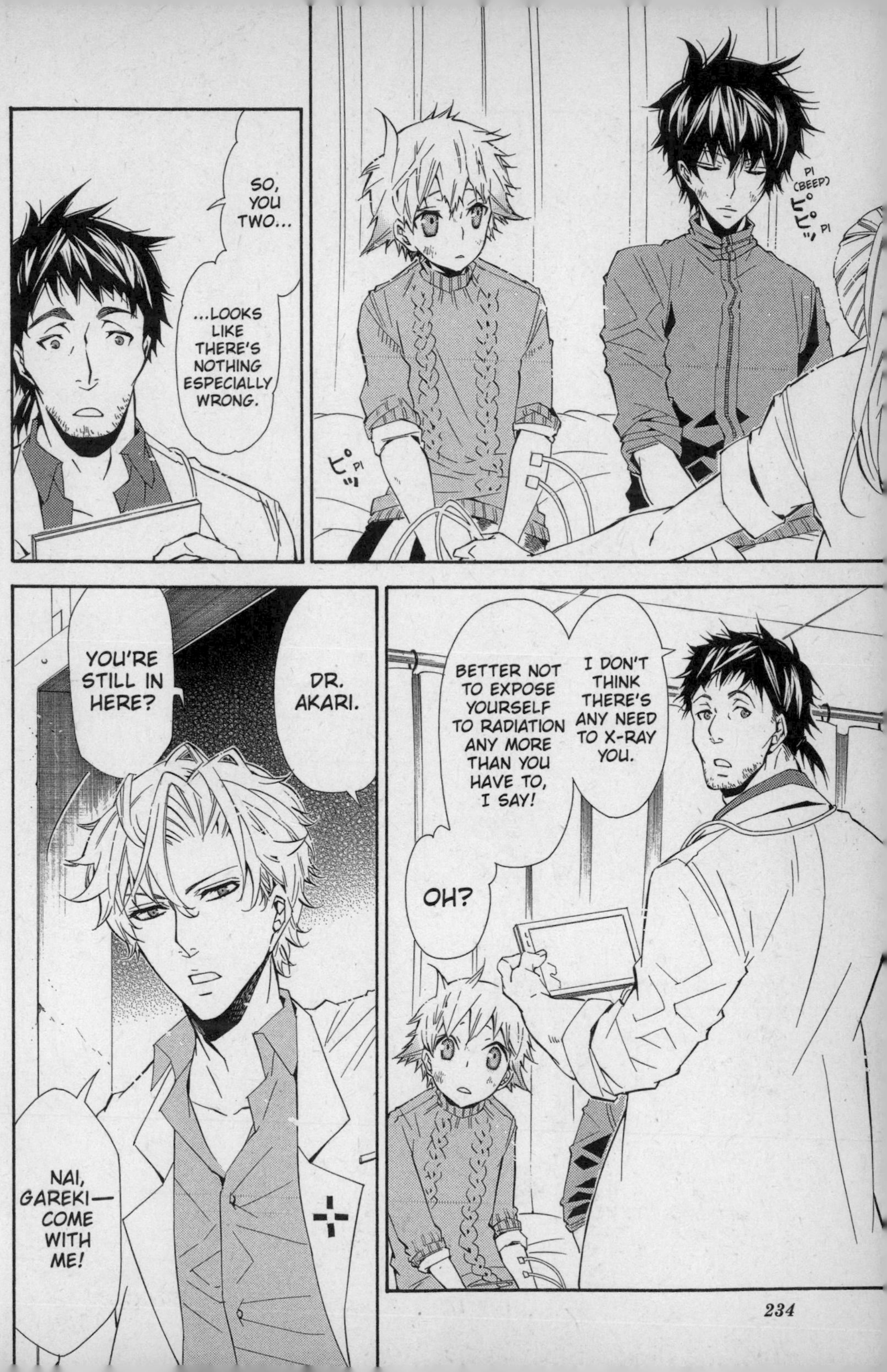
PI (BEEP)
PI
PI
SO, YOU TWO...
...LOOKS LIKE THERE'S NOTHING ESPECIALLY WRONG.
I DON'T THINK THERE'S ANY NEED TO X-RAY YOU.
BETTER NOT TO EXPOSE YOURSELF TO RADIATION ANY MORE THAN YOU HAVE TO, I SAY!
OH?
DR. AKARI.
YOU'RE STILL IN HERE?
NAI, GAREKI—COME WITH ME!

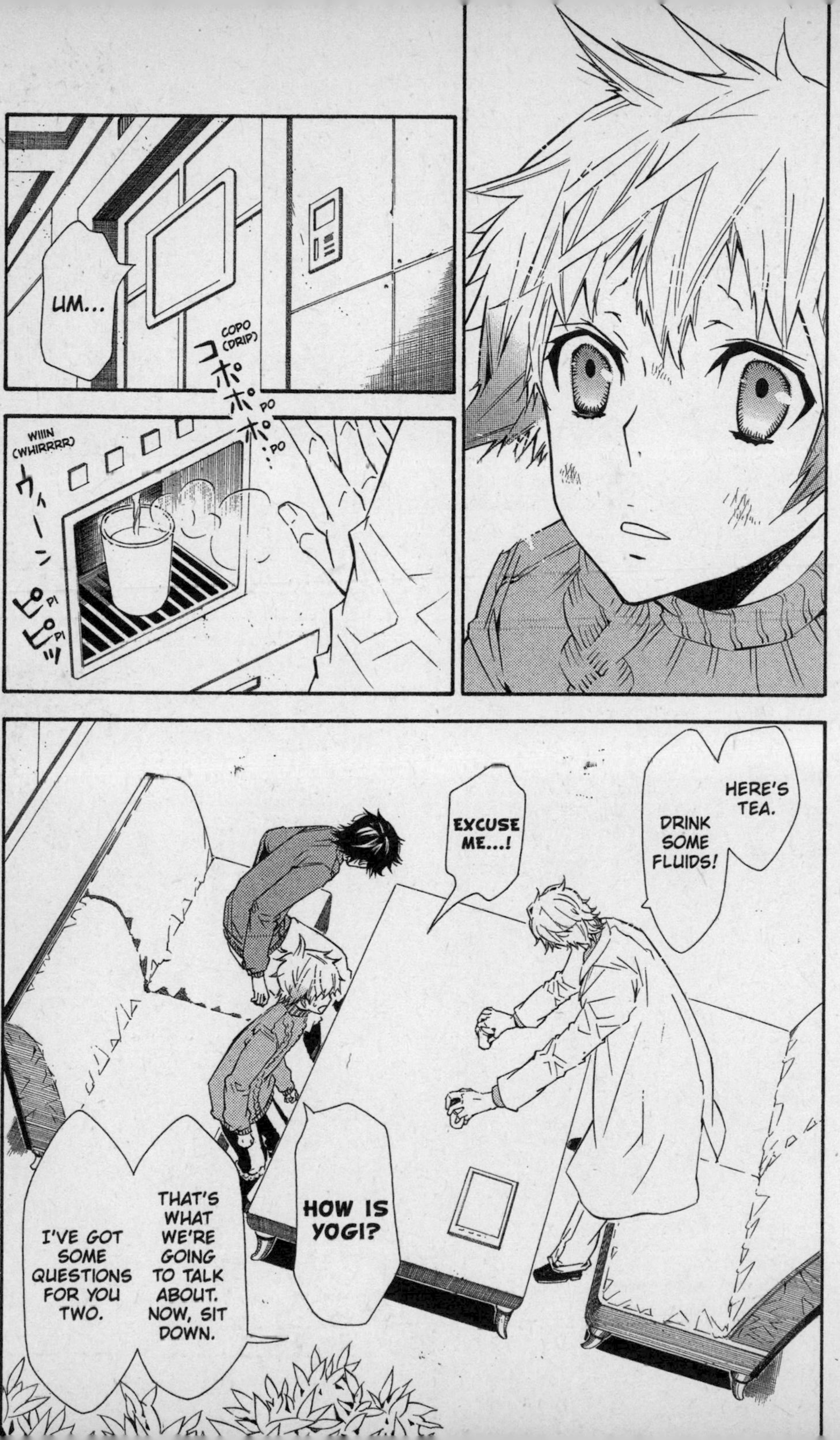
UM...
COPO (DRIP)
コポポポ…
PO
PO
WIIIN (WHIRRRR)
ウィーン
PI
PI
ピピッ
HERE'S TEA.
DRINK SOME FLUIDS!
EXCUSE ME...!
HOW IS YOGI?
THAT'S WHAT WE'RE GOING TO TALK ABOUT. NOW, SIT DOWN.
I'VE GOT SOME QUESTIONS FOR YOU TWO.

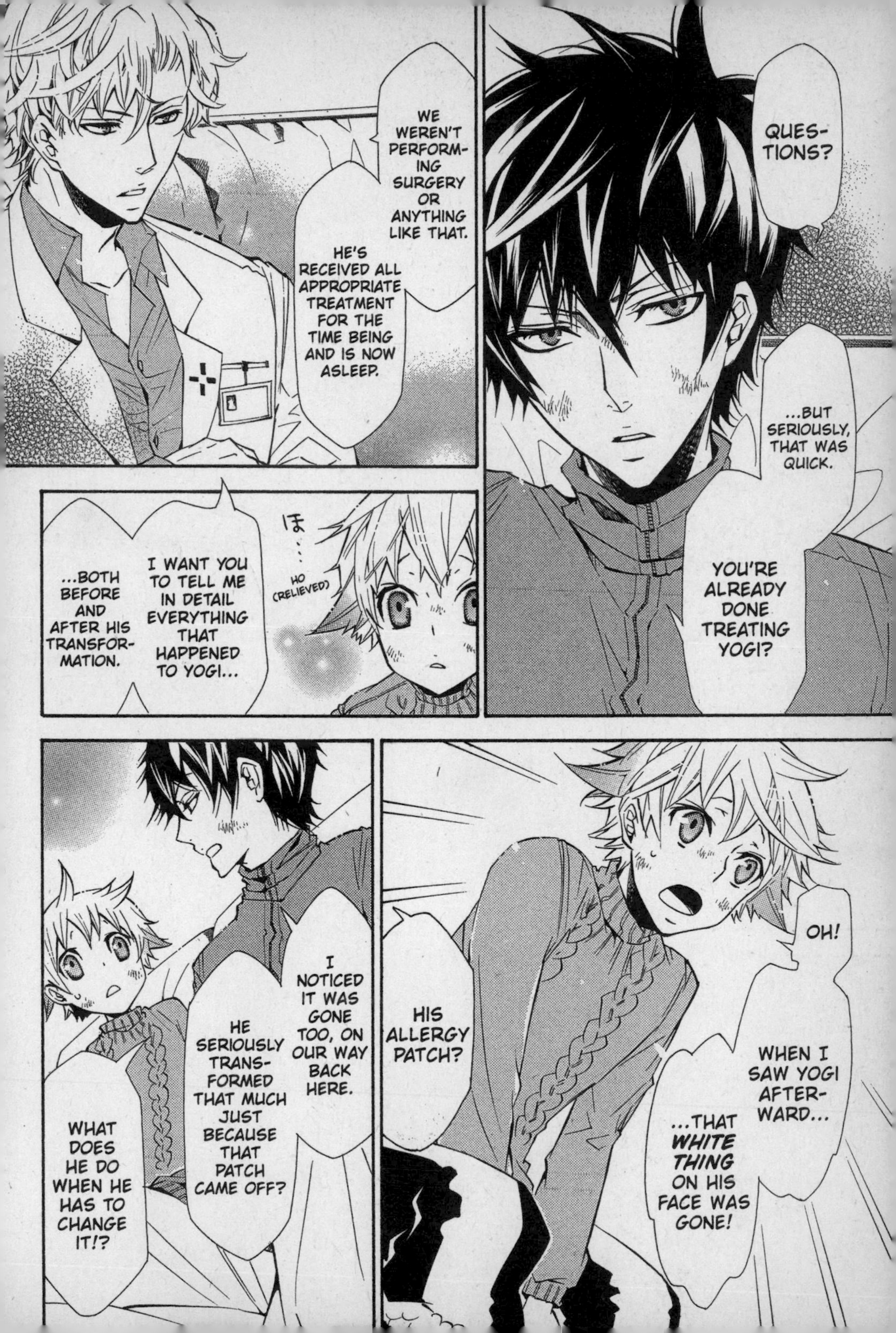

QUES-TIONS?
...BUT SERIOUSLY, THAT WAS QUICK.
YOU'RE ALREADY DONE TREATING YOGI?
WE WEREN'T PERFORM-ING SURGERY OR ANYTHING LIKE THAT.
HE'S RECEIVED ALL APPROPRIATE TREATMENT FOR THE TIME BEING AND IS NOW ASLEEP.
ほ…
HO (RELIEVED)
I WANT YOU TO TELL ME IN DETAIL EVERYTHING THAT HAPPENED TO YOGI...
...BOTH BEFORE AND AFTER HIS TRANSFOR-MATION.
OH!
WHEN I SAW YOGI AFTER-WARD...
...THAT *WHITE THING* ON HIS FACE WAS GONE!
HIS ALLERGY PATCH?
I NOTICED IT WAS GONE TOO, ON OUR WAY BACK HERE.
HE SERIOUSLY TRANS-FORMED THAT MUCH JUST BECAUSE THAT PATCH CAME OFF?
WHAT DOES HE DO WHEN HE HAS TO CHANGE IT!?

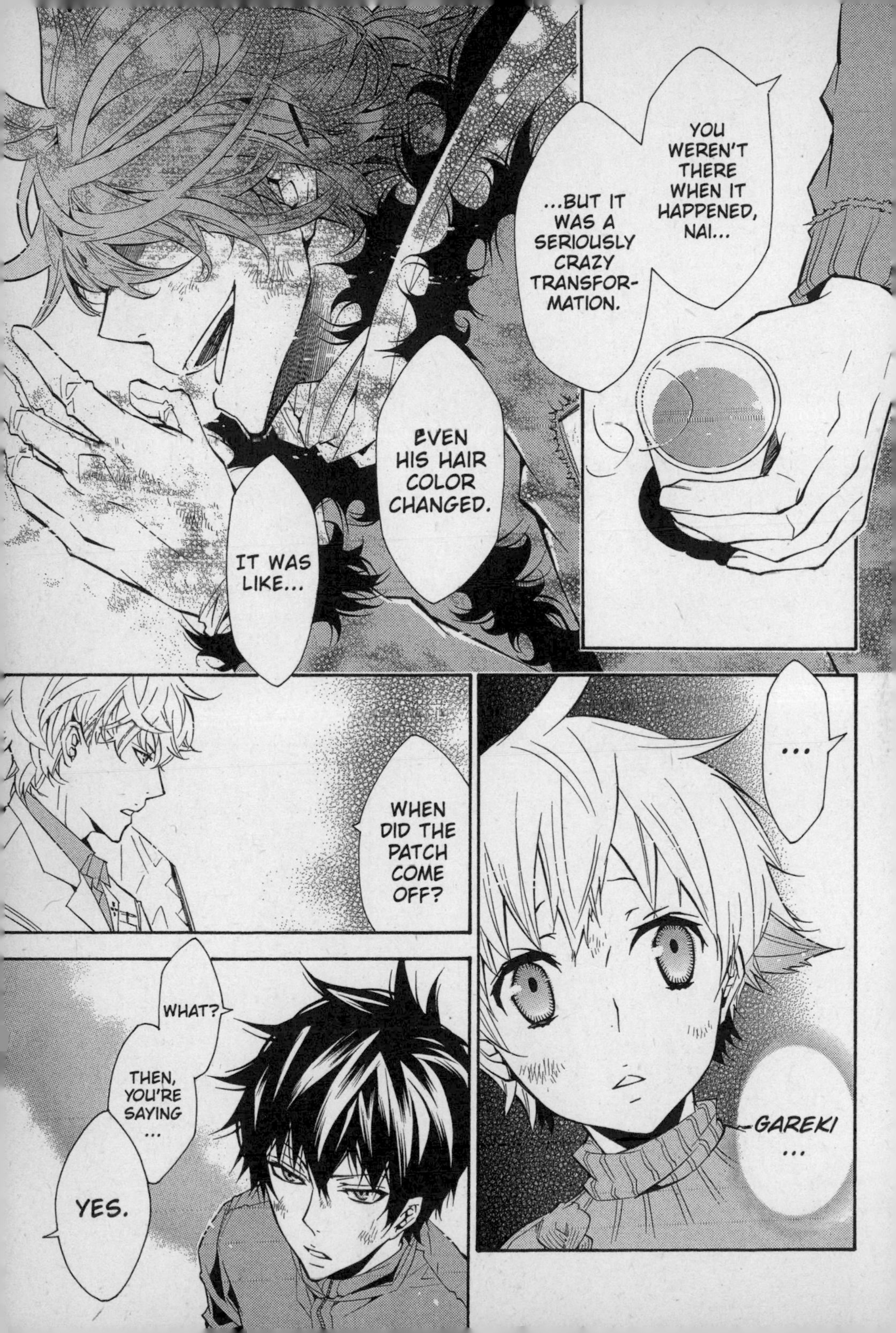

YOU WEREN'T THERE WHEN IT HAPPENED, NAI...
...BUT IT WAS A SERIOUSLY CRAZY TRANSFOR-MATION.
EVEN HIS HAIR COLOR CHANGED.
IT WAS LIKE...
...
GAREKI ...
WHEN DID THE PATCH COME OFF?
WHAT?
THEN, YOU'RE SAYING ...
YES.

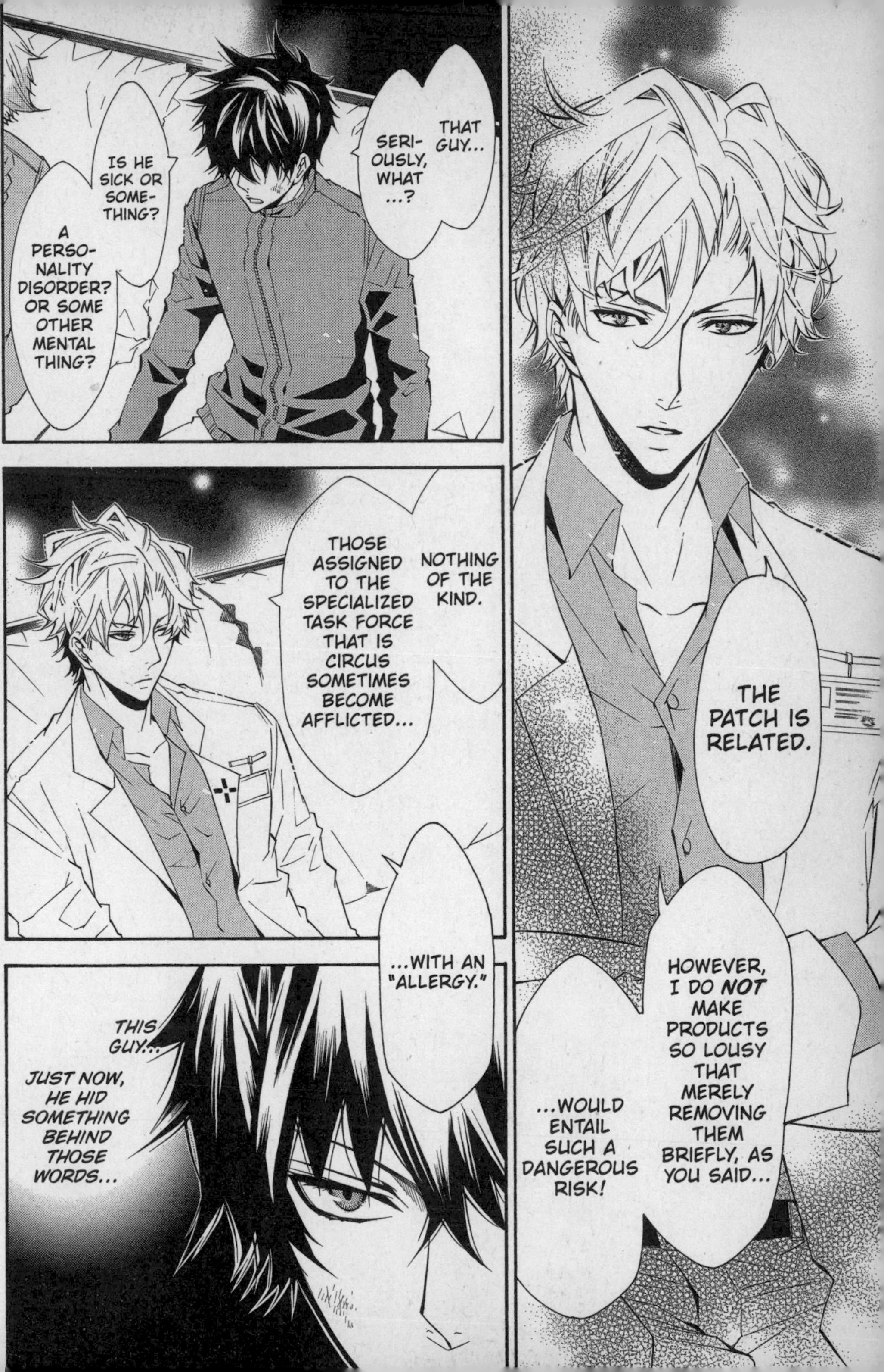
THE PATCH IS RELATED.
HOWEVER, I DO *NOT* MAKE PRODUCTS SO LOUSY THAT MERELY REMOVING THEM BRIEFLY, AS YOU SAID...
...WOULD ENTAIL SUCH A DANGEROUS RISK!
THAT GUY... SERIOUSLY, WHAT...?
IS HE SICK OR SOMETHING?
A PERSONALITY DISORDER? OR SOME OTHER MENTAL THING?
NOTHING OF THE KIND.
THOSE ASSIGNED TO THE SPECIALIZED TASK FORCE THAT IS CIRCUS SOMETIMES BECOME AFFLICTED...
...WITH AN "ALLERGY."
THIS GUY...
JUST NOW, HE HID SOMETHING BEHIND THOSE WORDS...

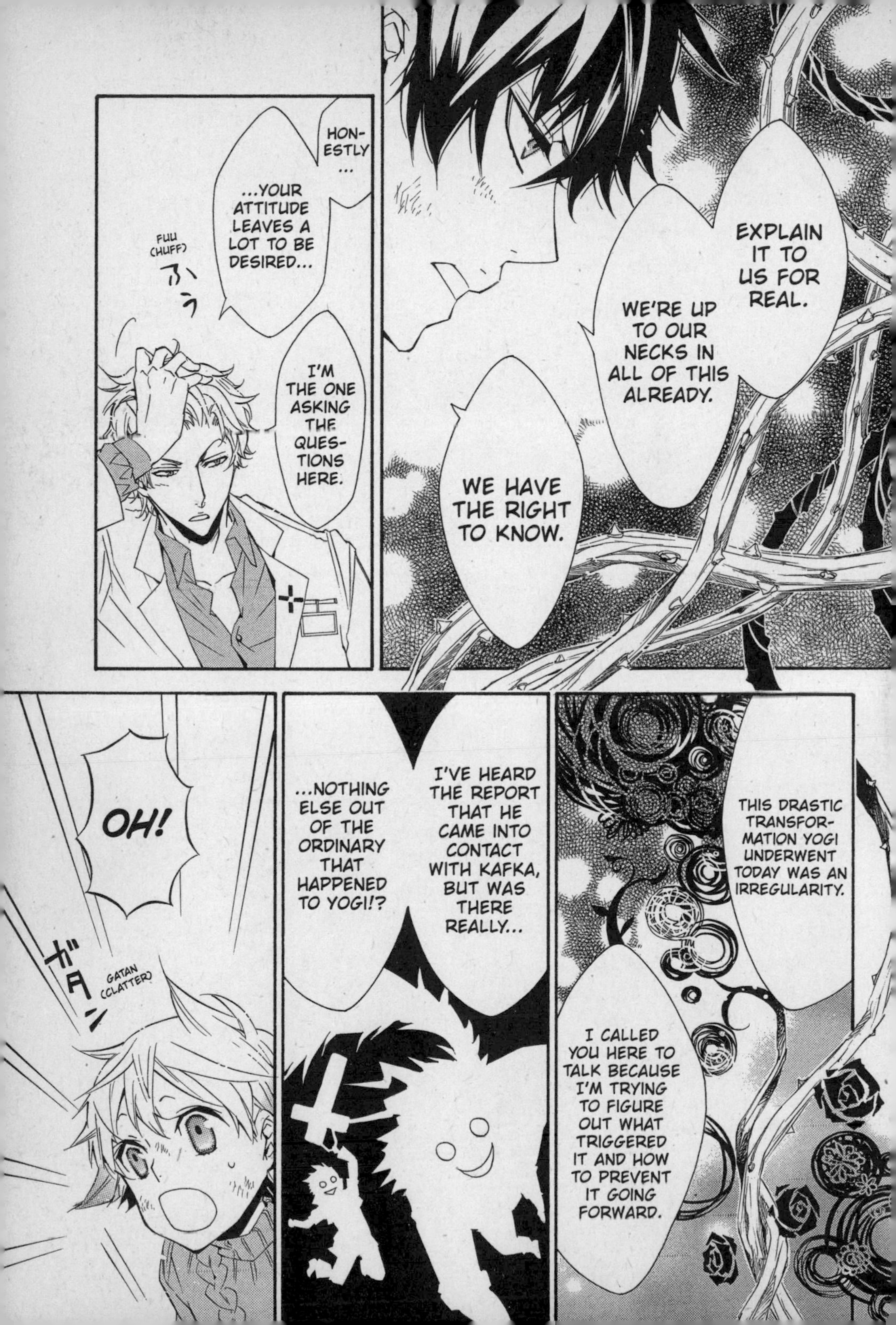
EXPLAIN IT TO US FOR REAL.
WE'RE UP TO OUR NECKS IN ALL OF THIS ALREADY.
WE HAVE THE RIGHT TO KNOW.
HON-ESTLY ...
...YOUR ATTITUDE LEAVES A LOT TO BE DESIRED...
ふぅ
FUU (CHUFF)
I'M THE ONE ASKING THE QUES-TIONS HERE.
THIS DRASTIC TRANSFOR-MATION YOGI UNDERWENT TODAY WAS AN IRREGULARITY.
I CALLED YOU HERE TO TALK BECAUSE I'M TRYING TO FIGURE OUT WHAT TRIGGERED IT AND HOW TO PREVENT IT GOING FORWARD.
I'VE HEARD THE REPORT THAT HE CAME INTO CONTACT WITH KAFKA, BUT WAS THERE REALLY...
...NOTHING ELSE OUT OF THE ORDINARY THAT HAPPENED TO YOGI!?
OH!
ガタン
GATAN (CLATTER)

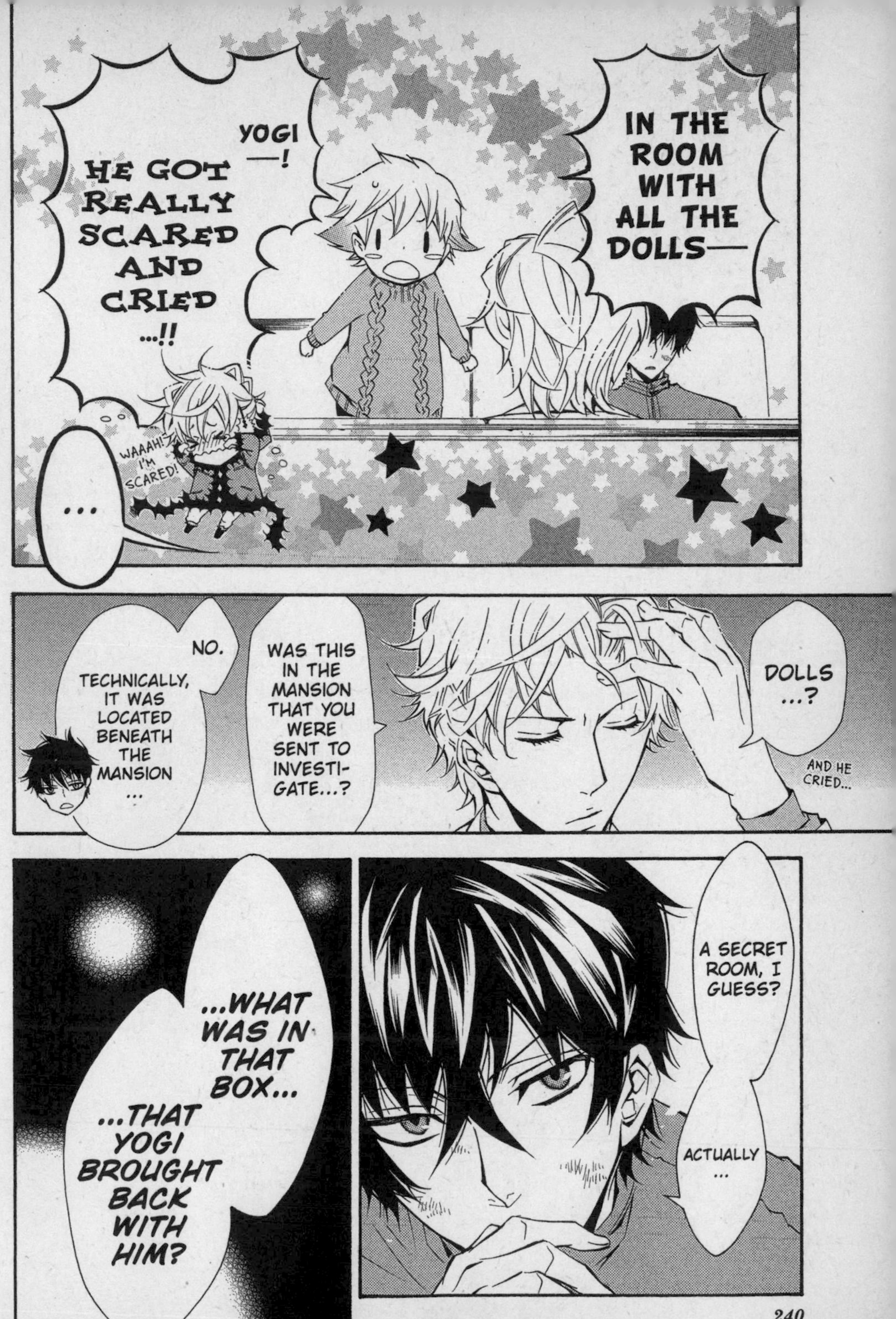
IN THE ROOM WITH ALL THE DOLLS—
YOGI —!
HE GOT REALLY SCARED AND CRIED ...!!
WAAAH! I'M SCARED!
...
DOLLS ...?
AND HE CRIED...
WAS THIS IN THE MANSION THAT YOU WERE SENT TO INVESTI-GATE...?
NO.
TECHNICALLY, IT WAS LOCATED BENEATH THE MANSION ...
A SECRET ROOM, I GUESS?
ACTUALLY ...
...WHAT WAS IN THAT BOX...
...THAT YOGI BROUGHT BACK WITH HIM?

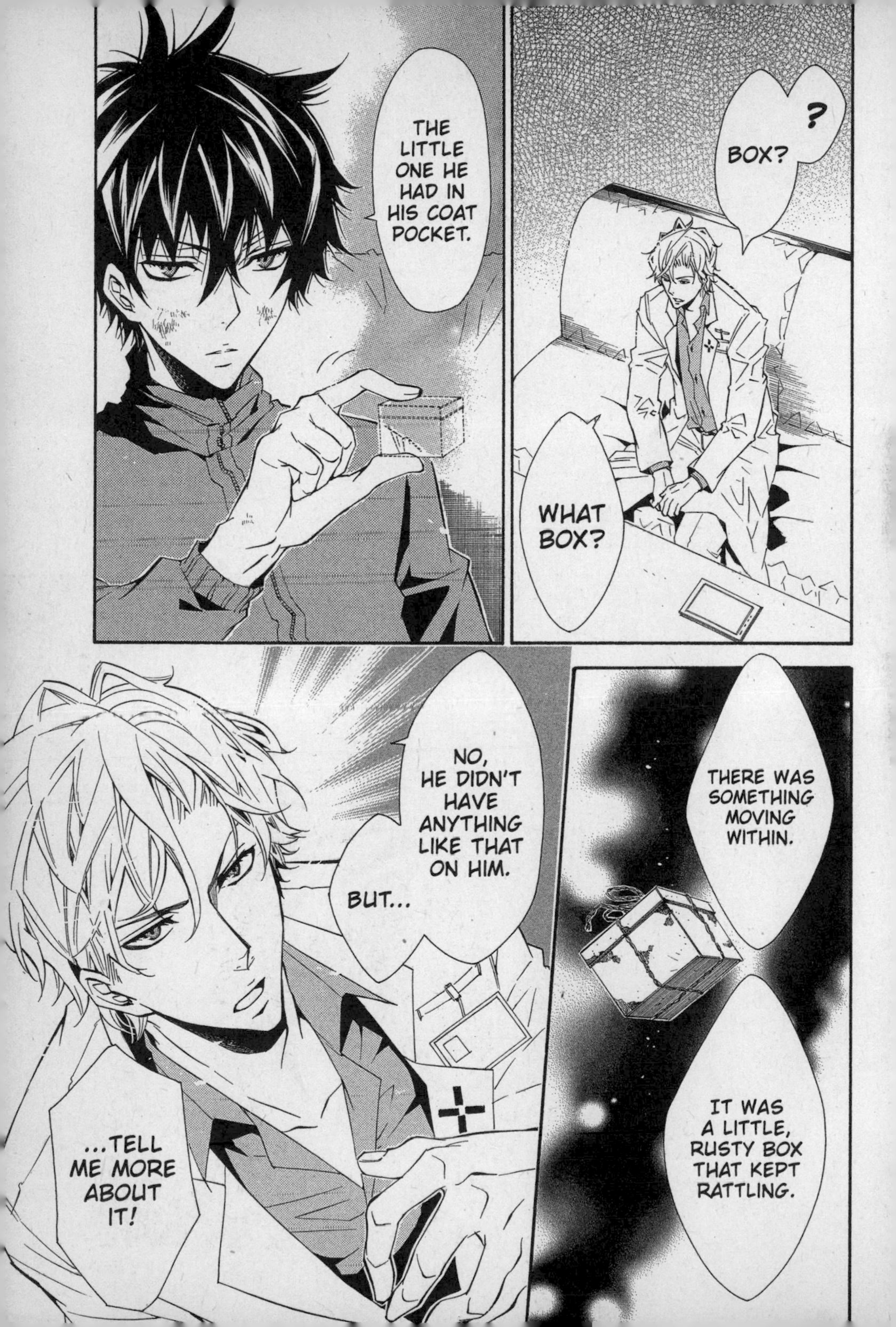
BOX? ?
WHAT BOX?
THE LITTLE ONE HE HAD IN HIS COAT POCKET.
THERE WAS SOMETHING MOVING WITHIN.
IT WAS A LITTLE, RUSTY BOX THAT KEPT RATTLING.
NO, HE DIDN'T HAVE ANYTHING LIKE THAT ON HIM.
BUT...
...TELL ME MORE ABOUT IT!

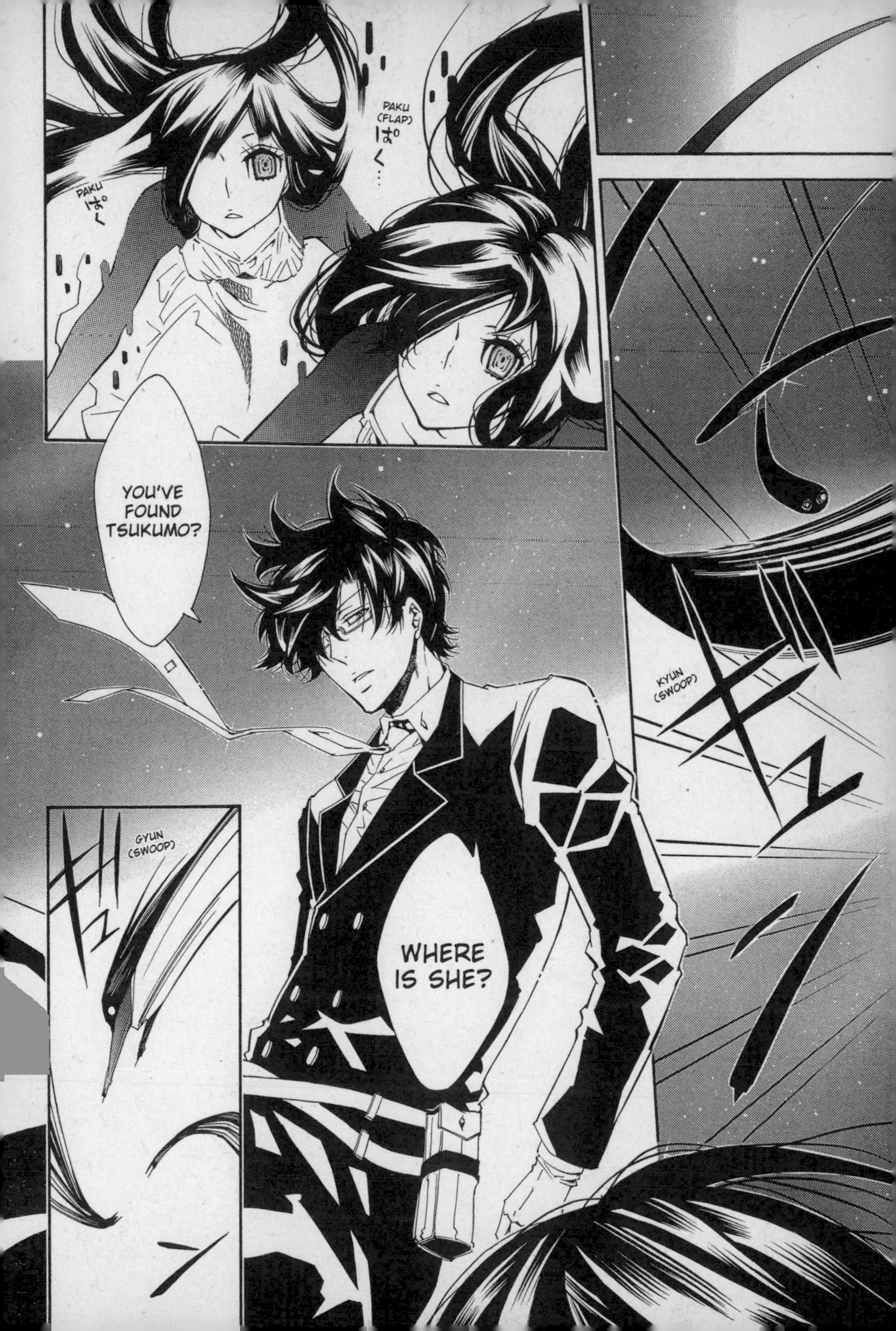
KYUN (SWOOP)
PAKU (FLAP) ぱく…
PAKU ぱく
YOU'VE FOUND TSUKUMO?
WHERE IS SHE?
GYUN (SWOOP)

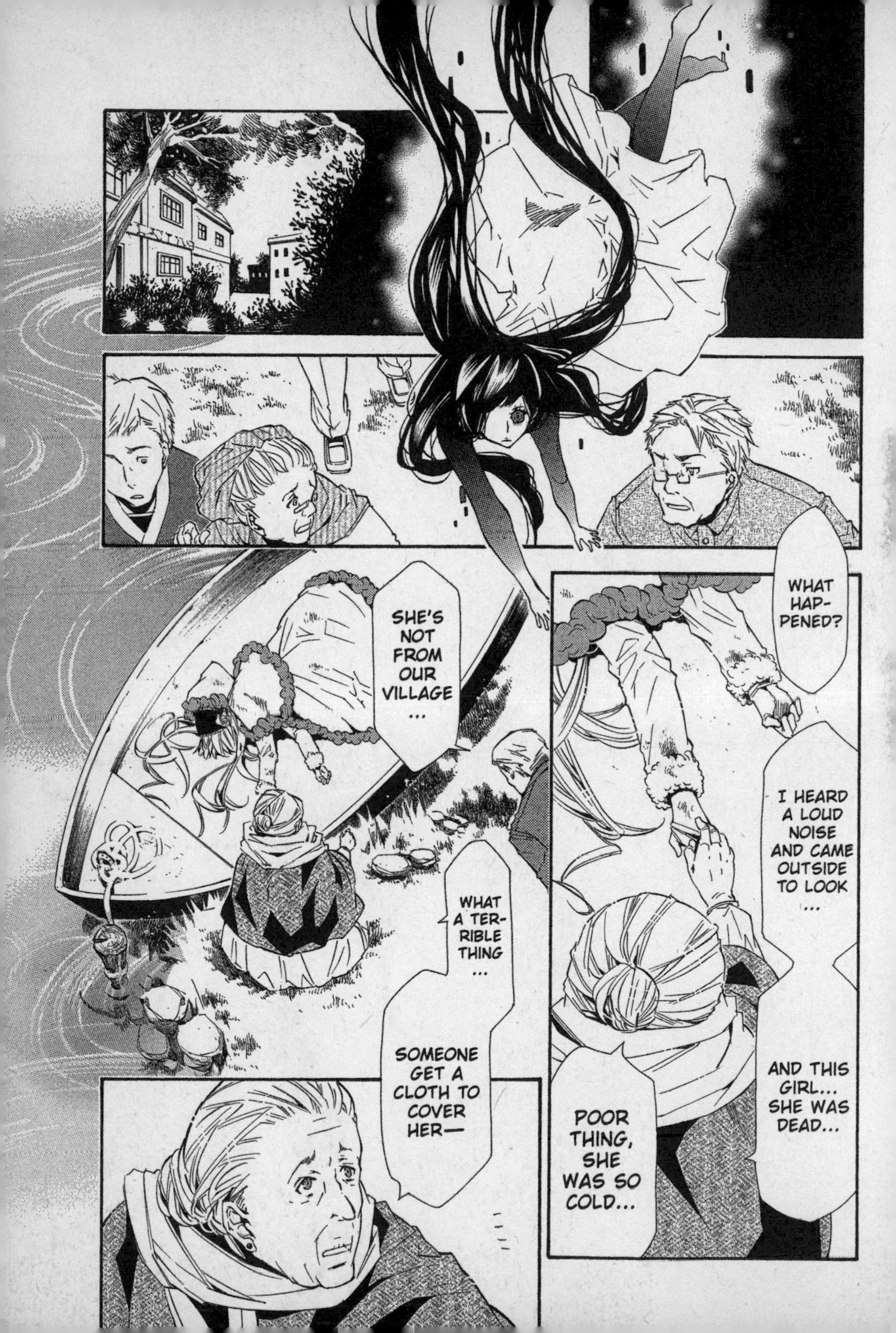
WHAT HAPPENED?
I HEARD A LOUD NOISE AND CAME OUTSIDE TO LOOK...
AND THIS GIRL... SHE WAS DEAD...
POOR THING, SHE WAS SO COLD...
SHE'S NOT FROM OUR VILLAGE...
WHAT A TERRIBLE THING...
SOMEONE GET A CLOTH TO COVER HER—

TSUKUMO
...

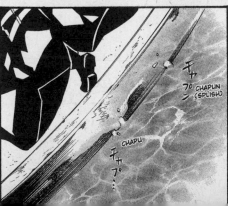

CHAPUN
(SPLISH)

CHAPU

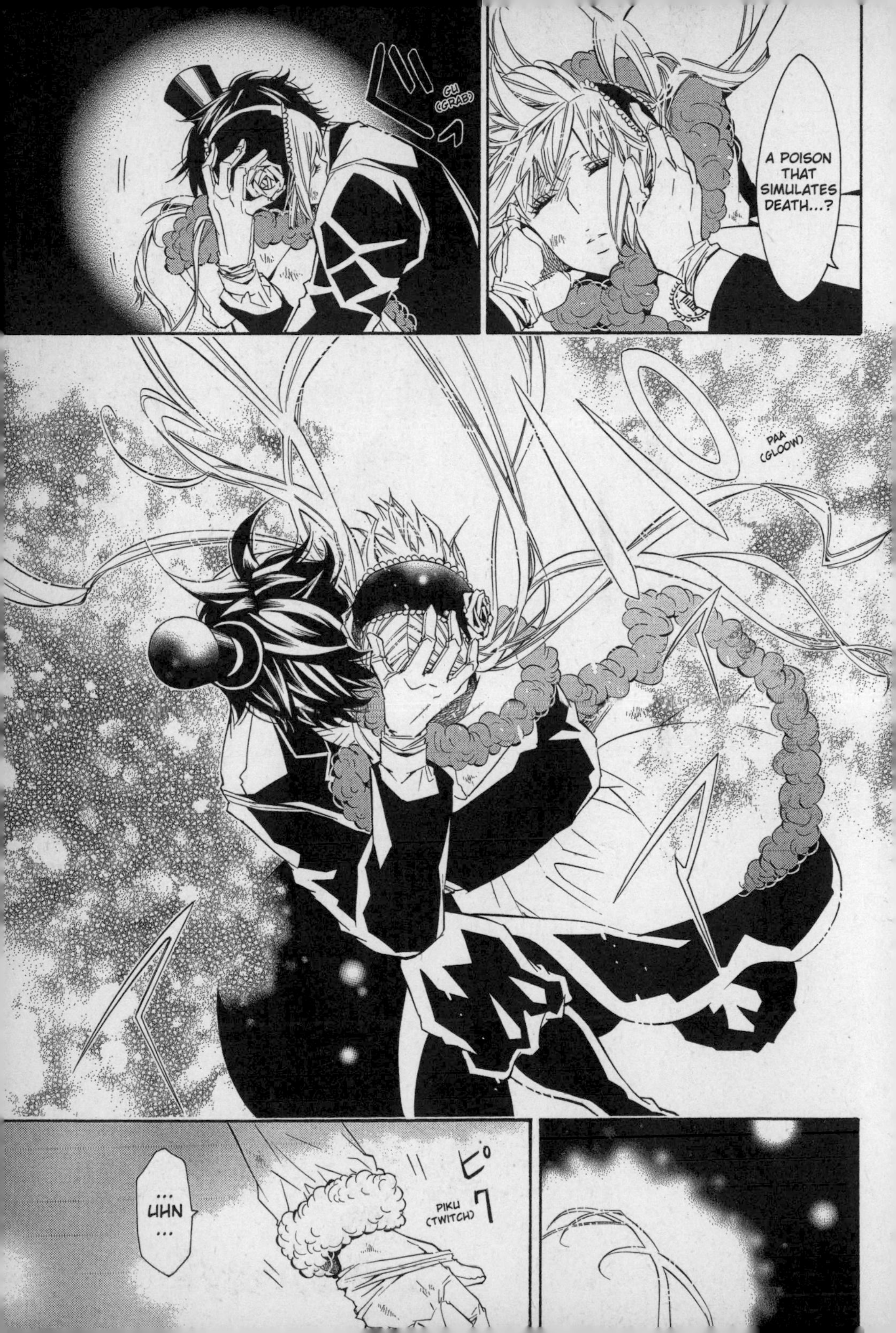
A POISON THAT SIMULATES DEATH...?
GU (GRAB)
PAA (GLOOW)
ピク
PIKU (TWITCH)
... UHN ...

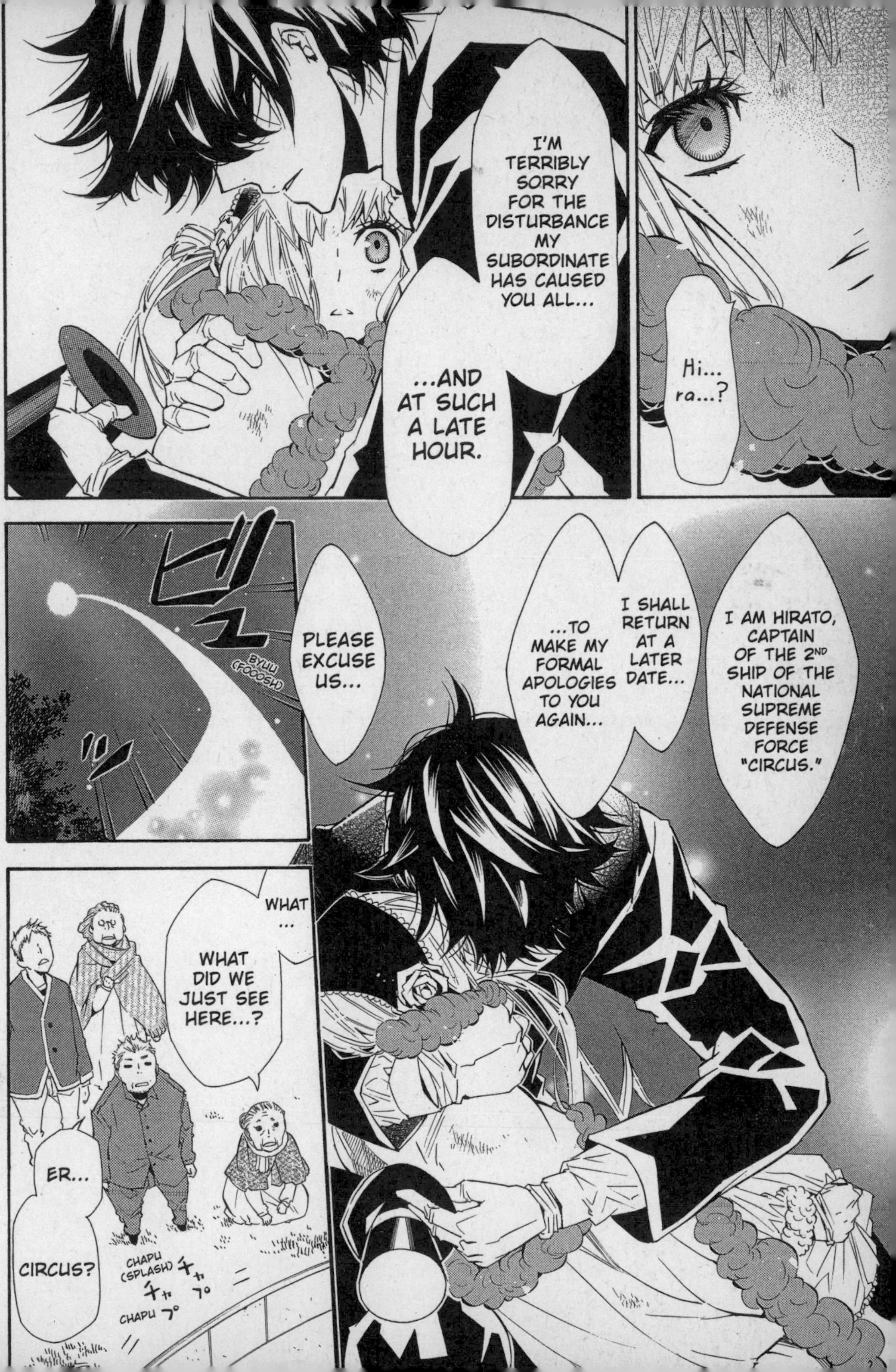

Hi... ra...?
I'M TERRIBLY SORRY FOR THE DISTURBANCE MY SUBORDINATE HAS CAUSED YOU ALL...
...AND AT SUCH A LATE HOUR.
I AM HIRATO, CAPTAIN OF THE 2ND SHIP OF THE NATIONAL SUPREME DEFENSE FORCE "CIRCUS."
I SHALL RETURN AT A LATER DATE...
...TO MAKE MY FORMAL APOLOGIES TO YOU AGAIN...
PLEASE EXCUSE US...
BYUU (FOOOSH)
WHAT ...
WHAT DID WE JUST SEE HERE...?
ER...
CIRCUS?
CHAPU (SPLASH)
CHAPU

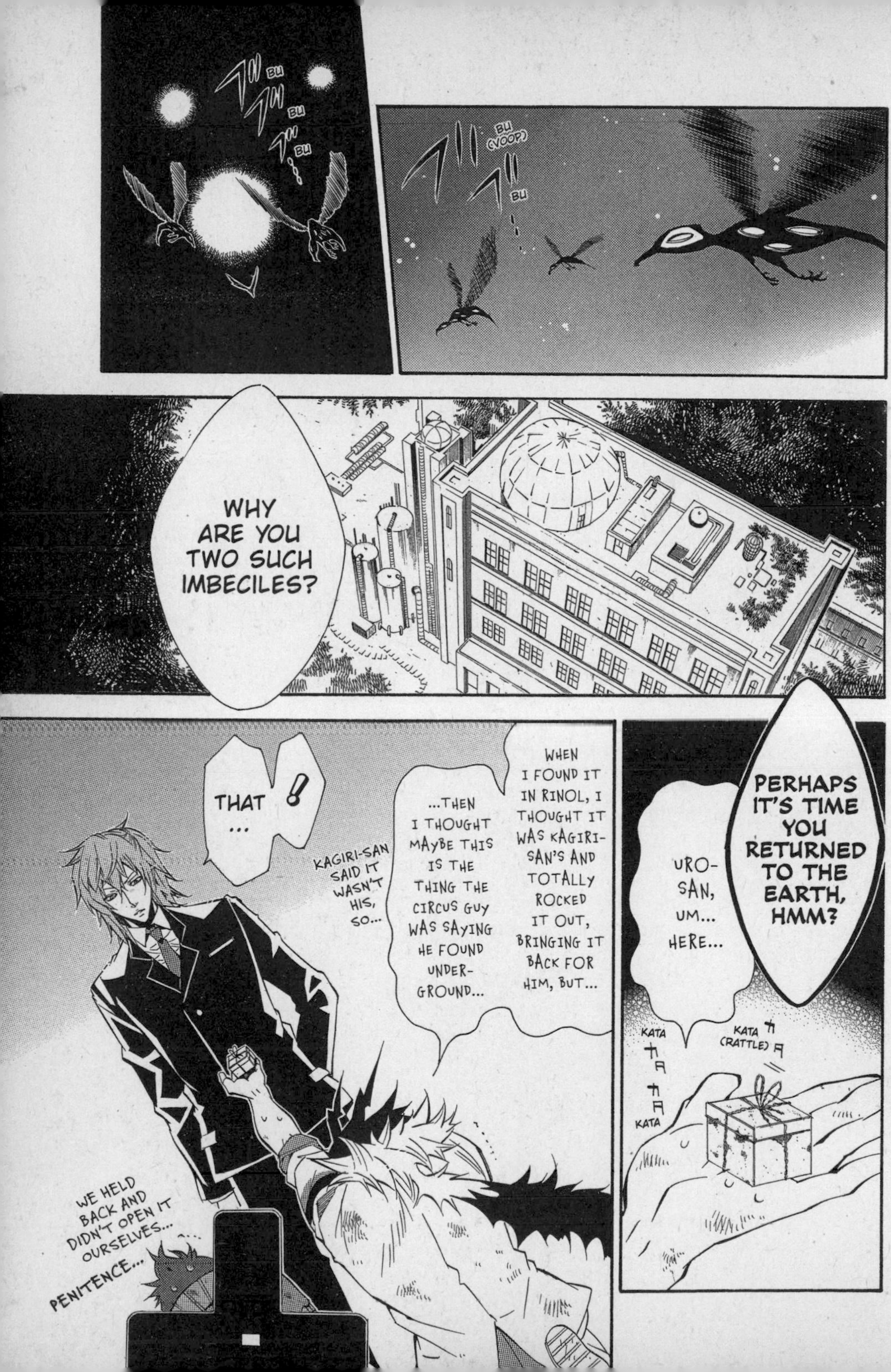
BU (VOOP)
BU
BU
BU
BU
WHY ARE YOU TWO SUCH IMBECILES?
PERHAPS IT'S TIME YOU RETURNED TO THE EARTH, HMM?
URO-SAN, UM... HERE...
KATA (RATTLE)
KATA
KATA
WHEN I FOUND IT IN RINOL, I THOUGHT IT WAS KAGIRI-SAN'S AND TOTALLY ROCKED IT OUT, BRINGING IT BACK FOR HIM, BUT...
...THEN I THOUGHT MAYBE THIS IS THE THING THE CIRCUS GUY WAS SAYING HE FOUND UNDER-GROUND...
KAGIRI-SAN SAID IT WASN'T HIS, SO...
THAT...!
WE HELD BACK AND DIDN'T OPEN IT OURSELVES...
PENITENCE...

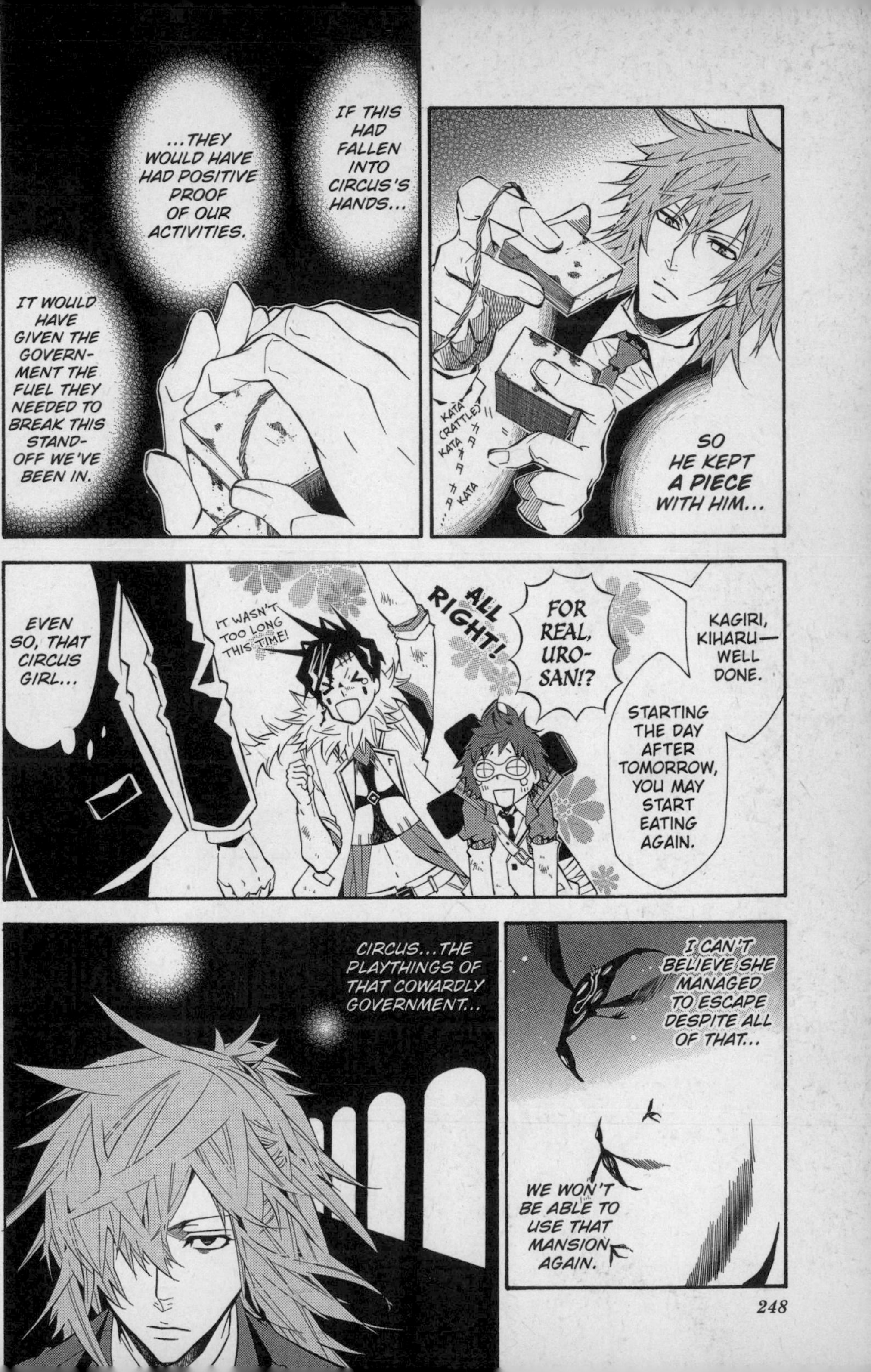
KATA (RATTLE) KATA KATA
SO HE KEPT A PIECE WITH HIM...
IF THIS HAD FALLEN INTO CIRCUS'S HANDS...
...THEY WOULD HAVE HAD POSITIVE PROOF OF OUR ACTIVITIES.
IT WOULD HAVE GIVEN THE GOVERNMENT THE FUEL THEY NEEDED TO BREAK THIS STANDOFF WE'VE BEEN IN.
KAGIRI, KIHARU—WELL DONE.
STARTING THE DAY AFTER TOMORROW, YOU MAY START EATING AGAIN.
FOR REAL, URO-SAN!?
ALL RIGHT!
IT WASN'T TOO LONG THIS TIME!
EVEN SO, THAT CIRCUS GIRL...
I CAN'T BELIEVE SHE MANAGED TO ESCAPE DESPITE ALL OF THAT...
WE WON'T BE ABLE TO USE THAT MANSION AGAIN.
CIRCUS...THE PLAYTHINGS OF THAT COWARDLY GOVERNMENT...

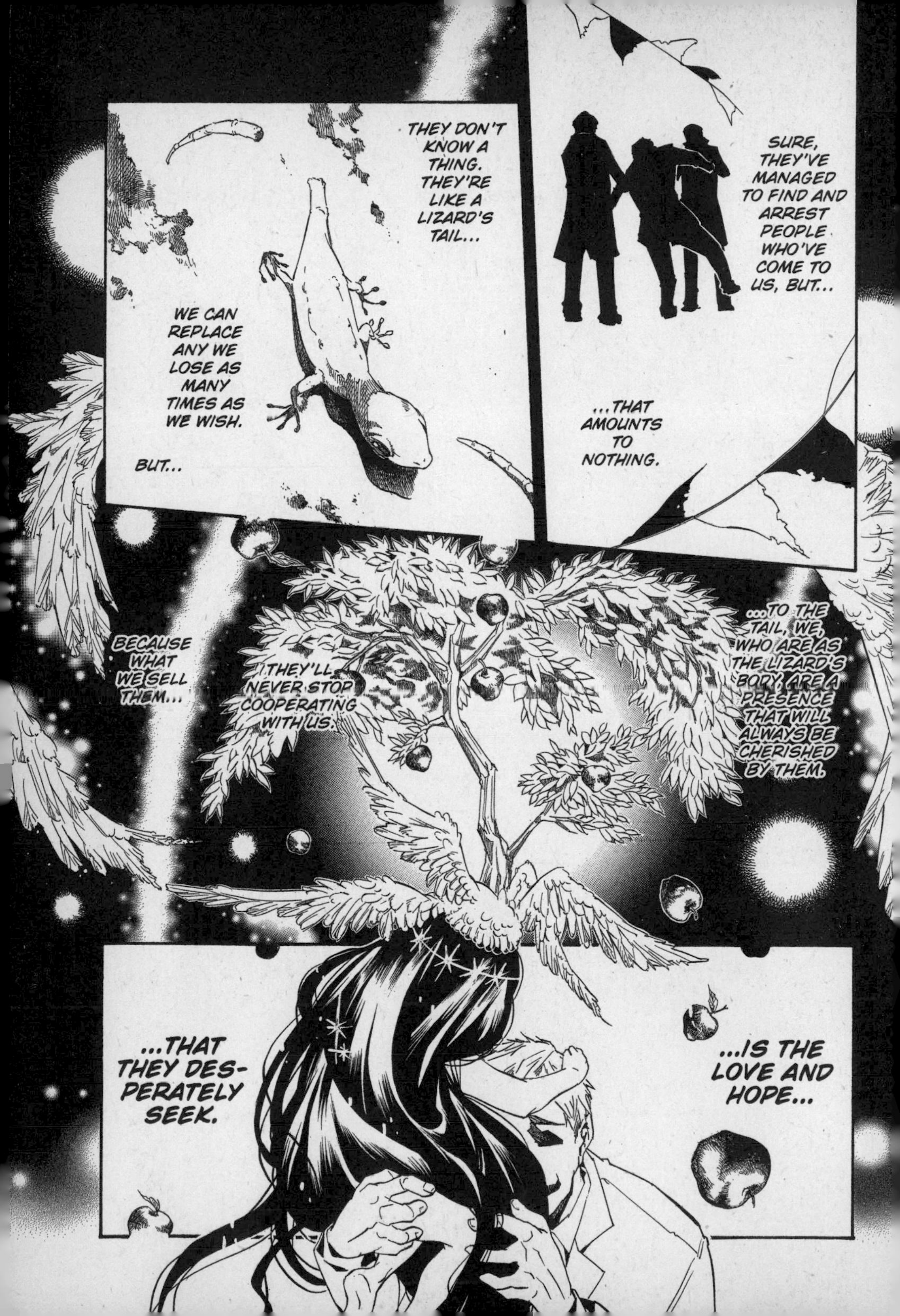
SURE, THEY'VE MANAGED TO FIND AND ARREST PEOPLE WHO'VE COME TO US, BUT...
...THAT AMOUNTS TO NOTHING.
THEY DON'T KNOW A THING. THEY'RE LIKE A LIZARD'S TAIL...
WE CAN REPLACE ANY WE LOSE AS MANY TIMES AS WE WISH.
BUT...
...TO THE TAIL, WE, WHO ARE AS THE LIZARD'S BODY, ARE A PRESENCE THAT WILL ALWAYS BE CHERISHED BY THEM.
THEY'LL NEVER STOP COOPERATING WITH US.
BECAUSE WHAT WE SELL THEM...
...IS THE LOVE AND HOPE...
...THAT THEY DES-PERATELY SEEK.

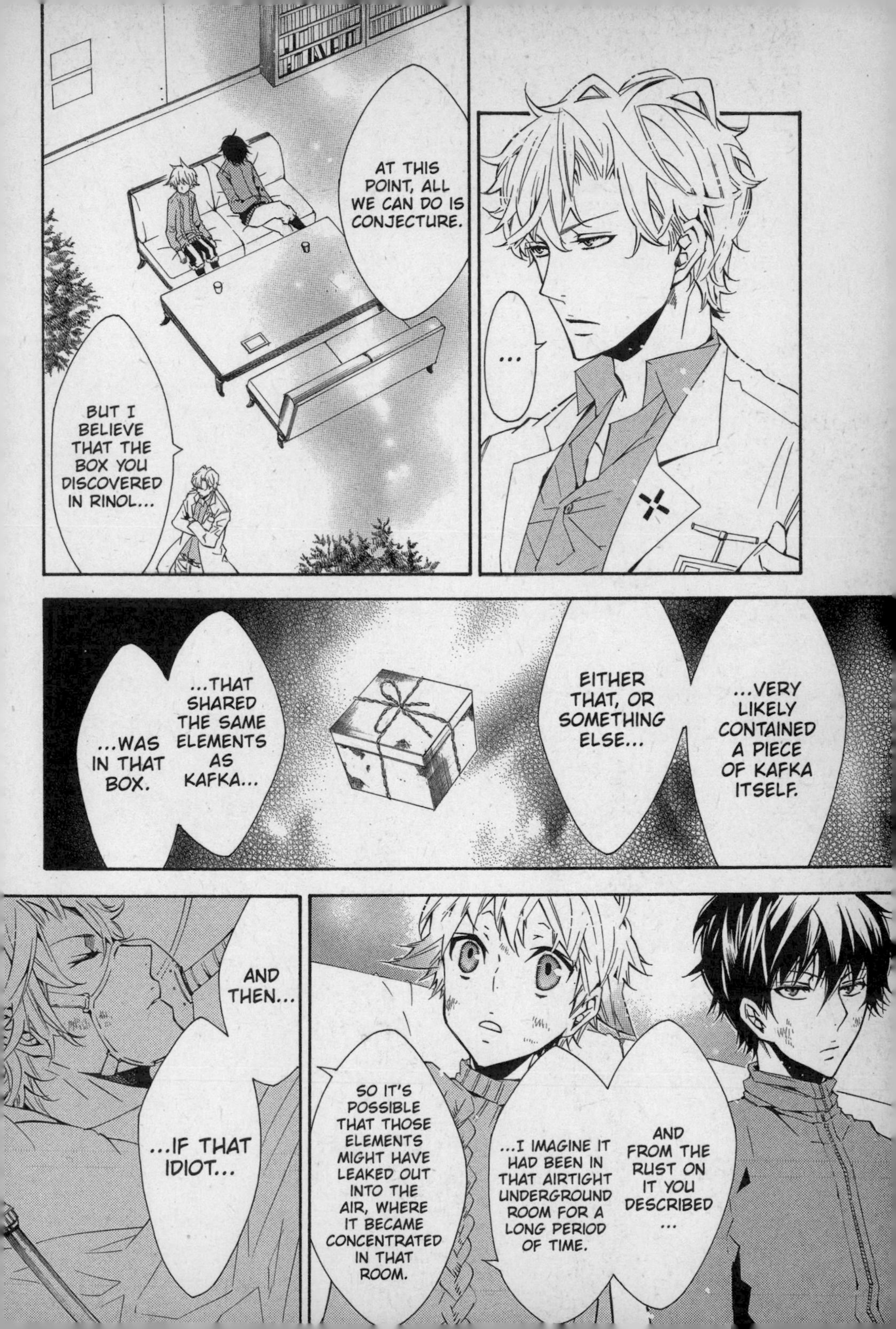
...
AT THIS POINT, ALL WE CAN DO IS CONJECTURE.
BUT I BELIEVE THAT THE BOX YOU DISCOVERED IN RINOL...
...VERY LIKELY CONTAINED A PIECE OF KAFKA ITSELF.
EITHER THAT, OR SOMETHING ELSE...
...THAT SHARED THE SAME ELEMENTS AS KAFKA...
...WAS IN THAT BOX.
AND FROM THE RUST ON IT YOU DESCRIBED ...
...I IMAGINE IT HAD BEEN IN THAT AIRTIGHT UNDERGROUND ROOM FOR A LONG PERIOD OF TIME.
SO IT'S POSSIBLE THAT THOSE ELEMENTS MIGHT HAVE LEAKED OUT INTO THE AIR, WHERE IT BECAME CONCENTRATED IN THAT ROOM.
AND THEN...
...IF THAT IDIOT...

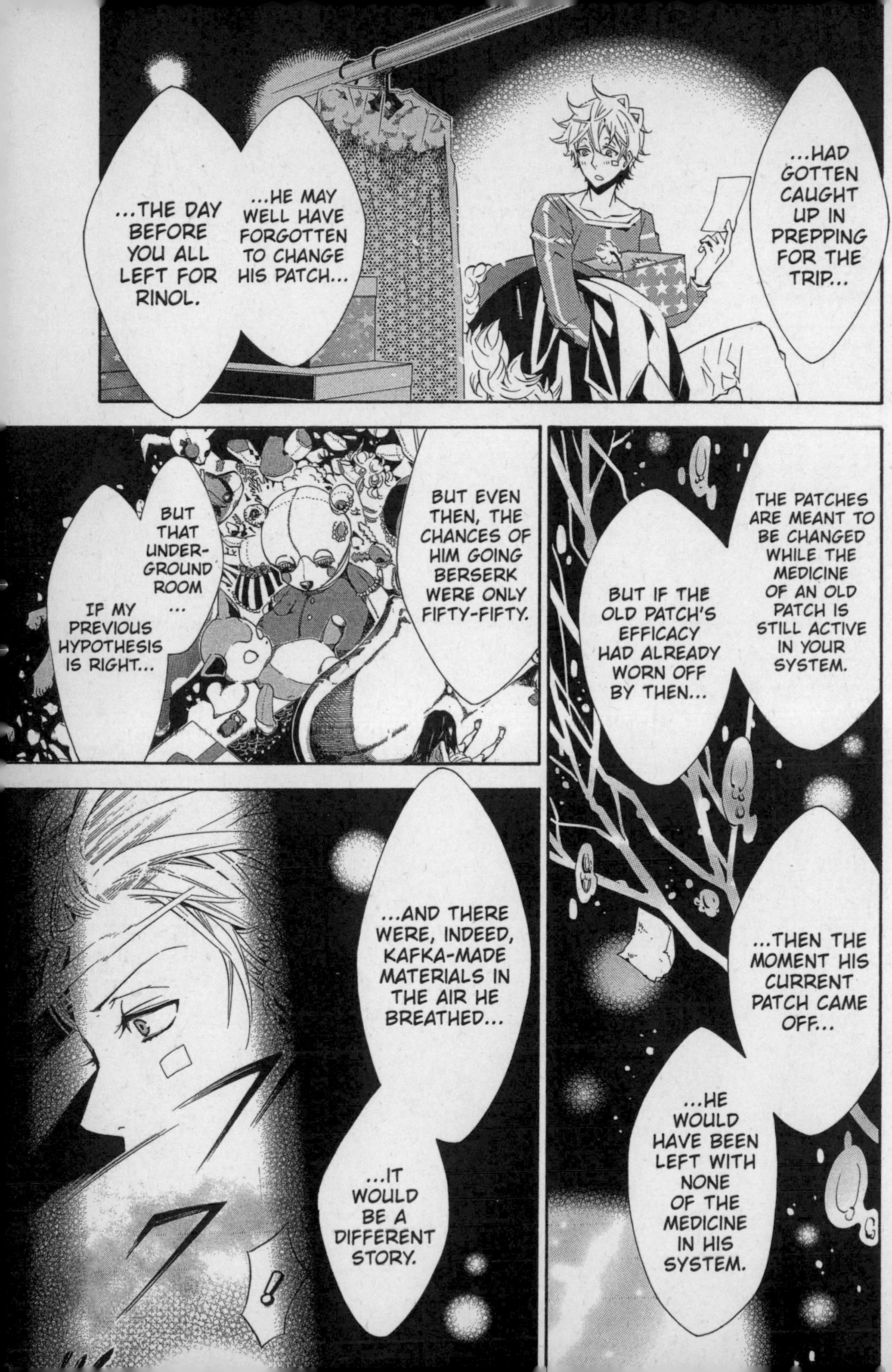
...HAD GOTTEN CAUGHT UP IN PREPPING FOR THE TRIP...
...HE MAY WELL HAVE FORGOTTEN TO CHANGE HIS PATCH...
...THE DAY BEFORE YOU ALL LEFT FOR RINOL.
THE PATCHES ARE MEANT TO BE CHANGED WHILE THE MEDICINE OF AN OLD PATCH IS STILL ACTIVE IN YOUR SYSTEM.
BUT IF THE OLD PATCH'S EFFICACY HAD ALREADY WORN OFF BY THEN...
...THEN THE MOMENT HIS CURRENT PATCH CAME OFF...
...HE WOULD HAVE BEEN LEFT WITH NONE OF THE MEDICINE IN HIS SYSTEM.
BUT THAT UNDERGROUND ROOM...
IF MY PREVIOUS HYPOTHESIS IS RIGHT...
BUT EVEN THEN, THE CHANCES OF HIM GOING BERSERK WERE ONLY FIFTY-FIFTY.
...AND THERE WERE, INDEED, KAFKA-MADE MATERIALS IN THE AIR HE BREATHED...
...IT WOULD BE A DIFFERENT STORY.
!

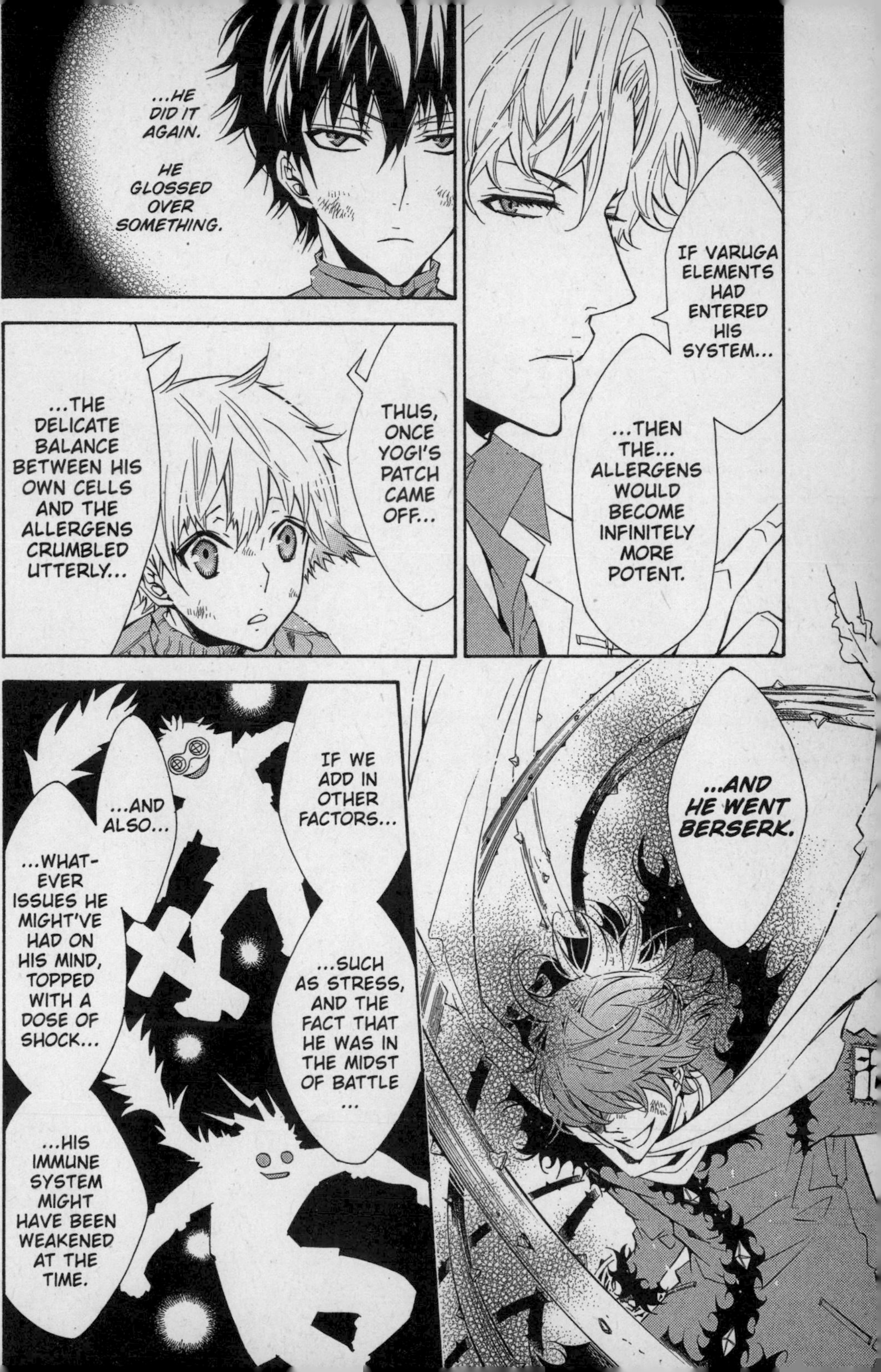
IF VARUGA ELEMENTS HAD ENTERED HIS SYSTEM...
...THEN THE... ALLERGENS WOULD BECOME INFINITELY MORE POTENT.
...HE DID IT AGAIN.
HE GLOSSED OVER SOMETHING.
THUS, ONCE YOGI'S PATCH CAME OFF...
...THE DELICATE BALANCE BETWEEN HIS OWN CELLS AND THE ALLERGENS CRUMBLED UTTERLY...
...AND HE WENT BERSERK.
IF WE ADD IN OTHER FACTORS...
...SUCH AS STRESS, AND THE FACT THAT HE WAS IN THE MIDST OF BATTLE ...
...AND ALSO...
...WHAT-EVER ISSUES HE MIGHT'VE HAD ON HIS MIND, TOPPED WITH A DOSE OF SHOCK...
...HIS IMMUNE SYSTEM MIGHT HAVE BEEN WEAKENED AT THE TIME.

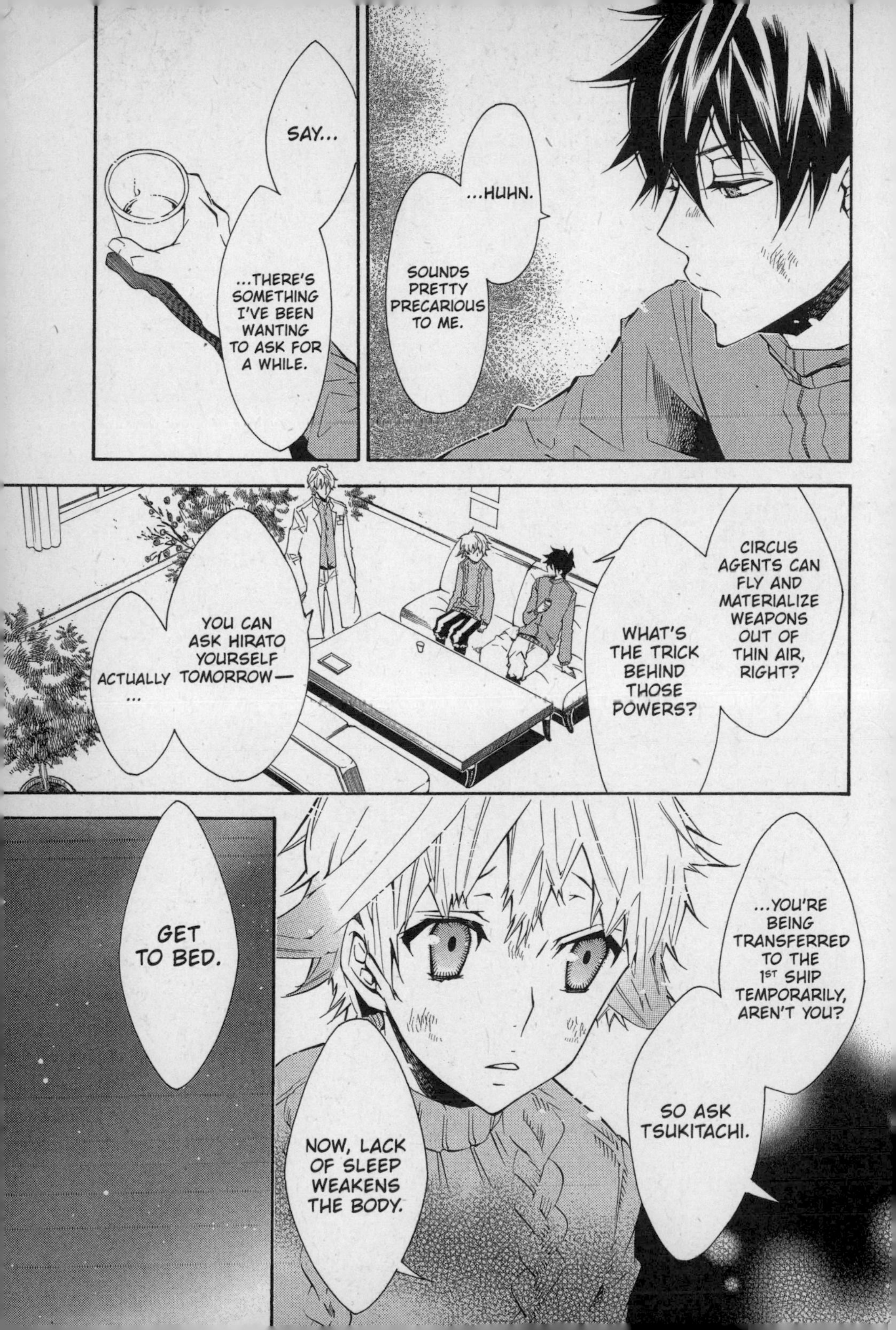
...HUHN.
SOUNDS PRETTY PRECARIOUS TO ME.
SAY...
...THERE'S SOMETHING I'VE BEEN WANTING TO ASK FOR A WHILE.
CIRCUS AGENTS CAN FLY AND MATERIALIZE WEAPONS OUT OF THIN AIR, RIGHT?
WHAT'S THE TRICK BEHIND THOSE POWERS?
YOU CAN ASK HIRATO YOURSELF TOMORROW—
ACTUALLY ...
...YOU'RE BEING TRANSFERRED TO THE 1ST SHIP TEMPORARILY, AREN'T YOU?
SO ASK TSUKITACHI.
NOW, LACK OF SLEEP WEAKENS THE BODY.
GET TO BED.

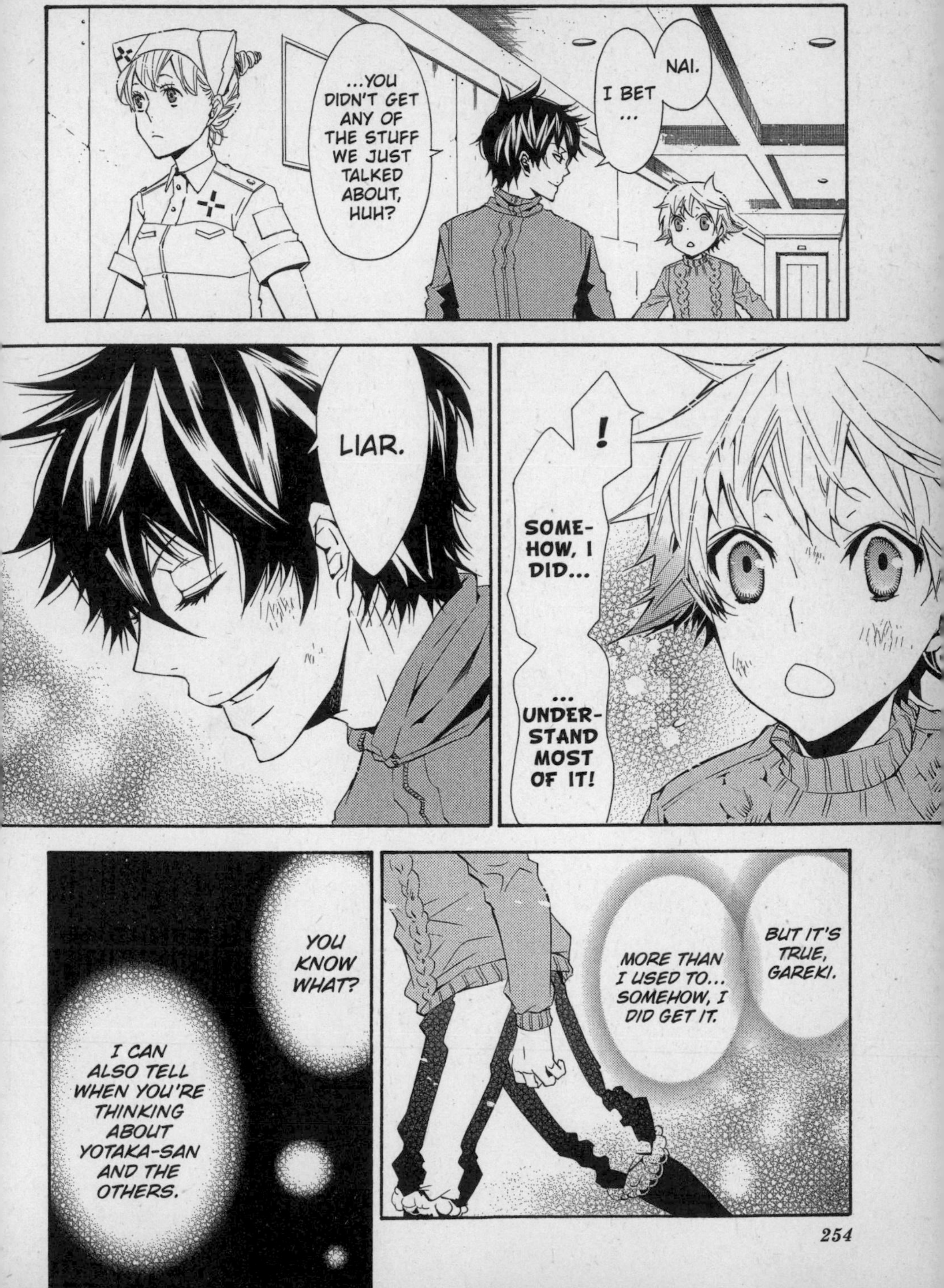
NAI.
I BET...
...YOU DIDN'T GET ANY OF THE STUFF WE JUST TALKED ABOUT, HUH?
!
SOMEHOW, I DID...
...UNDERSTAND MOST OF IT!
LIAR.
BUT IT'S TRUE, GAREKI.
MORE THAN I USED TO... SOMEHOW, I DID GET IT.
YOU KNOW WHAT?
I CAN ALSO TELL WHEN YOU'RE THINKING ABOUT YOTAKA-SAN AND THE OTHERS.

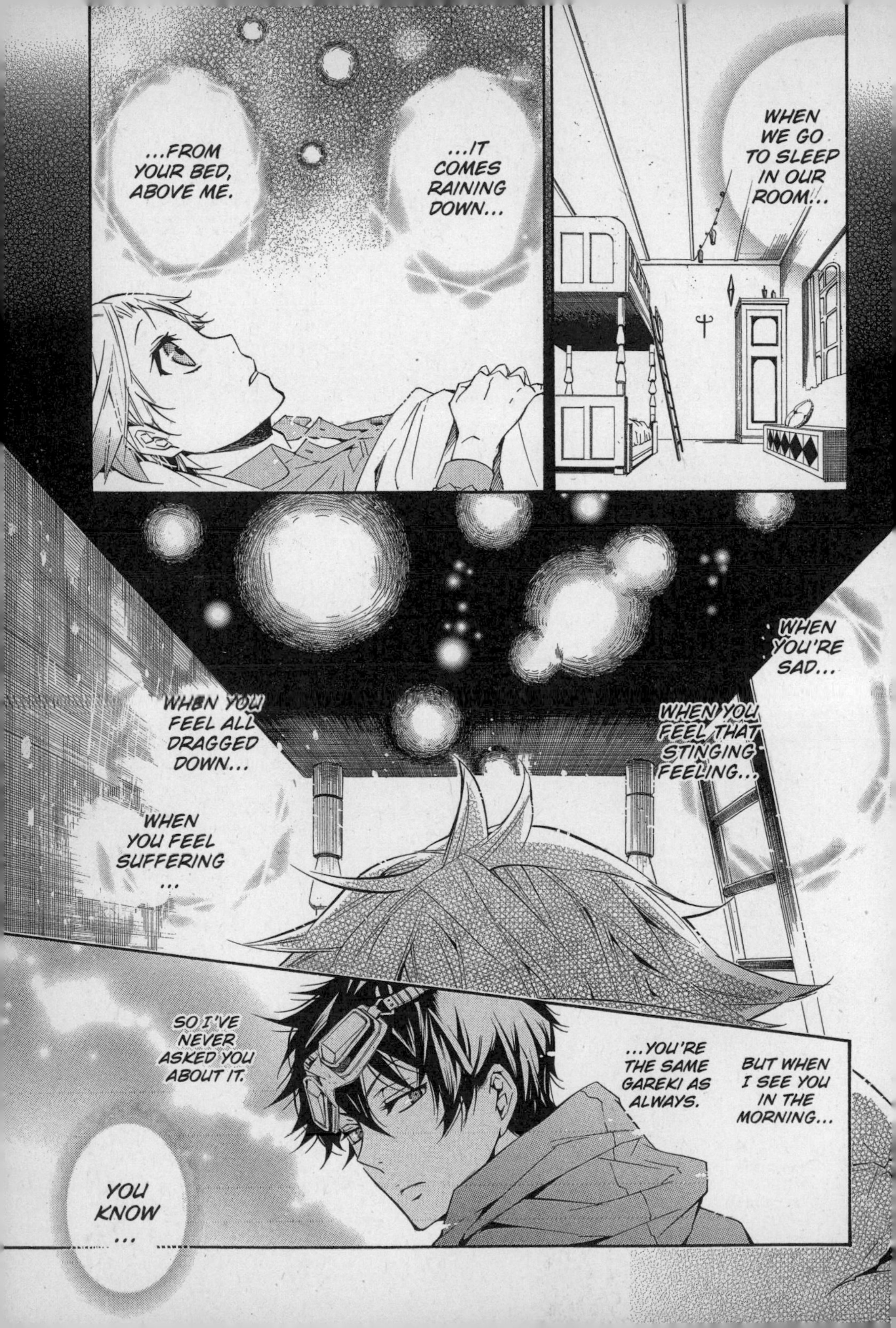
WHEN WE GO TO SLEEP IN OUR ROOM...
...IT COMES RAINING DOWN...
...FROM YOUR BED, ABOVE ME.
WHEN YOU'RE SAD...
WHEN YOU FEEL THAT STINGING FEELING...
WHEN YOU FEEL ALL DRAGGED DOWN...
WHEN YOU FEEL SUFFERING ...
BUT WHEN I SEE YOU IN THE MORNING...
...YOU'RE THE SAME GAREKI AS ALWAYS.
SO I'VE NEVER ASKED YOU ABOUT IT.
YOU KNOW ...

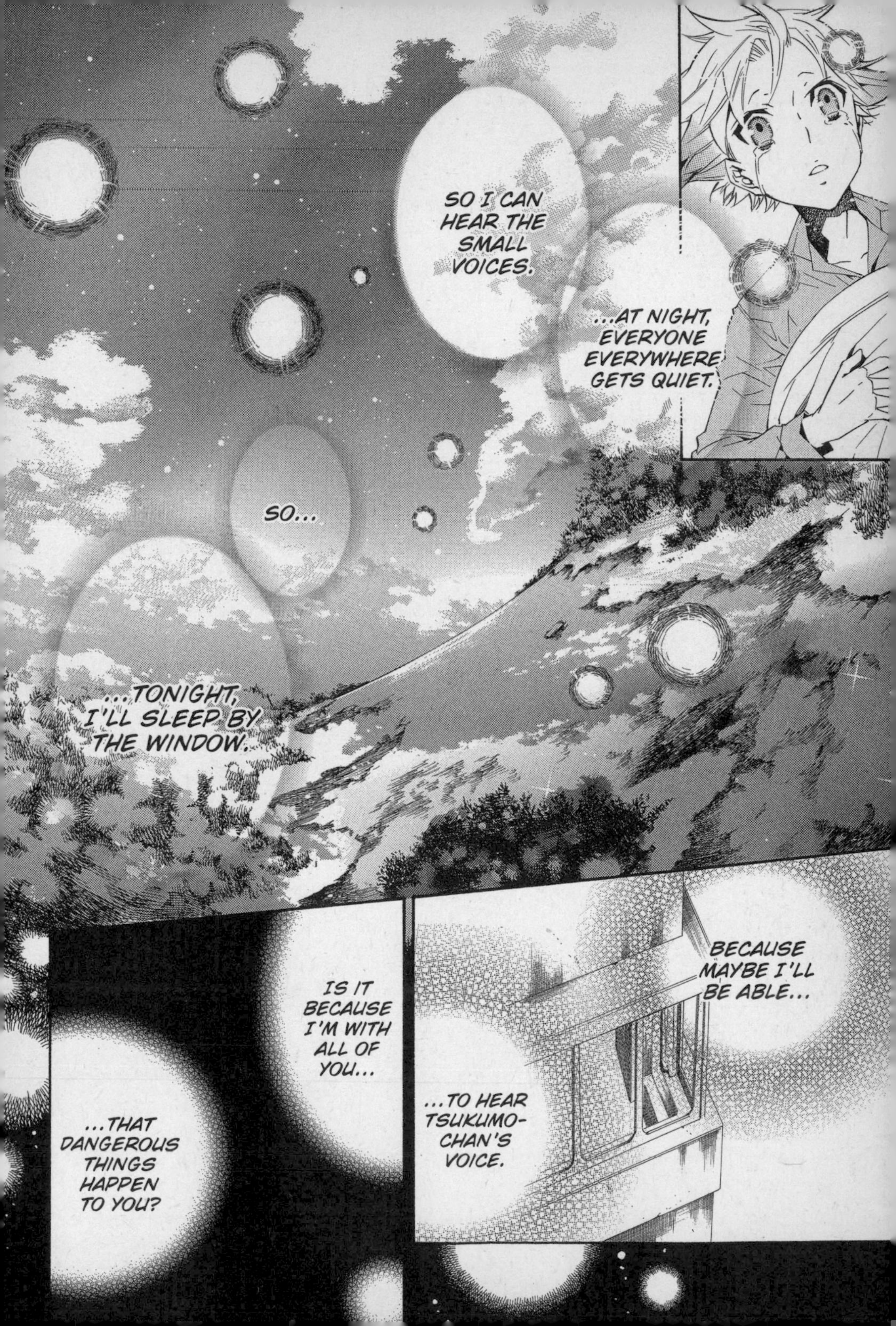
...AT NIGHT, EVERYONE EVERYWHERE GETS QUIET.
SO I CAN HEAR THE SMALL VOICES.
SO...
...TONIGHT, I'LL SLEEP BY THE WINDOW.
BECAUSE MAYBE I'LL BE ABLE...
...TO HEAR TSUKUMO-CHAN'S VOICE.
IS IT BECAUSE I'M WITH ALL OF YOU...
...THAT DANGEROUS THINGS HAPPEN TO YOU?

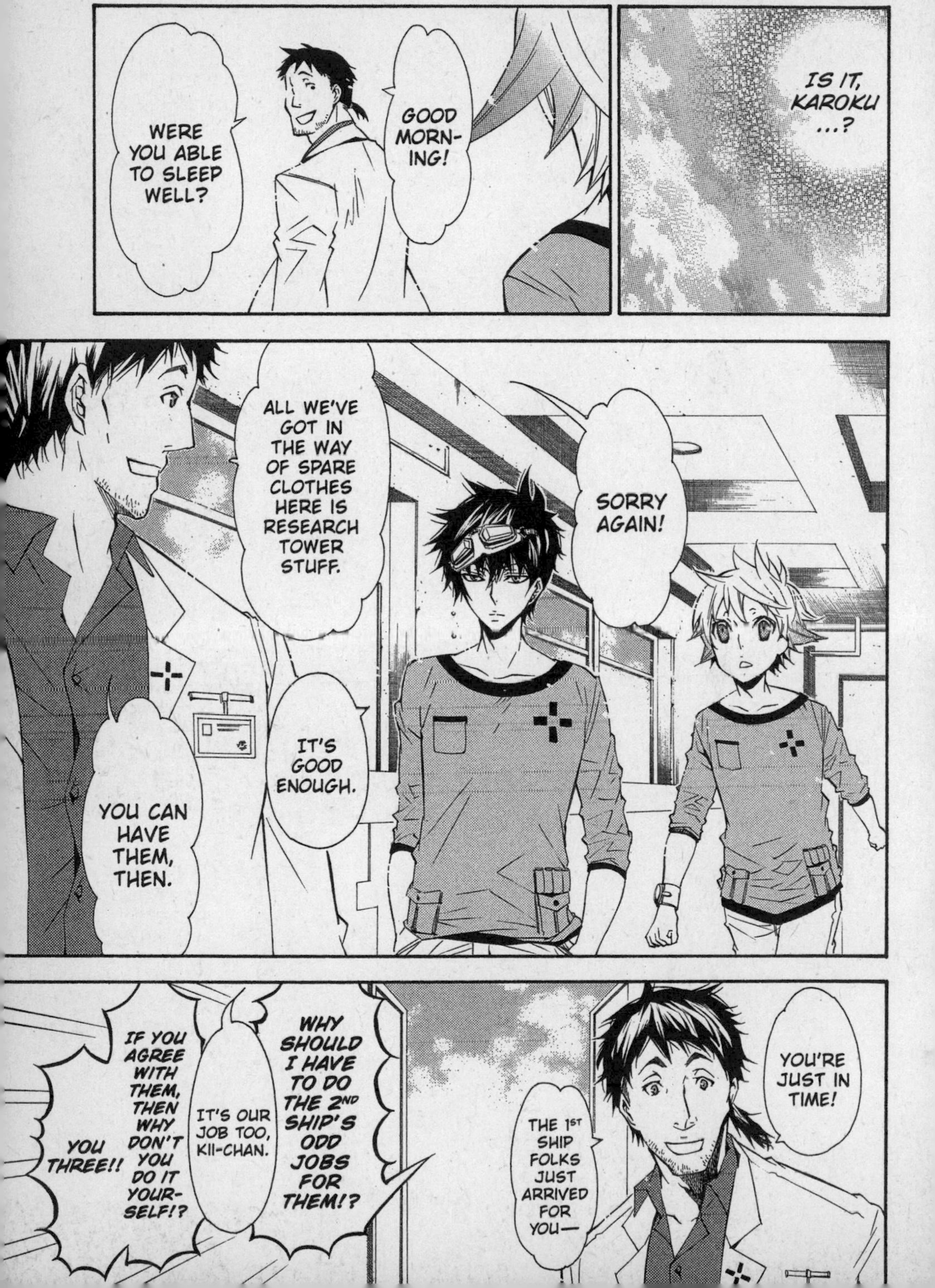
IS IT, KAROKU ...?
GOOD MORNING!
WERE YOU ABLE TO SLEEP WELL?
SORRY AGAIN!
ALL WE'VE GOT IN THE WAY OF SPARE CLOTHES HERE IS RESEARCH TOWER STUFF.
IT'S GOOD ENOUGH.
YOU CAN HAVE THEM, THEN.
YOU'RE JUST IN TIME!
THE 1ST SHIP FOLKS JUST ARRIVED FOR YOU—
WHY SHOULD I HAVE TO DO THE 2ND SHIP'S ODD JOBS FOR THEM!?
IT'S OUR JOB TOO, KII-CHAN.
IF YOU AGREE WITH THEM, THEN WHY DON'T YOU DO IT YOURSELF!?
YOU THREE!!

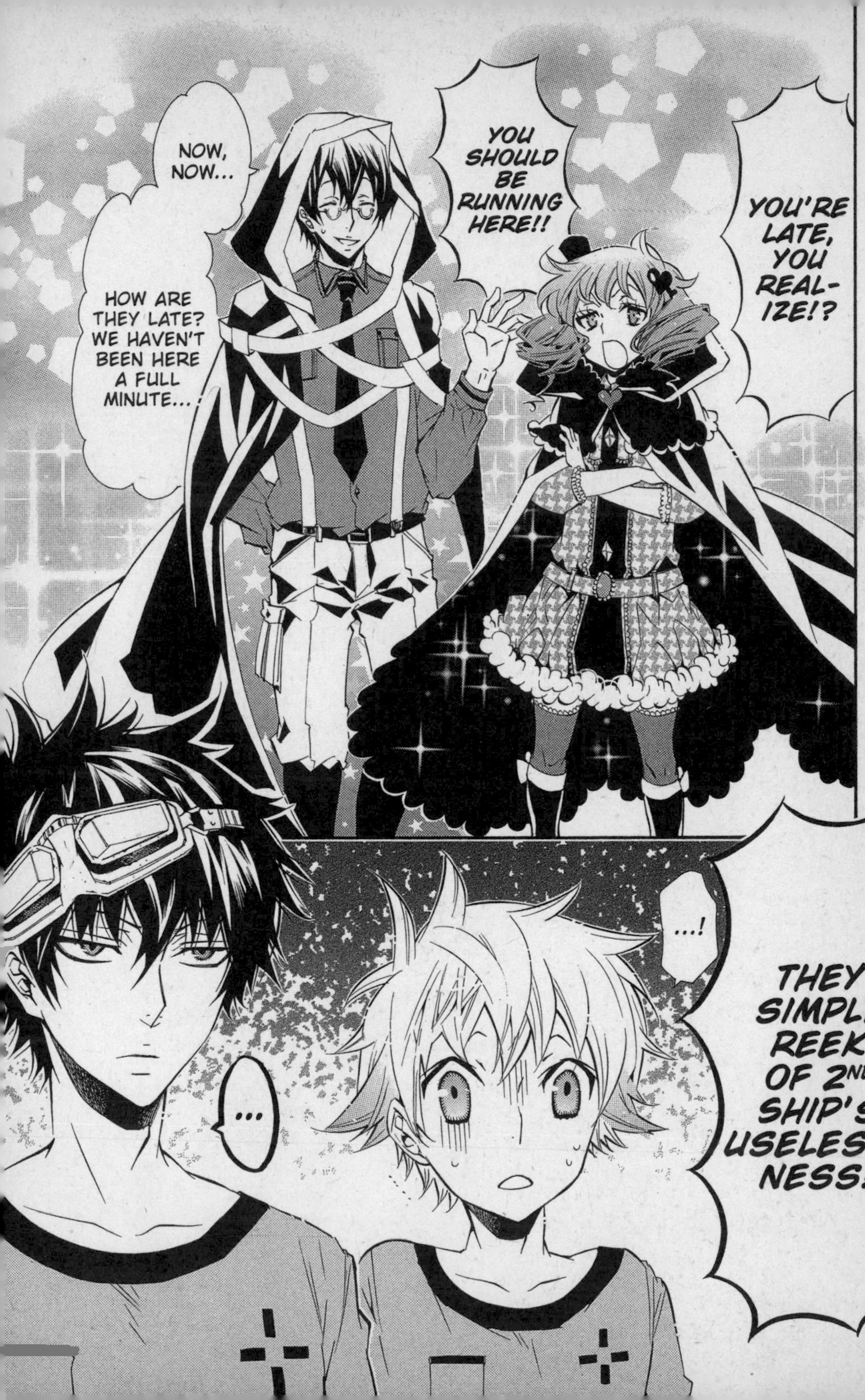
YOU'RE LATE, YOU REAL-IZE!?
YOU SHOULD BE RUNNING HERE!!
NOW, NOW...
HOW ARE THEY LATE? WE HAVEN'T BEEN HERE A FULL MINUTE...
...!
THEY SIMPLY REEK OF 2ND SHIP'S USELESS-NESS!
...

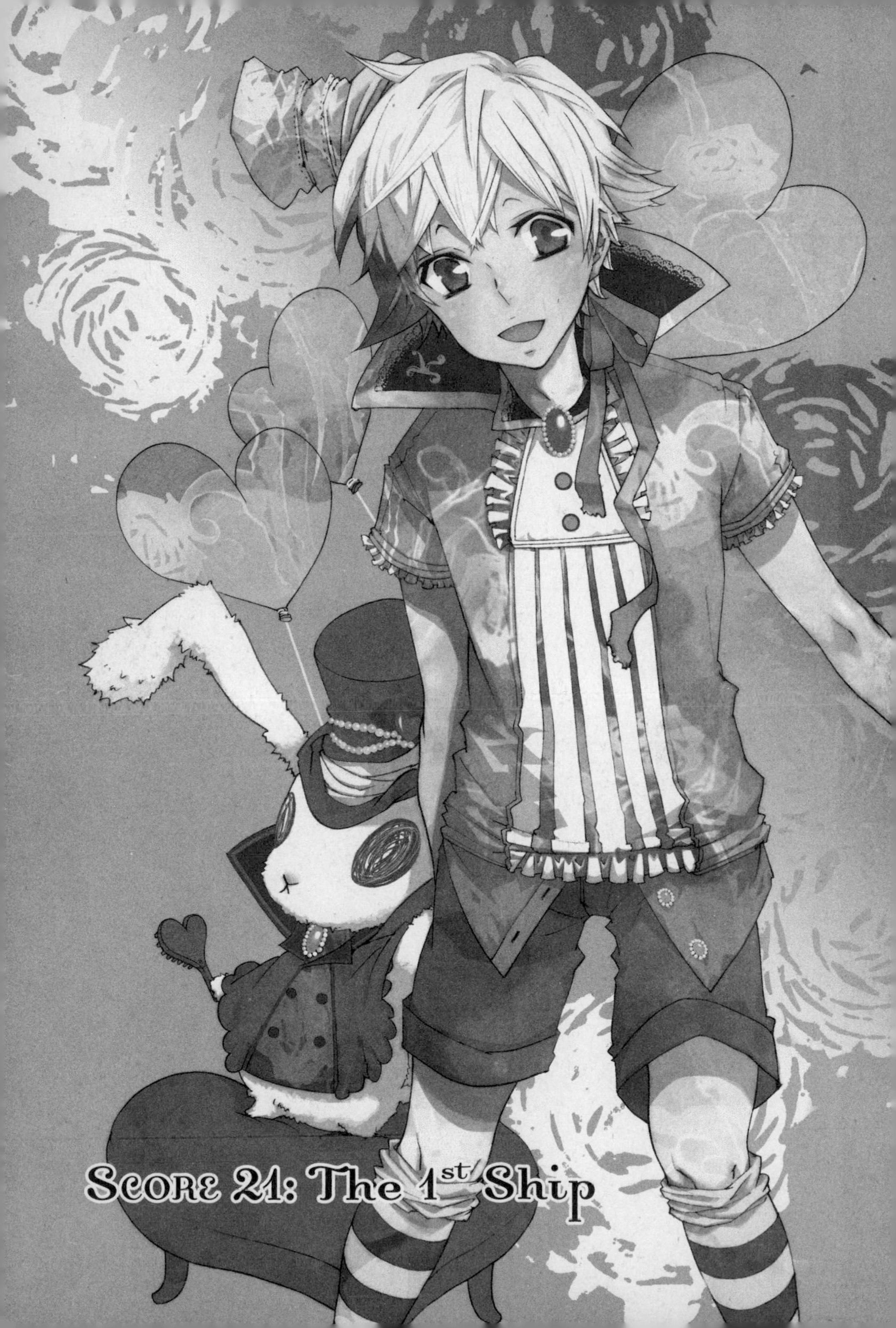

Score 21: The 1st Ship

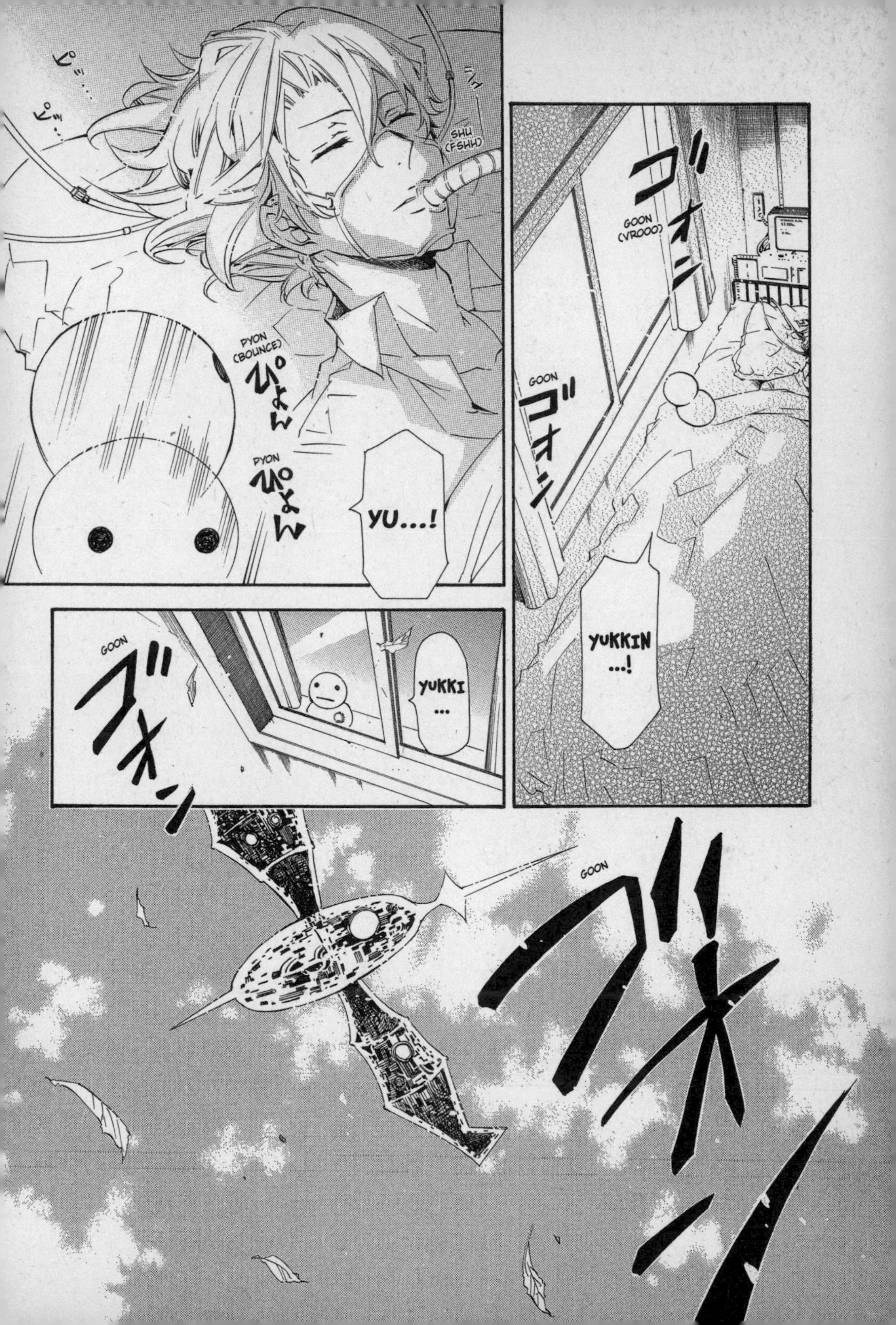
ゴォン
GOON (VROOO)
GOON
ゴォン
YUKKIN ...!
ピッ…
ピッ…
シュ
SHU (FSHH)
PYON (BOUNCE)
ぴょん
PYON
ぴょん
YU...!
GOON
ゴォン
YUKKI ...
GOON
ゴォン

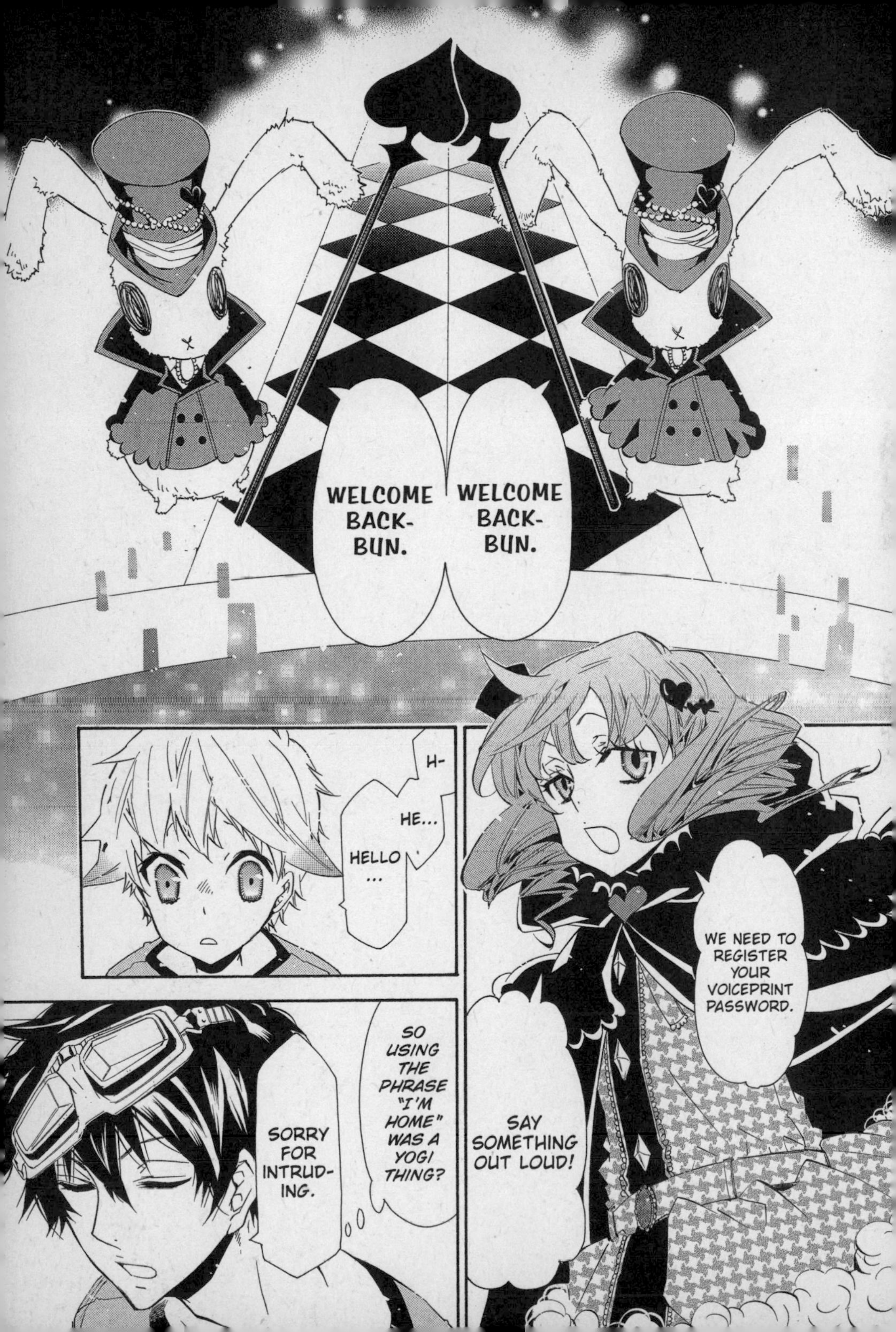
WELCOME BACK-BUN.
WELCOME BACK-BUN.
WE NEED TO REGISTER YOUR VOICEPRINT PASSWORD.
SAY SOMETHING OUT LOUD!
H-
HE...
HELLO...
SO USING THE PHRASE "I'M HOME" WAS A YOGI THING?
SORRY FOR INTRUD-ING.

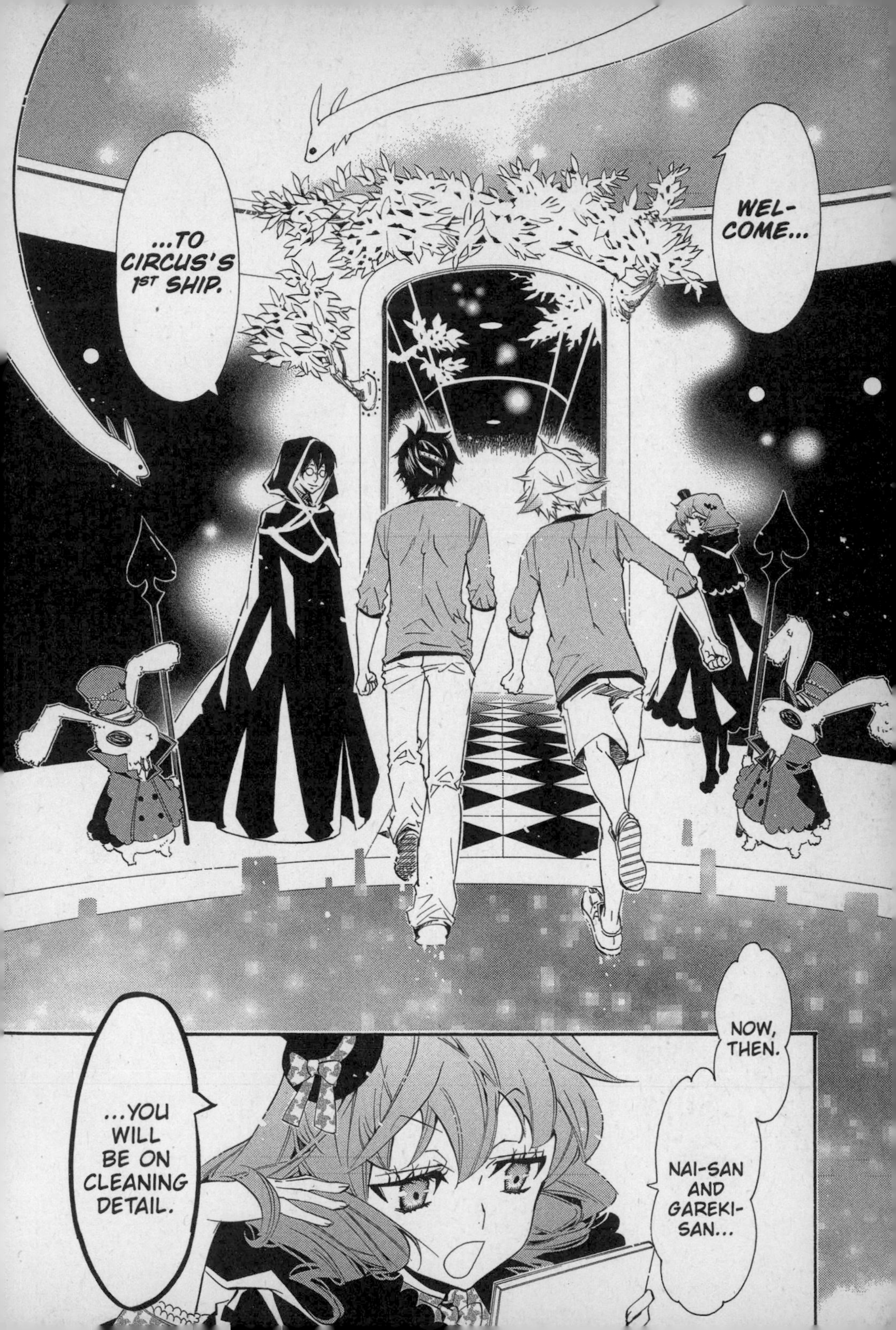
WEL-COME...
...TO CIRCUS'S 1ST SHIP.
NOW, THEN.
NAI-SAN AND GAREKI-SAN...
...YOU WILL BE ON CLEANING DETAIL.

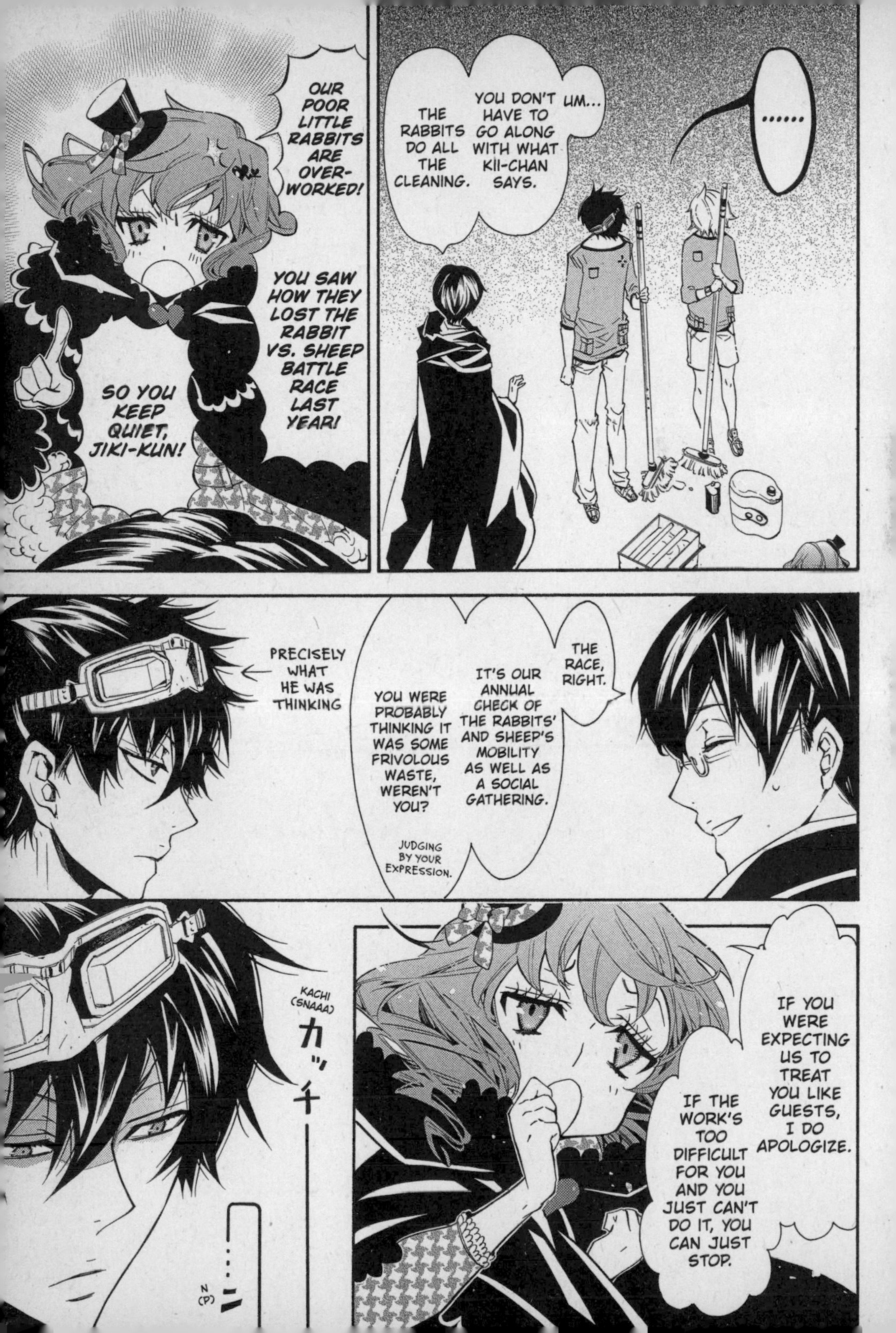
......
UM...
YOU DON'T HAVE TO GO ALONG WITH WHAT KII-CHAN SAYS.
THE RABBITS DO ALL THE CLEANING.
OUR POOR LITTLE RABBITS ARE OVER-WORKED!
YOU SAW HOW THEY LOST THE RABBIT VS. SHEEP BATTLE RACE LAST YEAR!
SO YOU KEEP QUIET, JIKI-KUN!
THE RACE, RIGHT.
IT'S OUR ANNUAL CHECK OF THE RABBITS' AND SHEEP'S MOBILITY AS WELL AS A SOCIAL GATHERING.
YOU WERE PROBABLY THINKING IT WAS SOME FRIVOLOUS WASTE, WEREN'T YOU?
JUDGING BY YOUR EXPRESSION.
PRECISELY WHAT HE WAS THINKING
IF YOU WERE EXPECTING US TO TREAT YOU LIKE GUESTS, I DO APOLOGIZE.
IF THE WORK'S TOO DIFFICULT FOR YOU AND YOU JUST CAN'T DO IT, YOU CAN JUST STOP.
KACHI (SNAAA)
カッチー
...
N (P)

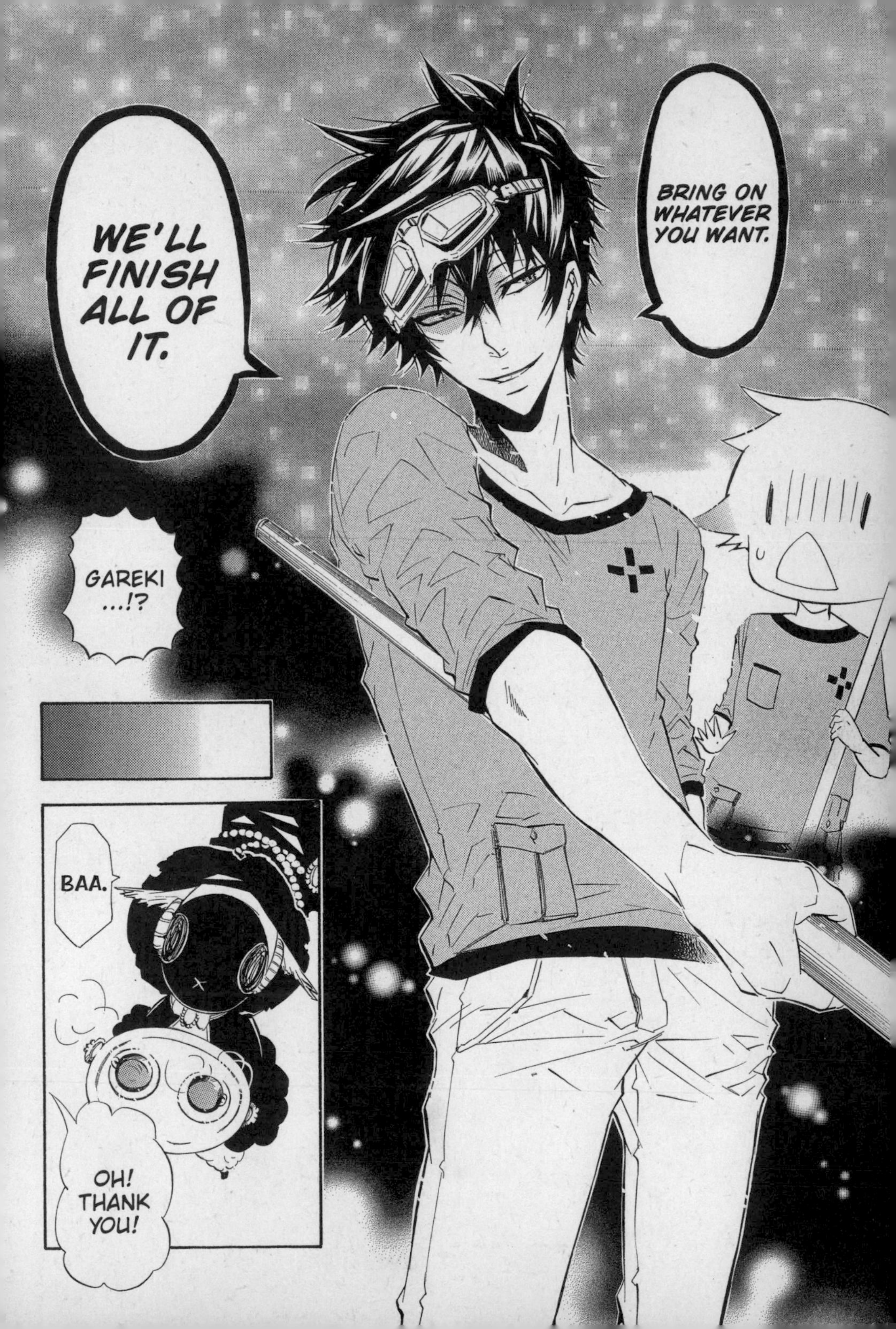
BRING ON WHATEVER YOU WANT.
WE'LL FINISH ALL OF IT.
GAREKI ...!?
BAA.
OH! THANK YOU!

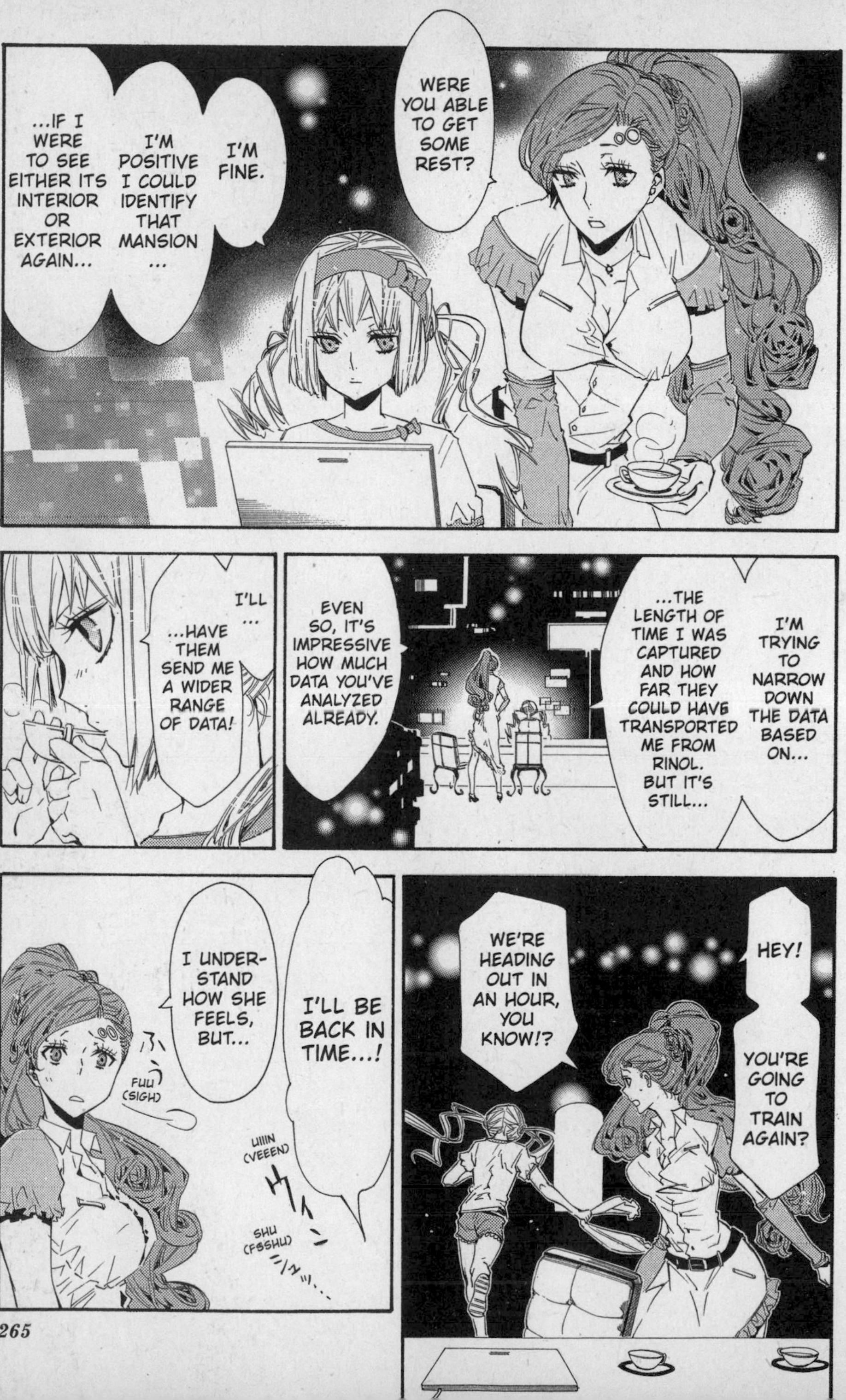

WERE YOU ABLE TO GET SOME REST?
I'M FINE.
I'M POSITIVE I COULD IDENTIFY THAT MANSION ...
...IF I WERE TO SEE EITHER ITS INTERIOR OR EXTERIOR AGAIN...
I'M TRYING TO NARROW DOWN THE DATA BASED ON...
...THE LENGTH OF TIME I WAS CAPTURED AND HOW FAR THEY COULD HAVE TRANSPORTED ME FROM RINOL. BUT IT'S STILL...
EVEN SO, IT'S IMPRESSIVE HOW MUCH DATA YOU'VE ANALYZED ALREADY.
I'LL ...
...HAVE THEM SEND ME A WIDER RANGE OF DATA!
HEY!
YOU'RE GOING TO TRAIN AGAIN?
WE'RE HEADING OUT IN AN HOUR, YOU KNOW!?
I'LL BE BACK IN TIME...!
UIIIN (VEEEND)
SHU (FSSHU)
I UNDER-STAND HOW SHE FEELS, BUT...
FUU (SIGH)

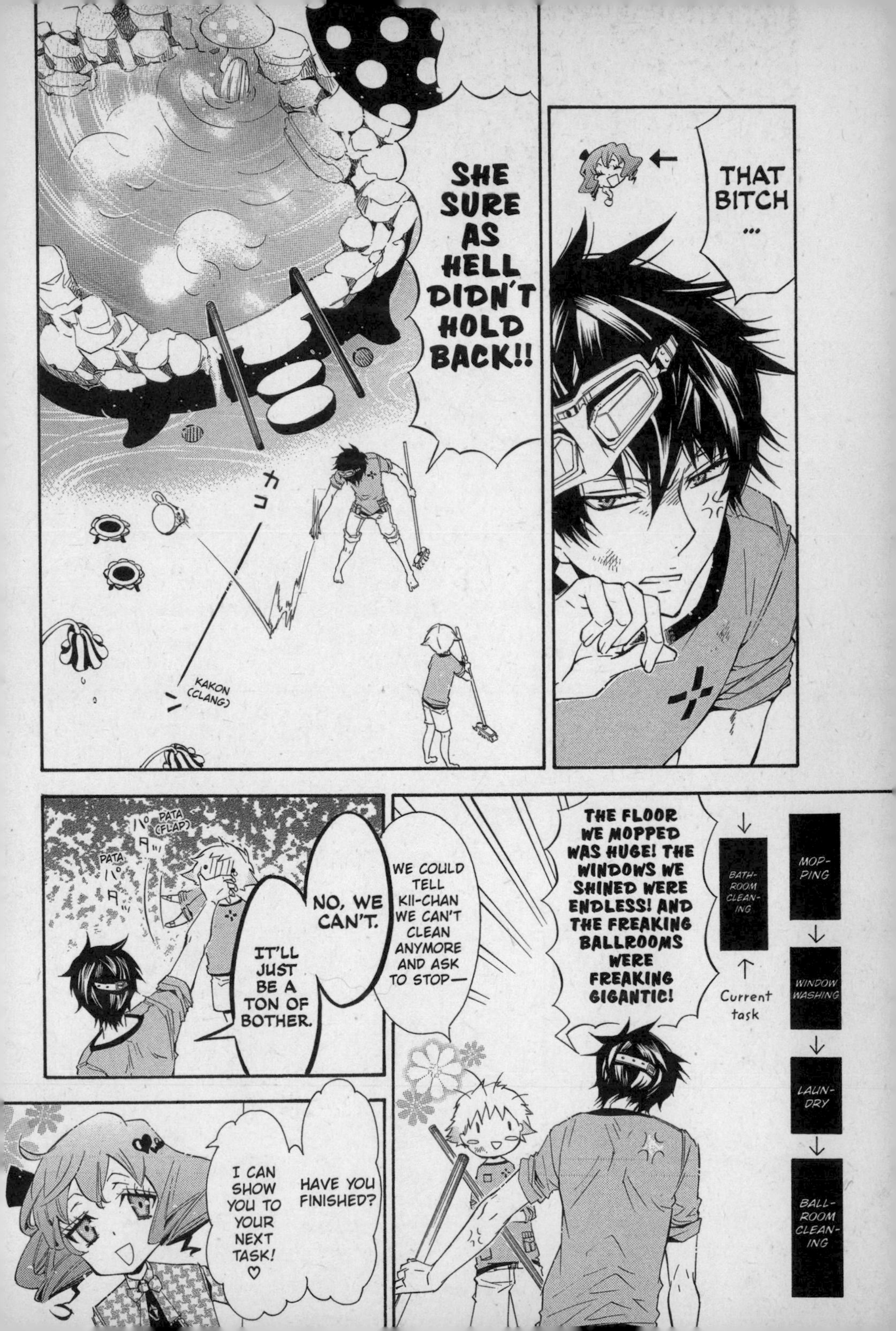
THAT BITCH ...
SHE SURE AS HELL DIDN'T HOLD BACK!!
カコ
KAKON (CLANG)
MOP-PING
WINDOW WASHING
LAUN-DRY
BALL-ROOM CLEAN-ING
BATH-ROOM CLEAN-ING
Current task
THE FLOOR WE MOPPED WAS HUGE! THE WINDOWS WE SHINED WERE ENDLESS! AND THE FREAKING BALLROOMS WERE FREAKING GIGANTIC!
WE COULD TELL KII-CHAN WE CAN'T CLEAN ANYMORE AND ASK TO STOP—
パタ
PATA (FLAP)
パタ
PATA
NO, WE CAN'T.
IT'LL JUST BE A TON OF BOTHER.
HAVE YOU FINISHED?
I CAN SHOW YOU TO YOUR NEXT TASK! ♡

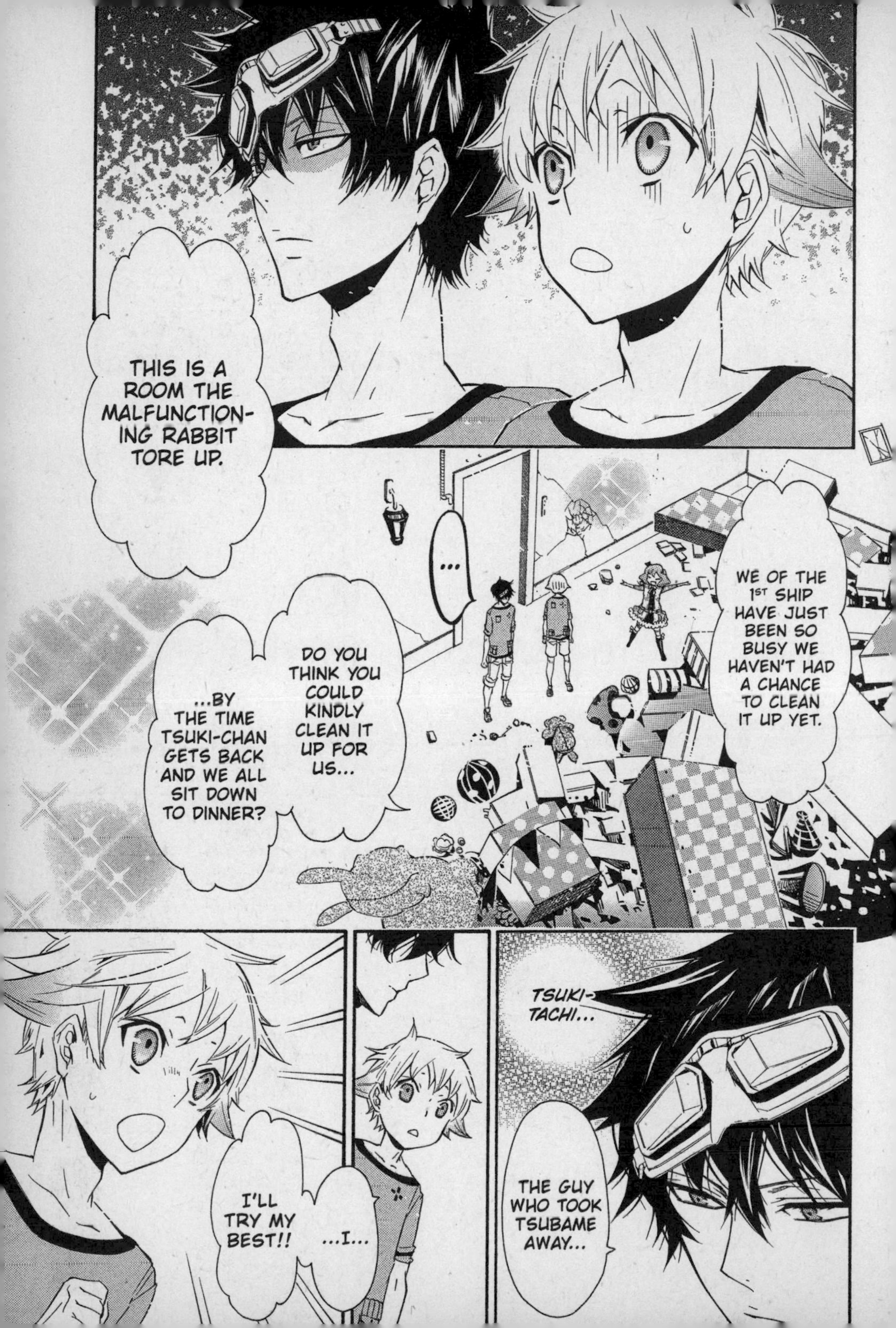
THIS IS A ROOM THE MALFUNCTIONING RABBIT TORE UP.
WE OF THE 1st SHIP HAVE JUST BEEN SO BUSY WE HAVEN'T HAD A CHANCE TO CLEAN IT UP YET.
...
DO YOU THINK YOU COULD KINDLY CLEAN IT UP FOR US...
...BY THE TIME TSUKI-CHAN GETS BACK AND WE ALL SIT DOWN TO DINNER?
TSUKI-TACHI...
THE GUY WHO TOOK TSUBAME AWAY...
...I...
I'LL TRY MY BEST!!

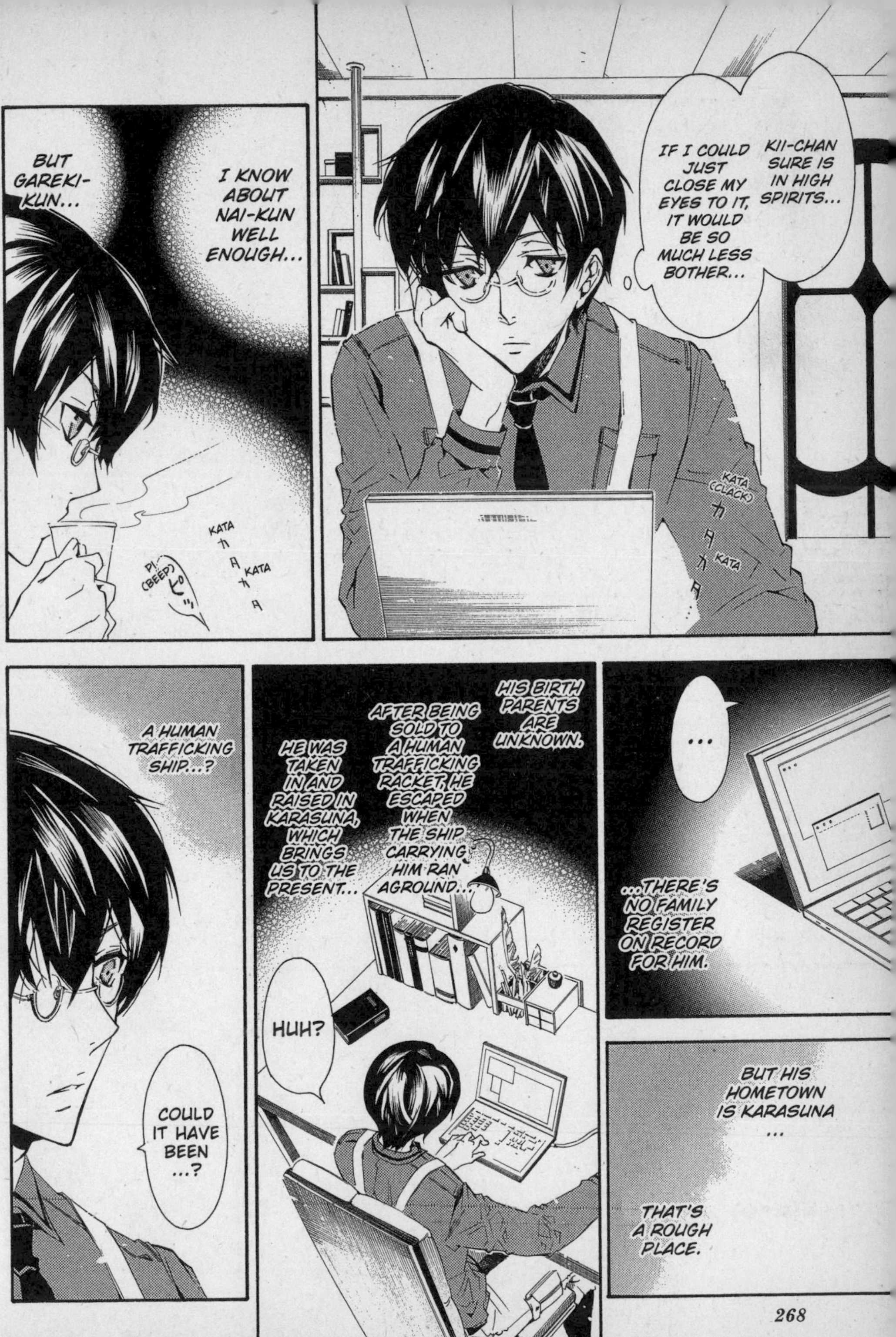
KII-CHAN SURE IS IN HIGH SPIRITS...
IF I COULD JUST CLOSE MY EYES TO IT, IT WOULD BE SO MUCH LESS BOTHER...
KATA (CLACK)
KATA
I KNOW ABOUT NAI-KUN WELL ENOUGH...
BUT GAREKI-KUN...
KATA
KATA
PI (BEEP)
...
...THERE'S NO FAMILY REGISTER ON RECORD FOR HIM.
BUT HIS HOMETOWN IS KARASUNA ...
THAT'S A ROUGH PLACE.
HIS BIRTH PARENTS ARE UNKNOWN.
AFTER BEING SOLD TO A HUMAN TRAFFICKING RACKET, HE ESCAPED WHEN THE SHIP CARRYING HIM RAN AGROUND...
HE WAS TAKEN IN AND RAISED IN KARASUNA, WHICH BRINGS US TO THE PRESENT...
HUH?
A HUMAN TRAFFICKING SHIP...?
COULD IT HAVE BEEN ...?

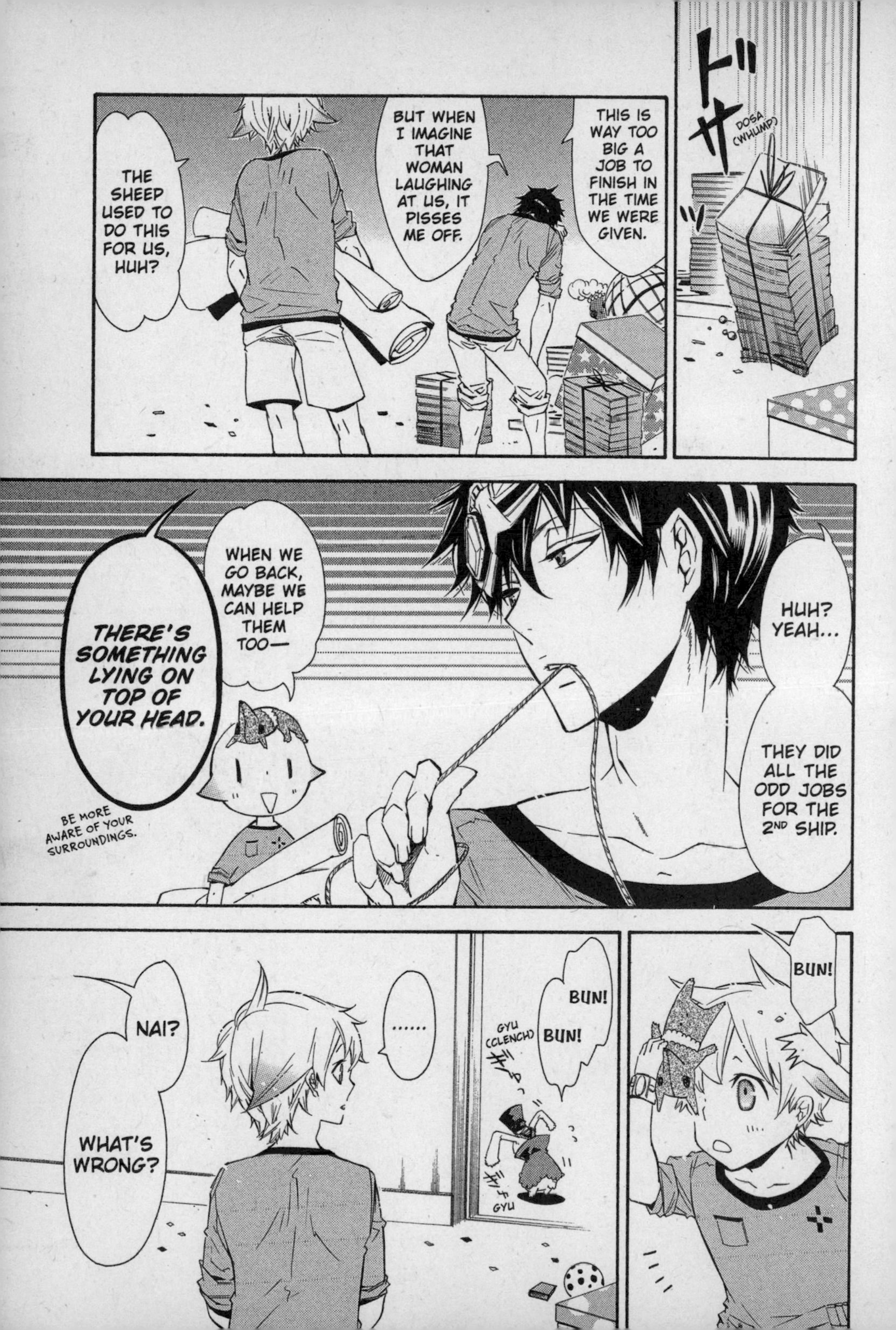
DOSA (WHUMP)
THIS IS WAY TOO BIG A JOB TO FINISH IN THE TIME WE WERE GIVEN.
BUT WHEN I IMAGINE THAT WOMAN LAUGHING AT US, IT PISSES ME OFF.
THE SHEEP USED TO DO THIS FOR US, HUH?
HUH? YEAH...
THEY DID ALL THE ODD JOBS FOR THE 2ND SHIP.
WHEN WE GO BACK, MAYBE WE CAN HELP THEM TOO—
THERE'S SOMETHING LYING ON TOP OF YOUR HEAD.
BE MORE AWARE OF YOUR SURROUNDINGS.
BUN!
BUN!
BUN!
GYU (CLENCH)
GYU
......
NAI?
WHAT'S WRONG?

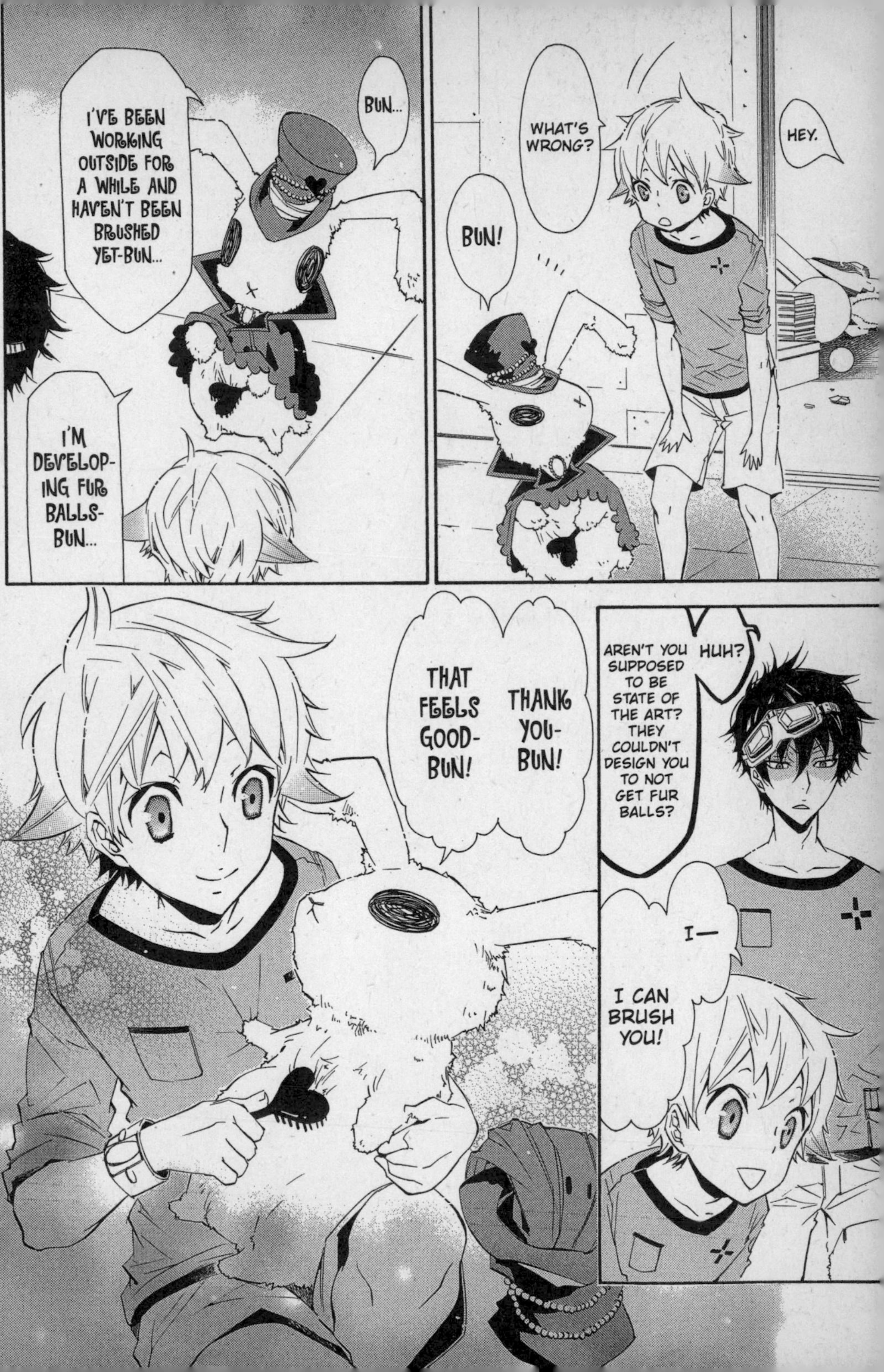
HEY.
WHAT'S WRONG?
BUN!
BUN...
I'VE BEEN WORKING OUTSIDE FOR A WHILE AND HAVEN'T BEEN BRUSHED YET-BUN...
I'M DEVELOP-ING FUR BALLS-BUN...
HUH?
AREN'T YOU SUPPOSED TO BE STATE OF THE ART? THEY COULDN'T DESIGN YOU TO NOT GET FUR BALLS?
I—
I CAN BRUSH YOU!
THANK YOU-BUN!
THAT FEELS GOOD-BUN!

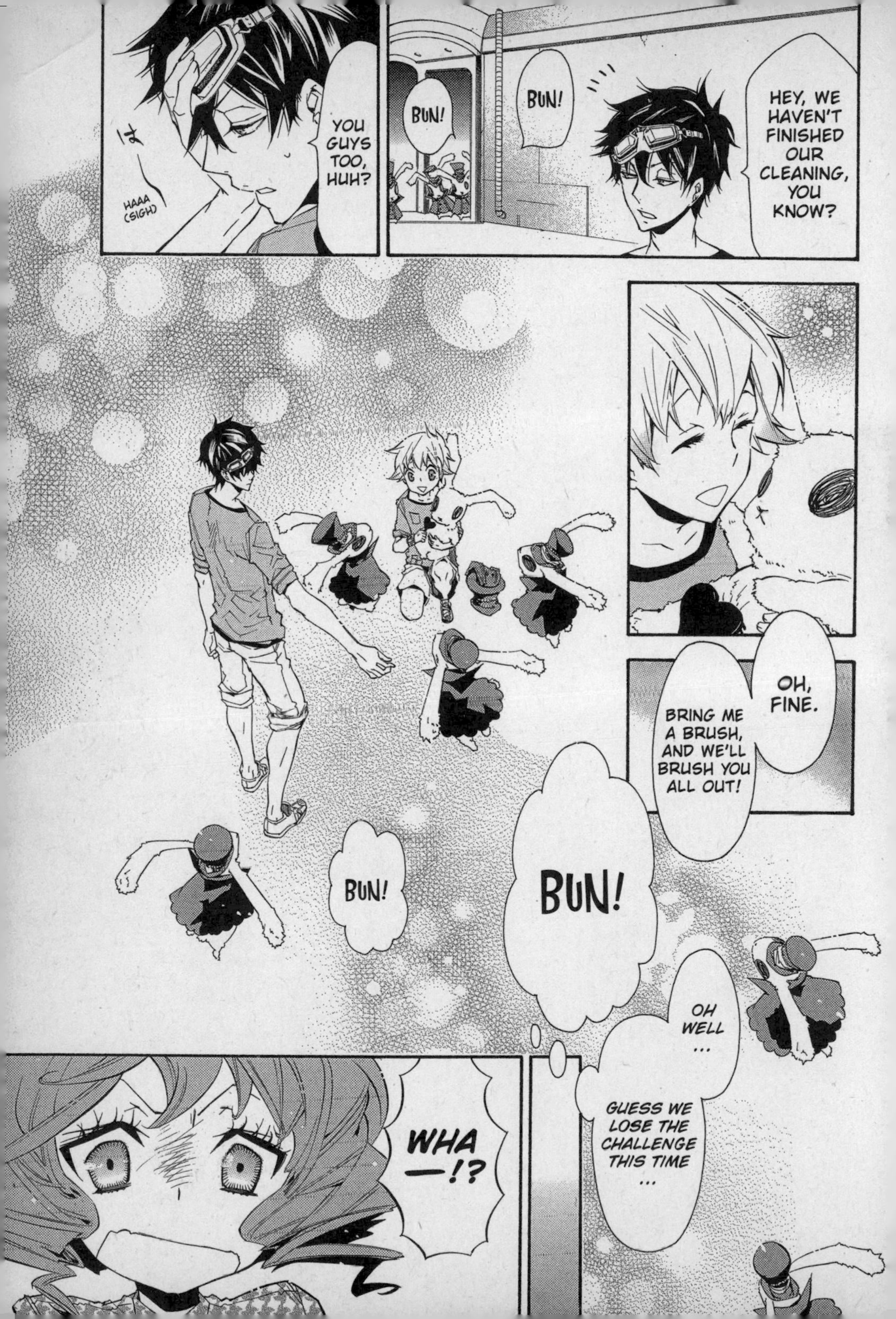
HEY, WE HAVEN'T FINISHED OUR CLEANING, YOU KNOW?
BUN!
BUN!
YOU GUYS TOO, HUH?
は
HAAA (SIGH)
OH, FINE.
BRING ME A BRUSH, AND WE'LL BRUSH YOU ALL OUT!
BUN!
BUN!
OH WELL ...
GUESS WE LOSE THE CHALLENGE THIS TIME ...
WHA—!?

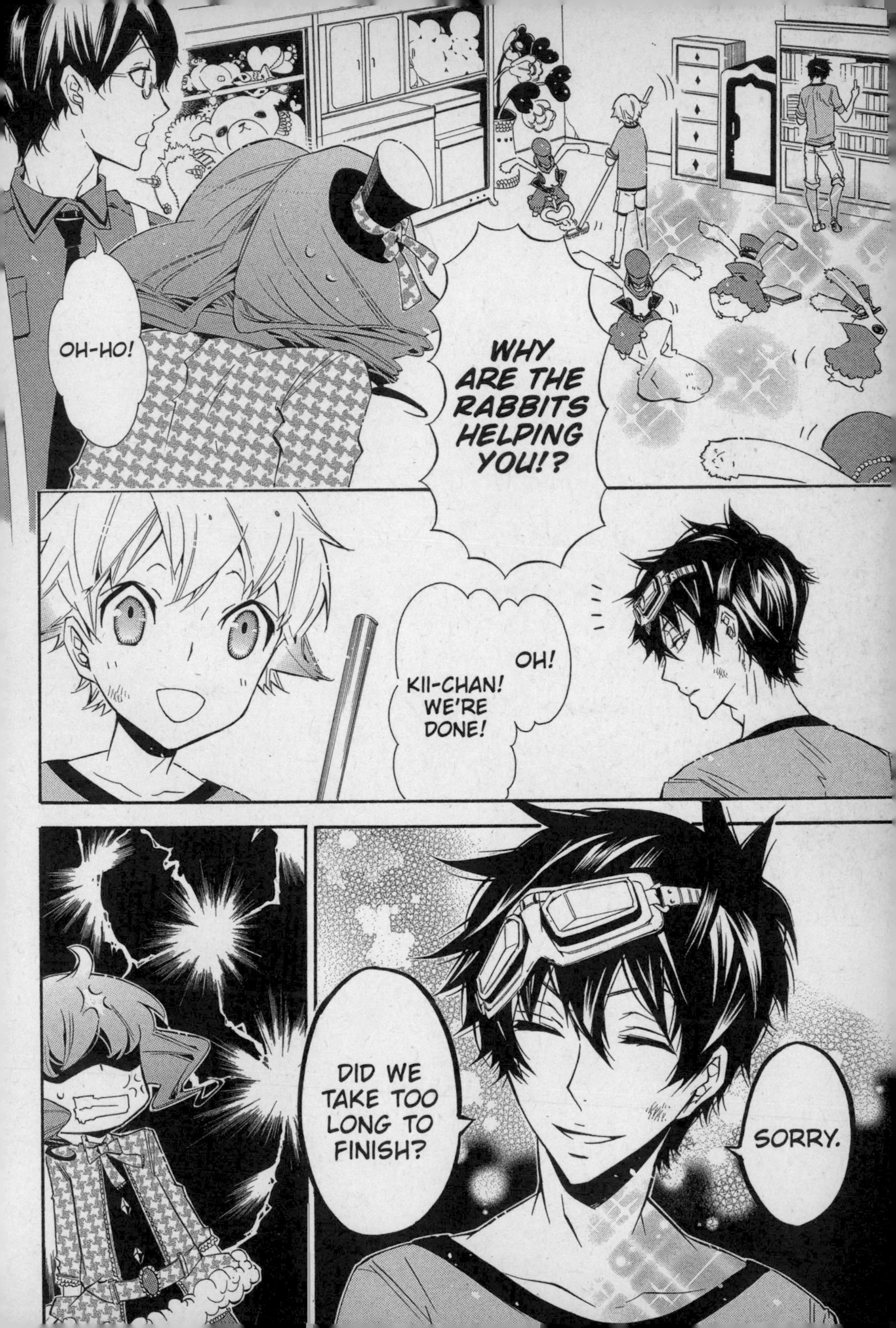
WHY ARE THE RABBITS HELPING YOU!?
OH-HO!
OH!
KII-CHAN! WE'RE DONE!
SORRY.
DID WE TAKE TOO LONG TO FINISH?

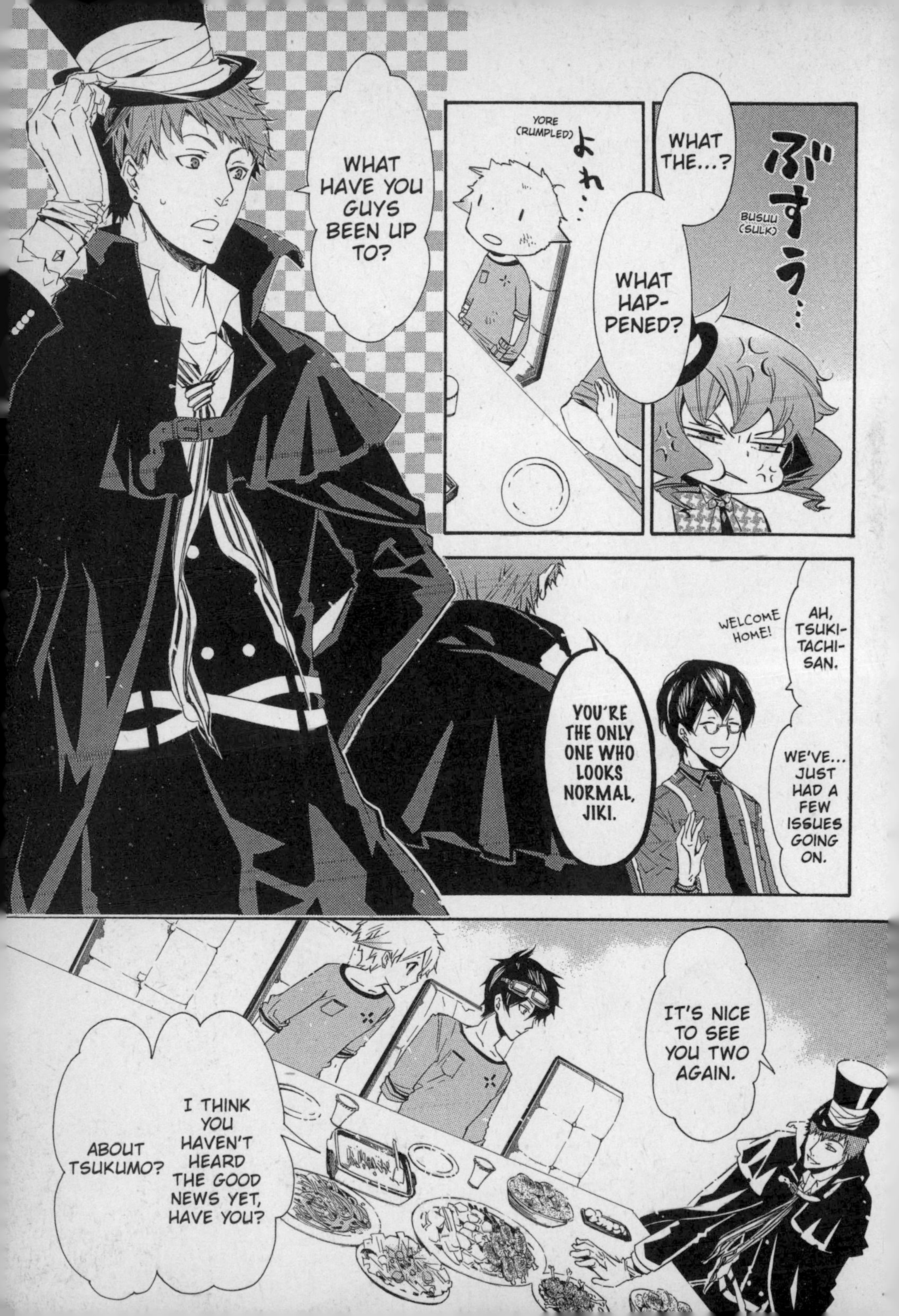
ぶすぅ…
BUSUU (SULK)
WHAT THE...?
WHAT HAP-PENED?
よれ…
YORE (RUMPLED)
AH, TSUKI-TACHI-SAN.
WELCOME HOME!
WE'VE... JUST HAD A FEW ISSUES GOING ON.
YOU'RE THE ONLY ONE WHO LOOKS NORMAL, JIKI.
WHAT HAVE YOU GUYS BEEN UP TO?
IT'S NICE TO SEE YOU TWO AGAIN.
I THINK YOU HAVEN'T HEARD THE GOOD NEWS YET, HAVE YOU?
ABOUT TSUKUMO?

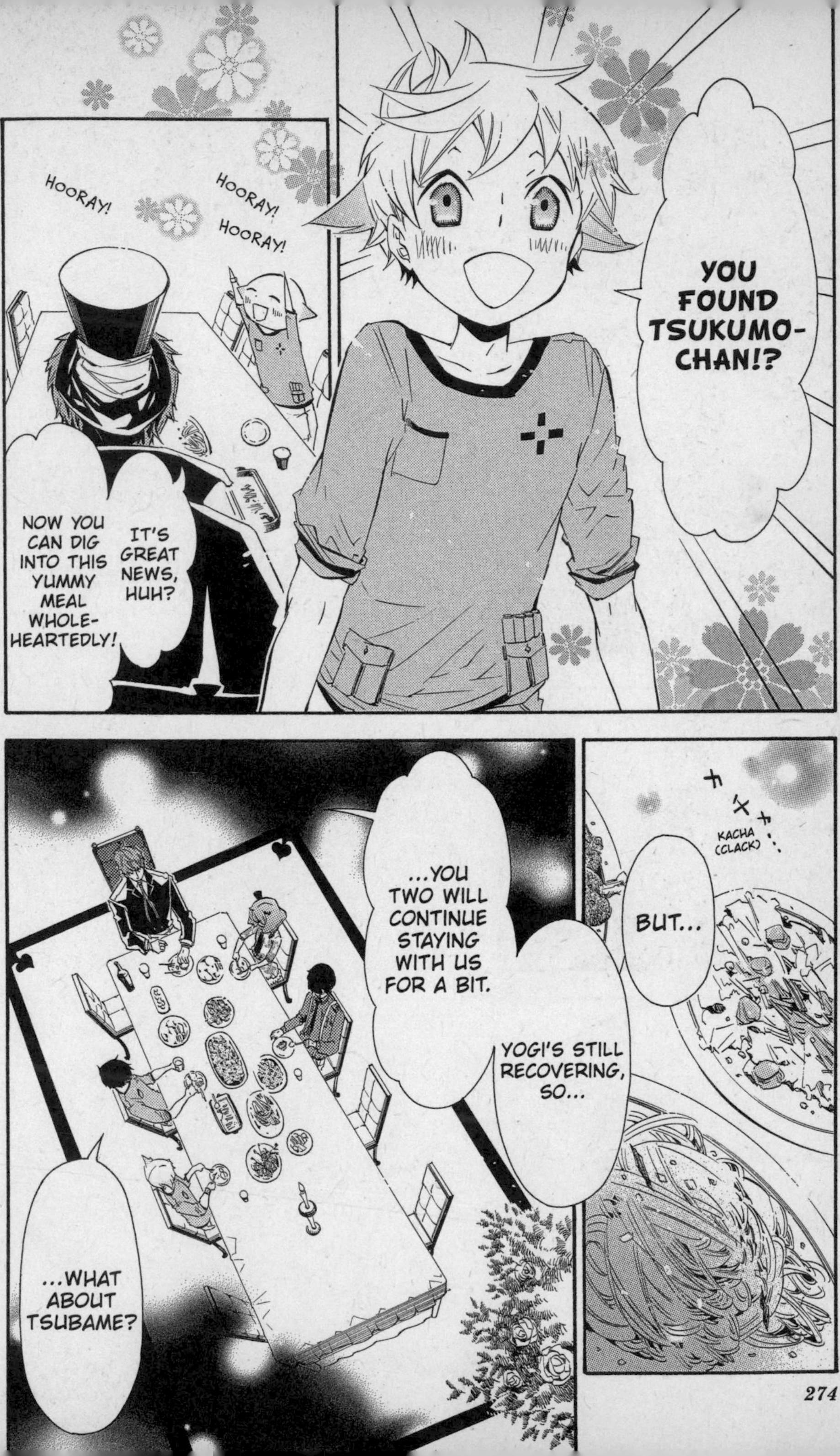
YOU FOUND TSUKUMO-CHAN!?
HOORAY!
HOORAY!
HOORAY!
IT'S GREAT NEWS, HUH?
NOW YOU CAN DIG INTO THIS YUMMY MEAL WHOLE-HEARTEDLY!
KACHA (CLACK)
BUT...
YOGI'S STILL RECOVERING, SO...
...YOU TWO WILL CONTINUE STAYING WITH US FOR A BIT.
...WHAT ABOUT TSUBAME?

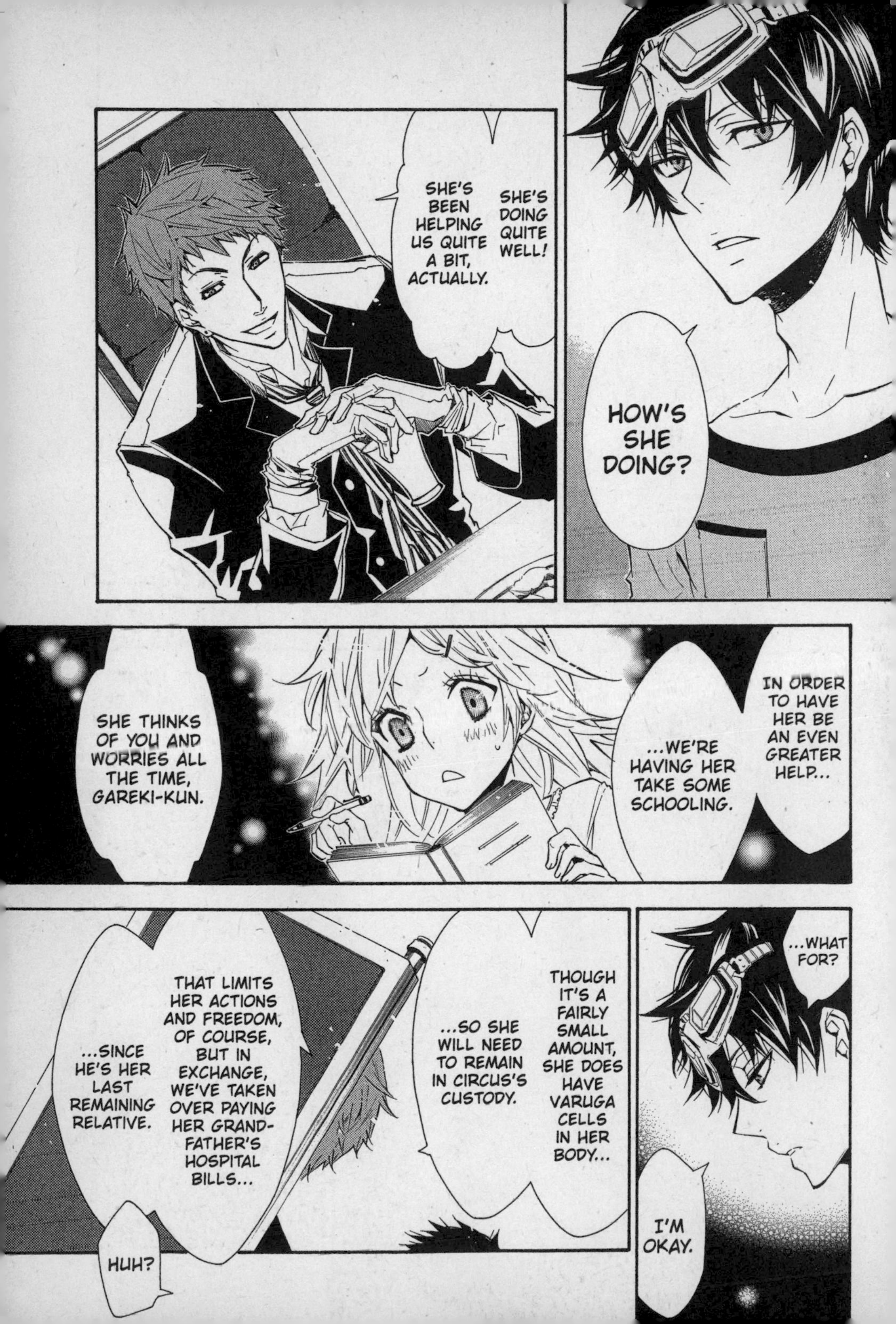
HOW'S SHE DOING?
SHE'S DOING QUITE WELL!
SHE'S BEEN HELPING US QUITE A BIT, ACTUALLY.
IN ORDER TO HAVE HER BE AN EVEN GREATER HELP...
...WE'RE HAVING HER TAKE SOME SCHOOLING.
SHE THINKS OF YOU AND WORRIES ALL THE TIME, GAREKI-KUN.
...WHAT FOR?
I'M OKAY.
THOUGH IT'S A FAIRLY SMALL AMOUNT, SHE DOES HAVE VARUGA CELLS IN HER BODY...
...SO SHE WILL NEED TO REMAIN IN CIRCUS'S CUSTODY.
THAT LIMITS HER ACTIONS AND FREEDOM, OF COURSE, BUT IN EXCHANGE, WE'VE TAKEN OVER PAYING HER GRAND-FATHER'S HOSPITAL BILLS...
...SINCE HE'S HER LAST REMAINING RELATIVE.
HUH?

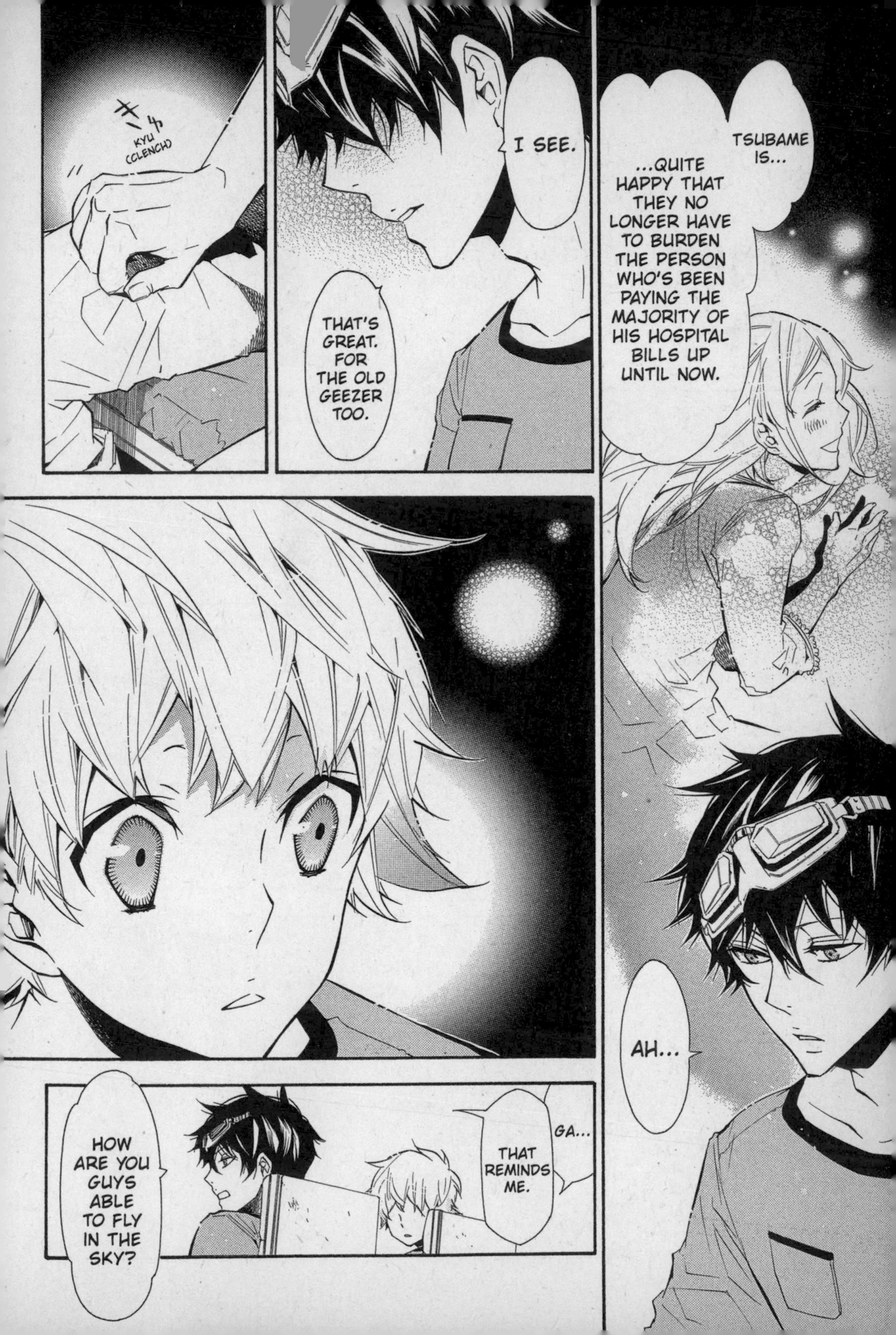
TSUBAME IS...
...QUITE HAPPY THAT THEY NO LONGER HAVE TO BURDEN THE PERSON WHO'S BEEN PAYING THE MAJORITY OF HIS HOSPITAL BILLS UP UNTIL NOW.
AH...
I SEE.
THAT'S GREAT. FOR THE OLD GEEZER TOO.
キュ
KYU (CLENCH)
GA...
THAT REMINDS ME.
HOW ARE YOU GUYS ABLE TO FLY IN THE SKY?

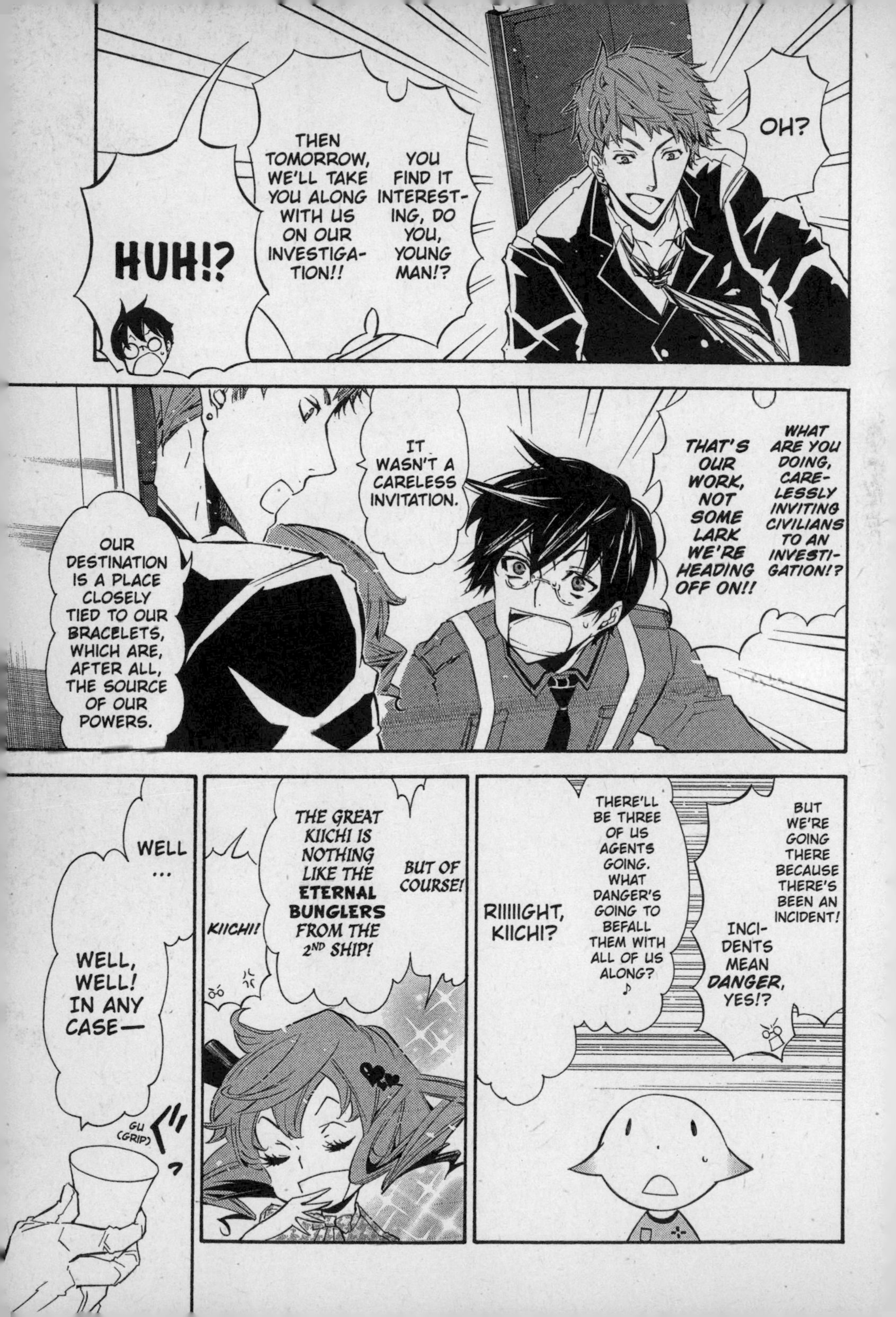
OH?
YOU FIND IT INTERESTING, DO YOU, YOUNG MAN!?
THEN TOMORROW, WE'LL TAKE YOU ALONG WITH US ON OUR INVESTIGATION!!
HUH!?
WHAT ARE YOU DOING, CARELESSLY INVITING CIVILIANS TO AN INVESTIGATION!?
THAT'S OUR WORK, NOT SOME LARK WE'RE HEADING OFF ON!!
IT WASN'T A CARELESS INVITATION.
OUR DESTINATION IS A PLACE CLOSELY TIED TO OUR BRACELETS, WHICH ARE, AFTER ALL, THE SOURCE OF OUR POWERS.
BUT WE'RE GOING THERE BECAUSE THERE'S BEEN AN INCIDENT!
INCIDENTS MEAN DANGER, YES!?
THERE'LL BE THREE OF US AGENTS GOING. WHAT DANGER'S GOING TO BEFALL THEM WITH ALL OF US ALONG? ♪
RIIIIIGHT, KIICHI?
BUT OF COURSE!
THE GREAT KIICHI IS NOTHING LIKE THE ETERNAL BUNGLERS FROM THE 2ND SHIP!
KIICHI!
WELL ...
WELL, WELL! IN ANY CASE—
GU (GRIP)

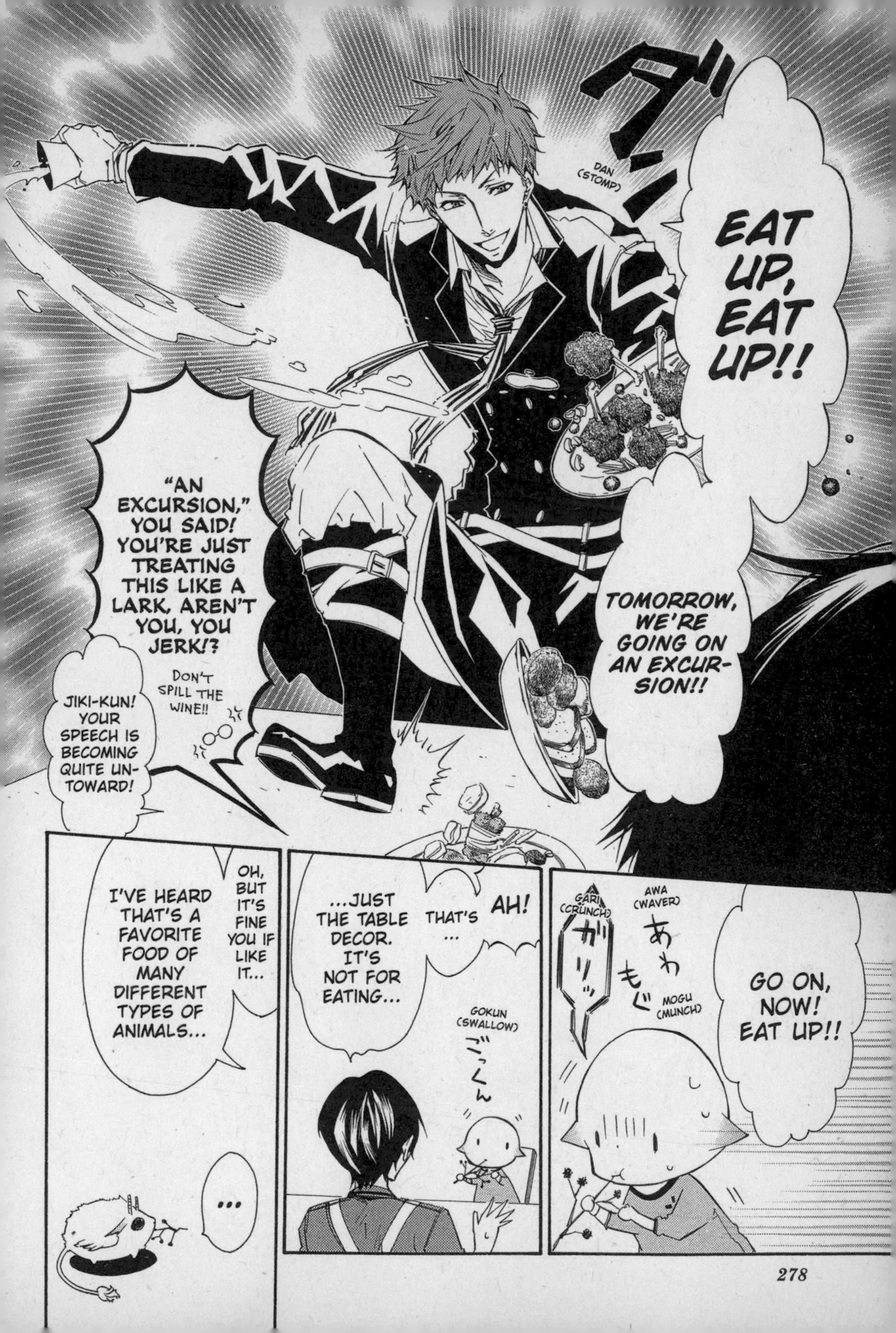
DAN (STOMP)
EAT UP, EAT UP!!
TOMORROW, WE'RE GOING ON AN EXCURSION!!
"AN EXCURSION," YOU SAID! YOU'RE JUST TREATING THIS LIKE A LARK, AREN'T YOU, YOU JERK!?
DON'T SPILL THE WINE!!
JIKI-KUN! YOUR SPEECH IS BECOMING QUITE UNTOWARD!
GO ON, NOW! EAT UP!!
AWA (WAVER)
あわ
GARI (CRUNCH)
ガリッッ
MOGU (MUNCH)
もぐ
AH!
THAT'S ...
...JUST THE TABLE DECOR. IT'S NOT FOR EATING...
GOKUN (SWALLOW)
ごっくん
OH, BUT IT'S FINE IF YOU LIKE IT...
I'VE HEARD THAT'S A FAVORITE FOOD OF MANY DIFFERENT TYPES OF ANIMALS...
...

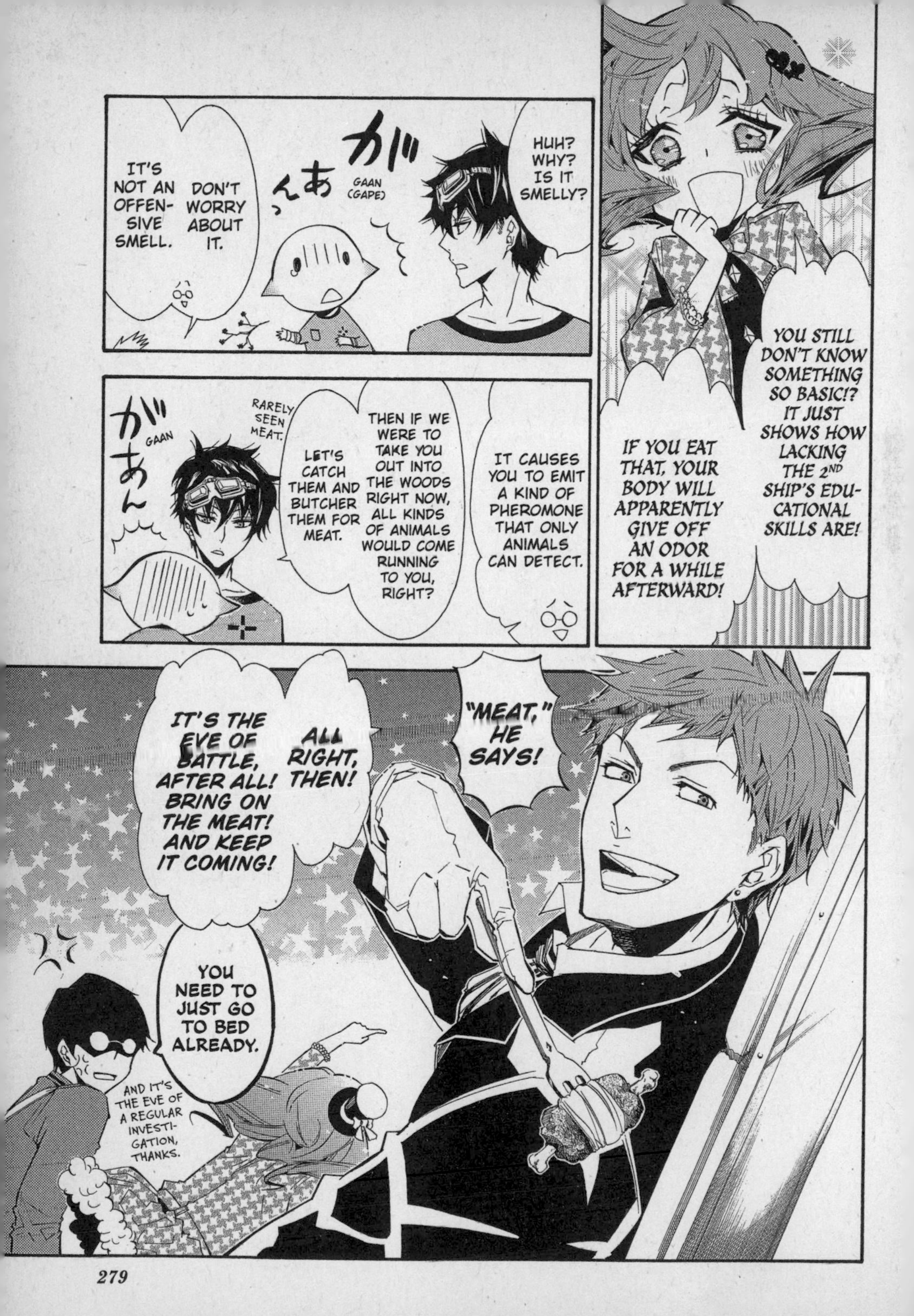
YOU STILL DON'T KNOW SOMETHING SO BASIC!? IT JUST SHOWS HOW LACKING THE 2nd SHIP'S EDU-CATIONAL SKILLS ARE!
IF YOU EAT THAT, YOUR BODY WILL APPARENTLY GIVE OFF AN ODOR FOR A WHILE AFTERWARD!
HUH? WHY? IS IT SMELLY?
GAAN (GAPE)
DON'T WORRY ABOUT IT.
IT'S NOT AN OFFEN-SIVE SMELL.
IT CAUSES YOU TO EMIT A KIND OF PHEROMONE THAT ONLY ANIMALS CAN DETECT.
THEN IF WE WERE TO TAKE YOU OUT INTO THE WOODS RIGHT NOW, ALL KINDS OF ANIMALS WOULD COME RUNNING TO YOU, RIGHT?
LET'S CATCH THEM AND BUTCHER THEM FOR MEAT.
RARELY SEEN MEAT.
GAAN
"MEAT," HE SAYS!
ALL RIGHT, THEN!
IT'S THE EVE OF BATTLE, AFTER ALL! BRING ON THE MEAT! AND KEEP IT COMING!
YOU NEED TO JUST GO TO BED ALREADY.
AND IT'S THE EVE OF A REGULAR INVESTI-GATION, THANKS.

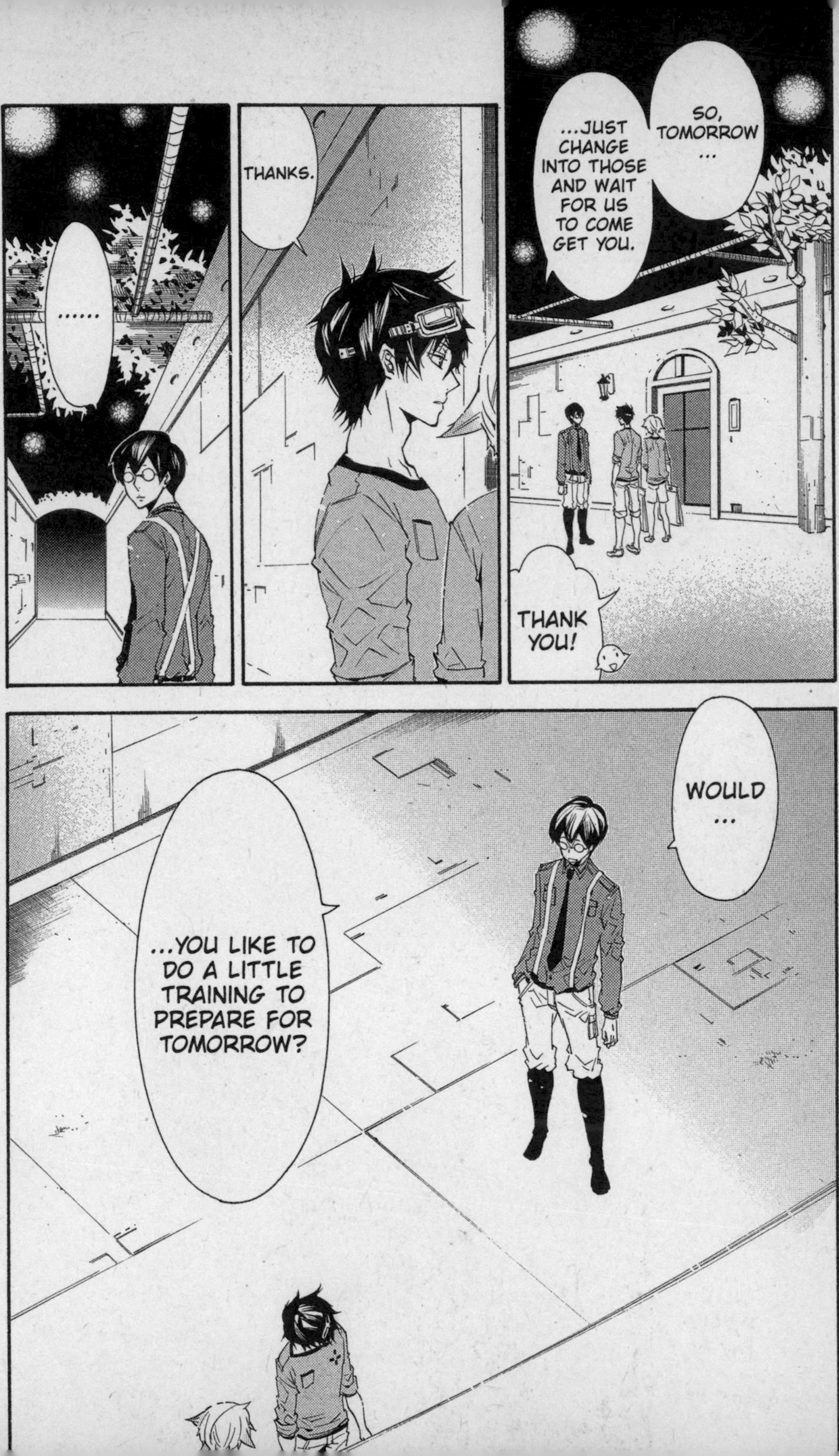
SO, TOMORROW ...
...JUST CHANGE INTO THOSE AND WAIT FOR US TO COME GET YOU.
THANK YOU!
THANKS.
......
WOULD ...
...YOU LIKE TO DO A LITTLE TRAINING TO PREPARE FOR TOMORROW?

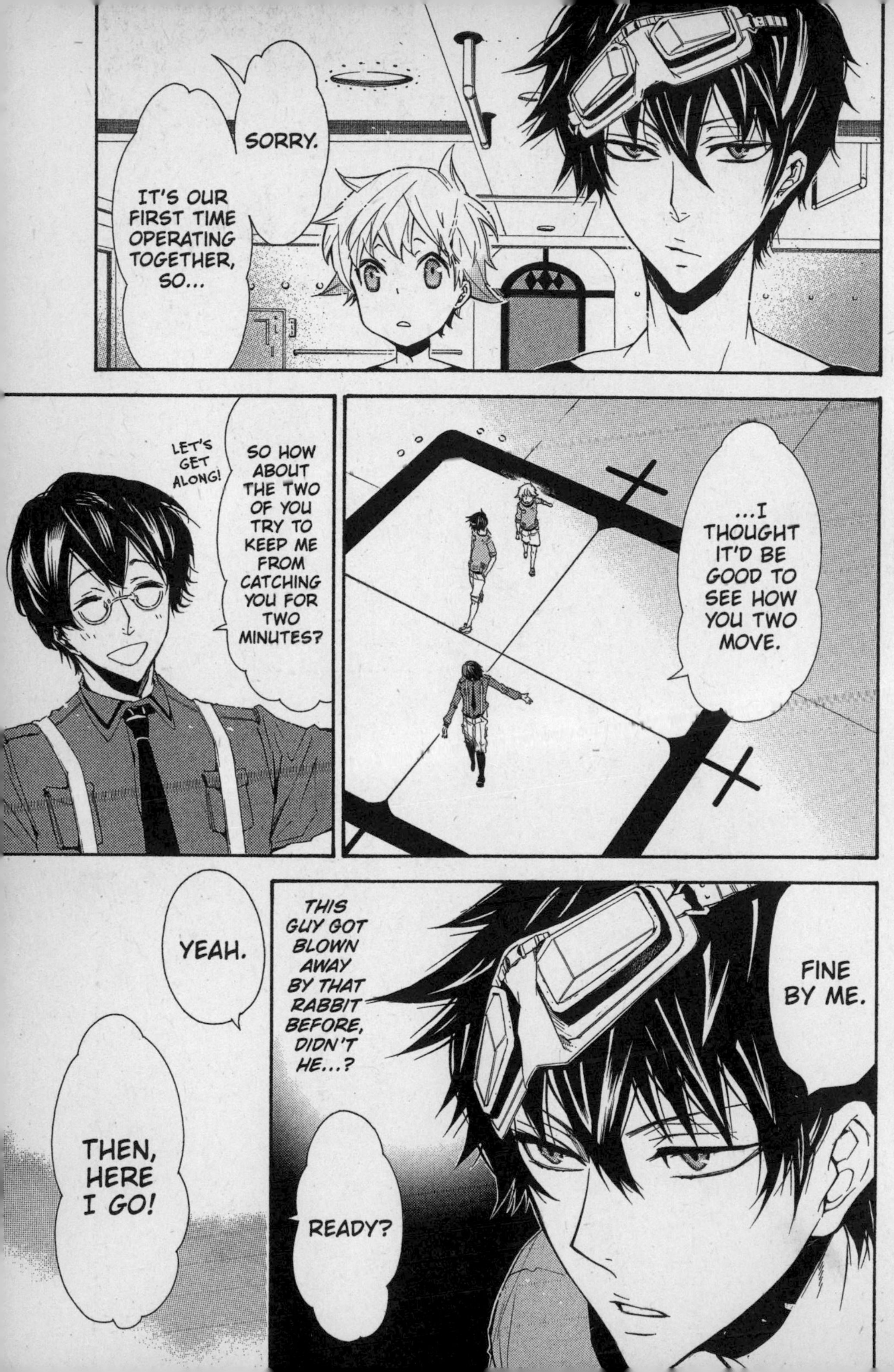
SORRY.
IT'S OUR FIRST TIME OPERATING TOGETHER, SO...
...I THOUGHT IT'D BE GOOD TO SEE HOW YOU TWO MOVE.
SO HOW ABOUT THE TWO OF YOU TRY TO KEEP ME FROM CATCHING YOU FOR TWO MINUTES?
LET'S GET ALONG!
FINE BY ME.
THIS GUY GOT BLOWN AWAY BY THAT RABBIT BEFORE, DIDN'T HE...?
READY?
YEAH.
THEN, HERE I GO!

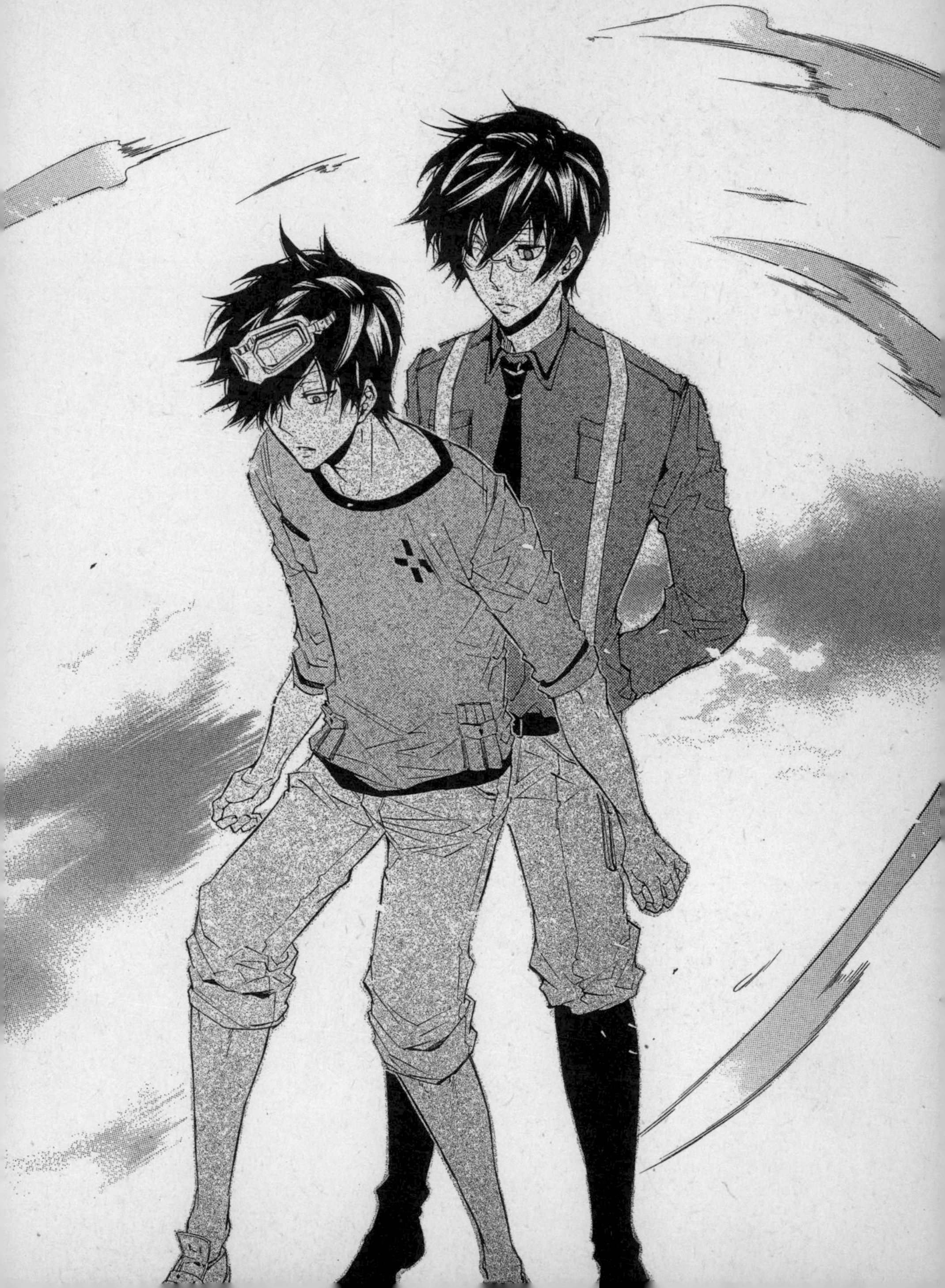

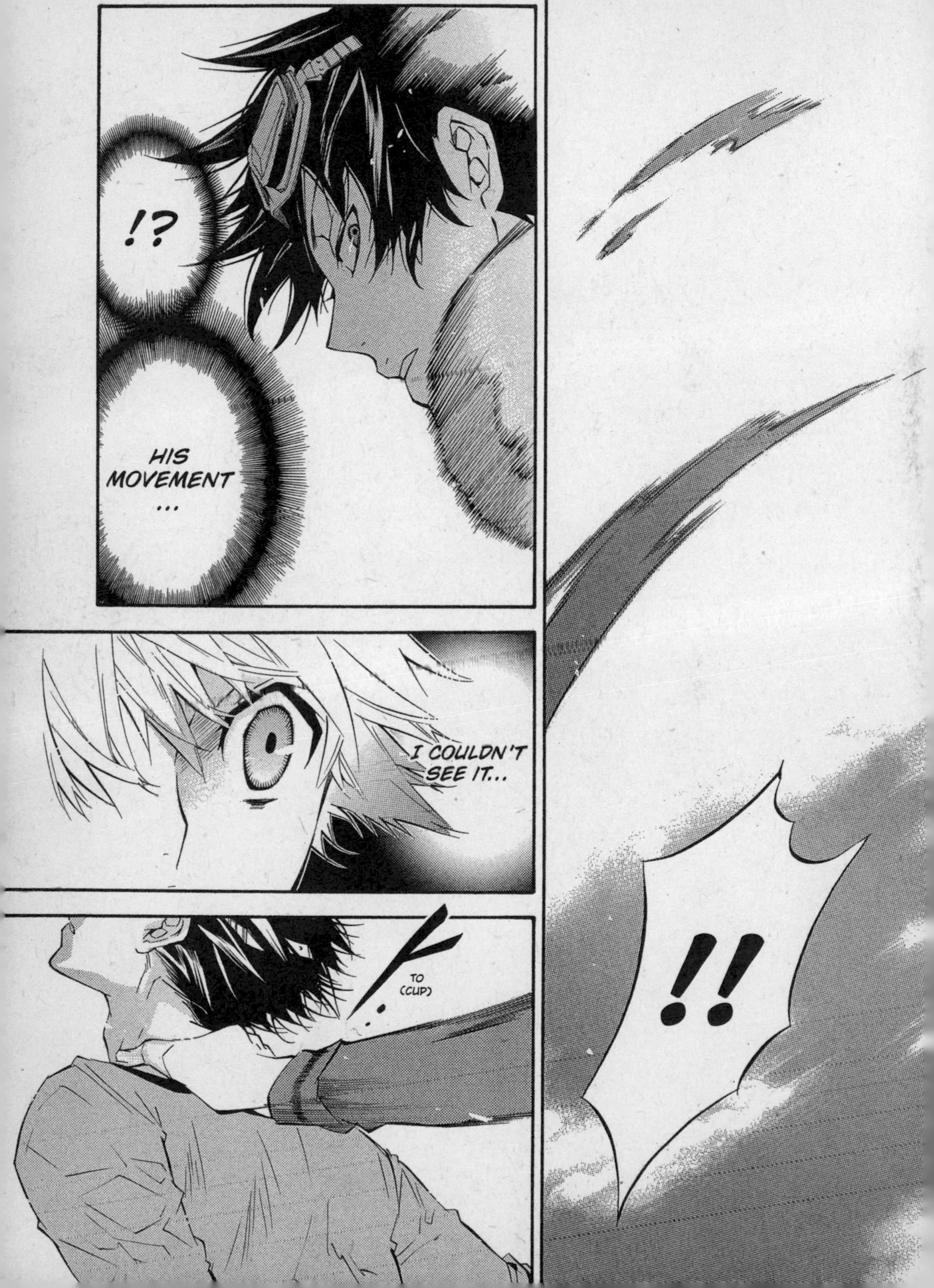
!!
!?
HIS MOVEMENT ...
I COULDN'T SEE IT...
TO (CUP)

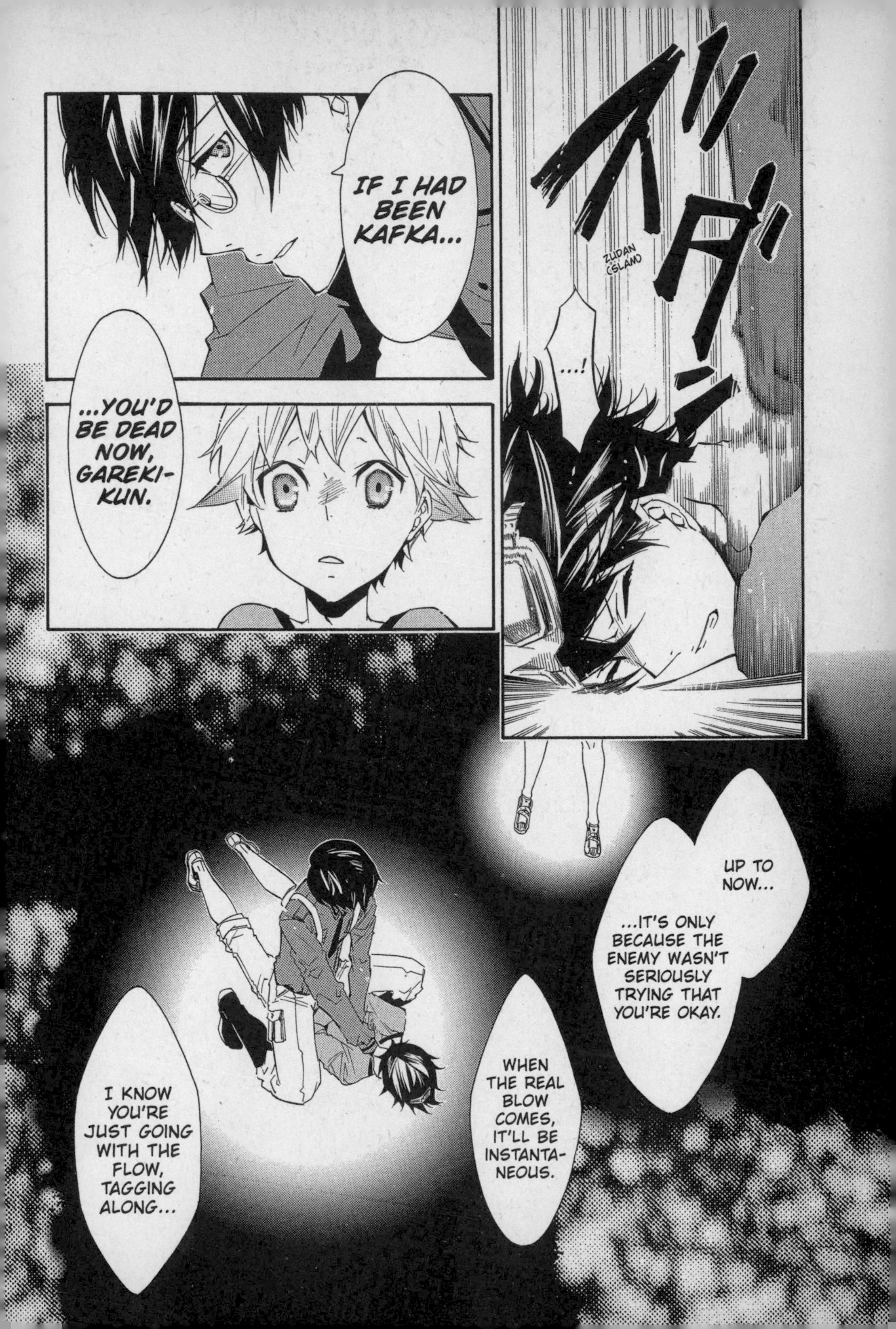
ZUDAN (SLAM)
...!
IF I HAD BEEN KAFKA...
...YOU'D BE DEAD NOW, GAREKI-KUN.
UP TO NOW...
...IT'S ONLY BECAUSE THE ENEMY WASN'T SERIOUSLY TRYING THAT YOU'RE OKAY.
WHEN THE REAL BLOW COMES, IT'LL BE INSTANTA-NEOUS.
I KNOW YOU'RE JUST GOING WITH THE FLOW, TAGGING ALONG...

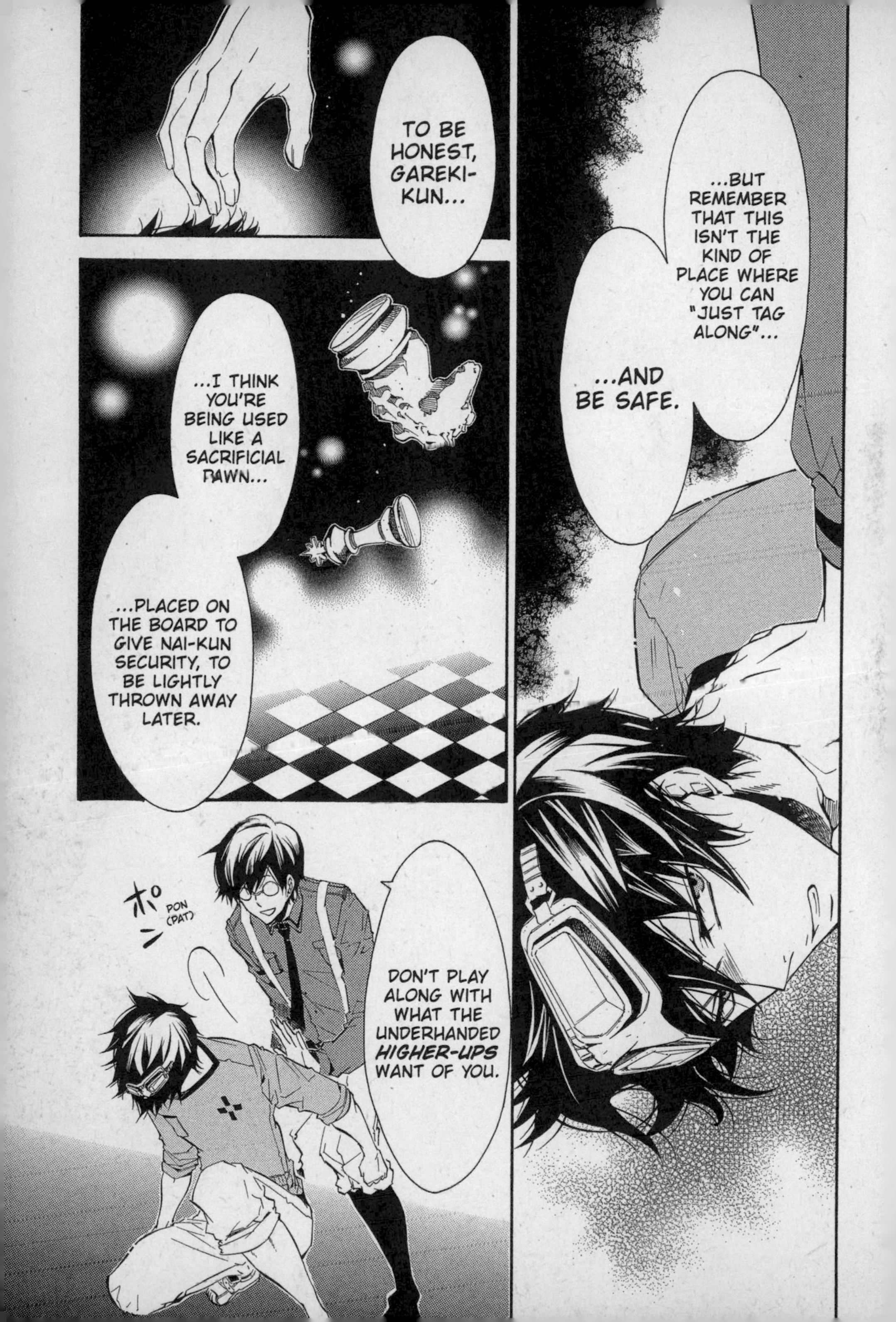
TO BE HONEST, GAREKI-KUN...
...I THINK YOU'RE BEING USED LIKE A SACRIFICIAL PAWN...
...PLACED ON THE BOARD TO GIVE NAI-KUN SECURITY, TO BE LIGHTLY THROWN AWAY LATER.
ポン PON (PAT)
DON'T PLAY ALONG WITH WHAT THE UNDERHANDED HIGHER-UPS WANT OF YOU.
...BUT REMEMBER THAT THIS ISN'T THE KIND OF PLACE WHERE YOU CAN "JUST TAG ALONG"...
...AND BE SAFE.

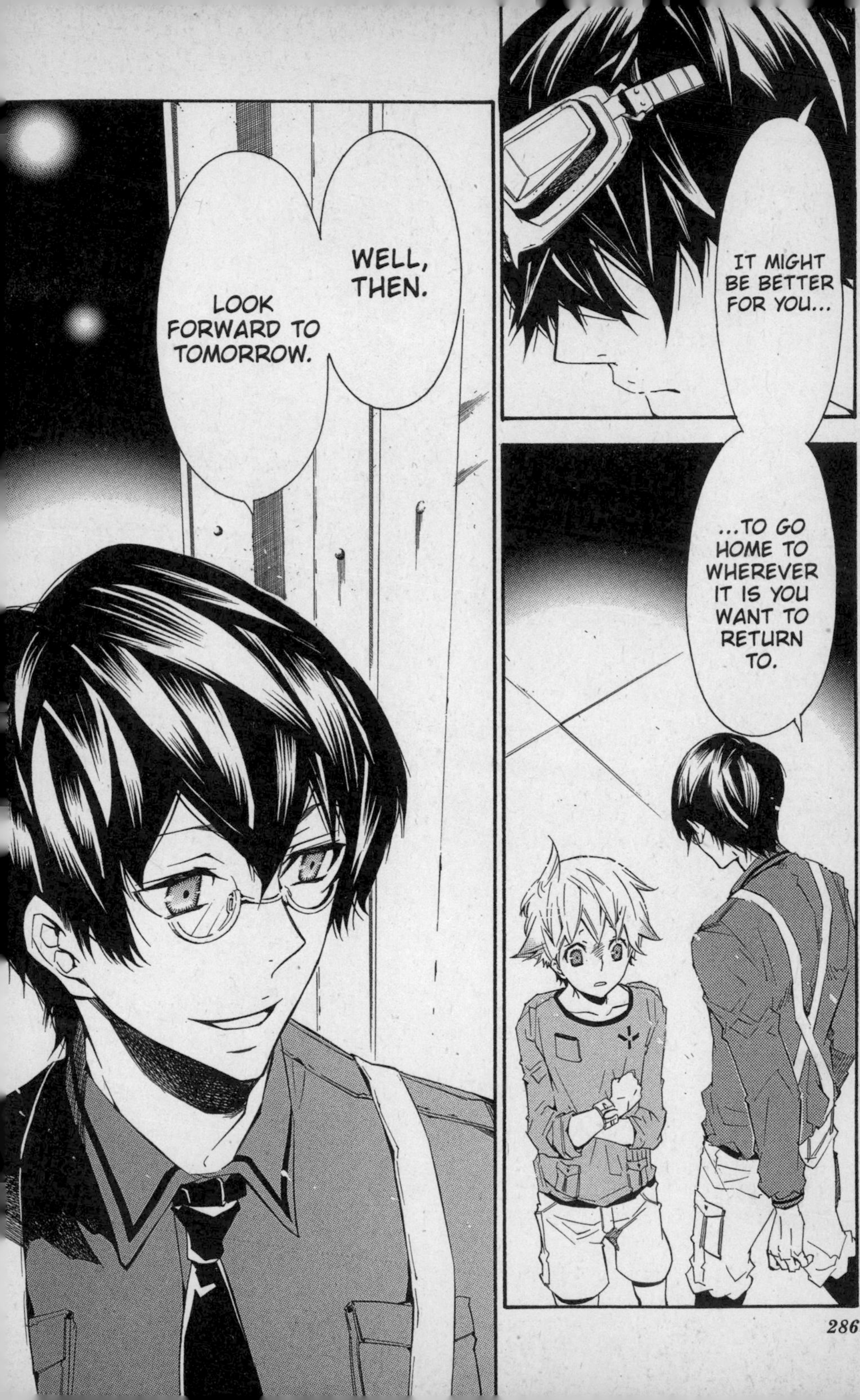
IT MIGHT BE BETTER FOR YOU...
...TO GO HOME TO WHEREVER IT IS YOU WANT TO RETURN TO.
WELL, THEN.
LOOK FORWARD TO TOMORROW.

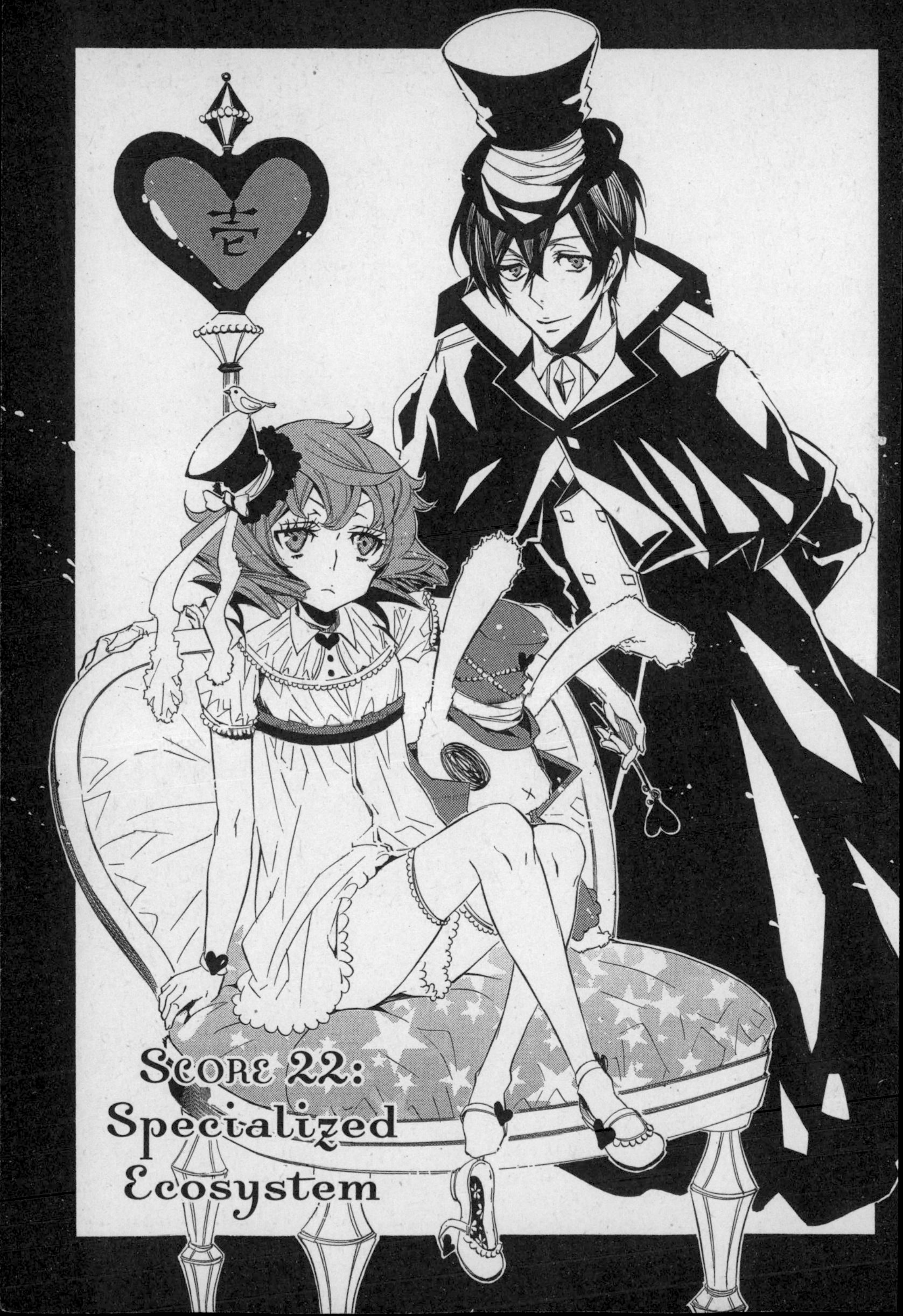
SCORE 22:
Specialized
Ecosystem

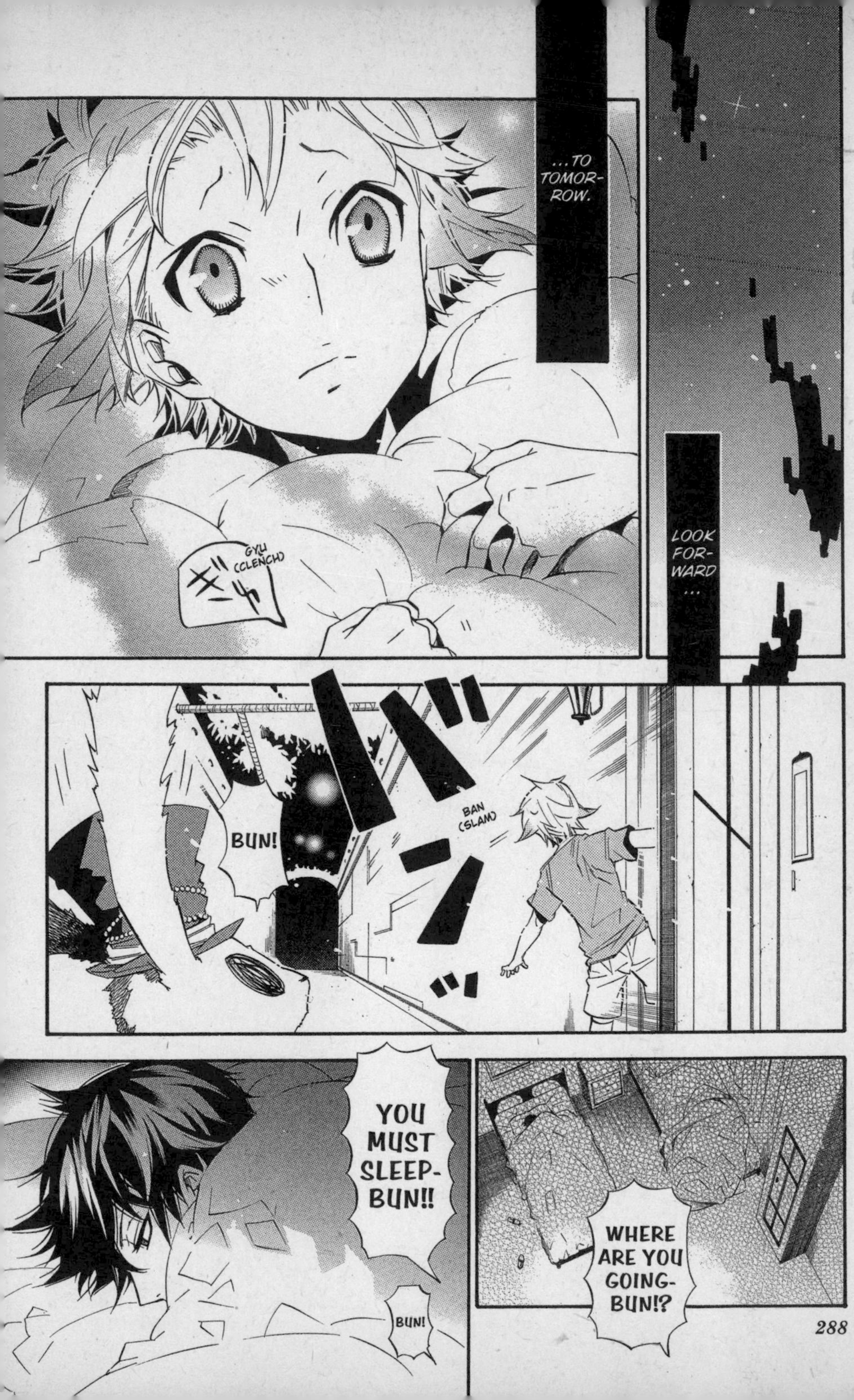

LOOK FORWARD...
...TO TOMORROW.
GYU (CLENCH)
BAN (SLAM)
BUN!
WHERE ARE YOU GOING-BUN!?
YOU MUST SLEEP-BUN!!
BUN!

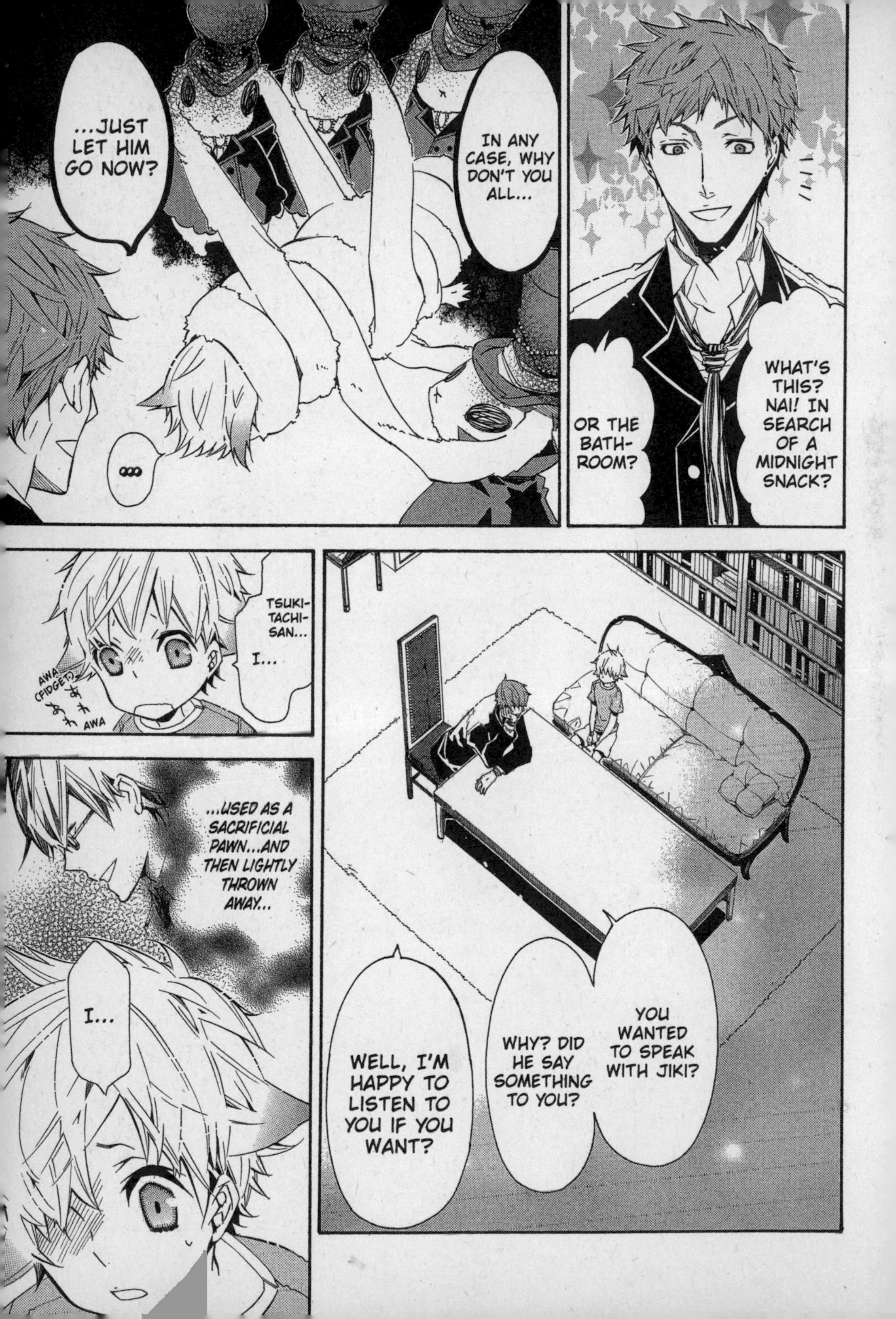
WHAT'S THIS? NAI! IN SEARCH OF A MIDNIGHT SNACK?
OR THE BATH-ROOM?
IN ANY CASE, WHY DON'T YOU ALL...
...JUST LET HIM GO NOW?
...
YOU WANTED TO SPEAK WITH JIKI?
WHY? DID HE SAY SOMETHING TO YOU?
WELL, I'M HAPPY TO LISTEN TO YOU IF YOU WANT?
TSUKI-TACHI-SAN...
I...
AWA (FIDGET) AWA
...USED AS A SACRIFICIAL PAWN...AND THEN LIGHTLY THROWN AWAY...
I...

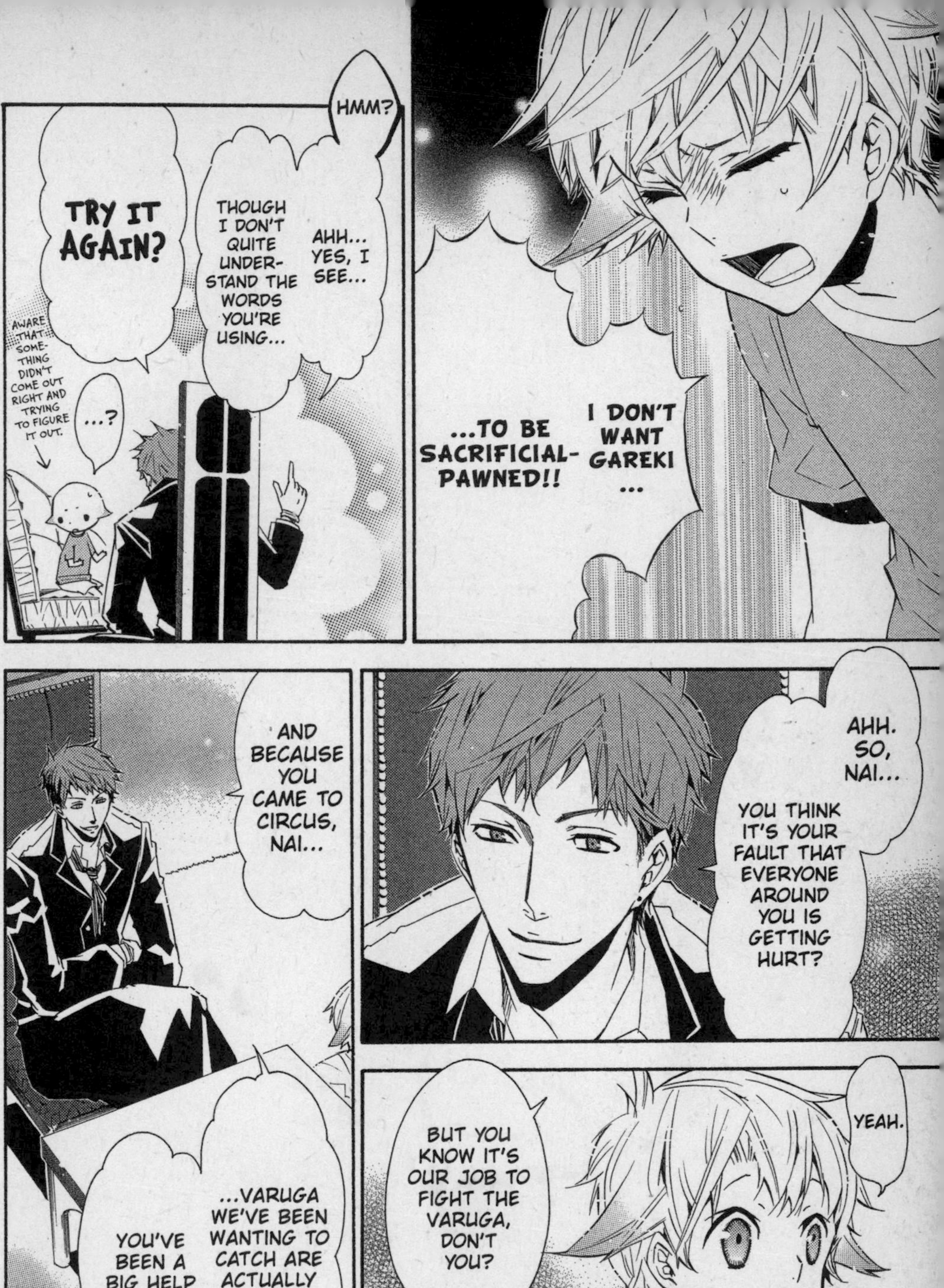
I DON'T WANT GAREKI ...
...TO BE SACRIFICIAL-PAWNED!!
HMM?
AHH... YES, I SEE...
THOUGH I DON'T QUITE UNDER-STAND THE WORDS YOU'RE USING...
TRY IT AGAIN?
...?
AWARE THAT SOME-THING DIDN'T COME OUT RIGHT AND TRYING TO FIGURE IT OUT.
AHH. SO, NAI...
YOU THINK IT'S YOUR FAULT THAT EVERYONE AROUND YOU IS GETTING HURT?
YEAH.
BUT YOU KNOW IT'S OUR JOB TO FIGHT THE VARUGA, DON'T YOU?
...
AND BECAUSE YOU CAME TO CIRCUS, NAI...
...VARUGA WE'VE BEEN WANTING TO CATCH ARE ACTUALLY SEEKING US OUT.
YOU'VE BEEN A BIG HELP IN LOTS OF WAYS! TO DR. AKARI TOO!

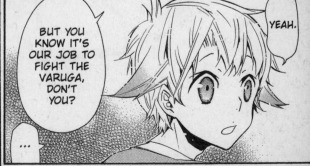

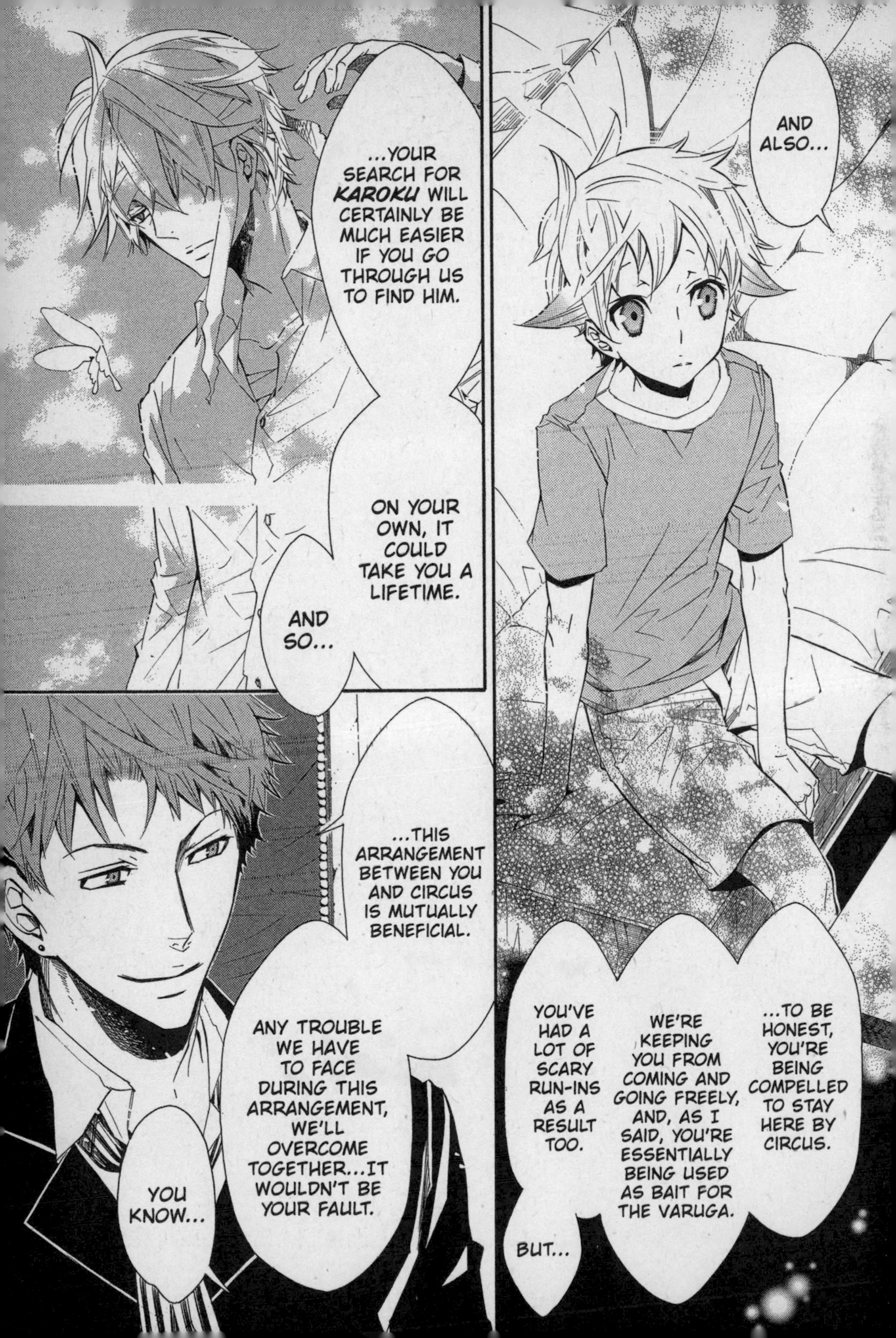
AND ALSO...
...TO BE HONEST, YOU'RE BEING COMPELLED TO STAY HERE BY CIRCUS.
WE'RE KEEPING YOU FROM COMING AND GOING FREELY, AND, AS I SAID, YOU'RE ESSENTIALLY BEING USED AS BAIT FOR THE VARUGA.
YOU'VE HAD A LOT OF SCARY RUN-INS AS A RESULT TOO.
BUT...
...YOUR SEARCH FOR KAROKU WILL CERTAINLY BE MUCH EASIER IF YOU GO THROUGH US TO FIND HIM.
ON YOUR OWN, IT COULD TAKE YOU A LIFETIME.
AND SO...
...THIS ARRANGEMENT BETWEEN YOU AND CIRCUS IS MUTUALLY BENEFICIAL.
ANY TROUBLE WE HAVE TO FACE DURING THIS ARRANGEMENT, WE'LL OVERCOME TOGETHER...IT WOULDN'T BE YOUR FAULT.
YOU KNOW...

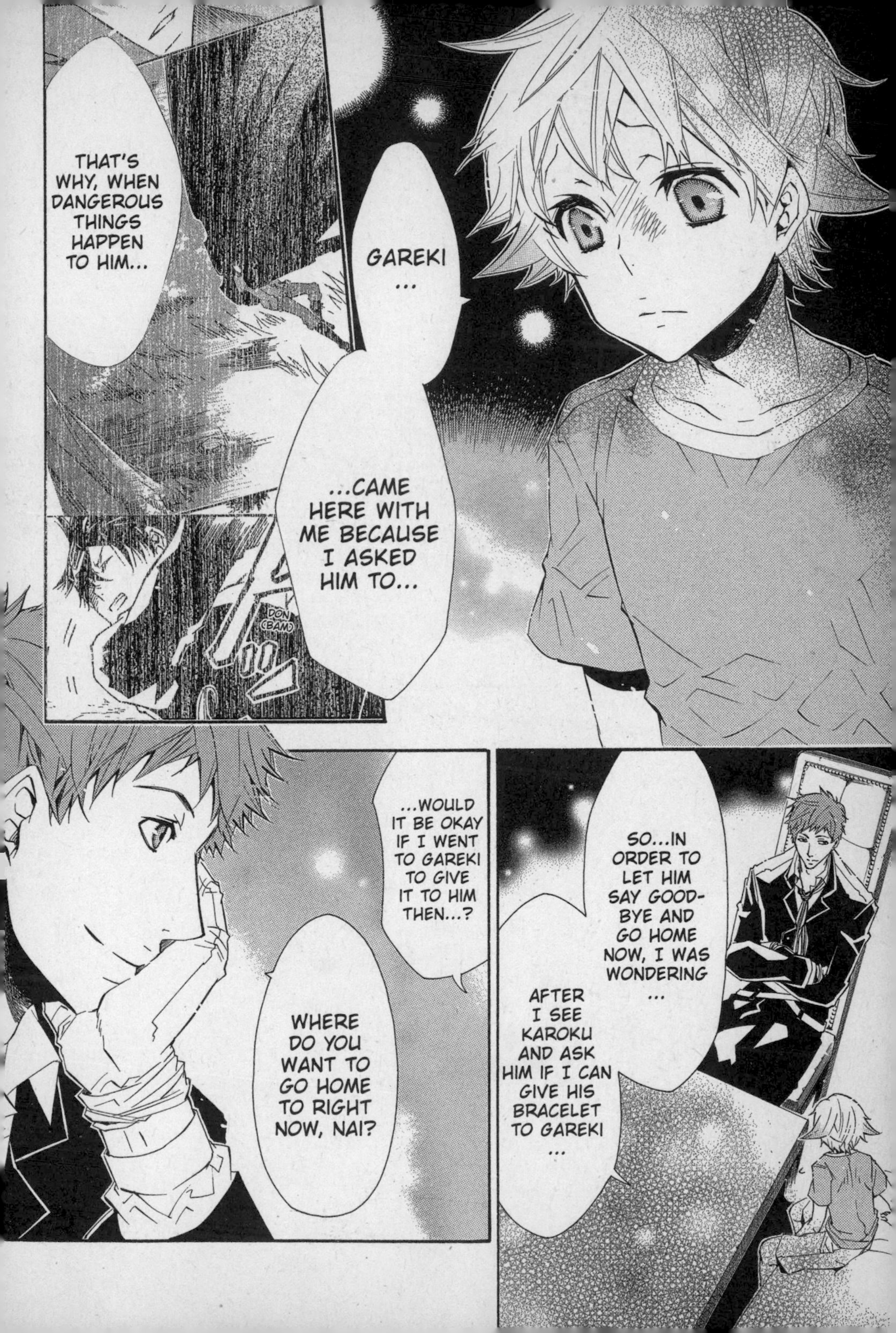
GAREKI ...
...CAME HERE WITH ME BECAUSE I ASKED HIM TO...
THAT'S WHY, WHEN DANGEROUS THINGS HAPPEN TO HIM...
DON (BAM)
SO...IN ORDER TO LET HIM SAY GOOD-BYE AND GO HOME NOW, I WAS WONDERING ...
AFTER I SEE KAROKU AND ASK HIM IF I CAN GIVE HIS BRACELET TO GAREKI ...
...WOULD IT BE OKAY IF I WENT TO GAREKI TO GIVE IT TO HIM THEN...?
WHERE DO YOU WANT TO GO HOME TO RIGHT NOW, NAI?

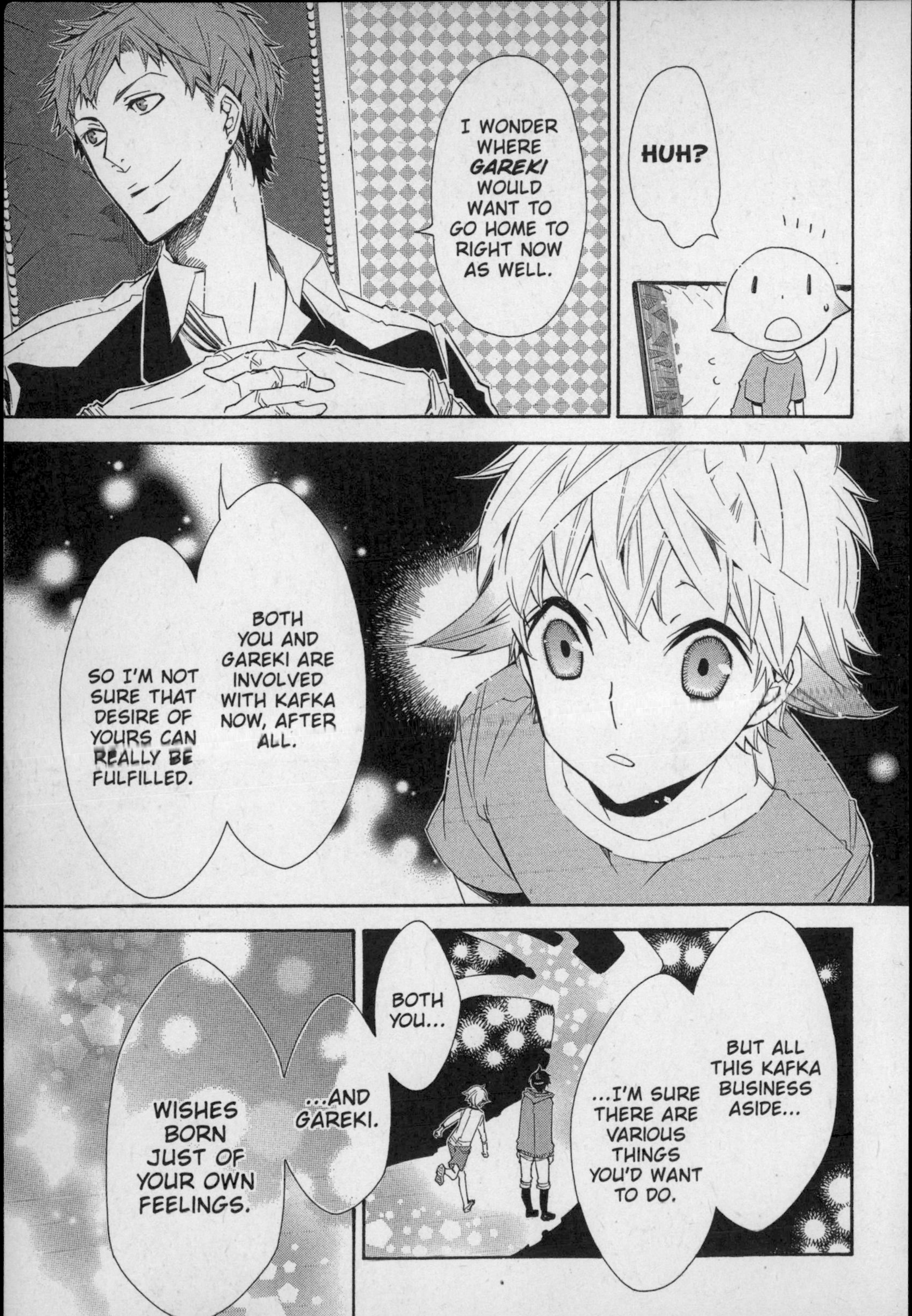
HUH?
I WONDER WHERE GAREKI WOULD WANT TO GO HOME TO RIGHT NOW AS WELL.
BOTH YOU AND GAREKI ARE INVOLVED WITH KAFKA NOW, AFTER ALL.
SO I'M NOT SURE THAT DESIRE OF YOURS CAN REALLY BE FULFILLED.
BUT ALL THIS KAFKA BUSINESS ASIDE...
...I'M SURE THERE ARE VARIOUS THINGS YOU'D WANT TO DO.
BOTH YOU...
...AND GAREKI.
WISHES BORN JUST OF YOUR OWN FEELINGS.

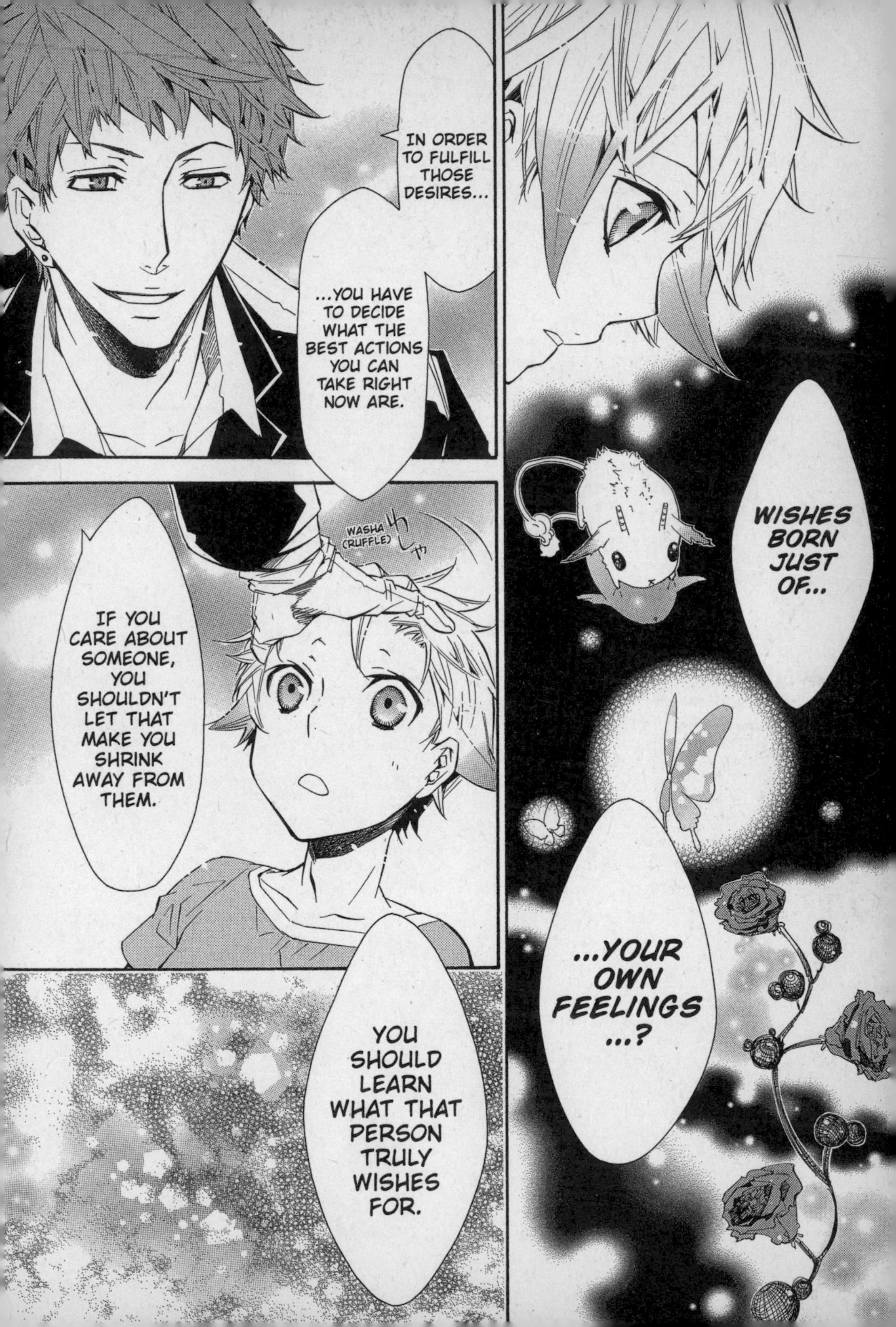
WISHES BORN JUST OF...
...YOUR OWN FEELINGS ...?
IN ORDER TO FULFILL THOSE DESIRES...
...YOU HAVE TO DECIDE WHAT THE BEST ACTIONS YOU CAN TAKE RIGHT NOW ARE.
WASHA (RUFFLE)
IF YOU CARE ABOUT SOMEONE, YOU SHOULDN'T LET THAT MAKE YOU SHRINK AWAY FROM THEM.
YOU SHOULD LEARN WHAT THAT PERSON TRULY WISHES FOR.

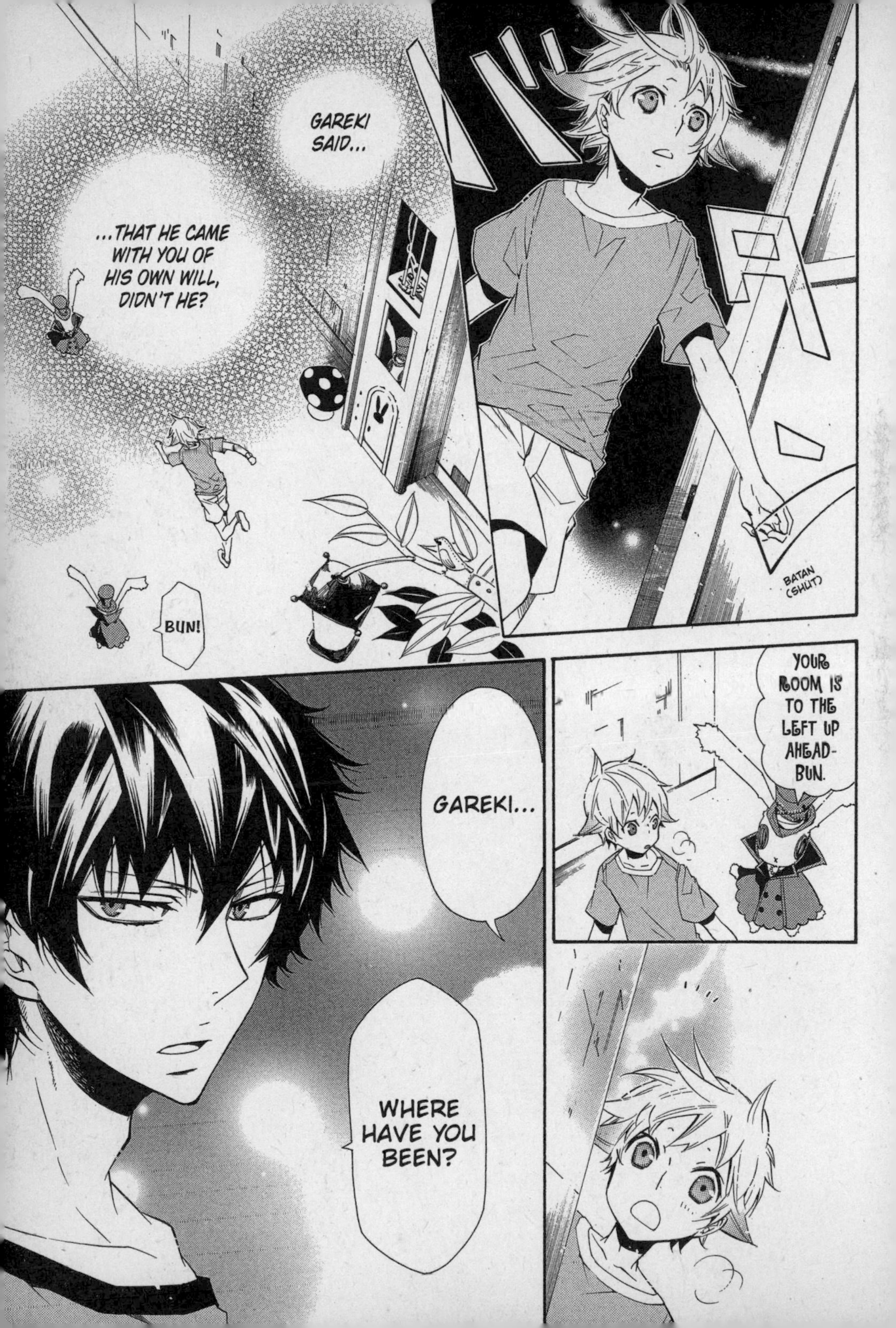
BATAN (SHUT)
GAREKI SAID...
...THAT HE CAME WITH YOU OF HIS OWN WILL, DIDN'T HE?
BUN!
YOUR ROOM IS TO THE LEFT UP AHEAD-BUN.
GAREKI...
WHERE HAVE YOU BEEN?

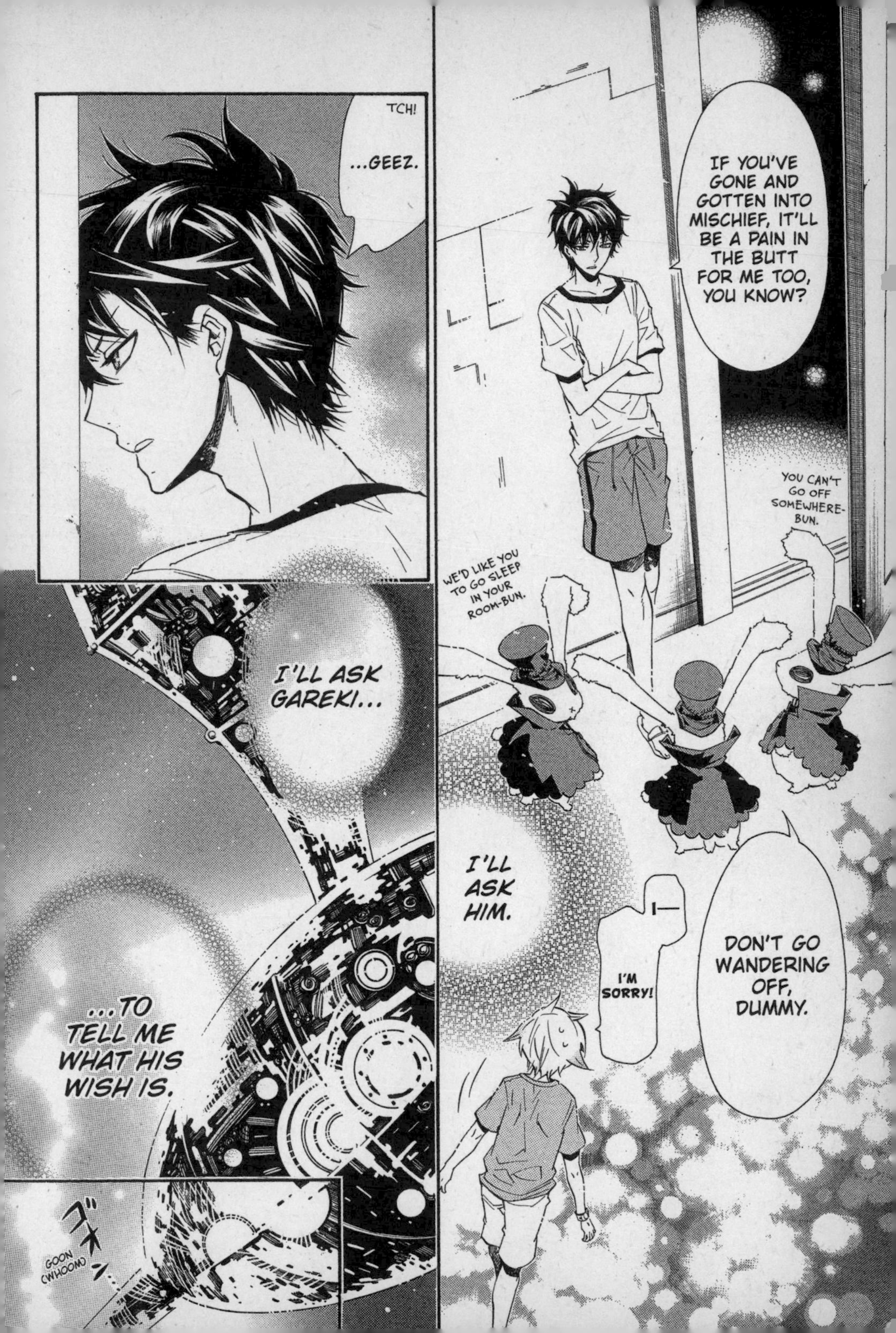
IF YOU'VE GONE AND GOTTEN INTO MISCHIEF, IT'LL BE A PAIN IN THE BUTT FOR ME TOO, YOU KNOW?
YOU CAN'T GO OFF SOMEWHERE-BUN.
WE'D LIKE YOU TO GO SLEEP IN YOUR ROOM-BUN.
DON'T GO WANDERING OFF, DUMMY.
I—
I'M SORRY!
I'LL ASK HIM.
TCH!
...GEEZ.
I'LL ASK GAREKI...
...TO TELL ME WHAT HIS WISH IS.
ゴオ
GOON (WHOOM)

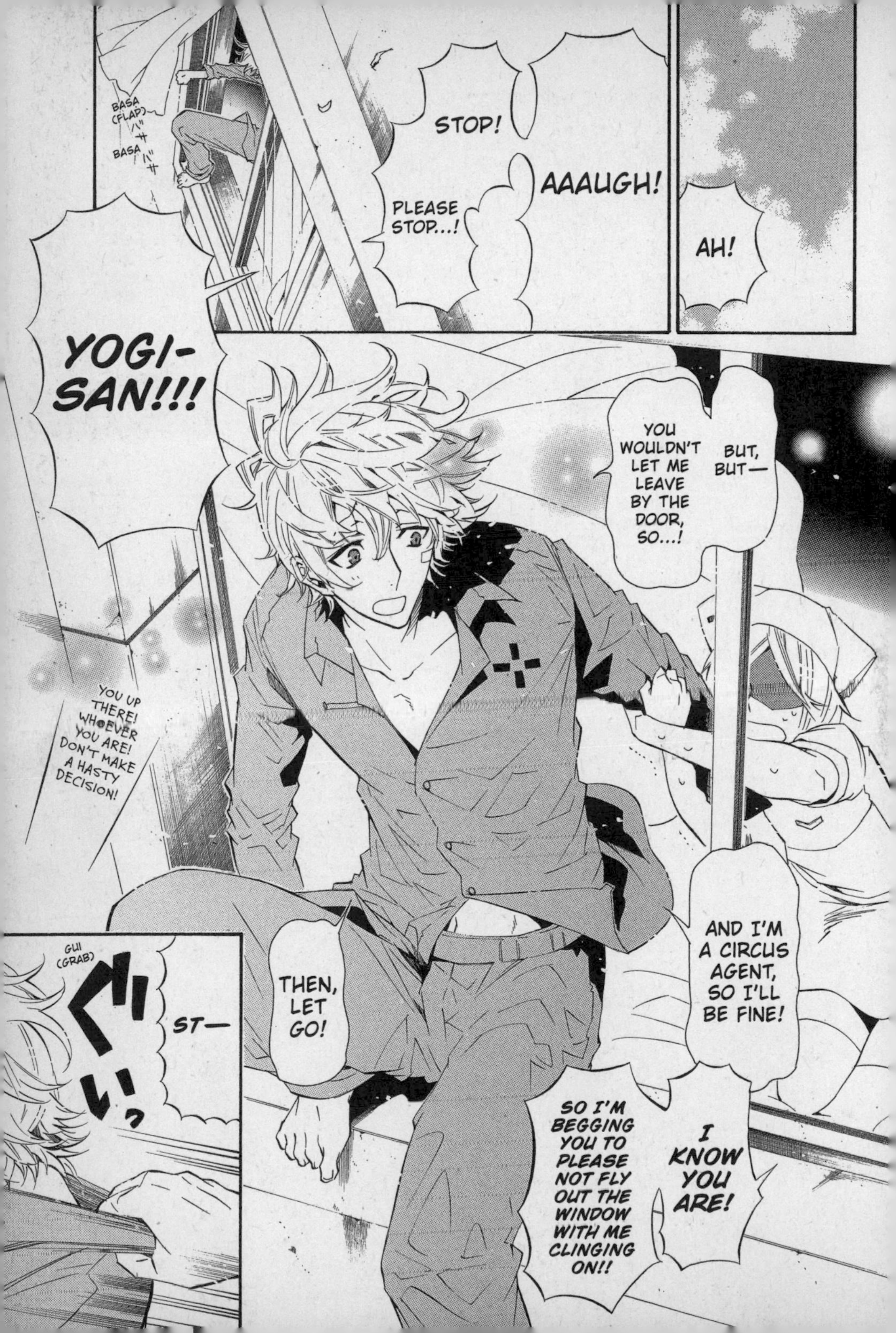
AH!
STOP!
AAAUGH!
PLEASE STOP...!
BASA (FLAP) バサ
BASA バサ
YOGI-SAN!!!
BUT, BUT—
YOU WOULDN'T LET ME LEAVE BY THE DOOR, SO...!
AND I'M A CIRCUS AGENT, SO I'LL BE FINE!
I KNOW YOU ARE!
SO I'M BEGGING YOU TO PLEASE NOT FLY OUT THE WINDOW WITH ME CLINGING ON!!
THEN, LET GO!
YOU UP THERE! WHOEVER YOU ARE! DON'T MAKE A HASTY DECISION!
ST—
GUI (GRAB) ぐいっ

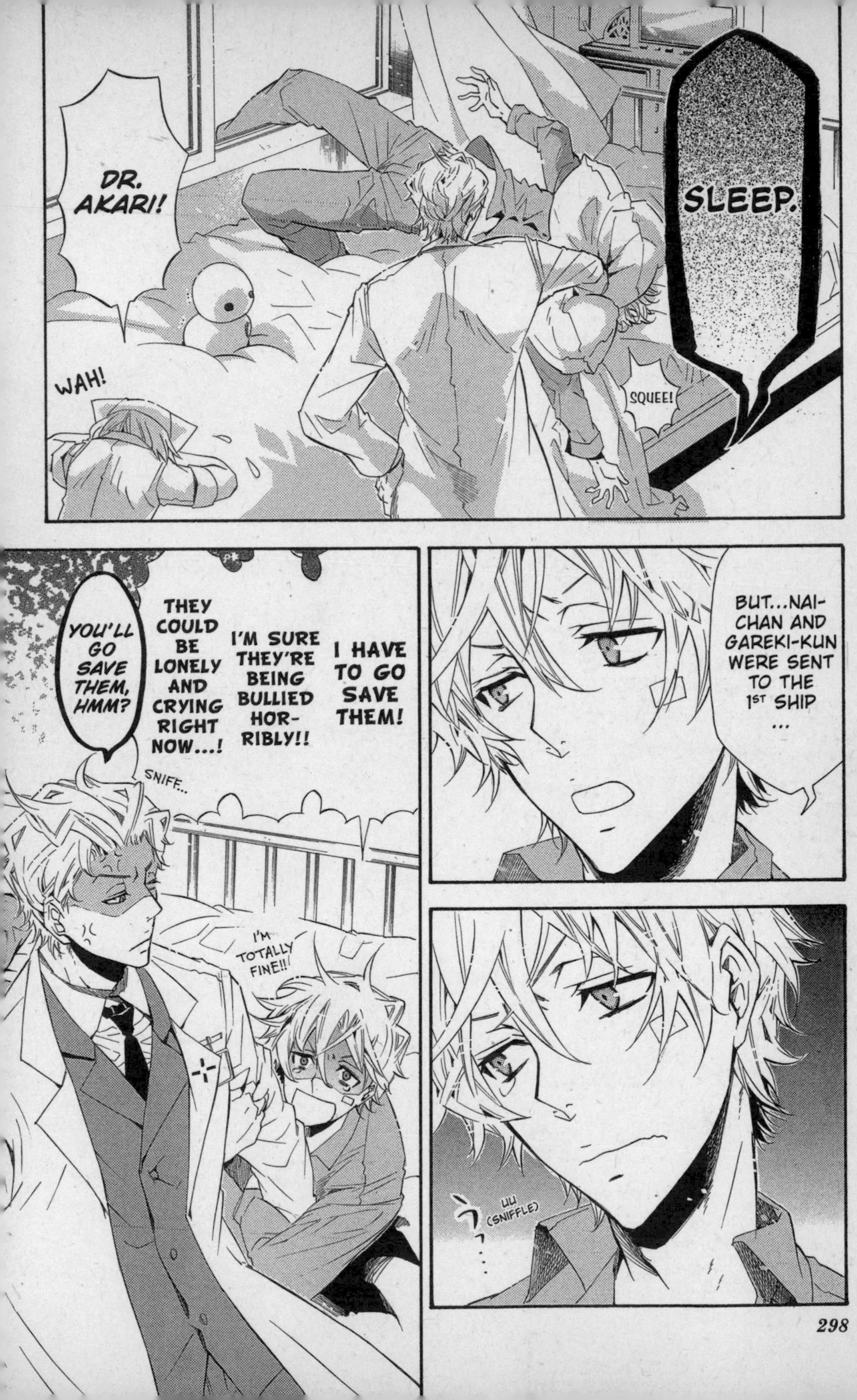
SLEEP.
SQUEE!
DR. AKARI!
WAH!
BUT...NAI-CHAN AND GAREKI-KUN WERE SENT TO THE 1st SHIP ...
UU (SNIFFLE)
I HAVE TO GO SAVE THEM!
I'M SURE THEY'RE BEING BULLIED HOR-RIBLY!!
THEY COULD BE LONELY AND CRYING RIGHT NOW...!
YOU'LL GO SAVE THEM, HMM?
SNIFF...
I'M TOTALLY FINE!!

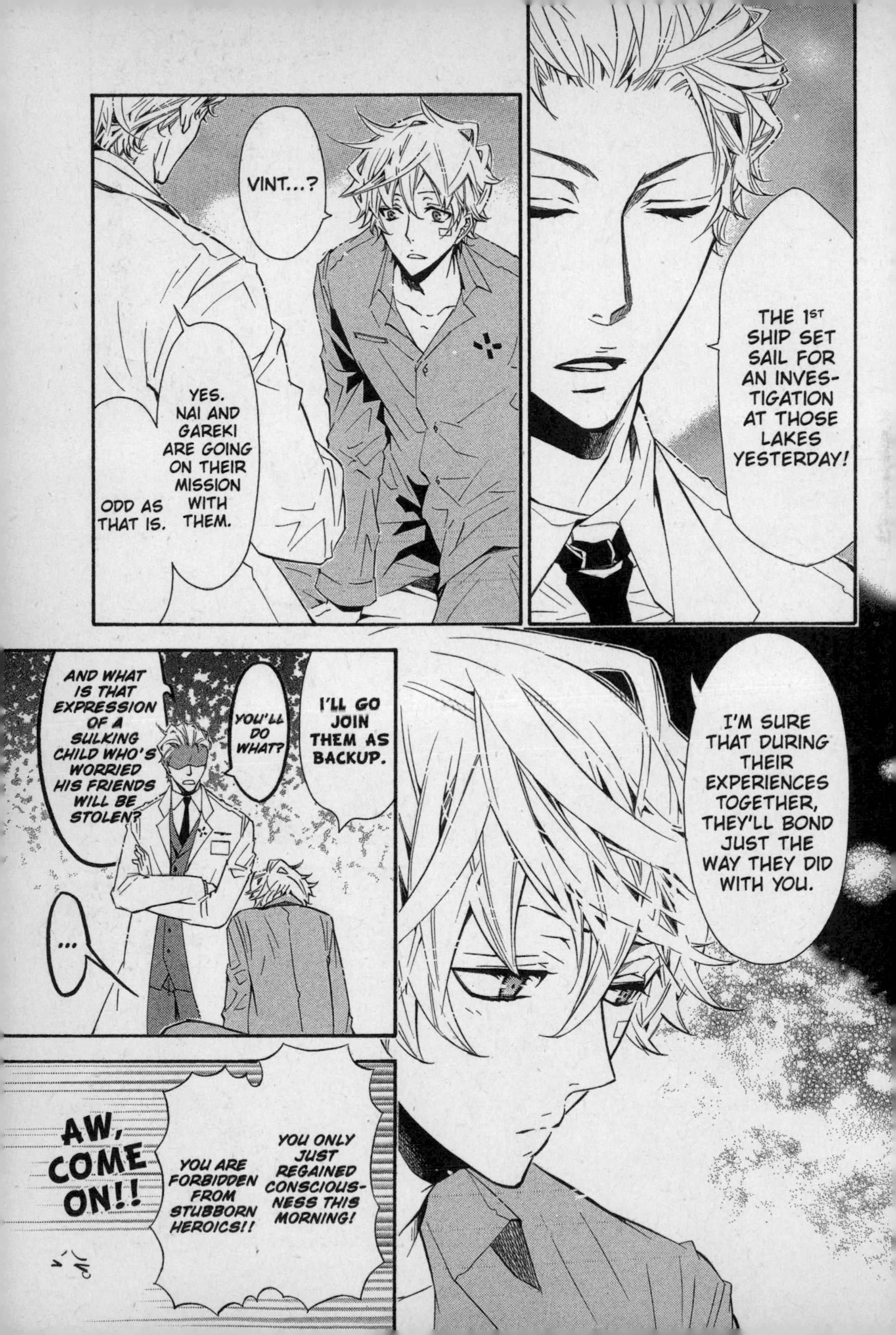

THE 1ST SHIP SET SAIL FOR AN INVESTIGATION AT THOSE LAKES YESTERDAY!
VINT...?
YES. NAI AND GAREKI ARE GOING ON THEIR MISSION WITH THEM.
ODD AS THAT IS.
I'M SURE THAT DURING THEIR EXPERIENCES TOGETHER, THEY'LL BOND JUST THE WAY THEY DID WITH YOU.
I'LL GO JOIN THEM AS BACKUP.
YOU'LL DO WHAT?
AND WHAT IS THAT EXPRESSION OF A SULKING CHILD WHO'S WORRIED HIS FRIENDS WILL BE STOLEN?
...
YOU ONLY JUST REGAINED CONSCIOUSNESS THIS MORNING!
YOU ARE FORBIDDEN FROM STUBBORN HEROICS!!
AW, COME ON!!

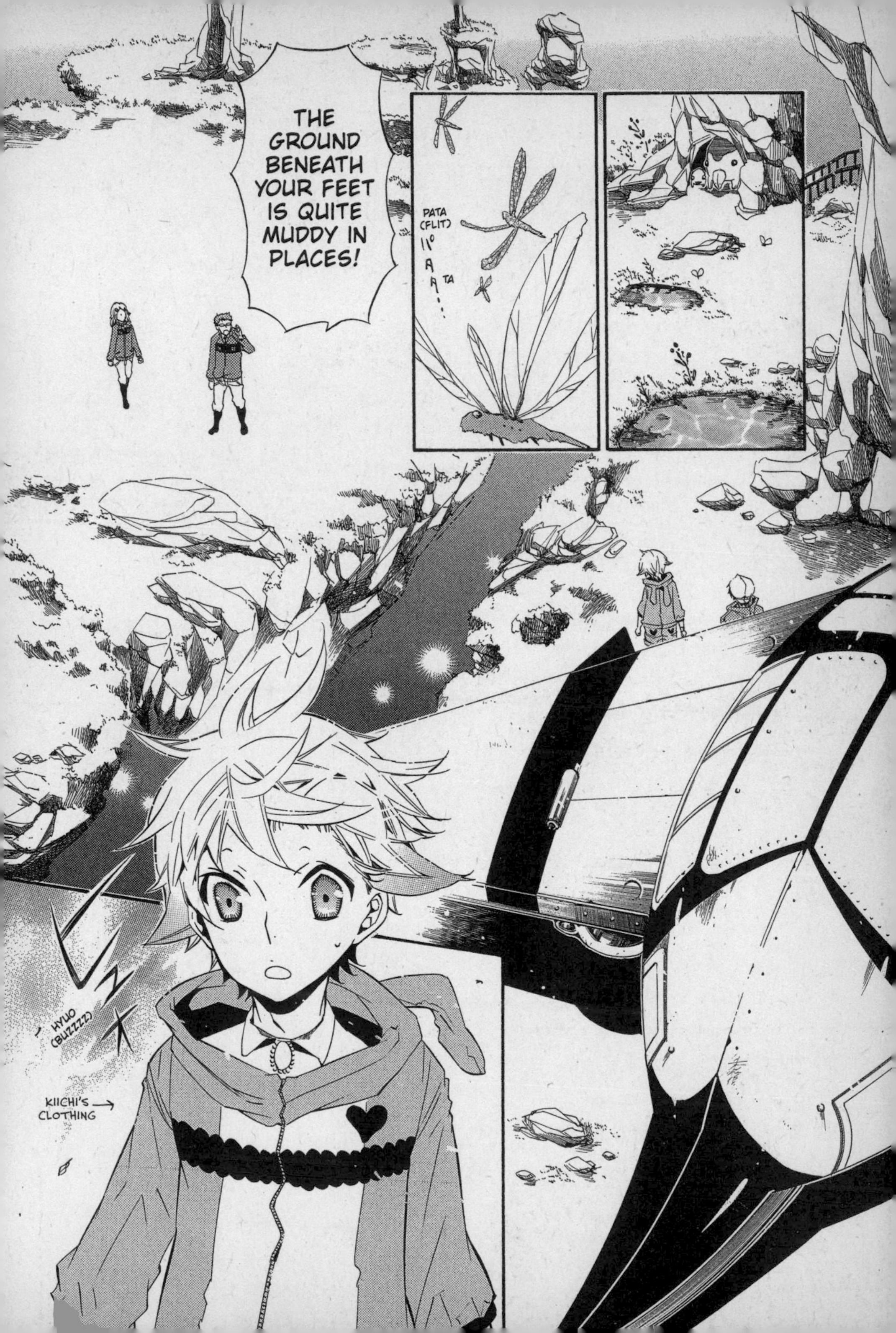
PATA (FLIT)
TA
THE GROUND BENEATH YOUR FEET IS QUITE MUDDY IN PLACES!
HYUO (BUZZZZ)
KIICHI'S CLOTHING

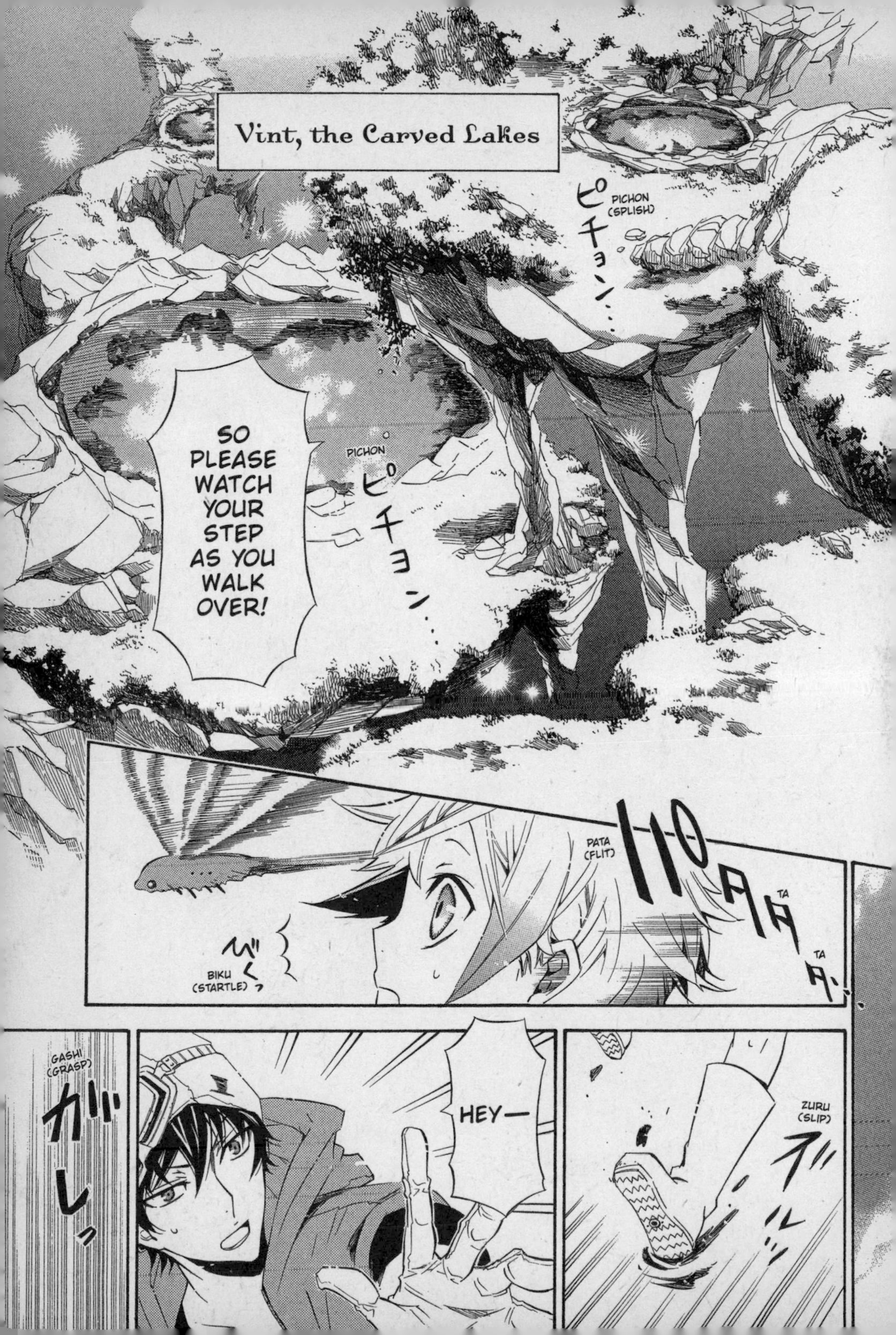
Vint, the Carved Lakes
ピチョン…
PICHON (SPLISH)
ピチョン…
PICHON
SO PLEASE WATCH YOUR STEP AS YOU WALK OVER!
TA
TA
PATA (FLIT)
びくっ
BIKU (STARTLE)
ズルッ
ZURU (SLIP)
HEY—
ガシッ
GASHI (GRASP)

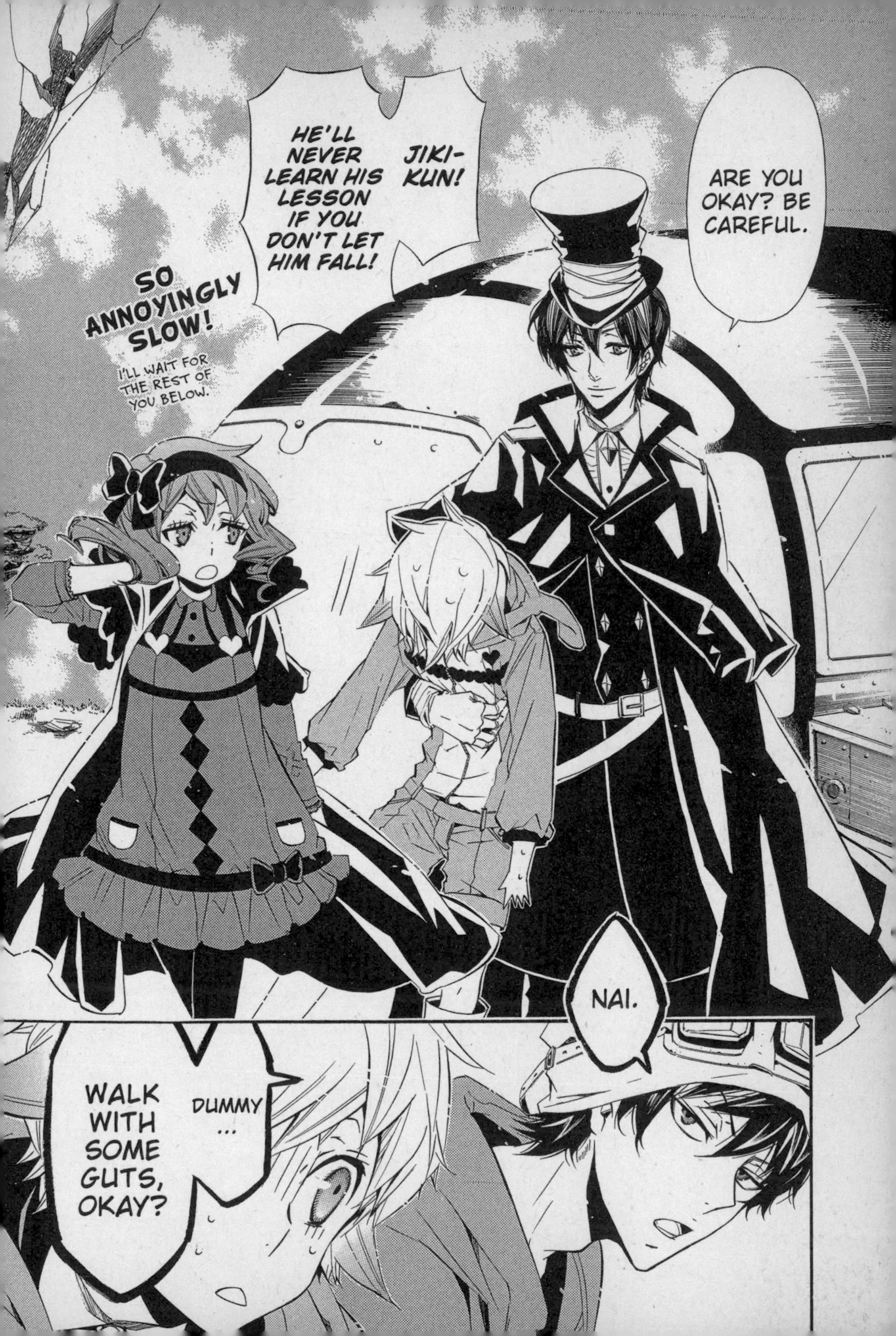
ARE YOU OKAY? BE CAREFUL.
JIKI-KUN!
HE'LL NEVER LEARN HIS LESSON IF YOU DON'T LET HIM FALL!
SO ANNOYINGLY SLOW!
I'LL WAIT FOR THE REST OF YOU BELOW.
NAI.
DUMMY ...
WALK WITH SOME GUTS, OKAY?

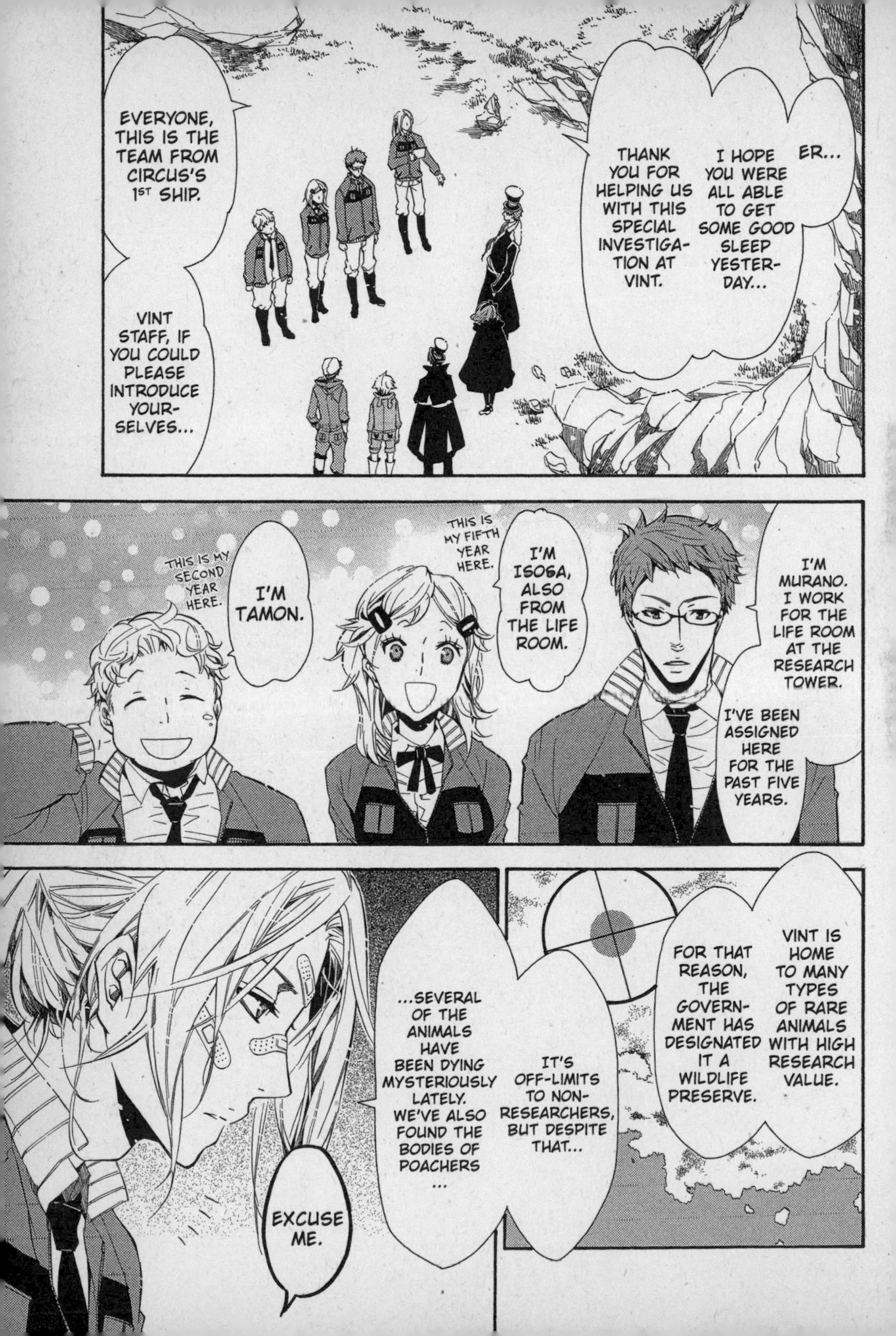
ER...
I HOPE YOU WERE ALL ABLE TO GET SOME GOOD SLEEP YESTERDAY...
THANK YOU FOR HELPING US WITH THIS SPECIAL INVESTIGATION AT VINT.
EVERYONE, THIS IS THE TEAM FROM CIRCUS'S 1ST SHIP.
VINT STAFF, IF YOU COULD PLEASE INTRODUCE YOURSELVES...
I'M MURANO. I WORK FOR THE LIFE ROOM AT THE RESEARCH TOWER.
I'VE BEEN ASSIGNED HERE FOR THE PAST FIVE YEARS.
I'M ISOGA, ALSO FROM THE LIFE ROOM.
THIS IS MY FIFTH YEAR HERE.
I'M TAMON.
THIS IS MY SECOND YEAR HERE.
VINT IS HOME TO MANY TYPES OF RARE ANIMALS WITH HIGH RESEARCH VALUE.
FOR THAT REASON, THE GOVERNMENT HAS DESIGNATED IT A WILDLIFE PRESERVE.
IT'S OFF-LIMITS TO NON-RESEARCHERS, BUT DESPITE THAT...
...SEVERAL OF THE ANIMALS HAVE BEEN DYING MYSTERIOUSLY LATELY. WE'VE ALSO FOUND THE BODIES OF POACHERS...
EXCUSE ME.

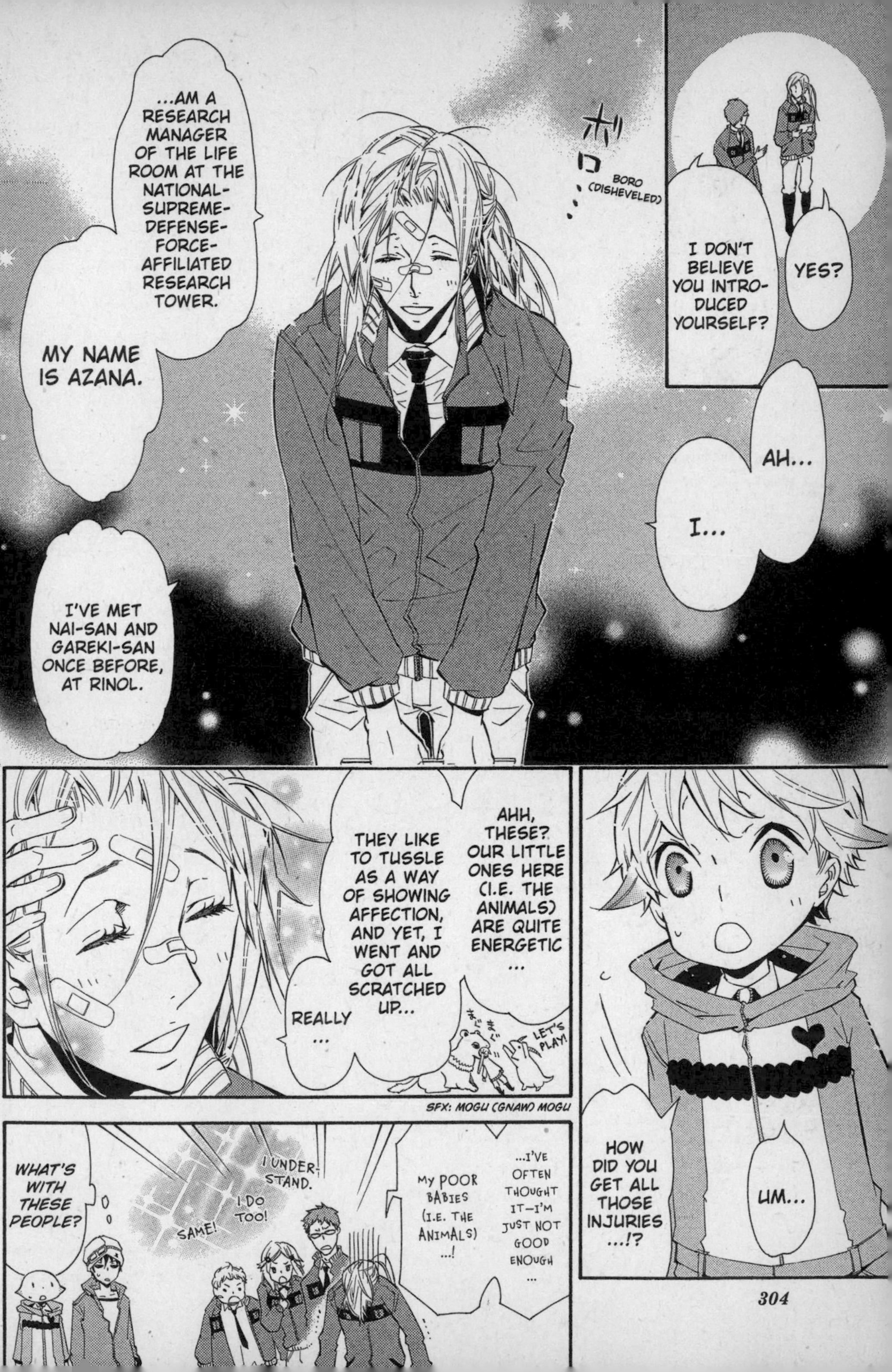
I DON'T BELIEVE YOU INTRODUCED YOURSELF?
YES?
AH...
I...
MY NAME IS AZANA.
...AM A RESEARCH MANAGER OF THE LIFE ROOM AT THE NATIONAL-SUPREME-DEFENSE-FORCE-AFFILIATED RESEARCH TOWER.
ボロ
BORO (DISHEVELED)
I'VE MET NAI-SAN AND GAREKI-SAN ONCE BEFORE, AT RINOL.
UM...
HOW DID YOU GET ALL THOSE INJURIES...!?
AHH, THESE? OUR LITTLE ONES HERE (I.E. THE ANIMALS) ARE QUITE ENERGETIC...
THEY LIKE TO TUSSLE AS A WAY OF SHOWING AFFECTION, AND YET, I WENT AND GOT ALL SCRATCHED UP...
REALLY...
LET'S PLAY!
SFX: MOGU (GNAW) MOGU
...I'VE OFTEN THOUGHT IT—I'M JUST NOT GOOD ENOUGH...
MY POOR BABIES (I.E. THE ANIMALS)...!
I UNDERSTAND.
I DO TOO!
SAME!
WHAT'S WITH THESE PEOPLE?

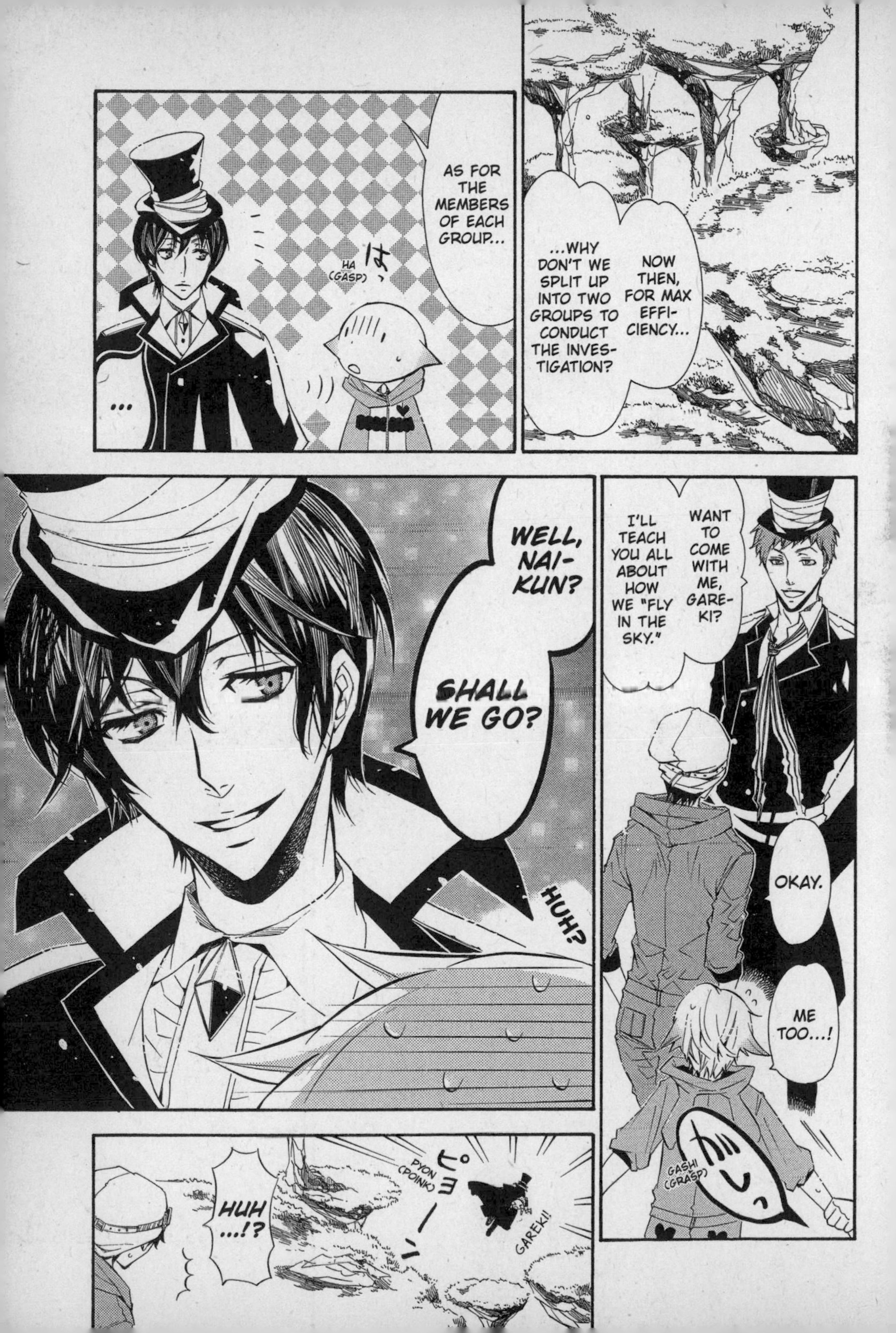
NOW THEN, FOR MAX EFFICIENCY...
...WHY DON'T WE SPLIT UP INTO TWO GROUPS TO CONDUCT THE INVESTIGATION?
AS FOR THE MEMBERS OF EACH GROUP...
は
HA (GASP)
...
WANT TO COME WITH ME, GAREKI?
I'LL TEACH YOU ALL ABOUT HOW WE "FLY IN THE SKY."
OKAY.
ME TOO...!
がしっ
GASHI (GRASP)
WELL, NAI-KUN?
SHALL WE GO?
HUH?
ピョーン
PYON (POINK)
GAREKI!!
HUH ...!?

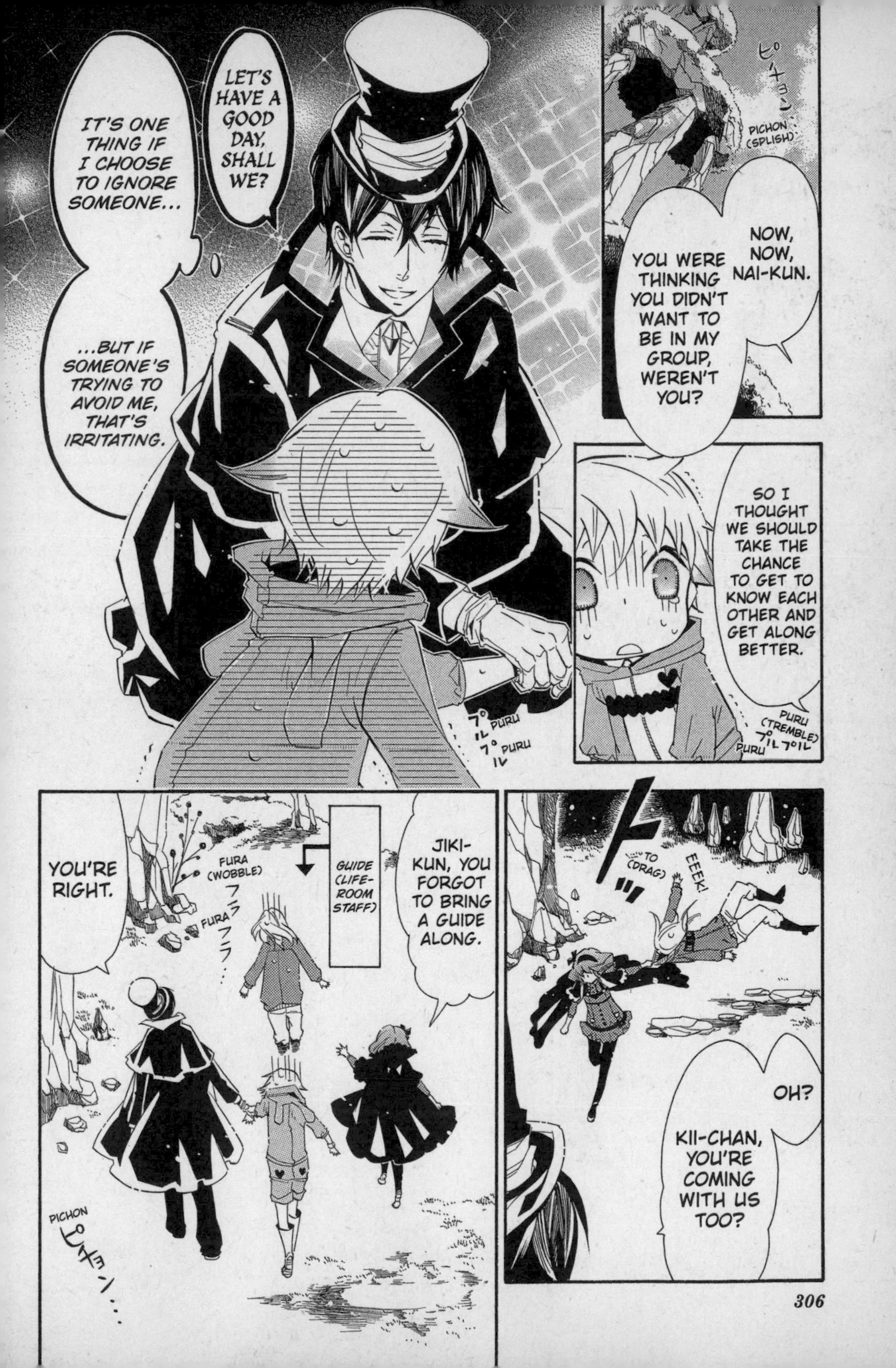
PICHON (SPLISH)
NOW, NOW, NAI-KUN.
YOU WERE THINKING YOU DIDN'T WANT TO BE IN MY GROUP, WEREN'T YOU?
SO I THOUGHT WE SHOULD TAKE THE CHANCE TO GET TO KNOW EACH OTHER AND GET ALONG BETTER.
PURU (TREMBLE) PURU
LET'S HAVE A GOOD DAY, SHALL WE?
IT'S ONE THING IF I CHOOSE TO IGNORE SOMEONE...
...BUT IF SOMEONE'S TRYING TO AVOID ME, THAT'S IRRITATING.
PURU PURU
TO (DRAG)
EEEK!
OH?
KII-CHAN, YOU'RE COMING WITH US TOO?
JIKI-KUN, YOU FORGOT TO BRING A GUIDE ALONG.
GUIDE (LIFE-ROOM STAFF)
YOU'RE RIGHT.
FURA (WOBBLE) FURA
PICHON

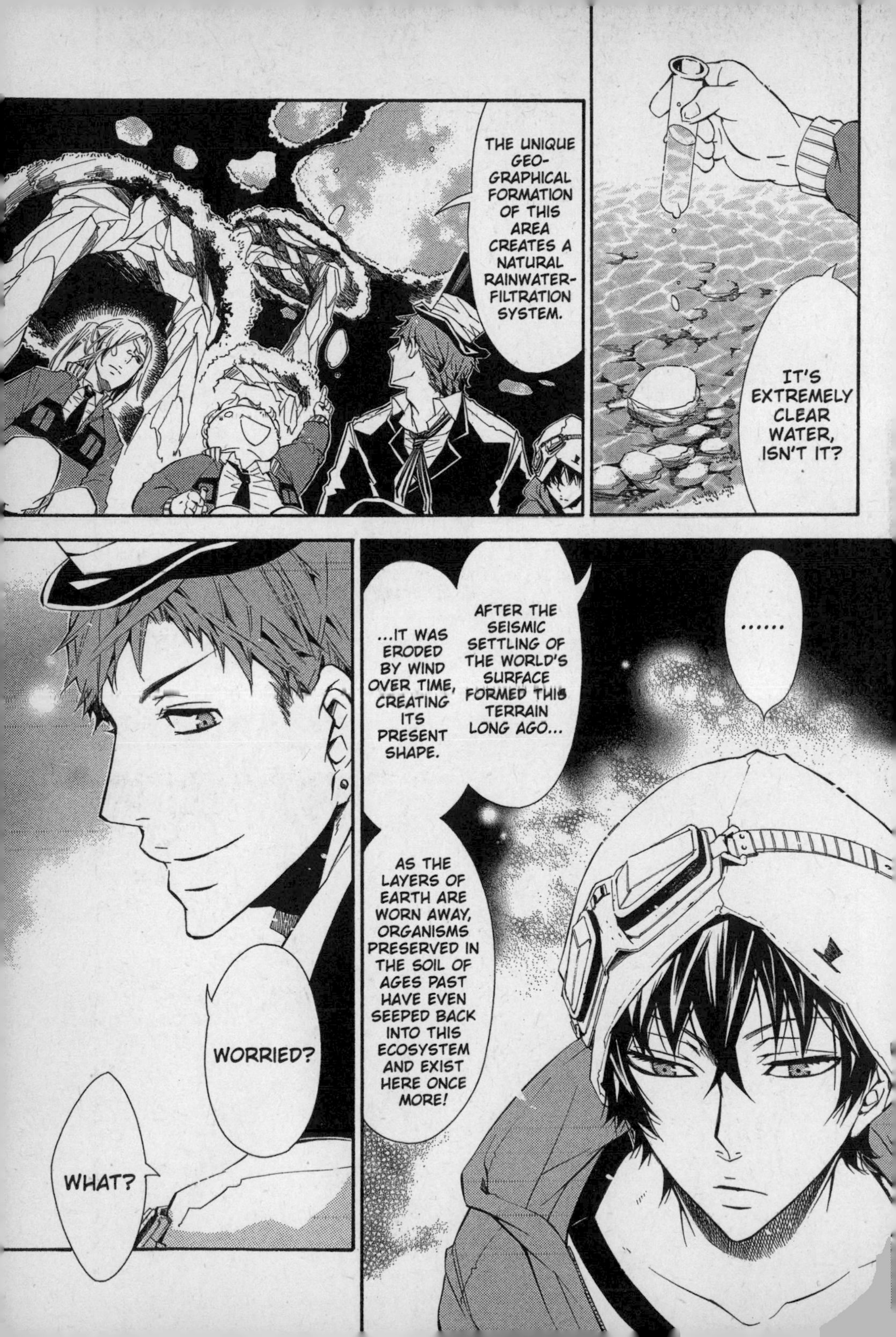
IT'S EXTREMELY CLEAR WATER, ISN'T IT?
THE UNIQUE GEO-GRAPHICAL FORMATION OF THIS AREA CREATES A NATURAL RAINWATER-FILTRATION SYSTEM.
......
AFTER THE SEISMIC SETTLING OF THE WORLD'S SURFACE FORMED THIS TERRAIN LONG AGO...
...IT WAS ERODED BY WIND OVER TIME, CREATING ITS PRESENT SHAPE.
AS THE LAYERS OF EARTH ARE WORN AWAY, ORGANISMS PRESERVED IN THE SOIL OF AGES PAST HAVE EVEN SEEPED BACK INTO THIS ECOSYSTEM AND EXIST HERE ONCE MORE!
WORRIED?
WHAT?

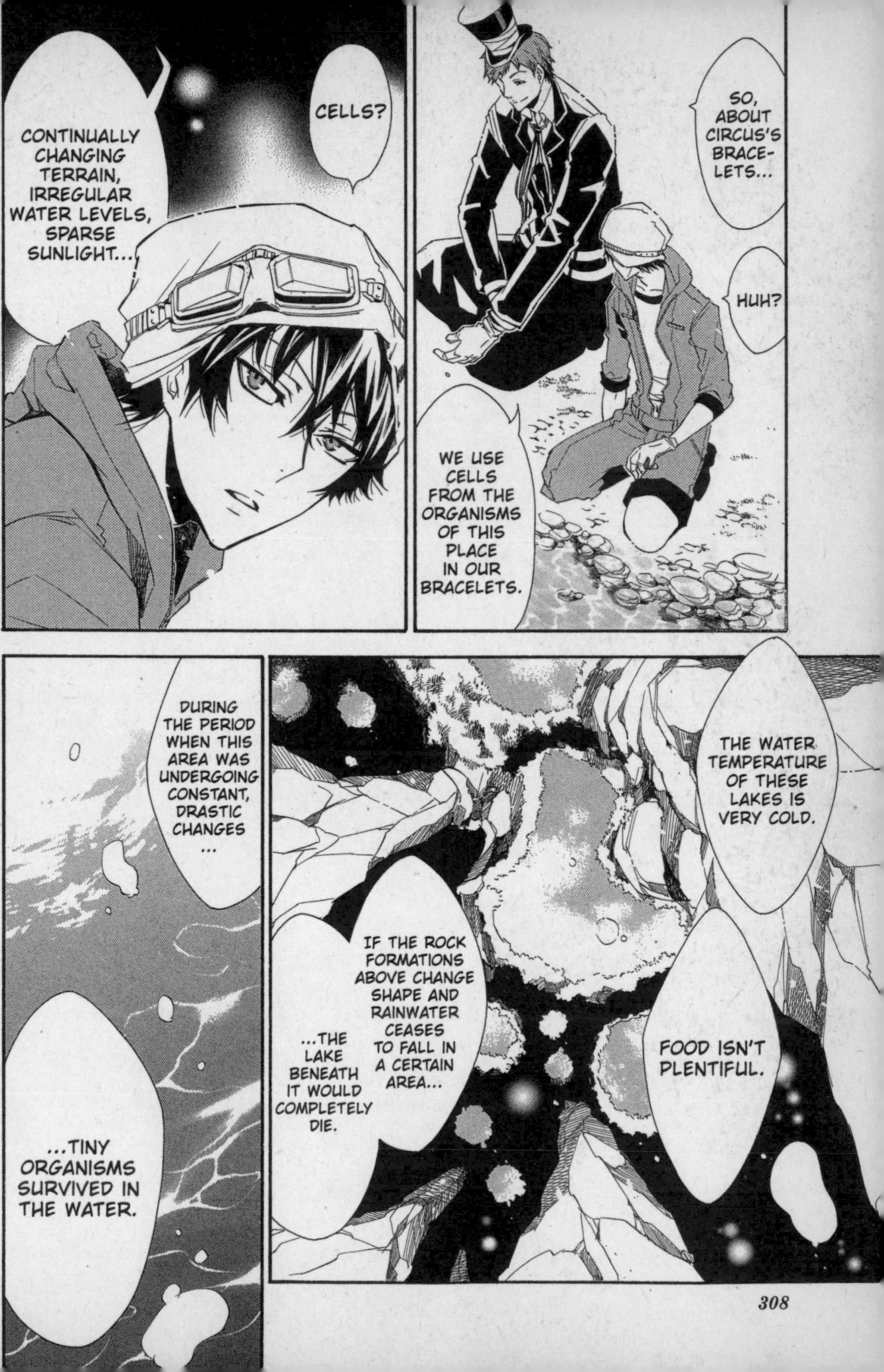
SO, ABOUT CIRCUS'S BRACE-LETS...
HUH?
WE USE CELLS FROM THE ORGANISMS OF THIS PLACE IN OUR BRACELETS.
CELLS?
CONTINUALLY CHANGING TERRAIN, IRREGULAR WATER LEVELS, SPARSE SUNLIGHT...
THE WATER TEMPERATURE OF THESE LAKES IS VERY COLD.
FOOD ISN'T PLENTIFUL.
IF THE ROCK FORMATIONS ABOVE CHANGE SHAPE AND RAINWATER CEASES TO FALL IN A CERTAIN AREA...
...THE LAKE BENEATH IT WOULD COMPLETELY DIE.
DURING THE PERIOD WHEN THIS AREA WAS UNDERGOING CONSTANT, DRASTIC CHANGES ...
...TINY ORGANISMS SURVIVED IN THE WATER.

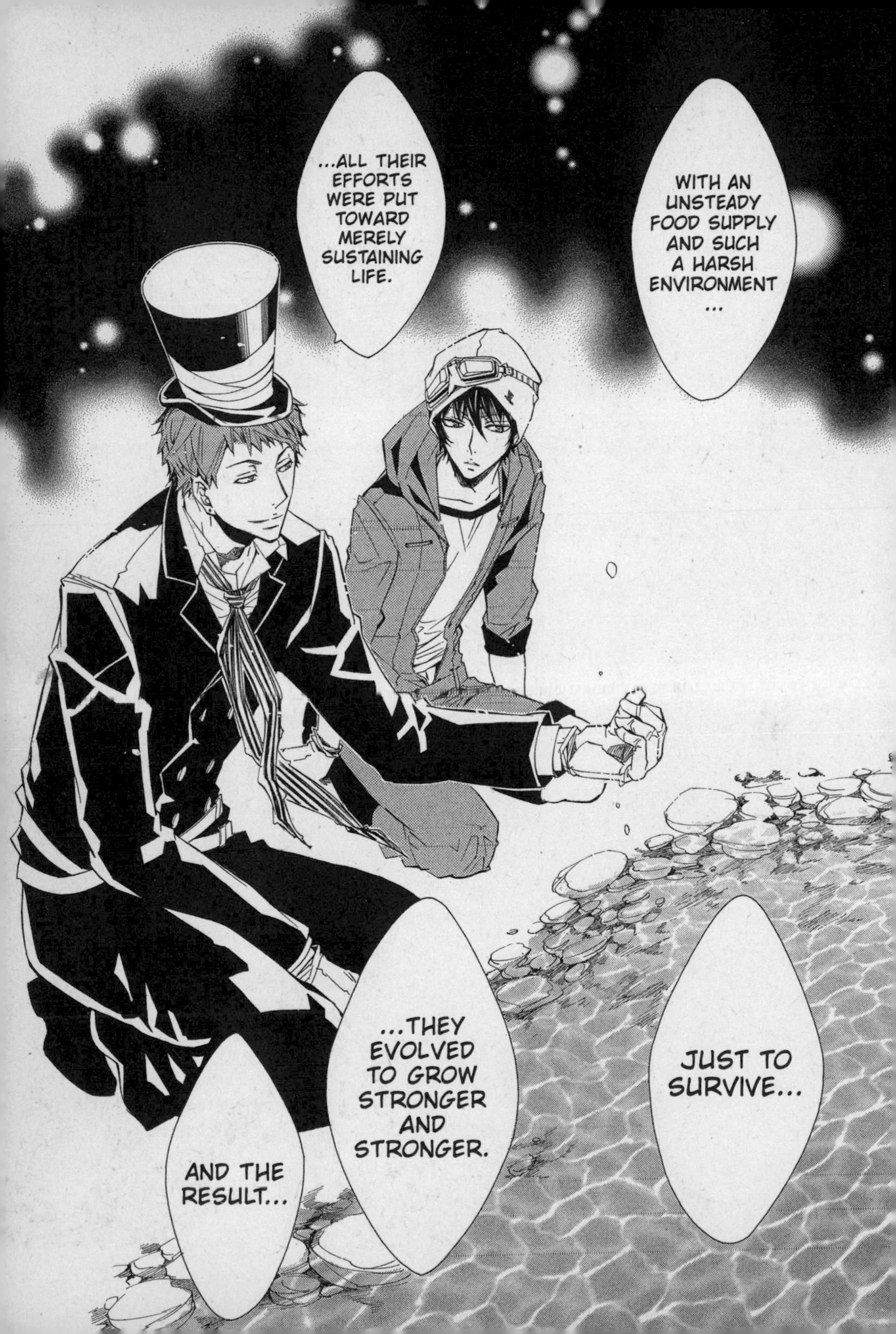
WITH AN UNSTEADY FOOD SUPPLY AND SUCH A HARSH ENVIRONMENT ...
...ALL THEIR EFFORTS WERE PUT TOWARD MERELY SUSTAINING LIFE.
JUST TO SURVIVE...
...THEY EVOLVED TO GROW STRONGER AND STRONGER.
AND THE RESULT...

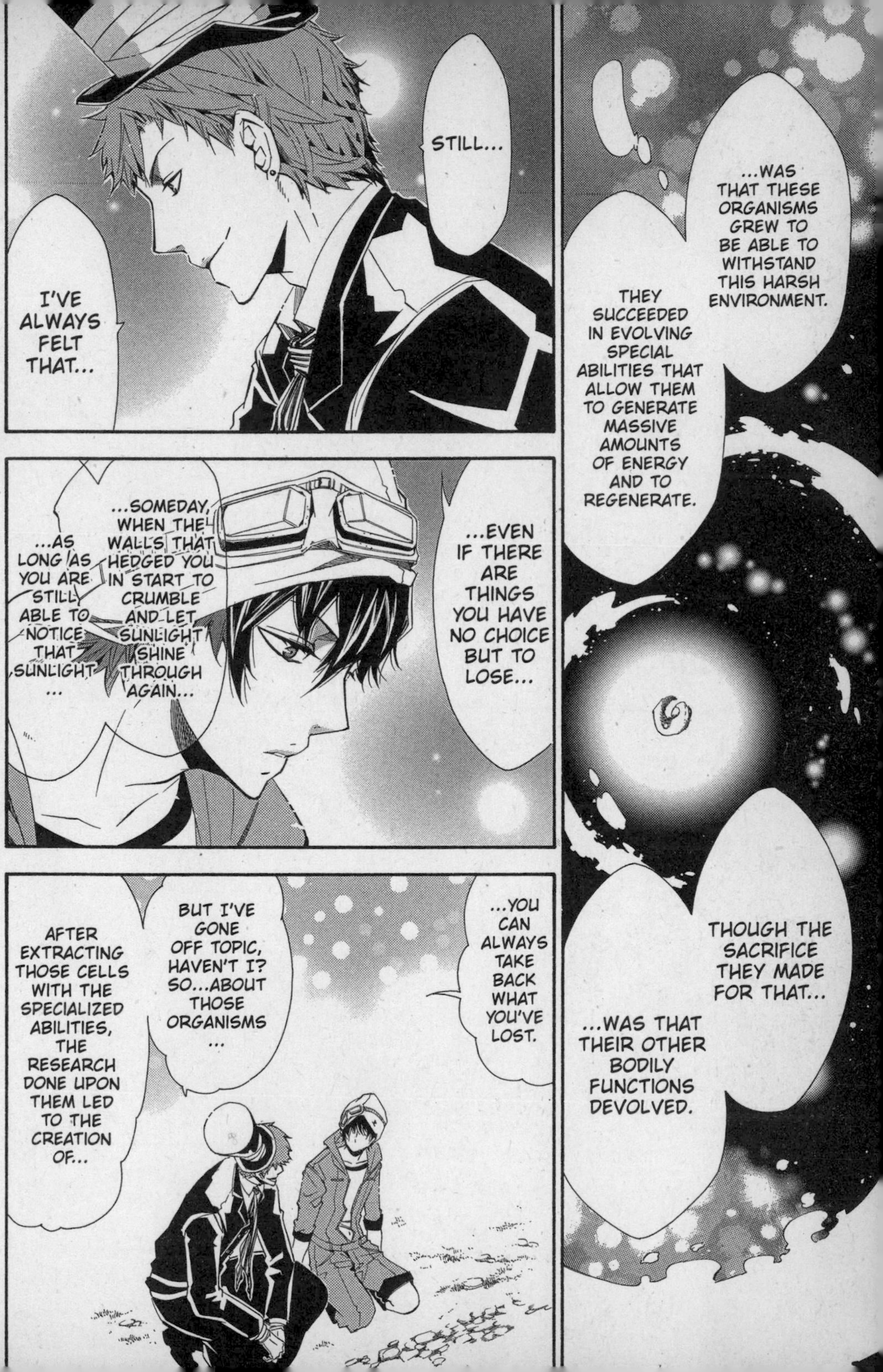
...WAS THAT THESE ORGANISMS GREW TO BE ABLE TO WITHSTAND THIS HARSH ENVIRONMENT.
THEY SUCCEEDED IN EVOLVING SPECIAL ABILITIES THAT ALLOW THEM TO GENERATE MASSIVE AMOUNTS OF ENERGY AND TO REGENERATE.
THOUGH THE SACRIFICE THEY MADE FOR THAT...
...WAS THAT THEIR OTHER BODILY FUNCTIONS DEVOLVED.
STILL...
I'VE ALWAYS FELT THAT...
...EVEN IF THERE ARE THINGS YOU HAVE NO CHOICE BUT TO LOSE...
...SOMEDAY, WHEN THE WALLS THAT HEDGED YOU IN START TO CRUMBLE AND LET SUNLIGHT SHINE THROUGH AGAIN...
...AS LONG AS YOU ARE STILL ABLE TO NOTICE THAT SUNLIGHT...
...YOU CAN ALWAYS TAKE BACK WHAT YOU'VE LOST.
BUT I'VE GONE OFF TOPIC, HAVEN'T I? SO...ABOUT THOSE ORGANISMS...
AFTER EXTRACTING THOSE CELLS WITH THE SPECIALIZED ABILITIES, THE RESEARCH DONE UPON THEM LED TO THE CREATION OF...

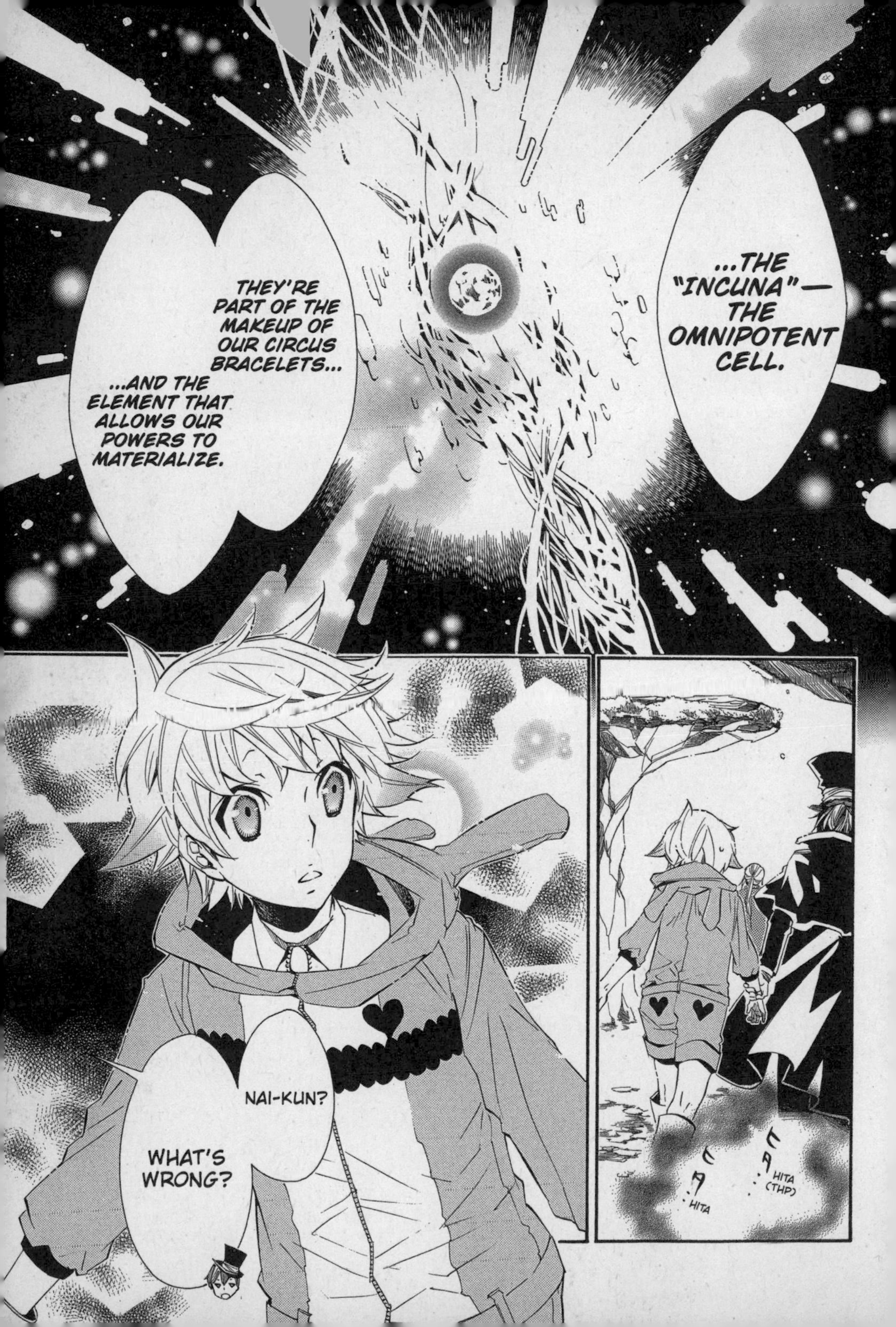
...THE "INCUNA"— THE OMNIPOTENT CELL.
THEY'RE PART OF THE MAKEUP OF OUR CIRCUS BRACELETS...
...AND THE ELEMENT THAT ALLOWS OUR POWERS TO MATERIALIZE.
HITA (THP)
HITA
NAI-KUN?
WHAT'S WRONG?

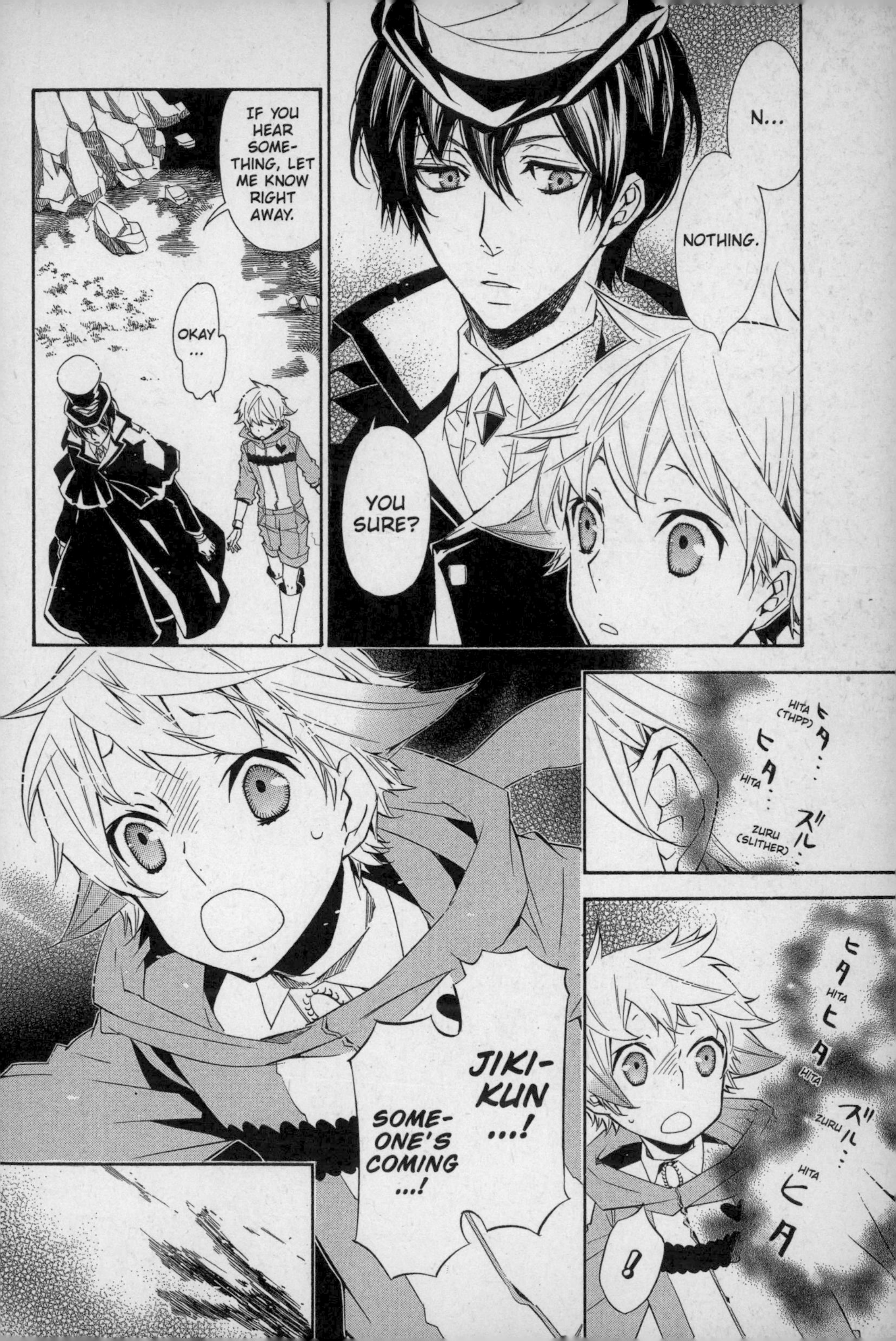
N...
NOTHING.
YOU SURE?
IF YOU HEAR SOME-THING, LET ME KNOW RIGHT AWAY.
OKAY...
ヒタ HITA (THPP)
ヒタ HITA
ズル ZURU (SLITHER)
ヒタ HITA
ヒタ HITA
ズル ZURU
ヒタ HITA
!
JIKI-KUN...!
SOME-ONE'S COMING...!

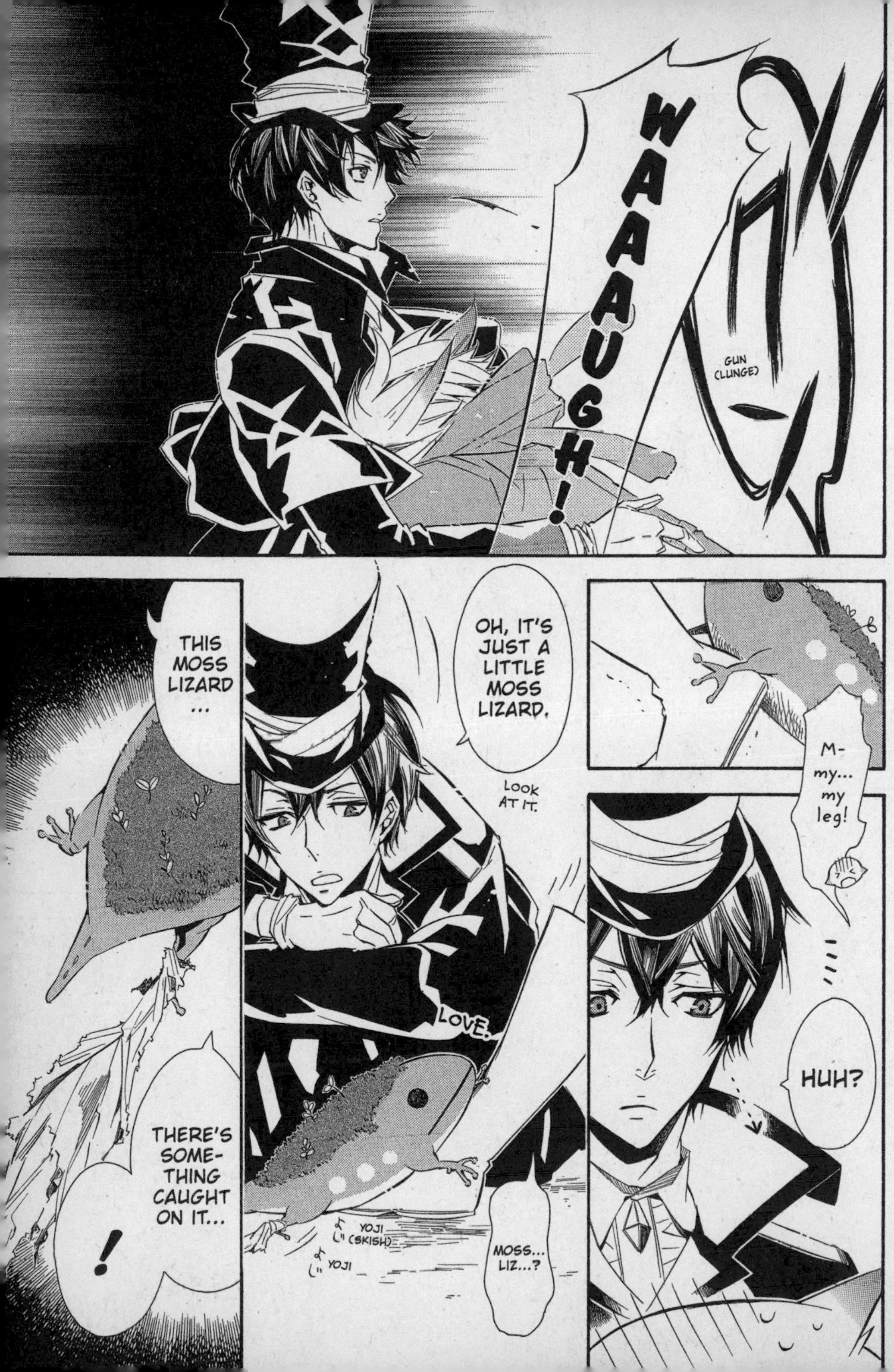
WAAAAUGH!
GUN (LUNGE)
M-my... my leg!
HUH?
MOSS... LIZ...?
OH, IT'S JUST A LITTLE MOSS LIZARD.
LOOK AT IT.
LOVE.
YOJI (SKISH)
YOJI
THIS MOSS LIZARD...
THERE'S SOME-THING CAUGHT ON IT...
!

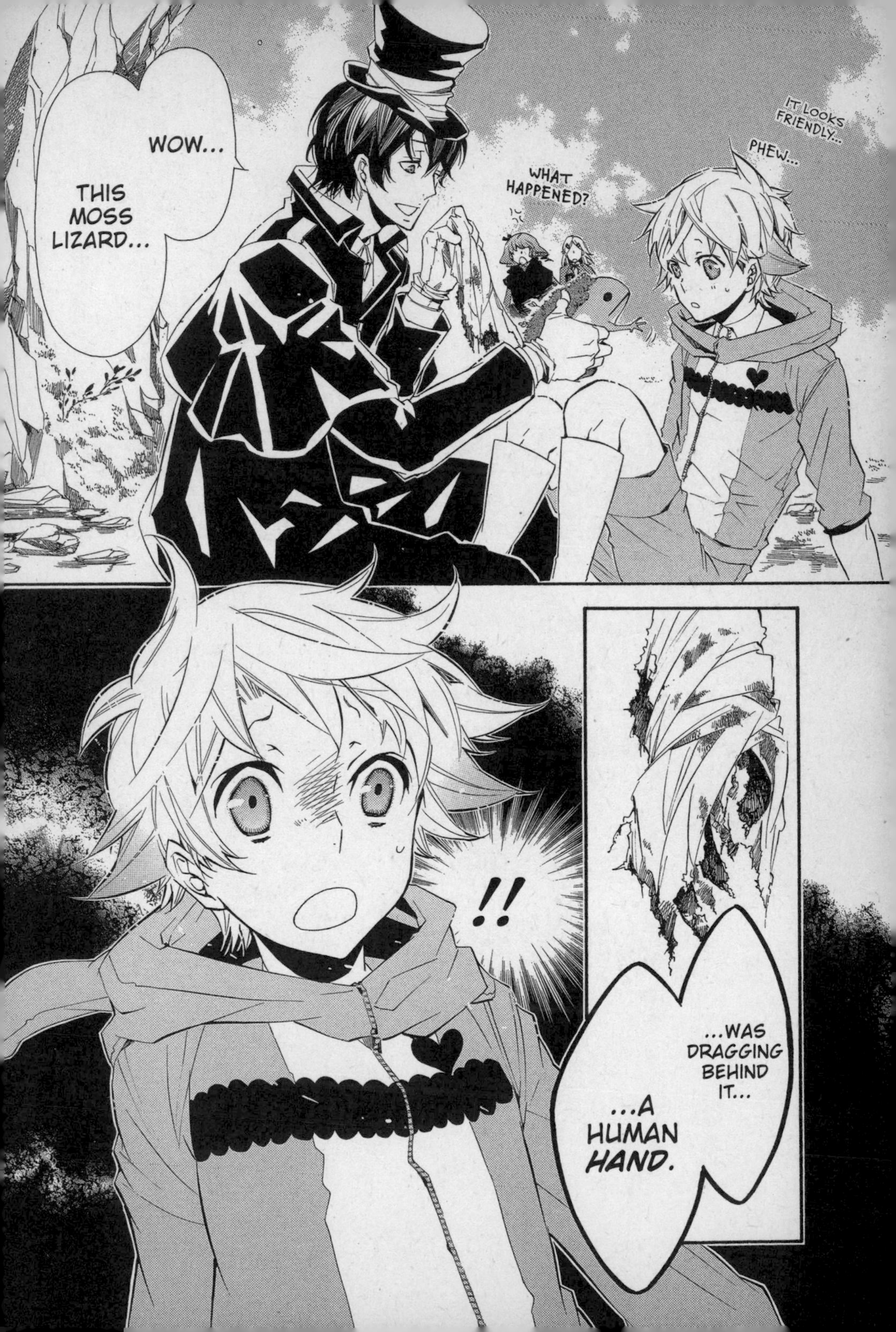
IT LOOKS FRIENDLY...
PHEW...
WHAT HAPPENED?
WOW... THIS MOSS LIZARD...
...WAS DRAGGING BEHIND IT...
...A HUMAN HAND.
!!

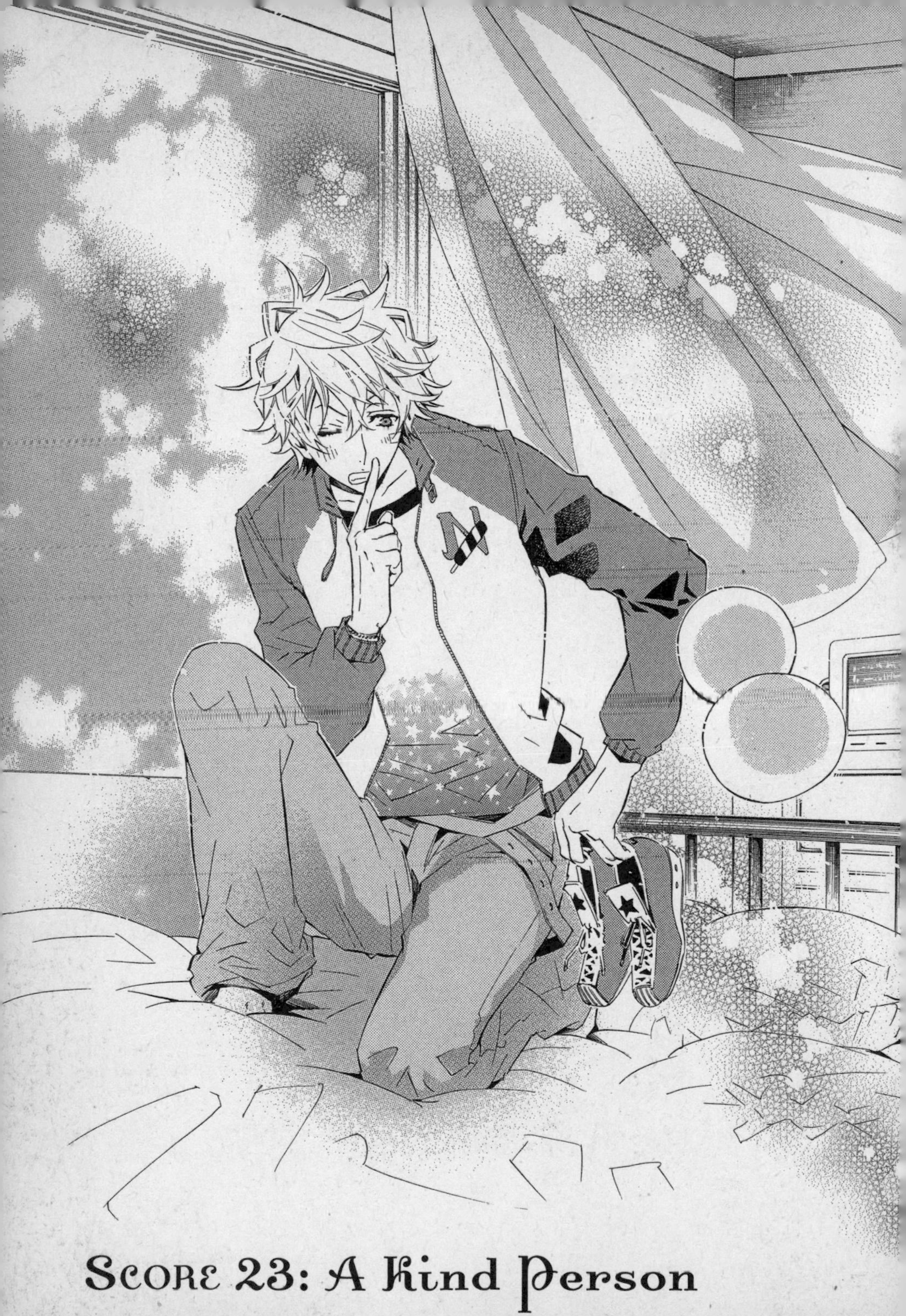

Score 23: A Kind Person

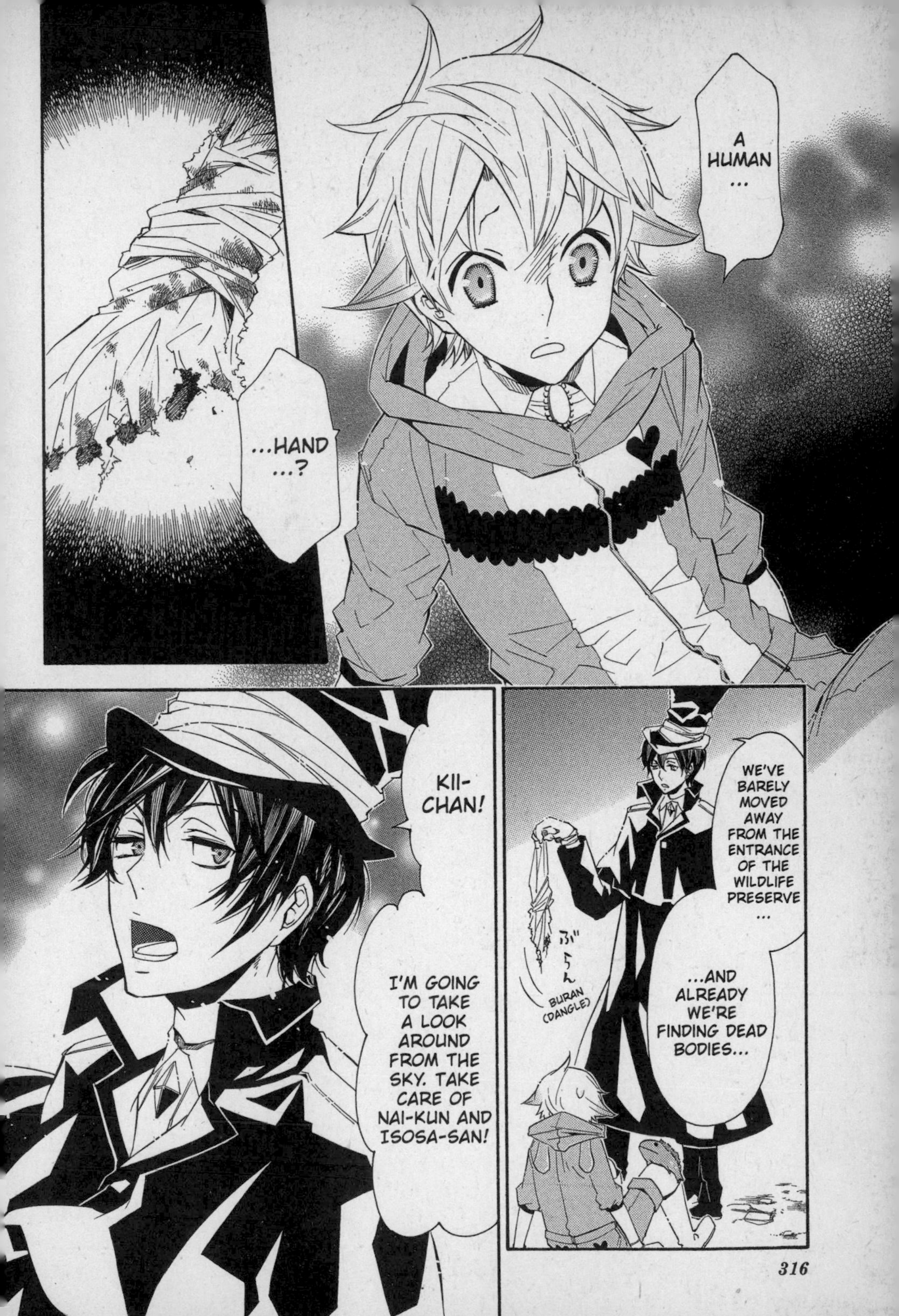
A HUMAN ...
...HAND ...?
WE'VE BARELY MOVED AWAY FROM THE ENTRANCE OF THE WILDLIFE PRESERVE ...
ぶらん
BURAN (DANGLE)
...AND ALREADY WE'RE FINDING DEAD BODIES...
KII-CHAN!
I'M GOING TO TAKE A LOOK AROUND FROM THE SKY. TAKE CARE OF NAI-KUN AND ISOSA-SAN!

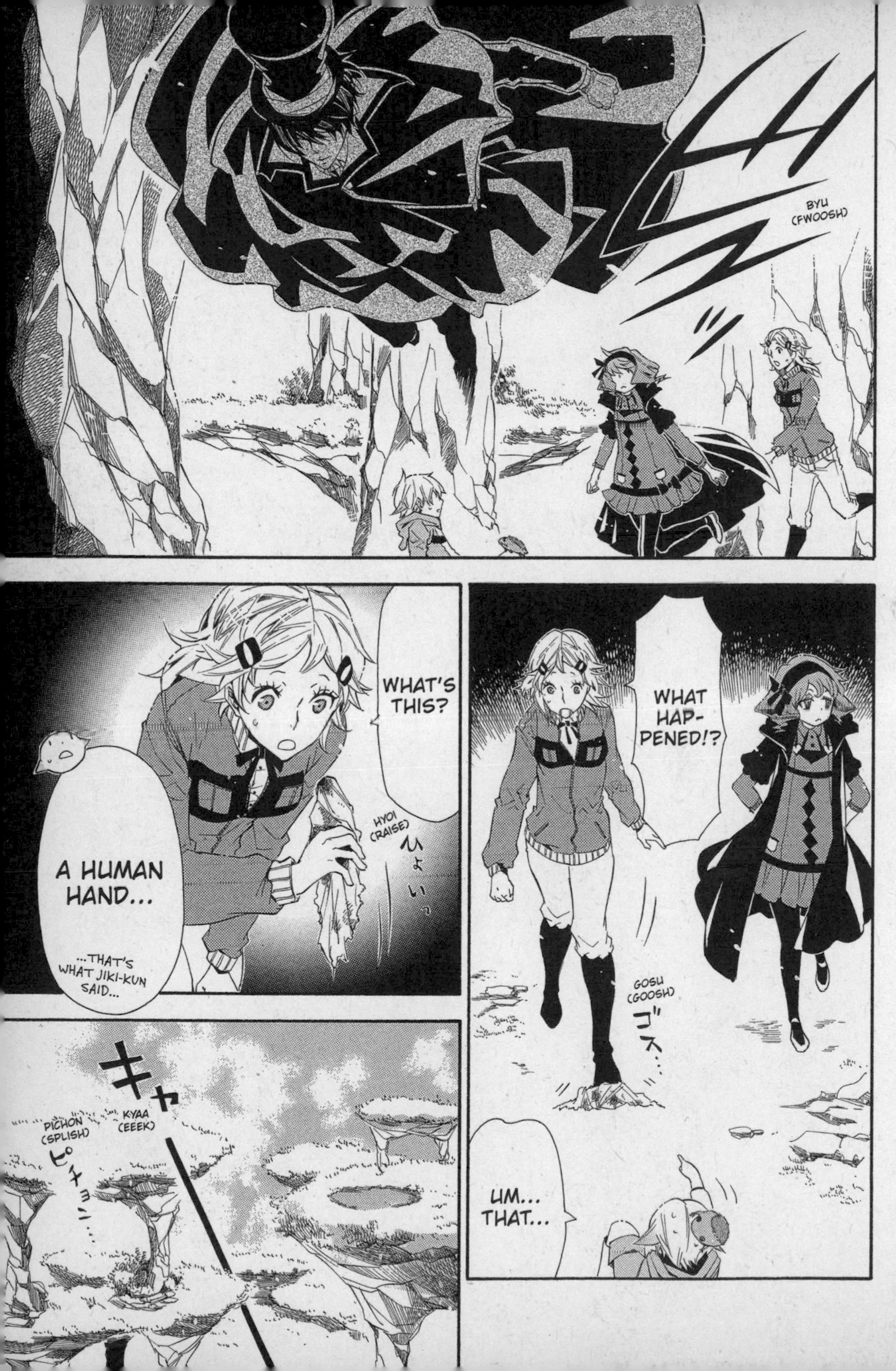
BYU
(FWOOSH)
WHAT HAP-PENED!?
GOSU (GOOSH)
ゴス…
UM... THAT...
WHAT'S THIS?
HYOI (RAISE)
ひょいっ
A HUMAN HAND...
...THAT'S WHAT JIKI-KUN SAID...
KYAA (EEEK)
キャ
PICHON (SPLISH)
ピチョン…

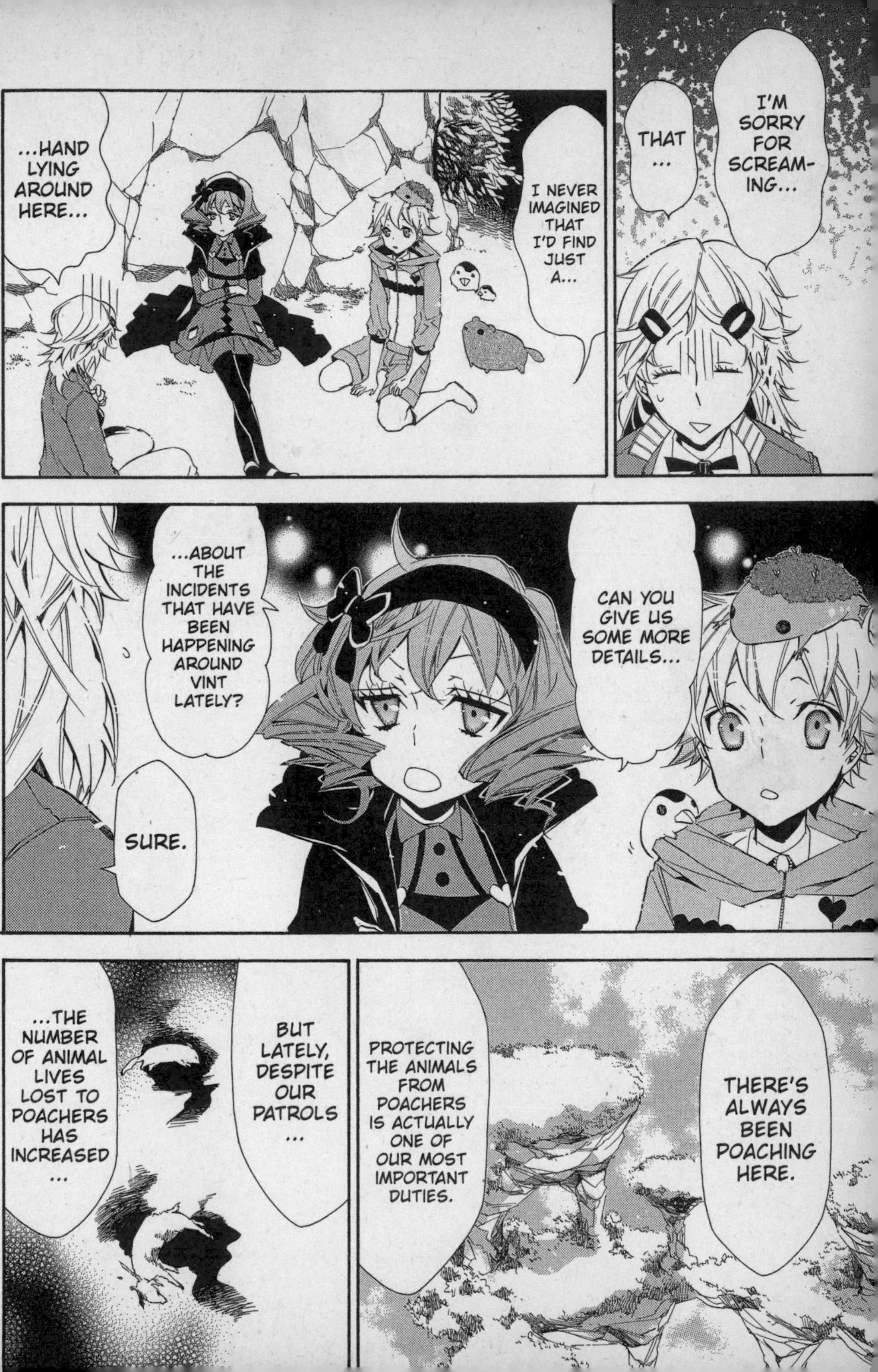
I'M SORRY FOR SCREAM-ING...
THAT...
I NEVER IMAGINED THAT I'D FIND JUST A...
...HAND LYING AROUND HERE...
CAN YOU GIVE US SOME MORE DETAILS...
...ABOUT THE INCIDENTS THAT HAVE BEEN HAPPENING AROUND VINT LATELY?
SURE.
THERE'S ALWAYS BEEN POACHING HERE.
PROTECTING THE ANIMALS FROM POACHERS IS ACTUALLY ONE OF OUR MOST IMPORTANT DUTIES.
BUT LATELY, DESPITE OUR PATROLS...
...THE NUMBER OF ANIMAL LIVES LOST TO POACHERS HAS INCREASED...

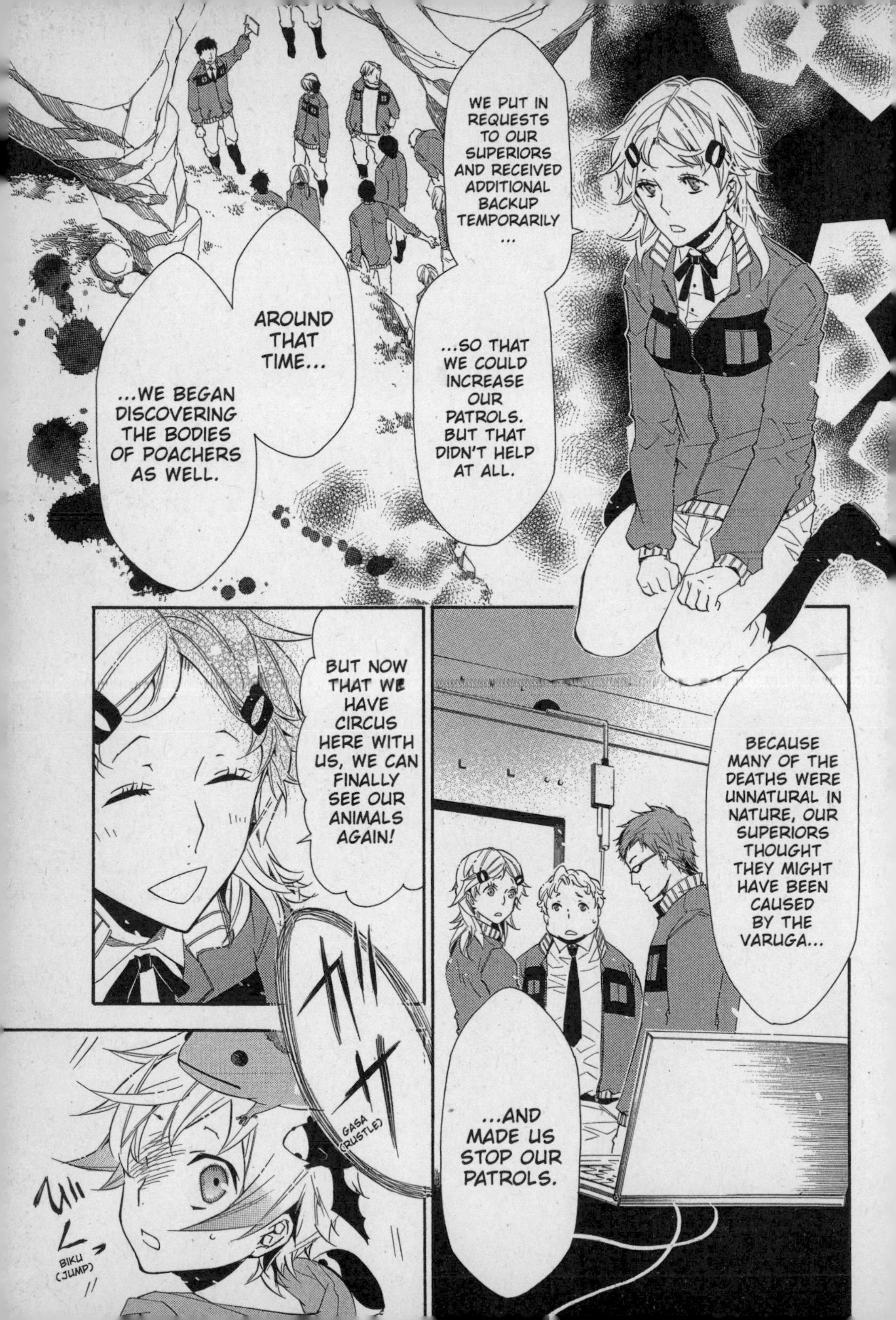
WE PUT IN REQUESTS TO OUR SUPERIORS AND RECEIVED ADDITIONAL BACKUP TEMPORARILY ...
...SO THAT WE COULD INCREASE OUR PATROLS. BUT THAT DIDN'T HELP AT ALL.
AROUND THAT TIME...
...WE BEGAN DISCOVERING THE BODIES OF POACHERS AS WELL.
BECAUSE MANY OF THE DEATHS WERE UNNATURAL IN NATURE, OUR SUPERIORS THOUGHT THEY MIGHT HAVE BEEN CAUSED BY THE VARUGA...
...AND MADE US STOP OUR PATROLS.
BUT NOW THAT WE HAVE CIRCUS HERE WITH US, WE CAN FINALLY SEE OUR ANIMALS AGAIN!
GASA (RUSTLE)
BIKU (JUMP)

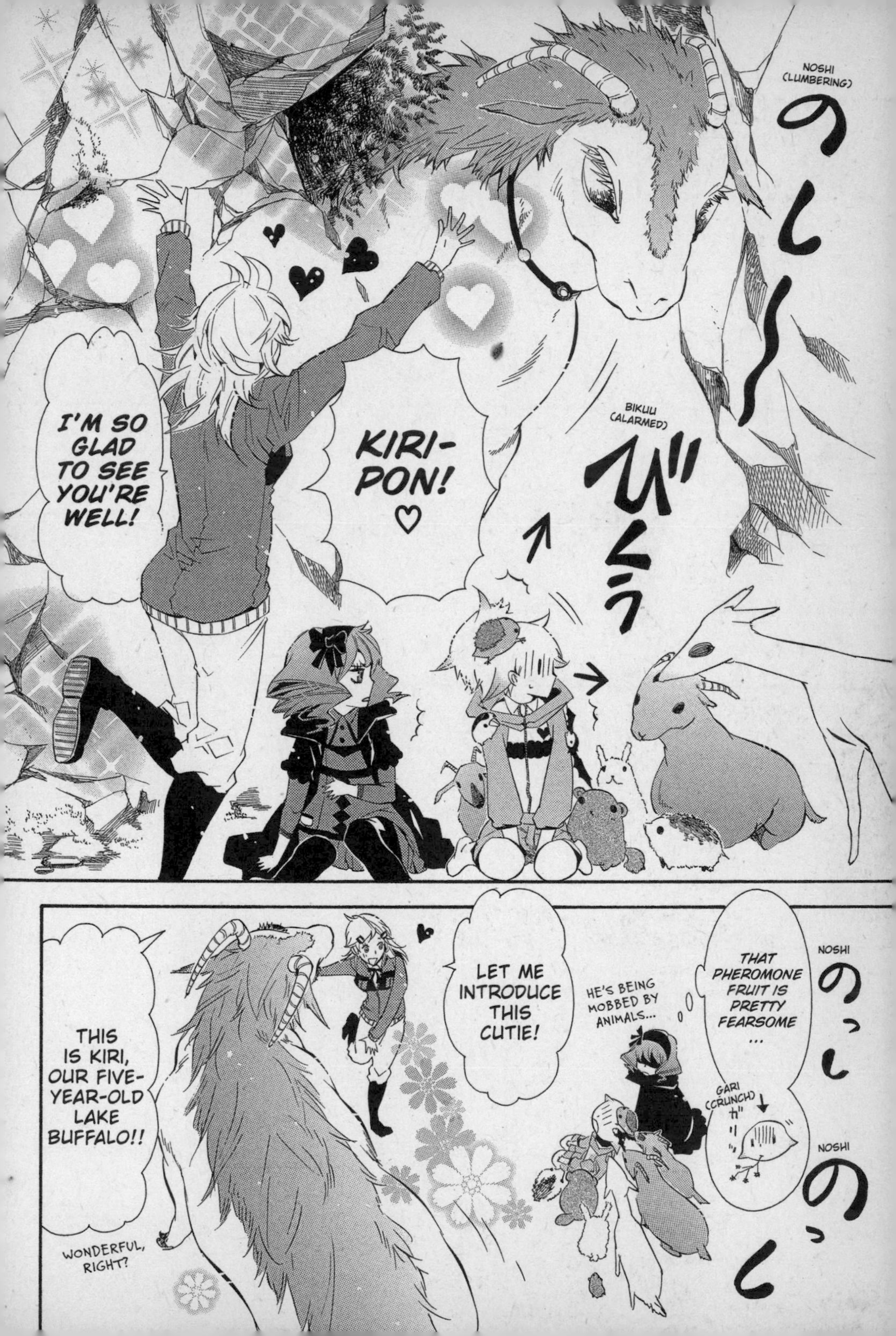
NOSHI (LUMBERING)
のし〜〜
BIKUU (ALARMED)
びくゥ
KIRI-PON! ♡
I'M SO GLAD TO SEE YOU'RE WELL!
NOSHI
のっし
THAT PHEROMONE FRUIT IS PRETTY FEARSOME ...
GARI (CRUNCH)
ガリ
NOSHI
のっし
HE'S BEING MOBBED BY ANIMALS...
LET ME INTRODUCE THIS CUTIE!
THIS IS KIRI, OUR FIVE-YEAR-OLD LAKE BUFFALO!!
WONDERFUL, RIGHT?

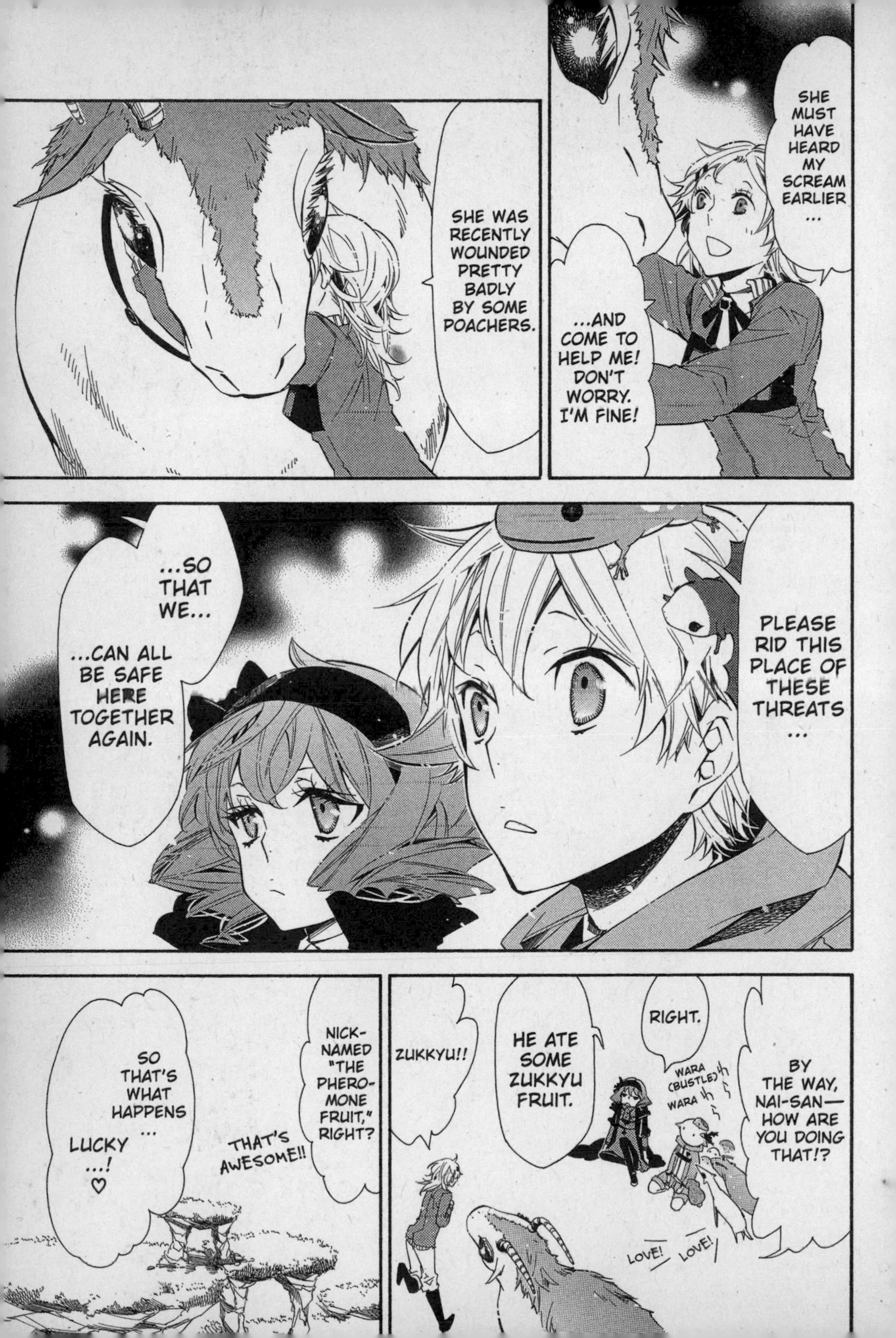
SHE MUST HAVE HEARD MY SCREAM EARLIER ...
...AND COME TO HELP ME! DON'T WORRY. I'M FINE!
SHE WAS RECENTLY WOUNDED PRETTY BADLY BY SOME POACHERS.
PLEASE RID THIS PLACE OF THESE THREATS ...
...SO THAT WE...
...CAN ALL BE SAFE HERE TOGETHER AGAIN.
BY THE WAY, NAI-SAN— HOW ARE YOU DOING THAT!?
WARA (BUSTLE) WARA
RIGHT.
HE ATE SOME ZUKKYU FRUIT.
ZUKKYU!!
LOVE! LOVE!
NICK-NAMED "THE PHERO-MONE FRUIT," RIGHT?
THAT'S AWESOME!!
SO THAT'S WHAT HAPPENS ...
LUCKY ...! ♡

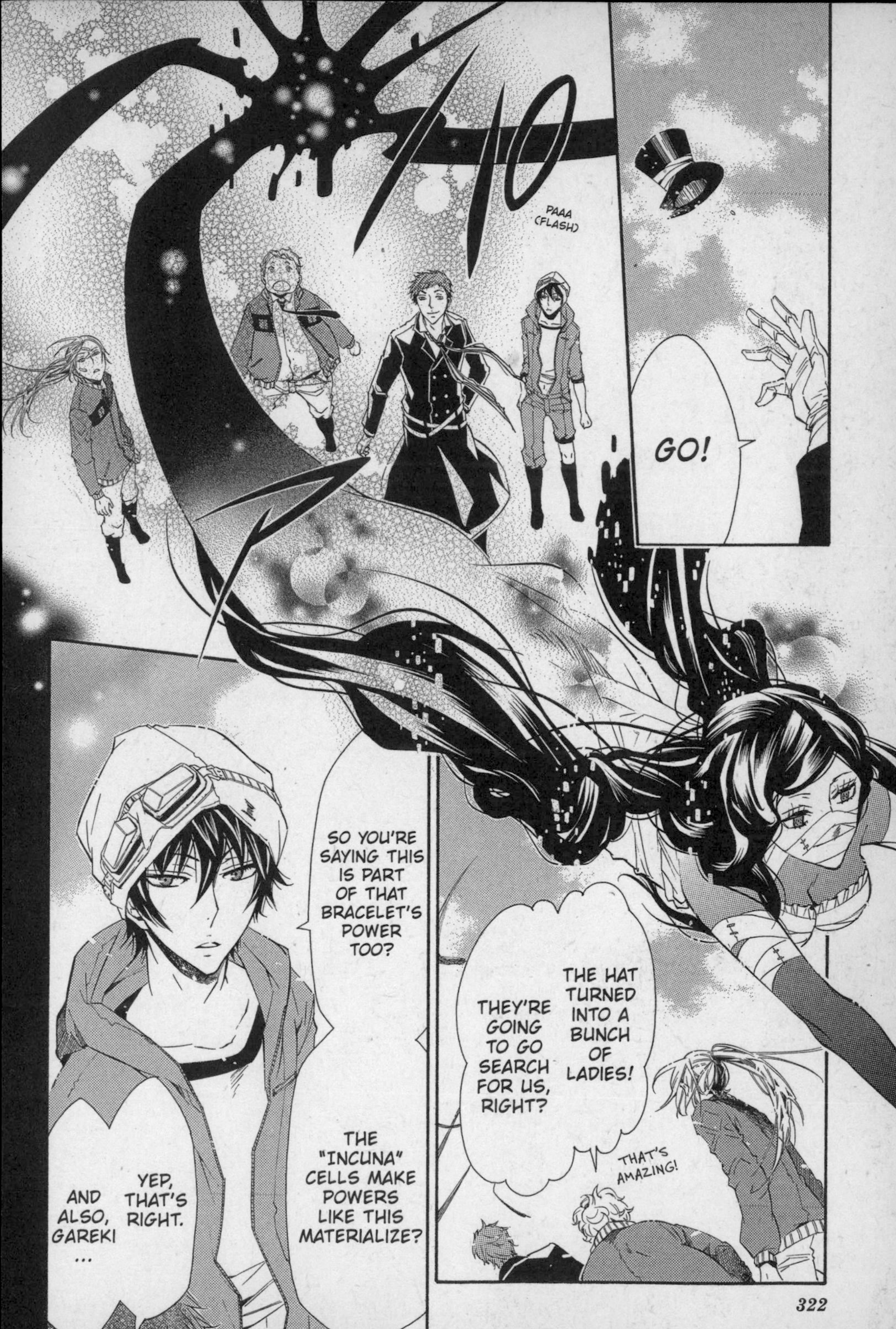
GO!
PAAA (FLASH)
THE HAT TURNED INTO A BUNCH OF LADIES!
THEY'RE GOING TO GO SEARCH FOR US, RIGHT?
THAT'S AMAZING!
SO YOU'RE SAYING THIS IS PART OF THAT BRACELET'S POWER TOO?
THE "INCUNA" CELLS MAKE POWERS LIKE THIS MATERIALIZE?
YEP, THAT'S RIGHT.
AND ALSO, GAREKI ...

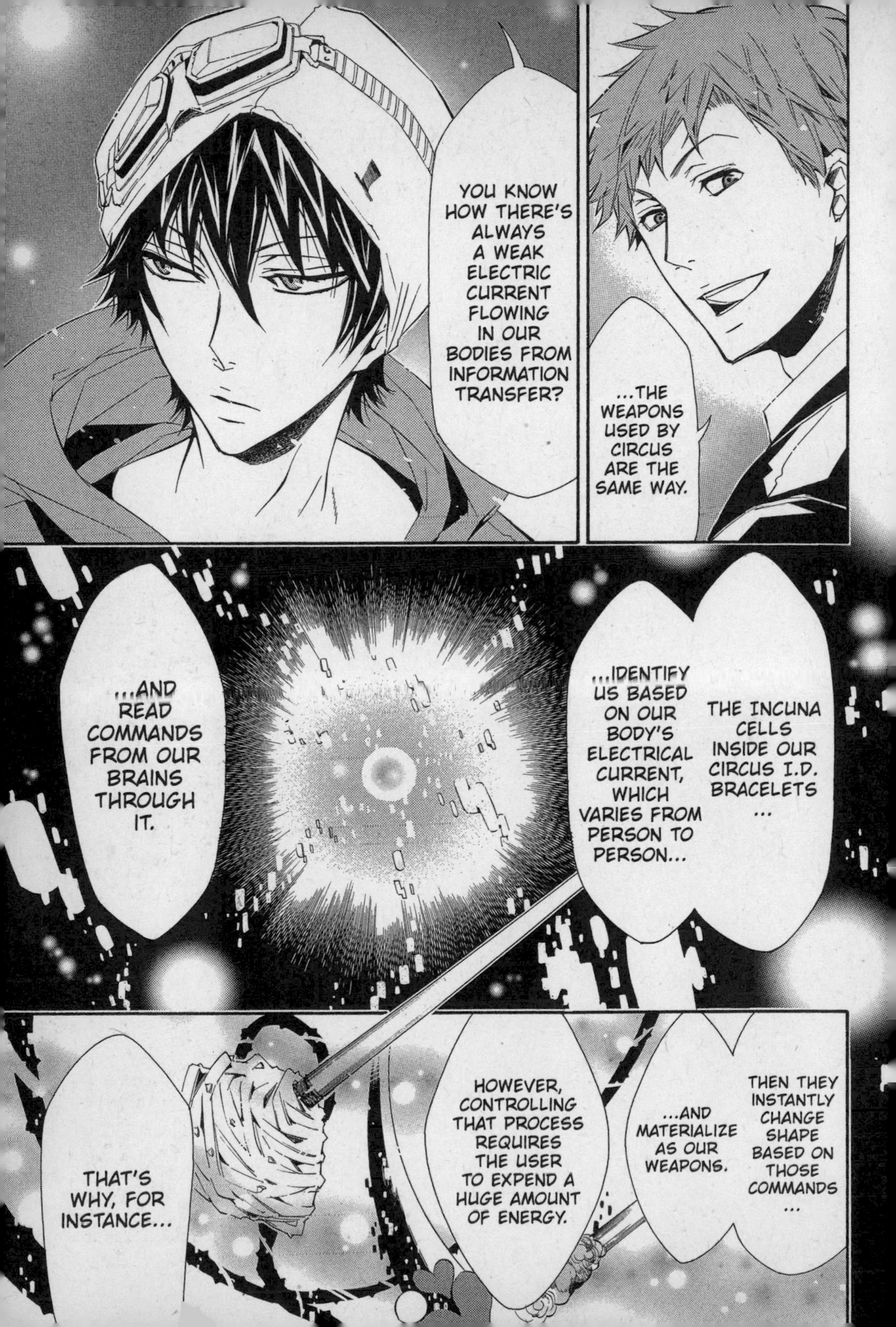
YOU KNOW HOW THERE'S ALWAYS A WEAK ELECTRIC CURRENT FLOWING IN OUR BODIES FROM INFORMATION TRANSFER?
...THE WEAPONS USED BY CIRCUS ARE THE SAME WAY.
THE INCUNA CELLS INSIDE OUR CIRCUS I.D. BRACELETS ...
...IDENTIFY US BASED ON OUR BODY'S ELECTRICAL CURRENT, WHICH VARIES FROM PERSON TO PERSON...
...AND READ COMMANDS FROM OUR BRAINS THROUGH IT.
THEN THEY INSTANTLY CHANGE SHAPE BASED ON THOSE COMMANDS ...
...AND MATERIALIZE AS OUR WEAPONS.
HOWEVER, CONTROLLING THAT PROCESS REQUIRES THE USER TO EXPEND A HUGE AMOUNT OF ENERGY.
THAT'S WHY, FOR INSTANCE...

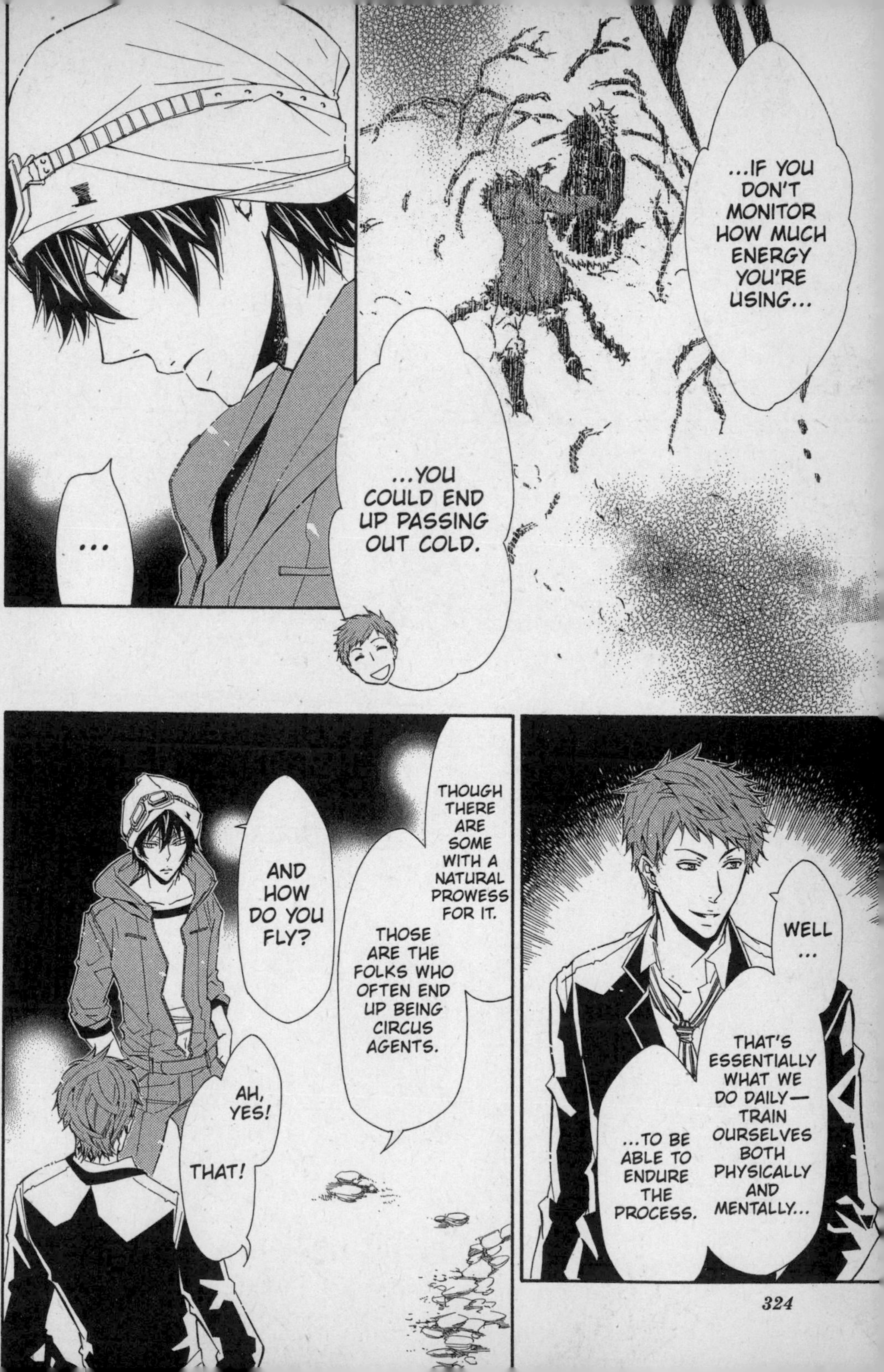
...IF YOU DON'T MONITOR HOW MUCH ENERGY YOU'RE USING...
...YOU COULD END UP PASSING OUT COLD.
...
WELL...
THAT'S ESSENTIALLY WHAT WE DO DAILY—TRAIN OURSELVES BOTH PHYSICALLY AND MENTALLY...
...TO BE ABLE TO ENDURE THE PROCESS.
THOUGH THERE ARE SOME WITH A NATURAL PROWESS FOR IT.
THOSE ARE THE FOLKS WHO OFTEN END UP BEING CIRCUS AGENTS.
AND HOW DO YOU FLY?
AH, YES!
THAT!

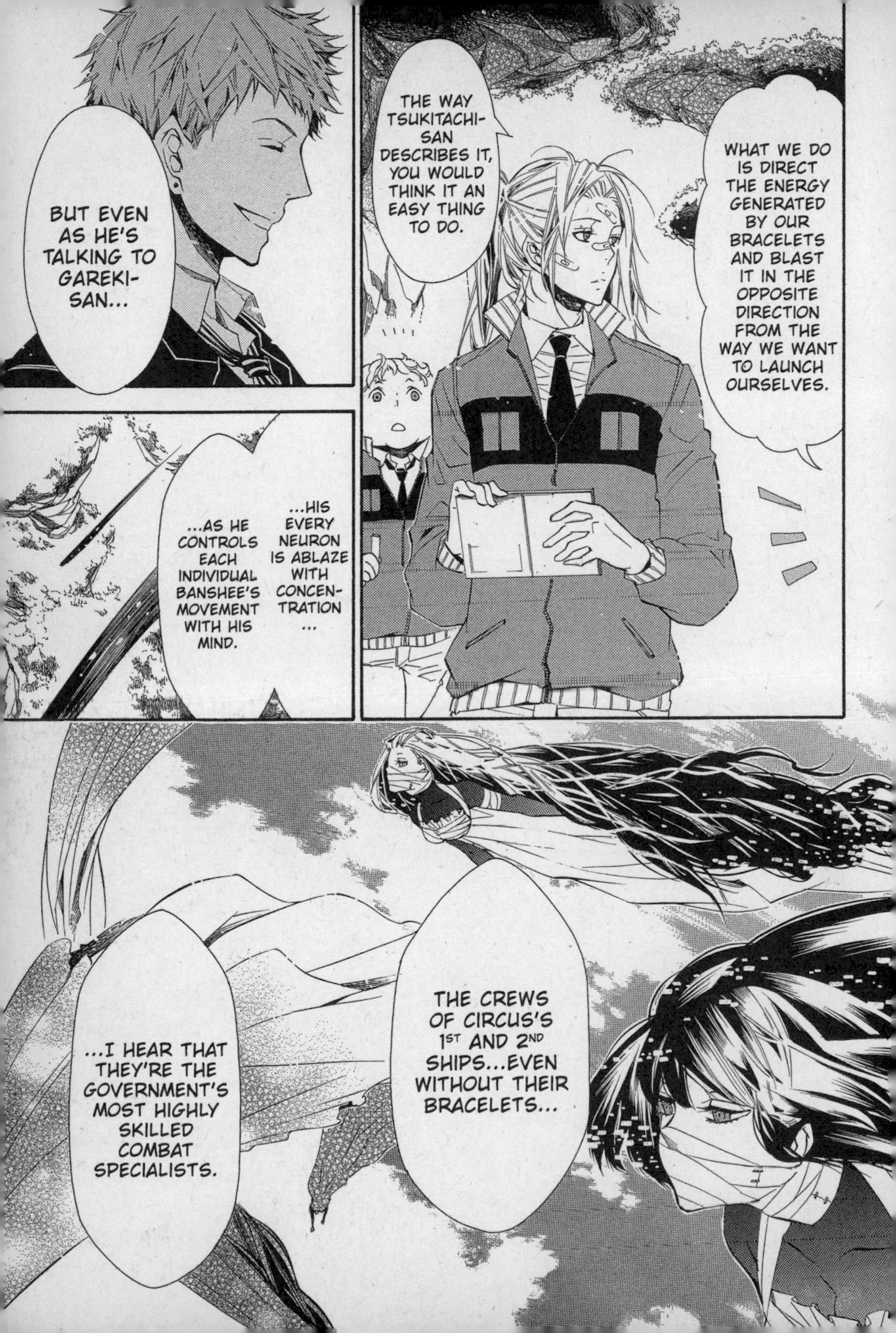
WHAT WE DO IS DIRECT THE ENERGY GENERATED BY OUR BRACELETS AND BLAST IT IN THE OPPOSITE DIRECTION FROM THE WAY WE WANT TO LAUNCH OURSELVES.
THE WAY TSUKITACHI-SAN DESCRIBES IT, YOU WOULD THINK IT AN EASY THING TO DO.
BUT EVEN AS HE'S TALKING TO GAREKI-SAN...
...HIS EVERY NEURON IS ABLAZE WITH CONCENTRATION...
...AS HE CONTROLS EACH INDIVIDUAL BANSHEE'S MOVEMENT WITH HIS MIND.
THE CREWS OF CIRCUS'S 1st AND 2nd SHIPS...EVEN WITHOUT THEIR BRACELETS...
...I HEAR THAT THEY'RE THE GOVERNMENT'S MOST HIGHLY SKILLED COMBAT SPECIALISTS.

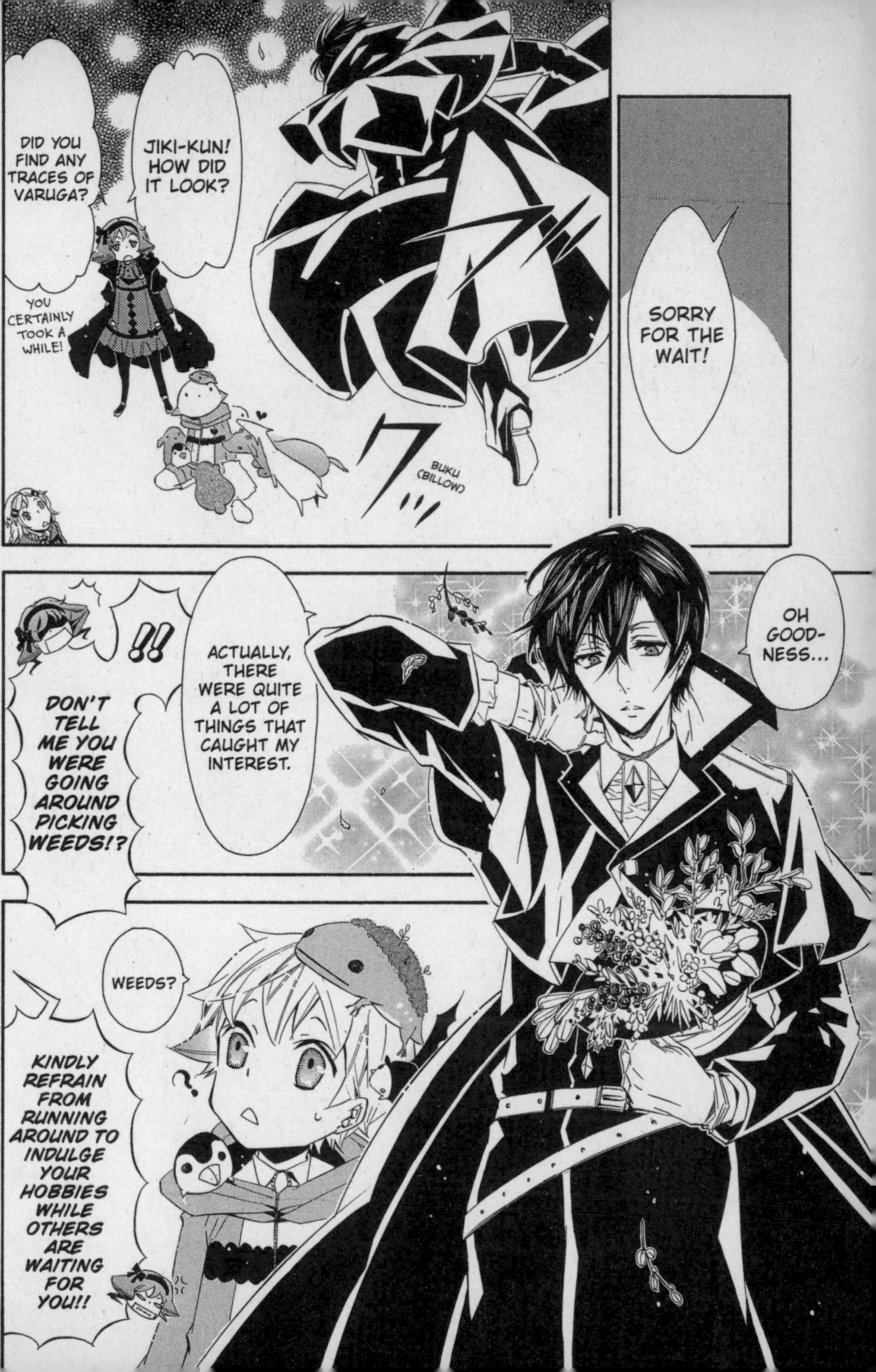
SORRY FOR THE WAIT!
JIKI-KUN! HOW DID IT LOOK?
DID YOU FIND ANY TRACES OF VARUGA?
BUKU (BILLOW)
YOU CERTAINLY TOOK A WHILE!
OH GOOD-NESS...
ACTUALLY, THERE WERE QUITE A LOT OF THINGS THAT CAUGHT MY INTEREST.
!!
DON'T TELL ME YOU WERE GOING AROUND PICKING WEEDS!?
WEEDS?
KINDLY REFRAIN FROM RUNNING AROUND TO INDULGE YOUR HOBBIES WHILE OTHERS ARE WAITING FOR YOU!!

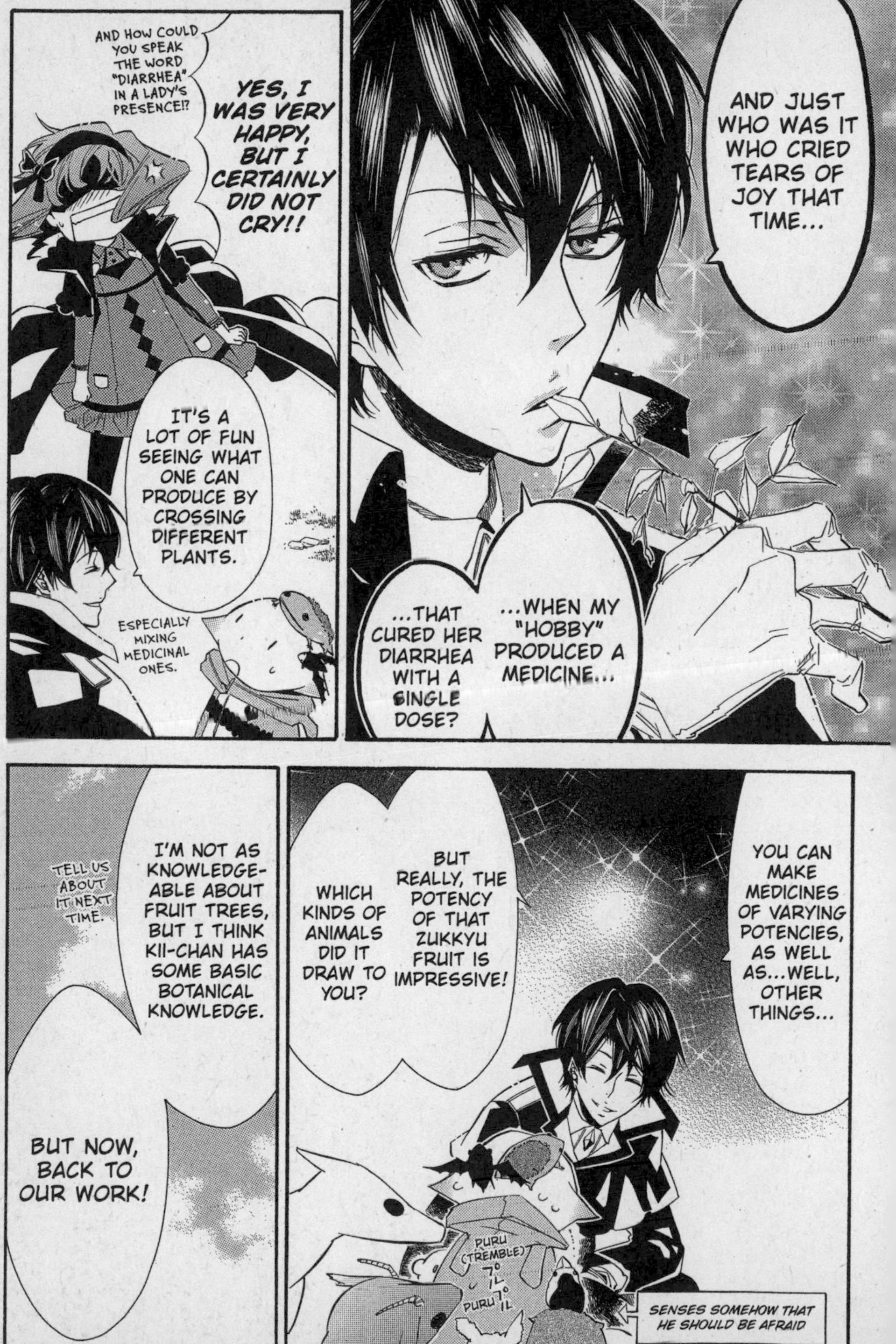
AND JUST WHO WAS IT WHO CRIED TEARS OF JOY THAT TIME...
...WHEN MY "HOBBY" PRODUCED A MEDICINE...
...THAT CURED HER DIARRHEA WITH A SINGLE DOSE?
YES, I WAS VERY HAPPY, BUT I CERTAINLY DID NOT CRY!!
AND HOW COULD YOU SPEAK THE WORD "DIARRHEA" IN A LADY'S PRESENCE!?
IT'S A LOT OF FUN SEEING WHAT ONE CAN PRODUCE BY CROSSING DIFFERENT PLANTS.
ESPECIALLY MIXING MEDICINAL ONES.
YOU CAN MAKE MEDICINES OF VARYING POTENCIES, AS WELL AS...WELL, OTHER THINGS...
BUT REALLY, THE POTENCY OF THAT ZUKKYU FRUIT IS IMPRESSIVE!
WHICH KINDS OF ANIMALS DID IT DRAW TO YOU?
PURU (TREMBLE) PURU
SENSES SOMEHOW THAT HE SHOULD BE AFRAID
I'M NOT AS KNOWLEDGE-ABLE ABOUT FRUIT TREES, BUT I THINK KII-CHAN HAS SOME BASIC BOTANICAL KNOWLEDGE.
TELL US ABOUT IT NEXT TIME.
BUT NOW, BACK TO OUR WORK!

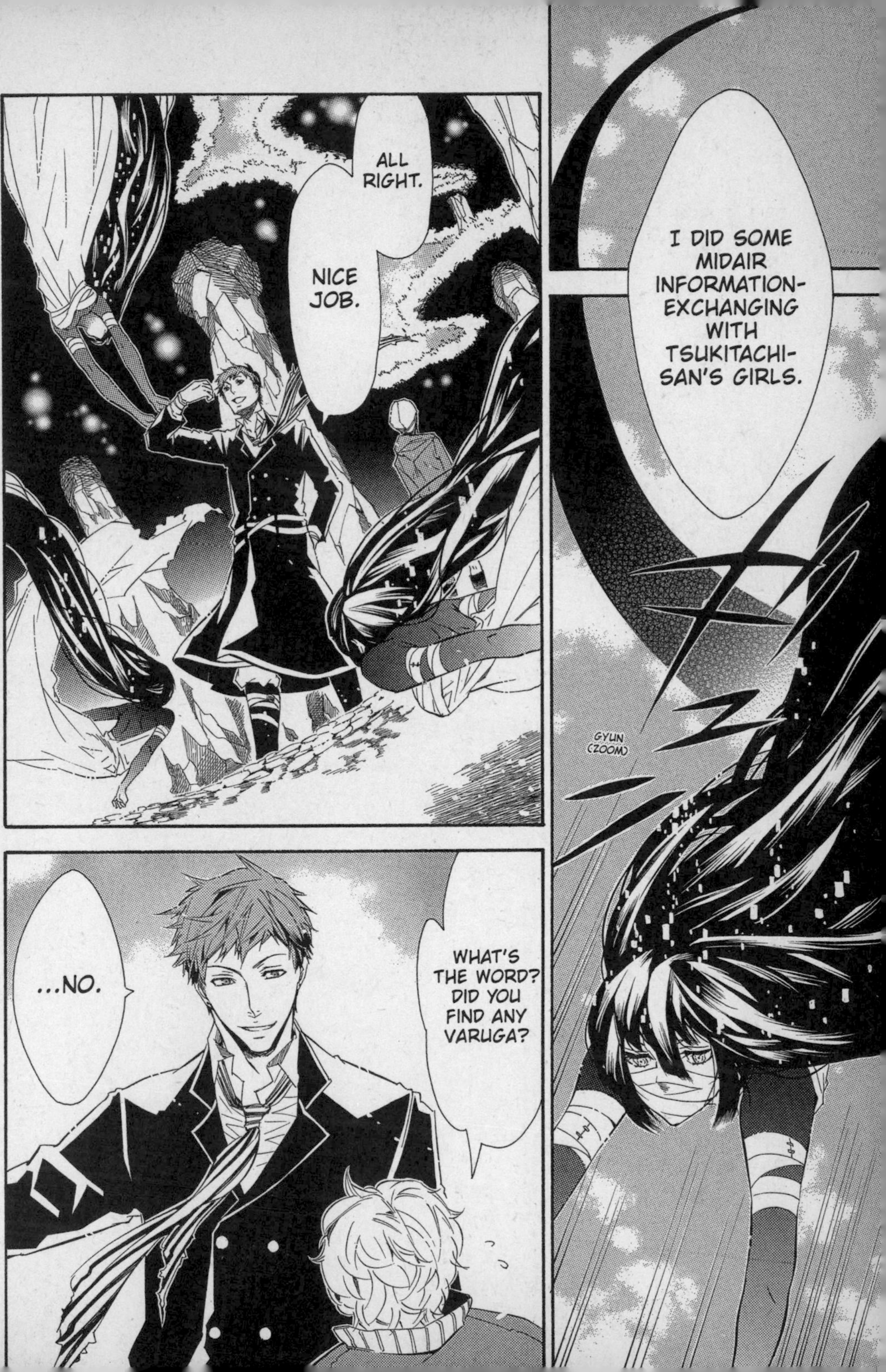
I DID SOME MIDAIR INFORMATION-EXCHANGING WITH TSUKITACHI-SAN'S GIRLS.
GYUN (ZOOM)
ALL RIGHT.
NICE JOB.
WHAT'S THE WORD? DID YOU FIND ANY VARUGA?
...NO.

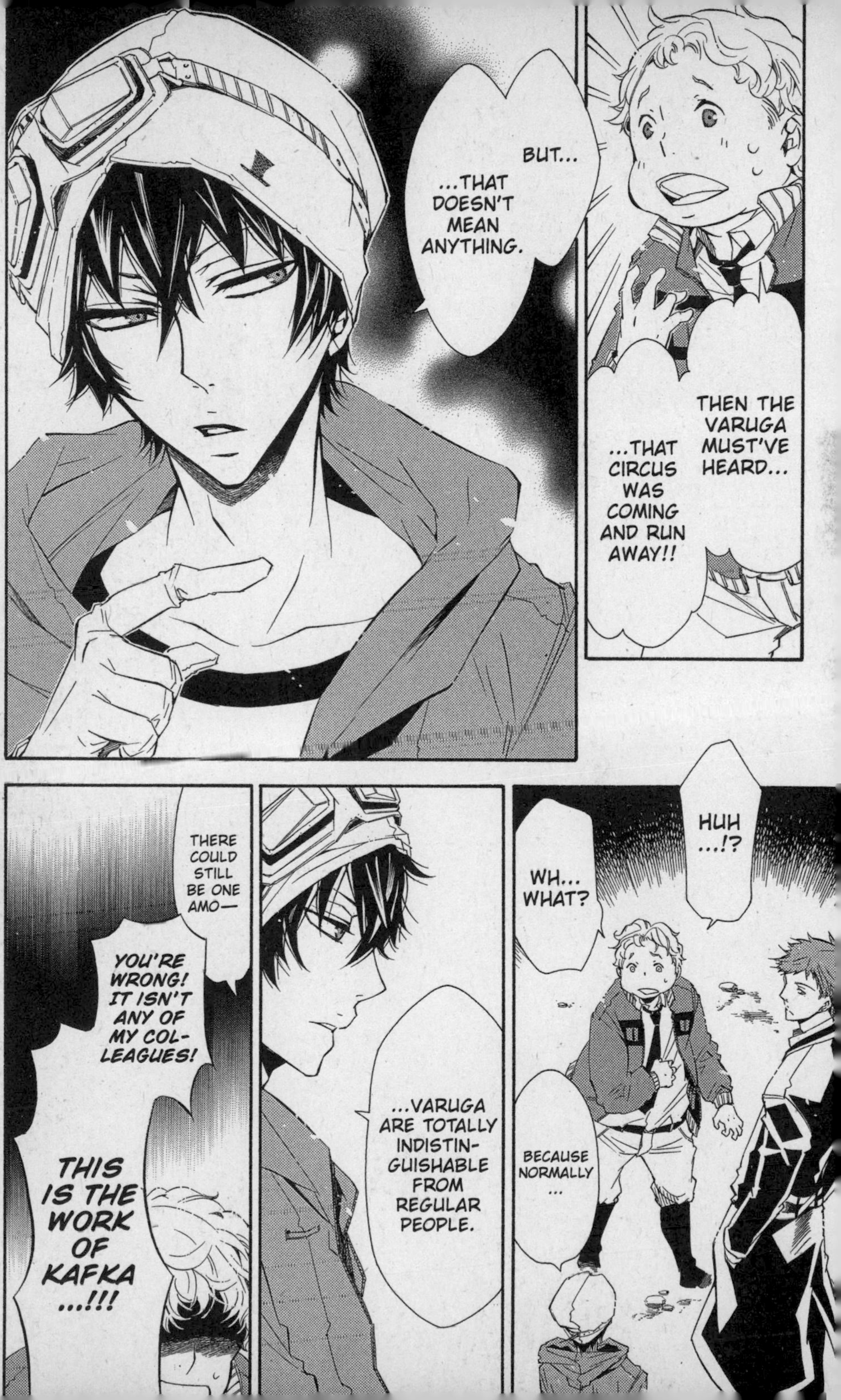
THEN THE VARUGA MUST'VE HEARD...
...THAT CIRCUS WAS COMING AND RUN AWAY!!
BUT...
...THAT DOESN'T MEAN ANYTHING.
HUH ...!?
WH... WHAT?
BECAUSE NORMALLY...
...VARUGA ARE TOTALLY INDISTIN-GUISHABLE FROM REGULAR PEOPLE.
THERE COULD STILL BE ONE AMO—
YOU'RE WRONG! IT ISN'T ANY OF MY COL-LEAGUES!
THIS IS THE WORK OF KAFKA ...!!!

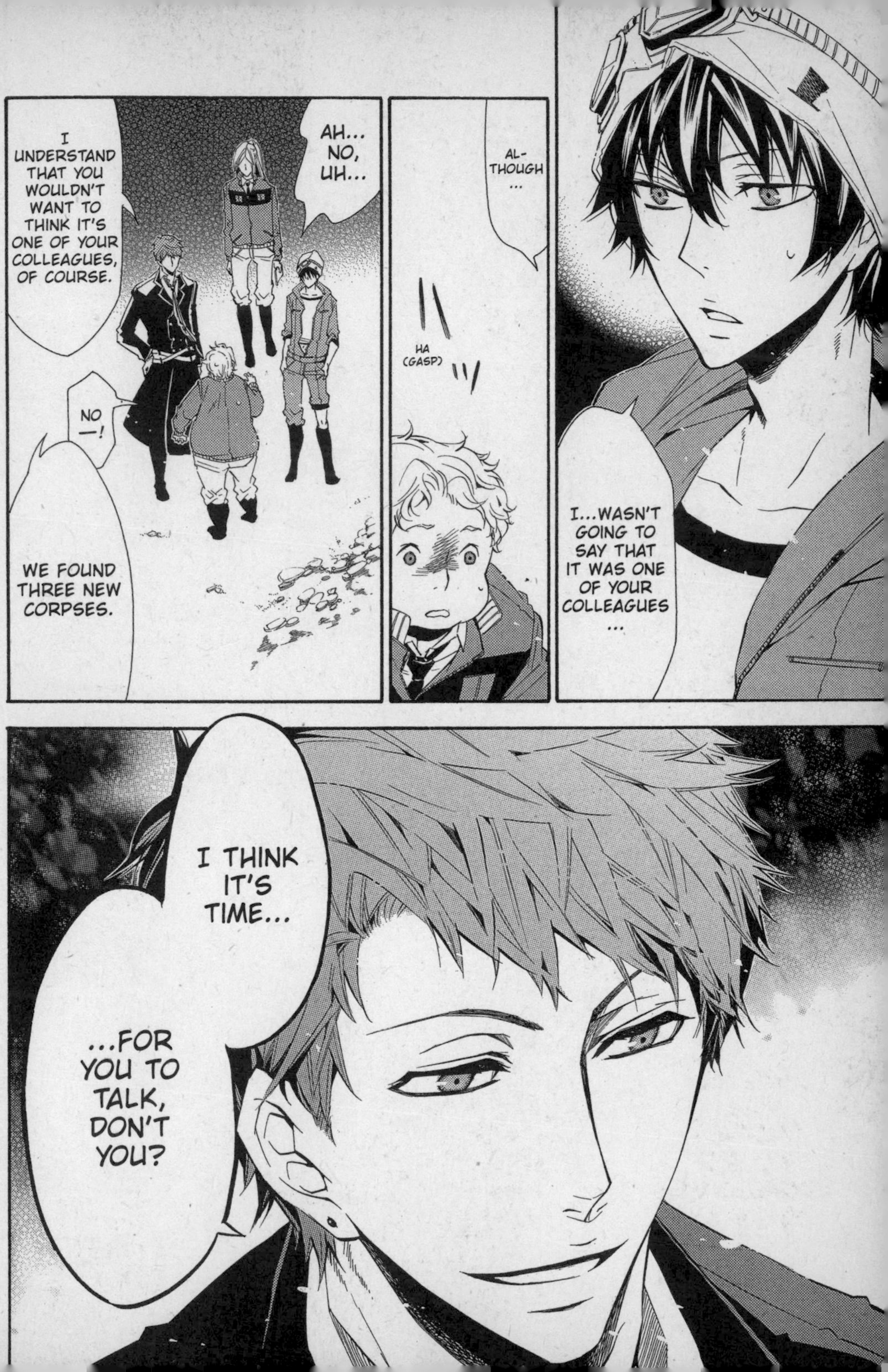
I...WASN'T GOING TO SAY THAT IT WAS ONE OF YOUR COLLEAGUES ...
AL-THOUGH ...
HA (GASP)
AH... NO, UH...
I UNDERSTAND THAT YOU WOULDN'T WANT TO THINK IT'S ONE OF YOUR COLLEAGUES, OF COURSE.
NO —!
WE FOUND THREE NEW CORPSES.
I THINK IT'S TIME...
...FOR YOU TO TALK, DON'T YOU?

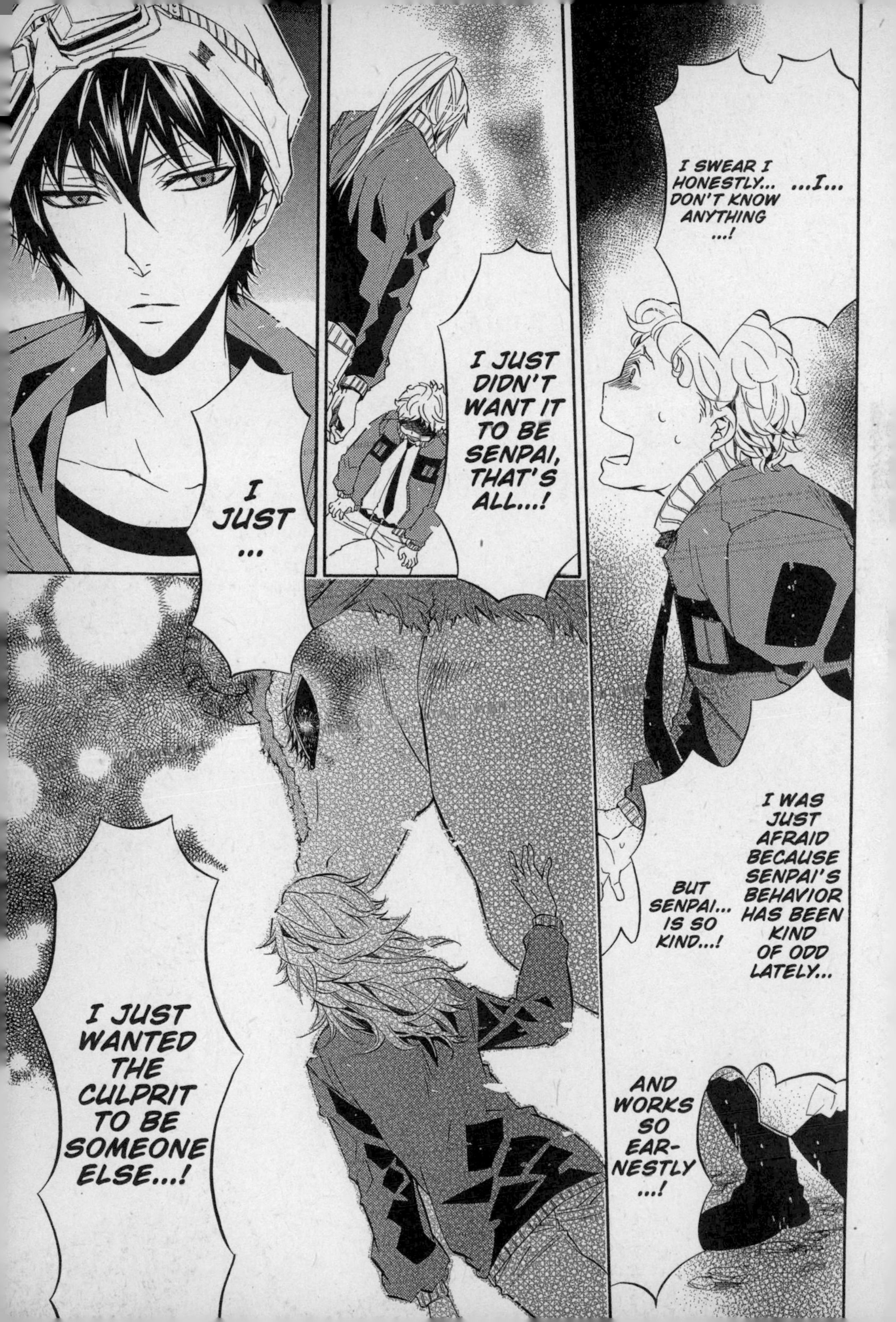
...I...
I SWEAR I HONESTLY... DON'T KNOW ANYTHING ...!
I WAS JUST AFRAID BECAUSE SENPAI'S BEHAVIOR HAS BEEN KIND OF ODD LATELY...
BUT SENPAI... IS SO KIND...!
AND WORKS SO EAR-NESTLY ...!
I JUST DIDN'T WANT IT TO BE SENPAI, THAT'S ALL...!
I JUST ...
I JUST WANTED THE CULPRIT TO BE SOMEONE ELSE...!

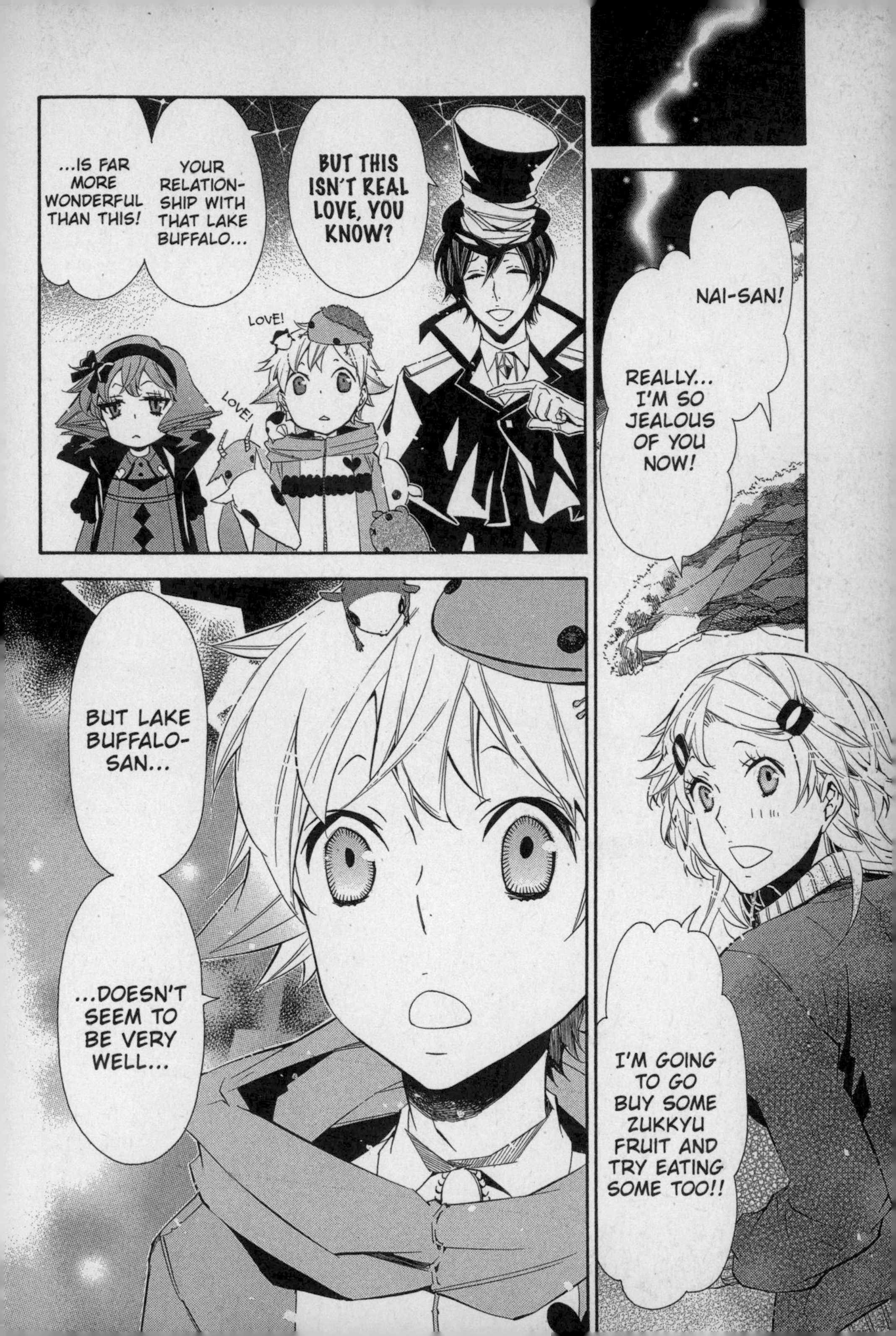
NAI-SAN!
REALLY... I'M SO JEALOUS OF YOU NOW!
I'M GOING TO GO BUY SOME ZUKKYU FRUIT AND TRY EATING SOME TOO!!
BUT THIS ISN'T REAL LOVE, YOU KNOW?
YOUR RELATION-SHIP WITH THAT LAKE BUFFALO...
...IS FAR MORE WONDERFUL THAN THIS!
LOVE!
LOVE!
BUT LAKE BUFFALO-SAN...
...DOESN'T SEEM TO BE VERY WELL...

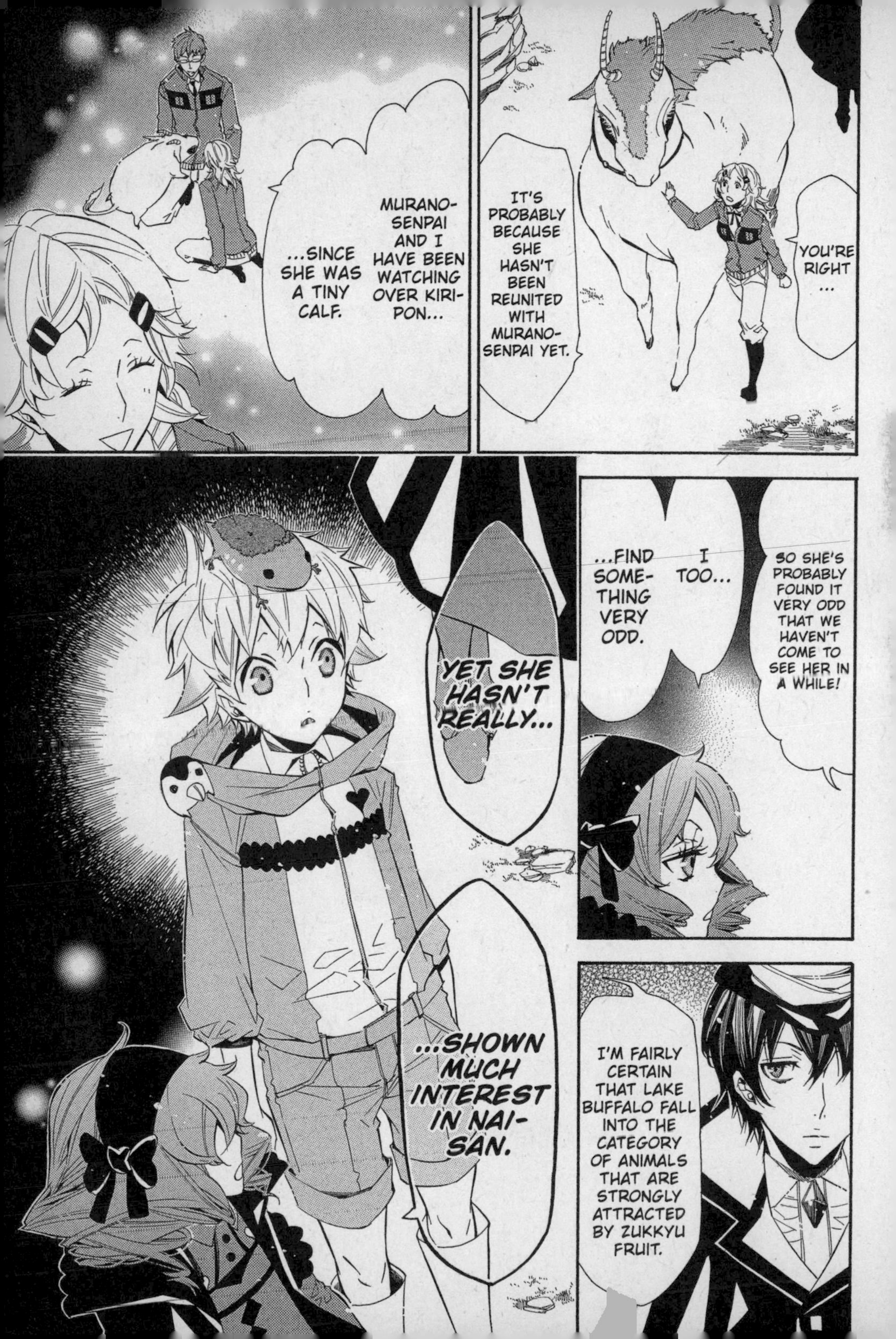
YOU'RE RIGHT ...
IT'S PROBABLY BECAUSE SHE HASN'T BEEN REUNITED WITH MURANO-SENPAI YET.
MURANO-SENPAI AND I HAVE BEEN WATCHING OVER KIRI-PON...
...SINCE SHE WAS A TINY CALF.
SO SHE'S PROBABLY FOUND IT VERY ODD THAT WE HAVEN'T COME TO SEE HER IN A WHILE!
I TOO...
...FIND SOMETHING VERY ODD.
I'M FAIRLY CERTAIN THAT LAKE BUFFALO FALL INTO THE CATEGORY OF ANIMALS THAT ARE STRONGLY ATTRACTED BY ZUKKYU FRUIT.
YET SHE HASN'T REALLY...
...SHOWN MUCH INTEREST IN NAI-SAN.

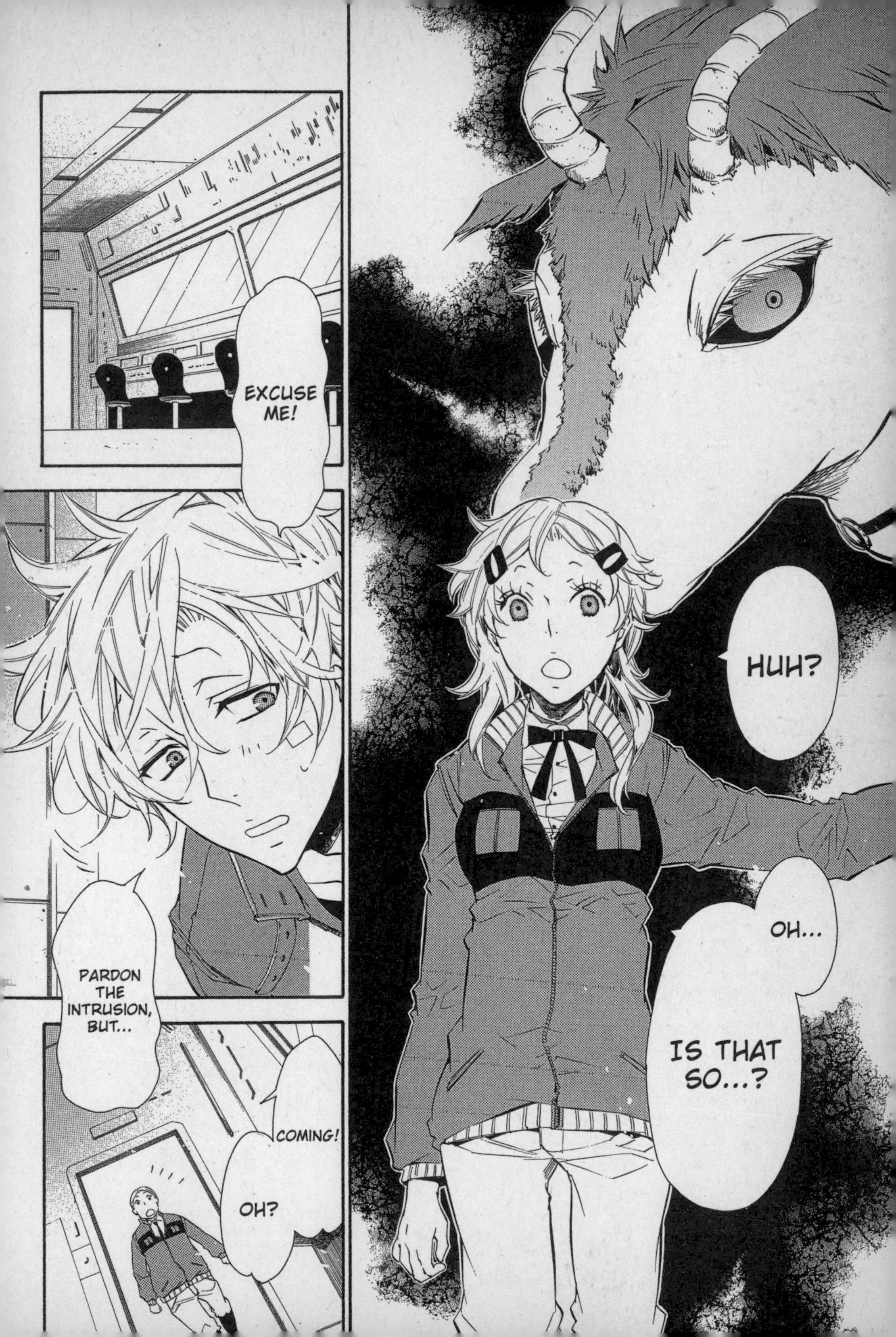
HUH?
OH...
IS THAT SO...?
EXCUSE ME!
PARDON THE INTRUSION, BUT...
COMING!
OH?

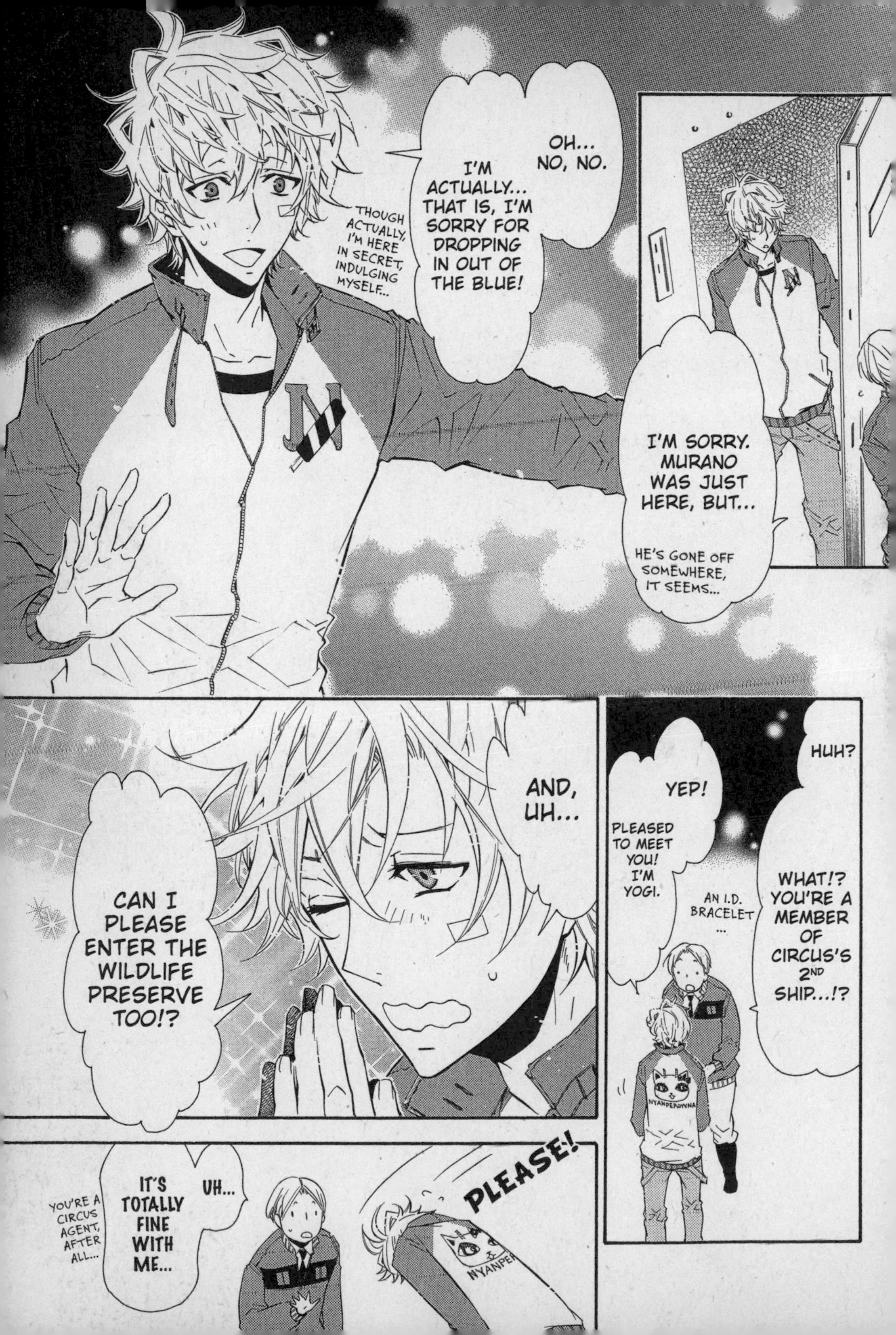
I'M SORRY. MURANO WAS JUST HERE, BUT...
HE'S GONE OFF SOMEWHERE, IT SEEMS...
OH... NO, NO.
I'M ACTUALLY... THAT IS, I'M SORRY FOR DROPPING IN OUT OF THE BLUE!
THOUGH ACTUALLY, I'M HERE IN SECRET, INDULGING MYSELF...
HUH?
WHAT!? YOU'RE A MEMBER OF CIRCUS'S 2ND SHIP...!?
YEP!
PLEASED TO MEET YOU! I'M YOGI.
AN I.D. BRACELET ...
AND, UH...
CAN I PLEASE ENTER THE WILDLIFE PRESERVE TOO!?
PLEASE!
UH...
IT'S TOTALLY FINE WITH ME...
YOU'RE A CIRCUS AGENT, AFTER ALL...

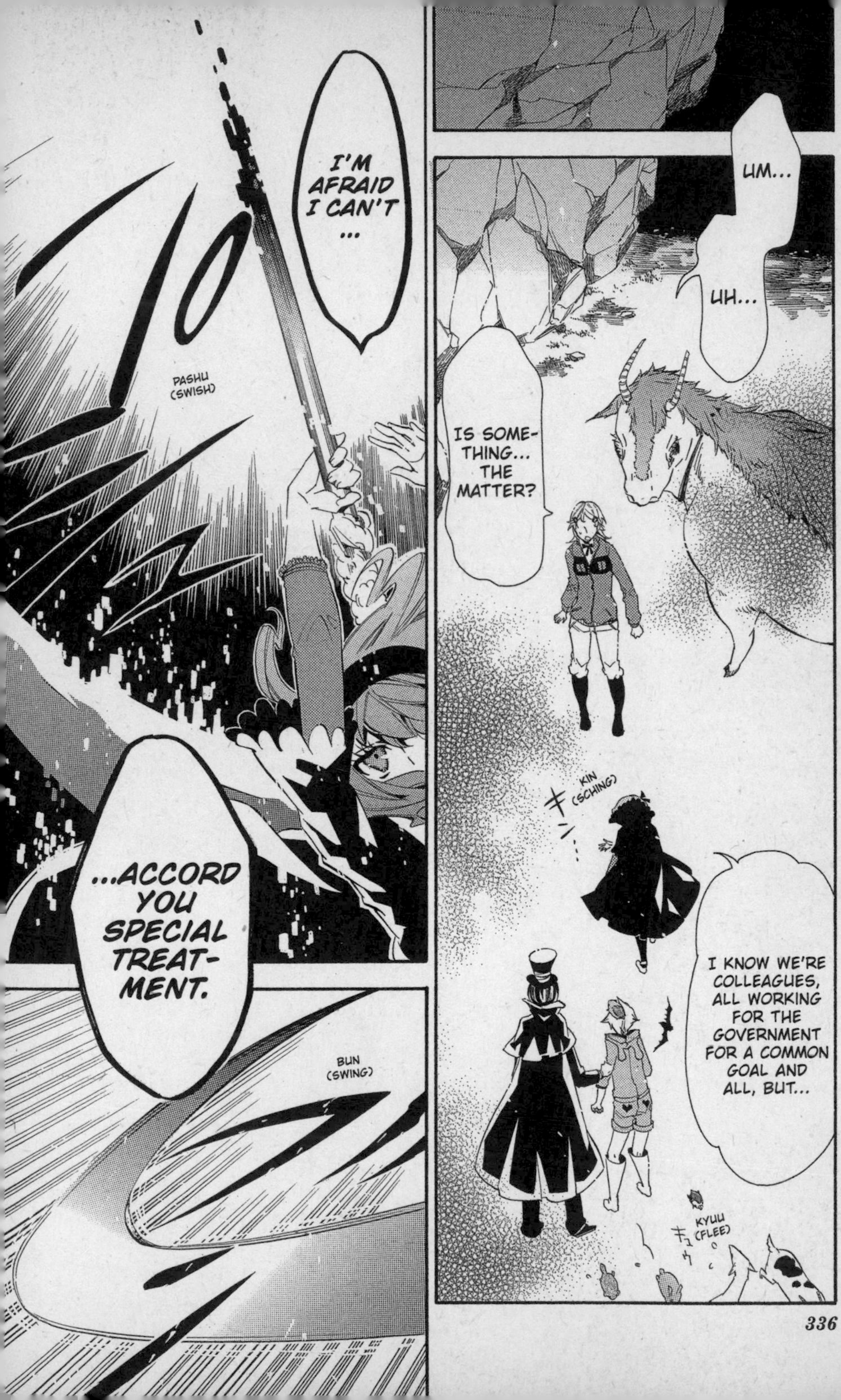
UM...
UH...
IS SOME-THING... THE MATTER?
KIN (SCHING)
I KNOW WE'RE COLLEAGUES, ALL WORKING FOR THE GOVERNMENT FOR A COMMON GOAL AND ALL, BUT...
KYUU (FLEE)
I'M AFRAID I CAN'T ...
PASHU (SWISH)
...ACCORD YOU SPECIAL TREAT-MENT.
BUN (SWING)

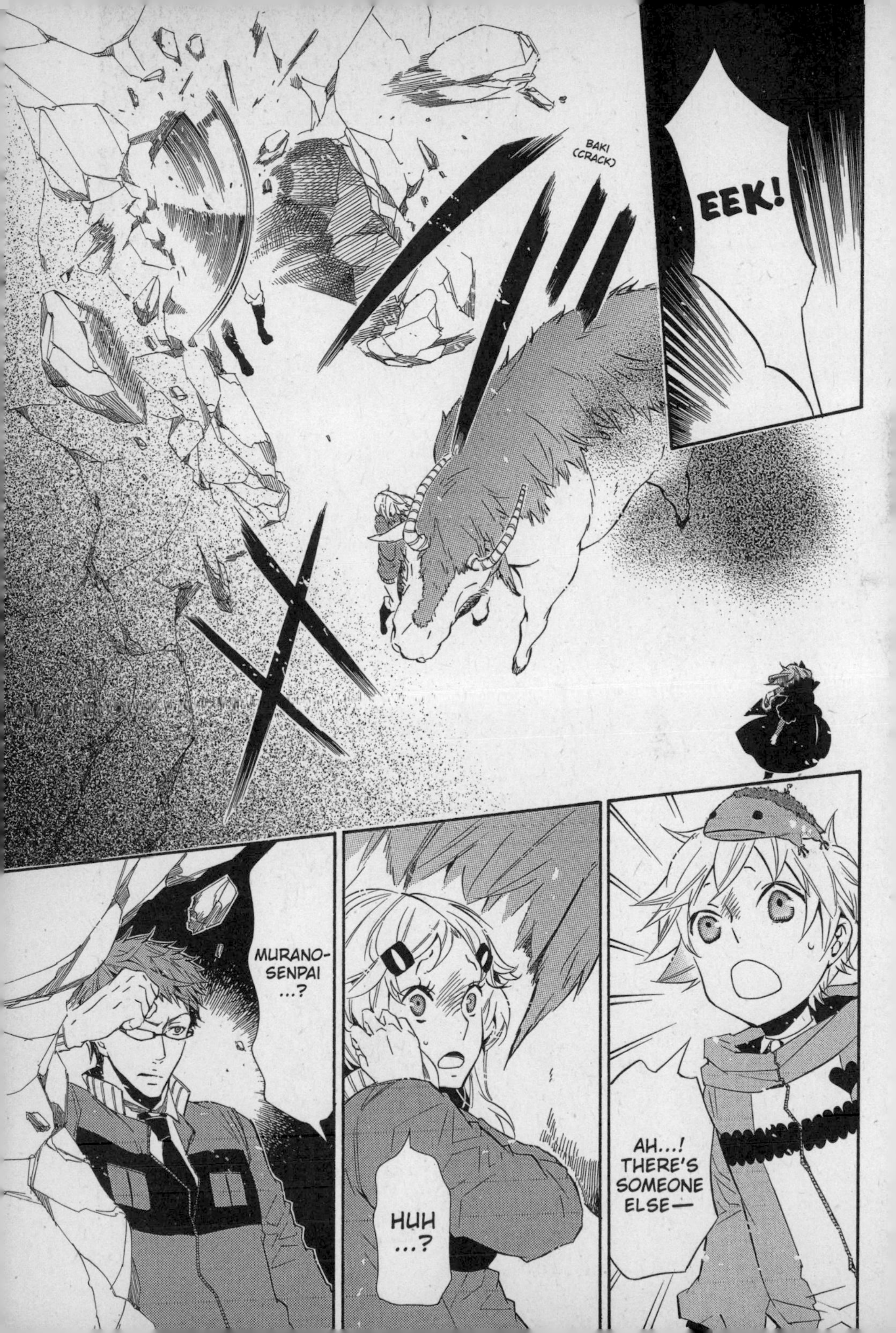
EEK!
BAKI (CRACK)
AH...! THERE'S SOMEONE ELSE—
HUH ...?
MURANO-SENPAI ...?

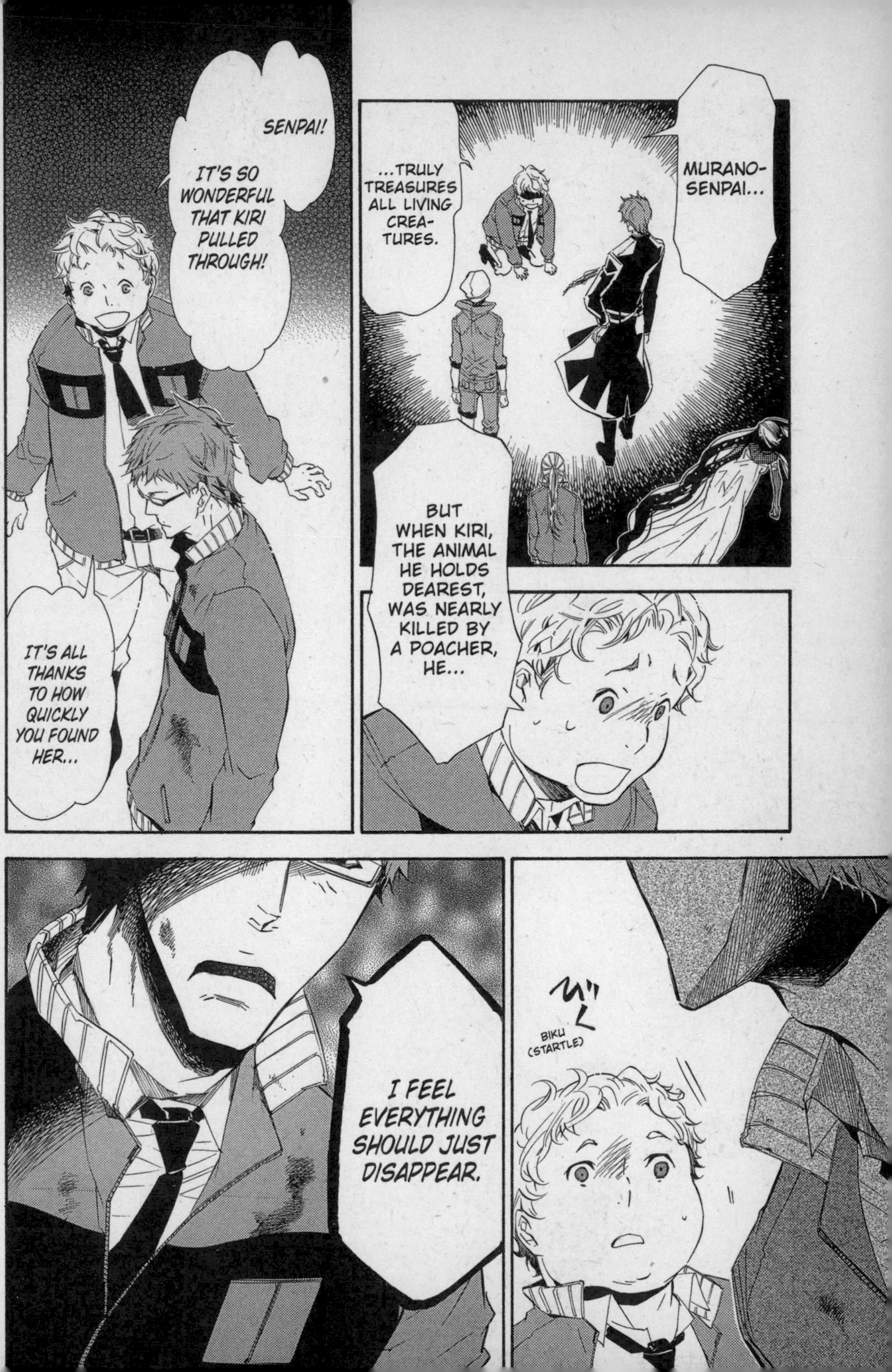
MURANO-SENPAI...
...TRULY TREASURES ALL LIVING CREATURES.
BUT WHEN KIRI, THE ANIMAL HE HOLDS DEAREST, WAS NEARLY KILLED BY A POACHER, HE...
SENPAI!
IT'S SO WONDERFUL THAT KIRI PULLED THROUGH!
IT'S ALL THANKS TO HOW QUICKLY YOU FOUND HER...
BIKU (STARTLE)
I FEEL EVERYTHING SHOULD JUST DISAPPEAR.

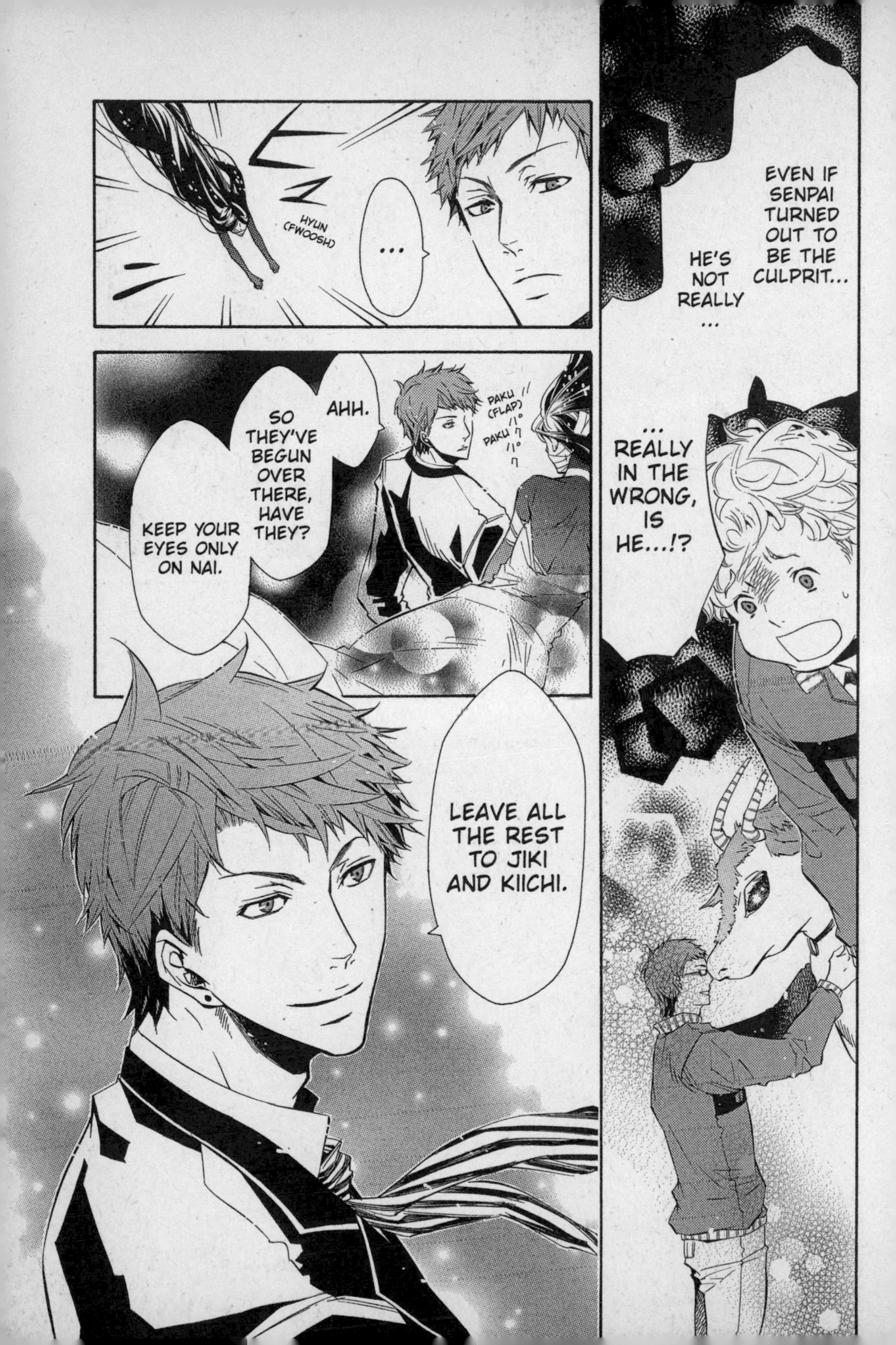
EVEN IF SENPAI TURNED OUT TO BE THE CULPRIT...
HE'S NOT REALLY ...
... REALLY IN THE WRONG, IS HE...!?
...
HYUN (FWOOSH)
PAKU (FLAP) PAKU
AHH.
SO THEY'VE BEGUN OVER THERE, HAVE THEY?
KEEP YOUR EYES ONLY ON NAI.
LEAVE ALL THE REST TO JIKI AND KIICHI.

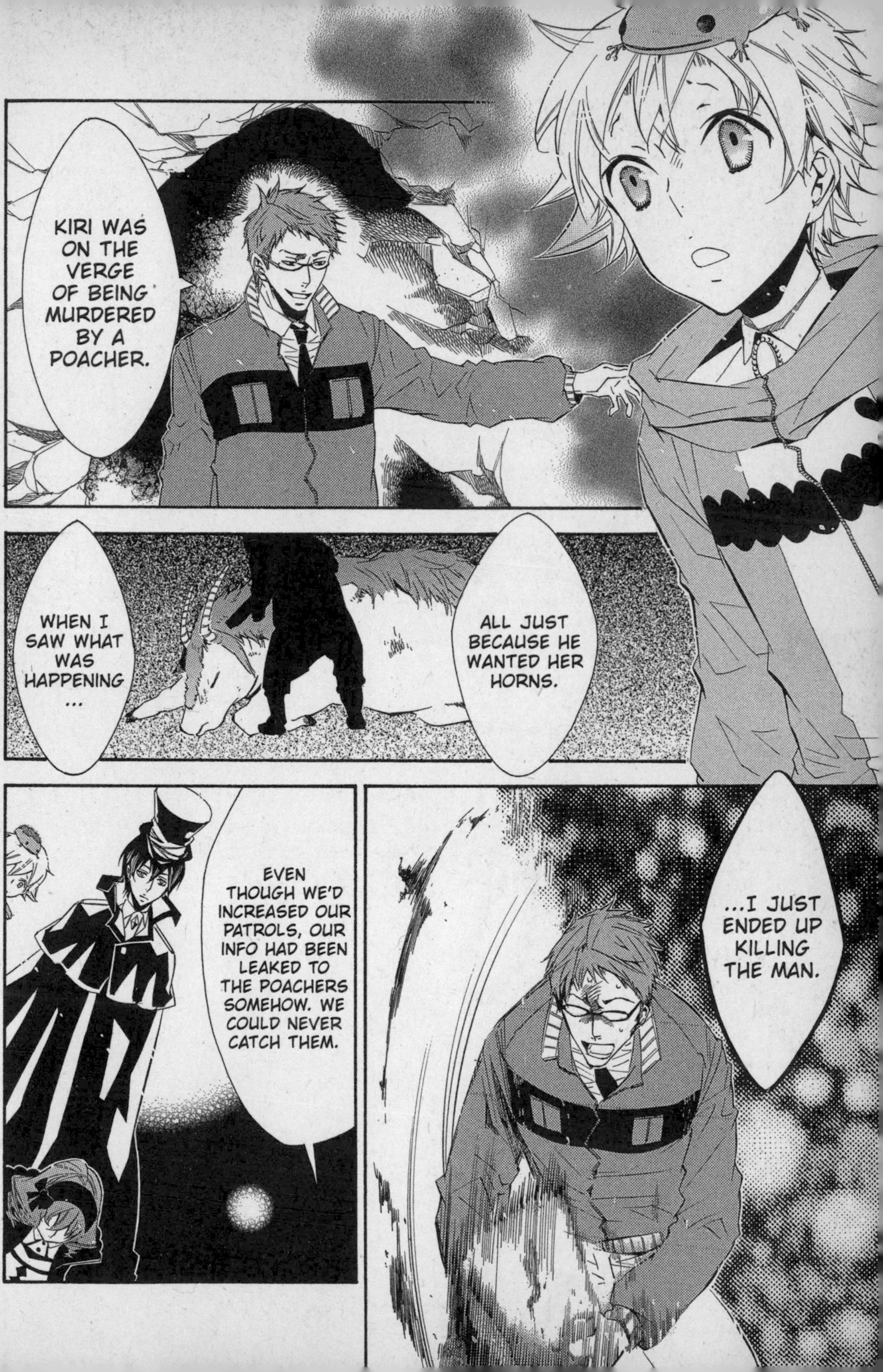
KIRI WAS ON THE VERGE OF BEING MURDERED BY A POACHER.
ALL JUST BECAUSE HE WANTED HER HORNS.
WHEN I SAW WHAT WAS HAPPENING ...
...I JUST ENDED UP KILLING THE MAN.
EVEN THOUGH WE'D INCREASED OUR PATROLS, OUR INFO HAD BEEN LEAKED TO THE POACHERS SOMEHOW. WE COULD NEVER CATCH THEM.

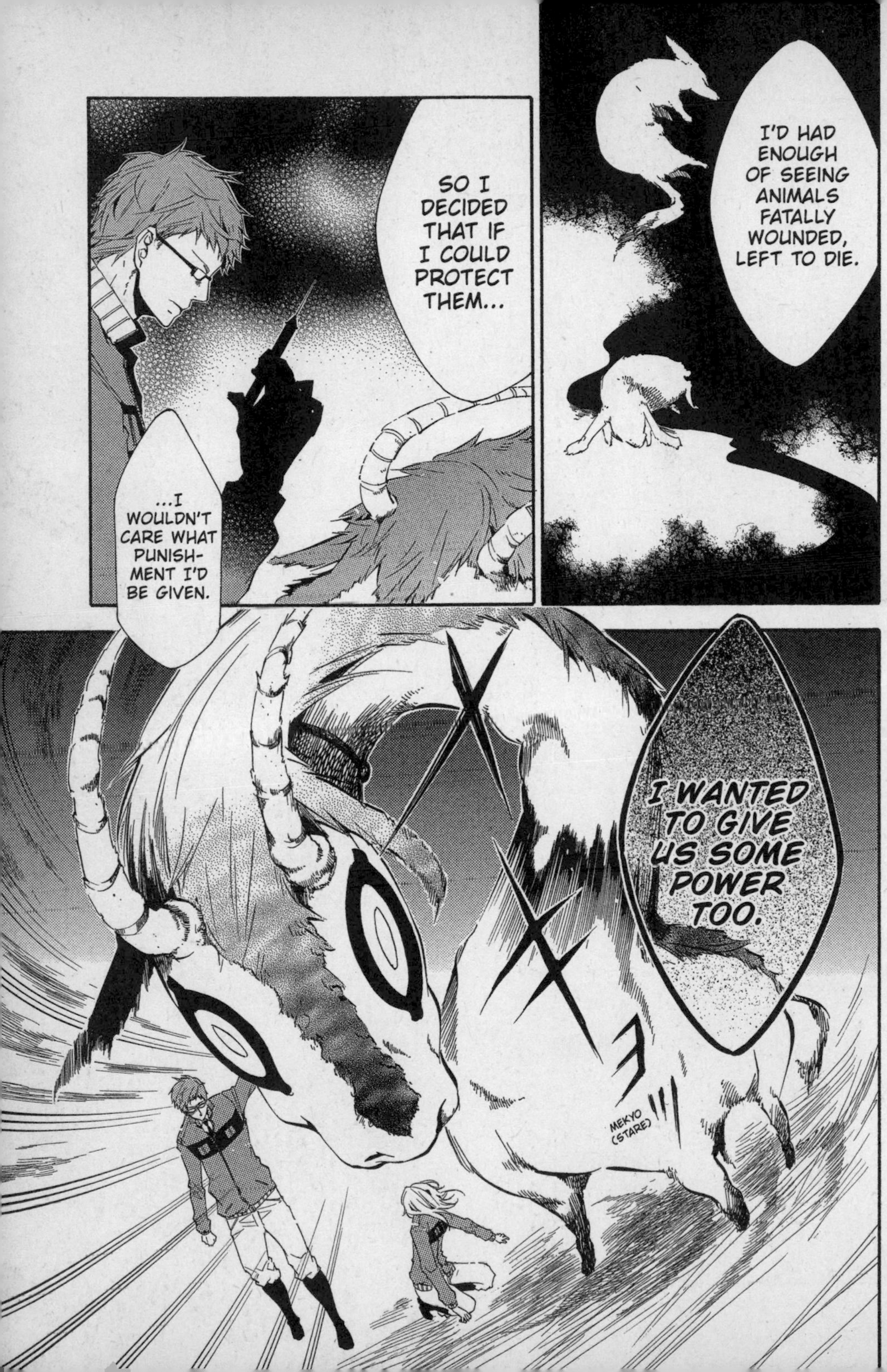

I'D HAD ENOUGH OF SEEING ANIMALS FATALLY WOUNDED, LEFT TO DIE.
SO I DECIDED THAT IF I COULD PROTECT THEM...
...I WOULDN'T CARE WHAT PUNISH-MENT I'D BE GIVEN.
I WANTED TO GIVE US SOME POWER TOO.
MEKYO (STARE)

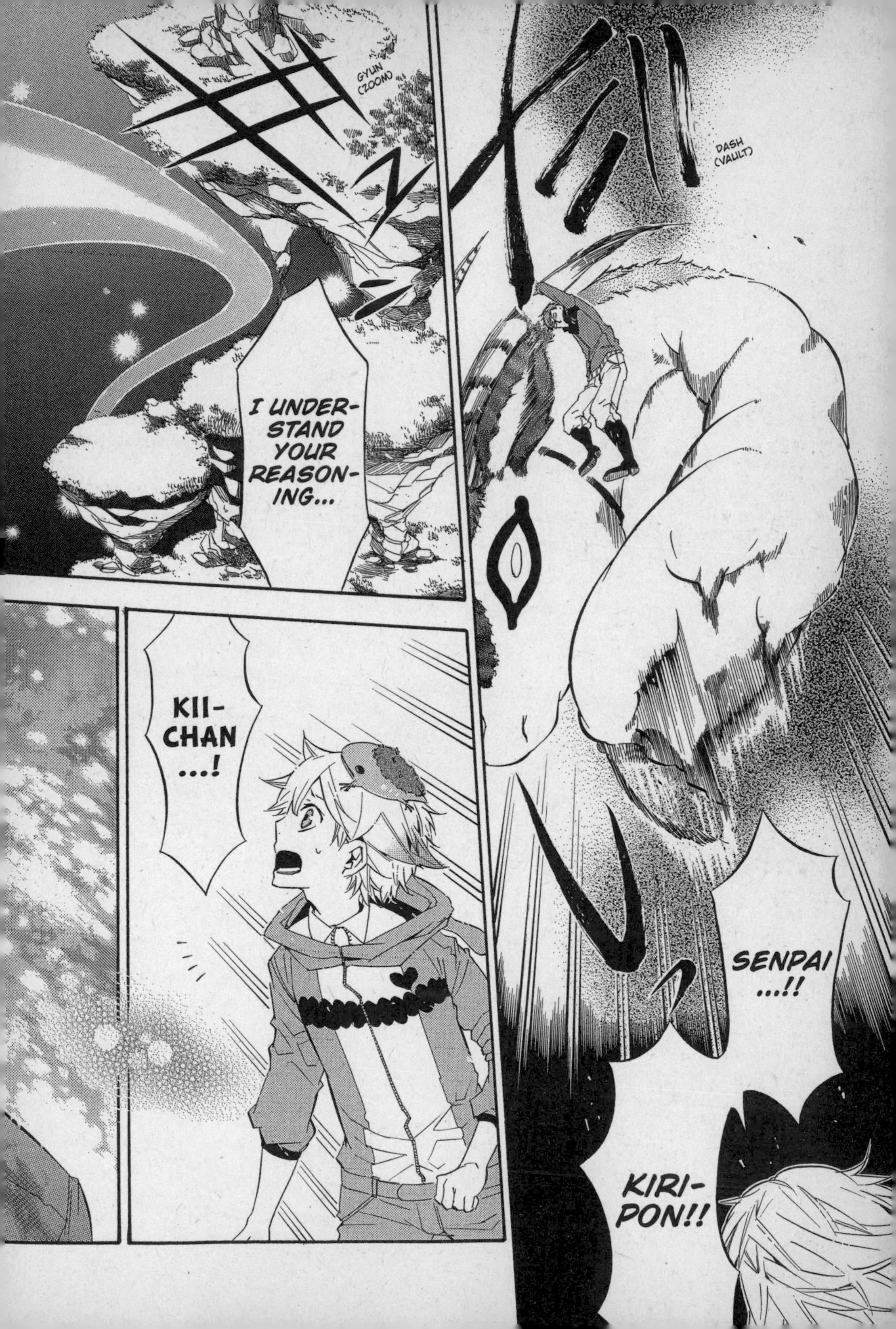
DASH
(VAULT)
SENPAI ...!!
KIRI-PON!!
GYUN
(ZOOM)
I UNDER-STAND YOUR REASON-ING...
KII-CHAN ...!

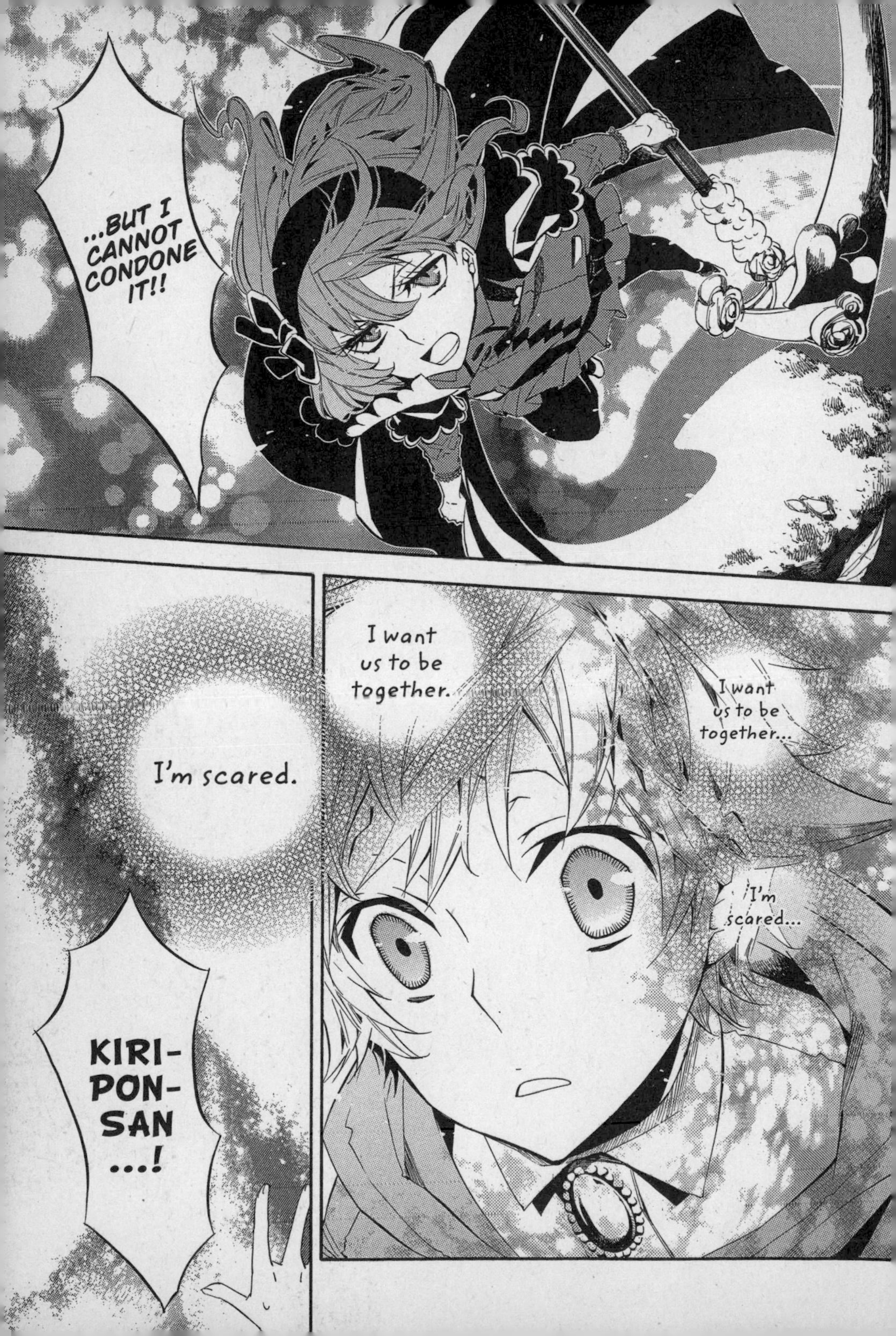
...BUT I CANNOT CONDONE IT!!
I want us to be together...
I'm scared...
I want us to be together.
I'm scared.
KIRI-PON-SAN...!

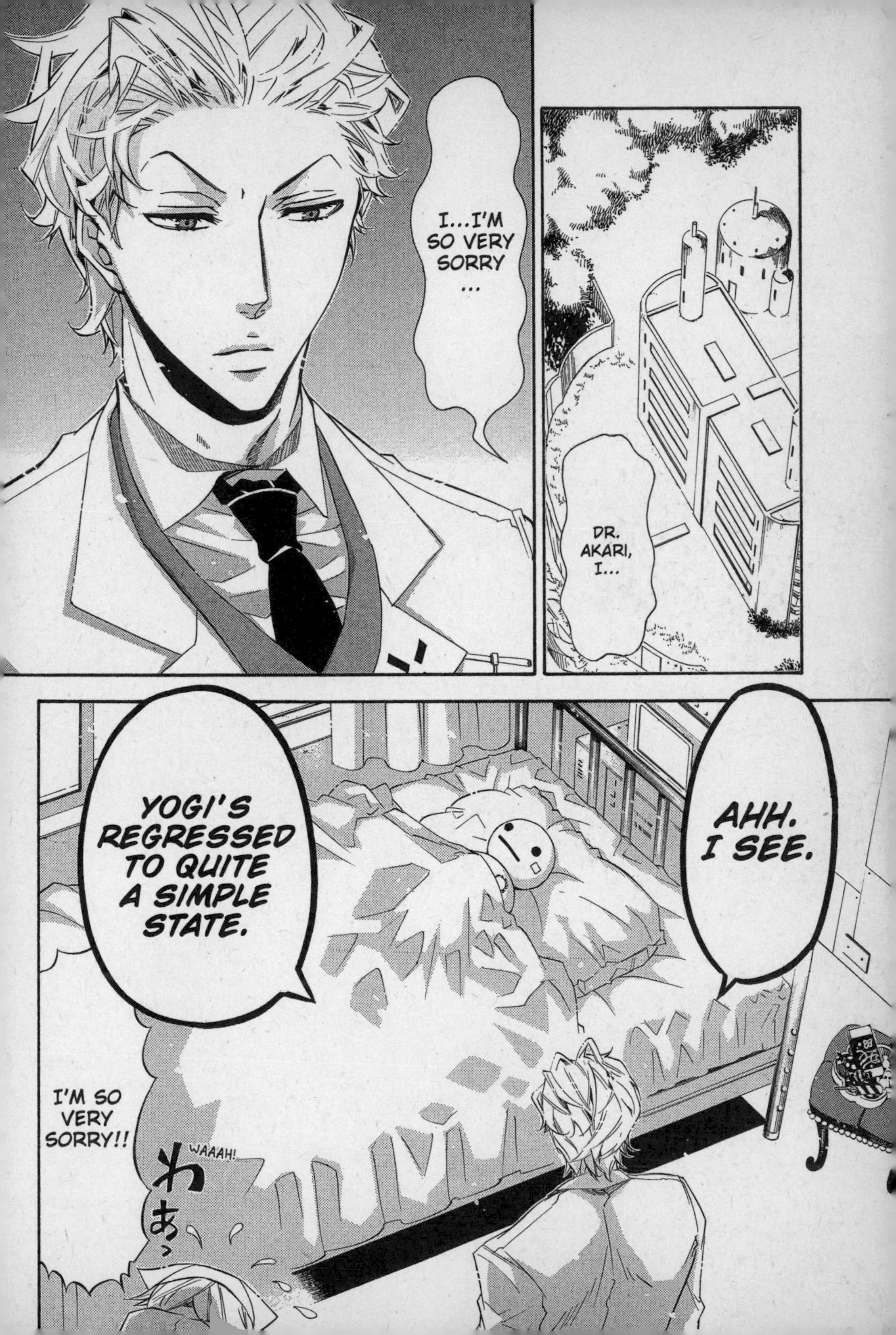
DR. AKARI, I...
I...I'M SO VERY SORRY ...
AHH. I SEE.
YOGI'S REGRESSED TO QUITE A SIMPLE STATE.
I'M SO VERY SORRY!!
WAAAH!
わあっ

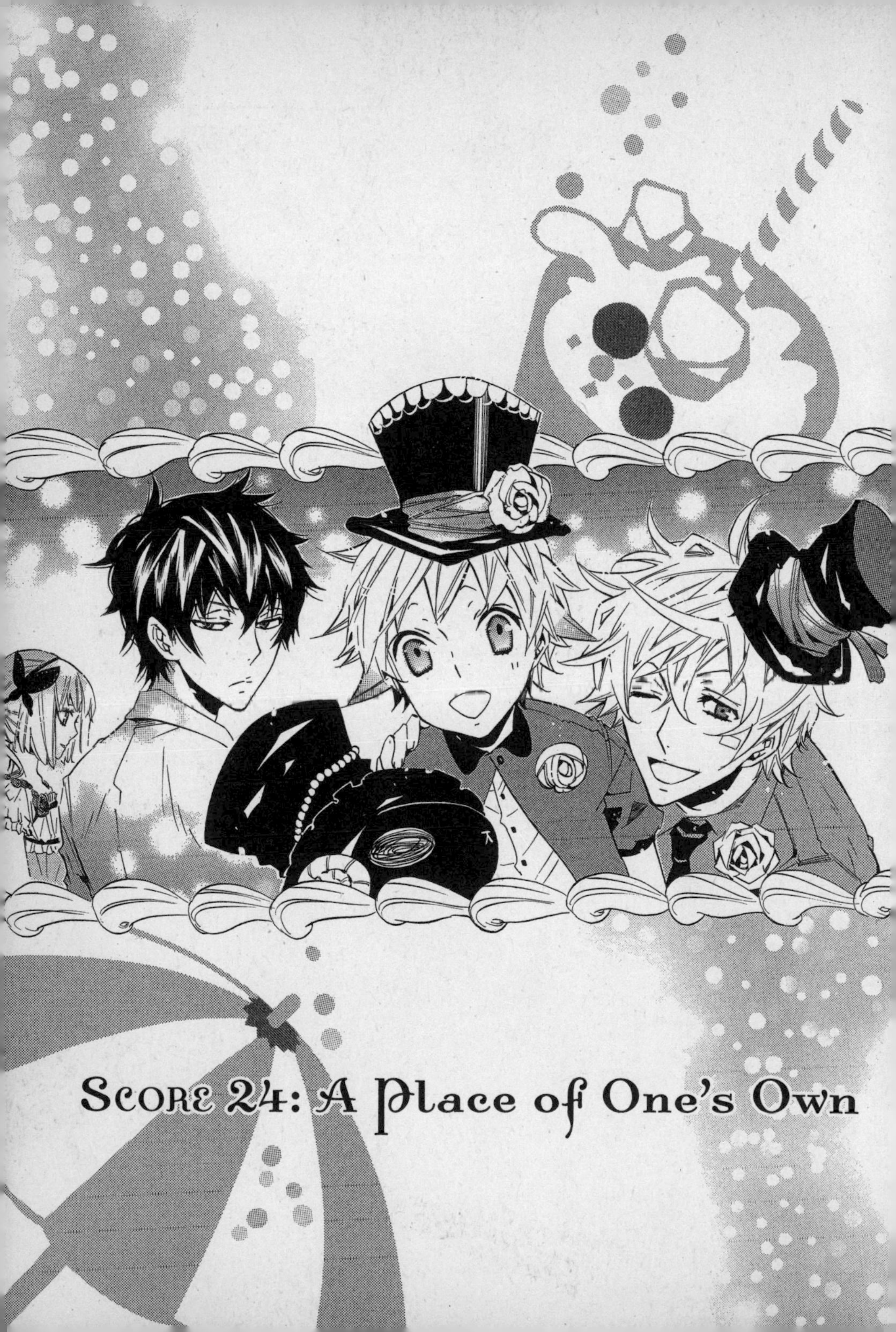
Score 24: A Place of One's Own

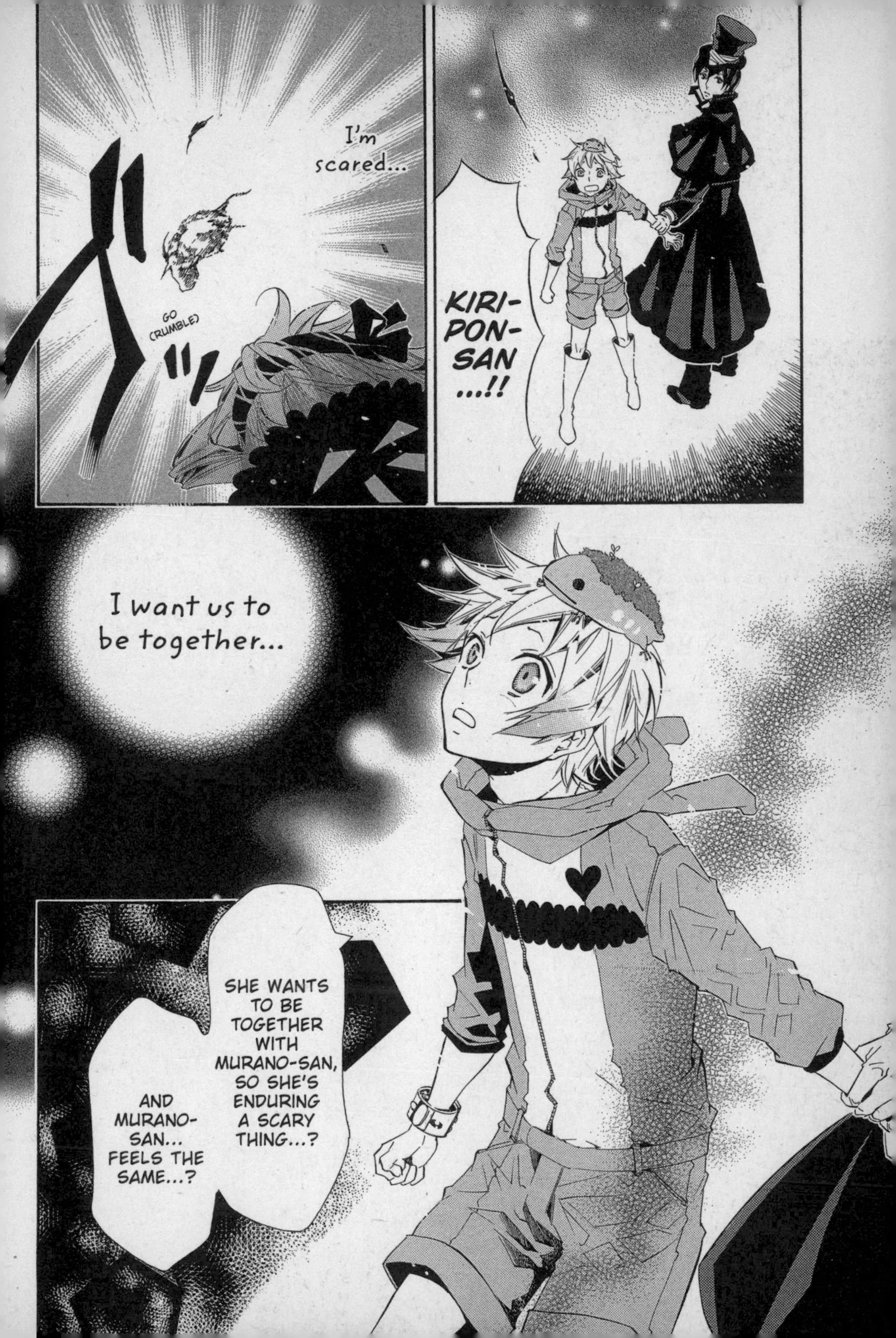
KIRI-PON-SAN...!!
I'm scared...
GO (RUMBLE)
I want us to be together...
SHE WANTS TO BE TOGETHER WITH MURANO-SAN, SO SHE'S ENDURING A SCARY THING...?
AND MURANO-SAN... FEELS THE SAME...?

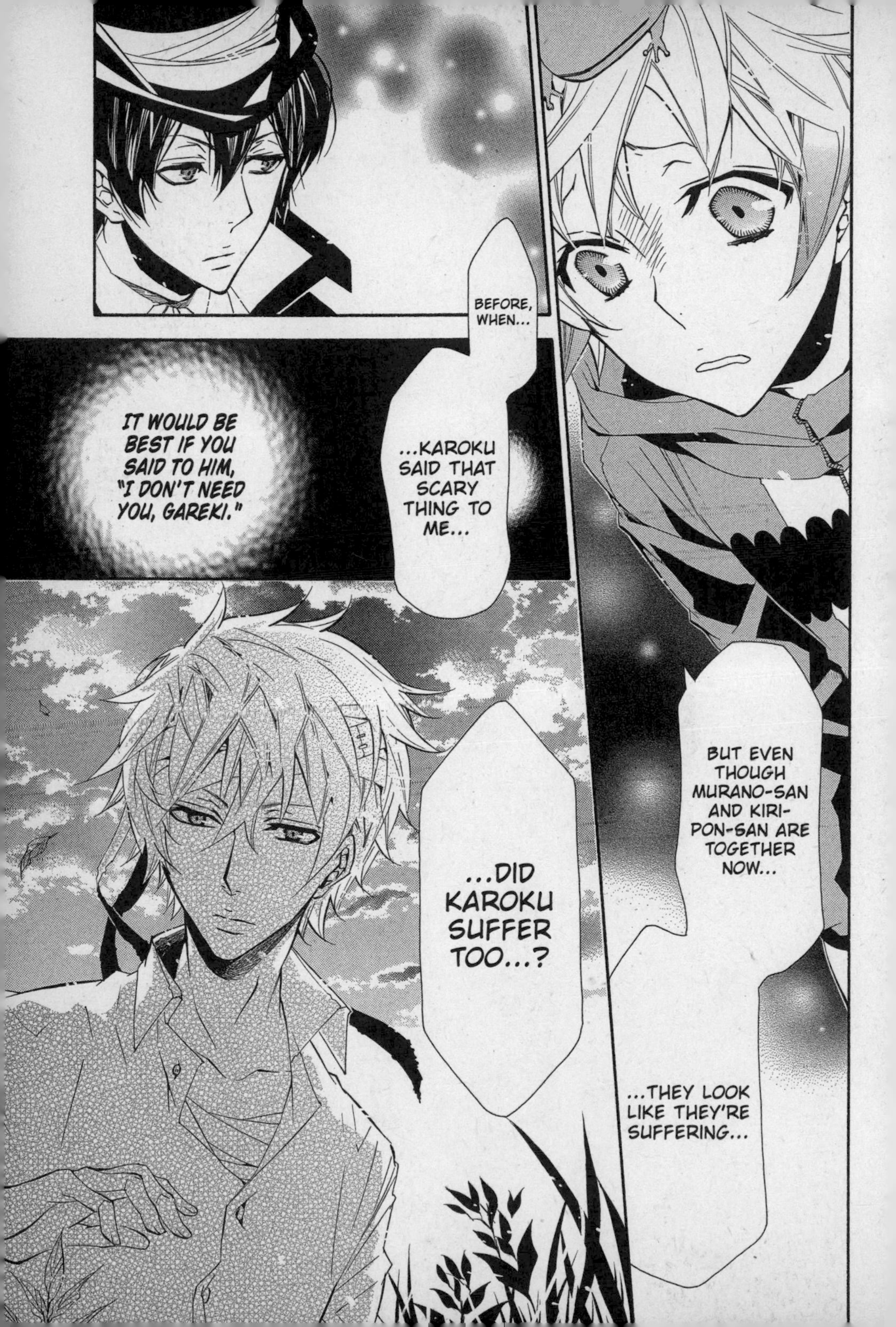
BEFORE, WHEN...
...KAROKU SAID THAT SCARY THING TO ME...
BUT EVEN THOUGH MURANO-SAN AND KIRI-PON-SAN ARE TOGETHER NOW...
...THEY LOOK LIKE THEY'RE SUFFERING...
IT WOULD BE BEST IF YOU SAID TO HIM, "I DON'T NEED YOU, GAREKI."
...DID KAROKU SUFFER TOO...?

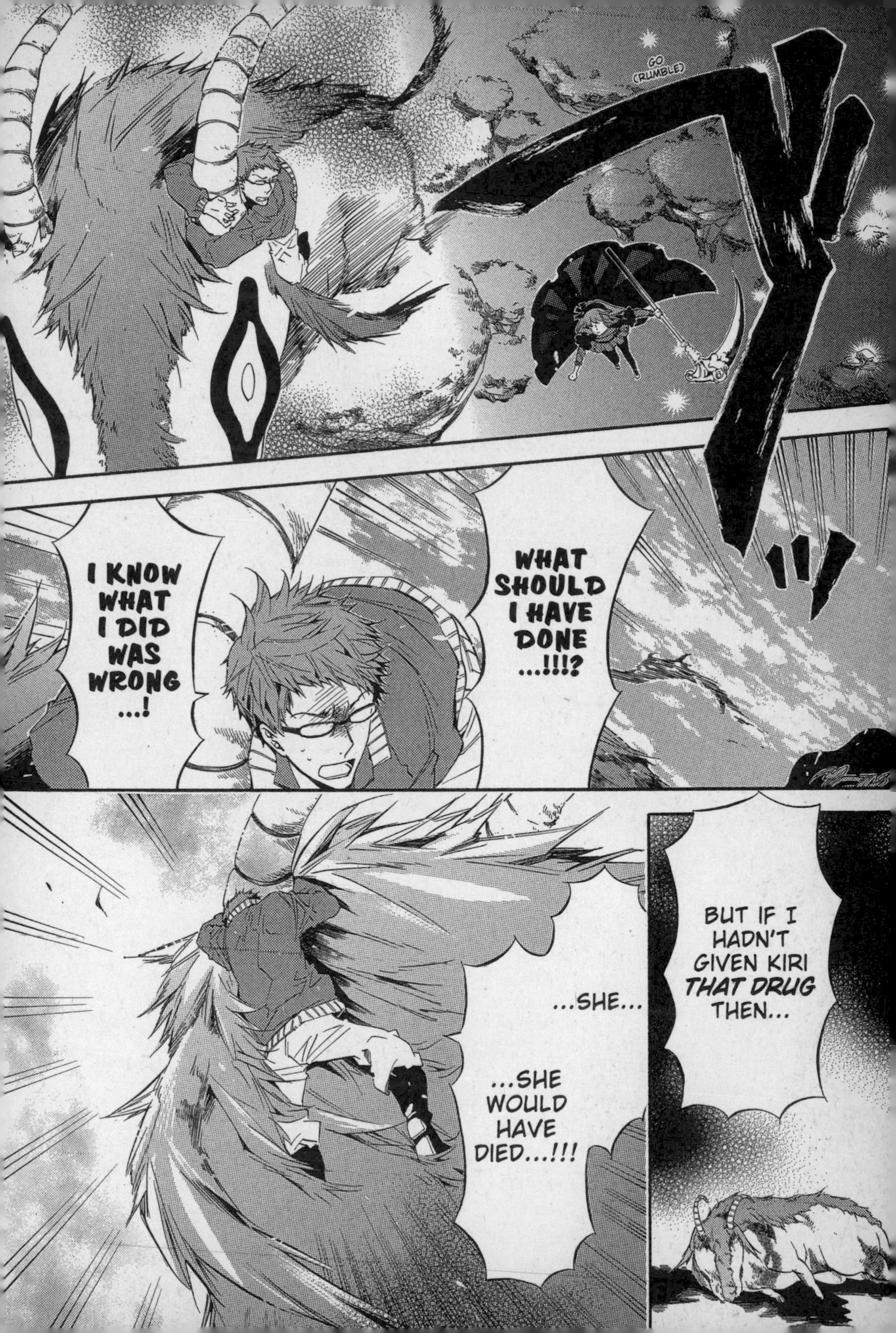
GO (RUMBLE)
WHAT SHOULD I HAVE DONE ...!!!?
I KNOW WHAT I DID WAS WRONG ...!
BUT IF I HADN'T GIVEN KIRI *THAT DRUG* THEN...
...SHE...
...SHE WOULD HAVE DIED...!!!

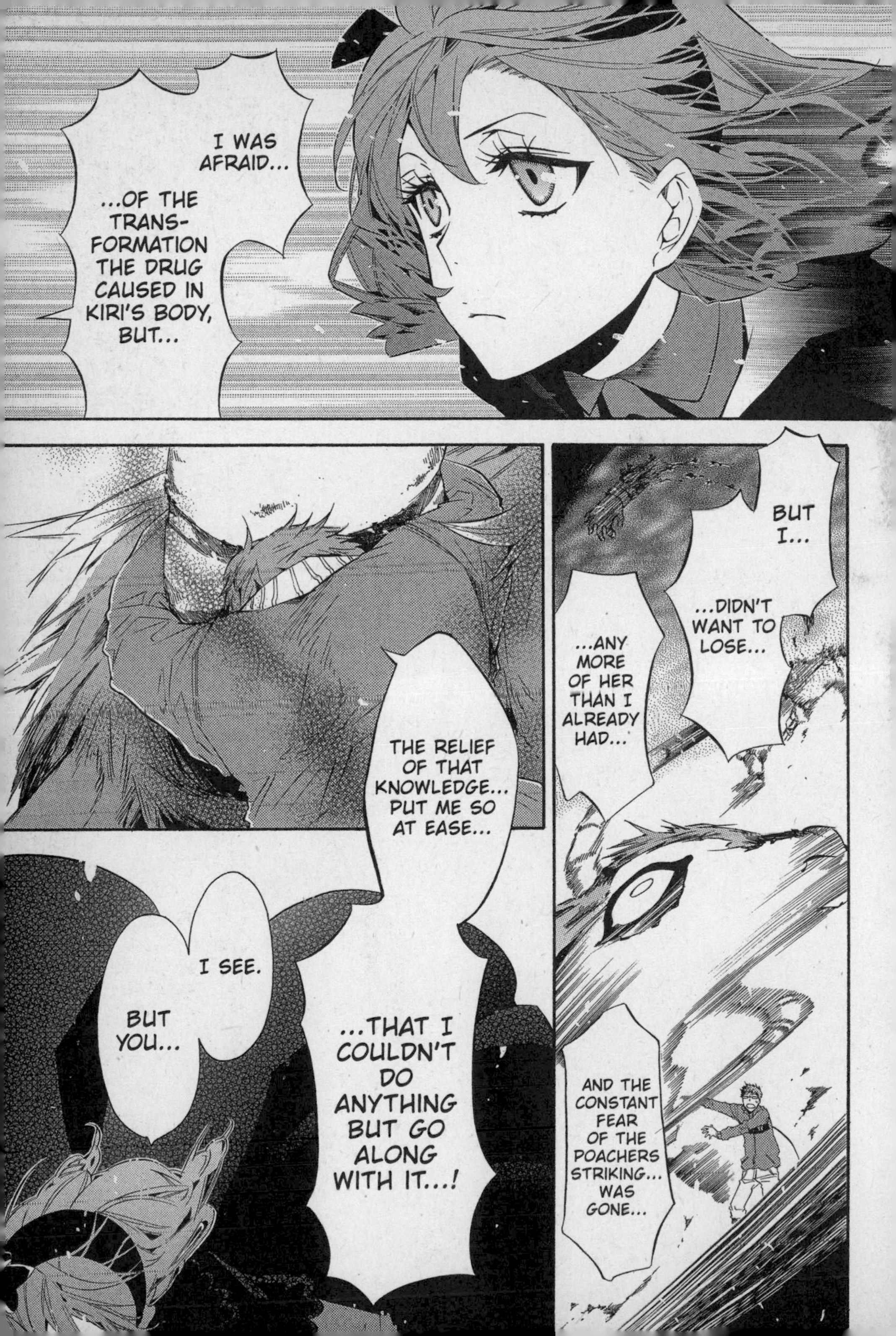
I WAS AFRAID...
...OF THE TRANS-FORMATION THE DRUG CAUSED IN KIRI'S BODY, BUT...
BUT I...
...DIDN'T WANT TO LOSE...
...ANY MORE OF HER THAN I ALREADY HAD...
AND THE CONSTANT FEAR OF THE POACHERS STRIKING... WAS GONE...
THE RELIEF OF THAT KNOWLEDGE... PUT ME SO AT EASE...
...THAT I COULDN'T DO ANYTHING BUT GO ALONG WITH IT...!
I SEE.
BUT YOU...

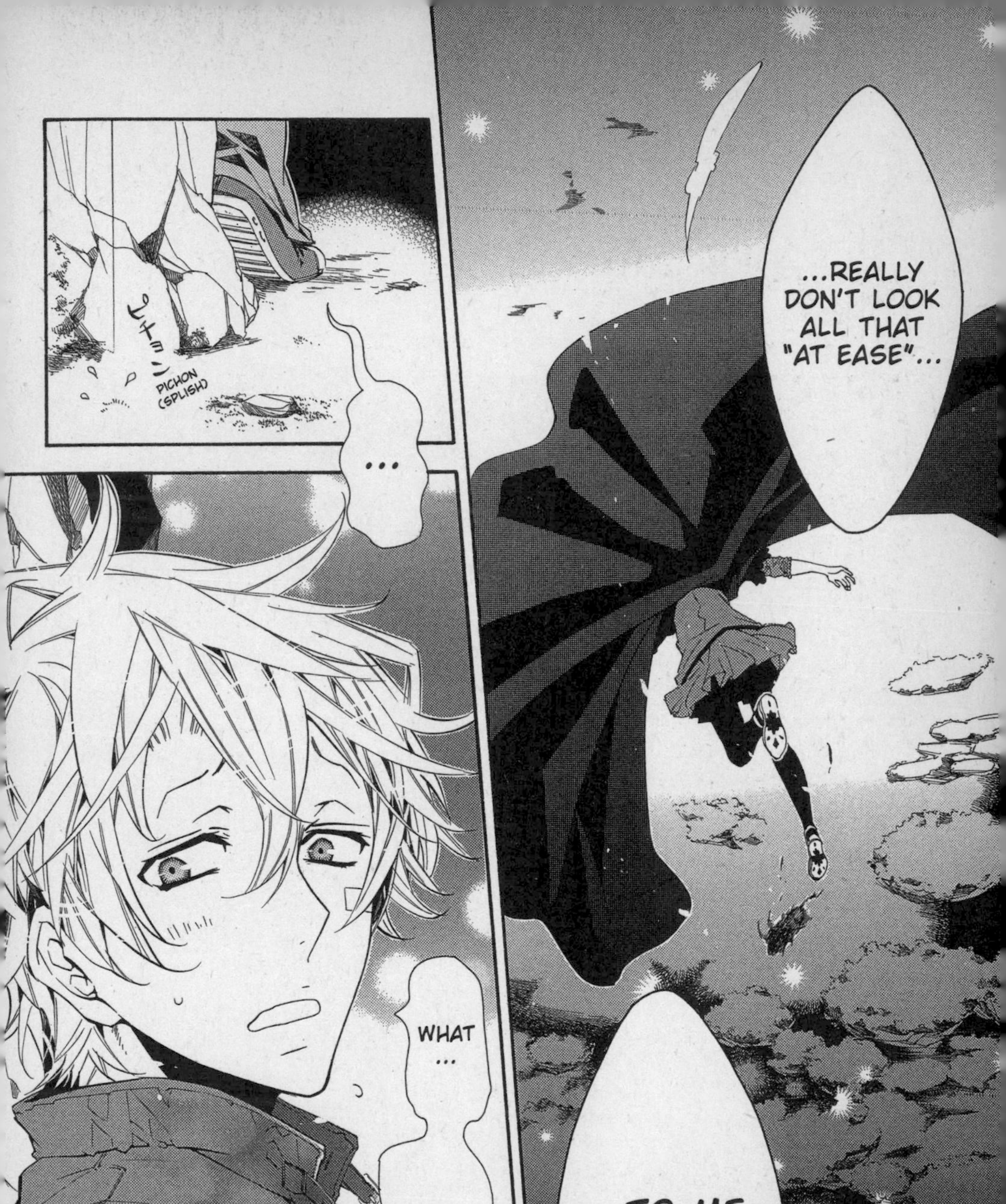

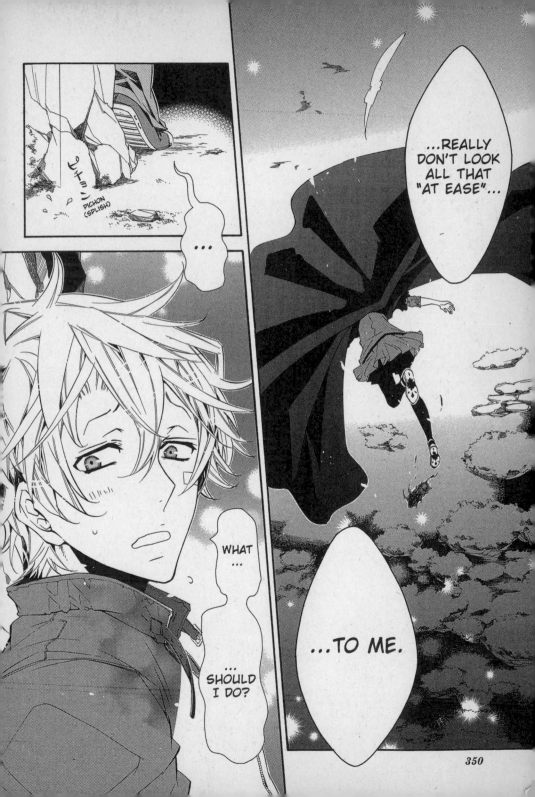

...REALLY DON'T LOOK ALL THAT "AT EASE"...
...TO ME.
ピチョン
PICHON (SPLISH)
...
WHAT ... ... SHOULD I DO?

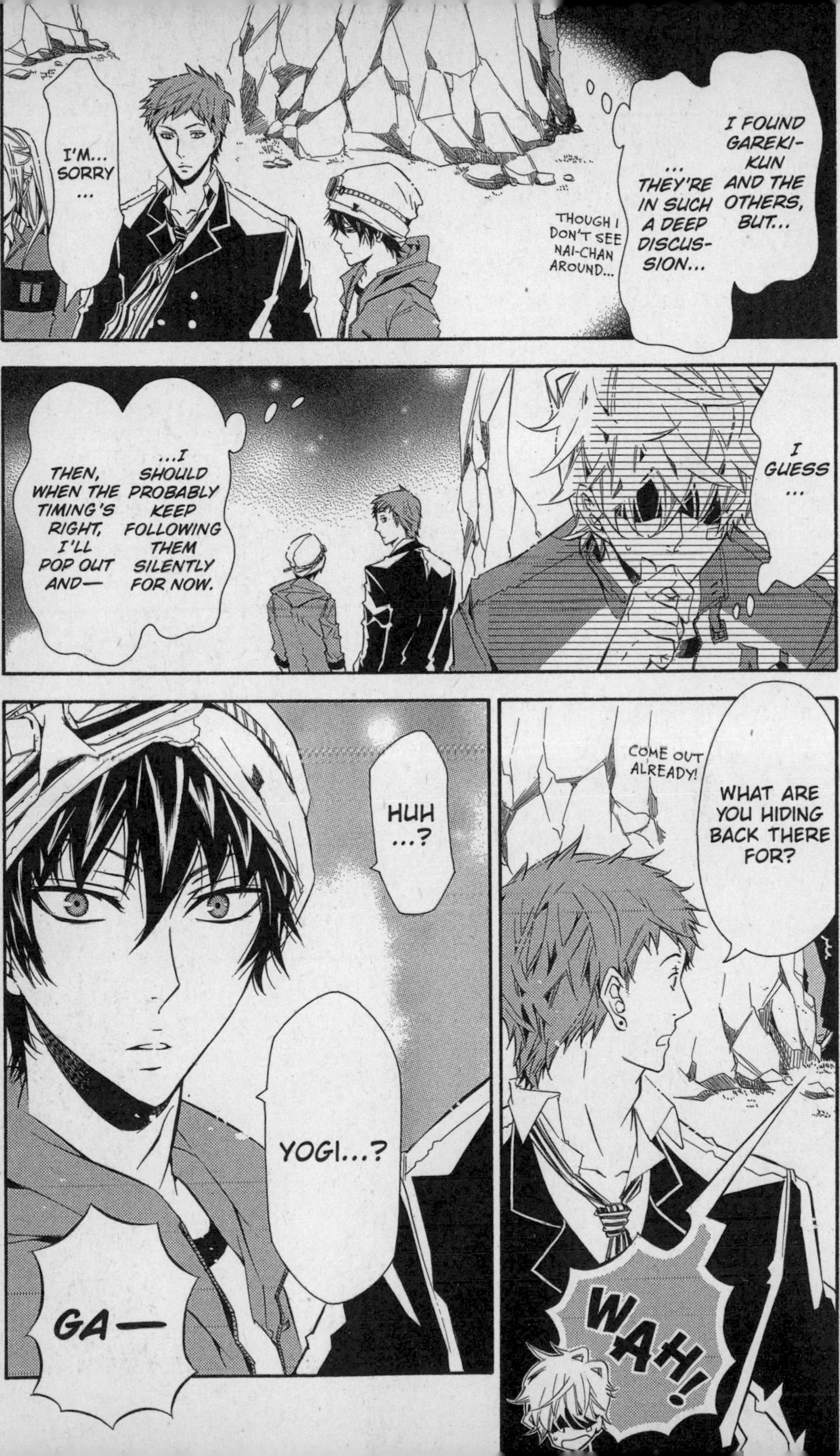
I FOUND GAREKI-KUN AND THE OTHERS, BUT...
...THEY'RE IN SUCH A DEEP DISCUSSION...
THOUGH I DON'T SEE NAI-CHAN AROUND...
I'M... SORRY...
I GUESS...
...I SHOULD PROBABLY KEEP FOLLOWING THEM SILENTLY FOR NOW.
THEN, WHEN THE TIMING'S RIGHT, I'LL POP OUT AND—
WHAT ARE YOU HIDING BACK THERE FOR?
COME OUT ALREADY!
WAH!
HUH...?
YOGI...?
GA—

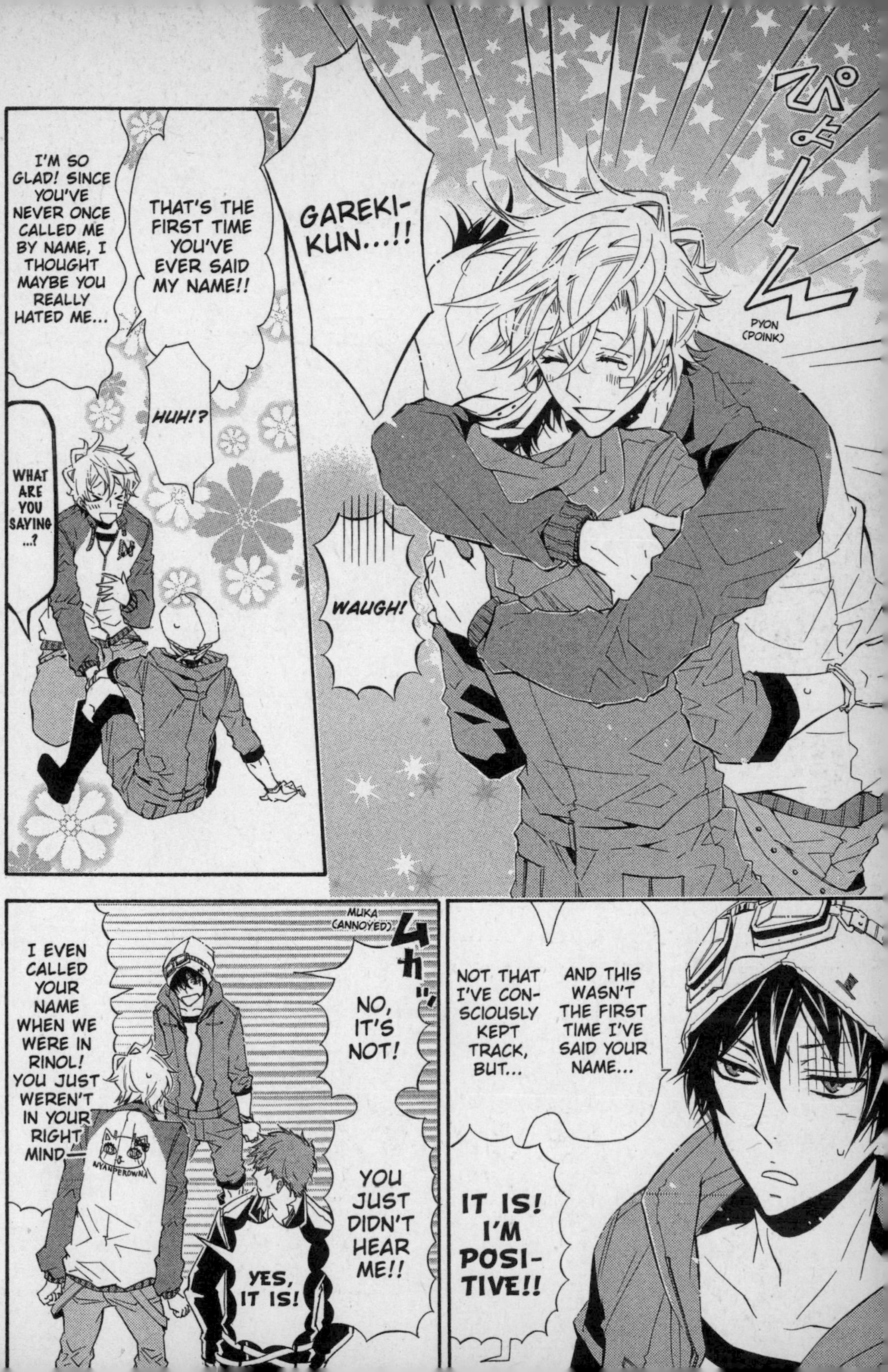
ぴょーん
PYON (POINK)
GAREKI-KUN...!!
WAUGH!
THAT'S THE FIRST TIME YOU'VE EVER SAID MY NAME!!
I'M SO GLAD! SINCE YOU'VE NEVER ONCE CALLED ME BY NAME, I THOUGHT MAYBE YOU REALLY HATED ME...
HUH!?
WHAT ARE YOU SAYING...?
AND THIS WASN'T THE FIRST TIME I'VE SAID YOUR NAME...
NOT THAT I'VE CONSCIOUSLY KEPT TRACK, BUT...
IT IS! I'M POSI-TIVE!!
ムカ
MUKA (ANNOYED)
NO, IT'S NOT!
I EVEN CALLED YOUR NAME WHEN WE WERE IN RINOL! YOU JUST WEREN'T IN YOUR RIGHT MIND—
NYANPEROWNA
YOU JUST DIDN'T HEAR ME!!
YES, IT IS!

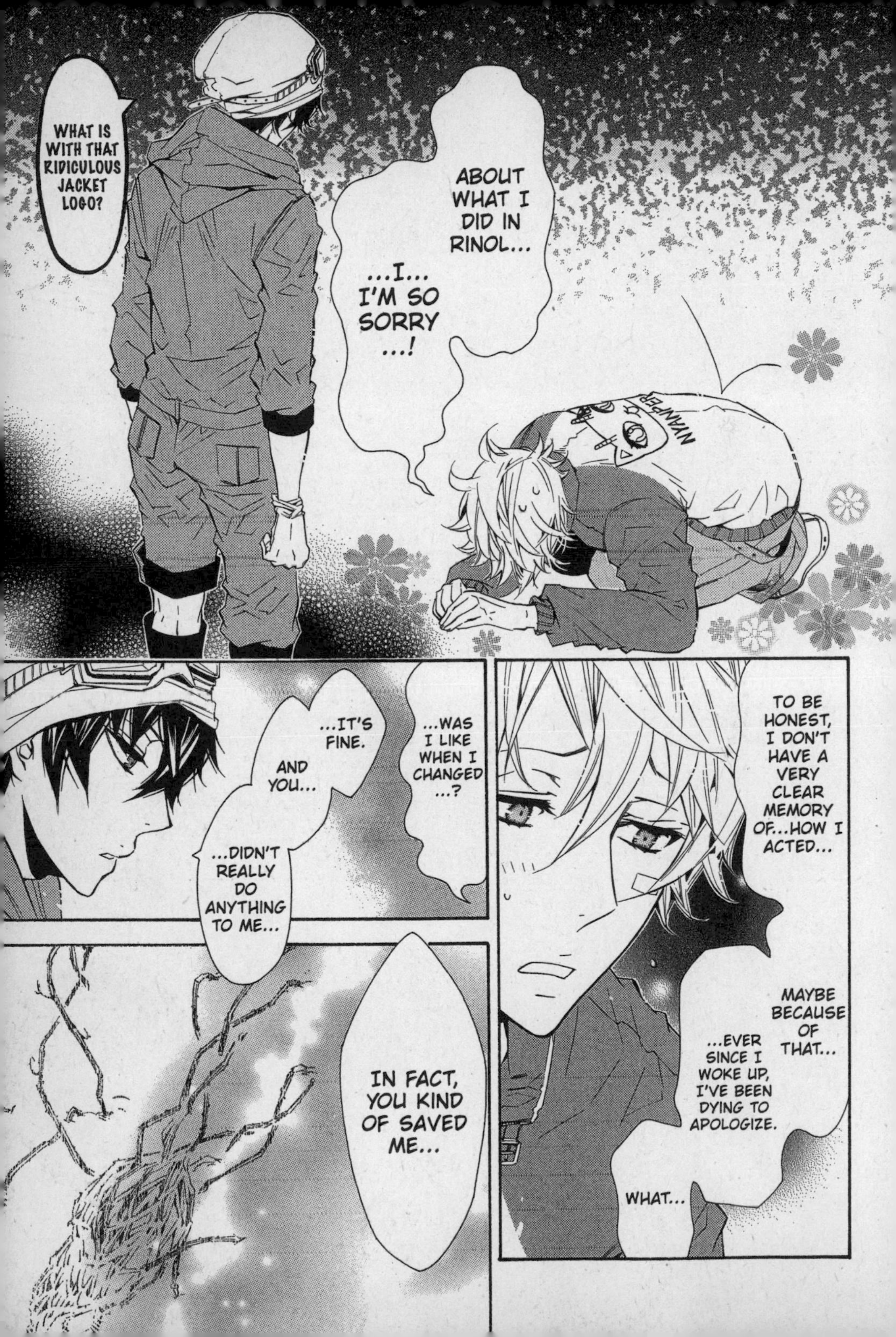
ABOUT WHAT I DID IN RINOL...
...I... I'M SO SORRY ...!
WHAT IS WITH THAT RIDICULOUS JACKET LOGO?
TO BE HONEST, I DON'T HAVE A VERY CLEAR MEMORY OF...HOW I ACTED...
...WAS I LIKE WHEN I CHANGED ...?
MAYBE BECAUSE OF THAT...
...EVER SINCE I WOKE UP, I'VE BEEN DYING TO APOLOGIZE.
WHAT...
...IT'S FINE.
AND YOU...
...DIDN'T REALLY DO ANYTHING TO ME...
IN FACT, YOU KIND OF SAVED ME...

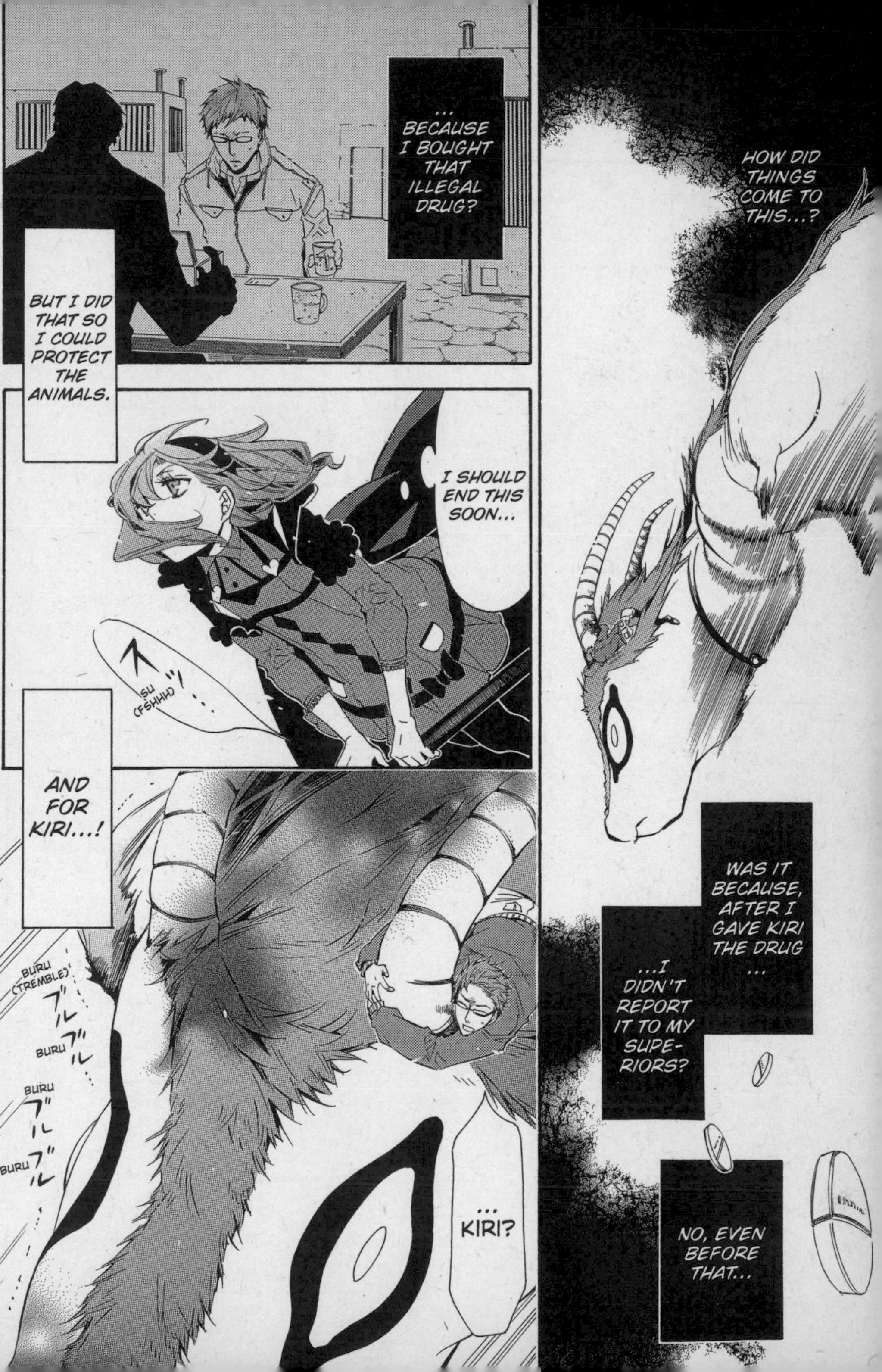
HOW DID THINGS COME TO THIS...?
WAS IT BECAUSE, AFTER I GAVE KIRI THE DRUG ...
...I DIDN'T REPORT IT TO MY SUPER-IORS?
NO, EVEN BEFORE THAT...
... BECAUSE I BOUGHT THAT ILLEGAL DRUG?
BUT I DID THAT SO I COULD PROTECT THE ANIMALS.
I SHOULD END THIS SOON...
SU (FSHHH)
AND FOR KIRI...!
BURU (TREMBLE)
BURU
BURU
BURU
... KIRI?

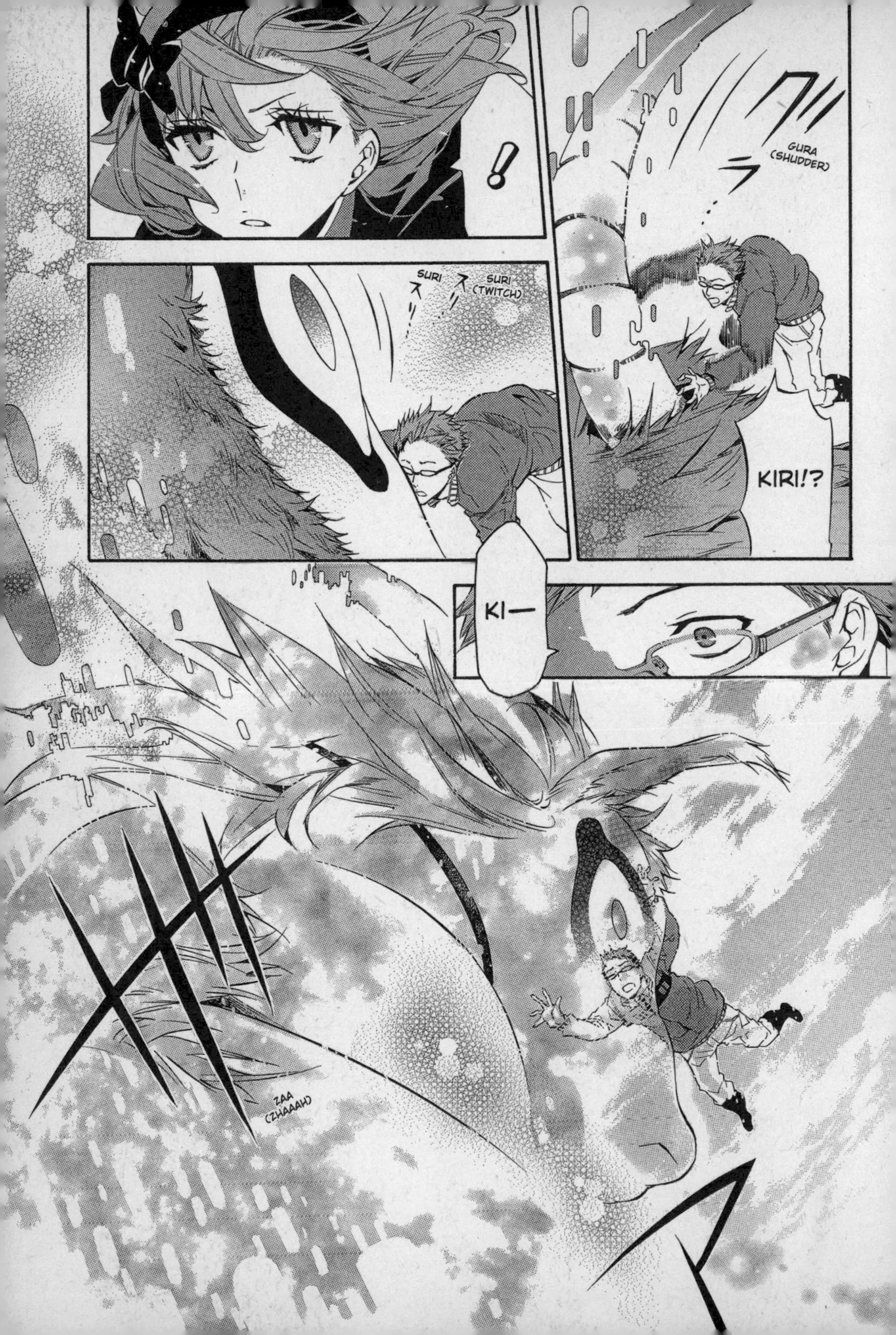
GURA (SHUDDER)
KIRI!?
SURI SURI (TWITCH)
!
KI—
ZAA (ZHAAAH)

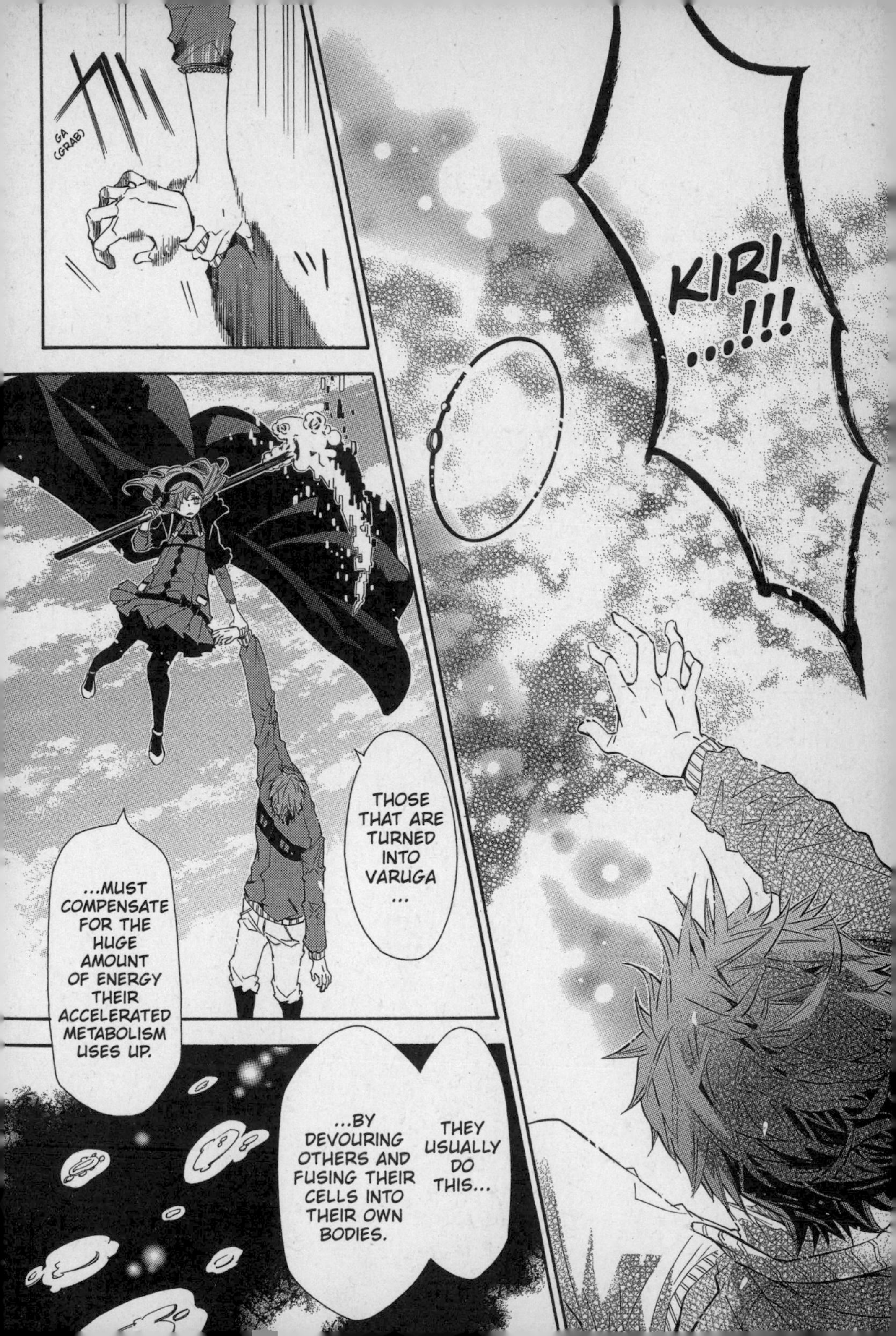
KIRI ...!!!
GA (GRAB)
THOSE THAT ARE TURNED INTO VARUGA ...
...MUST COMPENSATE FOR THE HUGE AMOUNT OF ENERGY THEIR ACCELERATED METABOLISM USES UP.
THEY USUALLY DO THIS...
...BY DEVOURING OTHERS AND FUSING THEIR CELLS INTO THEIR OWN BODIES.

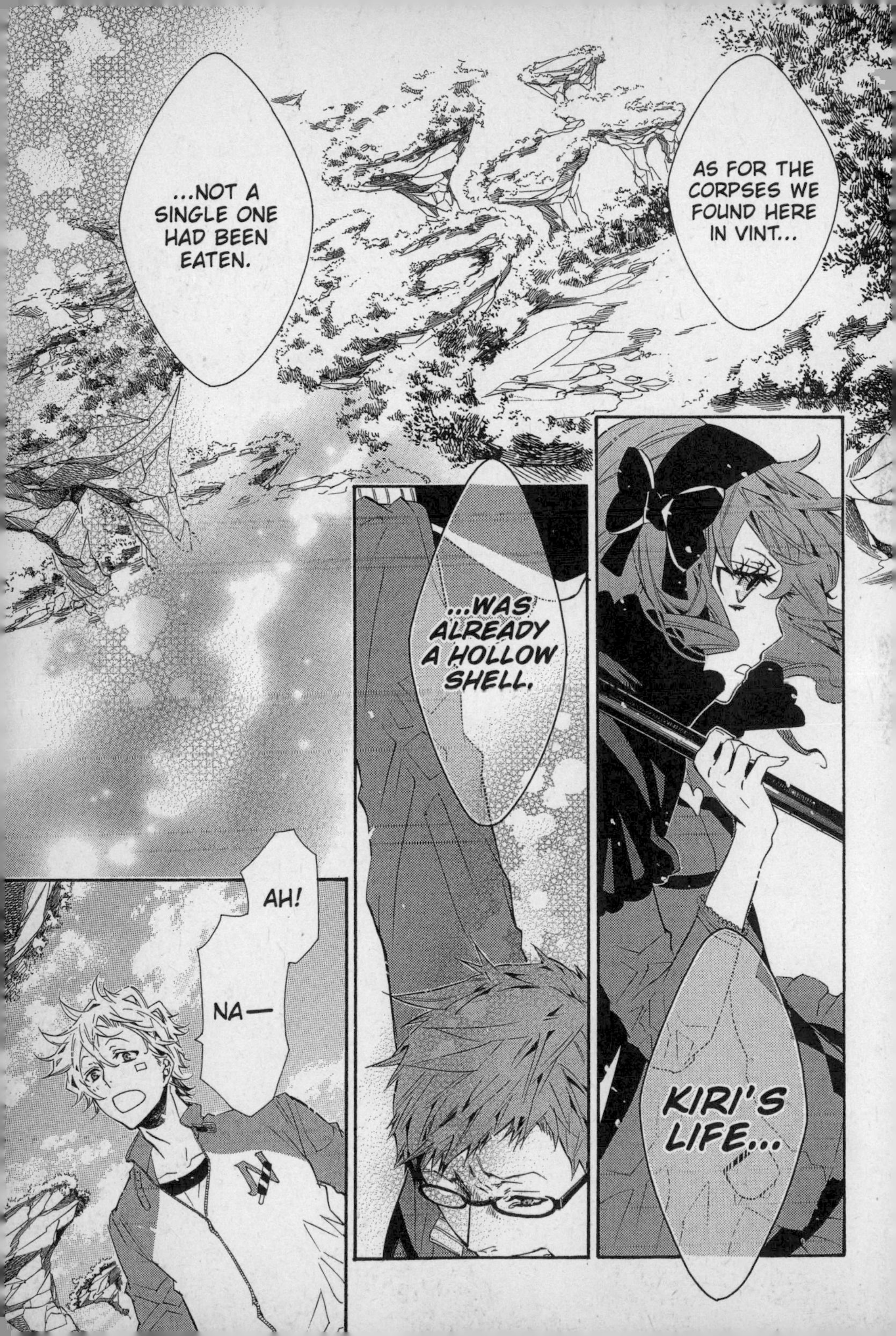
AS FOR THE CORPSES WE FOUND HERE IN VINT...
...NOT A SINGLE ONE HAD BEEN EATEN.
KIRI'S LIFE...
...WAS ALREADY A HOLLOW SHELL.
AH!
NA—

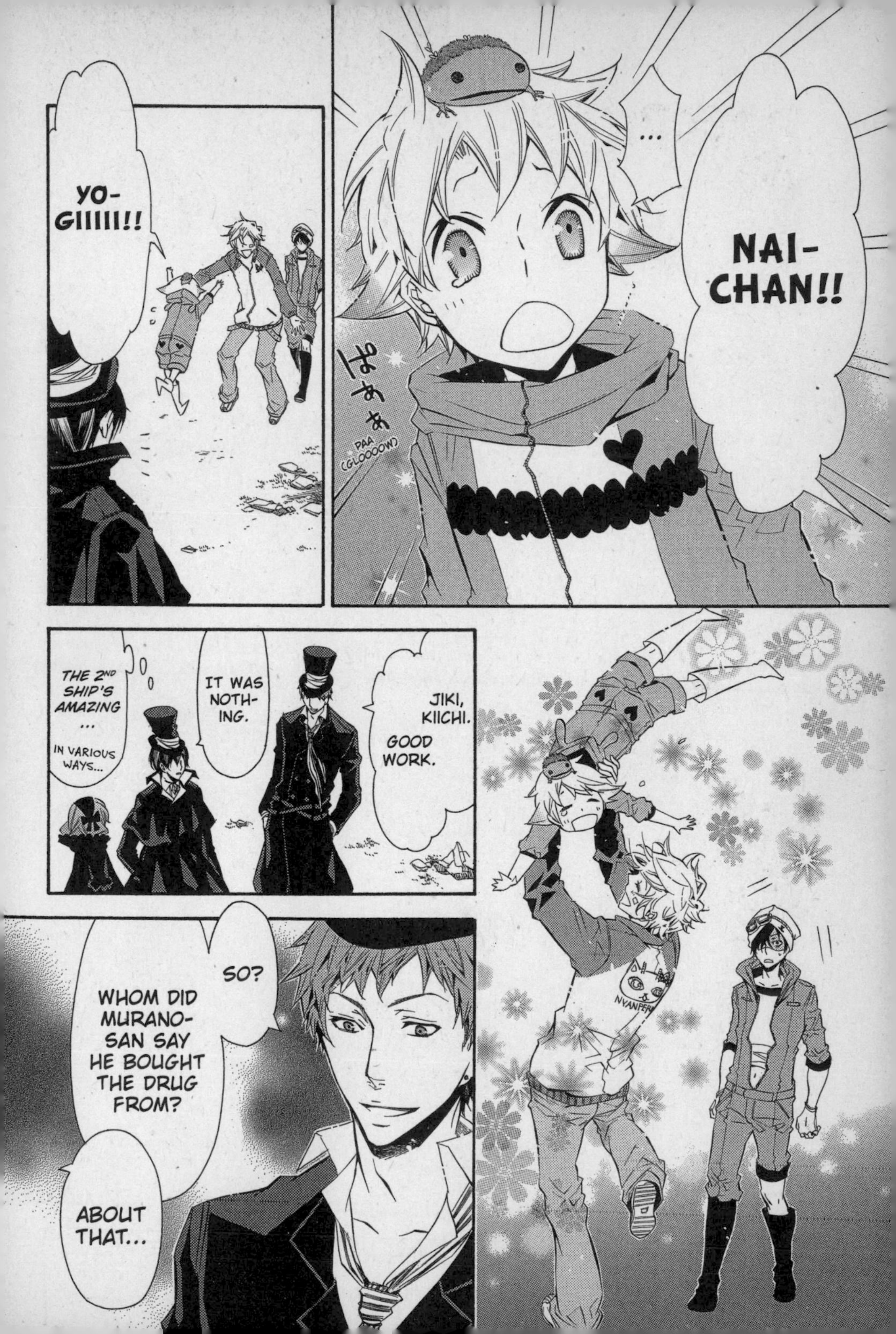

NAI-CHAN!!
...
ぱあぁ
PAA (GLOOOOW)
YO-GIIIIII!!
NYANPER
JIKI, KIICHI. GOOD WORK.
IT WAS NOTHING.
THE 2ND SHIP'S AMAZING ...
IN VARIOUS WAYS...
SO?
WHOM DID MURANO-SAN SAY HE BOUGHT THE DRUG FROM?
ABOUT THAT...

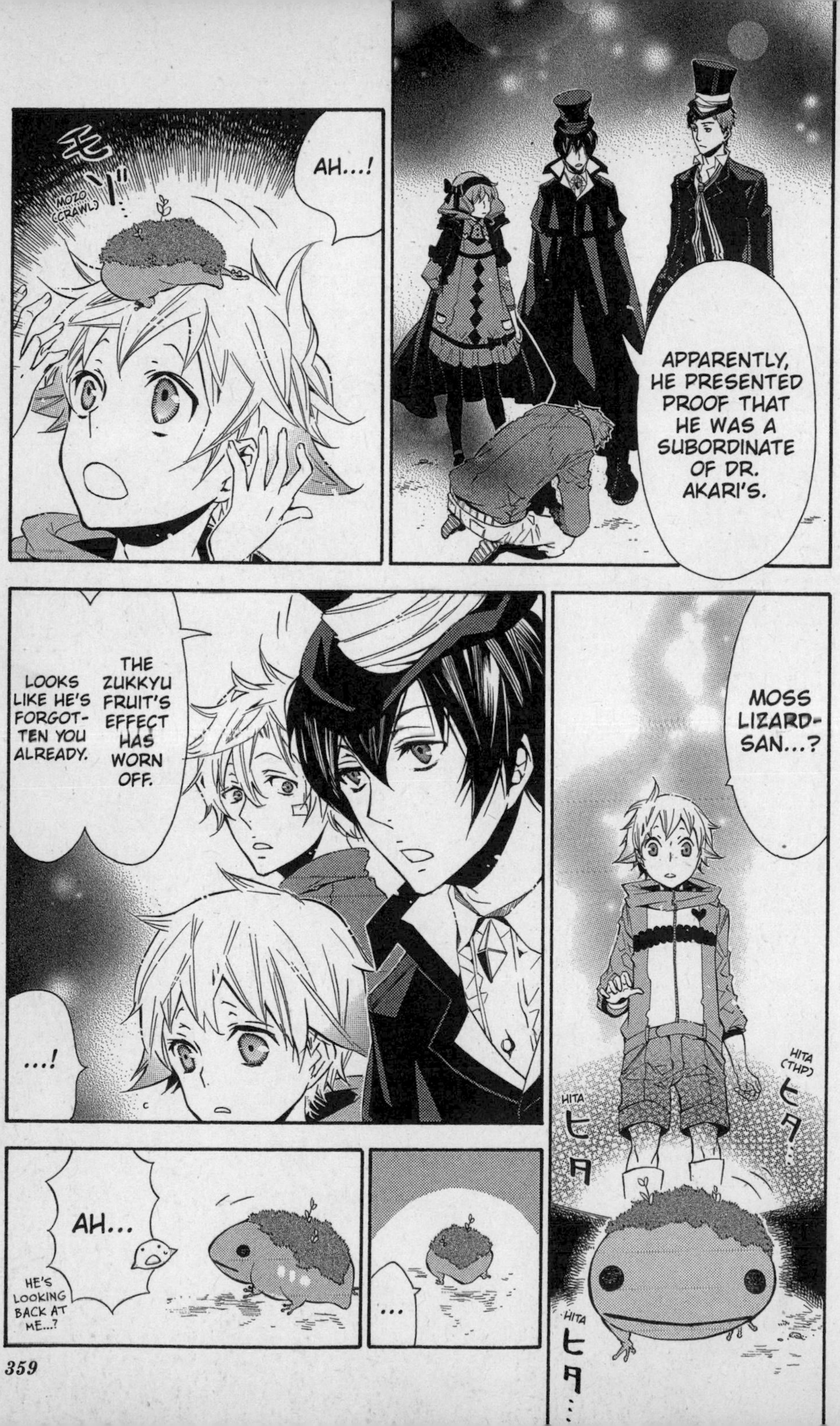
APPARENTLY, HE PRESENTED PROOF THAT HE WAS A SUBORDINATE OF DR. AKARI'S.
モゾ
MOZO (CRAWL)
AH...!
MOSS LIZARD-SAN...?
ヒタ
HITA (THP)
ヒタ
HITA
ヒタ
HITA
ヒタ...
THE ZUKKYU FRUIT'S EFFECT HAS WORN OFF.
LOOKS LIKE HE'S FORGOT-TEN YOU ALREADY.
...!
...
AH...
HE'S LOOKING BACK AT ME...?

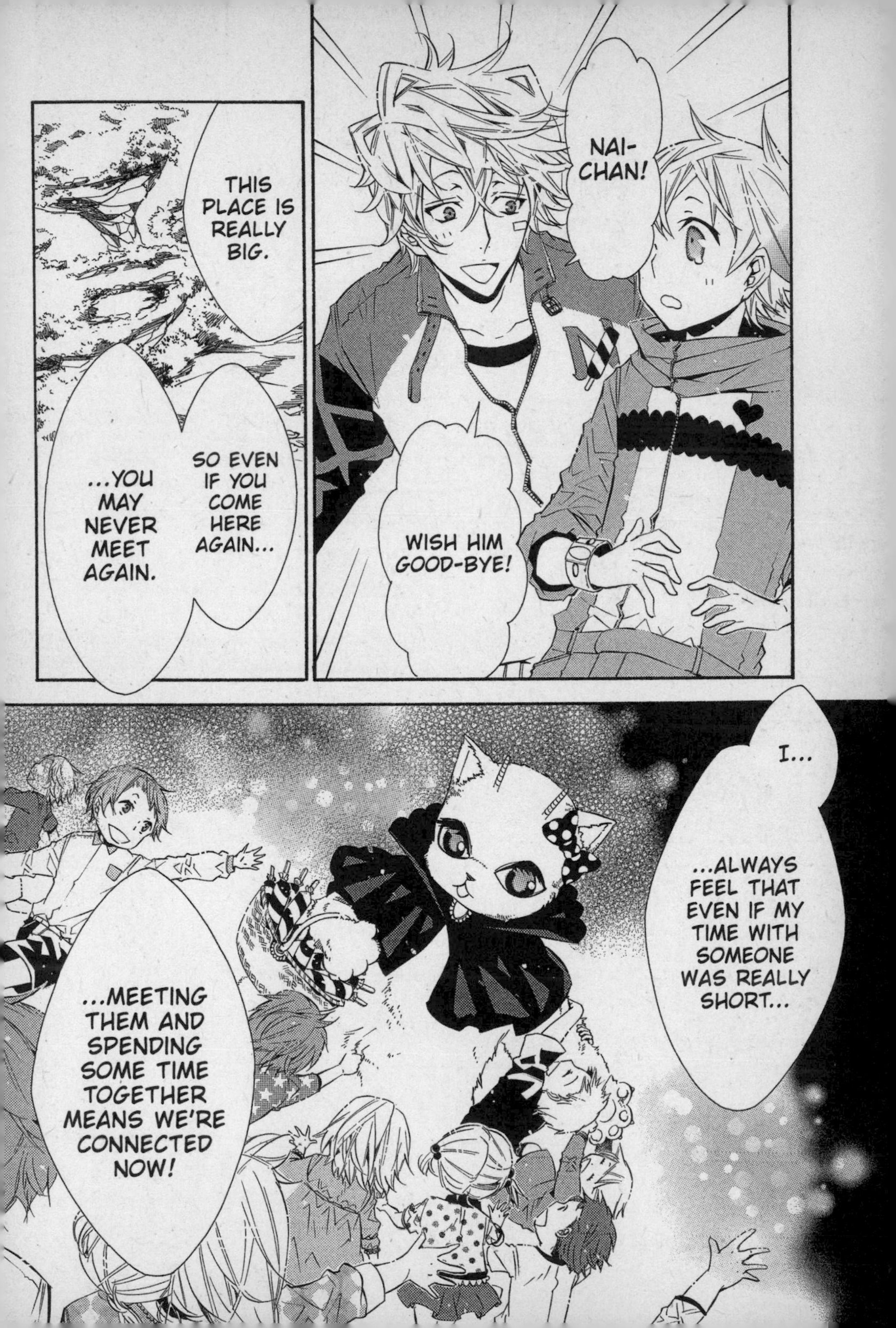
NAI-CHAN!
WISH HIM GOOD-BYE!
THIS PLACE IS REALLY BIG.
SO EVEN IF YOU COME HERE AGAIN...
...YOU MAY NEVER MEET AGAIN.
I...
...ALWAYS FEEL THAT EVEN IF MY TIME WITH SOMEONE WAS REALLY SHORT...
...MEETING THEM AND SPENDING SOME TIME TOGETHER MEANS WE'RE CONNECTED NOW!

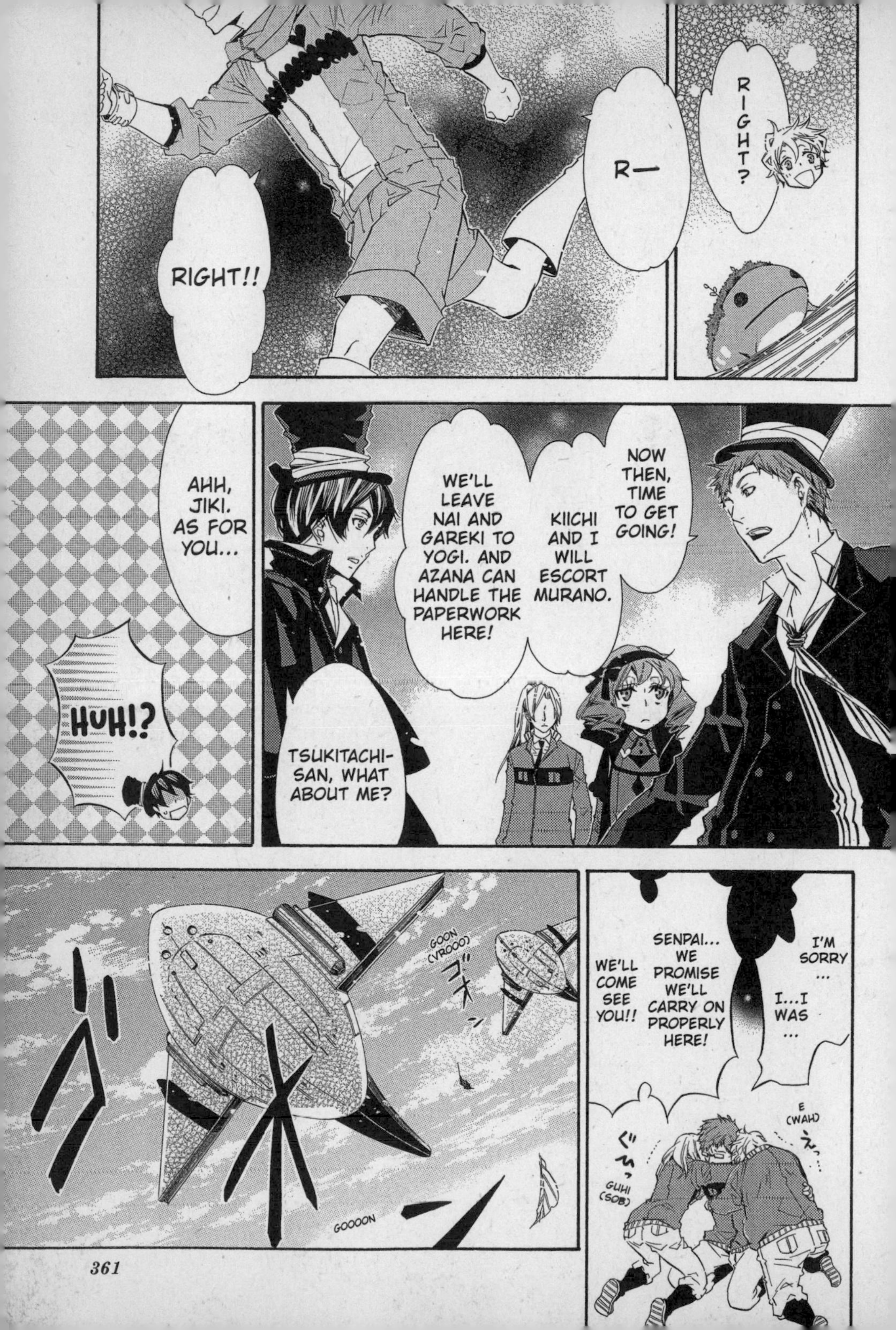
RIGHT?
R—
RIGHT!!
NOW THEN, TIME TO GET GOING!
KIICHI AND I WILL ESCORT MURANO.
WE'LL LEAVE NAI AND GAREKI TO YOGI. AND AZANA CAN HANDLE THE PAPERWORK HERE!
TSUKITACHI-SAN, WHAT ABOUT ME?
AHH, JIKI. AS FOR YOU...
HUH!?
I'M SORRY ... I...I WAS ...
SENPAI... WE PROMISE WE'LL CARRY ON PROPERLY HERE!
WE'LL COME SEE YOU!!
E (WAH)
GUHI (SOB)
GOON (VROOO)
GOOOON

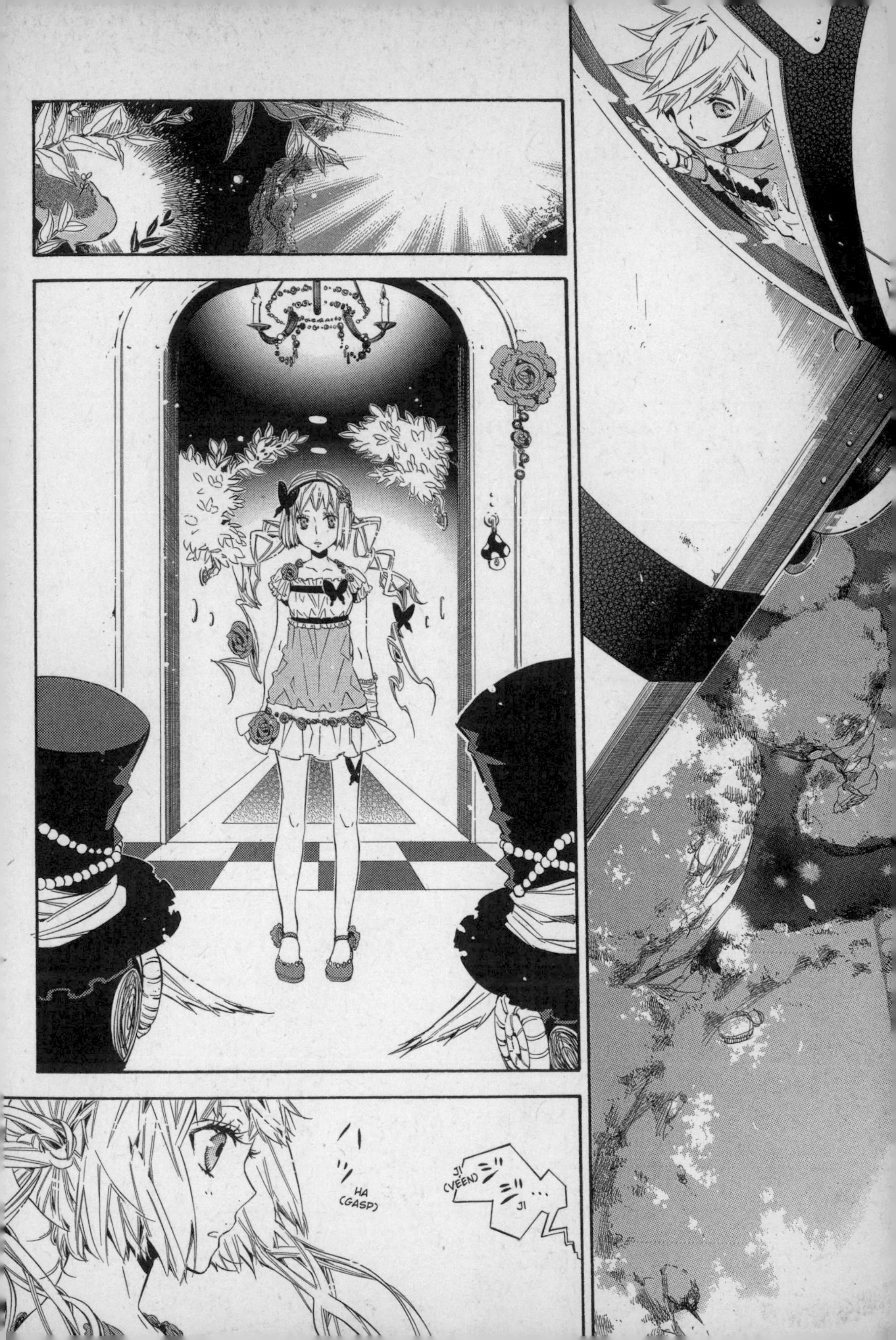
JI (VEEN) JI...
HA (GASP)

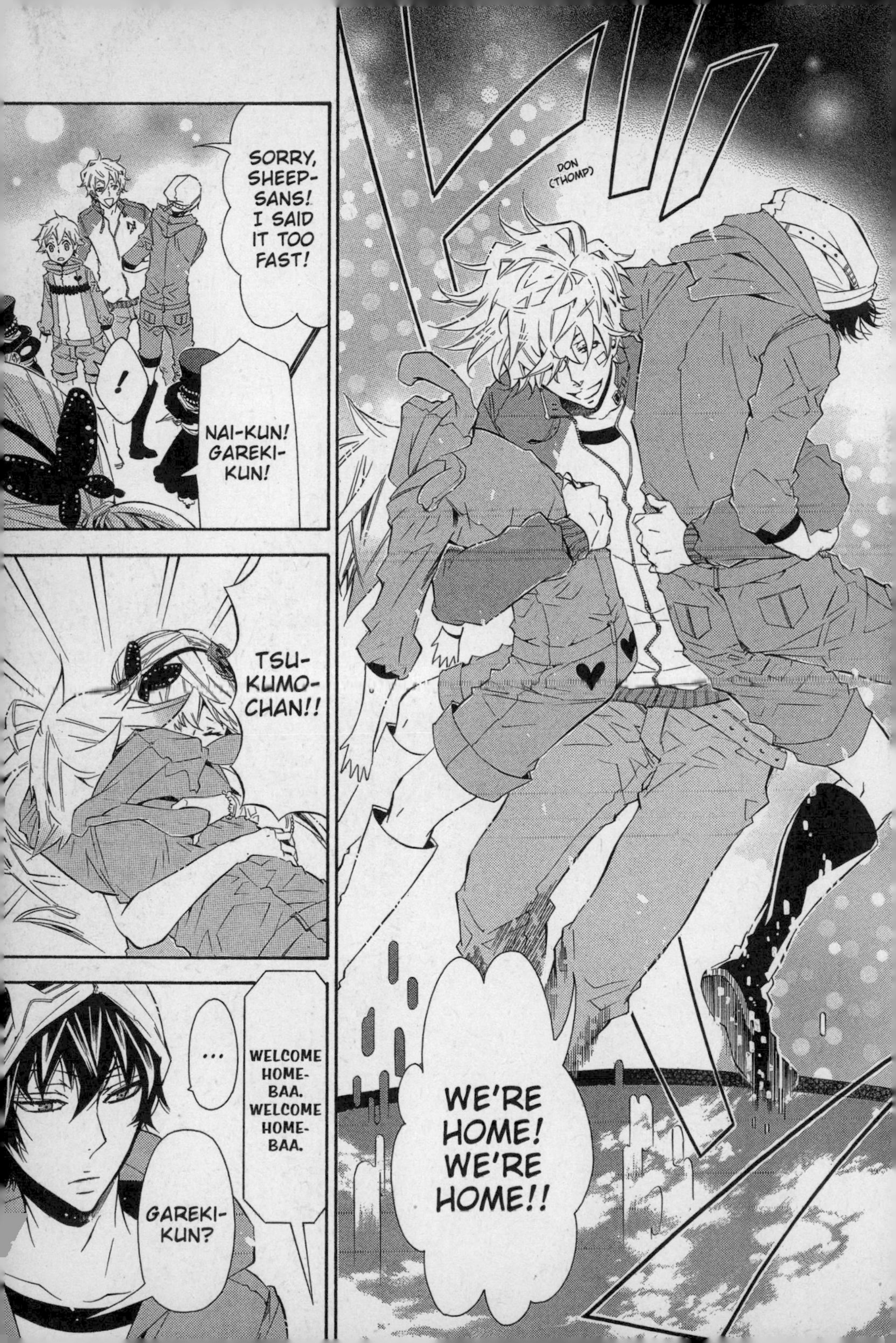
DON (THOMP)
WE'RE HOME! WE'RE HOME!!
SORRY, SHEEP-SANS! I SAID IT TOO FAST!
!
NAI-KUN! GAREKI-KUN!
TSU-KUMO-CHAN!!
WELCOME HOME-BAA. WELCOME HOME-BAA.
...
GAREKI-KUN?

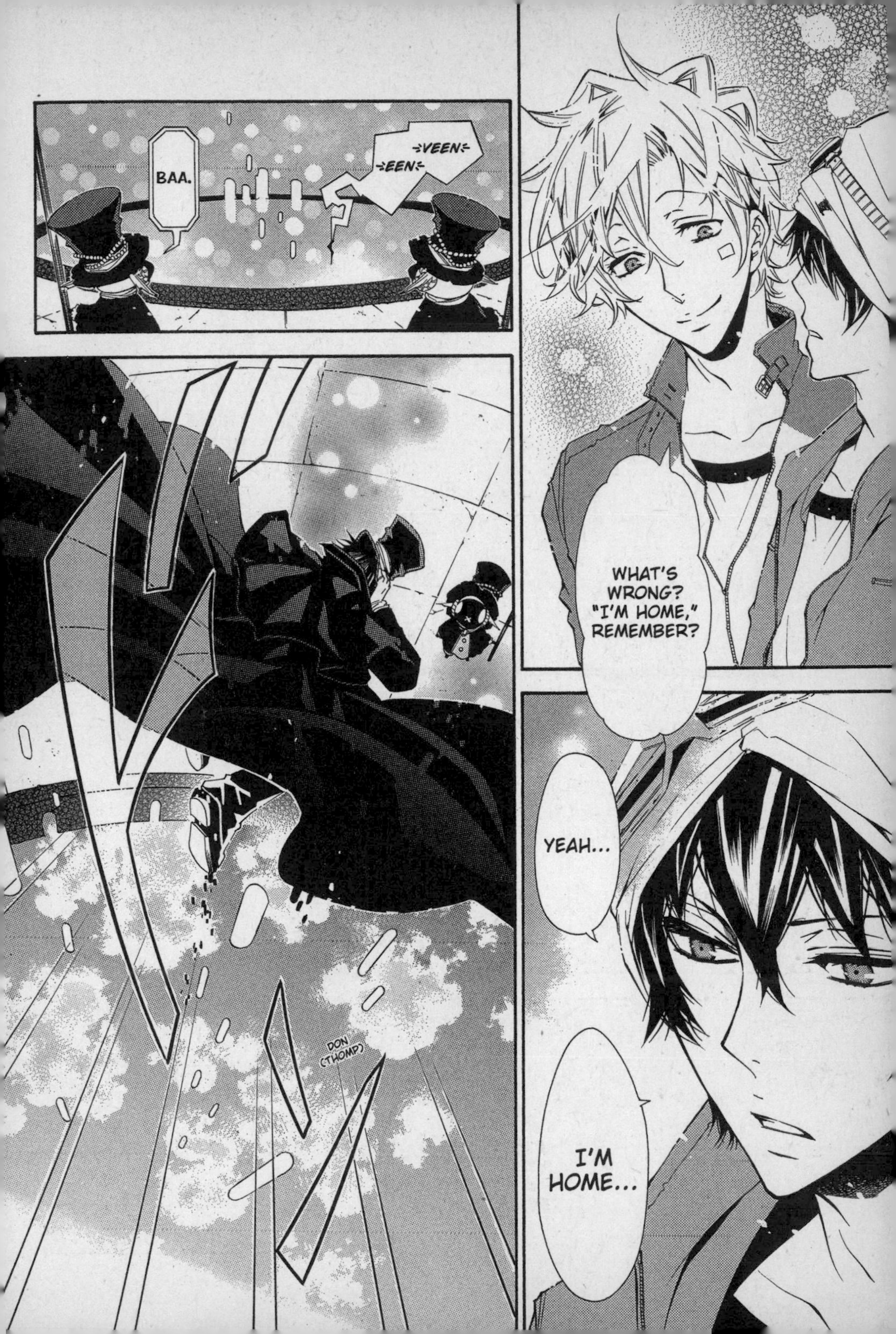
WHAT'S WRONG? "I'M HOME," REMEMBER?
YEAH...
I'M HOME...
VEEN
EEN
BAA.
DON (THOMP)

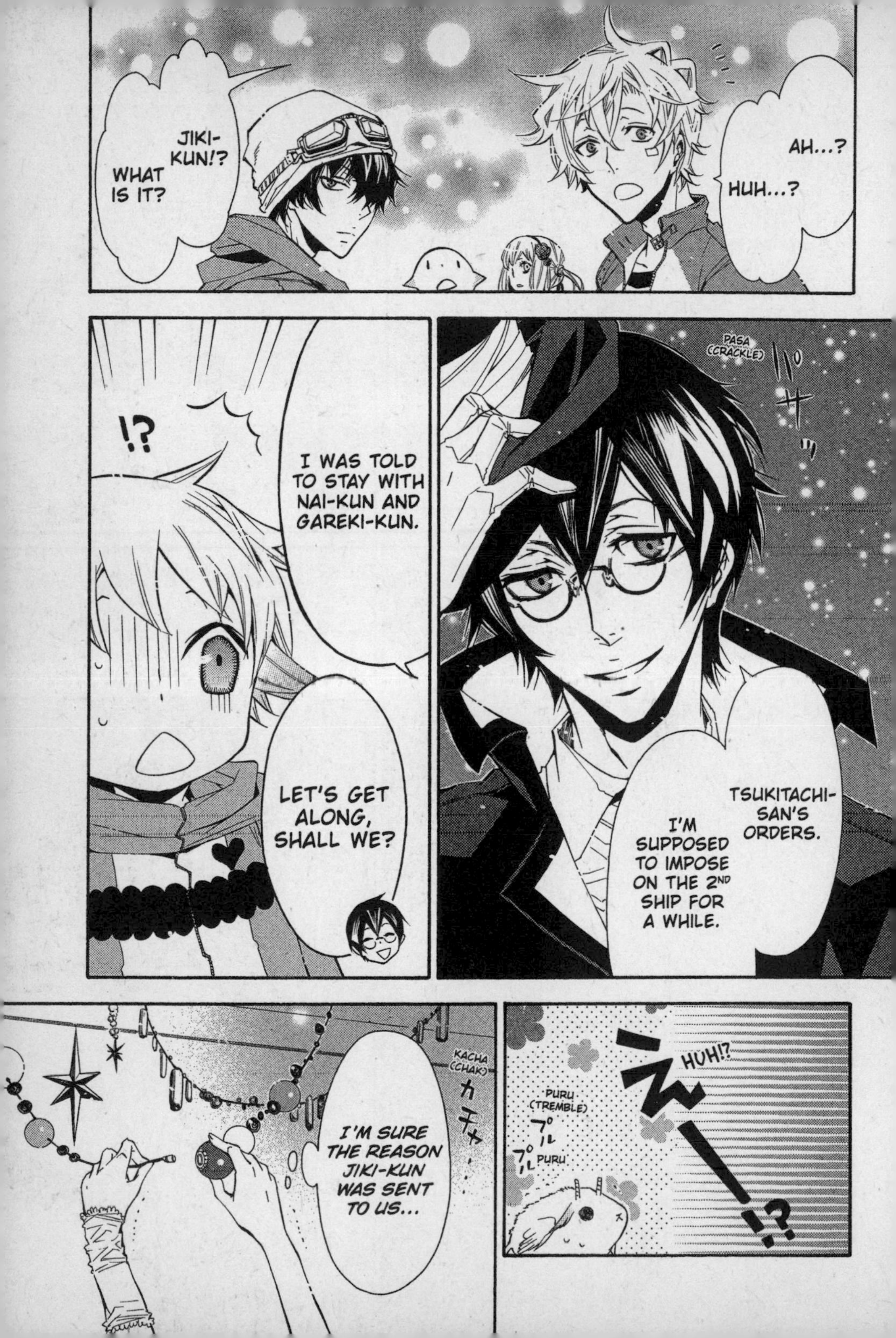
AH...? HUH...?
JIKI-KUN!? WHAT IS IT?
PASA (CRACKLE)
TSUKITACHI-SAN'S ORDERS.
I'M SUPPOSED TO IMPOSE ON THE 2ND SHIP FOR A WHILE.
I WAS TOLD TO STAY WITH NAI-KUN AND GAREKI-KUN.
!?
LET'S GET ALONG, SHALL WE?
HUH!?
PURU (TREMBLE)
PURU
KACHA (CHAK)
I'M SURE THE REASON JIKI-KUN WAS SENT TO US...

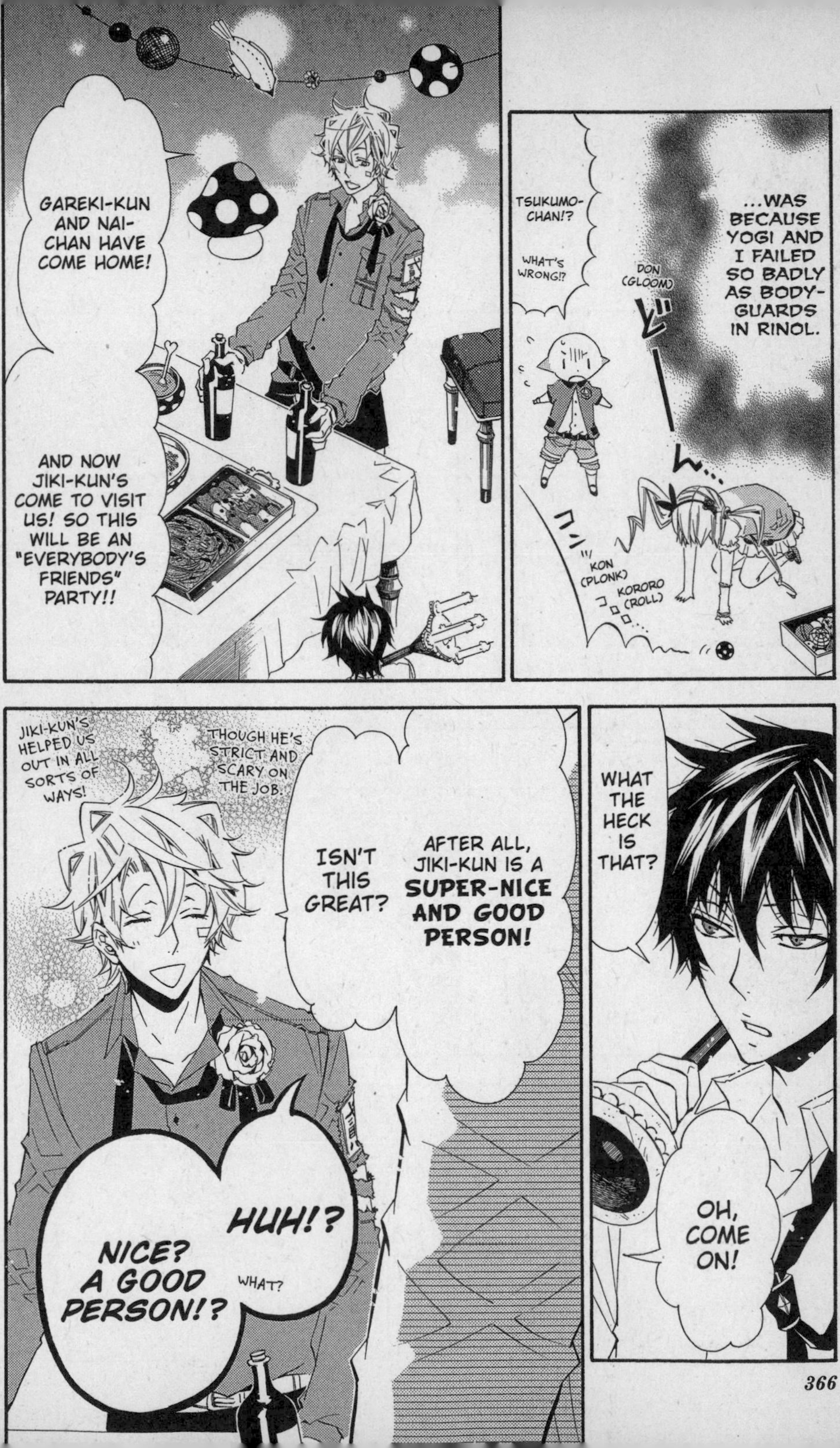
...WAS BECAUSE YOGI AND I FAILED SO BADLY AS BODY-GUARDS IN RINOL.
TSUKUMO-CHAN!?
WHAT'S WRONG!?
DON (GLOOM)
KON (PLONK)
KORORO (ROLL)
GAREKI-KUN AND NAI-CHAN HAVE COME HOME!
AND NOW JIKI-KUN'S COME TO VISIT US! SO THIS WILL BE AN "EVERYBODY'S FRIENDS" PARTY!!
WHAT THE HECK IS THAT?
OH, COME ON!
AFTER ALL, JIKI-KUN IS A SUPER-NICE AND GOOD PERSON!
THOUGH HE'S STRICT AND SCARY ON THE JOB.
ISN'T THIS GREAT?
JIKI-KUN'S HELPED US OUT IN ALL SORTS OF WAYS!
HUH!?
WHAT?
NICE? A GOOD PERSON!?

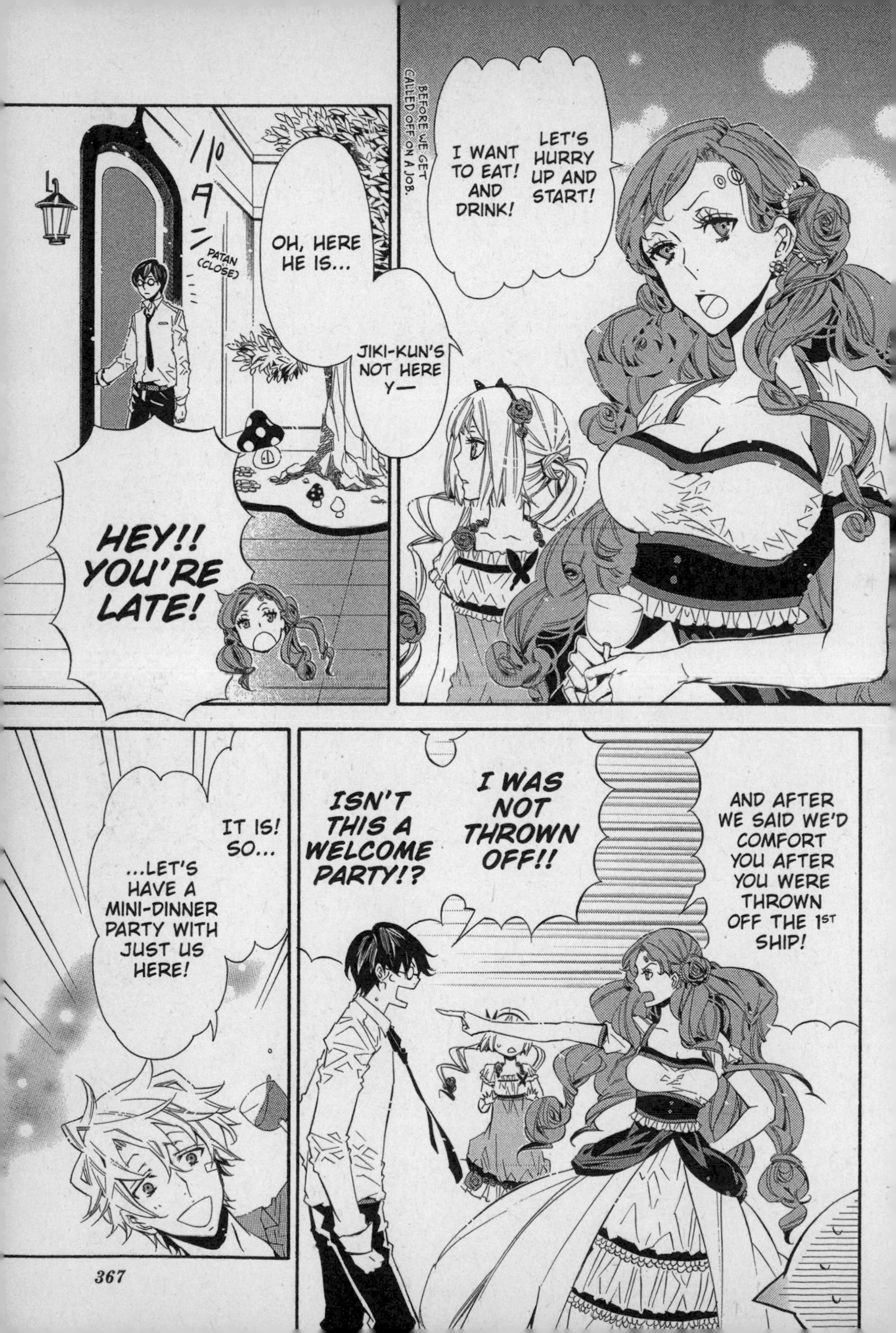
LET'S HURRY UP AND START!
I WANT TO EAT! AND DRINK!
BEFORE WE GET CALLED OFF ON A JOB.
JIKI-KUN'S NOT HERE Y—
OH, HERE HE IS...
PATAN (CLOSE)
HEY!! YOU'RE LATE!
AND AFTER WE SAID WE'D COMFORT YOU AFTER YOU WERE THROWN OFF THE 1ST SHIP!
I WAS NOT THROWN OFF!!
ISN'T THIS A WELCOME PARTY!?
IT IS! SO...
...LET'S HAVE A MINI-DINNER PARTY WITH JUST US HERE!

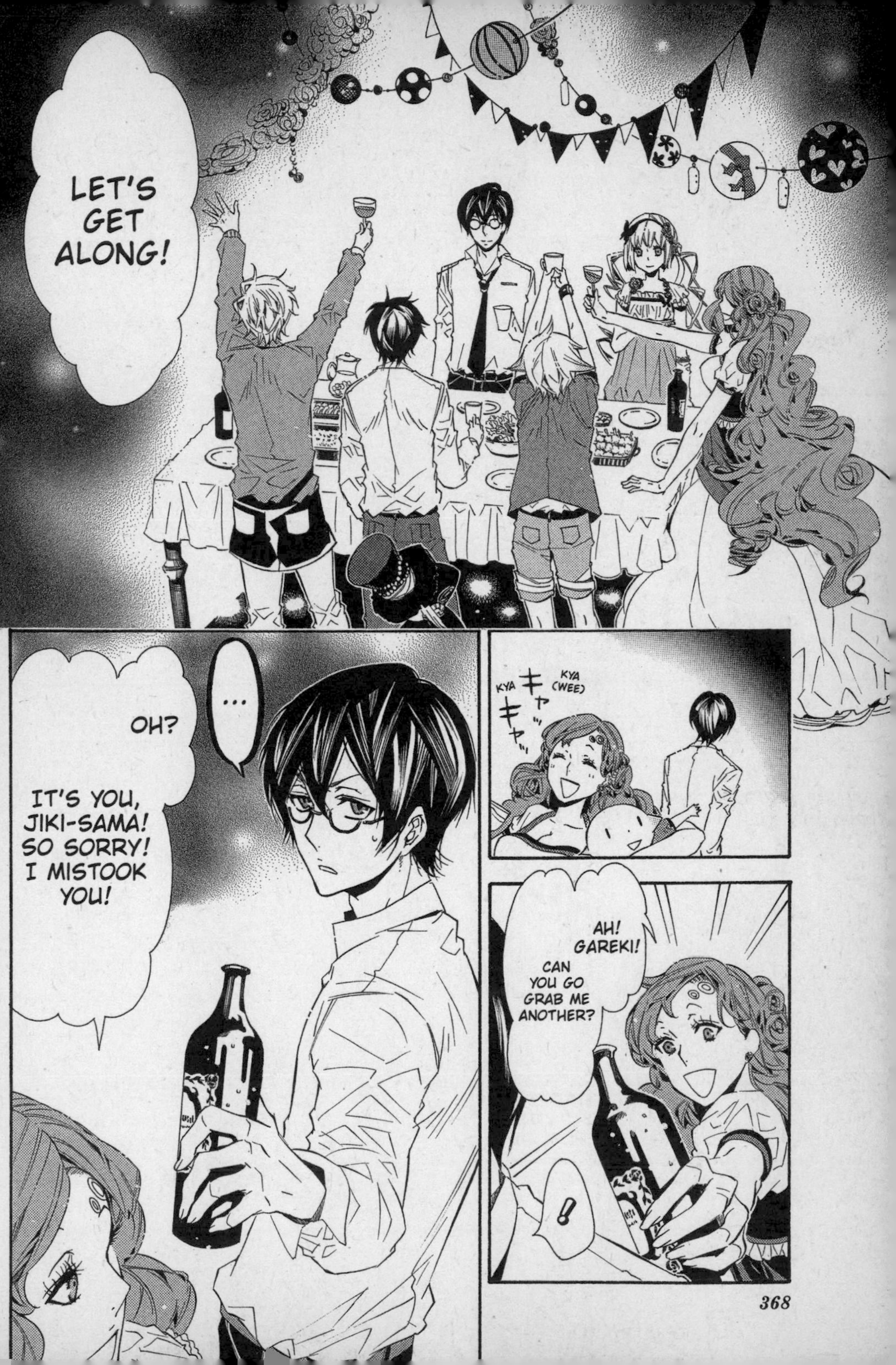
LET'S GET ALONG!
KYA (WEE)
KYA
キャ
キャッ
キャッ
AH! GAREKI!
CAN YOU GO GRAB ME ANOTHER?
!
...
OH?
IT'S YOU, JIKI-SAMA! SO SORRY! I MISTOOK YOU!

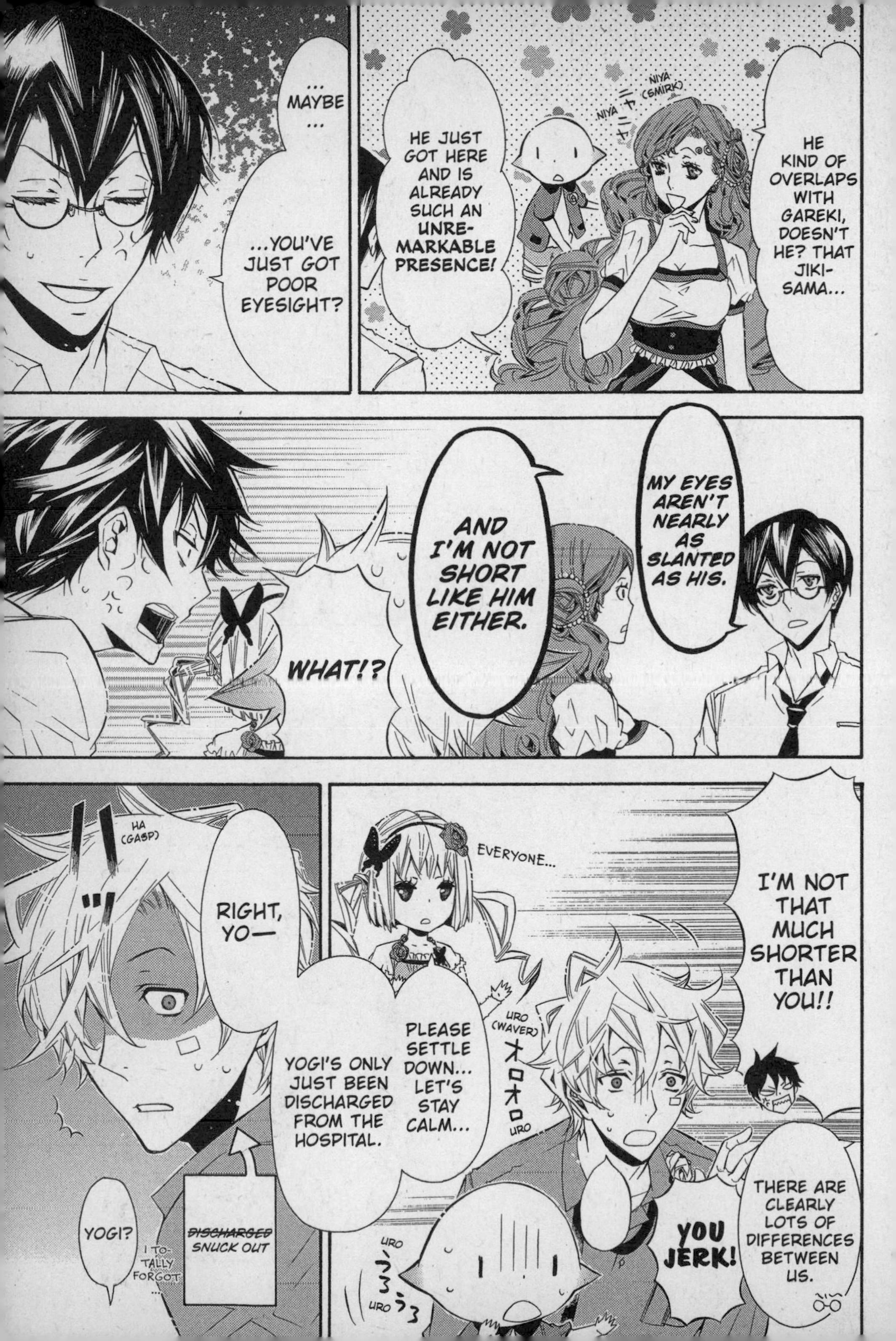
HE KIND OF OVERLAPS WITH GAREKI, DOESN'T HE? THAT JIKI-SAMA...
NIYA (SMIRK)
NIYA
HE JUST GOT HERE AND IS ALREADY SUCH AN UNRE-MARKABLE PRESENCE!
... MAYBE ...
...YOU'VE JUST GOT POOR EYESIGHT?
MY EYES AREN'T NEARLY AS SLANTED AS HIS.
AND I'M NOT SHORT LIKE HIM EITHER.
WHAT!?
I'M NOT THAT MUCH SHORTER THAN YOU!!
EVERYONE...
URO (WAVER)
URO
PLEASE SETTLE DOWN... LET'S STAY CALM...
YOGI'S ONLY JUST BEEN DISCHARGED FROM THE HOSPITAL.
THERE ARE CLEARLY LOTS OF DIFFERENCES BETWEEN US.
YOU JERK!
URO
URO
HA (GASP)
RIGHT, YO—
~~DISCHARGED~~ SNUCK OUT
I TO-TALLY FORGOT...
YOGI?

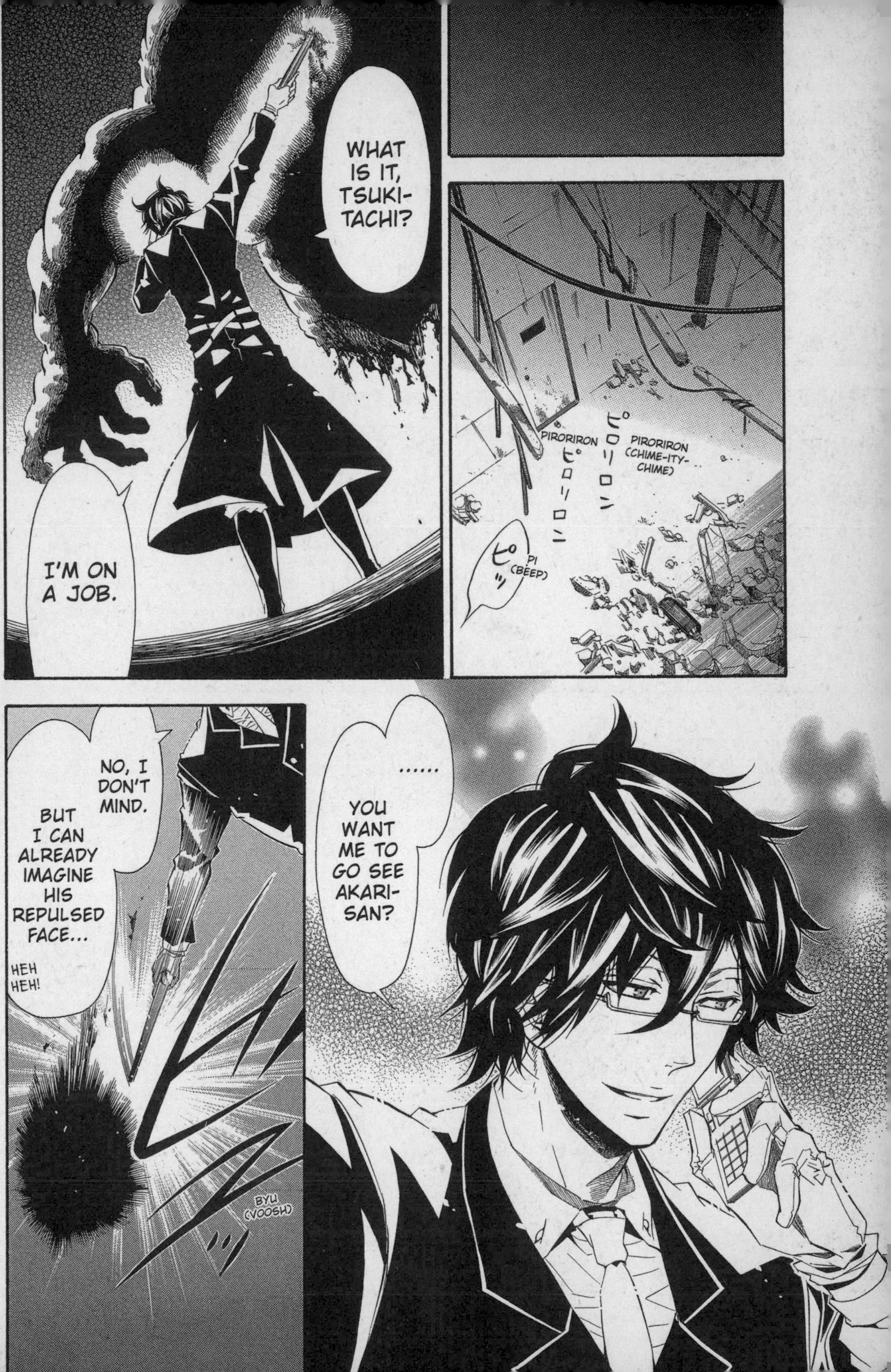
ピロリロン
ピロリロン
PIRORIRON
PIRORIRON (CHIME-ITY-CHIME)
ピッ
PI (BEEP)
WHAT IS IT, TSUKI-TACHI?
I'M ON A JOB.
......
YOU WANT ME TO GO SEE AKARI-SAN?
NO, I DON'T MIND.
BUT I CAN ALREADY IMAGINE HIS REPULSED FACE...
HEH HEH!
BYU (VOOSH)

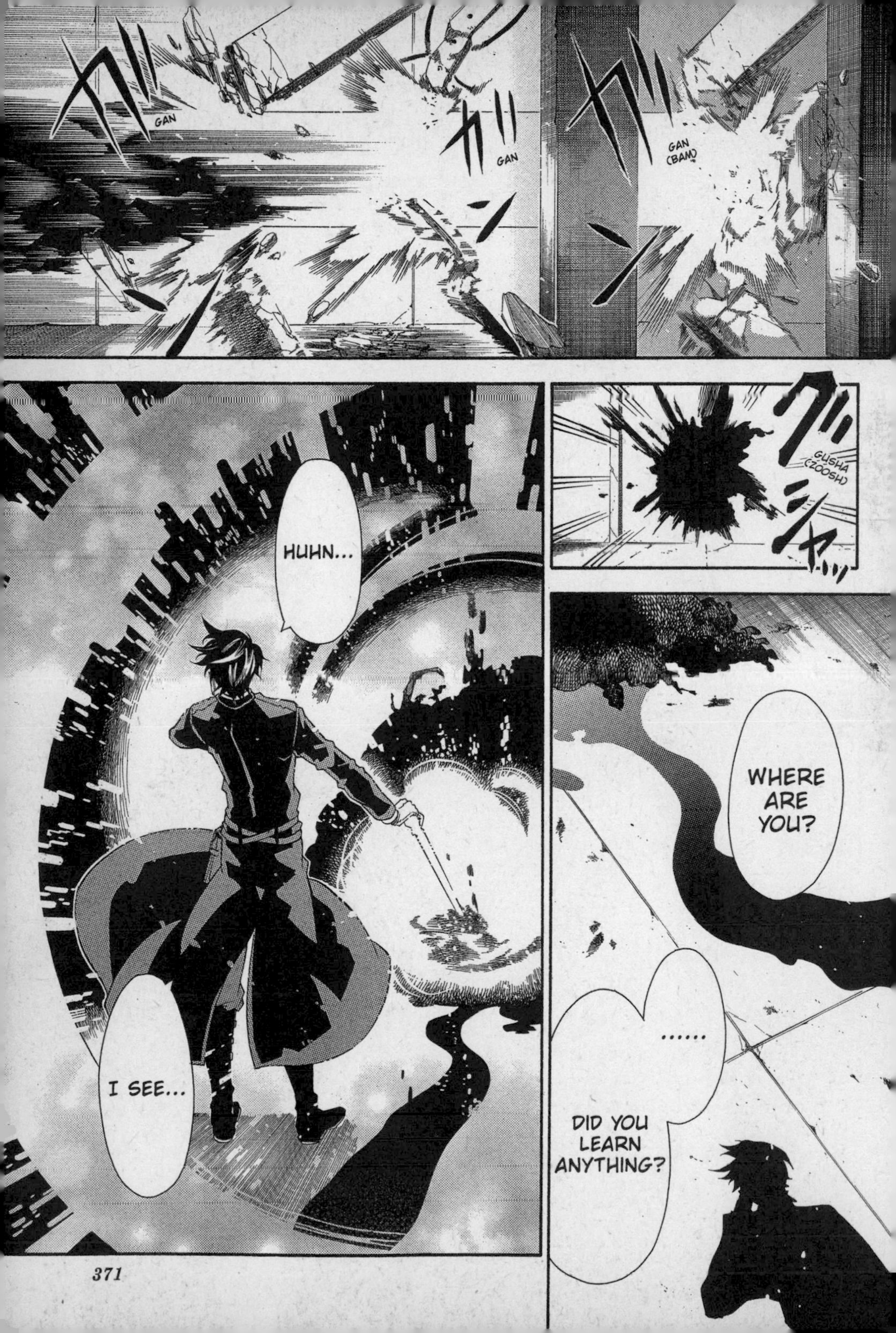
GAN
(BAM)
GAN
GAN
GUSHA
(ZOOSH)
WHERE ARE YOU?
......
DID YOU LEARN ANYTHING?
HUHN...
I SEE...

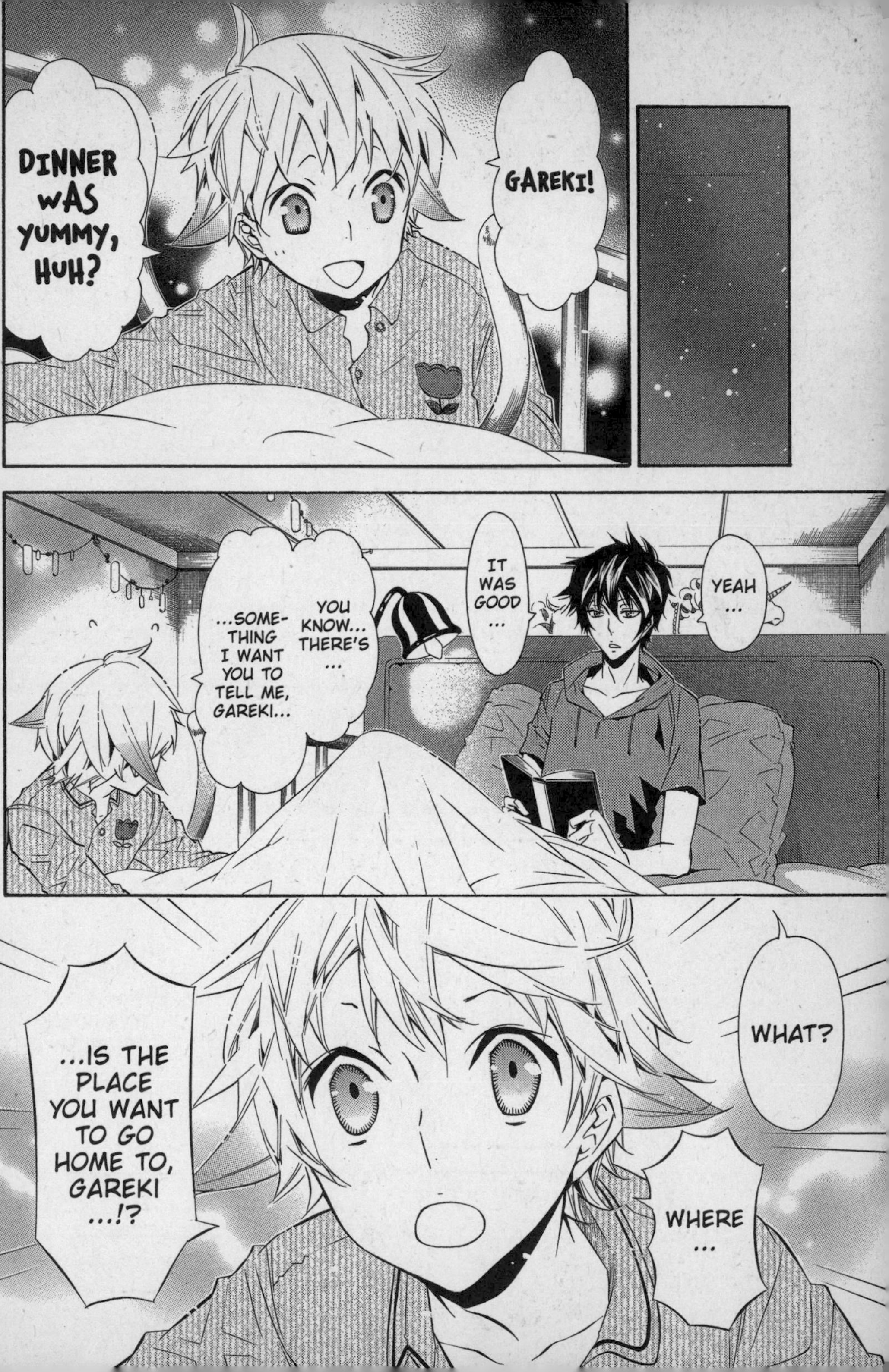
GAREKI!
DINNER WAS YUMMY, HUH?
YEAH...
IT WAS GOOD...
YOU KNOW... THERE'S...
...SOMETHING I WANT YOU TO TELL ME, GAREKI...
WHAT?
WHERE...
...IS THE PLACE YOU WANT TO GO HOME TO, GAREKI...!?

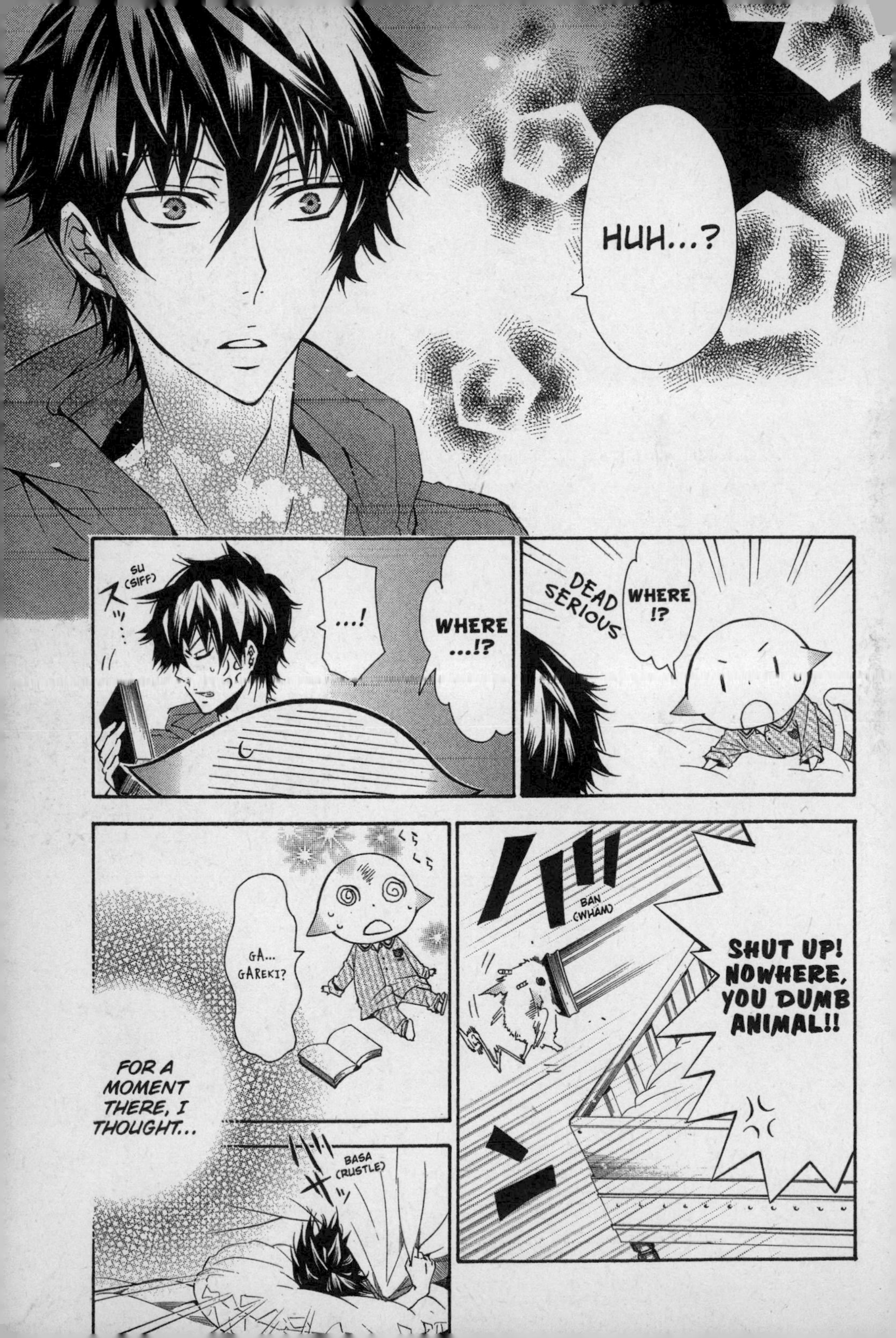
HUH...?
DEAD SERIOUS
WHERE !?
WHERE ...!?
...!
SU (SIFF)
BAN (WHAM)
SHUT UP! NOWHERE, YOU DUMB ANIMAL!!
GA... GAREKI?
FOR A MOMENT THERE, I THOUGHT...
BASA (RUSTLE)

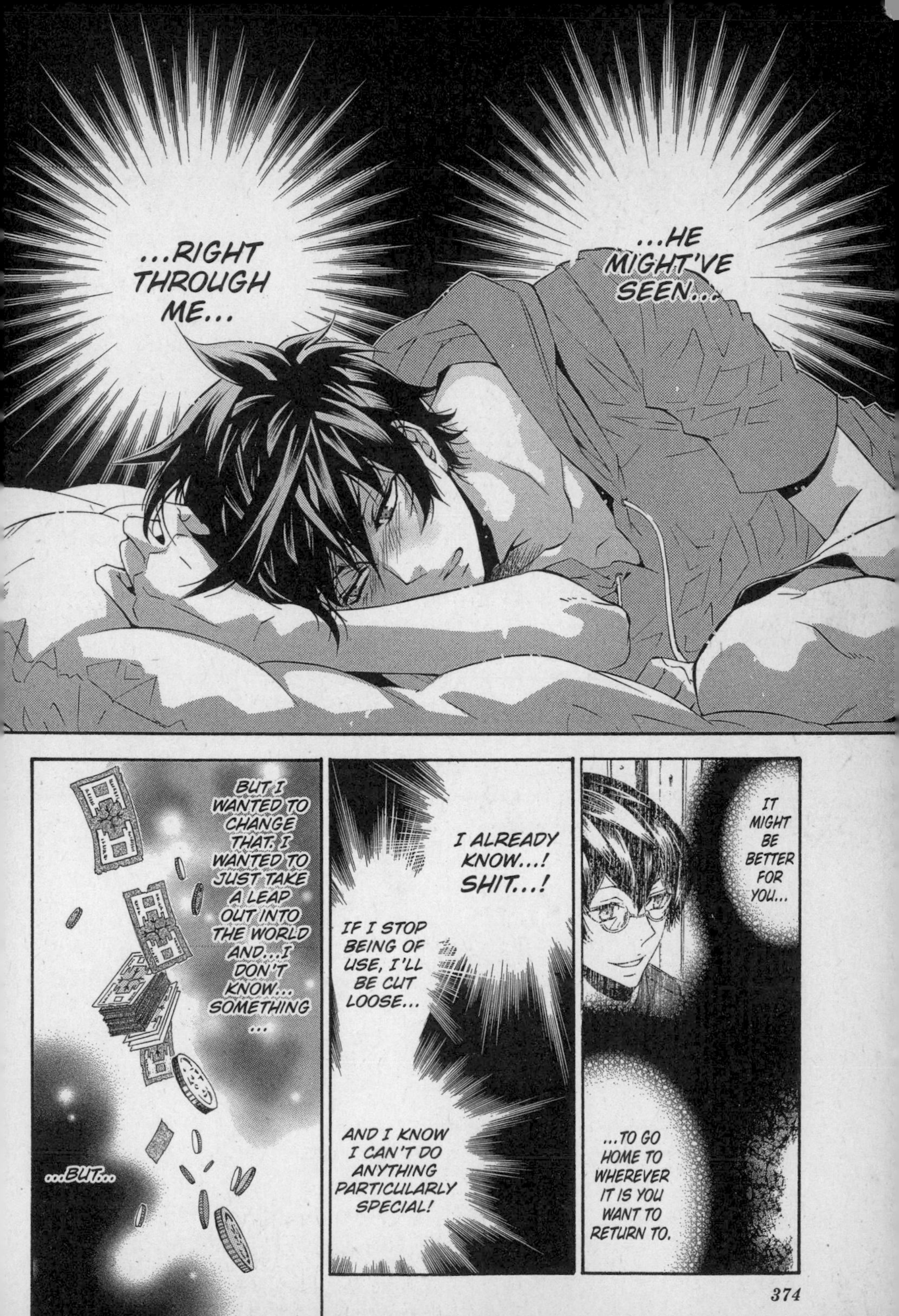
...HE MIGHT'VE SEEN...
...RIGHT THROUGH ME...
IT MIGHT BE BETTER FOR YOU...
...TO GO HOME TO WHEREVER IT IS YOU WANT TO RETURN TO.
I ALREADY KNOW...! SHIT...!
IF I STOP BEING OF USE, I'LL BE CUT LOOSE...
AND I KNOW I CAN'T DO ANYTHING PARTICULARLY SPECIAL!
BUT I WANTED TO CHANGE THAT. I WANTED TO JUST TAKE A LEAP OUT INTO THE WORLD AND...I DON'T KNOW... SOMETHING...
...BUT...

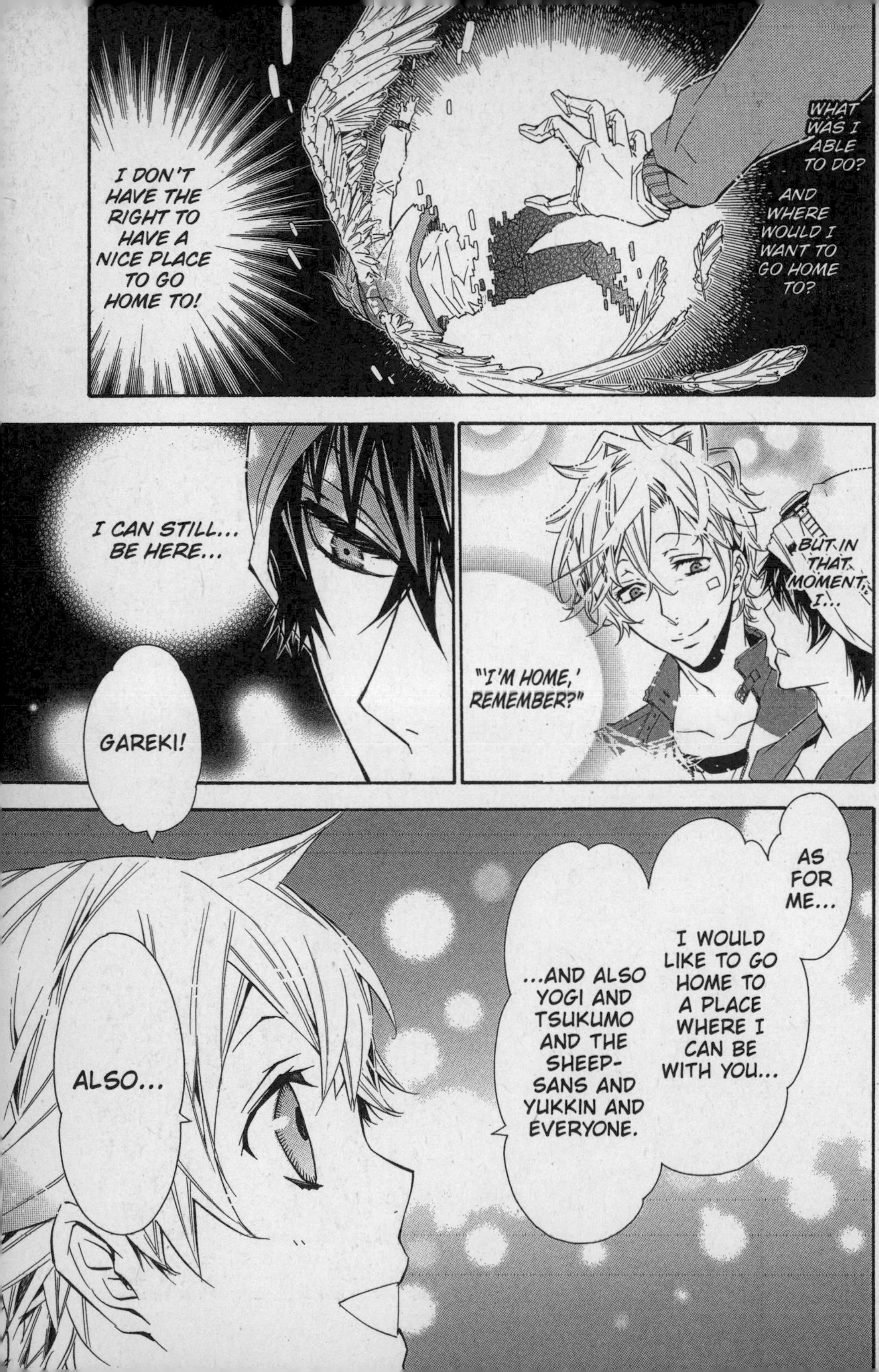
WHAT WAS I ABLE TO DO?
AND WHERE WOULD I WANT TO GO HOME TO?
I DON'T HAVE THE RIGHT TO HAVE A NICE PLACE TO GO HOME TO!
BUT IN THAT MOMENT, I...
"I'M HOME,' REMEMBER?"
I CAN STILL... BE HERE...
GAREKI!
AS FOR ME...
I WOULD LIKE TO GO HOME TO A PLACE WHERE I CAN BE WITH YOU...
...AND ALSO YOGI AND TSUKUMO AND THE SHEEP-SANS AND YUKKIN AND EVERYONE.
ALSO...

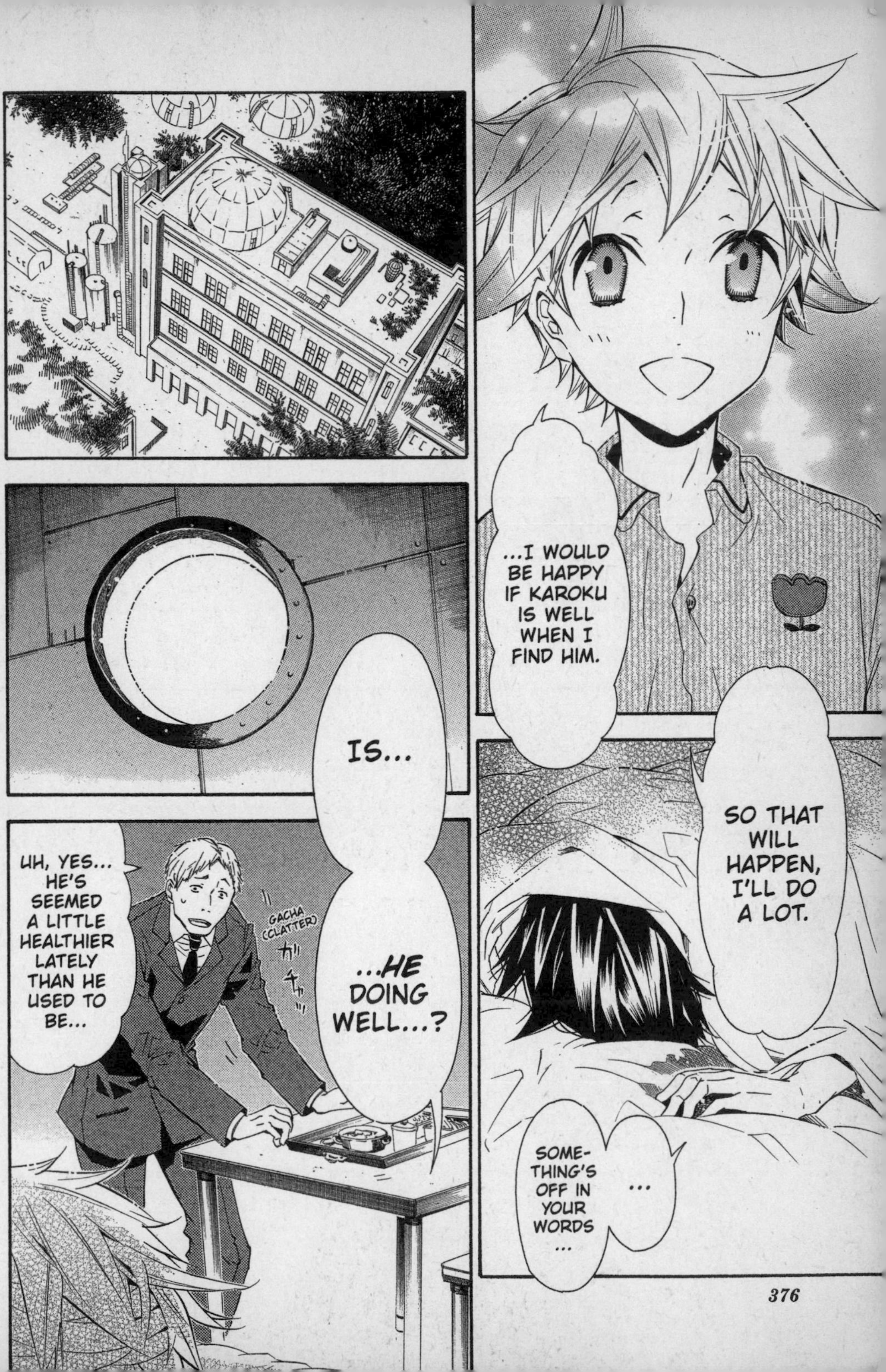

...I WOULD BE HAPPY IF KAROKU IS WELL WHEN I FIND HIM.
SO THAT WILL HAPPEN, I'LL DO A LOT.
...
SOME-THING'S OFF IN YOUR WORDS...
IS...
...HE DOING WELL...?
GACHA (CLATTER)
UH, YES... HE'S SEEMED A LITTLE HEALTHIER LATELY THAN HE USED TO BE...

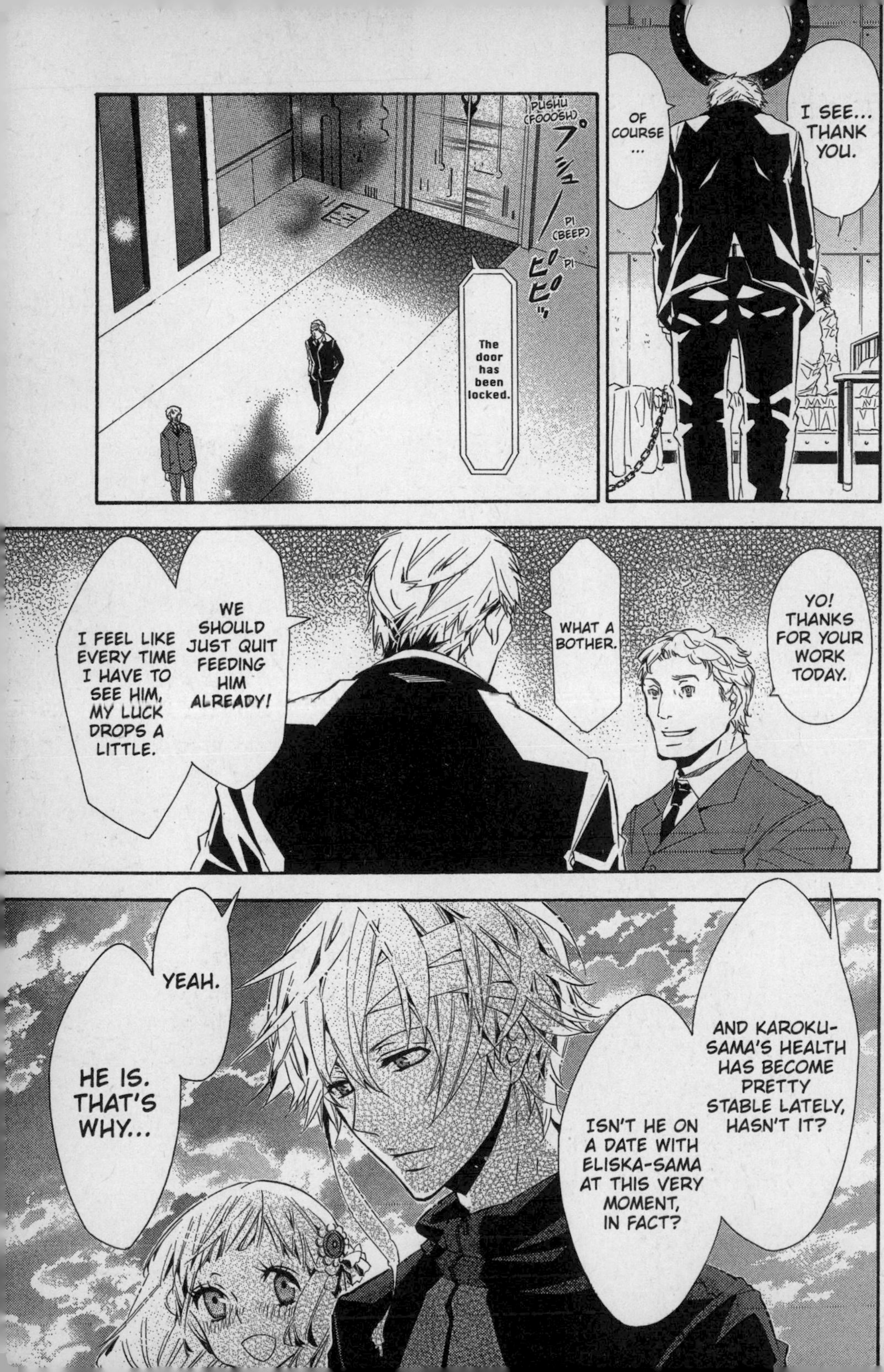
I SEE... THANK YOU.
OF COURSE...
PUSHU (FOOOSH)
PI (BEEP) PI
The door has been locked.
YO! THANKS FOR YOUR WORK TODAY.
WHAT A BOTHER.
WE SHOULD JUST QUIT FEEDING HIM ALREADY!
I FEEL LIKE EVERY TIME I HAVE TO SEE HIM, MY LUCK DROPS A LITTLE.
AND KAROKU-SAMA'S HEALTH HAS BECOME PRETTY STABLE LATELY, HASN'T IT?
ISN'T HE ON A DATE WITH ELISKA-SAMA AT THIS VERY MOMENT, IN FACT?
YEAH.
HE IS. THAT'S WHY...

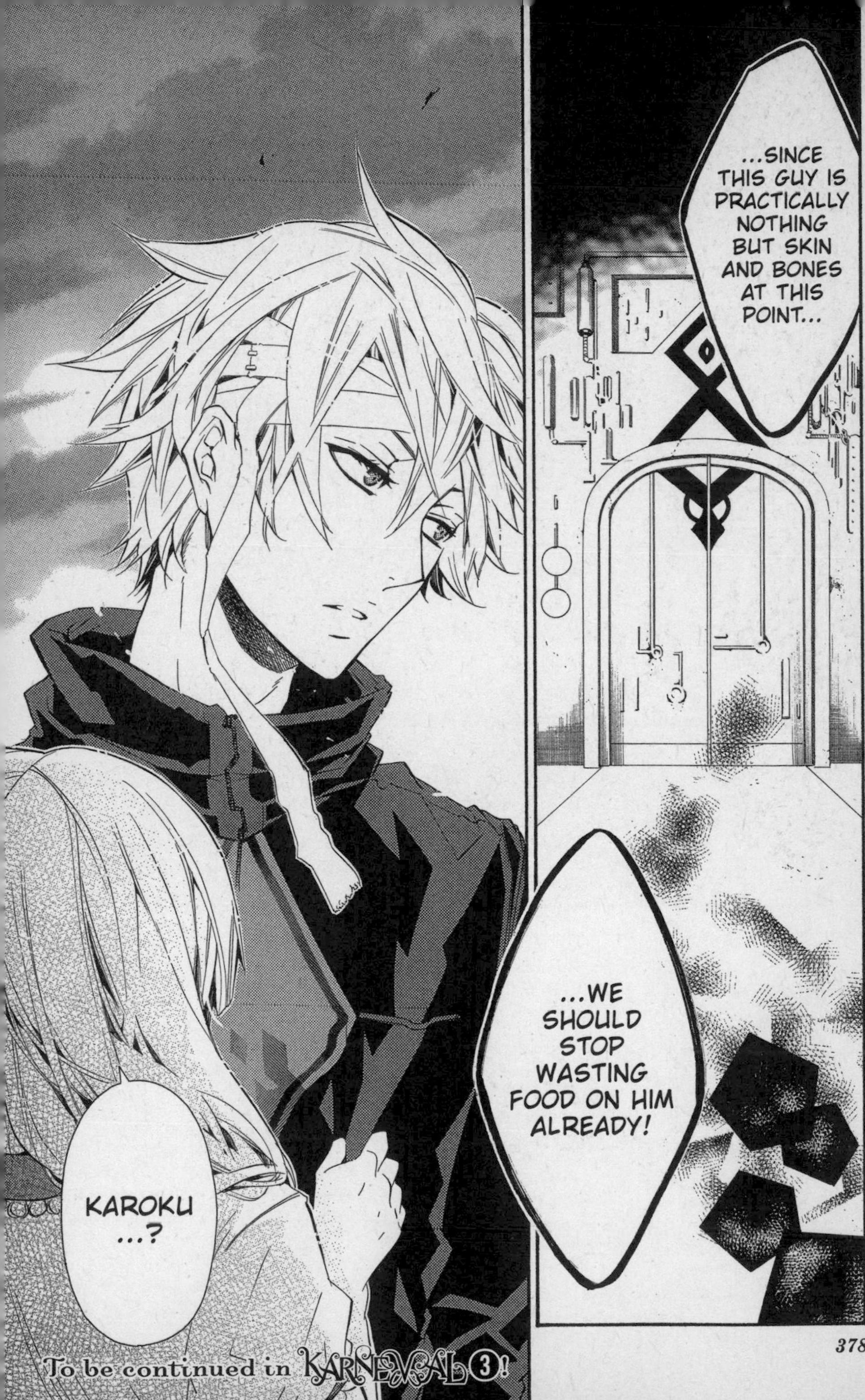
...SINCE THIS GUY IS PRACTICALLY NOTHING BUT SKIN AND BONES AT THIS POINT...
...WE SHOULD STOP WASTING FOOD ON HIM ALREADY!
KAROKU ...?

To be continued in KARNEVAL 3!

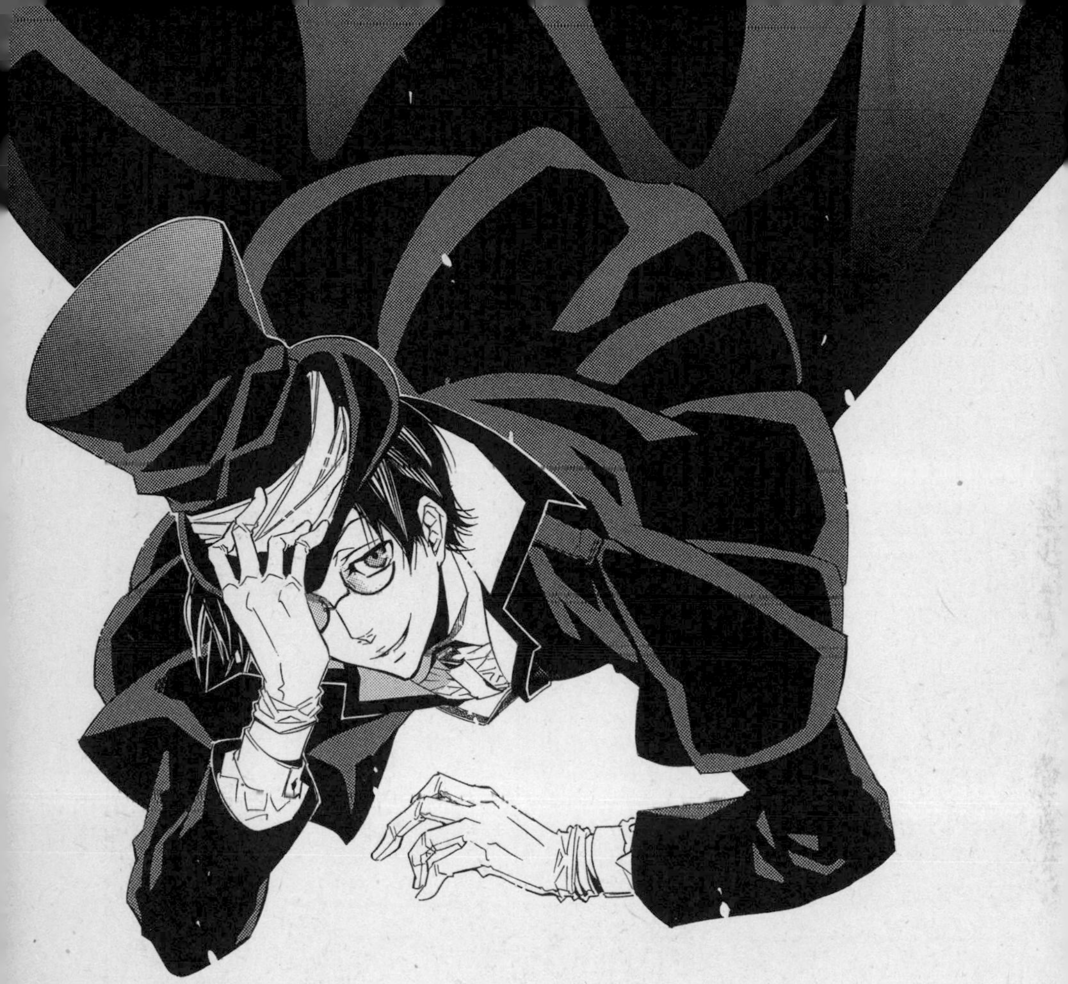

KARNEVAL

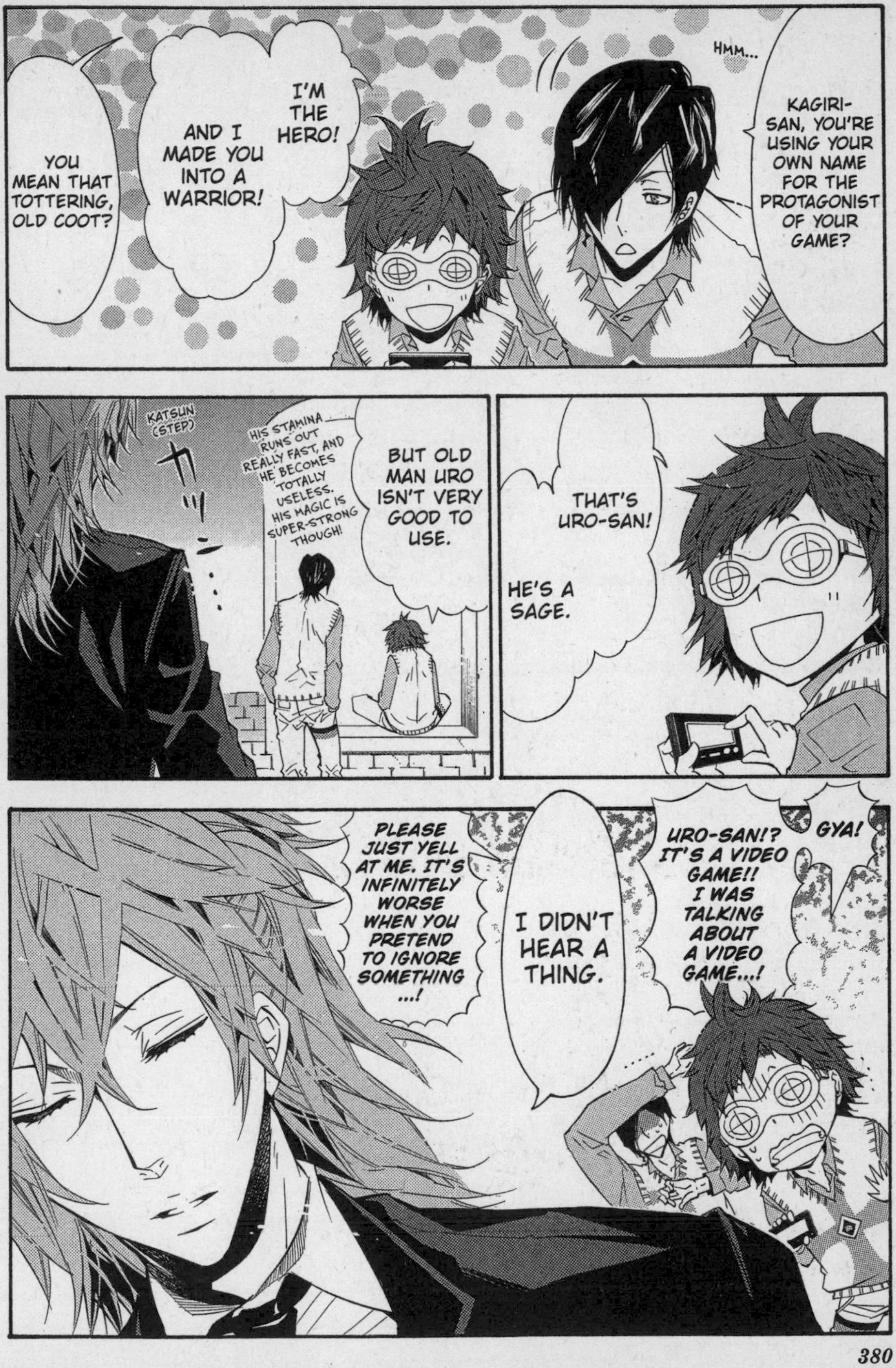
HMM...
KAGIRI-SAN, YOU'RE USING YOUR OWN NAME FOR THE PROTAGONIST OF YOUR GAME?
I'M THE HERO!
AND I MADE YOU INTO A WARRIOR!
YOU MEAN THAT TOTTERING, OLD COOT?
THAT'S URO-SAN!
HE'S A SAGE.
BUT OLD MAN URO ISN'T VERY GOOD TO USE.
HIS STAMINA RUNS OUT REALLY FAST, AND HE BECOMES TOTALLY USELESS. HIS MAGIC IS SUPER-STRONG THOUGH!
KATSUN (STEP)
GYA!
URO-SAN!? IT'S A VIDEO GAME!! I WAS TALKING ABOUT A VIDEO GAME...!
I DIDN'T HEAR A THING.
PLEASE JUST YELL AT ME. IT'S INFINITELY WORSE WHEN YOU PRETEND TO IGNORE SOMETHING...!

Bonus Comic 2 - The Fruits of His Studies ☆

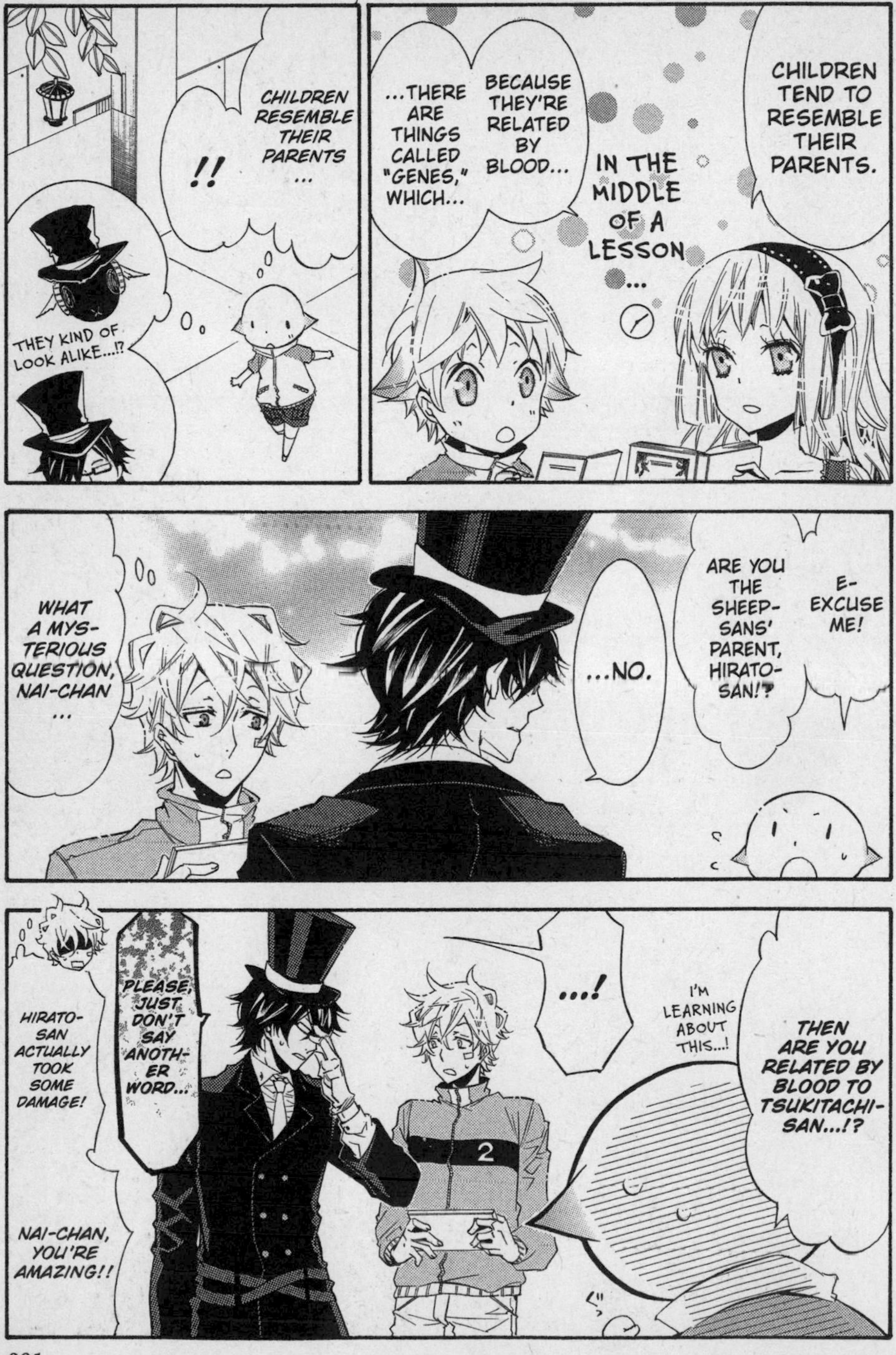
CHILDREN TEND TO RESEMBLE THEIR PARENTS.
IN THE MIDDLE OF A LESSON...
BECAUSE THEY'RE RELATED BY BLOOD...
...THERE ARE THINGS CALLED "GENES," WHICH...
CHILDREN RESEMBLE THEIR PARENTS...
!!
THEY KIND OF LOOK ALIKE...!?
E-EXCUSE ME!
ARE YOU THE SHEEP-SANS' PARENT, HIRATO-SAN!?
...NO.
WHAT A MYS-TERIOUS QUESTION, NAI-CHAN...
THEN ARE YOU RELATED BY BLOOD TO TSUKITACHI-SAN...!?
I'M LEARNING ABOUT THIS...!
...!
PLEASE, JUST DON'T SAY ANOTH-ER WORD...
HIRATO-SAN ACTUALLY TOOK SOME DAMAGE!
NAI-CHAN, YOU'RE AMAZING!!

Bonus Comic 3 - We're Not Recruiting Names Here.

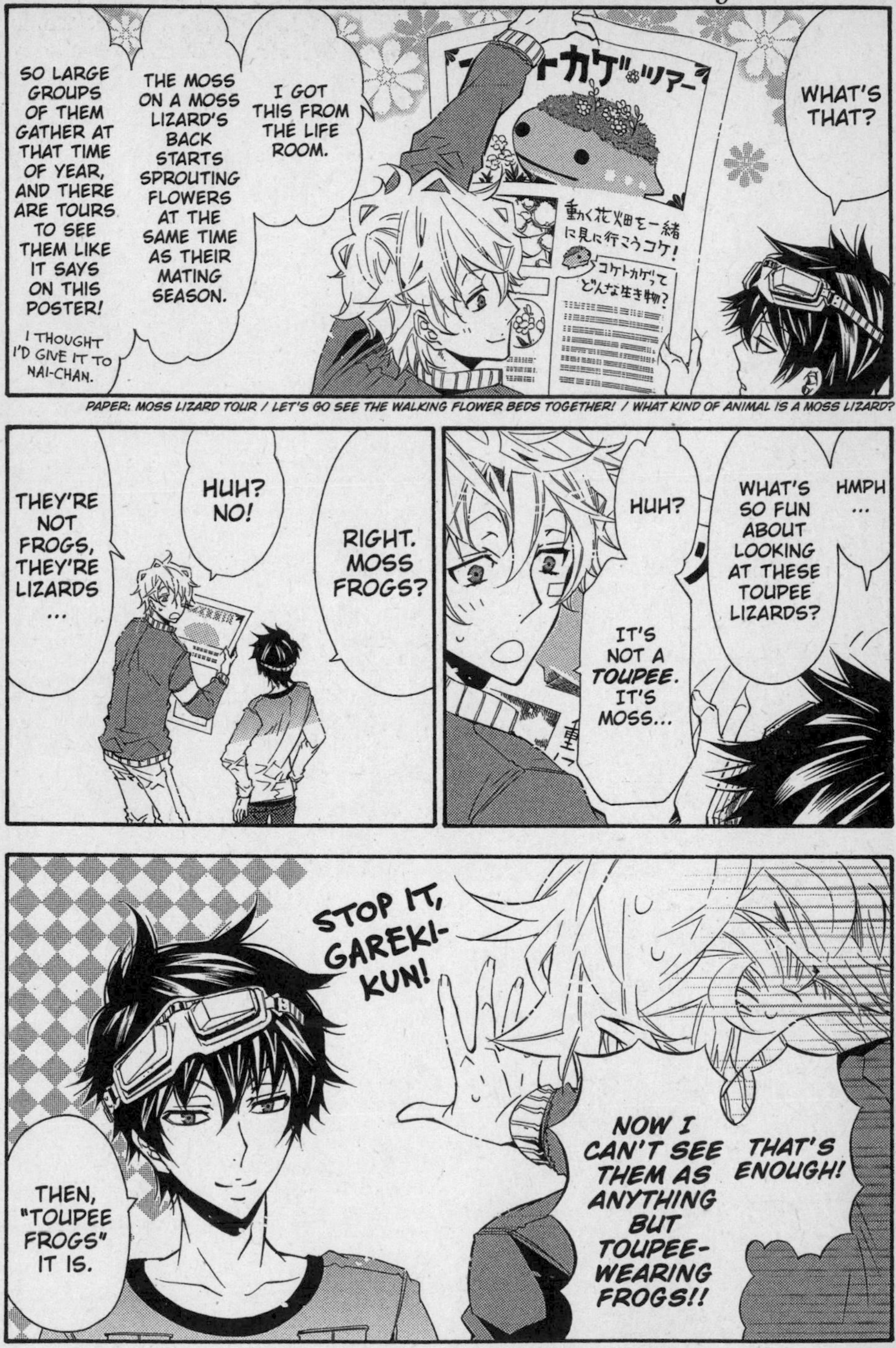
WHAT'S THAT?
ートカゲ ツアー
動く花畑を一緒に見に行こうコケ!
コケトカゲってどんな生き物?
I GOT THIS FROM THE LIFE ROOM.
THE MOSS ON A MOSS LIZARD'S BACK STARTS SPROUTING FLOWERS AT THE SAME TIME AS THEIR MATING SEASON.
SO LARGE GROUPS OF THEM GATHER AT THAT TIME OF YEAR, AND THERE ARE TOURS TO SEE THEM LIKE IT SAYS ON THIS POSTER!
I THOUGHT I'D GIVE IT TO NAI-CHAN.
PAPER: MOSS LIZARD TOUR / LET'S GO SEE THE WALKING FLOWER BEDS TOGETHER! / WHAT KIND OF ANIMAL IS A MOSS LIZARD?
HMPH...
WHAT'S SO FUN ABOUT LOOKING AT THESE TOUPEE LIZARDS?
HUH?
IT'S NOT A *TOUPEE*. IT'S MOSS...
RIGHT. MOSS FROGS?
HUH? NO!
THEY'RE NOT FROGS, THEY'RE LIZARDS...
STOP IT, GAREKI-KUN!
THAT'S ENOUGH!
NOW I CAN'T SEE THEM AS ANYTHING BUT TOUPEE-WEARING FROGS!!
THEN, "TOUPEE FROGS" IT IS.

THE DESTINATION OF OUR NEXT TOUR IS VOLUME 3! LET'S TAKE A TRIP THERE TOGETHER! ★ —YOGI

The End

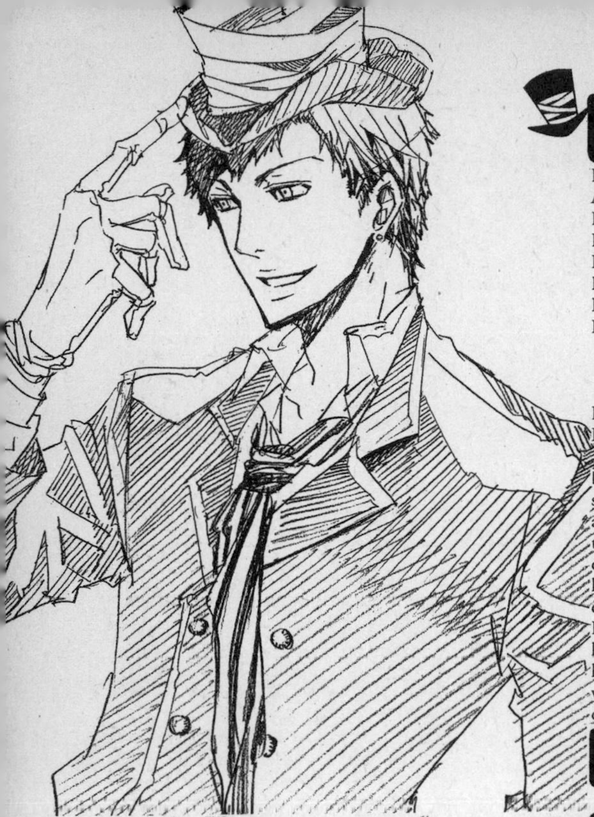

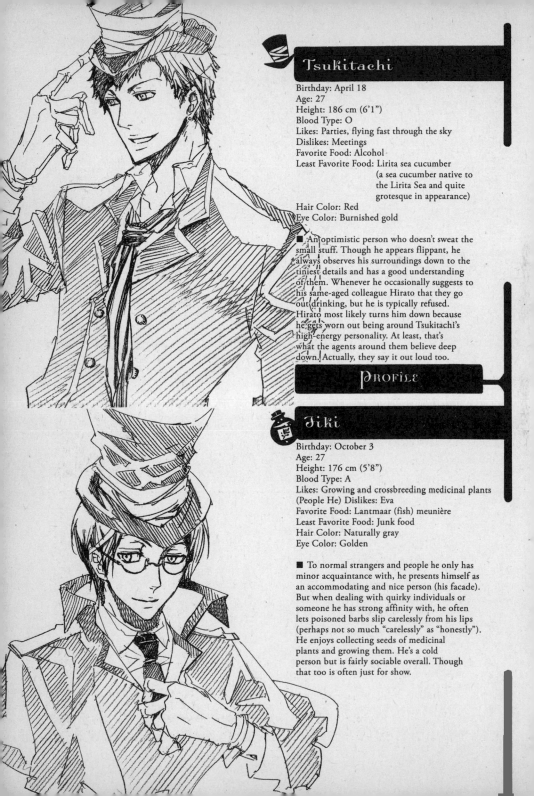

Tsukitachi

Birthday: April 18
Age: 27
Height: 186 cm (6'1")
Blood Type: O
Likes: Parties, flying fast through the sky
Dislikes: Meetings
Favorite Food: Alcohol
Least Favorite Food: Lirita sea cucumber (a sea cucumber native to the Lirita Sea and quite grotesque in appearance)
Hair Color: Red
Eye Color: Burnished gold

■ An optimistic person who doesn't sweat the small stuff. Though he appears flippant, he always observes his surroundings down to the tiniest details and has a good understanding of them. Whenever he occasionally suggests to his same-aged colleague Hirato that they go out drinking, but he is typically refused. Hirato most likely turns him down because he gets worn out being around Tsukitachi's high-energy personality. At least, that's what the agents around them believe deep down. Actually, they say it out loud too.

PROFILE

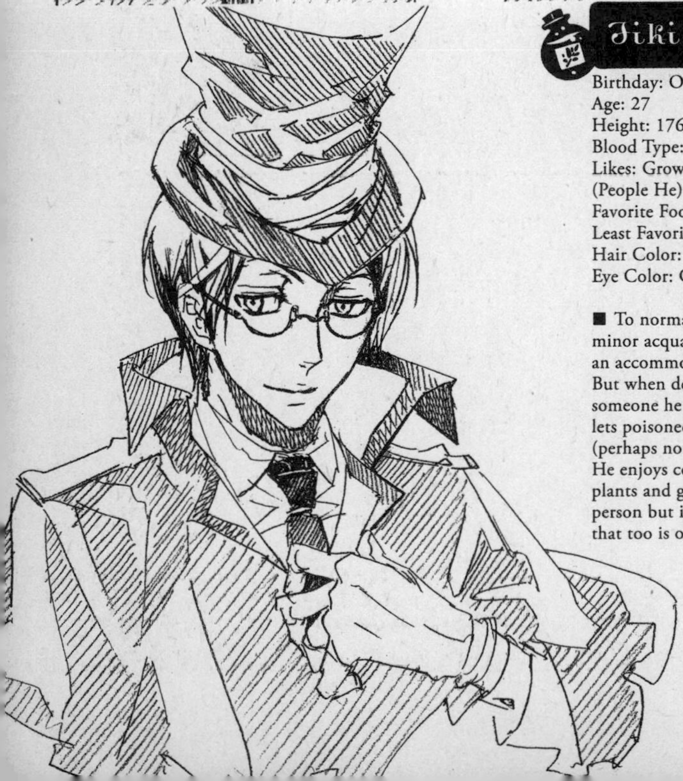

Jiki

Birthday: October 3
Age: 27
Height: 176 cm (5'8")
Blood Type: A
Likes: Growing and crossbreeding medicinal plants
(People He) Dislikes: Eva
Favorite Food: Lantmaar (fish) meunière
Least Favorite Food: Junk food
Hair Color: Naturally gray
Eye Color: Golden

■ To normal strangers and people he only has minor acquaintance with, he presents himself as an accommodating and nice person (his facade). But when dealing with quirky individuals or someone he has strong affinity with, he often lets poisoned barbs slip carelessly from his lips (perhaps not so much "carelessly" as "honestly"). He enjoys collecting seeds of medicinal plants and growing them. He's a cold person but is fairly sociable overall. Though that too is often just for show.

Kiichi

Birthday: November 25
Age: 15
Height: 151 cm (5'0")
Blood Type: O
Likes: Shopping, gourmet food
Dislikes: Being around children
Favorite Food: Sweets (especially creamy ones)
Least Favorite Food: Medicine made by Jiki
(in terms of taste)
Hair Color: Blue
Eye Color: Bright blue

■ Extremely proud and a complete
perfectionist—though there are times she
seems to miss things. At the prep school she
attended before joining Circus, Tsukumo
was her senior, and Kiichi still feels some
hostility toward her from that time (though
Tsukumo seems fairly unaware of it).
She is headstrong and hates losing, which are her
pluses in battle, and she can keep her composure
and accept circumstances calmly. She is seen
by most as having a bright future in Circus.

Eliska

Birthday: July 16
Age: 14
Height: 153 cm (5'0")
Blood Type: B
Likes: Going on dates with Karoku
Dislikes: Any time she can't spend with Karoku
Favorite Food: Prawn and ginruru (a type of
berry) cream salad
Least Favorite Food: Escargot
Hair Color: Peach
Eye Color: Peach

■ She is earnest about her feelings and
desires and is rather spoiled. Having grown up
surrounded by her grandfather's underlings,
she is used to being treated like a princess.
Since she was raised in an environment
where she didn't have to learn how to be
considerate of others, she never learned or
experienced proper communication with
people and has trouble building relationships
with others. Despite her spoiled attitude,
she does seem to depend on Uro. Her
relationship with Karoku is still unknown.

ZERO-SUM Magazine Drama CD Recording Report ☆
"I Can't Capture It All in Just Two Pages!"

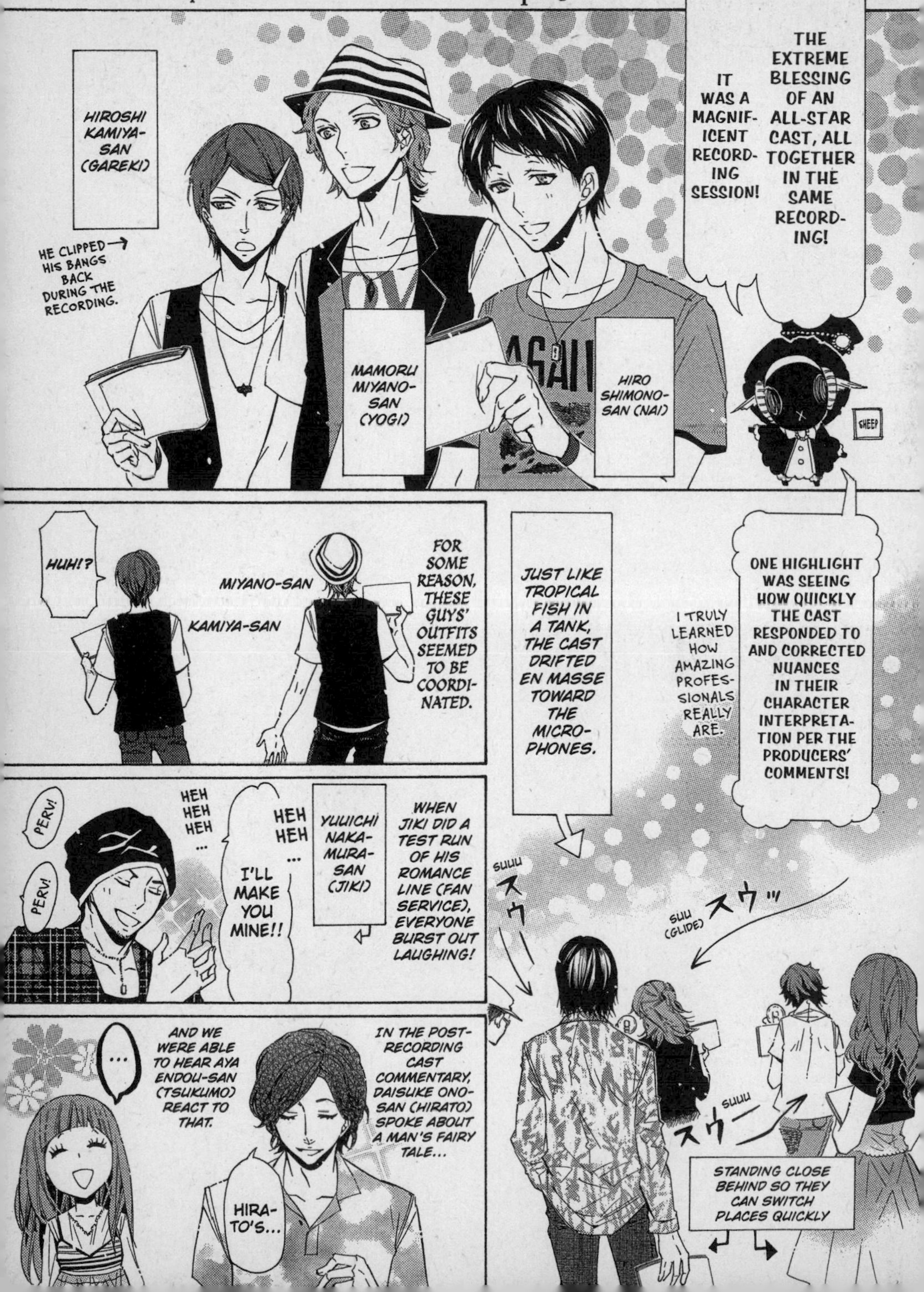
THE EXTREME BLESSING OF AN ALL-STAR CAST, ALL TOGETHER IN THE SAME RECORDING!
IT WAS A MAGNIFICENT RECORDING SESSION!
HIRO SHIMONO-SAN (NAI)
MAMORU MIYANO-SAN (YOGI)
HIROSHI KAMIYA-SAN (GAREKI)
HE CLIPPED HIS BANGS BACK DURING THE RECORDING.
SHEEP
ONE HIGHLIGHT WAS SEEING HOW QUICKLY THE CAST RESPONDED TO AND CORRECTED NUANCES IN THEIR CHARACTER INTERPRETATION PER THE PRODUCERS' COMMENTS!
I TRULY LEARNED HOW AMAZING PROFESSIONALS REALLY ARE.
JUST LIKE TROPICAL FISH IN A TANK, THE CAST DRIFTED EN MASSE TOWARD THE MICROPHONES.
SUU (GLIDE) スウッ
SUUU スウー
SUUU スウー
STANDING CLOSE BEHIND SO THEY CAN SWITCH PLACES QUICKLY
FOR SOME REASON, THESE GUYS' OUTFITS SEEMED TO BE COORDINATED.
MIYANO-SAN
KAMIYA-SAN
HUH!?
WHEN JIKI DID A TEST RUN OF HIS ROMANCE LINE (FAN SERVICE), EVERYONE BURST OUT LAUGHING!
YUUICHI NAKAMURA-SAN (JIKI)
HEH HEH...
I'LL MAKE YOU MINE!!
HEH HEH HEH...
PERV!
PERV!
IN THE POST-RECORDING CAST COMMENTARY, DAISUKE ONO-SAN (HIRATO) SPOKE ABOUT A MAN'S FAIRY TALE...
HIRATO'S...
AND WE WERE ABLE TO HEAR AYA ENDOU-SAN (TSUKUMO) REACT TO THAT.
...

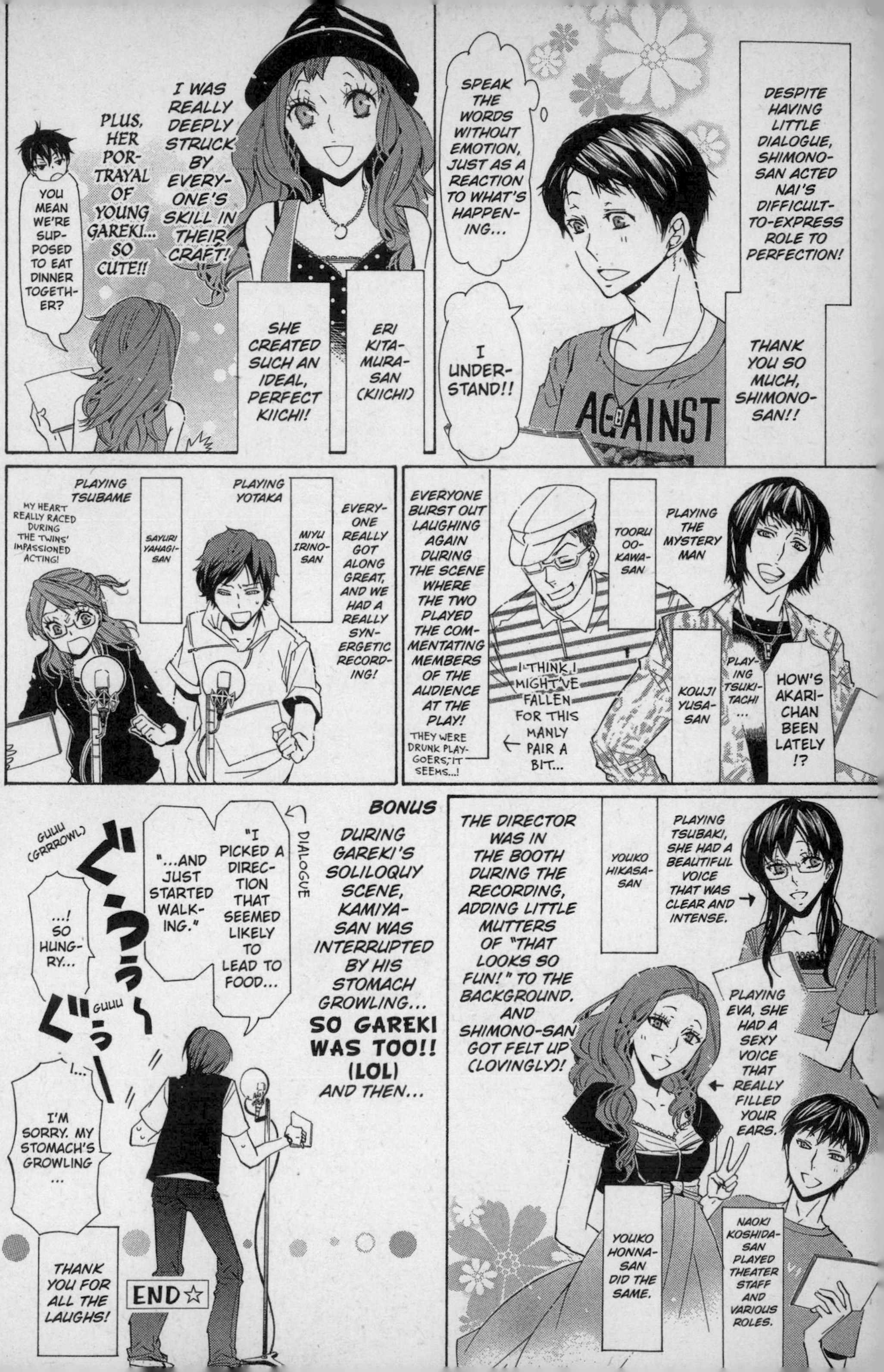

DESPITE HAVING LITTLE DIALOGUE, SHIMONO-SAN ACTED NAI'S DIFFICULT-TO-EXPRESS ROLE TO PERFECTION!
SPEAK THE WORDS WITHOUT EMOTION, JUST AS A REACTION TO WHAT'S HAPPENING...
I UNDERSTAND!!
AGAINST
THANK YOU SO MUCH, SHIMONO-SAN!!
I WAS REALLY DEEPLY STRUCK BY EVERYONE'S SKILL IN THEIR CRAFT!
ERI KITAMURA-SAN (KIICHI)
SHE CREATED SUCH AN IDEAL, PERFECT KIICHI!
PLUS, HER PORTRAYAL OF YOUNG GAREKI... SO CUTE!!
YOU MEAN WE'RE SUPPOSED TO EAT DINNER TOGETHER?
PLAYING THE MYSTERY MAN
TOORU OOKAWA-SAN
EVERYONE BURST OUT LAUGHING AGAIN DURING THE SCENE WHERE THE TWO PLAYED THE COMMENTATING MEMBERS OF THE AUDIENCE AT THE PLAY!
THEY WERE DRUNK PLAYGOERS, IT SEEMS...!
HOW'S AKARI-CHAN BEEN LATELY!?
PLAYING TSUKITACHI...
KOUJI YUSA-SAN
I THINK I MIGHT'VE FALLEN FOR THIS MANLY PAIR A BIT...
EVERYONE REALLY GOT ALONG GREAT, AND WE HAD A REALLY SYNERGETIC RECORDING!
PLAYING YOTAKA
MIYU IRINO-SAN
PLAYING TSUBAME
SAYURI YAHAGI-SAN
MY HEART REALLY RACED DURING THE TWINS' IMPASSIONED ACTING!
THE DIRECTOR WAS IN THE BOOTH DURING THE RECORDING, ADDING LITTLE MUTTERS OF "THAT LOOKS SO FUN!" TO THE BACKGROUND. AND SHIMONO-SAN GOT FELT UP (LOVINGLY)!
PLAYING TSUBAKI, SHE HAD A BEAUTIFUL VOICE THAT WAS CLEAR AND INTENSE.
YOUKO HIKASA-SAN
PLAYING EVA, SHE HAD A SEXY VOICE THAT REALLY FILLED YOUR EARS.
YOUKO HONNA-SAN DID THE SAME.
NAOKI KOSHIDA-SAN PLAYED THEATER STAFF AND VARIOUS ROLES.
BONUS
DURING GAREKI'S SOLILOQUY SCENE, KAMIYA-SAN WAS INTERRUPTED BY HIS STOMACH GROWLING... SO GAREKI WAS TOO!! (LOL) AND THEN...
DIALOGUE
"I PICKED A DIRECTION THAT SEEMED LIKELY TO LEAD TO FOOD..."
"...AND JUST STARTED WALKING."
GUUU (GRRROWL)
...! SO HUNGRY...
GUUU
I...
I'M SORRY. MY STOMACH'S GROWLING...
THANK YOU FOR ALL THE LAUGHS!
END☆

HELLO! IT'S ME, TOUYA. THANK YOU FOR READING VOLUME 4 OF *KARNEVAL*! WE GOT LOTS OF LETTERS AND MESSAGES FROM ALL OF YOU ASKING FOR A DRAMA CD, AND I'M THRILLED THAT WE WERE ACTUALLY ABLE TO GET ONE MADE. I'M SO GLAD! I REALLY DO READ YOUR LETTERS AND CONSIDER THEM PRECIOUS.

WHILE I WAS DRAWING THE MANUSCRIPT OF VOLUME 4, I HEARD THAT MY FIRST AUTOGRAPH EVENT WAS SCHEDULED, AND I'D HAVE MY VERY FIRST CHANCE TO MEET MY READERS DIRECTLY! EVEN IF IT WAS FOR WORK, I WAS ABLE TO MEET LOTS OF NEW PEOPLE AND HAD A WONDERFUL TIME.

SPEAKING OF WHICH, IN VOLUME 3, WE OFFERED A PROMOTIONAL GIFT OF "CANDID PHOTOS" OF ALL THE CHARACTERS, AND GAREKI WAS THE MOST POPULAR. HE ONLY BEAT YOGI BY A SLIM MARGIN, BUT ULTIMATELY, IT WAS THE FIFTEEN-YEAR-OLD WHO WON OUT (NOT THAT THEY WERE COMPETING FOR ANYTHING). MY EDITOR WAS SAYING THAT IF YOGI HAD WON, HE WOULD EXPRESS HIS FEELINGS EARNESTLY AND SAY SOMETHING LIKE, "WAAAH, THANK YOU!! I'M SO HAPPY!!" BUT GAREKI WOULDN'T EVEN CHANGE EXPRESSION AND WOULD JUST BE LIKE, "WHATEVER...THANKS."

I'M IN AGREEMENT. NAI, DO YOUR BEST!

— TOUYA MIKANAGI

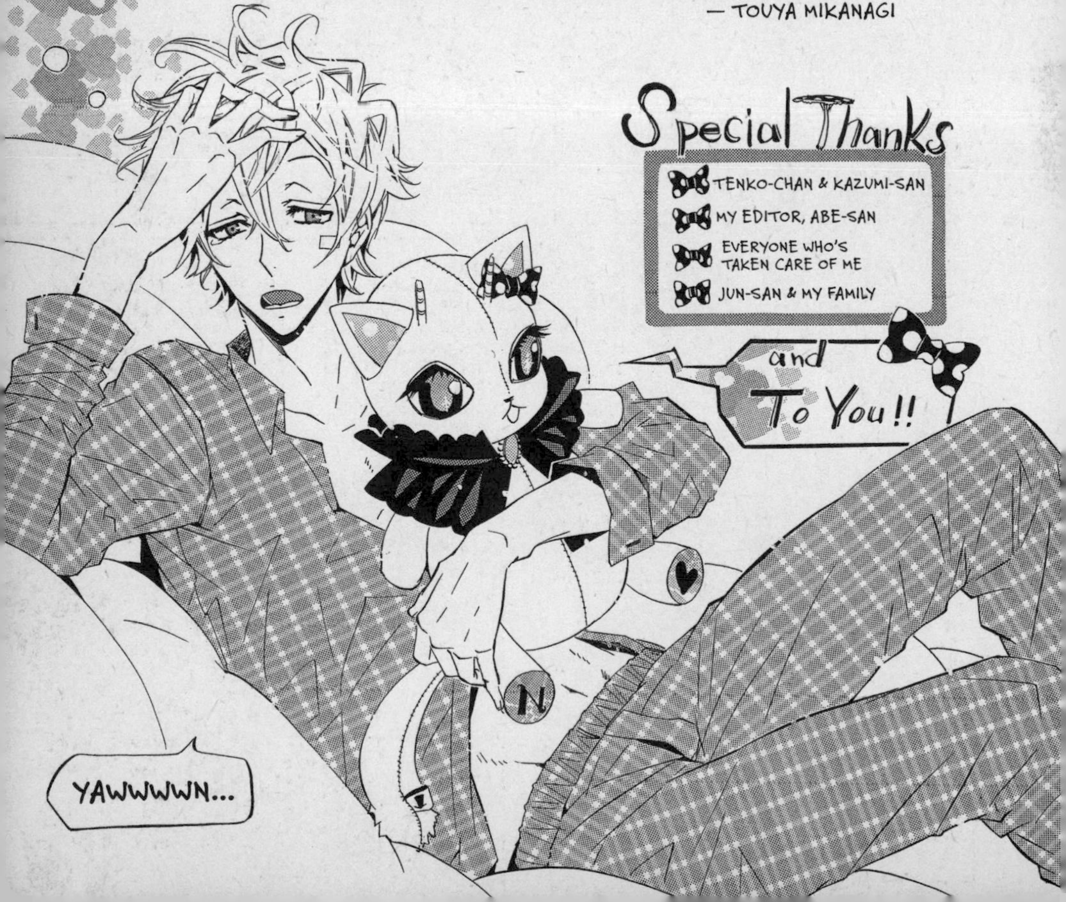
Special Thanks
TENKO-CHAN & KAZUMI-SAN
MY EDITOR, ABE-SAN
EVERYONE WHO'S TAKEN CARE OF ME
JUN-SAN & MY FAMILY
and
To You!!
YAWWWWN...

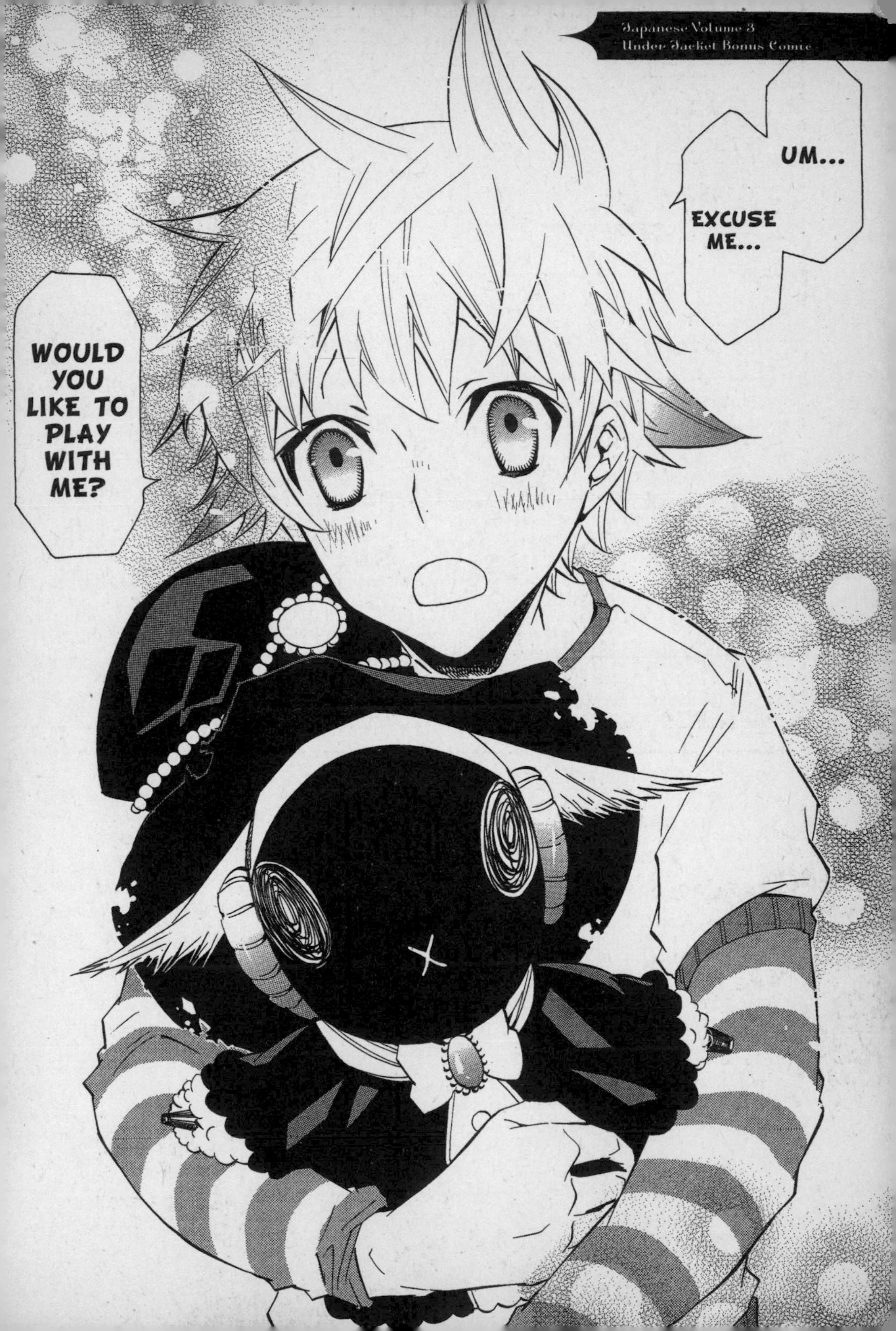
Japanese Volume 3
Under-Jacket Bonus Comic
UM...
EXCUSE ME...
WOULD YOU LIKE TO PLAY WITH ME?

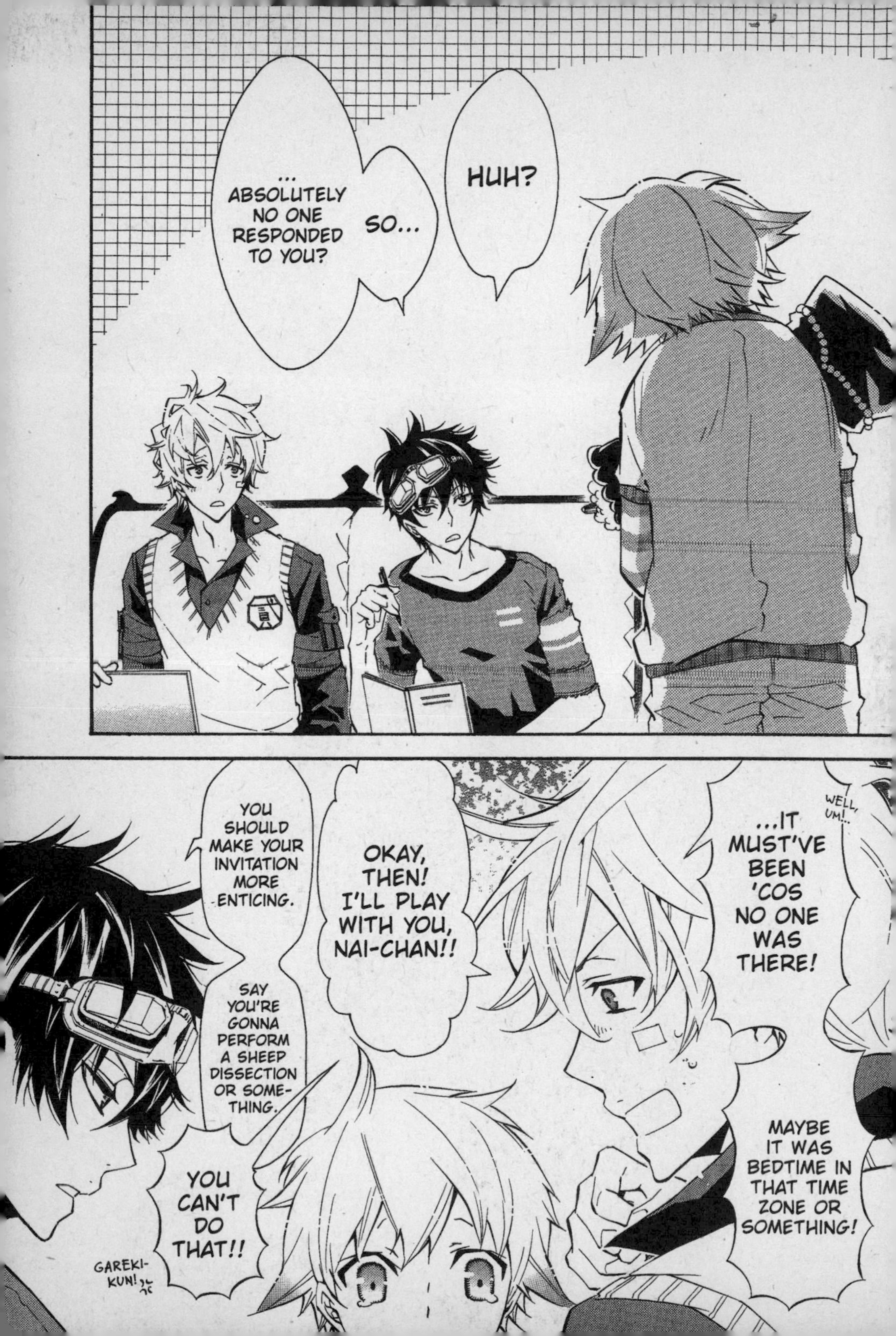
HUH?
SO...
...ABSOLUTELY NO ONE RESPONDED TO YOU?
WELL, UM!...
...IT MUST'VE BEEN 'COS NO ONE WAS THERE!
MAYBE IT WAS BEDTIME IN THAT TIME ZONE OR SOMETHING!
OKAY, THEN! I'LL PLAY WITH YOU, NAI-CHAN!!
YOU SHOULD MAKE YOUR INVITATION MORE ENTICING.
SAY YOU'RE GONNA PERFORM A SHEEP DISSECTION OR SOMETHING.
YOU CAN'T DO THAT!!
GAREKI-KUN!

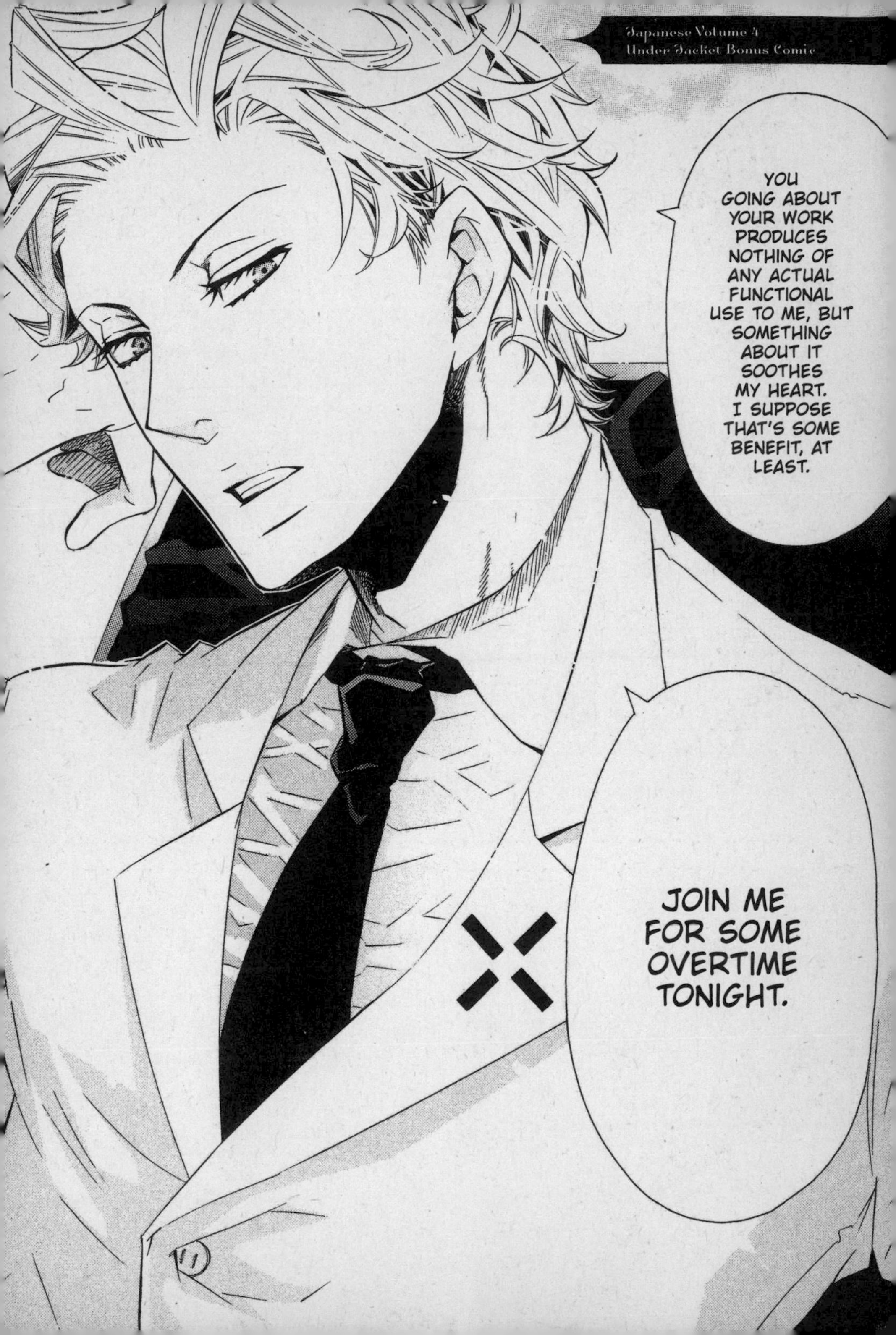
YOU GOING ABOUT YOUR WORK PRODUCES NOTHING OF ANY ACTUAL FUNCTIONAL USE TO ME, BUT SOMETHING ABOUT IT SOOTHES MY HEART. I SUPPOSE THAT'S SOME BENEFIT, AT LEAST.
JOIN ME FOR SOME OVERTIME TONIGHT.

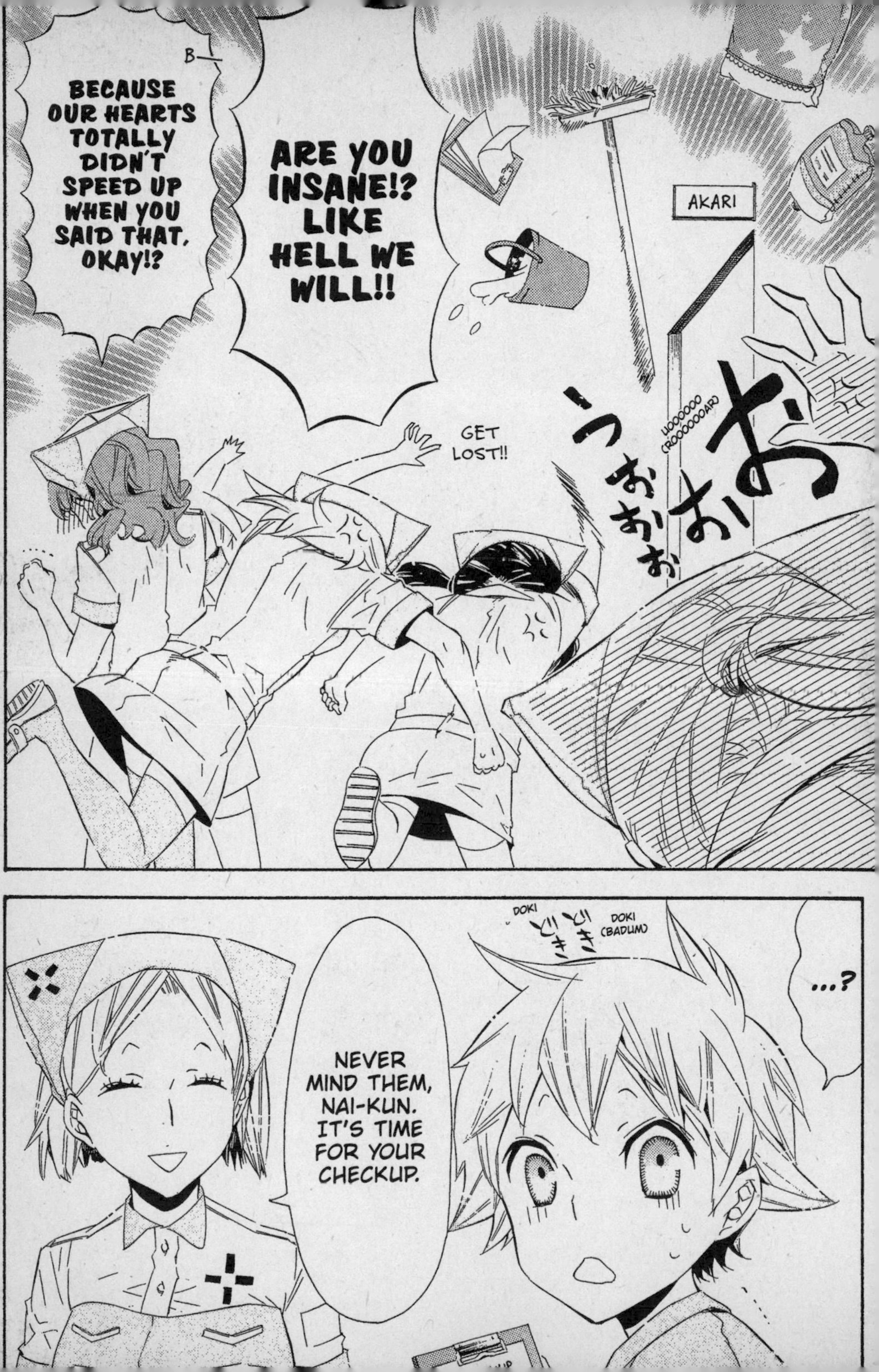
AKARI
うおおおおお
UOOOOOO (ROOOOOOAR)
ARE YOU INSANE!? LIKE HELL WE WILL!!
B—
BECAUSE OUR HEARTS TOTALLY DIDN'T SPEED UP WHEN YOU SAID THAT, OKAY!?
GET LOST!!
...?
どきどき
DOKI DOKI (BADUM)
NEVER MIND THEM, NAI-KUN. IT'S TIME FOR YOUR CHECKUP.

KARNEVAL

Read on for a preview of
the next volume!

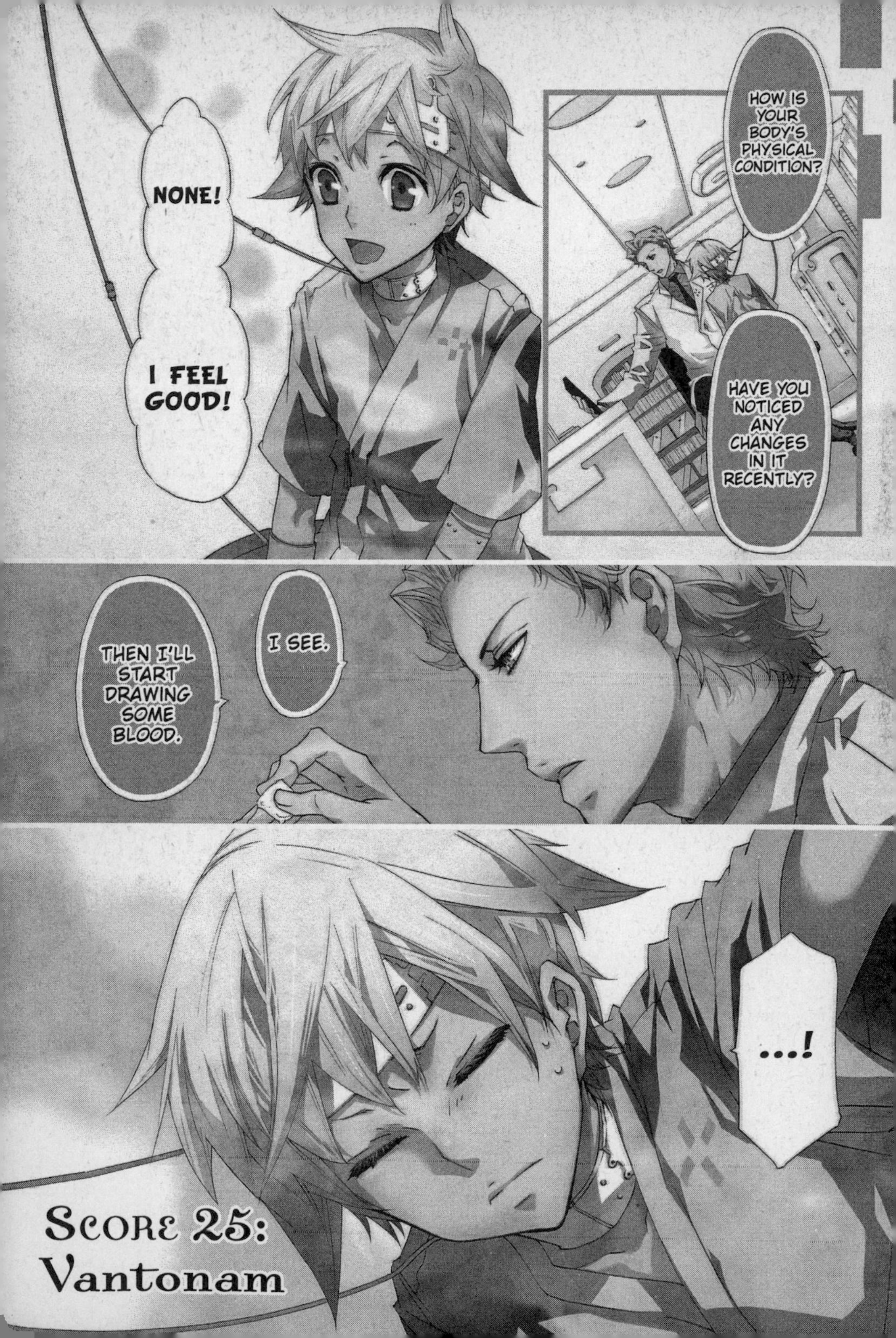
HOW IS YOUR BODY'S PHYSICAL CONDITION?
HAVE YOU NOTICED ANY CHANGES IN IT RECENTLY?
NONE!
I FEEL GOOD!
I SEE.
THEN I'LL START DRAWING SOME BLOOD.
...!
SCORE 25: Vantonam

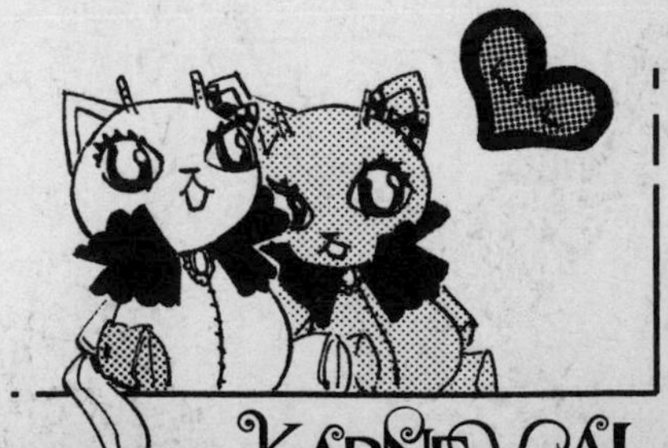
KARNEVAL

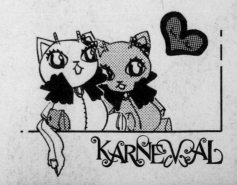

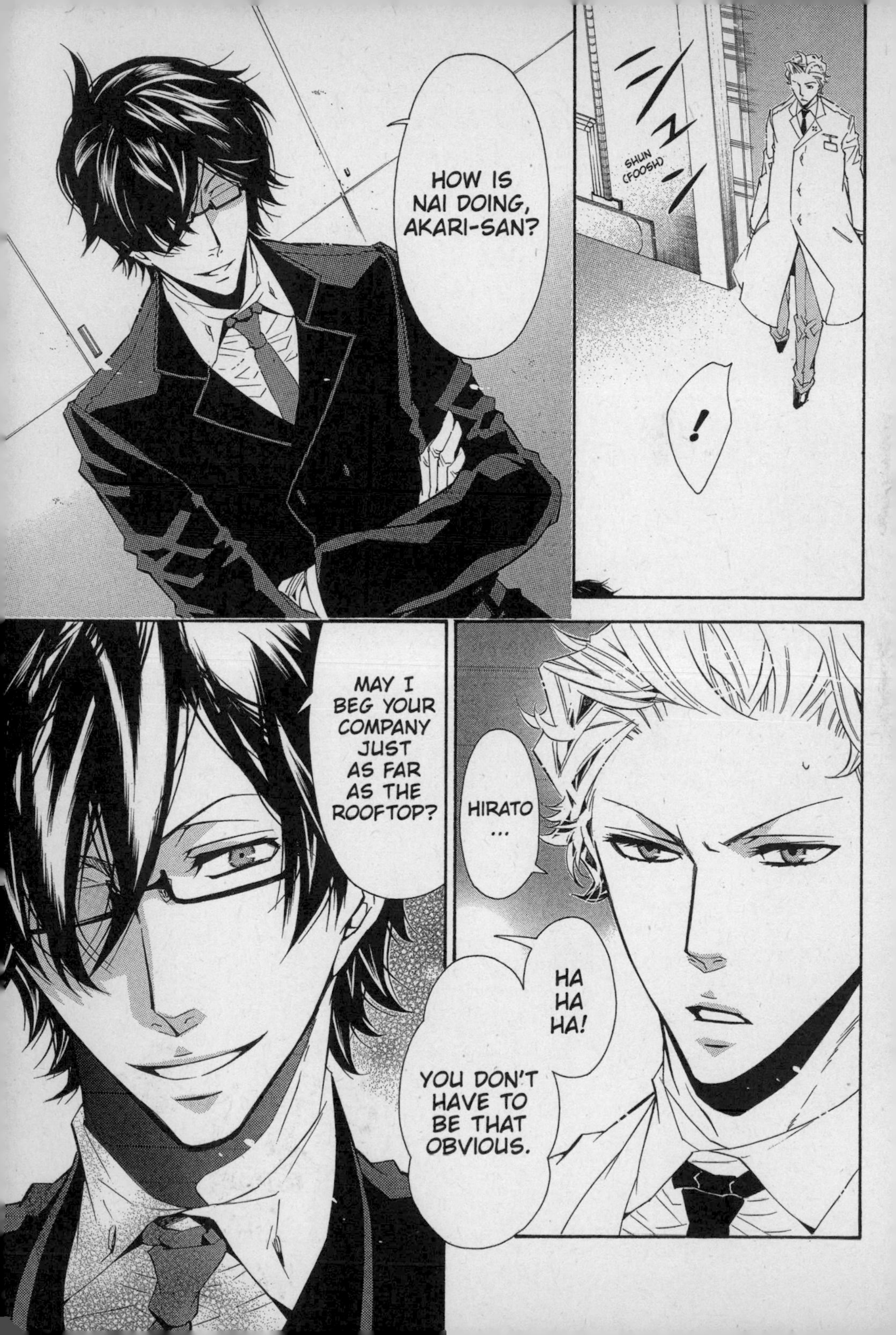
SHUN (FOOSH)
!
HOW IS NAI DOING, AKARI-SAN?
HIRATO ...
HA HA HA!
YOU DON'T HAVE TO BE THAT OBVIOUS.
MAY I BEG YOUR COMPANY JUST AS FAR AS THE ROOFTOP?

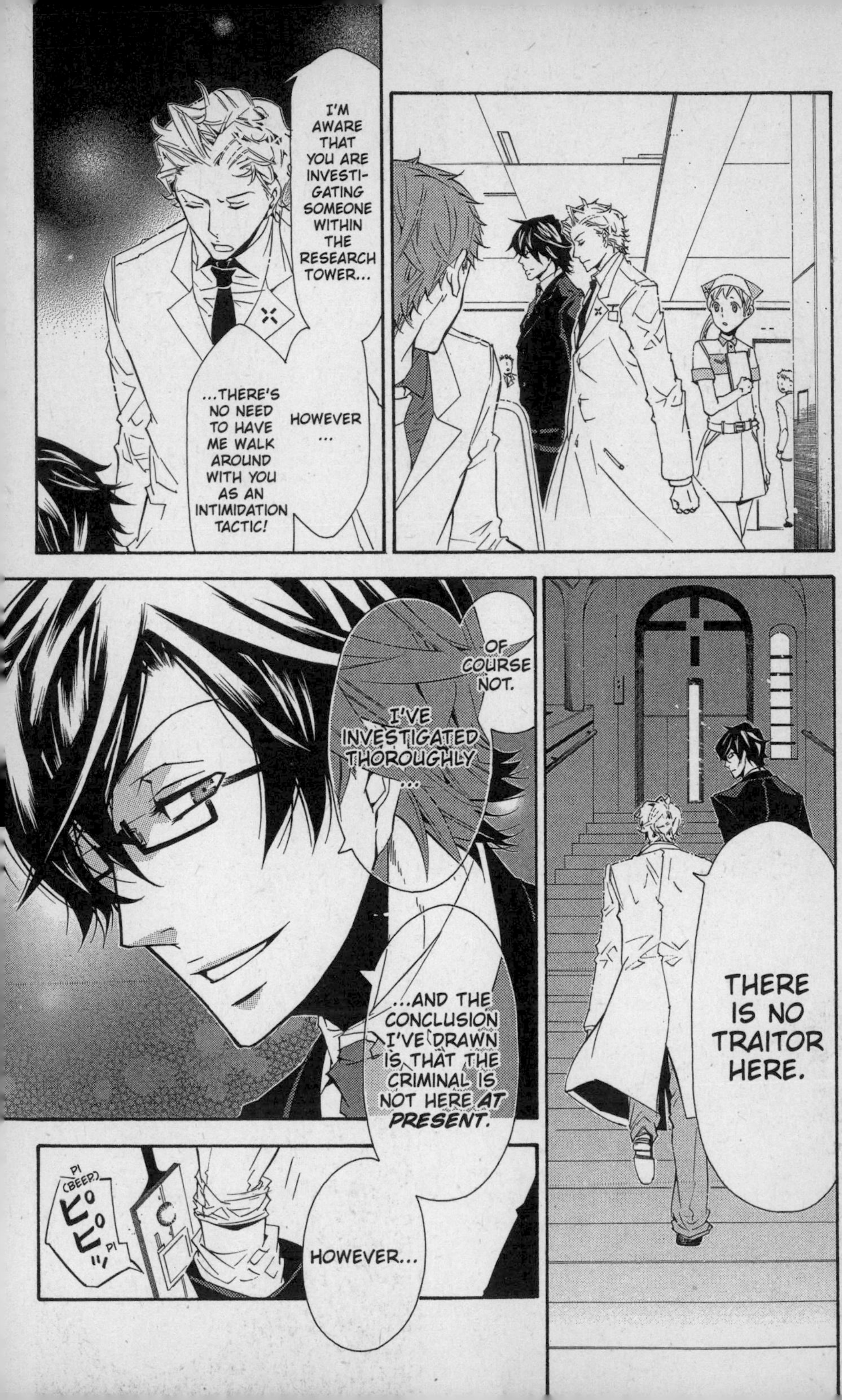
I'M AWARE THAT YOU ARE INVESTIGATING SOMEONE WITHIN THE RESEARCH TOWER...
HOWEVER...
...THERE'S NO NEED TO HAVE ME WALK AROUND WITH YOU AS AN INTIMIDATION TACTIC!
THERE IS NO TRAITOR HERE.
OF COURSE NOT.
I'VE INVESTIGATED THOROUGHLY...
...AND THE CONCLUSION I'VE DRAWN IS THAT THE CRIMINAL IS NOT HERE *AT PRESENT*.
PI PI (BEEP)
HOWEVER...

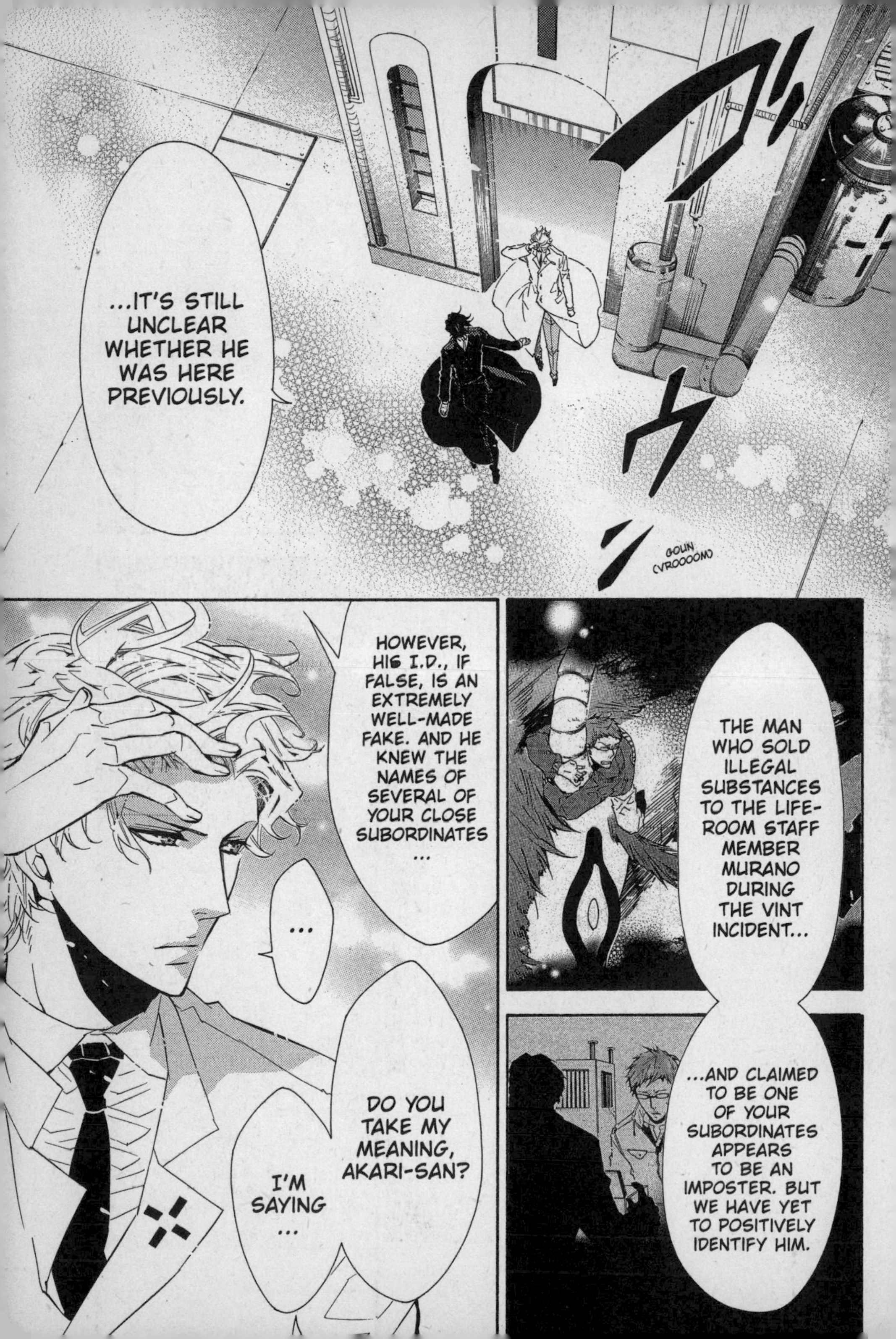
GOUN (VROOOOM)
...IT'S STILL UNCLEAR WHETHER HE WAS HERE PREVIOUSLY.
THE MAN WHO SOLD ILLEGAL SUBSTANCES TO THE LIFE-ROOM STAFF MEMBER MURANO DURING THE VINT INCIDENT...
...AND CLAIMED TO BE ONE OF YOUR SUBORDINATES APPEARS TO BE AN IMPOSTER. BUT WE HAVE YET TO POSITIVELY IDENTIFY HIM.
HOWEVER, HIS I.D., IF FALSE, IS AN EXTREMELY WELL-MADE FAKE. AND HE KNEW THE NAMES OF SEVERAL OF YOUR CLOSE SUBORDINATES ...
...
DO YOU TAKE MY MEANING, AKARI-SAN?
I'M SAYING ...

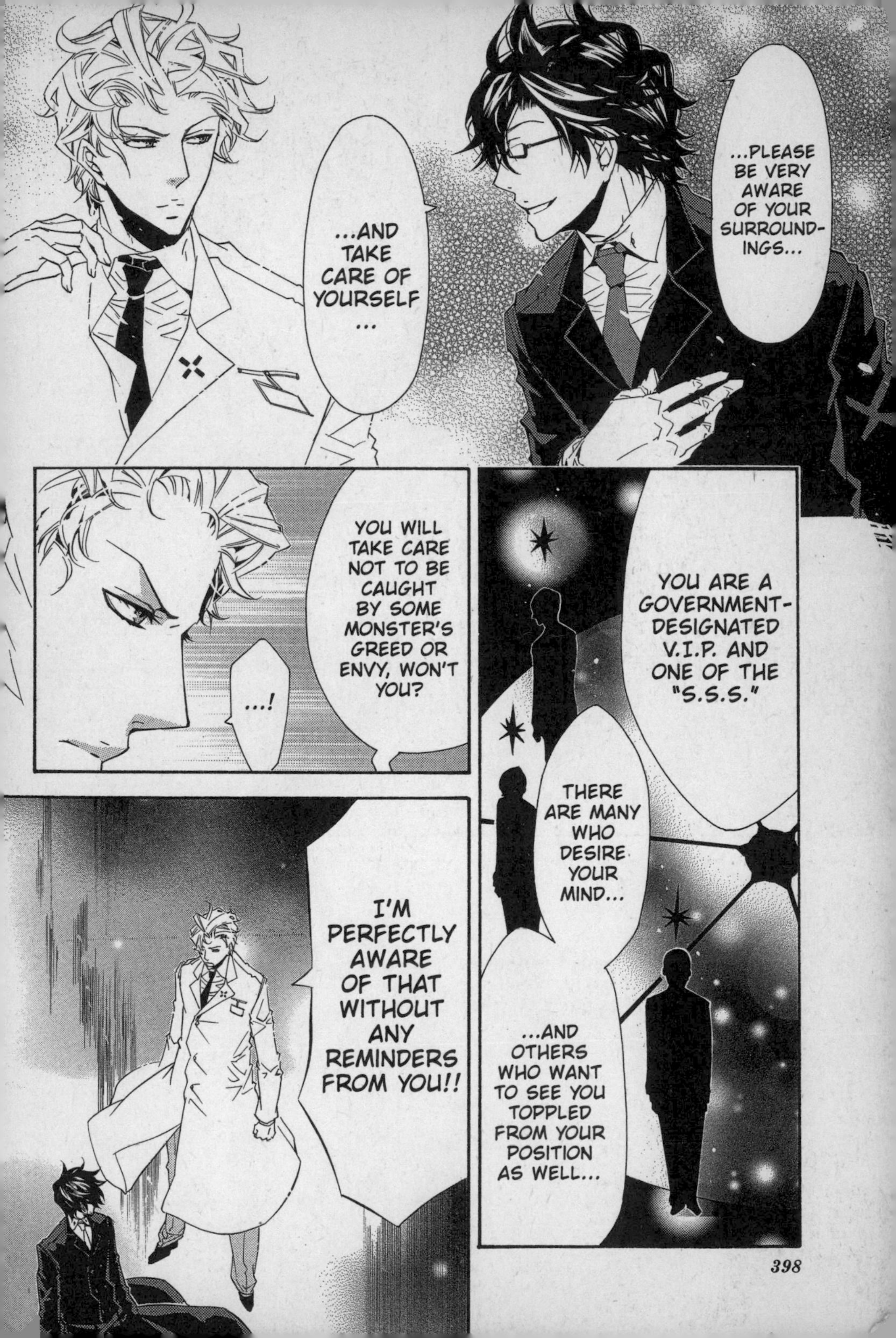
...PLEASE BE VERY AWARE OF YOUR SURROUND-INGS...
...AND TAKE CARE OF YOURSELF ...
YOU ARE A GOVERNMENT-DESIGNATED V.I.P. AND ONE OF THE "S.S.S."
THERE ARE MANY WHO DESIRE YOUR MIND...
...AND OTHERS WHO WANT TO SEE YOU TOPPLED FROM YOUR POSITION AS WELL...
YOU WILL TAKE CARE NOT TO BE CAUGHT BY SOME MONSTER'S GREED OR ENVY, WON'T YOU?
...!
I'M PERFECTLY AWARE OF THAT WITHOUT ANY REMINDERS FROM YOU!!

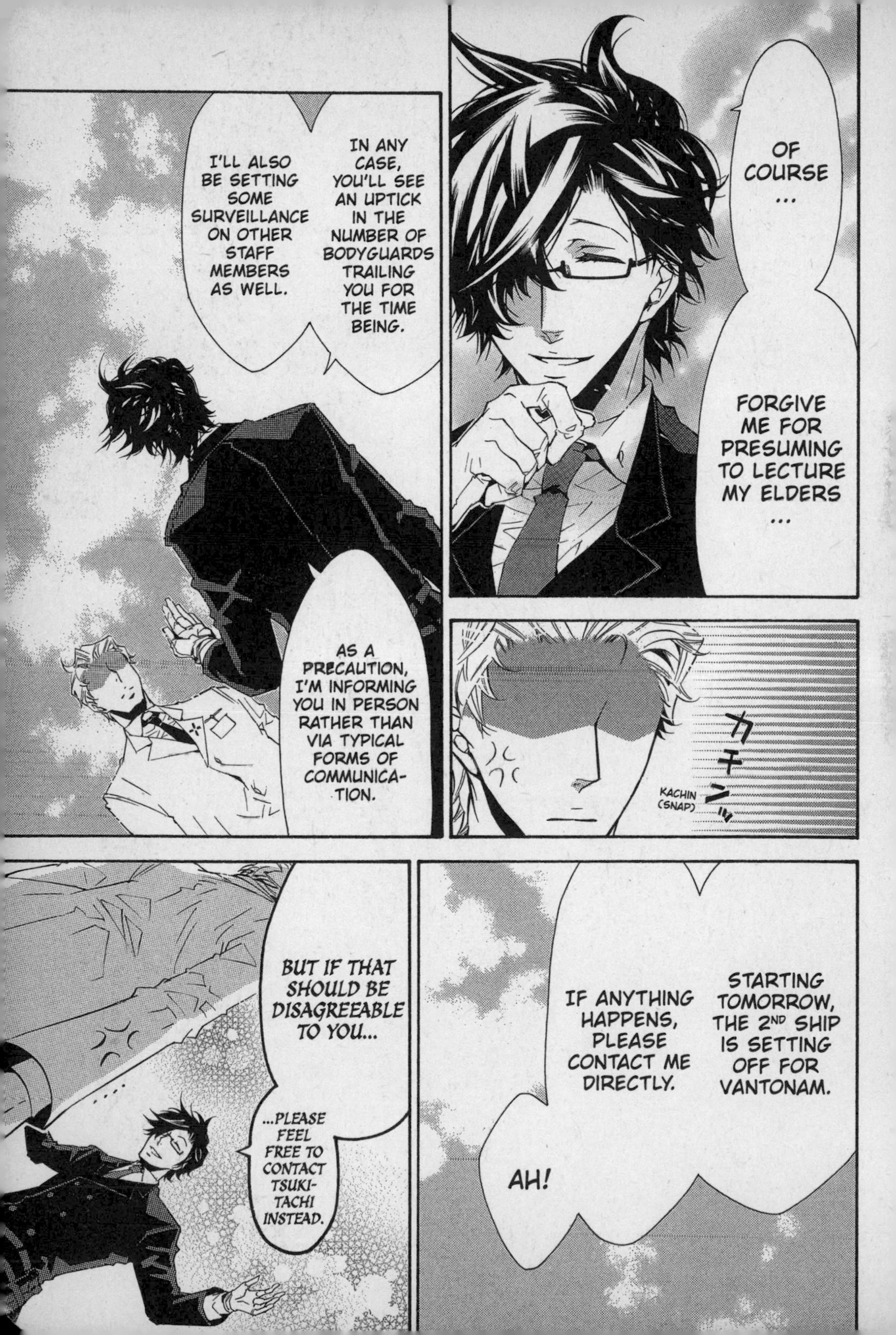
OF COURSE...
FORGIVE ME FOR PRESUMING TO LECTURE MY ELDERS...
KACHIN (SNAP)
IN ANY CASE, YOU'LL SEE AN UPTICK IN THE NUMBER OF BODYGUARDS TRAILING YOU FOR THE TIME BEING.
I'LL ALSO BE SETTING SOME SURVEILLANCE ON OTHER STAFF MEMBERS AS WELL.
AS A PRECAUTION, I'M INFORMING YOU IN PERSON RATHER THAN VIA TYPICAL FORMS OF COMMUNICA-TION.
STARTING TOMORROW, THE 2ND SHIP IS SETTING OFF FOR VANTONAM.
IF ANYTHING HAPPENS, PLEASE CONTACT ME DIRECTLY.
AH!
BUT IF THAT SHOULD BE DISAGREEABLE TO YOU...
...PLEASE FEEL FREE TO CONTACT TSUKI-TACHI INSTEAD.

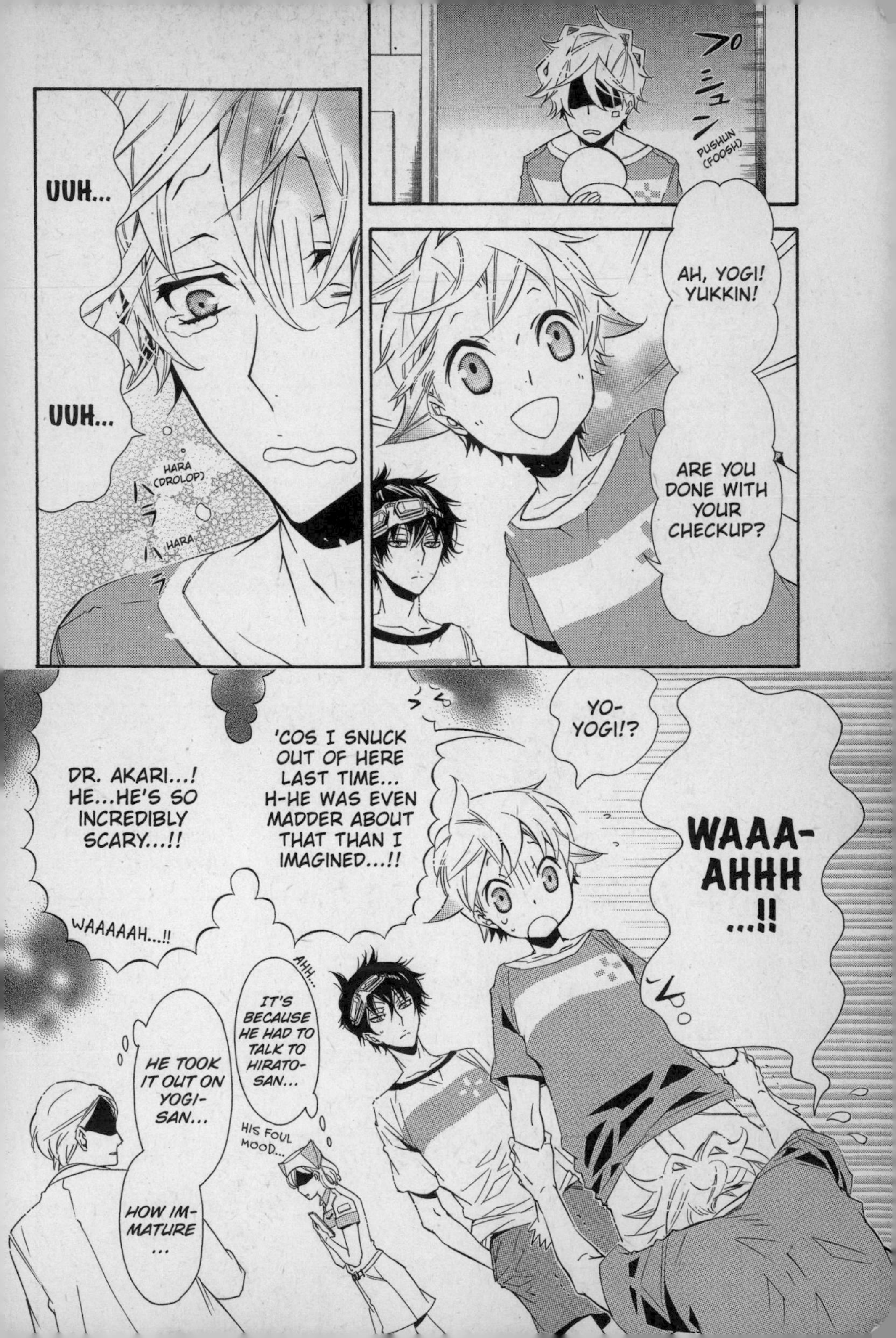
プシュン
PUSHUN (FOOSH)
AH, YOGI! YUKKIN!
ARE YOU DONE WITH YOUR CHECKUP?
UUH...
UUH...
HARA (DROLOP)
HARA
WAAA-AHHH ...!!
YO-YOGI!?
'COS I SNUCK OUT OF HERE LAST TIME... H-HE WAS EVEN MADDER ABOUT THAT THAN I IMAGINED...!!
DR. AKARI...! HE...HE'S SO INCREDIBLY SCARY...!!
WAAAAAH...!!
AHH...
IT'S BECAUSE HE HAD TO TALK TO HIRATO-SAN...
HIS FOUL MOOD...
HE TOOK IT OUT ON YOGI-SAN...
HOW IM-MATURE ...

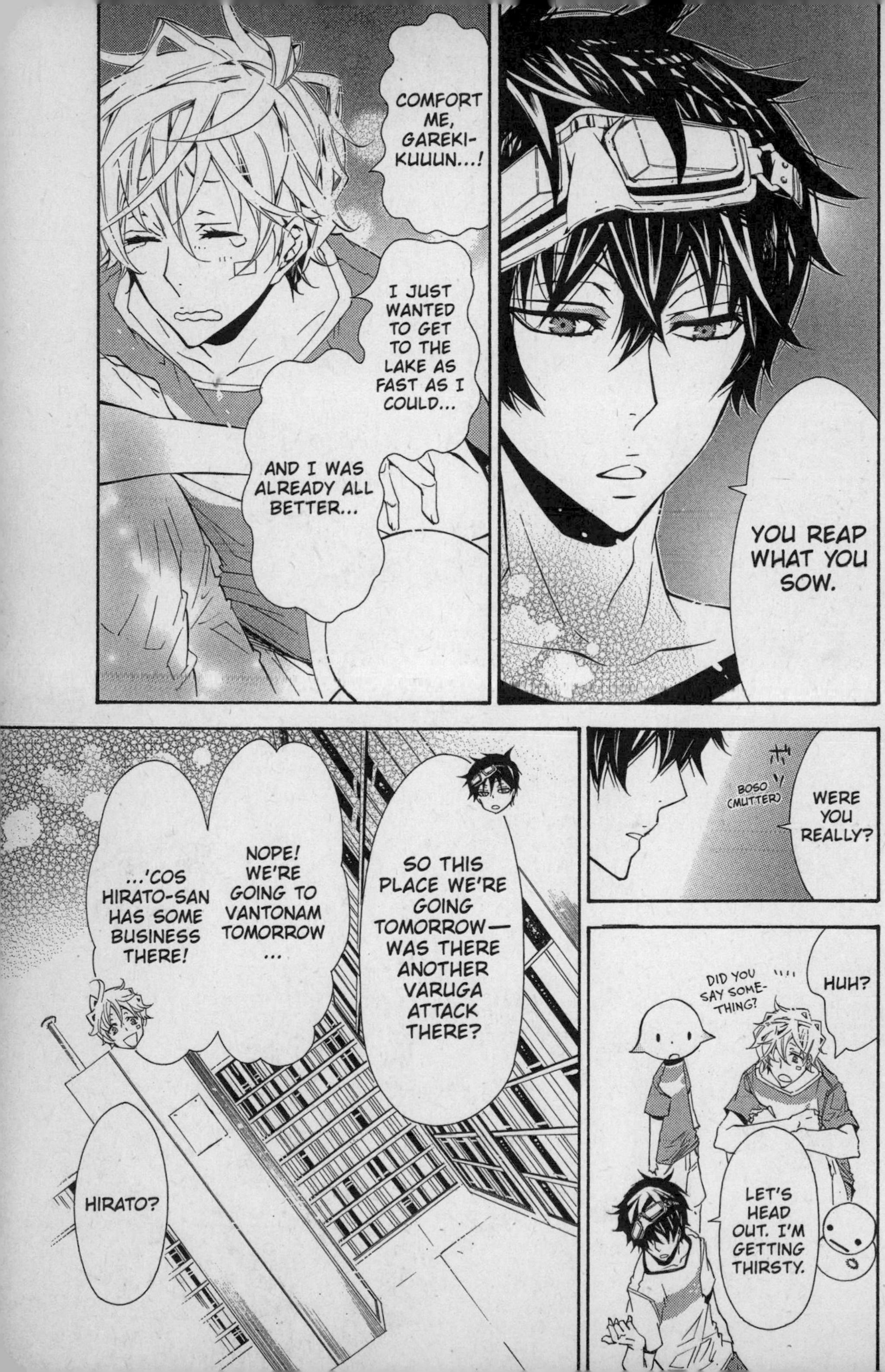
YOU REAP WHAT YOU SOW.
COMFORT ME, GAREKI-KUUUN...!
I JUST WANTED TO GET TO THE LAKE AS FAST AS I COULD...
AND I WAS ALREADY ALL BETTER...
BOSO (MUTTER)
WERE YOU REALLY?
HUH?
DID YOU SAY SOME-THING?
LET'S HEAD OUT. I'M GETTING THIRSTY.
SO THIS PLACE WE'RE GOING TOMORROW—WAS THERE ANOTHER VARUGA ATTACK THERE?
NOPE! WE'RE GOING TO VANTONAM TOMORROW...
...'COS HIRATO-SAN HAS SOME BUSINESS THERE!
HIRATO?

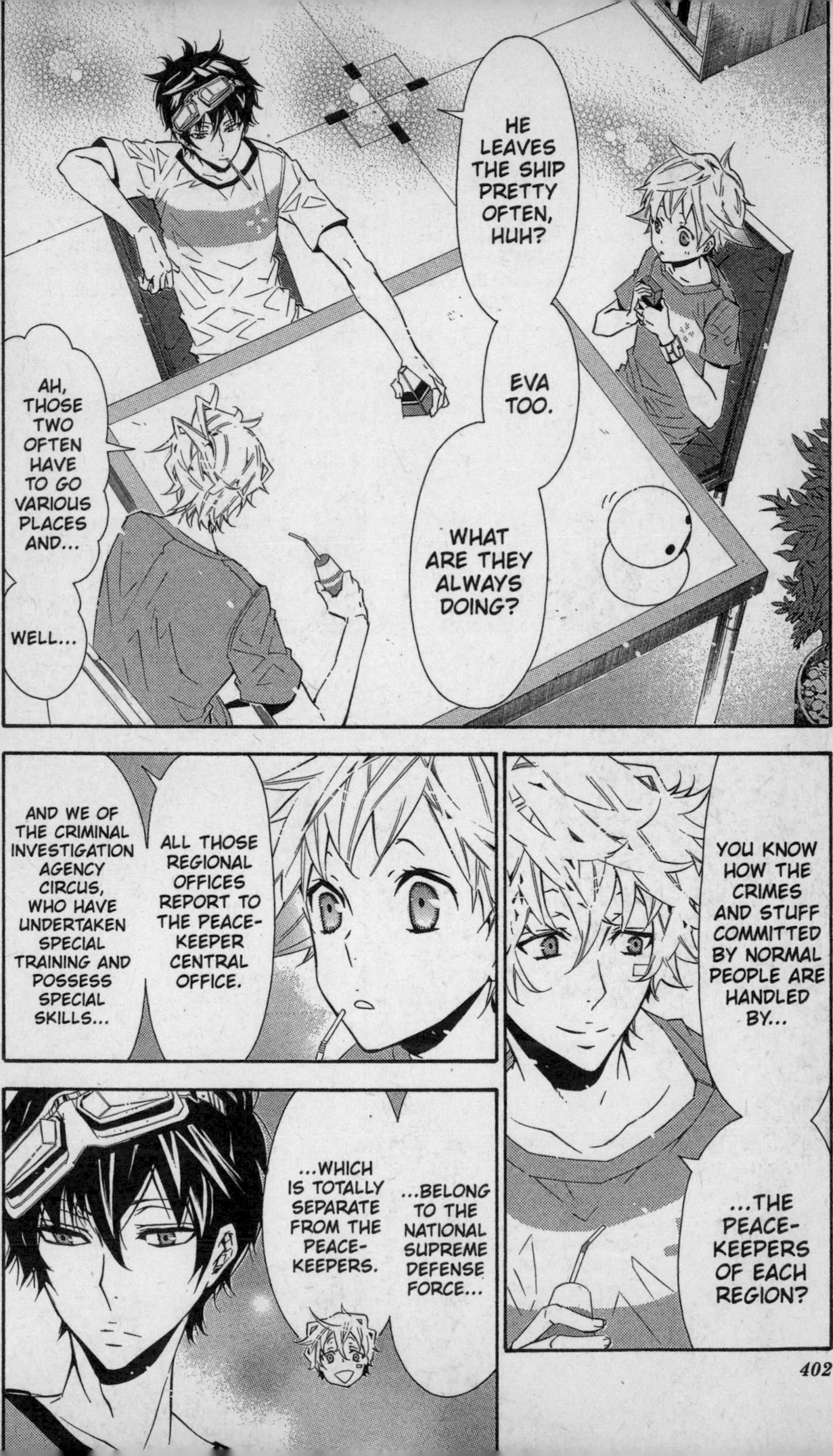
HE LEAVES THE SHIP PRETTY OFTEN, HUH?
EVA TOO.
WHAT ARE THEY ALWAYS DOING?
AH, THOSE TWO OFTEN HAVE TO GO VARIOUS PLACES AND...
WELL...
YOU KNOW HOW THE CRIMES AND STUFF COMMITTED BY NORMAL PEOPLE ARE HANDLED BY...
...THE PEACE-KEEPERS OF EACH REGION?
ALL THOSE REGIONAL OFFICES REPORT TO THE PEACE-KEEPER CENTRAL OFFICE.
AND WE OF THE CRIMINAL INVESTIGATION AGENCY CIRCUS, WHO HAVE UNDERTAKEN SPECIAL TRAINING AND POSSESS SPECIAL SKILLS...
...BELONG TO THE NATIONAL SUPREME DEFENSE FORCE...
...WHICH IS TOTALLY SEPARATE FROM THE PEACE-KEEPERS.

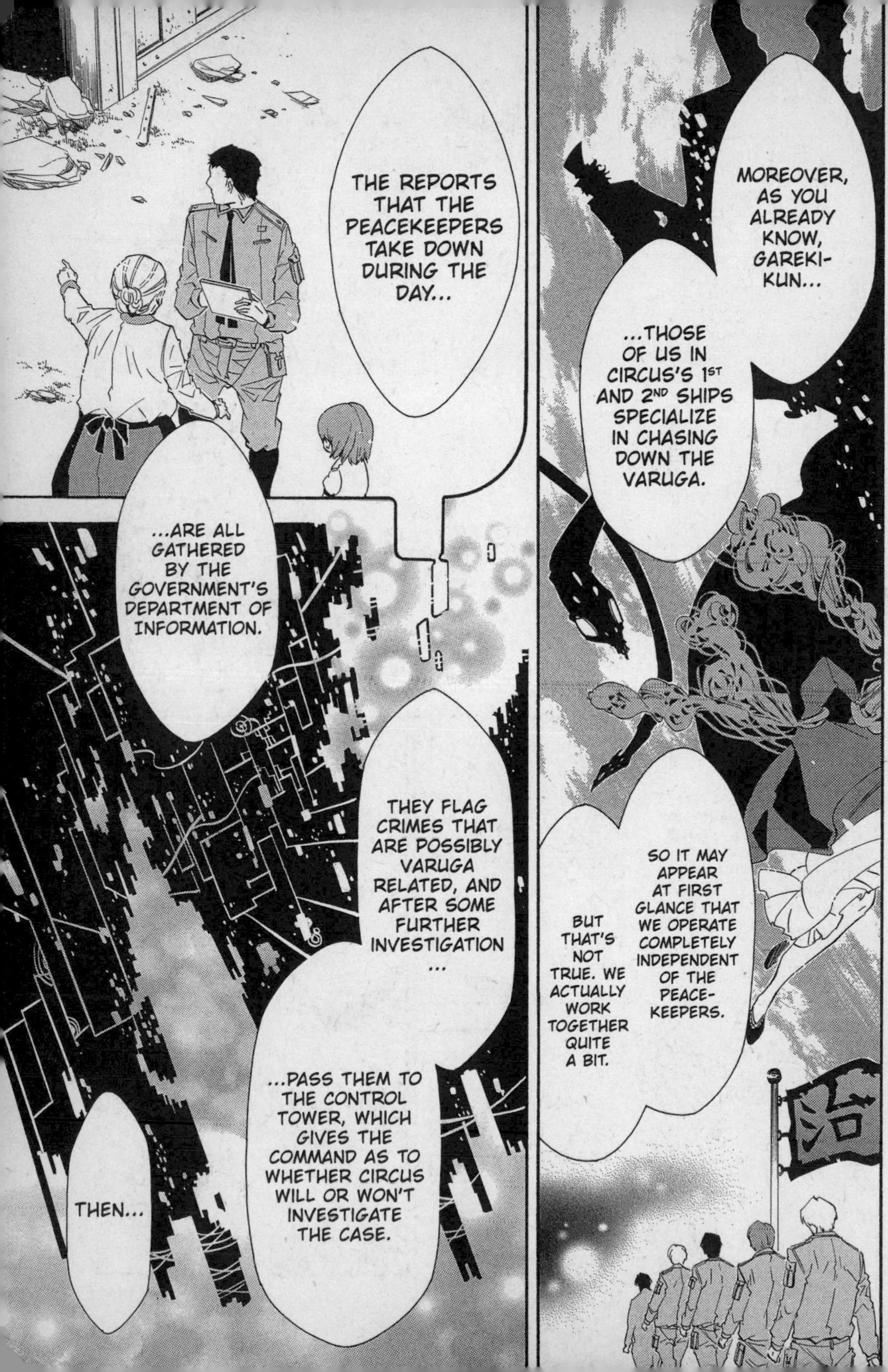
MOREOVER, AS YOU ALREADY KNOW, GAREKI-KUN...
...THOSE OF US IN CIRCUS'S 1ST AND 2ND SHIPS SPECIALIZE IN CHASING DOWN THE VARUGA.
SO IT MAY APPEAR AT FIRST GLANCE THAT WE OPERATE COMPLETELY INDEPENDENT OF THE PEACE-KEEPERS.
BUT THAT'S NOT TRUE. WE ACTUALLY WORK TOGETHER QUITE A BIT.
THE REPORTS THAT THE PEACEKEEPERS TAKE DOWN DURING THE DAY...
...ARE ALL GATHERED BY THE GOVERNMENT'S DEPARTMENT OF INFORMATION.
THEY FLAG CRIMES THAT ARE POSSIBLY VARUGA RELATED, AND AFTER SOME FURTHER INVESTIGATION...
...PASS THEM TO THE CONTROL TOWER, WHICH GIVES THE COMMAND AS TO WHETHER CIRCUS WILL OR WON'T INVESTIGATE THE CASE.
THEN...

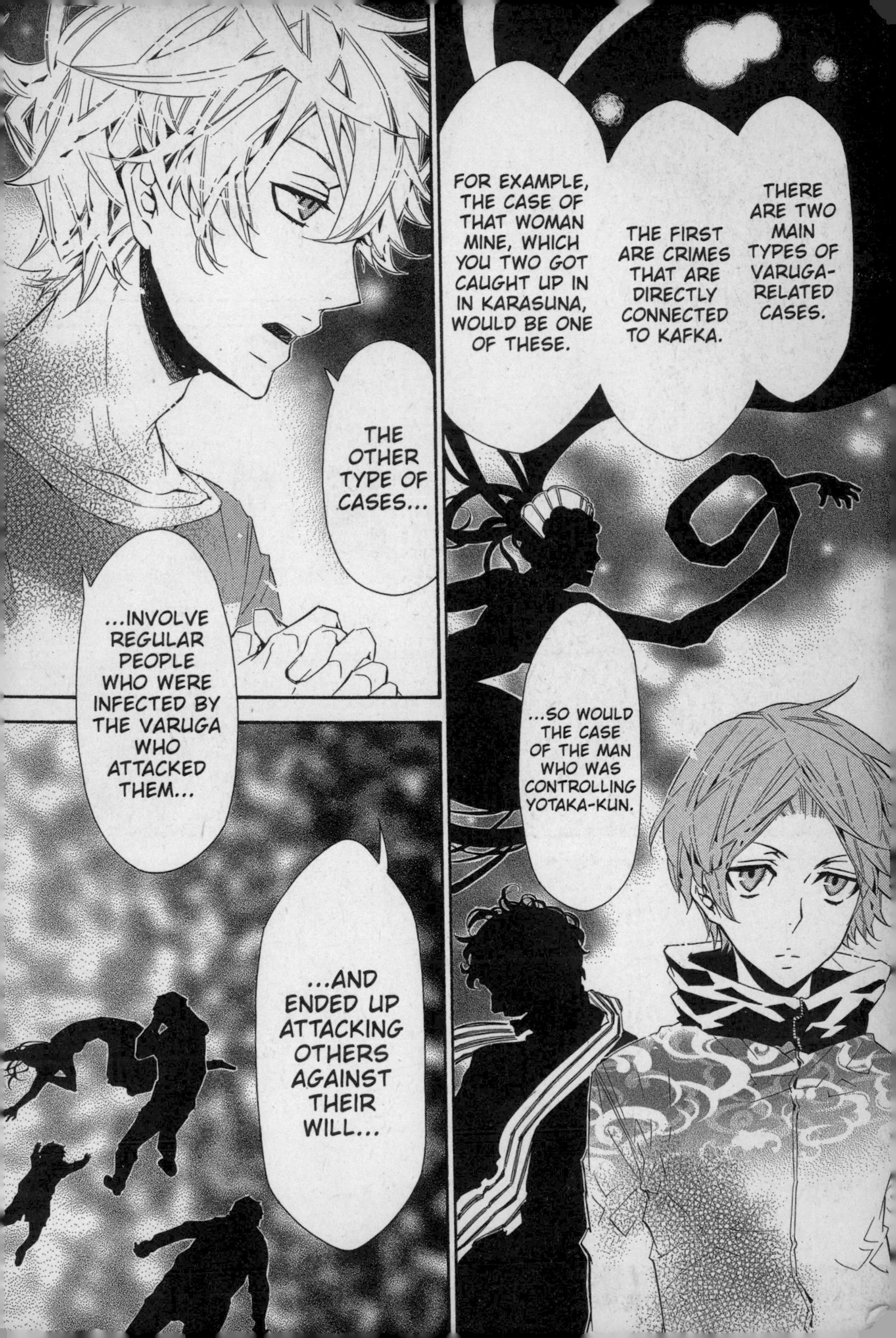
THERE ARE TWO MAIN TYPES OF VARUGA-RELATED CASES.
THE FIRST ARE CRIMES THAT ARE DIRECTLY CONNECTED TO KAFKA.
FOR EXAMPLE, THE CASE OF THAT WOMAN MINE, WHICH YOU TWO GOT CAUGHT UP IN IN KARASUNA, WOULD BE ONE OF THESE.
...SO WOULD THE CASE OF THE MAN WHO WAS CONTROLLING YOTAKA-KUN.
THE OTHER TYPE OF CASES...
...INVOLVE REGULAR PEOPLE WHO WERE INFECTED BY THE VARUGA WHO ATTACKED THEM...
...AND ENDED UP ATTACKING OTHERS AGAINST THEIR WILL...

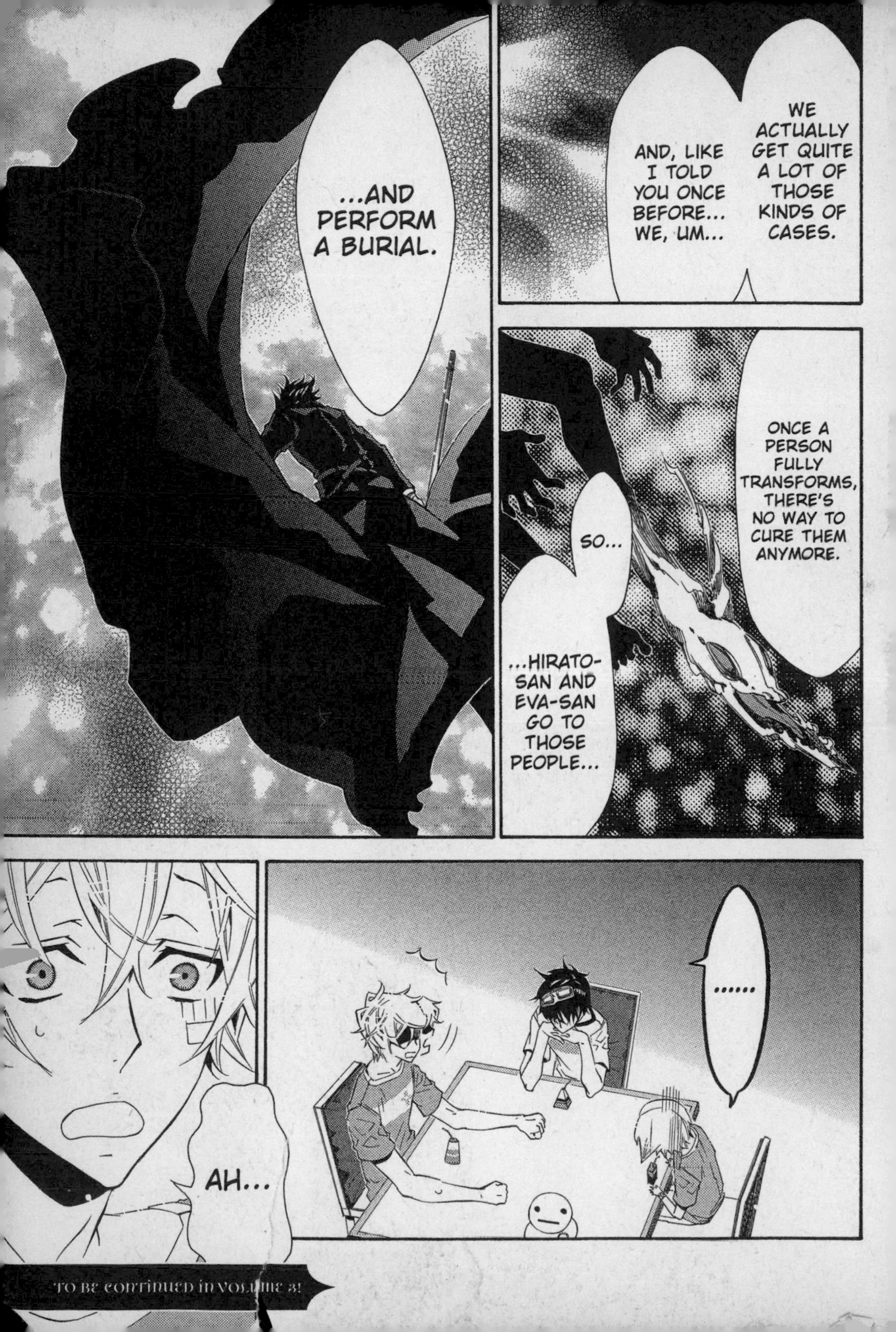
WE ACTUALLY GET QUITE A LOT OF THOSE KINDS OF CASES.
AND, LIKE I TOLD YOU ONCE BEFORE... WE, UM...
ONCE A PERSON FULLY TRANSFORMS, THERE'S NO WAY TO CURE THEM ANYMORE.
SO...
...HIRATO-SAN AND EVA-SAN GO TO THOSE PEOPLE...
...AND PERFORM A BURIAL.
......
AH...
TO BE CONTINUED IN VOLUME 3!

KARNEVAL 2

Touya Mikanagi

Translation: Su Mon Han   Lettering: Alexis Eckerman

Karneval vols. 3-4 © 2009 by Touya Mikanagi. All rights reserved. First published in Japan in 2009 by ICHIJINSHA. English translation rights arranged with ICHIJINSHA through Tuttle-Mori Agency, Inc., Tokyo.

Translation © 2015 by Hachette Book Group, Inc.

Yen Press
Hachette Book Group
1290 Avenue of the Americas
New York, NY 10104

www.HachetteBookGroup.com
www.YenPress.com

Yen Press is an imprint of Hachette Book Group, Inc.
The Yen Press name and logo are trademarks of Hachette Book Group, Inc.

The publisher is not responsible for websites (or their content)
that are not owned by the publisher.

First Yen Press Edition: July 2015

ISBN: 978-0-316-26347-4

10 9 8 7 6 5 4 3 2 1

BVG

Printed in the United States of America